CHALLENGES TO
WORLD PEACE

A GLOBAL
SOLUTION

John E. LaMuth M. S.

REFERENCE BOOKS OF AMERICA
Imprint for:
FAIRHAVEN BOOK PUBLISHERS

Library of Congress Catalog Card Number – 2009906623

Reference Books of America
Imprint for: Fairhaven Book Publishers
• 35425 Mojave Street – Suite B
Lucerne Valley, CA 92356 - USA

1-877-F.H.Books
• (877-342-6657)
Fax: 1-586-314-5960
values@charactervalues.com
www.global-solutions.org

Publisher's Cataloging-In-Publication Data

Challenges to world peace: a global solution / John E. LaMuth, Author.

  440 p. : ill. ; cm.
  ISBN: 978-1-929649-32-7

1. Virtues/values--Terminology. 2. Ethics--Terminology. 3. Affect (Psychology) 4. Criminality--Classification. 5. Ethical hierarchy--Technology. 6. World peace-- Moral and ethical aspects.
I. LaMuth, John E., author.

BF636 .L36 2009
158.4   2009906623

Printed on acid-free paper

Wholesale Distributor:
Ingram Book Group Inc.
La Vergne, Tennessee 37086

TABLE of CONTENTS

ACKNOWLEDGEMENTS

The Author gratefully wishes to acknowledge the many individuals that have contributed background material to *Challenges to World Peace: A Global Solution* including Maria Adamos PhD (envy-jealousy-shame-humiliation), and Matt Bowen M.A. (patience-scrupulousness-uprightness). Special appreciation is further extended to Al Mintzer of the Aim-Higher Curriculum Center for his numerous contributions relating to the character values (self-esteem-duty-compassion-sacrifice-perfection), as well as essays targeting the realm of excess (cynicism-pretentiousness-impetuosity). Further credit is duly noted with respect to *The Catholic Encyclopedia* primarily for themes of a religious nature: namely, Edward J. Hanna (penance-absolution-contrition), Herbert Thurston (benediction), G. H. Joyce (sanctity), Timothy Brosnahan (altruism), and John H. Stapleton (covetousness). Topics of a scriptural nature have gratefully been adapted from the *International Standard Bible Encyclopedia*: in particular, W. L. Walker (mercy-vanity-reproach), E. J. Forrester (reverence), Burton S. Easton (hospitality), William C. Morrow (forgiveness), Edward B. Pollard (tribulation), and Dwight M. Pratt (anguish), amongst others. Details relating to etymologies are credited to Douglas Harper: editor for the online resource: *etymonline.com*.

Acknowledgements in terms of photographic illustrations include the B. F. Skinner Foundation, Birmingham Museum of Art (Pesellino), British Museum (Papyrus of Ani), Prado Museum (Bosch), Founders Library (Hogarth), and Guildhall Library (Durer). Essays in relation to the topic of mental illness have gratefully been adapted from two major sources. Background material concerning the personality disorders and neuroses are credited to *Gale Encyclopedia of Psychology* - reprinted by permission of the Gale Group. Special appreciation is further extended to Mr. Irving Naiberg of Irvington Publishers with respect to his gracious permission to reproduce representative background material relating to the psychoses - from the Irvington publication: *The Classification of the Endogenous Psychoses - Fifth Edition*, by Karl Leonhard (1979). All other material not specifically acknowledged has been contributed by author John E. LaMuth, with special appreciation extended to Reference Books of America and Fairhaven Book Publishers for their gracious permission to reproduce excerpts from previous publications by the author in relation to the overall body of work.

ALSO BY THE AUTHOR ...

———————————

A Revolution in Family Values:
Tradition vs. Technology

———————————

Communication Breakdown:
Decoding the Riddle of Mental Illness

———————————

Character Values:
Promoting a Virtuous Lifestyle

———————————

A Diagnostic Classification of the
Emotions: A Three-Digit Coding
System for Affective Language

PREFACE

The revised and updated edition currently under consideration: *Challenges to World Peace: A Global Solution* proposes a master classificational system for themes of an ethical/emotional nature, promising key insights into preserving global peace and harmony. This all-inclusive ethical system incorporates the entire range of virtues, values, and vices specified within the Western ethical tradition. A fair portion of this virtuous tradition has historically been invested with religious overtones, an aspect that typically has been downplayed in today's modern secular culture. The newly proposed master three-digit coding system aims to remedy this crucial oversight, proposing a behaviorally-based system of moral classification that celebrates the enhanced degree of interconnectedness linking each of these ethical traditions. This technical innovation has only recently been made feasible through the introduction of the new science of Powerplay Politics™, an all-inclusive synthesis of the behavioral dynamics characterizing emotionally-charged language in general. This innovation is schematically organized in terms of a master three-digit coding system comprising *1,040* individual terms: the outline of which is partially depicted in the schematic table immediately below:

(300 – 399)	**(400 – 499)**
+ + VICES OF EXCESS	**MENTAL ILLNESS**
(Excessive Virtue)	**(Transitional Excess)**
(100 – 199)	**(200 – 299)**
+ MAJOR VIRTUES	**LESSER VIRTUES**
(Virtuous Mode)	**(Transitional Virtue)**

---

0 -	**NEUTRALITY STATUS**

(500 – 599)	**(600 – 699)**
- VICES OF DEFECT	**CRIMINALITY**
(Absence Of Virtue)	**(Transitional Defect)**
(700 – 799)	**(800 – 899)**
- - HYPERVIOLENCE	**HYPERCRIMINALITY**
(Excessive Defect)	**(Transit. Hyperviolence)**

The most salient feature of this master format is the centralized zone of neutrality status, the basic default setting for the entire conceptual system. It represents the initiation point for all new classes of relationship to follow, whether positive or negative in nature. The uppermost segments of the diagram represent the positive domain based upon cooperation, as reflected in the basic categories of the major and the lesser virtues. This dual formulation unites all of the traditional groupings of virtues, values, and ideals into a cohesive ten-level hierarchy: the first grand unified theory of its kind, as partially depicted below.

Glory • Prudence	**Honor • Justice**
Providence • Faith	**Liberty • Hope**
Grace • Beauty	**Free-Will • Truth**
Tranquility • Ecstasy	**Equality • Bliss**
Dignity • Temperance	**Integrity • Fortitude**
Civility • Charity	**Austerity • Decency**
Magnanim. • Goodness	**Equanimity • Wisdom**
Love • Joy	**Peace • Harmony**

The lower-most segments are alternately based within the realm of conflict/punishment: namely, Aristotle's vices of defect, as well as the affiliated sphere of criminality. For every virtue there necessarily exists a corresponding antonym (or vice): e.g., love vs. hate, good vs. evil, etc. permitting negative transactions to be analyzed according to their potential to be converted into the positive ones, and vice versa: a mirror-image reflection of the virtuous mode, as partially depicted below.

Infamy • Insurgency	**Dishonor • Vengeance**
Prodigality • Betrayal	**Slavery • Despair**
Wrath • Ugliness	**Tyranny • Hypocrisy**
Anger • Abomination	**Prejudice • Perdition**
Foolishness • Gluttony	**Caprice • Cowardice**
Vulgarity • Avarice	**Cruelty • Antagonism**
Oppression • Evil	**Persecution • Cunning**
Hatred • Iniquity	**Belligerence • Turpitude**

This basic core-nucleus of terms, in turn, serves as the foundation for the remaining layers of categories based upon the domain of excess. For the virtuous realm, this corresponds to Aristotle's vices of excess, as well as the communicational factors underlying the mental disorders. With respect to the darker realm of the vices of defect, this pattern further extends to the categorical extremes of hyperviolence and hypercriminality.

This grand-scale conceptual formulation of ethical categories represents an unprecedented addition to the field of ethical inquiry, expanding Aristotle's enduring "Theory of the Mean" into an all-inclusive theory of everything of an emotional nature. At the risk of appearing overly simplistic, each of these eight basic categories is further subdivided into much more detailed groupings of terms. For instance, the major virtues are further subdivided into *100* individual terms, whereas the lesser virtues are similarly specialized into *128* distinctive terms. When the six additional ethical categories are further added into the mix, the grand total summates to a staggering *1,040* individual terms.

The current work represents an updated edition of an earlier title by the author: *Character Values: Promoting a Virtuous Lifestyle* issued in 2005. For this initial edition, the issue of *character values* was specifically highlighted, although somewhat limiting in terms of the scope of its considerable international applications. In order to suitably broaden this range of perspectives, the current revised edition has purposely been retitled to reflect its more expanded focus on global solutions towards preserving international peace and harmony. Although much critical material has been retained from the earlier edition, a significant proportion of new material both clarifies and expands upon issues only briefly touched upon in the original edition. Indeed, the current edition represents a major expansion in terms of content, more than doubling the number of unique individual terms to a grand-total of *1,040* individual themes. The major overall focus, however, remains the promotion of a virtuous lifestyle through a more intimate examination of the cha-

racter values (and affiliated ethical categories), with applications fittingly extending to a global sphere of influence.

Far from remaining a purely academic exercise, this all-inclusive system addresses many issues of crucial import to modern culture. For instance, the realms of criminality and hypercriminality are examined in Part VI with considerable applications to political corruption and global international terrorism. Part VII, in turn, examines the range of communicational factors underlying mental illness: as specified for the overall symptom spectrum of the personality disorders, neuroses, mood disorders, and schizophrenia. This comprehensive examination of such an intriguing set of categories offers timely insights into the numerous conflicts facing modern culture today, as well as considerable inroads into information technology: most notably, a patented simulation of ethical artificial intelligence. Here, the formal dynamics of the three-digit coding system prove amenable to programming directly into a computer format, providing an intriguing new platform for ethical computer safeguards.

Perhaps the greatest potential for this breakthrough ethical coding system resides in its all-inclusive nature, accounting for virtually every major class of ethically-charged language presumed to exist. Indeed, based upon a limited number of elementary assumptions; namely, the principles of instrumental conditioning and the concept of the metaperspective, the ascending hierarchy of stepwise transformations ultimately accounts for the entire *1,040*-part complement of individual terms. It has been my great pleasure to aid in promoting this grand-scale undertaking, one that would have remained far more daunting without the efforts of a supportive cast of experts that have graciously contributed expertise to this ground-breaking new edition.

John E. LaMuth
August, 2009

PART-I

1

AN INTRODUCTION TO GLOBAL SOLUTIONS AND WORLD PEACE

A planetary system of ethics is an achievement that long has been anticipated on the world scene today. Although organized religion has long been regarded as the standard bearer for the promotion of a virtuous life style, the various conflicts that afflict the major world religions clearly expose the inherent weaknesses to such a simplistic interpretation. Ideally, a scientific foundation for such a global ethical perspective would prove exceedingly beneficial towards resolving many of these difficulties. The profound status of the scientific method effectively permeates the economic and social fabric of society as a whole. Here, a formal scientific tie-in with ethical principles should prove particularly effectively for removing many of the cultural stumbling blocks towards such a widespread global acceptance. In particular, a foundation within the scientific principles of behavioral psychology proves the most effective solution towards achieving worldwide acceptance: invoking instinctual principles shared in common as a human species (and with the rest of the animal kingdom) as a general unifying theme. When these elementary behavioral principles are further extended to encompass the more abstract social levels of group and universal authority, the affiliated relevant domain of the traditional groupings of virtues, values, and ideals rightfully enters the picture.

The upcoming Chapter 2 endeavors to provide the specific details for such a global ethical achievement, portraying the overall span of human culture as a ten-level ascending hierarchy of personal, group, universal, humanitarian, and transcendental classifications of authority/follower roles. Furthermore, this stepwise ascending authority/follower hierarchy formally invokes the systematic principles of Set Theory. Here, the elementary concepts of the one, the many, and

the absolute are specified in terms of the personal, the group, and the universal authority realms, respectively. Each of these distinctive conceptual levels is further associated with its own unique complement of ethical/motivational terms, extending (at the uppermost levels) to include the traditional listings of virtues and values relevant to a planetary system of ethics.

The subsequent Chapter 3 further addresses the related predicted goal of a strict behavioral foundation encompassing the principles of instrumental conditioning. This conceptual grounding within a purely secular (scientific) foundation fortuitously avoids offending the sensibilities of any particular world religion or culture in the process, wherein celebrating the commonalties embraced by all ethical traditions as a whole. Granted, the world's religions have enjoyed considerable long-term success in the promotion of a virtuous life-style, with origins considerably predating our modern technological age. For the vast majority of recorded history the existing complement of world religions have essentially co-existed more-or-less peacefully, although some degree of religious fanaticism has periodically instigated conflict amongst cultures. With the advent of our modern age of high technology, however, it would appear that mankind can no longer afford such a clash of cultures when extending to the realm of fanatical terrorism on a global scale. The newly proposed scientifically-based system of planetary ethics holds the greatest promise in this regard, and one with the potential to overcome the considerable threats to global peace and harmony.

The traditional realm of ethics and philosophy certainly plays a critical role in this respect, as reflected in the revered listings of virtues, values, and ideals. Indeed, the newly proposed science of Powerplay Politics provides the critical conceptual template for organizing this diverse range of motivational terms. This master ten-level hierarchy of authority/follower roles is correlated with a related complement of roughly one-thousand individual ethical terms including the major virtues and values, the vices of excess, the vices of defect, etc. Related applications include the lesser virtues, the realm of criminality and hypercriminality, as well as the communicational factors underlying mental illness. The traditional listings of virtues and values defined within this system all appear linked on an intuitive level, suggesting a clear sense of overall cohesiveness. When further contrasted with the related realm of the vices, the resultant master format expands to a grand total of *1,040* individual terms, the complete breakdown of which now will be described.

The key conceptual innovation arises as a direct outcome of the fledgling science of Communication Theory, borrowing the crucial concept of the metaperspective. It is defined as a higher-order perspective on the viewpoint held by another: schematically defined as "this is how I see you-seeing me." The higher-order groupings of virtues/values accumulate as subsets within this hierarchy of metaperspectives, each more abstract grouping building upon that which it supersedes. Take, for example, the cardinal virtues (prudence, justice, temperance, and fortitude), the theological virtues (faith-hope-charity-decency), and the classical Greek values (beauty-truth-goodness-wisdom). Each of these traditional groupings is further subdivided into four subordinate terms permitting precise point-for-point stacking within the hierarchy of metaperspectives. Additional listings of ethical terms can further be added to the mix: namely, the civil liberties (providence-liberty-civility-austerity), the humanistic values (peace-love-tranquility-equality), and the mystical values (ecstasy-bliss-joy-harmony). When taken in concert, the complete ten-level hierarchy of virtuous terms emerges in full detail, as partially reproduced in the compact table immediately below:

Nostalgia • Hero-Worship	Guilt • Blame
Glory • Prudence	Honor • Justice
Providence • Faith	Liberty • Hope
Grace • Beauty	Free-Will • Truth
Tranquility • Ecstasy	Equality • Bliss

Desire • Approval	Worry • Concern
Dignity • Temperance	Integrity • Fortitude
Civility • Charity	Austerity • Decency
Magnanim. • Goodness	Equanimity • Wisdom
Love • Joy	Peace • Harmony

This cohesive hierarchy of virtues, values, and ideals proves exceedingly comprehensive in scope, accounting for virtually every major term celebrated in the Western ethical tradition. It is particularly easy to gain a sense of the trend towards increasing abstraction when scanning the individual columns from top to bottom. The traditional sequences of terms line up seamlessly within this hierarchy of metaperspectives. Indeed, it proves exceedingly unlikely that this cohesive system could have arisen solely by chance. Furthermore, the ethical hierarchy mirrors the specialization of personal, group, spiritual, humanitarian, and transcendental realms within human society as a whole: which (when further specialized into authority/follower roles) accounts for the full ten-level span of ethical terms.

THE VICES OF DEFECT

Although a preferential emphasis on the virtues is certainly understandable, this virtuous mode can scarcely be considered solely in a vacuum. The truest applications for such a general ethical system derive precisely from a moral contrast with the related realm of the vices (where virtue and vice exist in concert with one another). Consequently, for every virtue there necessarily exists a corresponding antonym (or vice): namely, love vs. hate, peace vs. war, etc. The corresponding vices of defect represent the chief affective opposites of the respective virtuous counterparts, wherein providing an even sense of symmetry across the unified power hierarchy. The ten predicted categories for the vices of defect are arrayed in ten-level hierarchy similar to the pattern previously established for the virtuous mode.

Laziness • Treachery	Negligence • Vindictive.
Infamy • Insurgency	Dishonor • Vengeance
Prodigality • Betrayal	Slavery • Despair
Wrath • Ugliness	Tyranny • Hypocrisy
Anger • Abomination	Prejudice • Perdition

Apathy • Spite	Indifference • Malice
Foolishness • Gluttony	Caprice • Cowardice
Vulgarity • Avarice	Cruelty • Antagonism
Oppression • Evil	Persecution • Cunning
Hatred • Iniquity	Belligerence • Turpitude

This distinct ethical contrast allows negative transactions to be analyzed in terms of their potential for conversion into positive ones (and vice versa). The ten resultant categories of defect: such as the ecumenical vices (wrath, tyranny, persecution, and oppression), the moralistic vices (evil-cunning-ugliness-hypocrisy), and the humanistic vices (anger-hatred-prejudice-belligerence), etc., prove particularly significant for outlining this darker realm of the vices.

THE VICES OF EXCESS

The vices of defect, in turn, scarcely claim to be all-inclusive by any standard. Indeed, only half of the Seven Deadly Sins are formally accounted for in terms of the realm of defect. Here, pride, envy, and covetousness defy incorporation into the established realm of defect. This anomaly, in turn, is explained through aid of an additional class of the vices, known since ancient times as the vices of *excess*. In particular, Aristotle first described this dual system for the vice. The vices of defect (initially described) formally complement the respective vices of excess: defined as that range of extremes with respect to the virtues. Accordingly, Aristotle viewed the virtuous mode as a system of mean values (or norms) interposed between the vices of defect and vices of excess.

For instance, Aristotle cites the example of the virtue of courage. It represents the mean value interposed between the respective vice of defect (cowardice) and its excessive counterpart in foolhardiness. Virtue, accordingly, represents the middle-ground between defect and excess: wherein favoring moderation insofar as choosing a balance between this dual range of extremes. Indeed, it ultimately proves feasible to devise a parallel ten-level hierarchy for the realm of the vices of excess, mirroring point-for-point that previously established for the virtuous mode: although now extending to vanity, jealousy, shame, etc.

Pride • Flattery	Shame • Criticism
Vanity • Adulation	Humiliation • Ridicule
Conceit • Patronization	Mortification • Scorn
Pretention • Indulgence	Anguish • Mockery
Sanctimony • Sycophancy	Tribulation • Cynicism

Impudence • Envy	Insolence • Disdain
Arrogance • Jealousy	Audacity • Contempt
Impetuosity • Covetous.	Rashness • Reproach
Presumption • Longing	Boldness • Chagrin
Smugness • Affectation	Harshness • Bitterness

Curiously, the three-way specialization implied in Aristotle's Theory of the Mean fails to distinguish any parallel complement of extremes with respect to the vices of defect similar to that specified for the virtuous mode. This glaring lack of an even sense of symmetry is fortunately remedied through the introduction of an entirely new class

of affective terms: a terminology provisionally defined as the realm of *hyperviolence*. This new category is formally distinguished from the more routine realm of defect primarily in terms of the extremes by which it is expressed. Herein lies the formal prototype for the realm of hyperviolence; namely, that range of excess with respect to the vices of defect. The fact that Aristotle failed to distinguish this additional concept within his Theory of the Mean attests to the classical warrior ideal, where victory was to be achieved at any cost. The terminology for this extreme realm of hyperviolence scarcely enjoys the pedigree or tradition of the other listings of vices. Consequently, the respective listing of terms for the realm of hyperviolence is achieved through a prefix-style modification of the more basic realm of defect.

THE MASTER SCHEMATIC FORMAT LINKING VIRTUE AND VICE

In summary, through the formal additional of the realm of hyperviolence, a fully balanced symmetry finally becomes conceptually complete. Here, the four basic ethical categories: e.g., the virtues, vices of defect, vices of excess, and hyperviolence collectively account for the complete cross-section of emotionally charged language in general; as formally depicted in the master diagram immediately below:

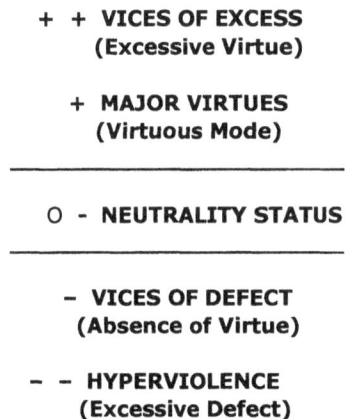

$$+ \ + \ \textbf{VICES OF EXCESS}$$
(Excessive Virtue)

$$+ \ \textbf{MAJOR VIRTUES}$$
(Virtuous Mode)

O - **NEUTRALITY STATUS**

$$- \ \textbf{VICES OF DEFECT}$$
(Absence of Virtue)

$$- \ - \ \textbf{HYPERVIOLENCE}$$
(Excessive Defect)

This schematic diagram is organized around the novel concept of "neutrality status," representing a neutral point of entry within the system (a default status from which all new relationships are formed). This neutral status is respectively defined as that benign sense of neglect we express towards strangers on the street: contacts that pose no meaningful sense of relationship, yet do not present any impending sense of harm.

Every new relationship (by definition) stems primarily from this zone of neutrality status, a potentiality that extends to the realm of the virtues, or alternately into the domain of defect. This ethical divergence is schematically depicted as the dual arrangement of terms immediately flanking the zone of neutrality. This pair of conflicting options represents an ethical "fork in the road," representing the basic core nucleus for the system. Most relationships are resolved through recourse to one option or the other (the basic thoroughfare for the system).

This dual interpretation can scarcely claim to be the total picture, for the parallel realm of excess lurks along the fringe boundaries of the core nucleus. For the virtuous realm, this corresponds to the related realm of the vices of excess. Furthermore, in terms of the vices of defect, this alternately targets the newly proposed realm of hyperviolence. These two extreme categories represent the figurative "fast lanes" of the relationship superhighway; namely, fringe areas exaggerated to the point of crossing over into the realm of excess. Fortunately, such forays into excess are typically somewhat limited. The enduring sense of stability within the social dynamic serves to lessen the unpredictable effects of such drastic mood swings.

THE TRANSITIONAL POWER MANEUVERS

The extended four-part hierarchy of virtue and vice, however, suffers one crucial shortcoming; namely, the respective authority/follower roles are fixed rigidly into place: allowing precious little flexibility to operate within the system. Versatility plays a key role in our modern mobile society, with continually shifting social coalitions placing ever-greater demands upon the individual. Each new adjustment within the social hierarchy calls for alternate mechanisms for integrating this new modification, an innovation that the established groupings of virtue/vice fail to take fully into account. In addition to the incremental pattern of maneuvering for power initially described, a more direct avenue, in turn, must exist for leapfrogging directly into the higher authority levels; e.g., the group, spiritual, and humanitarian levels, respectively. This further sequence of options is respectively termed the class of *transitional* power maneuvers, being that they "transition" the individual directly into new social contexts.

A number of key features distinguish this new class of transitional power maneuvers, whereby permitting a greater degree of versatility in terms of discrete transitional points across the entire ten-level span of the power hierarchy. These transitions represent direct motivational analogs of the main power maneuvers they serve to imitate. This often occurs in an exaggerated fashion in order to make the point more clearly. This flair for the dramatic can be either humorous (as in the realm of comedy), or tragic (as in the genre of melodrama). This strategy is the stock-in-trade for the standard "situation comedy," when the guest star intrudes upon the graces of the standard ensemble cast, typically with hilarious consequences. A similar pattern further holds true with respect to the more serious realm of melodrama, as particularly evident in the tradition of the daytime soap opera.

This transitional class of power maneuvers (as their name implies) refers to a relationship initiated for the first time. Here, the individual endeavors to establish a new transitional interaction within a pre-established social order. Indeed, the virtuous realm of humor/comedy is fully explained in terms of the dual transitional interplay of double-bind and counter double-bind maneuvers. Consequently, the distinctive classifications of *lesser* virtues represent transitional variations targeting the main virtuous realm. The pervasive human fascination with humor and comedy is fully explainable in terms of this versatile set of transitional power maneuvers, accounting for many of the lesser virtues (such as loyalty, responsibility, humility, etc.) not directly accounted for in terms of the major listings of virtues, values, and ideals.

Loyalty → Humility	Responsibility → Innocence
Fidelity → Majesty	Duty → Vindication
Piety → Magnificence	Allegiance → Exoneration
Felicity → Grandeur	Righteous. → Immaculate.

Discipline → Modesty	Vigilance → Meekness
Chivalry → Chastity	Courage → Obedience
Nobility → Purity	Valor → Conformity
Zeal → Perfection	Triumph → Pacifism

The comprehensive listing of lesser virtues depicted above actually represents just the most basic component within a much broader transitional format, a modification that formally expands upon the remaining categories specified within Aristotle's revised Theory of the Mean. This modification extends to the realms of criminality and hypercriminality as well as the communicational factors underlying mental illness. In concert with the initial class of lesser virtues, the four respective categories are depicted as the right-hand column of terms listed adjacent the major categories within the master diagram to follow.

```
+ +   VICES OF EXCESS      MENTAL ILLNESS
      (Excessive Virtue )   (Transitional Excess)

+     MAJOR VIRTUES        LESSER VIRTUES
      (Virtuous Mode)       (Transitional Virtue)
_____

0   ........   NEUTRALITY STATUS
_____

−     VICES OF DEFECT      CRIMINALITY
      (Absence of Virtue)   (Transitional Defect)

− −   HYPERVIOLENCE        HYPERCRIMINALITY
      (Excessive Defect)    (Transit. Hyperviolence)
```

In direct analogy to the main categories of terms, the transitional variations are similarly organized around the centralized zone of neutrality, wherein serving as direct transitional entry-points in relation to the major categories. The classifications of the lesser virtues are depicted immediately adjacent to the major virtuous realm. Similarly, the theme of criminality is depicted in concert with the respective vices of defect. Furthermore, in terms of the realm of excess, the theme of hypercriminality represents the transitional variation of hyperviolence, whereas the domain of mental illness, in turn, targets the vices of excess. The respective listings of individual terms, in turn, are depicted in the master schematic diagram comprising **Fig. 1A** (beginning overleaf).

The individual terminology for criminality and hypercriminality is fairly straightforward in terms of function: representing formal transitional variations with respect to the darker realm of defect. Criminality represents the ingrained tendency to initiate a relationship in a selfish or violent fashion, a contention echoed by many a criminologist. Consequently, a more detailed analysis of the terminology for both criminality/hypercriminality clearly remains beyond the scope of this introductory chapter, although a more comprehensive analysis is deferred until **Part VI**.

For sake of completeness, however, final reference must necessarily be made to the remaining transitional domain of mental illness. Here, mental illness is defined as that formal transitional sequence of double bind and counter double bind maneuvers targeting the realm of the vices of excess. Accordingly, each of the major classifications of the mental disorders (e.g., the personality disorders, neuroses, mood disorders, and schizophrenia) is fully explained in terms of the transitional model of mental illness predicted

in terms of the principles of Communications Theory. In keeping with its transitional relationship to the vices of excess (which are formally divorced from the domain of defect), mental illness appears fairly non-threatening in nature: as reflected in studies confirming the non-violent nature of the mentally ill in relation to the general population. This interpretation proves particularly insightful in terms the bizarre symptomology associated with the psychoses, a category of mental illness reflecting the extreme degree of disqualification characterizing the counter double-bind class of maneuvers. Indeed, the compact table listed below schematically depicts this dual interplay across the entire span of the psychoses, in addition to the personality disorders and forms of neurosis. This was chiefly permitted in terms of the preexisting system of terminology for the psychoses pioneered by German clinician, Karl Leonhard, as well as the nomenclature for the personality disorders and the neuroses contained in the *DSM–IV*.

Narcissistic Personality → Obsession Neurosis
Confabulatory Euphoria → Confab. Paraphrenia
Enthusiastic Euphoria → Proskinetic Catatonia
Non-Participatory Euphoria → Silly Hebephrenia

Borderline Personality → Phobia Neurosis
Suspicious Depression → Fantastic Paraphrenia
Self-Torturing Depression → Negativistic Cataton.
Non-Participatory Depression → Insipid Hebephr.

Dependent Personality → Compulsion Neurosis
Pure Mania → Expansive Paraphrenia
Unproductive Euphoria → Parakinetic Catatonia
Hypochondriacal Euphoria → Eccentric Hebephr.

Avoidant Personality → Anxiety Neurosis
Pure Melancholy → Incoherent Paraphrenia
Harried Depression → Affected Catatonia
Hypochondriacal Depression→ Autistic Hebeph.

This cohesive *32*-part complement of the mental disorders offers a preliminary overview of the transitional model of mental illness. It should further be noted that this dual model of the mental disorders essentially explains only the content/context of what is being communicated; namely, the transitional interplay of power maneuvers with respect to the vices of excess. Consequently, this newly proposed system is primarily meant to complement currently available treatment therapies (rather than supplanting them): wherefore aiding in the treatment and diagnosis of the mental disorders.

+ + VICES of EXCESS
(Excessive Virtue)

Pride - Flattery	Shame - Criticism
Vanity - Adulation	Humiliation - Ridicule
Conceit - Patronization	Mortification - Scorn
Pretention - Obsequious	Anguish - Mockery
Sanctimony - Sycophancy	Tribulat.- Cynicism
Impudence - Envy	Insolence - Disdain
Arrogance - Jealousy	Audacity - Contempt
Impetuosity - Covetous.	Rashness - Reproach
Presumption - Longing	Boldness - Chagrin
Smugness - Affectation	Harshness - Bitterness

+ MAJOR VIRTUES
(Virtuous Mode)

Nostalgia - Hero Worship	Guilt - Blame
Glory - Prudence	Honor - Justice
Providence - Faith	Liberty - Hope
Grace - Beauty	Free-will - Truth
Tranquility - Ecstasy	Equality - Bliss
Desire - Approval	Worry - Concern
Dignity - Temperance	Integrity - Fortitude
Civility - Charity	Austerity - Decency
Magnanim.- Goodness	Equan.- Wisdom
Love - Joy	Peace - Harmony

MENTAL ILLNESS – (B)
(Transitional Excess → Disqualified Excess)

Histrionic Personality → Dissociative Hysteria
Happiness Psychosis → Confabulatory A/L Paraphr.
Excited Confusion Psychosis → Excited Cataphasia

Paranoid Personality → Depersonalization Neurosis
Anxiety Psychosis → Fantastic A/L Paraphrenia
Inhibited Confusion Psych. → Inhibited Cataphasia

Passive/Aggressive Personal. → Conversion Hyster.
Manic/Depress. Disease → Manic A/L Paraphrenia
Hyperkin. Motility Psych.→Hyperkin. Periodic Cata.

Schizoid Personality → Neuraesthenic Neurosis
Manic/Depressive Disease → Confused A/L Paraphr.
Akinetic Motility Psychosis→ Akinetic Periodic Cata.

MENTAL ILLNESS – (A)
(Transitional Excess → Disqualified Excess)

Narcissistic Personality → Obsession Neurosis
Confabulatory Euphoria → Confab. Paraphrenia
Enthusiastic Euphoria → Proskinetic Catatonia
Non-Participatory Euphoria → Silly Hebephrenia
Borderline Personality → Phobia Neurosis
Suspicious Depression → Fantastic Paraphrenia
Self-Torturing Depression → Negativistic Catatonia
Non-Particip. Depression → Insipid Hebephrenia
Dependent Personality → Compulsion Neurosis
Pure Mania → Expansive Paraphrenia
Unproductive Euphoria → Parakinetic Catatonia
Hypochondriacal Euphoria → Eccentric Hebephren.
Avoidant Personality → Anxiety Neurosis
Pure Melancholy → Incoherent Paraphrenia
Harried Depression → Affected Catatonia
Hypochondriacal Depression → Autistic Hebephren.

LESSER VIRTUES (I)
(Transitional Virtue → Disqualified Virtue)

Loyalty → Humility	Responsibil. → Innocence
Fidelity → Majesty	Duty → Vindication
Piety→ Magnific.	Allegiance → Exoneration
Felicity → Grandeur	Righteous.→ Immaculat
Discipline → Modesty	Vigilance → Meekness
Chivalry → Chastity	Courage → Obedience
Nobility → Purity	Valor → Conformity
Zeal → Perfection	Triumph → Pacifism

LESSER VIRTUES (II)
(Transitional Virtue → Disqualified Virtue)

Self-Esteem → Reverence	Apology→ Clemency
Pomp → Veneration	Rectitude → Pardon
Sanctity → Homage	Penitence → Absolution
Dominion → Benediction	Contrition → Deliver.
Congeniality→Concess.	Appease.→Sympathy
Cordiality→Indulgence	Conciliate→Compass.
Hospitality→Gratitude	Accommodat→Mercy
Altruism → Goodwill	Sacrifice → Forgiveness

— VICES of DEFECT (Absence of Virtue)

Laziness - Treachery   Negligence - Vindictive.
Infamy - Insurgency   Dishonor - Vengeance
Prodigal - Betrayal   Slavery - Despair
Wrath - Ugliness   Tyranny - Hypocrisy
Anger - Abomination   Prejudice - Perdition

Apathy - Spite   Indifference - Malice
Foolishness - Gluttony   Caprice - Cowardice
Vulgarity - Avarice   Cruelty - Antagonism
Oppression - Evil   Persecution - Cunning
Hatred - Iniquity   Belligerence - Turpitude

CRIMINALITY (I) (Transitional Defect → Disqualified Defect)

t-Treachery → d-Laziness   t-Vindict. → d-Neglig.
t-Insurgency → d-Infamy   t-Vengeance → d-Dishon.
t-Betrayal → d-Prodigality   t-Despair → d-Slavery
t-Ugliness → d-Wrath   t-Hypocrisy → d-Tyranny

t-Spite → d-Apathy   t-Malice → d-Indifference
t-Gluttony → d-Foolish.   t-Cowardice → d-Caprice
t-Avarice → d-Vulgarity   t-Antagonism → d-Cruelty
t-Evil → d-Oppression   t-Cunning → d-Persecution

CRIMINALITY (II) (Transitional Defect → Disqualified Defect)

t-Laziness → d-Treachery   t-Negligence → d-Vindict.
t-Infamy → d-Insurgency   t-Dishon. → d-Vengeance
t-Prodigal → d-Betrayal   t-Slavery → d-Despair
t-Wrath → d-Ugliness   t-Tyranny → d-Hypocrisy

t-Apathy → d-Spite   t-Indifference → d-Malice
t-Foolish. → d-Gluttony   t-Caprice → d-Cowardice
t-Vulgarity → d-Avarice   t-Cruelty → d-Antag.
t-Oppression → d-Evil   t-Persecution → d-Cunning

— — HYPERVIOLENCE (Excessive Defect)

Indolence - Mutiny   Dereliction - Reprisal
Notoriety - Rebellion   Ignobility - Retribution
Licentious.- Treason   Savagery - Hopelessness
Fury - Hideousness   Despotism - Mendacity
Madness - Horror   Bigotry - Ruin

Languor - Grudging.   Callousness - Malignancy
Crassness - Voracity   Petulance - Cravenness
Rudeness - Greed   Hostility - Contentious.
Brutality - Heinous.   Barbarism - Ruthlessness
Vicious.- Balefulness   Atrocity - Fiendishness

HYPERCRIMINALITY (I) (Transitional Hyperviol. → Disqualified Hyperviol.)

t-Mutiny → d-Indolence
t-Rebellion → d-Notoriety
t-Treason → d-Licentiousness
t-Hideousness → d-Fury
t-Reprisal → d-Dereliction
t-Retribution → d-Ignobility
t-Hopelessness → d-Savagery
t-Mendacity → d-Despotism
t-Grudgingness → d-Languor
t-Voracity → d-Crassness
t-Greed → d-Rudeness
t-Heinousness → d-Brutality
t-Malignancy → d-Callousness
t-Cravenness → d-Petulance
t-Contentiousness → d-Hostility
t-Ruthlessness → d-Barbarism

HYPERCRIMINALITY (II) (Transitional Hyperviol. → Disqualified Hyperviol.)

t-Indolence → d-Mutiny
t-Notoriety → d-Rebellion
t-Licentiousness → d-Treason
t-Fury → d-Hideousness
t-Dereliction → d-Reprisal
t-Ignobility → d-Retribution
t-Savagery → d-Hopelessness
t-Despotism → d-Mendacity
t-Languor → d-Grudgingness
t-Crassness → d-Voracity
t-Rudeness → d-Greed
t-Brutality → d-Heinousness
t-Callousness → d-Malignancy
t-Petulance → d-Cravenness
t-Hostility → d-Contentiousness
t-Barbarism → d-Ruthlessness

Fig. 1A – Master Schematic Diagram Depicting the *408* Main Individual Terms

+ + ACC. VICES of EXCESS
(Excessive Accessory Virtue)

Narcissism - Blandish.   Ignominy - Reprehens.
Snobbery - Courtliness   Opprobrium - Denunci.
Vainglory - Condesc.   Despondency - Derision
Haughtiness - Servility   Agony - Sarcasm
Pietism - Subservience   Affliction - Satiricism

Impertinence - Invideous. Hubris - Despisal
Brazenness - Possessive.   Surliness - Repugn.
Brashness - Cravingness   Irascibility - Rebuke
Effrontery - Yearning   Temerity - Loathing
Gleefulness - Pretension   Rigor- Admonish.

ACC. MENTAL ILLNESS - (B)
(Transitional Acc. Excess → Disqualified Acc. Excess)

Histrionic Personality → Dissociative Hysteria
Happiness Psychosis → Confabulatory A/L Paraphr.
Excited Confusion Psychosis → Excited Cataphasia

Paranoid Personality → Depersonalization Neurosis
Anxiety Psychosis → Fantastic A/L Paraphrenia
Inhibited Confusion Psych. → Inhibited Cataphasia

Passive/Aggressive Personal. → Conversion Hyster.
Manic/Depress. Disease → Manic A/L Paraphrenia
Hyperkin. Motility Psych. → Hyperkin. Periodic Cata.

Schizoid Personality → Neuraesthenic Neurosis
Manic/Depressive Disease → Confused A/L Paraphr.
Akinetic Motility Psychosis→ Akinetic Periodic Cata.

ACC. MENTAL ILLNESS - (A)
(Transitional Acc. Excess → Disqualified Acc. Excess)

Narcissistic Personality → Obsession Neurosis
Confabulatory Euphoria → Confab. Paraphrenia
Enthusiastic Euphoria → Proskinetic Catatonia
Non-Participatory Euphoria → Silly Hebephrenia
Borderline Personality → Phobia Neurosis
Suspicious Depression → Fantastic Paraphrenia
Self-Torturing Depression → Negativistic Catatonia
Non-Particip. Depression → Insipid Hebephrenia
Dependent Personality → Compulsion Neurosis
Pure Mania → Expansive Paraphrenia
Unproductive Euphoria → Parakinetic Catatonia
Hypochondriacal Euphoria → Eccentric Hebephren.
Avoidant Personality → Anxiety Neurosis
Pure Melancholy → Incoherent Paraphrenia
Harried Depression → Affected Catatonia
Hypochondriacal Depression → Autistic Hebephren.

+ ACC. MAJOR VIRTUES
(Accessory Virtuous Mode)

Poignancy - Praise   Culpability - Censure
Exalt. - Circumspect. Uprightness - Equity
Bountiful. - Devotion Freedom - Fairness
Blessings - Charm   Conscience - Credence
Serenity - Rapture   Brotherhood - Content.

Passion - Admiration Apprehens. - Caring
Respect - Continence   Probity - Bravery
Courtesy - Kindness   Forbear. - Scruples
Gracious. - Benevol.   Patience - Shrewd.
Affection - Gladness   Amity - Accordance

ACC. LESSER VIRTUES (I)
(Transitional Acc. Virtue → Disqualified Acc. Virtue)

Fealty → Simplicity   Account. → Blameless.
Steadfast. → Loftiness Obligation→ Exculp.
Adoration → Sublimity   Obeisence → Aquittal
Happiness → Splendor   Commit. → Impeccabil.

Adherence → Demure.   Wariness → Timidity
Gallantry → Coyness   Intrepidity → Complais.
Stateliness → Wholesome. Stalwart. → Compli.
Fervor → Excellence   Victory → Amicableness

ACC. LESSER VIRTUES (II)
(Transitional Acc. Virtue → Disqualified Acc. Virtue)

Self-Respect → Esteem   Sorrow → Lenity
Ostentation → Acclaim   Remorse → Remittance
Holiness → Ardor   Regretful.→ Dispensation
Supremacy → Exultation   Grief → Redemption

Amiability → Favor   Placation → Empathy
Conviviality → Sanction   Concord. → Commiser.
Generosity → Thanksgiving   Consonance → Pity
Beneficence → Benignity   Propitiation → Remiss.

ACC. VICES of DEFECT
(Absence of Accessory Virtue)

Sloth - Traitorousness   Careless. - Retaliation
Disrepute - Sedition   Reprehension - Avengement
Profligacy - Perfidy   Bondage - Desperation
Indignation - Revulsion   Subjugate - Duplicity
Irateness - Abhorrence   Intolerance - Baneful.

Dispassion. - Resentment   Arbitrary- Malevolent
Preposterous. -Lechery   Fickleness- Pusillan.
Coarseness - Cupidity   Acrimony - Opposition
Animosity - Wickedness   Torment - Guilefulness
Enmity - Sinisterity   Militancy - Baseness

ACC. CRIMINALITY (I)
(Transitional Acc. Defect → Acc. Disqualified Defect)

t-traitor. →d-sloth   t-retaliation →d-careless.
t-sedition →d-disrepute   t-avenge. →d- reprehen
t-perfidy →d-profligacy   t-desper.→ d-bondage
t-revulsion→d-indign.   t-duplicity→ d-subjug.

t-resent. → d-dispassion   t-malev. → d-arbitrary
t-lechery → d-preposter.   t-pusillan. →d-fickle.
t-cupidity → d-coarse.   t-opposit. → d-acrimony
t-wicked.→ d-animosity   t-guileful. → d-torment

ACC. CRIMINALITY (II)
(Transitional Acc. Defect → Disqualified Acc. Defect)

t-sloth→ d-traitor.   t-careless. →d-retaliation
t-disrepute →d-sedition   t-reprehen. → d-avenge.
t-profligacy → d-perfidy   t- bondage→d-desper.
t-indign.→d-revulsion   t- subjug.→ d-duplicity

t-dispassion →d-resent.   t-arbitrary→ d-malev.
t-preposter. →d-lechery   t-fickle → d-pusillan.
t-coarse. → d-cupidity   t-acrimony → d-oppos.
t-animosity → d-wicked.   t-torment→ d-guileful.

ACC. HYPERVIOLENCE
(Excessive Accessory Defect)

Sluggish. - Untrustworthy   Laxity - Requital
Odium - Rebellion   Disgraceful. - Revenge
Debauchery - Disloyalty   Servitude - Grievous.
Outrage - Nastiness   Imperious. - Deceitful.
Enragement - Grotesque.   Discrim. - Damnation

Lethargy - Umbrage   Nonchalance - Peevish.
Absurdity - Ravenous.   Willfulness - Dastard.
Lewdness - Rapacious.   Rancor - Vexation
Discord - Badness   Ferocity - Deviousness.
Meanness - Nefarity   Truculency -Insideous.

ACC. HYPERCRIMINALITY (I)
(Transitional A-Hyperviol. → Disqualified A-Hyperviol.)

t-untrustworthy → d-sluggishness
t-rebellion → d-odium
t-disloyalty→ d-debauchery
t-nastiness→ d- outrage
t-requital→ d-laxity
t-revenge→ d-disgracefulness
t-grievousness→ d-servitude
t-deceitfulness→ d-imperiousness
t-umbrage → d-lethargy
t-ravenousness→ d-absurdity
t-rapaciousness→ d-lewdness
t-badness→ d-discord
t-peevishness→ d-nonchalance
t-dastardliness→ d-willfulness
t-vexation→ d-rancor
t-deviousness→ d-ferocity

ACC. HYPERCRIMINALITY (II)
(Transitional A-Hyperviol. → Disqualified A-Hypervoil.)

t- sluggishness→ d-untrustworthy
t-odium → d-rebellion
t-debauchery→ d-disloyalty
t-outrage→ d-nastiness
t-laxity→ d-requital
t-disgracefulness→ d-revenge
t-servitude→ d-grievousness
t-imperiousness→ d-deceitfulness
t-lethargy → d-umbrage
t-absurdity→ d-ravenousness
t-lewdness→ d-rapaciousness
t- discord→ d-badness
t-nonchalance → d-peevishness
t-willfulness→ d-dastardliness
t- rancor→ d-vexation
t-ferocity→ d-deviousness

Fig. 1B – Master Schematic Diagram Depicting the *408 Accessory Individual Terms*

THE THREE-DIGIT CODING SYSTEM

In summary, the newly proposed grand-unified system of affective categories represents an unprecedented contribution to the field of ethical inquiry, extending Aristotle's enduring *Theory of the Mean* into an all-inclusive theory of "everything" of an emotional nature. At the risk of appearing overly simplistic, each of these individual master categories is further subdivided into multiple groupings of individual terms. For instance, the major virtues are subdivided into *100* individual terms, whereas the lesser virtues are further split into *128* distinct terms. When the six remaining affective categories are further added into the mix, the grand total expands to an astonishing *1,040* individual terms.

With this all-encompassing ethical system firmly in place, it further proves crucial to devise a general system of numerical classification for distinguishing these emotions. The highly cohesive nature of the *1,040* individual terms permits an orderly style of three-digit coding system similar to that previously established for the *ICD-10* and (its offshoot) the *DSM*-series. In order to take full advantage of the ten-level span of the power hierarchy, this new decimal numbering system must necessarily remain at variance with its predecessors, rather functioning as an adjunct to these various systems. The current three-digit numbering system is organized as a three-stage process of progressive exclusion, where each successive digit progressively narrows the field so that a single term (from the initial field of *1040*) is ultimately specified.

The first digit within the numerical sequence proceeds to specify the eight individual master categories; namely, the major virtues, lesser virtues, vices of excess, etc. For instance, the major virtues are assigned the initial first-place digit of "1", enjoying a primary place of honor within the three-digit coding system. Furthermore, the lesser virtues are indicated by numbers beginning with "2," whereas the vices of excess and mental illness are specified by digits "3" and "4," respectively. The remaining numbers "5" through "8," in turn, shift the focus to the more negative aspects of the power hierarchy. Here, the vices of defect = 5, criminality = 6, hyperviolence = 7, and hypercriminality = 8. The remaining digits "9" and "0" leave ample room for further expansions to the three-digit coding system.

With the assignment of the first-digit formally accomplished, the second digit within the coding system further narrows the scope; in turn, specifying the ten individual levels within the power hierarchy. According to this numerical format, 1 = personal authority, 2 = personal follower, 3 = group authority, 4 = group representative, etc. Continuing to the uppermost end of the scale, 9 = transcendental authority, whereas the 10-spot represents the transcendental follower role (represented by zero as the second place digit). Indeed, reserving the zero for the upper end of the sequence permits a tidier pattern of organization. Here, the first level within the power hierarchy corresponds to a "one" in the 2nd-digit spot, allowing for less confusion in identifying the respective ascending levels. Furthermore, the uppermost levels are rarely an issue during most practical applications, making the "zero-spot" most effective at this terminal position.

With the initial two digits now formally defined, the remaining third-place digit now completes the coding system. For instance, should the first-place digit be a "1" (the major virtues), and the second digit is a "4" (for group representative), then the range of possibilities is respectively narrowed down to the single category of the cardinal virtues (prudence, justice, temperance, and fortitude). Indeed, each of the major listings of virtues, values, and ideals can further be specified in terms of such a two-digit combination. In order to specify each of the individual terms, the third digit is necessarily called into play. In terms of the ongoing example of the cardinal virtues, 140 = prudence, 141 = justice, 142 = temperance, and 143 = fortitude. Digits 4 through 7 in the three-slot, in turn, specify the *accessory* versions of the cardinal virtues, an aspect more adequately described in Chapter *8* of the current section. Here, 144 = circumspection, 145 = equitableness, 146 = continence, and 147 = bravery. The remaining third-place digits of 8 and 9 are alternately reserved for specifying the related class of general unifying themes. In terms of this example, these are identified as the main theme of the utilitarianism, as well as the accessory theme of practicality.

THE TRANSITIONAL POWER MANEUVERS

In summary, the three-digit coding system, when extended to the eight basic categories within the power hierarchy ultimately accounts for a grand total of *1,040* individual terms. Through a three-stage process of specification, the identity of any of the individual terms can be deduced solely in terms of its three-digit code. As is so often the case, however, an exception to the three-digit system necessarily exists; namely, that which applies to the *transitional* class of power maneuvers.

This latter set of categories is identified in terms of the use of *even* first place digits; e.g., 2 = the lesser virtues, 4 = mental illness, 6 = criminality, and 8 = hypercriminality. The initial class of transitional power maneuvers is actually completely explainable in terms of the requisite three-digit coding format. For instance, loyalty is coded as 220, responsibility is specified as 221, discipline = 222, etc.

The similar pattern, however, fails to hold true for the remaining counter double bind class of maneuvers. For instance, for the realm of the lesser virtues, the initial loyalty maneuver of the personal follower, in turn, is countered by the humility expressed by the personal authority. Furthermore, the related quest for responsibility is further countered by the disqualified sense of innocence expressed by the personal authority figure, etc. This remaining class of counter double bind maneuvers is necessarily distinguished through the aid of an additional decimal place. For instance, humility is specified as 210.1, whereas innocence is designated as 211.1, etc. The precise details for specifying this extra decimal place appear somewhat specialized in nature; hence, a topic more fittingly reserved for later sections of the book.

In summary, the current introductory chapter aimed to provide a general overview of the entire three-digit coding system. The following four pages of precise terminology offer a preliminary indication of the three-digit coding format, although the more minor categories 4, 6, 7, and 8 have deliberately been left out: deferred for subsequent treatment in their respective chapters. The discerning reader is encouraged to refer back to this extensive listing of terms (for easy reference) throughout the remainder of this book.

A further crucial innovation unique to the current revised edition invokes a radical expansion of the notion of the *accessory* perspectives of the general motivational themes. The inherent versatility of the human mind (by definition) allows for a subjective reflection on the objective perspectives of another, allowing crucial insights into affiliated feelings/motivations, an aspect traditionally known as *empathy*. This unique ability to attribute mental states to others is a key factor in what truly makes us human, an aspect that developmental psychologists refer to as *Theory of Mind*. This innate facility towards empathy depends primarily upon our ability to run cognitive simulations, whereby inferring the intentions and motivations of others by employing one's own mind as a conceptual template for that of others. This necessarily entails placing oneself in the role of another and further observing how one's mind resonates within such a mutually overlapping context. This reflective style of role reversal, in turn, specifies the existence of an entire parallel complement of ethical terms suitable for designating this dual degree of versatility. Indeed, the English language is richly blessed with a broad number of synonyms conducive to outlining this parallel complement of accessory terms.

A complete listing of accessory terms is depicted in **Fig. 1B**, a two-page layout immediately following the main complement of terms depicted in **Fig. 1A**. For instance, for the personal realm, the proposed accessory class of ego states (poignancy-culpability-passion-apprehension) is effectively complemented by the main virtuous listings of nostalgia-guilt-desire-worry. Furthermore, the accessory alter ego states of adoration-censure-admiration-caring) similarly reciprocate the respective main listings of terms (hero/worship-blame-approval-concern). This reciprocal interplay of both the main and accessory themes collectively permits a convincing simulation of empathic language in general, whereby the objective/subjective polarities are reversed through an inversion of the interplay of "you" and "I" roles. This key dual-directed dynamic for affective language provides crucial inroads towards an empathic model of human cooperation on an international scale of influence, promising fresh new insights into maintaining global peace and harmony.

A GENERAL OVERVIEW FOR *CHALLENGES TO WORLD PEACE*

In accordance with the considerable degree of detail ascribed to the three-digit coding system, the remaining sequence of chapters is divided into eight major sub-headings. The remainder of the current section is devoted entirely to the virtuous realm; in particular, the major groupings of virtues, values, and ideals representing the cardinal virtues, theological virtues, classical Greek values, etc. This initial **Part I** is further subdivided into nine separate chapters reflecting the personal, group, spiritual, humanitarian, and transcendental levels within the power hierarchy: defined in terms of code numbers spanning 100 to 199. In terms of **Part II**, Aristotle's enduring classifications of the vices of defect are alternately described, previously defined as the formal absence of virtue. This section further comprises six individual chapters (*10* through *15*), wherein reflecting the respective levels within the hierarchy of defect: defined in terms of code numbers 500 through 599.

THE MAJOR VIRTUES (100 – 199)

110 – Nostalgia	144 – Circumspection	178 – Ecumenism
111 – Guilt	145 – Equitableness	179 – Evangelism
112 – Desire	146 – Continence	180 – Beauty
113 – Worry	147 – Bravery	181 – Truth
114 – Poignance	148 – Utilitarianism	182 – Goodness
115 – Culpability	149 – Practicality	183 – Wisdom
116 – Passion	150 – Providence	184 – Charm
117 – Apprehension	151 – Liberty	185 – Credence
118 – Individualism	152 – Civility	186 – Benevolence
119 – Quintessentialism	153 – Austerity	187 – Shrewdness
120 – Hero-worship	154 – Bountifulness	188 – Eclecticism
121 – Blame	155 – Freedom	189 – Moralism
122 – Approval	156 – Courtesy	190 – Tranquility
123 – Concern	157 – Forbearance	191 – Equality
124 – Praise	158 – Romanticism	192 – Love
125 – Censure	159 – Charisma	193 – Peace
126 – Admiration	160 – Faith	194 – Serenity
127 – Caring	161 – Hope	195 – Brotherhood
128 – Pragmatism	162 – Charity	196 – Affection
129 – Expediency	163 – Decency	197 – Amity
130 – Glory	164 – Devotion	198 – Humanism
131 – Honor	165 – Fairness	199 – Cosmopolitanism
132 – Dignity	166 – Kindness	100 – Ecstasy
133 – Integrity	167 – Scrupulousness	101 – Bliss
134 – Exaltation	168 – Ecclesiasticism	102 – Joy
135 – Uprightness	169 – Orthodoxy	103 – Harmony
136 – Respectfulness	170 – Grace	104 – Rapture
137 – Probity	171 – Free-will	105 – Contentment
138 – Personalism	172 – Magnanimity	106 – Gladness
139 – Heroism	173 – Equanimity	107 – Accordance
140 – Prudence	174 – Blessings	108 – Mysticism
141 – Justice	175 – Conscientious.	109 – Spiritualism
142 – Temperance	176 – Graciousness	
143 – Fortitude	177 – Patience	

THE LESSER VIRTUES (200 – 299)

210 – Self-Esteem
210.1 – Humility
211 – Apology
211.1 – Innocence
212 – Congeniality
212.1 – Modesty
213 – Appeasement
213.1 – Meekness
214 – Self-Respect
214.1 – Simplicity
215 – Sorrow
215.1 – Blamelessness
216 – Amiability
216.1 – Demureness
217 – Placation
217.1 – Timidity
220 – Loyalty
220.1 – Reverence
221 – Responsibility
221.1 – Clemency
222 – Discipline
222.1 – Concession
223 – Vigilance
223.1 – Sympathy
224 – Fealty
224.1 – Esteem
225 – Accountability
225.1 – Lenity
226 – Adherence
226.1 – Favor
227 – Wariness
227.1 – Empathy
230 – Pomp
230.1 – Majesty
231 – Rectitude
231.1 – Vindication
232 – Cordiality
232.1 – Chastity
233 – Conciliation
233.1 – Obedience
234 – Ostentation
234.1 – Loftiness
235 – Remorse

235.1 – Exculpation
236 – Conviviality
236.1 – Coyness
237 – Concordance
237.1 – Complaisance
240 – Fidelity
240.1 – Veneration
241 – Duty
241.1 – Pardon
242 – Chivalry
242.1 – Indulgence
243 – Courage
243.1 – Compassion
244 – Steadfastness
244.1 – Acclaim
245 – Obligation
245.1 – Remittance
246 – Gallantry
246.1 – Sanction
247 – Intrepidity
247.1 – Commiseration
250 – Sanctity
250.1 – Magnificence
251 – Penitence
251.1 – Exoneration
252 – Hospitality
252.1 – Purity
253 – Accommodation
253.1 – Conformity
254 – Holiness
254.1 – Sublimeness
255 – Regretfulness
255.1 – Aquittal
256 – Generosity
256.1 – Wholesomeness
257 – Consonance
257.1 – Compliance
260 – Piety
260.1 – Homage
261 – Allegiance
261.1 – Absolution
262 – Nobility
262.1 – Gratitude

263 – Valor
263.1 – Mercy
264 – Adoration
264.1 – Ardor
265 – Obeisance
265.1 – Dispensation
266 – Stateliness
266.1 – Thanksgiving
267 – Stalwartness
267.1 – Pity
270 – Dominion
270.1 – Grandeur
271 – Contrition
271.1 – Immaculate.
272 – Altruism
272.1 – Perfection
273 – Sacrifice
273.1 – Pacifism
274 – Supremacy
274.1 – Splendor
275 – Grief
275.1 – Impeccability.
276 – Beneficence
276.1 – Excellence
277 – Propitiation
277.1 – Amicableness
280 – Felicity
280.1 – Benediction
281 – Righteousness
281.1 – Deliverance
282 – Zeal
282.1 – Goodwill
283 – Triumph
283.1 – Forgiveness
284 – Happiness
284.1 – Exultation
285 – Commitment
285.1 – Redemption
286 – Fervor
286.1 – Benignity
287 – Victory
287.1 – Remission

THE VICES OF EXCESS (300 – 399)

310 – Pride	344 – Courtliness	378 – Fanaticism
311 – Shame	345 – Denunciation	379 – Fundamentalism
312 – Impudence	346 – Possessiveness	380 – Obsequiousness
313 – Insolence	347 – Repugnance	381 – Mockery
314 – Narcissism	348 – Authoritarianism	382 – Longing
315 – Ignominy	349 – Absolutism	383 – Chagrin
316 – Impertinence	350 – Conceit	384 – Servility
317 – Hubris	351 – Mortification	385 – Sarcasm
318 – Egotism	352 – Impetuosity	386 – Yearning
319 – Egocentrism	353 – Rashness	387 – Loathing
320 – Flattery	354 – Vainglory	388 – Idealism
321 – Criticism	355 – Despondency	389 – Supremacism
322 – Envy	356 – Brashness	390 – Sanctimony
323 – Disdain	357 – Irascibility	391 – Tribulation
324 – Blandishment	358 – Ideology	392 – Smugness
325 – Reprehensibleness	359 – Pontification	393 – Harshness
326 – Invidiousness	360 – Patronization	394 – Pietism
327 – Despisal	361 – Scorn	395 – Affliction
328 – Officiousness	362 – Covetous	396 – Gleefulness
329 – Obtrusiveness	363 – Reproach	397 – Rigorousness
330 – Vanity	364 – Condescension	398 – Triumphalism
331 – Humiliation	365 – Derision	399 – Universalism
332 – Arrogance	366 – Cravingness	300 – Sycophancy
333 – Audacity	367 – Rebuke	301 – Cynicism
334 – Snobbery	368 – Clericalism	302 – Affectation
335 – Opprobrium	369 – Dogmatism	303 – Bitterness
336 – Brazenness	370 – Pretentiousness	304 – Subservience
337 – Surliness	371 – Anguish	305 – Satiricism
338 – Elitism	372 – Presumption	306 – Pretension
339 – Autocracy	373 – Boldness	307 – Admonishment
340 – Adulation	374 – Haughtiness	308 – Occultism
341 – Ridicule	375 – Agony	309 – Enigmatism
342 – Jealousy	376 – Effrontery	
343 – Contempt	377 – Temerity	

THE VICES OF DEFECT (500 – 599)

510 – Laziness	544 – Sedition	578 – Apostasy
511 – Negligence	545 – Avengement	579 – Infidelity
512 – Apathy	546 – Lechery	580 – Ugliness
513 – Indifference	547 – Pusillanimity	581 – Hypocrisy
514 – Slothfulness	548 – Corruption	582 – Evil
515 – Carelessness	549 – Venality	583 – Cunning
516 – Dispassion	550 – Prodigality	584 – Revulsion
517 – Arbitrariness	551 – Slavery	585 – Duplicity
518 – Knavery	552 – Vulgarity	586 – Wickedness
519 – Mischievousness	553 – Cruelty	587 – Guilefulness
520 – Treachery	554 – Profligacy	588 – Anarchism
521 – Vindictiveness	555 – Bondage	589 – Lawlessness
522 – Spite	556 – Coarseness	590 – Anger
523 – Malice	557 – Acrimony	591 – Prejudice
524 – Traitorousness	558 – Profanity	592 – Hatred
525 – Retaliation	559 – Scandalousness	593 – Belligerence
526 – Resentment	560 – Betrayal	594 – Irateness
527 – Malevolence	561 – Despair	595 – Intolerance
528 – Fraud	562 – Avarice	596 – Enmity
529 – Deception	563 – Antagonism	597 – Militancy
530 – Infamy	564 – Perfidy	598 – Nihilism
531 – Dishonor	565 – Desperation	599 – Alienation
532 – Foolishness	566 – Cupidity	500 – Abomination
533 – Capriciousness	567 – Opposition	501 – Perdition
534 – Disrepute	568 – Heresy	502 – Iniquity
535 – Reprehension	569 – Schismatism	503 – Turpitude
536 – Preposterousness	570 – Wrath	504 – Abhorrence
537 – Fickleness	571 – Tyranny	505 – Banefulness
538 – Villainy	572 – Oppression	506 – Sinisterity
539 – Licentiousness	573 – Persecution	507 – Baseness
540 – Insurgency	574 – Indignation	508 – Diabolism
541 – Vengeance	575 – Subjugation	509 – Sorcery
542 – Gluttony	576 – Animosity	
543 – Cowardice	577 – Torment	

This preliminary range of themes is further contrasted in **Parts III** and **IV** with respect to the related domain of excess: defined as that range of extremes targeting the virtuous mode, as well as the vices of defect. **Part III** is subdivided into three separate chapters that collectively specify the vices of excess, as well as a number of accessory issues that encompass code numbers spanning 300 through 399. **Part IV**, in turn, examines the realm of hyperviolence: a new ethical category defined as that range of excess targeting the vices of defect, spanning the sequence of code numbers 700 to 799.

This fundamental pattern of organization is fundamentally altered in **Part V** with respect to the transitional class of power maneuvers. This latter category was previously defined as a transitional variation upon the four major categories of terms outlined in **Parts I** through **IV**. **Part V** is devoted exclusively to an examination of the lesser virtues, which were initially defined as transitions targeting the virtuous mode. Following a short introductory chapter (that describes the transitional realm in general), **Part V** is further subdivided into four component chapters outlining the lesser virtues (I and II), as well as affiliated accessory issues. The completed description of lesser virtues from **Part V**, in turn, extends the transitional paradigm to the related themes of criminality and hypercriminality contained within **Part VI**. This section is further split into Chapters *27* and *28* devoted towards analyzing these specialized categories: as specified through the code numbers 600-699 and 800-899 respectively.

Skipping ahead to **Part VII** further spotlights the related set of transitional maneuvers targeting the vices of excess, an aspect previously defined as the communicational factors underlying the mental disorders. Indeed, this section represents the crowning achievement in terms of the three-digit coding system, being that these communicational factors have traditionally remained an elusive endeavor. The current coding system finally permits a comprehensive explanation for the riddle of mental illness. This section clearly varies from that which has gone before in that the terminology is rather more specialized in a clinical sense, as opposed to the more colloquial nature of the virtues, values, and vices. Consequently, **Part VII** relies primarily upon terminology employed within the mental-health field; namely, that outlined within *DSM-IV* as well as the nomenclature for the psychoses devised by German researcher, Karl Leonhard. The somewhat specialized nature of the respective terminology necessarily calls for a more comprehensive system of presentation, with **Part VII** subdivided into six component chapters devoted to the various clinical syndromes.

Chapter *29* begins this analysis with a general introduction to the study of mental illness, as well as the realm of the personality disorders and neuroses (Part-A). Chapter *30*, in turn, offers a preliminary overview of the psychoses as well as the general categories of the pure mood disorders. Chapter *31*, in turn, examines the systematic forms of schizophrenia as defined by Karl Leonhard. Chapter *32* provides a general examination of the personality disorders and forms of neurosis (Part-B). Chapter *33* takes a similar slant with respect to the cycloid forms of the mood disorders and unsystematic forms of schizophrenia. Finally, Chapter *34* formally evaluates the three-digit coding system in terms of its utility as an adjunct to the prevailing *DSM*-paradigm, wherein proposing critical insights into clinical diagnosis and counseling psychotherapy.

In terms a general overview, the final comprehensive **Part VIII** enters into speculation concerning global applications for the three-digit coding system. Chapter *35* formally outlines avenues for further research and development as well as intriguing modifications targeting a global sphere of influence. Chapter *36*, in turn, proposes applications relating to the darker realm of the ethical hierarchy; namely, those targeting the domain of criminality and hypercriminality. The three-digit coding system proves exceedingly effective with respect to the fields of criminal profiling and forensic psychology. Certainly with the ongoing trend towards global terrorism, this new technology proves particularly effective towards ameliorating the effects of such misguided motives.

Perhaps the most dramatic potential applications are detailed in Chapter *37* with respect to an ethical simulation of artificial intelligence, the basis for a recently approved US patent. This novel innovation employs the three-digit coding system as an aid to the programming of complex sets of ethical parameters. Through the aid of this computer technology, the task of detecting and cataloguing ethical behavior should greatly be simplified, eventually permitting the development of a master database of world literature eminently searchable in terms of affective content. Finally, an accessory Appendix – (A) further proposes many crucial applications to the rapidly expanding fields relating to the neurosciences. This master three-digit coding system, upon final analysis, should prove truly essential insights towards maintaining a peaceful status quo within a global sphere of international affairs.

2

THE TEN-LEVEL GLOBAL
POWER HIERARCHY

The major groupings of virtues, values, and ideals serve as the elementary foundation for the master three-digit coding system. This grand unification of ethical principles necessarily argues for a radical reinterpretation of the organizational principles currently under consideration. The key salient insight resides in viewing the individual as the rightful product of a diverse range of social and institutional influences. In addition to the most basic one-to-one style of personal interactions, the individual is further incorporated into a broad range of group contexts (namely, work, family, country, etc.), as well as an all-encompassing universal context. These distinctive contexts collectively summate into a unified authority hierarchy consistent with the theoretical principles governing the field of Set Theory. Set Theory remains in full agreement with the three-level model of the power hierarchy: with the unit set, the group set, and the universal set equating with the personal, group, and spiritual levels, respectively.

The concept of a three-level set hierarchy is actually nothing new, proposed centuries earlier by German philosopher, Emmanuel Kant. In his masterpiece, *Critique of Pure Reason*, Kant outlines a comprehensive system of conceptual categories he considers crucial to the formation of the human intellect. Most notable within this system is the relevant category of *quantity*: which Kant further subdivides into the concepts of unity, plurality, and totality. In a more basic conceptual sense, these three fundamental themes equate to the notions of the one, the many, and the absolute: equivalent (in a human social sense) to the personal, group, and spiritual levels within the power hierarchy.

This three-level social hierarchy, although appealing in its simplicity, clearly differs from Set Theory in that complex interactions between individuals do not exist solely in a vacuum, but rather

are further specialized into both authority/follower roles. For the personal realm, this amounts to the personal authority/personal follower roles, extending to the group realm as the group authority and group representative variations, ultimately culminating with respect to the spiritual authority and spiritual disciple roles. A brief description of each of these authority/follower roles definitely proves in order here, outlining the proposed grand unification of virtues, values, and ideals.

The most basic personal level of interaction refers to the one-to-one style of interaction occurring between individuals, much as typically encountered in one's personal friendships. This personal interplay, in turn, is specialized into either authority or follower roles. This is exemplified in the case of the master craftsman who typically remains dependent upon the services of his faithful apprentice. A similar scenario also holds true with respect to the hero and his sidekick, or the celebrity and his straight-man. Flexibility emerges as the key distinguishing feature, with the authority and follower roles complementing one another in terms of such an equitable balance of power. The authority figure formally depends upon the attentions of his follower (as much as the other way around), resulting in an equal balance of power within the personal power realm.

This elementary personal foundation, in turn, gives way to the equally pervasive notion of group authority. The group set surpasses the unit set in terms of its expansion to a multitude of elements (or class members) within this group-focused style of context. Personal concerns, accordingly, become subordinate to such a group power base, being that enough followers remain to continue group authority whether or not any single individual decides to desert. In a single stroke, the group authority sets himself well above any personal power struggles, an in-

110	111
Nostalgia	Guilt
112	**113**
Desire	Worry

EGO STATES
(Personal Authority)

120	121
Hero-Worship	Blame
122	**123**
Approval	Concern

ALTER EGO STATES
(Personal Follower)

130	131
Glory	Honor
132	**133**
Dignity	Integrity

PERSONAL IDEALS
(Group Authority)

140	141
Prudence	Justice
142	**143**
Temperance	Fortitude

CARDINAL VIRTUES
(Group Representative)

150	151
Providence	Liberty
152	**153**
Civility	Austerity

CIVIL LIBERTIES
(Spiritual Authority)

160	161
Faith	Hope
162	**163**
Charity	Decency

THEOLOGICAL VIRTUES
(Spiritual Disciple)

170	171
Grace	Free Will
172	**173**
Magnanimity	Equanimity

ECUMENICAL IDEALS
(Humanitarian Authority)

180	181
Beauty	Truth
182	**183**
Goodness	Wisdom

CLASSICAL GREEK VALUES
(Humanitarian Follower)

190	191
Tranquility	Equality
192	**193**
Love	Peace

HUMANISTIC VALUES
(Transcendental Authority)

100	101
Ecstasy	Bliss
102	**103**
Joy	Harmony

MYSTICAL VALUES
(Transcendental Follower)

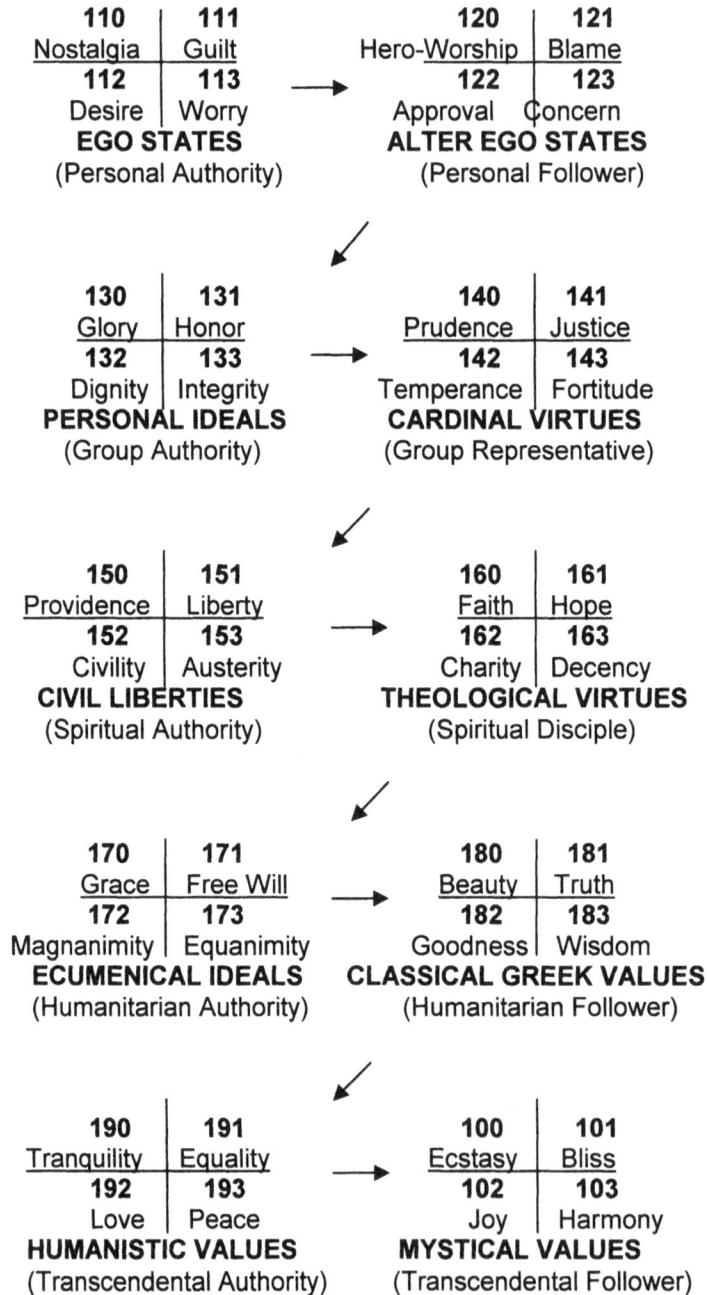

Figure 2 -- The Major Virtues, Values, and Ideals

novation exploited since ancient times as the well-established custom of tribal-based authority.

Group authority, in turn, is susceptible to its own unique form of follower countermaneuver: in this case, that expressed by the group representative. The latter's distinctive style of "strike" leverage is fully realized at this juncture, as witnessed in the modern trend towards collective bargaining. By organizing as a union collective, the rank-and-file nominates a shop steward to represent them in negotiations with management. The group representative, in essence, reminds the group authority that the cooperation of the labor pool is crucial for maintaining the group status quo. Here, the group authority (in concert with the group representative) shares an equal balance of power within the group power realm.

A similar pattern further holds true with respect to the remaining spiritual authority level, although this sense of "spiritual" is restricted to the universal sense of the term implicit in Set Theory. In this latter respect, the universal set clearly surpasses the multiplicity of the group domain: in essence, the sum-totality of all such groups within the universal realm. The universal set represents the "group of all potential group sets," a 3rd-order style of set-hierarchy (equivalent to the domain of all mankind). Indeed, whereas group authority surpasses the influence of its individual members, the spiritual authority similarly overrules the strike power of any of its constituent groups, wherein claiming authority over the sum-total of all mankind.

It is true (in practice) that each of the world's religions competes for the beliefs of the world's faithful. In principle, however, such religions vigilantly strive to convert all others, giving further credence to the universal sense of the term. This claim to universality is traditionally made binding through an appeal to God or Messiah-figure. This mystical style of sanction dates to the earliest of times. Here, a king could inspire the loyalty of his troops in the name of a "god of war" far in excess of what might be claimed as a mere mortal ruler.

Taking this trend to the limit, even a realm as abstract as the spiritual authority role must (by definition) be susceptible to its own unique form of follower maneuver: namely, that specified for the spiritual disciple. As spokesman for the spiritual congregation, the spiritual disciple reminds the spiritual authority that the blessings of the faithful are crucial for maintaining the spiritual status quo. Witness the power of the spiritual revolutionary for influencing such diverse historical events as the Protestant Reformation, and even the founding of the Christian movement, itself.

THE MASTER SCHEMATIC GROUPINGS OF VIRTUES, VALUES, AND IDEALS

In summary, the ascending three-level hierarchy of personal, group, and spiritual domains, when further viewed in terms of both authority and follower roles, provides the basic conceptual framework for explaining the grand unified system of virtuous terms. This format is schematically depicted in **Fig. 2**, including the respective three-digit codes for each of the individual virtues and values. This master schematic format (tentatively termed the *power pyramid* hierarchy) incorporates the major ethical classifications described so far (plus an equivalent number of new ones) for a grand total of ten: serving as the foundation for the remainder of the book to follow.

As the underlying captions serve to indicate, the uppermost three levels of this diagram are designated for the personal, group, and spiritual levels: accounting for the most basic groupings of virtues and ideals. The remaining lowermost pair of levels, in turn, introduce two hitherto unmentioned categories; namely, the humanitarian and transcendental realms, respectively. This additional set of authority levels is classified as uniquely abstract styles of power maneuvers, clearly surpassing the more basic organizational pattern previously established for the lower three levels. A brief description of these final two levels is definitely in order here, for the most abstract listings of virtues and values fall within these final two domains.

Although the spiritual realm is clearly the maximum level of organization (in keeping with the traditions of Set Theory), this very sense of chronological time permits the introduction of the more abstract notion of humanitarian authority. The great theoretical physicist, Albert Einstein defined time as the fourth dimension of the universe, making it exceedingly fitting that this humanitarian theme enters into consideration precisely at the 4th-order level within the power hierarchy. Humanitarian authority transcends the spiritual variety by claiming to speak for all generations of mankind, not just the current one: experienced as past traditionalism or future potentiality. Its extreme sense of generality precludes its identification within any singular social institution, its themes rather incorporated into the spiritual (and sometimes political) framework of society as a whole.

This extreme sense of the power of abstraction (when considered in its own right) ultimately serves as the basis for one final innovation within the power hierarchy; namely, the crowning tran-scendental authority level. Transcendental author-ity regains the upper hand by transcending the routine sense of concreteness shared in common by the lower levels, an innovation accounting for the most abstract listings of values within the au-thority hierarchy. The transcendental perspective enters freely into the realm of pure intuition and imagination, wherein forsaking the constraints of ordinary reality for the supreme and incontro-vertible realm of pure abstraction. This transcen-dental domain (in concert with its humanitarian counterpart) is also specialized into both authori-ty/follower roles, for a grand total of four catego-ries. In concert with the six respective roles cha-racterizing the personal, group, and spiritual le-vels, the master ten-level hierarchy emerges in full detail as depicted in **Fig. 2**.

Although basically only an introductory chap-ter, a few general observations necessarily can be made with respect to this distinctive schematic format. The ten individual categories of virtues, values, and ideals are organized as descending columns of five groupings each. The left-hand col-umn represents the hierarchy of authority roles, whereas the right specifies the corresponding fol-lower roles. This dual schematic format repre-sents the sum-totality of reciprocating interac-tions between the authority/follower roles, as the respective directional arrows serve to indicate.

The distinctive groupings of virtues and values for each individual level exhibit their own unique range of distinguishing characteristics. Each is represented as a quartet-style format depicted as quadrants in a pseudo-Cartesian system. The more traditional groupings (such as the cardinal virtues) are already established as four-part list-ings fitting quite nicely within the quartet-style format. Others (such as the theological virtues) have been supplemented beyond their traditional number in order to achieve a quartet-style status. A number of other groupings appear entirely new to the philosophical tradition, yet these too re-spect the quartet-style pattern characterizing the unified power hierarchy.

Similar to the reciprocating pattern of au-thority/follower roles (which build in a hierarchial fashion), the affiliated groupings of virtues, val-ues, and ideals similarly mirror this ascending pattern of organization. These ethical groupings build from the most elementary (the ego and alter ego states) clear up to the most abstract listings targeting the transcendental level (the humanistic and mystical values).

With respect to the rules for coding within the three-digit system, the first digit for the virtues,

by definition, is assigned the primary value of "1," as specified for the initial numbering pattern de-scribed in Chapter 1. The second digit further nar-rows the focus, in turn, specifying each of the ten individual levels within the power hierarchy: e.g., 1 = personal authority, 2 = personal follower, 3 = group authority, etc. In order to specify each of the individual terms, the third and final digit is ultimately called into play. For instance, 130 = glory, 131 = honor, 132 = dignity, and 133 = in-tegrity. Digits 4 through 7 in the three-slot, in turn, specify the accessory variations for the vir-tuous mode, as more extensively described in Chapter *8* of the current section. The final two third-place digits (8 and 9) are reserved for speci-fying the general unifying themes, as further de-scribed in Chapter 9. This virtuous realm runs the entire gamut of human experience, ranging from the instinctual to the sublime (and everything in between). A brief description of each of these in-dividual ethical groupings is definitely in order here, serving as a basic overview for the remain-ing detailed treatment to follow.

THE PERSONAL FOUNDATIONS FOR THE SCHEMATIC POWER HIERARCHY

The most rational point of initiation for this com-prehensive analysis is certainly the most basic personal level within the power hierarchy. Accord-ing to the upper-most level shown in **Fig. 2**, the dual categories are respectively listed as the ego states for the personal authority role (guilt-worry-nostalgia-desire) and the alter ego states for the follower role (hero-worship-blame-approval-concern). These groupings appear tailor-made for incorporation into the personal power realm, adapted from the traditions of self-help psychol-ogy, including *Your Erroneous Zones* by Dr. Wayne Dyer. The intensely personal nature of this self-help genre makes its respective terminology particularly effective for specifying the interper-sonal dynamics underlying this elementary level. The specific rationale behind their particular as-signment, as well as the related distinction be-tween the authority and follower roles is an un-dertaking best reserved for a more detailed treatment in Chapter *3*.

Although only briefly outlined, this initial complement of ego/alter ego states, in turn, serves as the foundation for the remaining listings of virtues, values, and ideals outlined in **Fig. 2**. Indeed, a general pattern of organization emerges from this schematic diagram; namely, the left-hand column is characterized by what are termed the authority ideals: read downwards as the personal ideals, civil liberties, ecumenical ideals, and humanistic values. The right-hand column of follower roles, in turn, specifies a parallel trend based upon the virtues; namely, the cardinal virtues, theological virtues, classical Greek values, and mystical values. For sake of consistency, the initial authority trend will be examined in its entirety first, followed, in turn, by an equally comprehensive treatment of the respective sequence of follower roles.

THE AUTHORITY IDEALS

The first mentioned sequence of authority ideals begins with the group authority level; namely, the provisionally termed class of "personal ideals" (glory-honor-dignity-integrity). The personal designation for this grouping might appear somewhat of a misnomer although more properly viewed as ideals within the group sense of the term. These personal ideals, in turn, build directly upon the ego states previously established for the personal authority role, wherein accounting for the hybrid quality of the grouping. In this latter respect, the group authority *gloriously* acts in a nostalgic fashion or *honorably* acts in a guilty fashion towards the personal follower figure. Similarly, he might *dignifiedly* act in a desirous fashion or worrisomely act with *integrity*, again building on the elementary foundation in the ego states.

The personal ideals collectively derive from the Latin tradition, effectively highlighting the Roman's fascination with the heroic principles governing group leadership. This enduring group focus is primarily expressed in the many symbolisms for royalty and nobility; as in the heraldic traditions of the circle of *glory*, the *honor* point, the cap of *dignity*, and the social symbolisms for *integrity*. Guided by such lofty ideals, the group authority rightly aspires to such noble themes, an undertaking befitting leaders in society.

The next higher level of spiritual authority rates a similar treatment indicative of the respective class of "civil liberties" (providence-liberty-civility-austerity). Each of these themes is prominently featured in the founding of the United States, as collectively celebrated in the precepts of the *Declaration of Independence*. This revolutionary document celebrates divine authority as one of its central premises, invoking the universal rights of man to overrule the tyrannical edicts of English monarch, King George III. Although this designation of *civil liberties* might appear to suggest somewhat of a political context, further analysis reveals the deep spiritual underpinnings for these four basic themes. Indeed, each of these

themes was traditionally worshipped as a classical deity in its own right; namely, Providentia, Libertas, Civitas, and Auster. In terms of this "universal" context, *providence* represents a more advanced counterpart of glory, whereas *liberty* makes a similar correspondence to honor. Furthermore, *civility* amounts to a spiritual refinement of dignity, whereas *austerity* denotes integrity from a universal perspective.

The universal prerequisites for spiritual authority, in turn, serve as the foundation for the related concept of humanitarian authority, an innovation firmly rooted within the concept of "historical" time. This enduring humanitarian focus is directly reflected in the abstract listing of ethical terms, provisionally termed the *ecumenical* ideals (grace-freewill-magnanimity-equanimity). The enduring significance of this grouping certainly fits a common stereotype; namely, timeless themes in keeping with such a grand humanitarian perspective. Although closely affiliated with spiritual concerns, a more detailed analysis clearly reveals a grand humanitarian focus: as reflected in the long tradition of ecumenical councils where generational issues were thrust into focus.

This grouping enjoyed particular favor during the Protestant Reformation. According to the basic tenet of Martin Luther: "By *grace* are thee are saved through faith." These ecumenical ideals add a more enduring historical dimension to the civil liberties previously established for the spiritual tradition. For example, *grace* imparts a more enduring humanitarian significance to providence, whereas *free will* provides a historical perspective for liberty. Similarly, the remaining ecumenical ideals of *magnanimity* and *equanimity* extend a similar traditionalist mindset to the spiritual themes of civility and austerity.

The crowning transcendental level ultimately rounds out the stepwise description of authority roles. This transcendental perspective formally appeals to the idealized realm of pure abstraction, in essence, transcending the more concrete nature of the four initial levels. The respective grouping of *humanistic* values (peace-love-tranquility-equality) rightfully enters into consideration here: ideal themes befitting such a lofty transcendental perspective. Each of these terms fits such a supremely abstract perspective, ideals attuned to realms wholly transcending routine experience. This distinctive set of values dates at least to classical times, worshipped as abstract deities in their own right: namely, Pax (peace), Cupid (love), Quies (tranquility), and Aequitas (equality). These themes, in turn, served as the inspiration for many modern movements, as in the New England Transcendentalists and the Peace Protest against the Vietnam War.

THE ETHICAL TRADITIONS FOR THE FOLLOWER ROLES

The completed description of the authority ideals, in turn, sets the stage for a discussion of the remaining sequence of the follower roles. Whereas the authority hierarchy was based upon the ego states, the remaining follower sequence alternately targets the alter ego states, further extending to the well-established traditions of the cardinal and theological virtues. These two basic categories of virtue have collectively enjoyed a distinguished place of honor in the Western ethical tradition. As their qualifiers imply, the theological virtues (faith-hope-charity-decency) are specific to the spiritual disciple role, whereas the cardinal virtues (prudence-justice-temperance-fortitude), by default, target the group follower perspective.

The latter cardinal virtues directly serve to initiate the follower trend, derived from the Latin *cardos* (hinge): based upon the belief that all higher virtues hinge upon these basic four. Accordingly, the cardinal virtues exhibit distinct parallels to the more elementary class of alter ego states; in this case, prudent-worship, just-blame, temperate-approval, or fortitudinous-concern. The enduring tradition of cardinal virtues figures prominently in the writings of the Greek philosopher Plato, particularly his fanciful dialogue, *The Republic*. These cardinal virtues provide an effective focal point within the dialogue, promoted as codes of conduct befitting Plato's ideal concept of the Greek city-state.

The even more advanced grouping of theological virtues (faith-hope-charity-decency), in turn, builds upon an elementary foundation within the cardinal virtues. The great Church theologian, St. Thomas Aquinas, viewed the theological virtues as divinely inspired. This directly contrasts with the more elementary nature of the cardinal virtues, which were more widely regarded as naturally occurring, social predispositions. Befitting their exalted moral status, the theological virtues remain an enduring theme in New Testament scripture, particularly celebrated by St. Paul as supreme moral principles governing the virtuous conduct of a true disciple of Christ.

Although the formal designation of "theological" originally applied only to the first three basic terms, the addition of the fourth related theme of *decency* effectively modifies this grouping into a form consistent with the schematic power hierarchy. This traditional shortfall in the full complement of terms further appears to account for the great theoretical insight missed throughout the ages; namely, the theological virtues represent the higher spiritual analogues of the subordinate class of cardinal virtues (just as the latter are based upon the alter ego states). Here, one acknowledges the prudent-*faith* or blameful-*hope* for justice professed by the spiritual disciple figure, in addition to the temperate sense of the *charitableness* or fortitudinous sense of *decency* germane to the discussion.

The completed description of the group/spiritual levels, in turn, extends to the humanitarian domain with respect to the "representative member of humanity" role. More properly termed the philosopher's maneuver, this perspective invokes the prestige of speaking for all generations of mankind (not just the current one). In essence, the representative member of humanity reminds the humanitarian authority of his formal sanction from humanity, lest he lose prestige in such matters. The humanitarian authority perspective is initially seen as more of a policy-making strategy than any immediate style of power perspective. The humanitarian follower, in turn, retains the option of rejecting humanitarian policy; hence, maintaining an equal balance of power within the humanitarian power realm.

The traditionally revered grouping of classical Greek values (beauty-truth-goodness-wisdom) rightfully enters into consideration here, the major groupings of virtues already accounted for at the lower levels. This enduring notion of value invokes precisely such a humanitarian focus, the more immediate sense of virtue now extending to the timeless quality of value. Indeed, the classical Greek values date to the most ancient of times, celebrated by Plato as pure forms (or essences) that transcend the variability of the natural world. Each of these values was worshiped as an abstract deity in its own right; namely, Venus (beauty), Veritas (truth), Bonus Eventus (goodness), and Sapientia (wisdom). This classical sense of value, in turn, fulfills the trend previously established with respect to the cardinal/theological virtues. This formal correspondence extends to the *beauteous*-faith or just-hope for the *truth*, as well as the charitable sense of *goodness* or decent sense of *wisdom* expressed by the humanitarian follower figure.

Even a follower level as abstract as the transcendental must (by definition) be invested with its own unique form of follower countermaneuver, in this case, that invoked by the transcendental follower. Despite this extreme level of abstraction, it still proves feasible to distinguish a respective listing of ethical terms provisionally termed the mystical values (ecstasy-bliss-joy-harmony). Although the formal specifics of this grouping are scarcely warranted at this juncture, suffice it to say they encompass the enigmatic realm of religious mysticism tuned to realms wholly transcending routine experience. This crowning mystical level effectively closes out the "nameable" realm of the power hierarchy, although it is still possible to postulate the existence of a supernatural extension to the power hierarchy: a topic best reserved for the more detailed examination of mysticism contained in Chapter 7.

THE POWER PYRAMID HIERARCHY

In summary, the completed cursory analysis of the ten-level hierarchy of virtuous terms aimed to provide a suitably comprehensive overview of virtuous realm, a mere glimpse of the detailed terminology to follow. At the heart of this system lies the unified power hierarchy shown in **Fig. 2**, a confluence of authority/follower roles spanning the personal, group, spiritual, humanitarian, and transcendental realms. In tribute to this dramatic scope, this new conceptual paradigm is respectively termed the *power pyramid* hierarchy, in direct analogy to the exponential expansion of total membership at each successive level. This notion is suggestive of the "pyramid" money schemes of the late 1970's, when profits were achieved by recruiting from an ever-expanding base of investors. This figurative metaphor (perhaps more than any other) reflects the ascending sense of interactivity within the unified power hierarchy.

Although this ascending hierarchy of authority/follower roles emerges as a direct outcome of the principles governing Set Theory, the true value of this system emerges in terms of the respective listings of individual terms, intriguing in their quartet style of organization. This basic pattern formally reflects the cohesiveness of the individual terms, as previously established with respect to the cardinal virtues, theological virtues, and classical Greek values. Returning to **Fig. 2**, in the left-hand column denoting the authority roles, the first quadrant lists the ascending sequence of nostalgia-glory-providence-grace-tranquility. All five terms share a common past-directed focus stressing past notable achievements. The same quadrant within the right-hand column of follower roles yields the related sequence of hero worship-prudence-faith-beauty-ecstasy: themes that reciprocate the authority trend through the reinforcement of such past notable perspectives by the follower figure.

A similar pattern further holds true with respect to the upper right-hand quadrants of **Fig. 2**. The respective authority roles lead to the sequence of guilt-honor-liberty-freewill-equality: themes all sharing a past-directed focus although now specifying a more submissive sense. The remaining follower trend (blame-justice-hope-truth-bliss) further verifies this contention, a sequence mirroring that based on hero worship with the exception that negative reinforcement is now called into focus. Indeed, it proves particularly amazing that these ethical trends should exist at all, each lining up so perfectly within its respective quadrant of the power hierarchy. This grand scale organization is certainly a major selling point, its perfect symmetry and cohesiveness far too intricate to have arisen solely by chance. Indeed, these ten basic ethical groupings actually turn-out to be a skeleton framework for the much broader system of terminology covering the entire range of emotionally-charged language in general: an issue clearly warranting further investigation.

GLOBAL APPLICATIONS RELATING TO THE TEN-LEVEL ETHICAL HIERARCHY

This grand-scale organization of the major ethical traditions within the virtuous realm proves a fitting launch-point for applications relating to world peace and global harmony. The majority of the distinctive listings of virtues/values are invested with well-established literary traditions permitting the stepwise construction of the ascending power hierarchy, a feat unheralded on the world scene today. These well-established ethical traditions prove particularly amenable to widespread acceptance on the world international scene, their classical and contemporary roots serving as an elementary foundation for most major political institutions invested with preserving order and stability across human society in general.

For instance, the legal system celebrates the traditions of the cardinal virtues, where the enduring ideal of jurisprudence derives directly from this classical arrangement of themes. The Declaration of Independence, in turn, celebrates the classifications of civil liberties, which appeal to the universal rights of man through the ideals of providence and liberty maintained through civil discourse. The world economy is similarly based upon a cooperative sense of international trust with respect to currency exchange, as exemplified in the group ideals of honor in fair business dealings, and dignity and integrity with regard to a mutually equitable array of commercial practices across the board.

This highly interdependent system of global economic cooperation would remain entirely untenable without such enduring virtuous underpinnings, an ethical dynamic that has marched hand in hand with the dramatic ascent of global international trade. These solid virtuous foundations need to constantly be renewed as a check on unbridled western capitalism, particularly in times of considerable upheaval, such as regrettably occurring during the current global economic downturn. The more abstract virtues and values characterizing a humanitarian perspective traditionally celebrate a long-term course of action targeting a more stable global infrastructure, a lesson seemingly lost on the self-serving droves of investors/speculators that sacrificed global economic stability on the altar of short-term financial gains of a highly speculative nature.

This lesson favoring long-term goals is similarly applicable to the career politician class, which is often similarly shortsighted in terms of partisan politics and self-serving reelection concerns, all the while delaying critical action on long-term issues concerning budgetary irresponsibility that threaten national growth and prosperity. Indeed, US politicians (in cooperation with major financial institutions) collaborated to remove the regulatory safeguards that ultimately precipitated the proliferation of so-called toxic assets that contributed to the current global meltdown.

A move towards resurrecting our traditional virtuous roots proves crucial towards reining-in the free exercise of our capitalist impulses, a welcome global perspective with the potential for preventing further such destabilizing scenarios. Indeed, there are very few social institutions: whether legal, political, or religious that could not gain substantially from the dramatic new insights contained within the unprecedented ten-level hierarchy of the major virtuous traditions. Furthermore, this cohesive virtuous foundation, in turn, serves as a major conceptual framework for the addition of many related applications to the darker realms of ethical inquiry. These include novel inroads into understanding the domain of the vices of defect, as well as a conceptual revolution in comprehending the troubling motives underlying criminality and international terrorism. This grand-scale ethical system has arrived on the world scene at perhaps its greatest hour of need, a glimmer of hope for those that might endeavor to put such a versatile innovation into action.

The following chapter launches this grand-scale endeavor with respect to a detailed examination of the personal authority/follower roles. Indeed, it is precisely at this most basic level that the technical rationale behind the quartet-style organization of ethical terms is finally adequately addressed, ultimately explained in terms of the behavioral terminology of operant conditioning. The psychological field of behaviorism is devoted to the study of instinctual styles of goal-seeking behaviors, an undertaking definitely suggestive of the more abstract focus of the virtues, values, and ideals. The father of modern behaviorism, B. F. Skinner, proposed a similar correlation of behavioral and ethical principles in his quest for an all-encompassing "Technology of Behavior."

In his masterpiece, *Beyond Freedom and Dignity* (1971), Skinner examined the behavioral correlates for a broad range of ethical terms (such as freedom and dignity), although with a limited degree of success. Through the aid of the unified power hierarchy, however, this motivational style of analysis can be carried to its logical conclusion, incorporating virtually every major term within the Western ethical tradition. Indeed, it proves particularly crucial to view the ascending hierarchy of virtues/values as based entirely within behavioral principles and terminology, as indicated in the elementary nature of the ego/alter ego states. The science of behaviorism, therefore, serves as the rational launch-point for any further ethical analysis, beginning with the detailed chapter to follow. A brief history of the behavioral movement is definitely in order at this juncture, for herein lie the keys to outlining the instinctual foundations for the entire ten-level hierarchy.

3

THE BEHAVIORAL FOUNDATIONS
FOR THE VIRTUOUS REALM

To the casual student of psychology, the mention of conditioning theory typically brings to mind the classical variety pioneered by Russian behaviorist, Ivan Pavlov. Pavlov was the first to discover that dogs could be trained to salivate to the sound of a neutral conditioned stimulus (such as a ticking metronome) provided it was extensively paired beforehand with a food reward (the unconditioned stimulus). Subsequent researchers extended these results to various other types of reflexive behavior amenable to laboratory investigation. These automatic types of behavior, however, are typically at odds with the more deliberate goal-seeking styles of behavior characterizing mature human endeavor. For the adult, behavior typically precedes reinforcement, instead of following it (as in the classical sense).

Descriptions of this latter type of conditioning first come to light in the writings of Bekhterev, a fellow countryman of Pavlov. This variation was termed *instrumental* conditioning, in that goal-seeking behavior was said to be instrumental in procuring reinforcement from the environment. Indeed, Bekhterev further demonstrated that the strength of instrumental behaviors can greatly be enhanced by increasing the frequency/amplitude of the contingent reinforcement.

Instrumental conditioning soon rivaled classical conditioning in the field of learning theory, only reaching its greatest potential through the efforts of American psychologist B. F. Skinner. Skinner expanded upon traditional "instrumental" theory by developing his own radical variation respectively termed *operant* conditioning. According to Skinner, goal-seeking behaviors "operate" on the environment to produce reinforcement; hence, the operant sense of the term. Skinner actually distinguishes two distinct forms of operant conditioning, designated for his parallel con-

cepts of positive and negative reinforcement. Positive reinforcement (as its name implies) refers to a rewarding aspect within the environment targeted through solicitous types of behavior. A widely cited example of positive reinforcement concerns the plight of the wilderness bear cub, which in the course of foraging overturns a fallen log concealing a wild honeycomb. The rewarding consequences of such a honey bonanza directly encourage further such log-turning behavior in the future, particularly when such efforts are periodically re-rewarded.

Negative reinforcement, on the other hand, refers to the avoidance of some unpleasant aspect within the environment through aversive types of behavior; as in fleeing from predators or stepping around pitfalls. Returning to the previous example, the bear cub might jump into a lake to avoid the unpleasant consequences of a hot summer day, or a swarm of angry bees for that matter. Although distinct mechanisms are clearly involved, both positive and negative variations are similarly reinforcing to the individual, encouraging approach / avoidance types of behavior in relation to the environment.

Skinner's most enduring contribution to the field of behaviorism involves his ingenious experimental designs, allowing for degrees of precision unheard of in the natural state. Employing various animal models, Skinner perfected clever automated set-ups for simulating the interaction of learned operant behaviors (such as depressing a lever) and subsequent reinforcement: as in the delivery of a food pellet (+R), or the avoidance of floor shocks (−R). Within such a controlled laboratory setting, Skinner was effectively able to calculate how different schedules of reinforcement affect the overall behavior of the organism, contrasting the effects of strictly measured reinforcement to that of randomly intermittent or variable reinforcement modes.

CONDITIONING IN A SOCIAL SETTING

The observation of similar types of instinctual behavior in humans invites many practical comparisons that (for the most part) prove quite enlightening. Nature studies, indeed, have confirmed the stabilizing effects of operant conditioning within certain naturally occurring animal societies. For instance the grooming behaviors observed within the wild baboon troop serve to cement the bonds between dominant and subordinate members. The subordinate baboons groom the coats of the troop leaders in exchange for their outward approval. A similar set of circumstances is further seen with respect to breeding behaviors between the sexes.

These distinct interactions find further parallels within human society, where mankind's symbolic use of language permits approval to be expressed in more dramatic formats; namely, praise, commendation, etc. Symbolism also gives meaning to what Skinner terms the secondary reinforcers; e.g., money, power, etc. Although paper currency is not intrinsically pleasing in itself, it is secondarily reinforcing in that it can be exchanged for any of the primary reinforcers: as in food, shelter, etc. These secondary reinforcers directly encourage procurement behaviors in complex types of situations where rewards are customarily delayed. Herein lies the basis for the Protestant work ethic; e.g., no work - no pay!

Although the effectiveness of rewards clearly remains without question, social hierarchies are rarely so idyllic as to be ruled entirely through positive reinforcement. Grooming behaviors are typically restricted to members of the opposite sex, or members of the same sex that are not a serious challenge to each other. The drive to become the dominant member of the troop is alternately determined through aggressive types of behavior. Such power skirmishes, unfortunately, can prove detrimental to the cooperative social unit, particularly in terms of the threat of serious injury or fatalities. Most social species, accordingly, have evolved stereotypical submissive behaviors serving to terminate the conflict well ahead of any permanent damage. Instead of continuing to act contentiously, the loser switches to appeasement to escape further punishment.

In the highly competitive wolf pack, for example, the defeated wolf bares its throat to the victor in an overt plea for mercy. This submissive display effectively serves as a visual cue to the dominant wolf to leniently terminate the conflict well ahead of any permanent damage. For the primate troop, this aspect is alternately seen in the crouching/appeasement postures assumed by the subordinate member. Such actions are similarly suggestive of the "prisoner of war" mentality, where waving a white flag is a cue to the victors to forgo the certain extermination bound to occur in a fight to the death; e.g., "Remember the Alamo!"

THE HUMAN CONNECTION

Although such ethological observations prove extremely enlightening, their extrapolation to the human condition proves infinitely more complex. In particular, the extreme degree of complexity separating human and animal societies renders any direct comparisons tentative at best. In contrast to animal societies, mankind is essentially a product of his supportive culture, which cooperatively permits the effective management of environmental factors. Whereas lower animal societies remain at the mercy of the environment for their reinforcement (or lack thereof), mankind's facility for taming the forces of nature has led to the unique reassignment of reinforcement to specialized agencies within the social hierarchy. This is particularly evident in the traditional work place setting, where the employee performs a service function in exchange for secondary reinforcers; namely, money, praise, prestige, etc. Individuals in the enviable position of controlling reinforcement typically enjoy coveted positions of power or authority within the social hierarchy, employing rewards to encourage the procurement behaviors of the subordinate staff of laborers.

The human sphere of operant conditioning, accordingly, is viewed as a two-stage process; namely, goal-seeking behaviors followed by subsequent reinforcement. In particular, the individual initially acts in a procurement fashion (appetite or aversion) in order to be positively rewarded or leniently spared punishment. The employee works industriously in order to earn the praise of his boss, or acts submissively in order to avoid being fired. When (X) is defined as procurement and (Y) is specified as reinforcement, the complete operant interaction is respectively defined as $X \rightarrow Y$.

THE DUAL CONDITIONED SEQUENCE

This formal behavioral model further brings to light the major paradox of the conditioned relationship; namely, as a two-stage sequential

The Late B. F. Skinner: Photographed at Work in his Lab - Courtesy of the B. F. Skinner Foundation

process, only one role can occur in the present at any given time. In particular, when procurement is actively occurring, reinforcement remains a future potentiality. Similarly, when reinforcement finally comes to pass, procurement is effectively reduced to a passive memory status. This dual style of conditioned interaction is schematically represented in **Fig. 3A** (depicted overleaf): with procurement again represented as the letter (X), whereas reinforcement is alternately specified by the letter (Y). The complete scale of time is further represented by paired (oppositely-facing) "wedges" denoting both past and future time frames, with the gap separating the two representing the present. This dual wedge format was purposely chosen in reference to the observation that the measure of time increases as a direct function of its distance from the present.

According to Part A of **Fig. 3A**, when procurement (X) is immediately occurring, reinforcement (Y) remains a future potentiality. This particular interaction is formally based upon the successful completion of previous interactions from the past, formally represented by the X → Y (small type) notation depicted within the past-directed time wedge. Indeed, this previous experience serves as the basic motivational template for the current ongoing interaction, promoting active procurement (X), in hopes of future reinforcement (Y).

According to Part B, the inevitable passage of time further relegates procurement (X) to a memory role prompted by the active bestowal of reinforcement (Y) in the present. This current reinforcement now targets the formerly active procurement role, promoting an effective sense of closure to the completed operant sequence. This

(A)

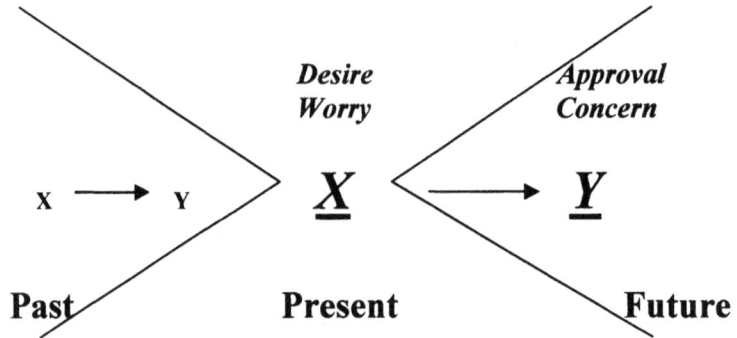

(B)

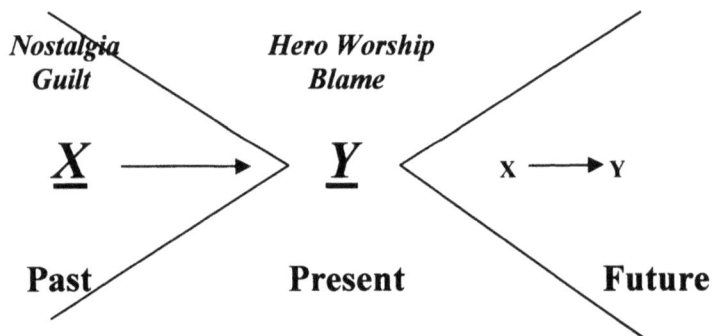

Fig. 3A - The Two-Stage Schematic for Operant Conditioning

circumstance further serves as the active template upon which all future operant sequences are based, as represented by the X → Y (small type) notation depicted in the future-directed time wedge. Through this systematic interplay of sequences (A) and (B), both procurement and reinforcement share an equal spotlight in the present, along with their subsequent displacement into either past or future timeframes respectively. In fact, the completion of Part B formally sets the stage for further cycles within the operant sequence; for if configuration (B) is phase shifted one step further into the past, one returns back to the identical configuration depicted in Part A !

This cyclic periodicity is certainly a key feature of this formal model, for (in the real world) these motivational interchanges accumulate in a seamless fashion over real time. Indeed, it is chiefly through this systematic style of analysis (isolated through stages over time) that the conditioned relationship is respectively seen as punctuated from either the procurement or reinforcement perspectives.

THE INTROSPECTIVE SIDE TO CONDITIONING THEORY

This dual "staggered" model of the conditioned relationship, although suitably comprehensive in scope, unfortunately is limited by a strict reliance upon behavioral terminology. Although procurement and reinforcement retain their objective significance within an active time frame, their extension to either past or future dimensions respectively begs for a corresponding distinction in meaning. Although behavioral terminology (true to its objective prerequisites) proves effectively inadequate in this regard, colloquial English is infinitely better equipped, particularly with respect to categories dealing with subjective motivations. For clues to these specifics, it ultimately proves fruitful to redirect the focus of this analysis to the literature of "self-help" psychology, a genre generally specializing in such personalized motivational themes.

The most fitting launch-point for such an examination concerns the very initiation of the operant sequence, where active procurement behaviors (appetite or aversive) anticipate the future bestowal of reinforcement; namely, rewarding or lenient behaviors, respectively. As schematically depicted in Part-A of **Fig. 3A**, the operant sequence X → Y represents a future-directed style of interaction, with active procurement (X) directly aimed towards securing a measure of future reinforcement (Y).

112 – DESIRE

This active sense of procurement (in a solicitous sense) is colloquially equated with *desire*, a forward-looking emotion that anticipates the contingent bestowal of approval or rewards. For instance, the celebrity entertainer, through his polished stage-act, solicits a rewarding sense of approval from his retinue of admiring fans. His desirous quest for approval represents the driving force behind his entertaining routine, the eventual bestowal of applause further spurring his quest for suitable fanfare. The celebrity bears a certain risk in assuming that reinforcement will eventually be forthcoming. He can, however, be reasonably assured by the wealth of previous cycles of reinforcement over the past, wherein spurring hopes for similar acclaim in the future.

122 – APPROVAL

The reinforcing aspects of the related theme of *approval* are formally reflected in its respective derivation, tracing its origins to the Latin *probus* (good). It is traditionally defined as an act of sanction or commendation, also synonymous with "approbation" (of similar derivation). According to the preceding celebrity example, the devoted fan rewardingly expresses approval through a hearty round of applause, or other such expression of goodwill. In this expanded sense, the fan's reinforcing sense of approval directly reciprocates the desirous perspective initially expressed by the personal authority figure.

113 – WORRY

A similar style of analysis further holds true with respect to the avoidance types of behavior, a variation colloquially equated with *worry*. In keeping with the preceding celebrity example, the celebrity worrisomely acts in a submissive fashion, wherein fully expecting a lenient sense of concern from his peer group. This worrisome perspective is particularly suggested in the throat-baring behaviors initially described for the wolf pack, where the submissive pack member exaggerates his degree of vulnerability in anticipation of a speedy sense of relief. In a more advanced verbal respect, worry operates in a similar fashion: a vocal expression of submissiveness aimed at eliciting a lenient sense of concern. Indeed, it would clearly appear risky to express such an extreme degree of vulnerability without a reasonable assurance of upcoming leniency. Past conditioned cycles again come into play, where previous instances of leniency further justify such a radical act of faith.

123 – CONCERN

The affiliated concept of concern certainly fits the general profile of leniency, conventionally defined as the act of troubling oneself or professing an interest in another. In direct response to the personal authority's apprehensive sense of worry, the personal follower leniently acts in a concerned fashion, wherein acting to alleviate such an aversive perspective. Although the broad range of connotations associated with concern might suggest other possible interpretations, the current (more restricted) perspective certainly fits the prerequisites specified for the conditioned relationship, a factor further verified for the more abstract levels established within the ascending authority hierarchy.

THE AUTHORITY / FOLLOWER ROLES

The preliminary style of conditioned interaction (namely, desire/approval and worry/concern), in turn, allows further crucial insights into the distinctive dichotomy between the authority and follower roles within the power hierarchy. In a strictly formal sense, the personal authority is defined as that role which comes first in the operant sequence. The respective desirous/worrisome perspectives effectively dictate the upcoming bestowal of reinforcement by the personal follower figure. This latter follower role (as its title implies) directly *follows* the preliminary perspective of the personal authority figure, further playing up the potential for the forthcoming reinforcement. Indeed, without this ultimate bestowal of reinforcement, the personal authority's preliminary procurement behaviors will all have been in vain, similar to the case previously established for the celebrity and his fan base.

This respective interplay of authority/follower roles, in turn, is modified with respect to the second stage of the conditioned interaction. This subsequent phase represents the active bestowal of reinforcement by the personal follower, as schematically represented in Part-B of **Fig. 3A**. This second stage is phase-shifted one step further into the past. Reinforcement (Y) now occupies the present, whereas procurement (X) is displaced into the past-directed time wedge. In essence, the personal follower is respectively thrust into an immediately active role, directly reinforcing the past worthy deeds initiated by the personal authority figure.

THE ERRONEOUS ZONES

For clues to the specifics of this follower-based terminology, it ultimately proves crucial to return to the literature of self-help psychology, a genre specializing in such personalized emotional themes. Take, for example, the runaway bestseller, *Your Erroneous Zones*, by Dr. Wayne Dyer. The clever title (a play on the sensationalism of the erogenous zones) piqued the interest of an entire generation, although its more profound themes ensured its enduring significance. This work specifically examines the phenomenon of emotional dependencies and how they can become damaging to one's personal self-esteem. The fact that Dr. Dyer considers them to be "erroneous" is based upon his personal value judgement of what constitutes a truly self-actualized individual.

In Chapter VII, Breaking the Barrier of Convention, Dr. Dyer introduces the novel concept of the focusing-on-others-line, cleverly abbreviated "f.o.o.l." It alludes to the foolishness of looking outside oneself for sole advice on how to feel or act. It represents a conceptual continuum linking the affiliated erroneous zones of hero-worship and blame, both of which represent externally directed behaviors that focus upon others to the exclusion of taking responsibility for oneself. According to Dr. Dyer, there is nothing inherently self-defeating about appreciating others or their achievements so long as this tendency does not repudiate of one's individual self-worth. For instance, the hero-worshipper warmly exalts the lofty standards set by another, becoming "erroneous" only when one's personal hero becomes significantly more important. In a related sense, blamefulness aims to direct the focus away from oneself, seeking external reasons for one's feelings of helplessness or frustration.

120 – HERO WORSHIP

As the first term within the focusing-on-others-line, hero-worship colloquially represents a rewarding style of positive reinforcement bestowed by the personal follower. It specifically rewards the past notable achievements of the personal authority, experienced as a poignant sense of nostalgia. For instance, in the familiar example of the "autograph hound," the personal follower worshipfully acts in a rewarding fashion towards his authority figure in hopes of receiving an autograph or other such token of acknowledgement. This worshipful perspective, expressed in terms of a glowing sense of adulation, is generally sufficient to elicit a modest acknowledgement of appreciation from the respective authority figure.

110 – NOSTALGIA

The celebrity figure (from the preceding example), in turn, is reciprocally dependent upon his retinue of admiring fans. Indeed, any nostalgia perspective remains entirely meaningless without such suitable fanfare. This poignant acknowledgement of past worthy achievements is certainly warranted within such a worshipful context, a role directly in keeping with such a grand authority status. The personal authority, accordingly, is someone the personal follower looks to for personal direction/guidance, providing a fitting sense of purpose to the latter's hero-worship role.

121 – BLAME

A similar circumstance further holds true with respect to the remaining sequence of terms based upon guilt/blame. As the opposite pole on the focusing-on-others-line, blame exhibits distinct similarities to hero-worship with the exception that leniency (rather than rewards) is now called into focus. Similar to hero-worship, blame is essentially a verbal perspective, wherein impugning the sensibilities of one's authority figure in a censuring display of concern. In spelling-out grievances in terms of such blameful expression of censure, the personal follower, in turn, solicits the sincere acknowledgement of culpability from the personal authority figure. In this latter respect, the personal follower leniently acts blamefully, wherein prompting the guilt perspective of the personal authority figure.

111 – GUILT

In response to the blameful treatment of the personal follower, the personal authority guiltily acts submissively: a verbal expression of culpability along the lines of an appeasement perspective. Through such a submissive stance, the personal authority plays-up his vulnerability within the conditioned interaction in response to the lenient treatment of the personal follower figure. In essence, his professed sense of guilt effectively cuts short the potential for any further conflict. Any subsequent action taken against the guilty party is now motivated out of a blameful sense of concern. According to this more moderate strategy, lenient rehabilitation (rather than vengeful retribution) now remains the order of the day.

THE EGO AND ALTER EGO STATES

In this highly interdependent sense, the personal authority and personal follower effectively complement one another within the conditioned relationship, wherein formally maintaining an equal balance of power. Indeed, the hero is equally dependent upon the attentions of his sidekick. Similarly, the master craftsman is essentially lost without the cooperation of his apprentice. Herein lies the fundamental paradox underlying the authority/follower interaction: namely, one hand is definitely needed to wash the other. The old Zen Buddhist adage describing how the follower leads the leader (as much as the other way around) certainly rings true in this basic respect.

It remains only a further minor step to formally label this dual complement of colloquial terms for both authority and follower roles. The choice of the "erroneous zones" (I & II) was an initial consideration in deference to Dr. Dyer's considerable contribution to the field. In addition to hero worship and blame, Dr. Dyer also discusses both guilt and worry in *Your Erroneous Zones*. In order to avoid confounding these two basic groupings, the ultimate designation of the ego and alter ego states was ultimately selected.

The first-mentioned listing of ego states (guilt-worry-nostalgia-desire) formally specifies the motivations specific to the personal authority role. This initial complement of terms directly confirms the basic observation that procurement behaviors serve to initiate the two-stage operant sequence. The *ego* is defined as the most basic sense of self to emerge through self-reflection. Accordingly, the elementary character of this respective class of ego states directly bears out this interpretation. The ego states prove equally applicable with respect to inanimate objects within the environment (such as in desiring a cup of water), further verifying their elementary status.

The remaining listing of alter ego states, in turn, refers to motivations specific to the personal follower role: e.g., hero/worship-blame-approval-concern. As their name implies, the alter ego states represent higher-order perspectives on the more elementary complement of ego states. For instance, the *blame* perspective of the personal follower builds directly upon the guilt expressed by the personal authority figure. Furthermore, *approval* complements desire, whereas *hero worship* reciprocates nostalgia. Generally speaking, the personal follower consummates the sequence initially established by the personal authority figure: in essence, objectifying the role of the latter, wherein lending credence to the term "alter ego."

THE METAPERSPECTIVE SCHEMATIC FORMAT

The higher-order paradigm of the alter ego states is further reminiscent of a similar concept pioneered in the emerging field of Communication Theory; most notably, the *metaperspective* format pioneered by R. D. Laing and P. I. Watzlawick. In *Interpersonal Perception* (1966) Laing (et al) researched the dynamics of interpersonal communication, characterized as "the spiral of reciprocal perspectives." In his *Pragmatics of Human Communication* (1967) Watzlawick (and associates) alternately focused upon the informational aspects of communication, defined as a "hierarchy of metaperspectives." Both of these formulations share a common theme; namely, communication between individuals is generally compounded by abstract "meta" messages that define how the relationship is to be conducted. The metaperspective, from the Greek *meta* (above), is defined as a higher-order perspective on a viewpoint held by another: schematically described as "this is how I see you seeing me." Spontaneous forms of communication are objectified as formal objects of discourse, adding both a sense of content and context to a given verbal interaction.

In addition to this initial class of metaperspective, even more abstract perspectives are theoretically feasible, leading to what Communication Theorists term the *meta-metaperspective*. This more advanced perspective is one meta-level further removed from the more basic metaperspective format, schematically defined as: "this is how I see you - seeing me - seeing you." Indeed, there does not appear to be any barrier limiting the degree to which reflection can serve as a basis for itself, resulting in a multi-level model of meta-communication in general. This metaperspective format, depicted in **Fig. 3B**, provides a schematic interpretation of the unified power hierarchy, culminating in an unprecedented 10th-order level of meta-abstraction.

A REVIEW OF CONDITIONING THEORY

In summary, the completed description of the ego and alter ego states effectively rounds out the stepwise description of the personal power realm. The somewhat technical tone for this introductory chapter proved particularly crucial here. Indeed, a sturdy foundation is crucial to the construction of any higher-level structure. It proves particularly fruitful, therefore, to formally summarize what has been proposed in this somewhat technical

style of chapter. First proposed were the instinctual types of conditioned behavior so eloquently categorized in B. F. Skinner's terminology of operant conditioning. This instinctual foundation, in turn, proved applicable to a human sphere of influence, a model of motivation taking full account of mankind's heritage within the animal kingdom. Skinner's elementary principles of positive and negative reinforcement certainly proved well suited to the task, providing the elementary framework for the subsequent hierarchy of virtues, values, and ideals.

Further described were the two-stage dynamics of operant conditioning, offering crucial insights into sequences that extends to the alternate time dimensions. Human society is uniquely specialized to operate within such alternate time dimensions: namely, the tendency to learn from past experience, as well as the ability to plan for future contingencies. Operant terminology proved inadequate in terms of such introspectively derived perspectives, wherein necessitating the introduction of colloquial terms into the mix. With minor modification, the "erroneous zones" introduced by Dr. Wayne Dyer proved adequate to the task consistent with their revised designations as ego/alter ego states. These colloquial groupings add a crucial introspective dimension to the strictly objective nature of behavioral terminology, serving as the subjective foundation for the remaining higher-order listings of virtues, values, and ideals.

This resultant ten-level hierarchy of ethical terms, in turn, redirects the focus of the current analysis, effectively specifying the repetition of both the authority and follower roles within the power hierarchy. Being that the personal authority acts first within the operant sequence, it seems only fitting that he would be the first to repeat in the modified sense of group authority. The group authority perspective, in turn, is countered by the meta-meta-metaperspective of the group representative. Indeed, this ascending hierarchy of authority/follower roles ultimately extends to the confluence of spiritual, humanitarian, and transcendental levels: culminating in an unprecedented 10th-order level of meta-abstraction, reflected in the respective categories of virtues, values, and ideals.

One might rightfully question the capacity of the human mind to entertain such an advanced multiplicity of metaperspectives, particularly at the most abstract meta-order levels. The mind is apparently able to selectively focus-in upon the immediately relevant levels within the ascending power hierarchy similar to the analogy of a ten-

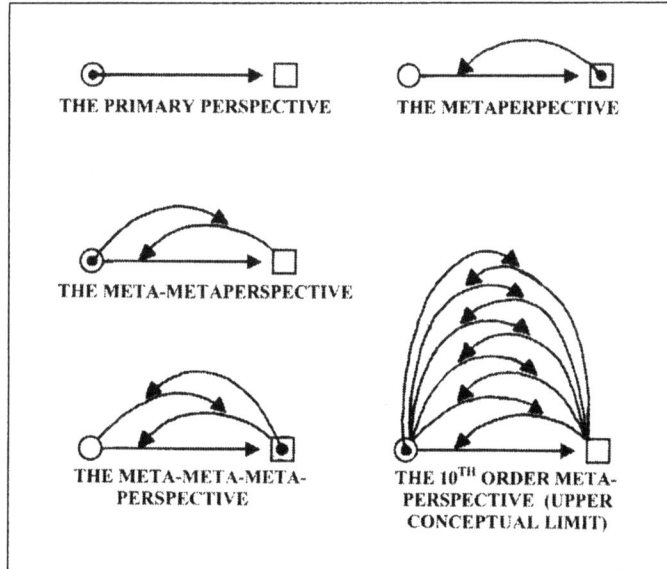

Fig. 3B - The Ten-Level Hierarchy of Metaperspectives
The Schematic Foundation for the Ten-Level Hierarchy of Virtues, Values, and Ideals

level flight of stairs. The process of rising to the next higher step implies the primacy of the immediately adjoining levels, amounting to a span of three individual levels (equivalent to the meta-metaperspective): quite a modest task for the versatile human mind.

THE SCHEMATIC DEFINITIONS FOR THE VIRTUES, VALUES, AND IDEALS

Although the preceding style of virtuous hierarchy proves convincing on an intuitive level, its enhanced degree of detail necessitates an even more comprehensive degree of precision than has currently been demonstrated. In this latter respect, the systematic organization of the authority hierarchy formally permits the construction of what must necessarily be termed the "schematic definitions" of the power hierarchy. This crucial innovation spells out in longhand the precise location of each virtue/value within the linguistic matrix while simultaneously preserving the correct orientation of the respective authority/follower roles. Each such definition is formally constructed along the lines of a two-stage sequential format; namely, (A) the formal recognition of the preliminary power maneuver, and (B) the countermaneuver currently being employed and, hence, labeled. Take, for example, the schematic definition for the representative cardinal virtue of *justice*, reproduced below from the comprehensive series

of definitions depicted in **Tables A-1** to **A-4**.

> Previously, I (as your group authority) have honorably acted in a guilty fashion towards you: countering your (as PF) blameful treatment of me.
> But now, you, (as group representative) will justly-blame me: overruling my (as GA) honorable sense of guilt.

According to this specific "justice" example, the honorable sense of guilt expressed by the group authority represents the preliminary power maneuver, wherein countered by the *just*-blaming of the group representative. Note how the polarity of authority/follower roles is effectively preserved equivalent to their original polarity outlined in **Fig. 2**. In terms of this two-stage schematic format, the preliminary power perspective represents the "one-down" power maneuver, whereas the current power maneuver designates the "one-up" variety. Power leverage, accordingly, is secured by rising to a "one-up" power status; namely, ascending to the next higher metaperspectival level. This comprehensive hierarchy of schematic definitions is essentially viewed as a motivational style of calculus replete with the transformational rules governing how each level meshes with those above or below it. In keeping

NOSTALGIA	HERO WORSHIP
Previously, you (as reinforcer) have rewardingly acted in a reinforcing fashion towards me: overriding my (as procurer) solicitous treatment of you. But now, I (as personal authority) will *nostalgically* act in a solicitous fashion towards you: overruling your rewarding treatment of me.	Previously, I (as personal authority) have nostalgically acted in solicitous fashion towards you: overriding your (as reinforcer) rewarding treatment of me. But now, you (as personal follower) will *worshipfully* act in a rewarding fashion towards me: overruling my (as PA) nostalgic treatment of you.
GLORY	**PRUDENCE**
Previously, you (as my personal follower) have worshipfully acted in a rewarding fashion towards me: overriding my (as PA) nostalgic treatment of you. But now, I (as group authority) will *gloriously* act in a nostalgic fashion towards you: overruling your (as PF) worshipful treatment of me.	Previously, I (as group authority) have gloriously acted in a nostalgic fashion towards you: overriding your (as PF) worshipful treatment of me. But now, you (as group representative) will *prudently* act worshipfully towards me: overruling my (as GA) glorious treatment of you.
PROVIDENCE	**FAITH**
Previously, you (as group representative) have prudently acted in a worshipful fashion towards me: overriding my (as GA) gloriously-nostalgic treatment of you. But now, I (as spiritual authority) will gloriously act in a *provident* fashion towards you: overruling your (as GR) prudent-worship of me.	Previously, I (as spiritual authority) have gloriously acted in a provident fashion towards you: overriding your (as GR) prudent-worship of me. But now, you (as my spiritual disciple) will prudently act in a *faithful* fashion towards me: overruling my (as SA) provident treatment of you.
GRACE	**BEAUTY**
Previously, you (as my spiritual disciple) have prudently acted in a faithful fashion towards me: overriding my (as SA) gloriously-provident treatment of you. But now, I (as humanitarian authority) will providently act in a *graceful* fashion towards you: overruling your (as SD) prudent-faith in me.	Previously, I (as your humanitarian authority) have providently acted gracefully towards you: overriding your (as SD) prudent-faith in me. But now, you (as representative member of humanity) will *beauteously* act in a faithful fashion towards me: overruling my (as HA) graceful treatment of you.
TRANQUILITY	**ECSTASY**
Previously, you (as representative member of humanity) have beauteously acted in a faithful fashion towards me: overriding my (as HA) providently-graceful treatment of you. But now, I (as transcendental authority) will *tranquilly* act in a graceful fashion towards you: overruling your (as RH) beauteous-faith in me.	Previously, I (as your transcendental authority) have tranquilly acted gracefully towards you: overriding your (as RH) beauteous-faith in me. But now, you (as my transcendental follower) will beauteously act in an *ecstatic* fashion towards me: overruling my (as TA) tranquil sense of gracefulness.

Table A-1 - The Definitions Based on Nostalgia/Hero-Worship

GUILT	BLAME
Previously, you (as reinforcer) have leniently acted in a reinforcing fashion towards me: overriding my (as procurer) submissive treatment of you. But now, I (as personal authority) will *guiltily* act in a submissive fashion towards you: overruling your lenient treatment of me.	Previously, I (as personal authority) have guiltily acted in a submissive fashion towards you: overriding your (as reinforcer) lenient treatment of me. But now, you (as my personal follower) will *blamefully* act in a lenient fashion towards me: overruling my (as PA) guilty treatment of you.
HONOR	JUSTICE
Previously, you (as my personal follower) have blamefully acted in a lenient fashion towards me: overriding my (as PA) guilty treatment of you. But now, I (as group authority) will *honorably* act in a guilty fashion towards you: overruling your (as PF) blameful treatment of me.	Previously, I (as group authority) have honorably acted in a guilty fashion towards you: overriding your (as PF) blameful treatment of me. But now, you (as group representative) will *justly*-blame me: overruling my (as GA) honorable sense of guilt.
LIBERTY	HOPE
Previously, you (as group representative) have justly-blamed me: overriding my (as GA) honorable sense of guilt. But now, I (as spiritual authority) will honorably act in a *libertarian* fashion towards you: overruling your just-blaming of me.	Previously, I (as spiritual authority) have honorably acted in a libertarian fashion towards you: overriding your (as GR) just-blaming of me. But now, you (as my spiritual disciple) will blamefully-*hope* for justice: overruling my (as SA) libertarian sense of honor.
FREE WILL	TRUTH
Previously, you (as my spiritual disciple) have blamefully-hoped for justice: overriding my (as SA) libertarian sense of honor. But now, I (as humanitarian authority) will honorably act in a *freely willed* fashion towards you: overruling your (as SD) blameful-hope for justice.	Previously, I (as humanitarian authority) have honorably acted in a freely-willed fashion towards you: overriding your (as SD) blameful-hope for justice. But now, you (as representative member of humanity) will justly-hope for the *truth*: overruling my (as HA) libertarian sense of free will.
EQUALITY	BLISS
Previously, you (as representative member of humanity) have justly-hoped for the truth: overriding my (as HA) libertarian sense of free will. But now, I (as transcendental authority) will freely-willed act in an *egalitarian* fashion towards you: overruling your (as RH) just-hope for the truth.	Previously, I (as transcendental authority) have freely-willed acted in an egalitarian fashion towards you: overriding your (as RH) just-hope for the truth. But now, you (as my transcendental follower) will *blissfully* hope for the truth: overruling my (as TA) egalitarian treatment of you.

Table A-2 – The Definitions Based Upon Guilt/Blame

DESIRE	APPROVAL
Previously, I (as reinforcer) have rewardingly acted in a reinforcing fashion towards you: overriding your (as procurer) solicitous treatment of me. But now, you (as personal authority) will *desirously* act in a solicitous fashion towards me: overruling my rewarding treatment of you.	Previously, you (as personal authority) have desirously acted in a solicitous fashion towards me: overriding my (as reinforcer) rewarding treatment of you. But now, I (as your personal follower) will rewardingly act in an *approving* fashion towards you: overruling your (as PA) desirous treatment of me.
DIGNITY	**TEMPERANCE**
Previously, I (as your personal follower) have rewardingly acted in an approving fashion towards you: overriding your (as PA) desirous treatment of me. But now, you (as group authority) will *dignifiedly* act in a desirous fashion towards me: overruling my (as PF) approving treatment of you.	Previously, you (as my group authority) have dignifiedly acted in a desirous fashion towards me: overriding my (as PF) approving treatment of you. But now, I (as group representative) will *temperately* act in an approving fashion towards you: overruling your (as GA) dignified-desire for me.
CIVILITY	**CHARITY**
Previously, I (as group representative) have temperately acted in an approving fashion towards you: overriding your (as GA) dignified-desire for me. But now, you (as spiritual authority) will dignifiedly act in a *civil* fashion towards me: overruling my (as GR) temperate-approval of you	Previously, you (as my spiritual authority) have dignifiedly acted in a civil fashion towards me: overriding my (as GR) temperate approval of you. But now, I (as spiritual disciple) will temperately act *charitably* towards you: overruling your (as SA) civilly-dignified treatment of me.
MAGNANIMITY	**GOODNESS**
Previously, I (as your spiritual disciple) have temperately acted in a charitable fashion towards you: overriding your (as SA) civilly-dignified treatment of me. But now, you (as humanitarian authority) will civilly act *magnanimously* towards me overruling my (as SD) charitable treatment of you.	Previously, you (as humanitarian authority) have civilly acted magnanimously towards me: overriding my (as SD) charitable treatment of you. But now, I (as representative member of humanity) will charitably act with *goodness* towards you: overruling your (as HA) magnanimous treatment of me.
LOVE	**JOY**
Previously, I (as representative member of humanity) have charitably acted with goodness towards you: overriding your (as HA) civilly-magnanimous treatment of me. But now, you (as transcendental authority) will magnanimously act *lovingly* towards me: overruling my (as RH) goodly treatment of you.	Previously, you (as transcendental authority) have magnanimously acted lovingly towards me: overriding my (as RH) goodly treatment of you. But now, I (as your transcendental follower) will goodly act in a *joyous* fashion towards you: overruling your (as TA) magnanimously-loving treatment of me.

Table A-3 – The Definitions Based Upon Desire/Approval

WORRY	CONCERN
Previously, I (as reinforcer) have leniently acted in a reinforcing fashion towards you: overriding your (as procurer) submissive treatment of me. But now, you (as personal authority) will *worrisomely* act in a submissive fashion towards me: overruling my lenient treatment of you.	Previously, you (as my personal authority) have worrisomely acted in a submissive fashion towards me: overriding my (as reinforcer) lenient treatment of you. But now, I (as your personal follower) will leniently act in a *concerned* fashion towards you: overruling your (as PA) worrisome treatment of me.
INTEGRITY	**FORTITUDE**
Previously, I (as your personal follower) have leniently acted in a concerned fashion towards you: overriding your (as PA) worrisome treatment of me. But now, you (as group authority) will worrisomely act with *integrity* towards me: overruling my (as PF) concerned treatment of you.	Previously, you (as group authority) have worrisomely acted in an integrity-filled fashion towards me: overriding my (as PF) concerned treatment of you. But now, I (as group representative) will *fortitudinously* act with concern towards you: overruling your (as GA) worrisome sense of integrity.
AUSTERITY	**DECENCY**
Previously, I (as group representative) have fortitudinously acted in a concerned fashion towards you: overriding your (as GA) worrisome sense of integrity. But now, you (as spiritual authority) will *austerely* act with integrity towards me: overruling my (as GR) fortitudinous sense of concern.	Previously, you (as spiritual authority) have austerely acted with integrity towards me: overriding my (as GR) fortitudinous sense of concern. But now, I (as spiritual disciple) will fortitudinously act in a *decent* fashion towards you: overruling your (as SA) austere sense of integrity.
EQUANIMITY	**WISDOM**
Previously, I (as your spiritual disciple) have fortitudinously acted in a decent fashion towards you: overriding your (as SA) austere sense of integrity. But now, you (as humanitarian authority) will austerely act with *equanimity* towards me: overruling my (as SD) decent treatment of you.	Previously, you (as humanitarian authority) have austerely acted with equanimity towards me: overriding my (as SD) decent treatment of you. But now, I (as representative member of humanity) will decently act in a *wise* fashion towards you: overruling your (as HA) austere sense of equanimity.
PEACE	**HARMONY**
Previously, I (as representative member of humanity) have decently acted in a wise fashion towards you: overriding your (as HA) austere sense of equanimity. But now, you (as transcendental authority) will *peaceably* act with equanimity towards me: overruling my (as RH) decent sense of wisdom.	Previously, you (as transcendental authority) have peaceably acted with equanimity towards me: overriding my (as RH) decent sense of wisdom. But now, I (as transcendental follower) will wisely act in a *harmonious* fashion towards you: overruling your (as TA) peaceable treatment of me.

Table A-4 – The Definitions Based Upon Worry/Concern

with the principles of a numerical calculus, the integral is viewed as a "one-up" power maneuver, whereas the differential is seen as the "one-down" variety.

In terms of **Tables A-1** to **A-4**, the complete forty-part listing of schematic definitions for the virtuous realm covers the entire ten-level span of the power hierarchy. The instinctual terminology for operant conditioning dominates the preliminary levels, replaced in due fashion by the virtues/values specific to the higher authority levels. For each succeeding level, a new term (distinguished through *italics*) denotes the power maneuver currently under consideration. Beginning with the group level, certain of the preliminary terms begin to drop out of the equation, freeing-up space for the terms currently under consideration, wherein maintaining a stable buffer of terms. The affiliated authority/follower roles similarly remain consistent throughout the ten-level hierarchy, although systematically abbreviated (for the sake of brevity) at non-critical positions. Here, PA stands for personal authority, PF represents the personal follower, etc. Several of the more atypical abbreviations are GR (group representative), SD (spiritual disciple), and RH (representative member of humanity).

The reciprocal interplay of the "you" and "I" roles proves equally crucial, maintaining a stable platform of objective/subjective perspectives, wherein simulating the reciprocal interplay of authority/follower roles. This dual interplay follows a strict set of guidelines; namely, the objective "you" roles are restricted to those immediately occurring in the present, whereas the subjective "I" roles are limited to the past/future time dimensions. In this latter respect, the "I" ego serves as a bookmark for a subjective sense of self characterizing the alternate time dimensions. The objective "you" role, in contrast, is overtly apparent to all in attendance, a real time objectification of the immediately active roles.

This subjective/objective trade-off ultimately permits a more stable sense of role security within the schematic definitions, schematically defined as: "if you, then I" (and vice versa). Consequently, both the authority and follower roles share an equal degree of influence: namely, half are designated from the subjective "I" role, whereas the remainder are specified from the objective "you" status. The corresponding virtuous terms, in turn, verify the specifics of the overall definition format. The discerning reader is encouraged to refer-back to the four tables of schematic definitions through the remainder of the current section, wherein allowing each individual term to be viewed in the global schematic context of the unified power hierarchy.

The remainder of the current **Part I** is devoted to systematically outlining the formal dynamics of the individual virtuous realm. Accordingly, each succeeding chapter is devoted exclusively to a specific authority/follower domain within the power hierarchy, replete with a description of the individual ethical terms. Chapter *4* initiates this analysis with a detailed examination of the group authority/follower roles, introducing the personal ideals and cardinal virtues, respectively. Chapter *5*, in turn, focuses on the spiritual authority/disciple roles, providing an in-depth analysis of the civil liberties and theological virtues. Chapter *6* further examines the corresponding humanitarian roles, introducing the classical Greek values and ecumenical ideals, respectively. Chapter *7*, in turn, targets the transcendental realm, offering an in-depth examination of the humanistic values and mystical values. Finally, Chapters *8* and *9* round out the current section with a discussion of a number of supplementary issues relating to the virtues; namely, the accessory virtues and values along with the general unifying themes. Each of these respective chapters is further enhanced with an extensive body of excerpts from both classical and contemporary literature, adding a further entertaining dimension to such a grand-scale undertaking.

The scope of this background material is essentially eclectic in nature, not favoring any one cultural tradition over another. True to its general foundations in Western thought, many of the ethical terms have originally developed within the Christian tradition, a feature not always compatible with the more secular focus of modern academia. The spirited literary excerpts from Church theologians and Bible scripture, nevertheless, were left intact: for to qualify these historical documents in hindsight would greatly diminish the impact of the background material. This eclectic strategy, however, should not be construed as favoring one faith-based system over another; for the virtuous perspective is effectively a global phenomenon. With this caveat firmly in place, the objective prerequisites for the current reference work should satisfy even the most stringent of critics, a resource that should remain applicable even on a global stage. This grand undertaking is hereby initiated with a detailed analysis of the group power realm, an institution virtually synonymous with many collective forms of human endeavor.

4

THE GROUP ETHICAL REALM

Group (or tribal) authority is certainly one of mankind's most time-honored traditions. Prior to the dawning of our modern agricultural age, primitive hunter tribes wandered the earth following the uneven distribution of game animals, much as occurs in the remote outposts of the world today. In a purely organizational sense, the human tribe shows many similarities to the primitive social order of the lion pride or the wolf pack, although a closer examination reveals many finer distinctions. In particular, the human tribe is distinguished through its symbolic use of verbal communication over and beyond any instinctual form of body language. Lower animal societies are limited almost exclusively to this gestural style of communication, as suggested in the grooming and throat-baring types of behavior previously described. Although vocalization is often a key feature in many complex animal societies, it is chiefly employed in a guttural fashion without any consensus sense of form or meaning.

Although these instinctual forms of communication (by definition) occur chiefly between individuals, such personal interactions, in turn, are summated across the extent of the social hierarchy: resulting in a "round-robin" style of pecking order. This dominance hierarchy only superficially conforms to true tribal authority in that it promotes a single dominant leader overseeing a descending hierarchy of less powerful individuals. This arrangement further makes little provision for any enduring sense of permanence, resulting in a frequent reshuffling of power within the pecking order. The human tribe, in contrast, picks a single consensus leader overseeing a collective of virtually equal followers. Although jockeying for position is not entirely abandoned, it ultimately is made subordinate to this group power leverage.

This distinction between the simple pecking order and true group authority is chiefly made possible through mankind's innovative use of verbal symbolism. Nonverbal communication is meaningful only in immediate types of contexts, allowing only for one obvious means of interpretation; namely, the most basic pecking order sense. Human language, in contrast, is distinguished by its ability to communicate symbolically about abstract or motivational issues: permitting verbal communication not formally tied to such immediate concerns. Through this verbal refinement, mankind is essentially able to distinguish the more abstract style of group authority from its more elementary foundation in the personal pecking order, setting the stage for the cooperative social structure so crucial on the world scene today.

The group authority achieves this enhanced authority status by countering the more limited partisan concerns of the personal follower. The "side kick" style of strike leverage employed by the personal follower no longer proves effective against the group authority, who announces that individual members are now expendable when it comes down to a personal challenge for power. According to this third-order metaperspectival format, enough followers always remain to perpetuate group authority whether or not any individual should decide to desert. In a single stroke, the group authority is elevated well above any personal power struggles, an innovation that has endured as the familiar tradition of civic authority.

Although group authority has undergone many refinements down through the ages, its basic dynamics have remained fairly consistent in nature. Originally the tribal chiefdom was organized along familial lines, with related clan members answering to a single dominant patriarch or matriarch. Similarities in language and culture eventually brought related clans together, resulting in the enduring trend towards the nation state. Originally, nationalism implied the leadership of a regal monarch, with royal power passed down (in tribal fashion) through inheritance. This regal authority was celebrated through the potent use of ritual symbolisms: as reflected in the enduring Western traditions of the scepter, throne, crown, etc. The supportive cast of influential dukes and nobles relied upon a similar use of heraldic symbolisms for maintaining their accessory authority status.

The Western tradition of heraldry dates at least to medieval times, expressed in the development of the hereditary "coat of arms." This latter term derives from the military custom of embroidering the emblem of the knight directly upon the surcoat covering the armor. The protective function of the armor complicated the identification of friend or foe during the heat of battle, leading to the invention of personal heraldic symbolisms inscribed upon the shield. Originally, these symbols were personally selected, generally commemorating a defining episode during the knight's military career. Confusion ultimately arose concerning the duplication of designs, leading to the formal appointment of *heralds*, whose supervision of the art form gave rise to the general sense of the term. The introduction of gunpowder eventually rendered protective armor obsolete, reducing heraldry to its current formality of tracing family ancestry.

The traditional coat of arms is formally composed of a shield, crest, and motto. The descriptive terms employed in heraldry are assigned specific meanings in order to avoid confusion amongst the various authorities. A number of key heraldic terms with regal overtones particularly come to mind, in keeping with the four affective dimensions predicted for the group authority perspective. Colorful terms such as the circle of *glory* (or halo), the *honor*-point (on the shield), and the cap of *dignity* (or chapeau) abound within the heraldic literature. Add to these the animal symbolisms associated with *integrity* and the cohesive listing of "personal ideals" falls neatly into place.

This four-part grouping of glory-honor-dignity-integrity collectively traces its origins to the classical Latin tradition. Indeed, the Romans celebrated group leadership to perhaps its grandest degree of style. The personal ideals represent the more advanced group analogues of the subordinate class of ego states (they serve to supercede). Although their personal designation might seem to suggest somewhat of a misnomer, the group authority maneuver directly maneuvers upon the personal follower perspective, wherein accounting for the hybrid quality of the grouping. Accordingly, *glory* represents the group analogue of nostalgia, whereas *honor* denotes a similar

modification of guilt. Furthermore, *dignity* redefines desire from a group perspective, whereas *integrity* denotes a more idealized form of worry. The remainder of the current chapter offers a detailed examination of the personal ideals in concert with their corresponding literary traditions.

130 – GLORY

The first of the personal ideals, *glory*, enjoys a rather broad range of meanings: from exalted praise/honor to heightened achievement or distinction. Its modern spelling derives from the Latin *gloria* (of similar meaning and usage). As with so many of their abstract concepts, the Romans divinely worshipped glory as a deity: as witnessed in a dedicatory inscription to *Gloria* unearthed at Numidia in Northern Africa. She also appears as Gloria Exercitus (training, exercise) on medallions of the Roman emperor Constantius II, and simply as *Gloria* on other imperial coins.

The classical Greeks also worshipped this aspect in the guise of their abstract goddess *Eucleia*. Originally, Eucleia had been a surname of Artemis (the Greek Goddess of the Hunt), although this qualifier eventually came to be worshipped as a deity in its own right. She was particularly worshipped in the city-state of Athens, where a sanctuary was dedicated to her from the spoils-of-war seized at the Battle of Marathon. This battle was the greatest military triumph for the brave Athenians, with a reported *6,400* Persian casualties vs. *192* fatalities for the Athenians. Eucleia, accordingly, symbolized the exalted state of glory the Athenians enjoyed on their exalted victory day.

During the subsequent Christian era, glory retained its grand pretensions, as reflected in the symbolisms associated with the circle of glory (or halo). The halo is traditionally defined as a translucent disc of light surrounding the heads of revered religious figures. It also takes the form of brilliant rays of light or an illuminated cloud (the nimbus). The circle of glory originally appears to have been a Roman invention, signifying the divine power wielded by pagan deities, although eventually emerging as a key feature of Christian art. For the early Christian Church the halo was restricted to depictions of Divinity; only later extending to angels, saints, and martyrs. In certain depictions of the Trinity, the trio of halos is embellished with intersecting bars of light suggestive of a crucifix, bejeweled in a style fitting a king. Indeed, some representations are inscribed with the letters of the Latin *Rex* (king) within the bars of the cruciform halo denoting nobility.

The Heraldic Symbolisms for the Personal Ideals
In Clockwise Order: Circle of Glory – Honor Point – Rampant – Cap of Dignity

These group symbolisms for glory also figure prominently in the classical traditions of Eucleia, where the victorious Greeks were bountifully rewarded through the corresponding spoils of war. Similarly, the halo is a fitting artistic device for depicting divinely bestowed glory. Even in our modern era, glory still figures prominently in prestigious sporting events such as the Olympics, where great performances by winning athletes are acknowledged in glorious medal presentation ceremonies attended by throngs of admiring fans. The fact that such athletes are classified as amateurs (competing without pay) only further serves to magnify the symbolic glory they bow to receive upon the presentation stand.

131 – HONOR

Any discussion of glory must necessarily remain incomplete without mention of the related theme of *honor*. Honor is similarly invested with a broad range of meaning: from admiration and esteem to nobility and honesty. Its modern spelling derives from the classical Latin term of similar spelling and meaning. Similar to the case previously made for glory, honor was also worshipped as a deity by the Romans, personified by their abstract god Honos. On Roman coins and medals, Honos is depicted as a handsome youth holding a spear in his right hand and a "horn of plenty" in his left. He is crowned with a wreath of bay leaves and his chest is exposed. His chief temple was situated outside the Porta Capena in Rome, in close proximity to the temple of Mars, the Roman God of War. An even more ancient altar was dedicated to Honos outside the Colline gate. Persons sacrificing here were obliged to have their heads uncovered: a custom still widely followed today in the swearing of oaths.

The early Middle Ages further preserved such classical considerations, with honor figuring prominently in the Codes of Courtesy and Chivalry, also known as the Court of Venus and the Field of Mars. Indeed, in medieval heraldry, the honor point refers to the high center point on the shield, the field where the crowning symbolisms of nobility are most likely to occur. The heraldic sense of the term actually spans a much broader range of meaning, implying primacy and/or seniority. It also suggests (like honesty) a sense of what is rightfully expected with respect to one's civic obligations.

This upright quality comes through most clearly with respect to the tradition of the Code of Honor: namely, that system of reciprocal rights and obligations governing a particular trade or profession. It typically takes the form of honesty in one's business dealings, as well as loyalty to one's fraternal organizations. It frequently was compounded by the themes of etiquette and good breeding consistent with such a refined social context. Consequently, this code eventually came to be associated with many stylized rituals: most notably, the time-honored custom of dueling to restore one's honor (or that of one's family).

132 – DIGNITY

The third of the personal ideals, *dignity*, continues the spirit of the group authority perspective, although now shifting the focus to a more active perspective. Its modern spelling derives from the Latin *dignitas* (merit or worth), from *dignus* (worthy): the same root for the Latin *decorum* (propriety). The great Roman statesman Cicero directly mentions dignity within the context of his rhetorical treatment of decorum. In the course of his dissertation, Cicero restricted this term exclusively to the brotherhood of man: defining dignity as that crucial quality which distinguishes man from lower animals. He further states that mankind's intellect is superior in its capacity for rational insight, in direct contrast to the more shortsighted pursuits of the rest of the animal kingdom. These classical themes underwent a significant revival during the Renaissance, when Italian humanists (following Cicero's precedent) equated the dignity of man with the tradition of the humanities. Dignity, accordingly, was associated with the *art* of being human, instilled through the study of the liberal arts and sciences.

These classical overtones further extended to the Middle Ages with respect to the heraldic symbolisms affiliated with dignity. These were particularly apparent with respect to the stylized *chapeau*, also known as the cap of dignity or estate. As the chief heraldic emblem of dignity, the chapeau was elegantly constructed of red velvet: sporting a flat crown and an ermine rim in a regal style reminiscent of the halo. The cap originally was worn by barons and nobles of the British Parliament, formally specifying their elevated rank and status. Around the time of Charles II, the chapeau was further embellished with precious metal around its base, giving rise to the coronet (or crown) of British royalty. Indeed, the velvet cap contained within the British royal crown is directly traceable to this original cap of dignity.

These noble connotations of the chapeau rate further consideration in light of its designation as the cap of maintenance (or estate). According to medieval tradition, the noble enjoyed exclusive control over his feudal estate, accompanied by the attendant responsibilities of maintaining the general welfare of the serfs. In times of trouble, the noble often provided his subjects protection within the walls of his stockade in exchange for their faithful labors on the estate. Indeed, the great power and dignity enjoyed by the noble stemmed directly from his shrewd encouragement of his loyal workforce.

133 – INTEGRITY

The final of the personal ideals, *integrity*, directly parallels the related theme of dignity with the exception that submissiveness (rather than solicitousness) is now called into focus. This basic interpretation is directly reflected in the traditional connotations of the term; namely, moral probity and ethical steadfastness. Its modern spelling derives from the Latin *integritas* (completeness, purity), from *integer* (whole). In this steadfast respect, integrity is figuratively symbolized as the domestic dog consistent with the latter's enduring reputation as "man's best friend."

Perhaps the most celebrated dog in classical mythology was Sirius, the ever-faithful companion of Orion the Hunter. Accordingly, Sirius was honored with a prominent place in the heavens, featured within the constellation *Canis Major* as Sirius, the Dogstar. This name is said to derive from the Greek *seirios* (hot, scorching), alluding to the fact that this star annually appeared in the dawn sky during the hottest time of the year. This fortuitous timing further contributed to the belief that such heat was chiefly accounted for by the brilliance of Sirius. The ancient Egyptians similarly welcomed its morning appearance as a sign that the annual Nile flood would soon be forthcoming. The classical Romans sacrificed red-haired dogs to Sirius, perhaps due to the reddish flashes sometimes seen due to refraction near the horizon. In fact, the Romans affectionately worshipped Sirius as Canicula (Little Dog), which in conjunction with his "warm" reputation led to the common expression "the dog days of summer."

This unswerving devotion for the integrity of the domestic dog is further reflected in its traditionally given name "*Fido*," from the Latin *fideo*

(I believe). Other carnivores with strong social instincts (such as the lion) are also esteemed as paragons of integrity in classical mythology. Indeed, according to Old Testament scripture, the lion and the wolf were respectively revered as the symbolic emblems of the Jewish tribes of Judah and Benjamin. In medieval heraldry, one of the most popular shield arrangements was the *rampant*: namely, a lion standing upright in profile with its front paws splayed (as if warding off a blow). The rampaging lion was sometimes depicted sporting a regal crown, a factor further in keeping with the group overtones of integrity. Indeed, this regal sense of integrity for the group authority (under adverse circumstances) directly complements the more dignified demeanor initially seen in more positive contexts.

THE CARDINAL VIRTUES: THE ESSENCE OF GROUP COHESIVENESS

The completed description of the personal ideals effectively rounds out the stepwise description of the group authority perspective. These four basic themes all derived from Latin roots, accentuating the Roman's enduring fascination with group leadership. The group authority perspective, accordingly, promotes these four basic themes; namely, dignified purpose tempered by integrity, accompanied by a sense of glory/honor in one's civic endeavors. This distinctive group power base effectively allows the group authority to overrule the more shortsighted concerns of the personal follower, in turn, regaining the upper hand within the ascending power hierarchy. In light of the more elementary form of personal authority (which it supersedes), the group authority figure is similarly susceptible to his own unique form of follower countermaneuver: in this case, that expressed by the group representative.

The group follower perspective is essentially as ancient as group authority itself, serving as a crucial counterpoint to the power of the group authority figure. Similar to the personal follower role (that it supercedes), the group representative shares the distinctive style of "strike" leverage characterizing the follower role. Indeed, it is chiefly with through this more advanced (group) context that the strike power of the follower figure reaches its greatest degree of potential. Although this basic strike leverage traces its origins to classical times, it only recently has truly come of age with respect to the dramatic rise of unions and collective bargaining. Prior to the turn of the century the typical factory worker suffered many indignities at the whim of his employer, yet was powerless to resist out of fear of being replaced. By playing one employee against another, management effectively maximized the power leverage implicit for the group authority perspective.

A corresponding rise in power within the group, however, forced management to come to a more equal footing with labor. Through the latter's reorganization as a "union collective," the rank-and-file picked a consensus spokesman (the shop steward) to represent them in their dealings with management. The most powerful leverage in collective bargaining, however, resides in the much publicized (and all too often wielded) strike clause within the union contract. According to this group power tactic, the group representative informs the group authority that without the cooperation of the labor pool, there will be no one left to justify his authority status. Through the judicious use of the strike option, the group representative effectively evens the score in job-related conflicts, as witnessed in the modern-day standoff between labor and management.

This enduring reliance on the strike option for pressing militant demands is generally invoked in only most intractable situations; namely, those negative conflicts where both parties suffer to some degree. It is ultimately possible, however, to invoke a more positive slant on the group follower perspective, as exemplified in the principles governing group *cohesiveness*. According to Group Theory, the theme of cohesiveness refers to a general preponderance of attractive vs. repulsive forces within the group. Cartwright and Zander (1960) identified five attractive forces within the successful group: respectively defined as (1) a strong feeling of "we"ness rather than "I"ness, (2) friendliness and loyalty to fellow members, (3) collective work towards a common goal, (4) willingness to endure pain or frustration for the sake of the group, and (5) a common defense against criticism. According to these same researchers, members attracted to a group are more likely to exhibit congruent attitudes: namely, responsible action, interpersonal harmony, similarity of values, and an emphasis on security within the group.

It still remains to be determined, however, which precise combination of terms goes towards satisfying the requisite four-part complement of affective dimensions predicted for the group representative perspective. Being that the group representative reprises the role originally undertaken as personal follower, this new format, accordingly, should represent a more abstract variation on the initial complement of alter ego states; namely, hero-worship, blame, approval, and concern.

Consequently, it proves fitting to return to the writings of Dr. Wayne Dyer for clues to the identity of this additional class of terms. In *Your Erroneous Zones*, Dr. Dyer hints at a higher class of terms distinguished by their group (rather than personal) sphere of influence. For instance, in Chapter VIII, "The Justice Trap," Dr. Dyer examines the "erroneous zone" of justice in its naive sense of expecting life always to be fair. Indeed, it further proves fitting to draw parallels between justice and its more elementary sense of blame. The outlook for the remaining dimensions, however, proves scarcely as clear. Justice, however, was already specified as one of the four cardinal virtues; namely, prudence-justice-temperance-fortitude. Indeed, this distinctive grouping conveniently appears tailor-made for satisfying the four affective dimensions predicted for the group representative perspective.

THE CLASSICAL TRADITIONS FOR THE CARDINAL VIRTUES

The English spellings for the cardinal virtues all collectively derive from Latin roots, although earlier precedents clearly exist in the Greek tradition. They first appear as a definitive grouping in Plato's dialogue *The Republic*, although Plato intimates that they were already a tradition even in his own day. The lyrical poet Pindar is credited with their first recorded reference in his *Eighth Isthmian Ode* (478 BCE): where Peleus and his fellow Aeacids are cited as models of justice, courage, temperance, prudence, and piety (a fifth virtue originally included within this grouping). In his *Republic*, however, Plato eliminates the somewhat extraneous concept of piety, focusing on the remaining four as the central core for his enduring system of ethical philosophy.

For Plato, virtue played a preeminent role in securing the health and harmony of the soul. In his dialogue *The Republic*, Plato (speaking through Socrates) proposes his utopian vision of the Greek city-state: one wishfully compensating for the weakness plaguing the troubled Athens of his day. Plato's ideal city-state was organized along the lines of a three-part caste system consisting of a ruling elite of guardians, a military class of warriors, and a mercantile class of workers (respectively symbolized as gold, silver, and bronze). The guardian class enjoyed an extensive degree of education accentuating the virtues of *prudence* and wisdom. The warrior class was subject to exhaustive military training selecting for the qualities of *fortitude* and courage in defense of the city. Furthermore, the economic focus of the worker/craftsman class selected for the virtue of *temperance* concerning such economic matters. Finally, the virtue of *justice* was ultimately found in the truth that each caste performed the task for which it was best suited; namely, duties consistent with its respective virtuous mode. The city-state, accordingly, is prudent, just, temperate, and brave: directly amplifying those noble qualities professed by its three supportive castes.

The subsequent rise to power of the Roman Empire brought further consideration to the Latin versions of the cardinal virtues. The Romans greatly admired classical Greek culture, borrowing extensively from their rhetoric and philosophy (including the enduring canon of cardinal virtues). One of the most influential Latin expositions in this regard was Cicero's *De Officiis*, a stirring tribute to the Latinized grouping of prudentia, justitia, temperatus, and fortitio. An early distrust of pagan philosophy initially led many Christians to reject the validity of this Latin complement of cardinal virtues. With the eventual Roman acceptance of Christianity, however, Clement and Origen among the Greeks, as well as Lactantius and Ambrose among the Romans, began freely adapting pagan virtues to fit emerging Christian morality. Origen was among the first to draw attention to the preeminence of the cardinal virtues, describing them as indispensable to moral development. Although not specifically mentioned as a grouping in the New Testament, they nevertheless enjoyed widespread individual appeal. They are also listed as a cohesive grouping in the OT *Wisdom of Solomon*, a book further incorporated into the Apocrypha included within the Roman Catholic Bible.

It remained to the efforts of St. Ambrose (of Milan) to give this classical listing its traditional designation: deriving from the Latin *cardos* (hinge), deriving from the basic belief that all of mankind's more noble tendencies *hinge* upon these basic four virtues. This perspective, indeed, is prophetic in light of the pivotal role these virtues play at the group level within the ascending power hierarchy. These Christian perspectives on the cardinal virtues ensured their enduring significance in later Western culture, celebrated as moralistic standards in their own right. These themes enjoy considerable prestige even in our modern age, particularly when impassioned calls to service and duty remain the order of the day. The true significance of the cardinal virtues, however, ultimately stems from their direct foundation within the respective alter ego states. In this latter respect, *prudence* represents the group analogue of hero worship, whereas *justice* desig-

Personifications of the Four Cardinal Virtues (Clockwise: P-T-J-F) - circa 1295
Somme le Roi - ms. 6329, folio 96v, Paris Arsenal, Photo courtesy Bibliotheque Nationale, Paris

nates a similar refinement of blame. Furthermore, *temperance* adds a public sense of moderation to approval, whereas *fortitude* defines concern from a civic perspective. Although this dual degree of correspondence proves intuitively convincing, its true validity is ultimately verified within the expanded context of their respective literary traditions.

140 – PRUDENCE

The first mentioned of the cardinal virtues, *prudence*, is traditionally defined as sound judgement or discretionary conduct in practical affairs. Its modern spelling derives from the Latin *prudens*

(denoting wisdom and foresight). According to classical Greek mythology, the goddess Metis was revered as the divine personification of prudence and foresight. Metis (a Titan and mother of Zeus) aided Zeus in the liberation of his elder siblings, facilitating their dramatic rise to power. Indeed, Zeus was proclaimed their leader in gratitude for spurring their deliverance. In acknowledgement of her assistance, Zeus spared Metis the vanquished fate of the other Titans. She faithfully remained by his side, celebrated as the most wise of all of the divinities.

These mythological interpretations found further expression in the classical philosophy of the day. In Plato's *Republic*, prudence is specifically singled out as the foremost of the four cardinal virtues. This theme was similarly celebrated by Plato's contemporary Aristotle, who viewed it as a key factor in the moral development of the individual conscience. These pagan perspectives, in turn, extended to the Christian era, although modified to fit emerging Christian sensibilities. Accordingly, prudence is defined as a deep spiritual insight into one's moral duties, as well as the concrete means towards their fulfillment. Furthermore, prudence remains the cardinal virtue most allied to practical reason, a key motivation behind all virtuous acts.

This foresightful aspect of Christian prudence finds parallel consideration in the medieval tradition of cathedral art. Through the dramatic medium of stained glass, each of the cardinal virtues was visually personified using a stylized set of human attributes. Prudence, for instance, is depicted as a seated maiden holding a book, sometimes pointing to a globe at her feet. She is also shown holding a compass (a symbol of direction) or a mirror intertwined by serpents (signifying personal intuition). She is sometimes depicted with two faces (or even three) signifying her consideration of past, present, and future contexts. Prudence eventually became synonymous with courtly behavior, particularly the pronounced degree of decorum expressed towards the royal family. The magnificent palaces of Europe certainly fostered such a grand cast of supportive characters, an entourage that gloried in the majesty of the regal monarch. In particular, prudence gained considerable popularity as a femininely given name, reflecting the courtly spirit characterizing the royal "ladies-in-waiting."

141 – JUSTICE

Jurisprudence dictates that any description of prudence must necessarily remain incomplete without mention of the related theme of *justice*. This latter theme derives from the Latin *justitia*, from *jus* (the law). Just as Metis was revered as the divine personification of prudence, so the Greek goddess, Themis, symbolized the related theme of justice. As the most abstract of all of the Titans, Themis symbolized law, order, and custom (as well as justice). She is depicted as a flowingly garbed maiden holding aloft a balanced set of scales upon which she weighs the claims of opposing parties. She is sometimes shown holding a cornucopia (horn of plenty) signifying the abundant blessings affiliated with law and order. She is generally depicted presiding at the right hand of

Zeus, offering counsel in matters relating to divine justice.

In the Roman tradition, Jupiter mirrors Zeus' role as the defender of righteous causes. Themis similarly gives way to Justitia, the Roman goddess of justice. In direct parallels to Themis, Justitia is traditionally depicted as a flowingly draped maiden holding aloft a balanced set of scales, although now also brandishing a sword (signifying the enforcement of the law). In contrast to the "all-seeing" eye of Themis, Justitia is alternately depicted as blindfolded, signifying complete impartiality under the law. Indeed, medieval representations of her (as the second cardinal virtue) rely heavily upon such classical attributes: namely, raised sword, scales, blindfold, etc.

These classical overtones are further consistent with the legal administration of the Roman Empire. In particular, the Justinian Code of Law specifically defines justice as: "the constant and firm willingness to render every man his due." This basic conviction was further echoed centuries later by St. Thomas Aquinas in his comprehensive discussion of justice contained within his *Summa Theologica*. These general interpretations of justice appear to share a common theme; namely, the subordination of one's personal self-interests to the collective welfare comprising the group. Indeed, justice certainly fulfills its status as a group follower perspective, a fact amply documented in the modern-day institution of the *jury* trial.

True to its origins in British Common Law, the jury trial has remained a prominent American standard since colonial times. The American variation preserves the basic features of the Common Law jury; namely, a twelve-member panel presided over by a judge empowered to determine a unanimous verdict. This group focus is particularly evident during the jury selection process, where complete impartiality is sought across a broad cross-section of the general population. The public is similarly invited to witness the courtroom proceedings, with criminal cases referenced using the formula: The People vs. John Doe.

Following the systematic presentation of evidence, the jury ultimately deliberates in private over the presumed guilt or innocence of the accused, tempering the letter of the law with personal intuition and insight. The jury foreman (as representative of the group) submits the final verdict to the judge, who (as spokesman for the court) reads the decision to the defendant. The lack of a unanimous verdict is figuratively termed a "hung jury," being that complete agreement is necessary for establishing the guilt or innocence of the accused. The sentencing phase focuses on the moral rehabilitation of the individual, a factor that aims to avoid any personal quest for retribution. Although fines or jail-time are typically pronounced at this juncture, such punitive measures are primarily meant to protect the general public (as well as providing restitution to the injured party). A penitent attitude on the part of the defendant generally secures a greater degree of leniency from the judge. Indeed, an honorable admission of guilt is rightfully expected if justice is truly said to have been done.

142 – TEMPERANCE

The third of the cardinal virtues, *temperance*, is traditionally defined as restraint or moderation in the indulgence of the appetites. Its modern spelling derives from the Latin *temperantia* (moderation), from the Latin root *tempos* (extent or measure). It is certainly ironic that the true value of this virtue was often overlooked during the classical era, particularly in light of the sensual excesses characterizing the imperial Roman era. The more austere Greeks, in contrast, worshipped this theme as their abstract goddess Sophrosyne, the divine personification of moderation and self-control. Indeed, her name is defined as a Greek compound denoting "safe-mindedness." Sophrosyne, accordingly, is depicted as a comely maiden in flowing garb, holding a *ewer* (pitcher) and *cantharos* (a libation cup employed in drinking rituals).

According to Plato's masterpiece, *The Republic,* temperance is defined as the rational restraint of the physical appetites: particularly, food, drink, and sexual indulgence. In his later dialogue, *Laws,* Plato intimates that temperance aspires to a likeness to God, a theme further professed by early Church theologians in their pursuit of the virtuous lifestyle. Medieval artisans, in turn, symbolized temperance in the classical style reminiscent of Sophrosyne. Some stained glass representations portray Temperance with a torch and a jug. Others include a vessel of water for mixing with the wine (wherein diluting its inebriating effects). Related depictions feature a scourge and a bridle (sometimes with the bit in place) signifying the restraint of the passions.

In our modern age, this trend towards alcoholic restraint found ready expression in terms of the emergence of the temperance movement. Although the problems associated with the overconsumption of wine and ale had long been acknowledged, they only reached glaring proportions with respect to the easy availability of distilled spirits during the Industrial Revolution. Initially, the shortcomings associated with intemperance were largely overlooked, pure alcohol being revered as a divine essence consistent with its medieval designation as the "water of life." Beginning with the 19th century, however, such naive assumptions eventually gave way to a more enlightened recognition of alcohol's inherent health risks, resulting in the emergence of the organized temperance movements in Europe and the United States. Indeed, during an era that searched for simplistic solutions to the evils of society, total abstinence from alcohol was seen as a major remedy for poverty, crime, and marital discord.

Granted, the sedative properties of alcohol prove immediately reinforcing to the individual, although personal concerns are not the overriding issue here. Rather, the temperance movement focused on the threat to the traditional family unit, particularly that affecting the male wage-earner. The neighborhood pubs of the day were widely prized as havens for the off-duty crowd, stealing time perhaps more properly spent with the wife and children. When the "bread winner" finally did stagger home, he typically was too inebriated to offer much meaningful companionship, a factor often compounded by a violent lowering of inhibitions. The hard-core alcoholic further experienced difficulty holding down a job, gravely threatening the stability of the family.

It is scarcely surprising, then, that the women of the times were so insistent upon the success of the temperance movement, their emerging power to vote providing fertile inroads towards these ends. As representatives of the family unit, the wives petitioned their husbands to forgo their personal gratification in deference to the welfare of the group. Such noble aspirations celebrated the restraint implicit in temperate consumption, directly condemning the uncontrolled gratification characterizing the personal perspective. When such voluntary restrictions proved difficult to enforce, the temperance movement opted for (and amazingly achieved) the total abstinence provisions outlined in the Prohibition Amendment to the U. S. Constitution. Although this ambitious experiment failed in the long run, it foundered primarily on the absoluteness of its demands. Then (as now) education on the value of moderation still proves the most effective strategy for regulating such highly addictive substances.

143 – FORTITUDE

The final of the cardinal virtues, *fortitude*, is typically listed ahead of temperance in the traditional listing of virtues: a reversal attesting to its crucial role in the violent exploits of the ancient world.

Accordingly, it is defined as the patient endurance of trouble or pain: courage and bravery are cited as its major synonyms. Its modern spelling derives from the Latin *fortitutio*, from *fortis* (strength or power). During the classical era, fortitude was directly identified with Virtus, the Roman personification of manly courage and valor: from the Latin *vir* (man). Patriarchal philosophers primarily identified manliness with godliness, with *virtu* becoming synonymous with moral goodness, along with other terms hinting at male potency (such as rectitude and uprightness). V*irtu* eventually came to be identified with moral competency in general, as suggested in the broader sense of the term.

As was customary for other virtues of the day, Virtus was worshipped as the goddess of courage by the Romans; her unconventional gender directly at odds with the masculine sense of the term. She is traditionally portrayed as a youthful warrior attired in a short tunic draped so that her right breast is exposed (a necessary precaution during the practice of archery). She wears a richly ornamented helmet upon her head, while another helmet (representing the enemy) is pressed underfoot. She holds a spear in her left hand and a sword in her right in a style reminiscent of the legendary race of Amazon women.

These military connotations of fortitude endured the decline of the classical era, remaining one of the dominant themes throughout the Medieval Age. During the ensuing age of chivalry, fortitude fired the hopes and aspirations of all knights within the realm. It served to subjugate the emotions of fear and cowardice while inspiring dutiful behavior in perilous or treacherous situations. It is traditionally ordered to prudence, effectively moderating the tendency towards reckless bravado. These moral overtones are further reflected in the cathedral art of the day, incorporating many of the classical attributes traditionally associated with Virtus. In addition to the upright sword, shield, and armor, fortitude is variously depicted tearing open the jaws of a lion, or chained to a column suggestive of the biblical story of Samson. In one portrayal, fortitude is shown holding a miniature tower entwined by a dragon (the neck of which she grasps), an allusion to the perpetual struggle between the contrasting themes of good and evil.

Accordingly, fortitude is listed (along with temperance) as one of the Seven Gifts of the Holy Spirit (Gal. 5:22). The heroic overtones typically associated with martyrdom certainly support such a pacifistic interpretation; namely, patient and unflinching devotion even in the face of death. True fortitude, however, is also invested with a strategic defensive slant, the military *fort* deriving from the same Latin root-stem. In truth, it might be judged just as noble to stand fast under entrenched attack as to lead the charge, further underscoring this dual aspect of the term. This potential risk of life-and-limb calls for sacrifice on the order of true "intestinal" fortitude; namely, the figurative ability to *stomach* adversity. Indeed, whether one aspires to military glory or martyrdom, one's personal concerns pale in significance to the welfare of the group.

Similar to the preceding example of temperance, the brave warrior is totally dedicated to the cause of duty and allegiance within his military unit. Even in our modern age of mechanistic warfare, the courage of the brave soldier knows no bounds: ranging from vexing personal hardships to the perilous risk of life or limb. This overriding sense of duty is particularly evident on the eve of a great battle, when a stirring call to courage is made by the general-in-command: wherein alleviating any lingering sense of doubt on the part of his enlisted men. The general ultimately reminds his soldiers of the peril to their free way of life (and that of their loved ones), directly appealing to their crucial role towards restoring the political status quo.

In conclusion, the group follower perspective offers a fitting counterpoint to the preliminary power leverage expressed by the group authority figure. As chief spokesman for the group, the group representative proceeds to establish an equal balance of power with respect to his group authority figure. The main power leverage stems primarily from the shrewd reinforcement of his authority figure; namely, *prudent*-worship, *just*-blaming, *temperate*-approval, and *fortitudinous*-concern. The virtuous themes of Plato's *Republic* certainly ring true in this regard, each member of the group fully cognizant of their proper role therein; namely, to be prudent, just, temperate, or brave. When ultimately faced with such a potent challenge to his authority status, the group authority endeavors to regain the upper hand within the ascending power hierarchy; namely, rising again to the next higher *spiritual* authority level.

5

THE SPIRITUAL / UNIVERSAL REALM

Similar to the case previously established for the group authority role, spiritual (or universal) authority is essentially as ancient as civilization itself, serving an analogous stabilizing function in many primitive cultures. Prior to our modern age of scientific inquiry, primitive man relied almost exclusively on religious belief and superstition to explain the bewildering complexities of the natural world. The typically violent forces of earth, wind, and fire served as a source of both awe and amazement, inspiring an enduring sense of sacredness within the primitive mentality. The orderly rhythms governing the procession of the sun, moon, and stars must have similarly invoked feelings of amazement, eventually identified with an enduring pantheon of celestial gods. This complex constellation of myth and ritual eventually gave rise to a specialized clan of tribal shamans, extending to the priestly castes characterizing many early civilizations. According to this early mentality, the priest's ritual appeal to divinity spelled the difference between illness and health, fortune and disaster: a welcome hedge in an uncertain world.

In ancient Egypt, the pharaoh and the priestly class shared more-or-less equally in the power of the kingdom, each magnifying the power of the other in the eyes of the people. First and foremost, the pharaoh represented the supreme political figurehead for the Egyptian people. Egypt's prosperous economy served as a powerful magnet for refugees throughout the region. In order to counteract this multi-cultural challenge to his native authority, the pharaoh took full advantage of the much broader cloak of spiritual authority; namely, that binding over the group of all groups (or all mankind). By claiming direct lineage from the gods, the pharaoh proclaimed supreme authority over all groups within his domain regardless of any partisan concerns therein. The spiritual authority figure served clear notice that

plenty of groups remained to perpetuate his authority status whether or not any particular group would decide to desert. Consequently, the spiritual authority transcends the limitations plaguing partisan politics, wherein assuming the maximum degree of power leverage characterizing the universal perspective.

The Western tradition of spiritual authority has remained virtually synonymous with Christian principles since the decline of the classical Roman era. As founder of the Christian movement, Christ made direct claim to the role of Messiah (or Anointed One) within the Jewish tradition. His reputed claim to divinity (as the Son of God) established Christ as the premier spiritual authority figure of his day. Indeed, Christ was particularly well versed in the spiritual authority maneuver, as witnessed in his many encounters with the hypocritical Pharisees of his day. In one instance, the Pharisees attempted to trap Jesus into an act of treason, questioning whether it was lawful to give tribute unto Caesar? Invoking the spiritual authority countermaneuver, Christ cleverly replied: "Render unto Caesar the things that are Caesar's, and unto God the things that are God's." Certainly, these scriptural precedents echo the modern-day separation of church and state, a cornerstone of the American legal system.

MODERN PERSPECTIVES WITH RESPECT TO SPIRITUAL AUTHORITY

From a historical perspective, the establishment of the United States of America arose as a direct consequence of the power struggle pitting the Colonials against the oppressive rule of the British Crown. A long line of English monarchs (leading to King George III) relentlessly oppressed the American colonists, including a plan to proclaim the Church of England as the official state religion throughout the Colonies (conflicting with the diverse spiritual foundations of the latter). This outrage, compounded by other economic policies, resulted in the *Declaration of Independence* and subsequent Revolutionary War. The *Declaration* represented an unprecedented appeal to spiritual authority overruling the more partisan concerns promulgated by the British crown. In keeping with the common Christian heritage of the colonies, the *Declaration of Independence* proclaimed: "All men are created equal, endowed by their Creator with certain unalienable rights; namely, life, liberty, and the pursuit of happiness." In contrast to the prevailing royalist perspective, the colonials viewed government as instituted through man's consent to protect fundamental human rights.

Historical precedent dictates that the *Declaration's* author, Thomas Jefferson, borrowed extensively from earlier British theorists on the subject. In *On Civil Government, the Second Treatise* (1690) John Locke proposed that no one should harm another with respect to life, health, liberty, or possessions. Furthermore, should one actually be harmed, the injured party would enjoy full right to compensation. Locke's treatise was published shortly after the Glorious Revolution of 1688, which witnessed the expulsion of King James II from the British throne. Four generations later, the American colonist's similar dissatisfaction with British policies encouraged a revival in social conscience. Jefferson adopted Locke's principles of life and liberty, while modifying the remaining theme of property (for aesthetic reasons) into "pursuit of happiness."

Although the spirited literary style of the *Declaration* provided some measure of consolation to the disgruntled colonials, they soon became embroiled in the long and brutal War of Independence. The ultimate victory of the revolutionary forces lead to the subsequent adoption of the *Constitution* of the United States. In a curious oversight, the framers of the *Constitution* failed to include adequate guarantees of the civil liberties so eloquently proclaimed in the *Declaration of Independence*. Indeed, the people rightfully rejected Federalist claims that such guarantees exceeded the limits of constitutional authority.

This shortcoming fortunately was remedied during the first regular meeting of Congress chiefly through the efforts of James Madison. The Madison Amendments stemmed from numerous proposals gleaned from the various state conventions. The final ten amendments (comprising the *Bill of Rights*) included guarantees on freedom of speech, religion, and the press. Further safeguards include the right to a speedy trial, reasonable bail, and the power to confront one's accus-

ers. Other amendments protected against mandatory self-incrimination, unreasonable search-and-seizure, as well as cruel and unusual punishment. None of these rights were absolute, however, for the amendments never were meant to conflict with the general public welfare. Indeed, the *Bill of Rights* only limited the power of the federal government, the states being clearly reluctant to diminish their individual autonomy.

With respect to the individual groupings of virtues and values examined to date, the diverse range of civil liberties guaranteed in the *Bill of Rights* can scarcely claim the pedigree or tradition essential for incorporation into the unified power hierarchy. It proves effective, however, to view the generic concept of "civil liberty" as the confluence of two supportive concepts; namely, *civility* and *liberty*. Add to these the related themes of *providence* and *austerity* and the master grouping of spiritual authority themes falls neatly into focus. In this expanded sense, the master four-part listing of providence-liberty-civility-austerity collectively comprises what is termed the class of *civil liberties*, in direct acknowledgement of their enduring moralistic precedents. According to this more abstract context, the civil liberties represent the higher spiritual analogues of the more basic group class of personal ideals (glory-honor-dignity-integrity). Here, *providence* represents a spiritual refinement of glory, whereas *liberty* makes a parallel analogy to honor. Similarly, *civility* redefines dignity from a spiritual perspective, whereas *austerity* represents a more idealized form of integrity. Although the political applications of the civil liberties might seem to belie their spiritual significance, recall that the spiritual authority maneuver builds directly upon the group follower perspective, wherein accounting for the "hybrid" quality of the grouping. Indeed, this dual correspondence is adequately reflected in the expanded context of the respective literary traditions.

150 – PROVIDENCE

The first of the civil liberties, *providence*, is a theme of virtually universal appeal. Its modern spelling derives from the Latin *providentia* (the power to see in advance), from *pro-* (before) and *videre* (to see). The ancient Romans specifically worshipped Providentia as their divine personification of the foresight guiding the fortunes of the empire. Certain Roman coins depict Providentia as a stylized eagle holding the scepter of Rome in its beak descending to the throne of the emperor in a peaceful transition of power. Providentia further came to signify the nourishing and protective power of the classical gods in general. This providential favor allowed the earth to bloom with grain in the spring, aided by an ample supply of rain throughout the growing season. Extreme ritual devotion was considered crucial for securing the fortuitous favor of the gods.

These classical connotations of providence are particularly suggestive of the visual symbolisms associated with the *cornucopia*, literally, the "horn of plenty." According to Roman mythology, the cornucopia traced its origins to Achelous the River God, who transformed himself into a raging bull in order to gain the upper hand in a violent struggle against Hercules. Achelous lost one of his horns during the struggle, eventually retrieved by river nymphs who reverently filled it with fruits and flowers of the season. Henceforth, it was magically said to perpetually overflow with all manner of bountiful blessings from the earth.

In keeping with this bountiful character, the cornucopia was depicted as a major attribute for many gods and goddesses of the period. Chief among these was Fortuna, the goddess of fortune, and Copia, handmaiden to Fortuna (and goddess of plenty). Plutus, the Roman god of wealth, was also depicted cradling a horn of plenty. It is respectively portrayed as a gently curving spiral horn overflowing with fruit and grain, a symbolism traditionally associated with the modern day celebration of Thanksgiving. The cornucopia signified the providential favor the Pilgrims enjoyed in the form of a bountiful harvest, commemorating the Pilgrims' brave adaptation to life in the New World. Here the cornucopia represents one of the most potent metaphors for Divine Providence, being that the supply of blessings remains virtually unlimited in principle. Through hard work (and some assistance from the natives), the Pilgrims succeeded in harvesting enough surplus to insure their survival through the harsh winter. These devout Pilgrims undoubtedly considered their success as divinely inspired, in direct contrast to the holiday's current (more secular) focus. Indeed, these spiritual themes were the founding principles for the establishment of the thirteen original colonies.

151 – LIBERTY

Allied to any discussion of providence is the related theme of *liberty*, defined as the right to act without interference within the limits of the law. The term traces its origins to the Latin *libertas*, from *liber* (free). In the early days of the Roman Republic, liberty was regarded as a constitutional mandate, in contrast to tyranny or dictatorship. In keeping with many of the other classical themes, Libertas was worshipped as a deity, with several temples dedicated to her in Rome alone. She is traditionally depicted as a lightly attired matron holding a broken scepter in one hand and a staff hung with a felt cap in the other. The staff (the *vindicta*) played a role in the ceremonial freeing of slaves. The felt cap (the *pilleus*) was further bestowed upon the heads of freed slaves following completion of this ceremony. It originally had been placed upon the heads of troublesome slaves at auction, wherein absolving the vendor of any subsequent liability. Towards the end of the Republic (circa the assassination of Julius Caesar) portrayals of Libertas often included a stylized dagger signifying the blood that is often shed in her defense.

In a more contemporary sense, liberty has enjoyed a special place of honor within the American system of government, one of the treasured principles upon which this great country was founded. In a debt of gratitude from the world as a whole, the Frenchman Auguste Bartholdi commemorated this spirit of freedom in his monumental sculpture, the Statue of Liberty. Bartholdi's aesthetic vision of Liberty blends clear classical overtones with innovative technical design. It features a flowingly garbed personification of the goddess depicted in the act of gaining her freedom. Her right hand holds aloft a burning torch, while her left cradles a book of law inscribed July 4, 1776. The classical tradition of the liberty cap is curiously lacking, replaced by a striking crown of stylized rays of light. Broken shackles lie at her feet as she strides forward towards liberation.

Similar to the case previously established for providence, liberty is clearly a past-directed form of the authority perspective, an interpretation entirely in keeping with the classical overtones associated with the Statue of Liberty. This spiritual focus is particularly evident in the abstract principles embodied in the *Declaration of Independence*, where liberty is specifically singled out as one of the three God-given rights guaranteed to all individuals. Through this libertarian perspective, the spiritual authority directly expands upon the honor perspective of the group authority figure, further countering the justice maneuver expressed by the group representative. These spiritual overtones are extremely suggestive of the "larger than life" attributes of the Statue of Liberty. Liberty's mild (but commanding) demeanor must surely have enthralled the uninitiated as one of the many wonders America had to offer. Towards these ends, it was Liberty's outstretched torch that figuratively served to light the way for the perpetual throngs of hopeful refugees, an endeavor that many immigrants hoped to realize in this golden land of opportunity.

152 – CIVILITY

The third of the civil liberties, *civility*, certainly rates its title role within this grouping. As the chief spiritual analogue of dignity, civility is traditionally defined as a sense of courtesy or chivalry in a civic context. Its modern spelling derives from the Latin *civilitas*, from *civis* (citizen). Indeed, limited archaeological evidence suggests that the Romans worshipped this theme as a deity, as indicated in a dedicatory inscription to Civitas unearthed in Rome. Although *civitas* initially referred to the art of skilled governance, it eventually came to signify the refinements of polite society in general.

In its alternate legal sense, the concept of Civil Law originally applied to the sum-body of the Roman Code, particularly that applicable to the private citizen. According to the Common Law traditions of the English speaking world, Civil Law refers to the personal and property rights of the individual, a residual category that exceeds the scope of Criminal, Military, and International Law. In this latter sense, the *U. S. Bill of Rights* makes clear provisions for such individual civil rights, although unforeseen ambiguities plague the wording of virtually every key passage. It ultimately fell to the judiciary/legislature to derive legally binding interpretations for each of these civil rights provisions.

The current body of civil rights precedents emerged over a long series of legal decisions. The *Bill of Rights* originally applied only to freemen, although modified through the abolition of slavery as formalized in the *Emancipation Proclamation*. The subsequent Civil Rights Acts of 1866 and 1870 allowed all citizens the free right to engage in legal transactions; as in owning property or entering into lawsuits. The Civil Rights Act of 1871 further made it unlawful to deny any citizen equal protection under the law, whether through force, threat, or intimidation. The Act of 1875 guaranteed the free use of public accommodations, although this legislation was later reversed as unconstitutional. This latter reactionary trend culminated in 1896 with the Supreme Court ruling of Plessy vs. Ferguson, upholding the principle of "separate but equal" facilities for people of color.

The midpoint of the current century, however, again ushered in the winds of change, as witnessed in the 1954 Supreme Court Decision of Brown vs. Topeka Board of Education. This historic ruling overturned the legal precedent of segregation in public schools, citing the inherent inequality of such a forced arrangement. Many related aspects of racial segregation soon followed as targets of reform. On December 1, 1955, Rosa Parks was arrested in Montgomery, Alabama for refusing to surrender her bus seat to a white passenger. The black seamstress' courageous act of defiance touched off a year-long boycott of the city transit system, a cause further championed by civil rights leader, Rev. Martin Luther King Jr. As a spokesman for the Southern Christian Leadership Conference, King preached a message of non-violent resistance: culminating in the Civil Rights March from Selma to Montgomery, Alabama with a turn-out estimated at *25,000* strong. Faced with such intense public scrutiny, Congress soon passed a flurry of new legislation aimed at barring racial segregation. The Civil Rights Act of 1964 banned discrimination in employment and public accommodations, whereas the Civil Rights Act of 1968 extended these guarantees to real estate and private housing.

Civility represents a spiritual ideal within the dignity tradition, although clearly surpassing the more limited group focus of the latter. For instance, Rosa Parks solicitously boarded the bus, fully expecting a civil environment en route to her destination. As the agent for the bus-company, the driver was rightfully expected to respect her civil rights consistent with the routine expectations of the paying patrons. The civil atmosphere inherent to the public conveyance would necessarily specify the principles of equality under the law were it not for the prejudicial undercurrents plaguing the Deep South of the day. The bus driver maliciously ejected Rosa Parks from the bus employing ingrained racial prejudice as the rationale for compromising her civil rights. Indeed, it would truly appear ironic to resort to such an inverted example for now illustrating the dynamics of civility, so much do we take such rights for granted. The government fortunately remedied such an appalling circumstance, passing a rapid sequence of civil rights ordinances targeting such prejudicial treatment. These fundamental human standards are now effectively safeguarded throughout the public sector, ensuring uniform standards of trade and commerce across the land.

153 – AUSTERITY

The fourth and final of the civil liberties, *austerity*, extends the group theme of integrity into a higher *spiritual* sphere of influence. Its modern spelling derives from the Greek *austeros* (denoting dryness or harshness). Accordingly, it is traditionally defined as the endurance of pain, hardship, or misfortune, often in a mortified fashion. It can also suggest a sense of harshness or strictness in the bestowal of discipline. In the Latin tradition, this distinctive theme is identified with the Roman god Auster, the divine personification of the South Wind. Auster, accordingly, is described as the dry and sultry south wind, the *sirocco* of the modern-day Italians. It is the harbinger of hot and dry weather consistent with Italy's close proximity to the Sahara Desert. Indeed, some historians trace its origins to the Latin root-stem *uro-* (denoting the tendency to burn).

In its alternate philosophical sense, austerity's traditions establish it as one of the fundamental principles governing the strict Code of Sparta (a powerful city-state to the south of Athens). Sparta maintained its military might primarily through an elaborate system of state-enforced regimentation and disciple. At the tender age of seven, male children were separated from their parents and raised in state sanctioned military academies. The recruits slept year round in open barracks on reeds harvested from the banks of the river Eurota. Family life, again, was reinstated only upon reaching the age of thirty, when the individual was finally accorded the full rights and privileges of a citizen of Sparta.

These classical connotations of harshness and discipline have similarly endured to our modern age, as exemplified in the recurring traditions of the *austerity* budget. This political policy has long been employed to bolster faltering economies chiefly through increased production and the export of capital goods (wherein improving the overall balance of trade). It also offered a stopgap solution to temporary economic problems such as financing a military campaign or balancing the federal budget. The United Kingdom, in particular, has instituted austerity budgets throughout its history, ensuring its enduring influence in modern economic theory.

In the United States, this theme definitely brings to mind the price controls instituted by President Nixon during the mid-70's: a strategy aimed at controlling skyrocketing inflation. The truest sense of the term, however, extends to the early 1980's with the advent of "Reaganomics." President Reagan deliberately resurrected the theme of the austerity budget to describe his revolutionary program to revitalize the national economy. The lack-luster state of affairs characterized by runaway inflation and high unemployment called for a bold set of economic measures; namely, sharp budget cutting to shrink the public sector, as well as a broad retreat from business and environmental regulations. This policy of "supply side" economics promised (and eventually delivered) a surge in non-inflationary economic growth, although initially to the detriment of the more underprivileged economic classes.

On the opposing side of the ledger, the general public rightfully expected that their submissive attempts at economic cooperation would be rewarded with the desired results. The traditional austerity budget generally calls for such cooperative measures; namely, reduced consumption and resource conservation. In exchange for this collective sacrifice, the government rightfully was expected to improve the economy to the point where such austerity measures would no longer be necessary. Critics of the plan argued that the economic sacrifices demanded of the public were disproportionately severe at the lower end of the spectrum, a premise all too evident during the early years of the Reagan Plan. Fortunately such hardships quickly ran their course, resulting in the healthier and happier economy currently in force today.

THE THEOLOGICAL VIRTUES

The completed description of the civil liberties paints a rather moralistic picture of the spiritual authority perspective. In particular, each of the civil liberties was prominently featured in the *Declaration of Independence*, a document formally invoking such spiritual themes in its struggle against the tyranny of the British crown. In our modern age, this universal perspective generally transcends such strict religious overtones, as particularly evident in the thoroughly secularized charters of world-governing bodies such as the United Nations, the World Trade Organization, or the World Court. The U. N. clearly employs such a universal perspective in that the wishes of member nations are expendable should they dare challenge global peace and harmony (a lesson forcefully taught to Iraq during the First Gulf War). The spiritual authority figure clearly overrules the more limited partisan concerns of the group representative, effectively regaining the upper hand in the perpetual power struggle. Similar to the initial forms of authority (that it supersedes), spiritual authority is also susceptible to its own unique form of follower countermaneuver; namely, that claimed by the spiritual disciple.

The spiritual disciple maneuver is essentially as ancient as spiritual authority itself, restoring an equal balance of power to the universal power realm. Similar to the other follower maneuvers (that it supercedes), the spiritual disciple maneuver shares the distinctive style of "strike" leverage so effective in confrontations with the authority figure. For the spiritual disciple, this generally takes the form of a universal style of strike leverage, as traditionally seen in the emergence of schisms or heresies. Although the extreme degree of abstraction encountered at this level might appear to invalidate any meaningful degree of effectiveness, witness the power of the revolutionary for influencing such enduring historical events as the Protestant Reformation; and, indeed, the very founding of Christianity itself.

In his designated role of spokesman for the spiritual congregation, the spiritual disciple informs the spiritual authority that the blessings of the faithful are crucial for preserving his authority status. Fortified by this formal "strike" leverage, the spiritual disciple can wield a considerable degree of influence within the spiritual congregation. History certainly abounds with many such dramatic twists of fate, as witnessed in the emergence of the Protestant Reformation. Here the unassuming monk, Martin Luther dared to speak out against the corrupt practices of the Roman Catholic Church, a schism destined to forever change the face of Western civilization. Although this drastic style of strike leverage is typically effective only in negative circumstances, a more positive slant may alternately be gained with respect to the cohesiveness of the spiritual congregation. Although group cohesiveness was previously defined in terms of the four cardinal virtues, the congregational variety is further specified within the tradition of the theological virtues.

The theological virtues (faith, hope, and charity) have enjoyed a long and distinguished religious tradition, rivaling that previously established for the cardinal virtues. Although individually mentioned throughout the Old Testament, they are first listed as a cohesive grouping in the New Testament particularly in the writings of St. Paul. Paul is certainly the most prolific contributor to the New Testament, a factor entirely in keeping with the considerable influence the theological virtues play in many of his epistles. These virtues are most prominently featured in Chapter 13 of his First Letter to the Corinthians where he finishes with the stirring admonition: "And now abideth faith, hope, and charity, these three; but the greatest of these is charity." These same three virtues are also listed as a cohesive grouping in the First Epistle of St. Peter (1:21-22). Their designation as *theological* dates to the influence of St. Gregory the Great, who celebrated the supreme moral foundations of these three basic virtues, while also acknowledging their intimate connection to the cardinal virtues.

This enduring theme extended to the writings of later Church theologians, most notably, St. Thomas Aquinas (1225-1274). In his *Summa Theologica*, St. Thomas specifically distinguishes the cardinal (or natural) virtues from the theological (or supernatural) versions. According to Aquinas, the cardinal virtues are rooted within the psychological nature of man, developed primarily through concerted moral effort. They perfect mankind's natural dispositions, wherein defending against instinctual types of excess. In contrast, the theological virtues are alternately viewed as supernatural, divinely serving to spur on our true spiritual nature. They are said to rule our moral life, infusing it with a divine sense of inspiration.

In keeping with his illustrious predecessors, St. Thomas limited his treatment of the theological virtues to the first basic three. This circumstance, however, leaves the complement one term short of satisfying the overall four-part listing predicted for the spiritual disciple perspective. Historical precedent has certainly favored such a technical shortcoming, particularly in light of the fact that medieval theologians traditionally grouped the theological and cardinal virtues together summating to the mystical number of "seven." This seven-fold listing was magically said to counteract the evil influence of the Seven Deadly Sins; namely, pride, anger, envy, lust, gluttony, covetousness, and sloth. This theme first appears in the writings of Psychomachia of Prudentius (circa 400 CE), picturing in vivid verse the inner conflict pitting virtue against vice.

Despite these theological interpretations, it ultimately proves crucial to return to the original scriptural sources for clues to the identity of the missing theological virtue. It is particularly significant to note that Chapter 13 of St. Paul's First Letter to the Corinthians is curiously the shortest chapter of the entire epistle, more or less arbitrarily separated from the adjoining chapters. St. Paul fittingly sums up the theme of the subsequent Chapter 14 with the quotation: "Let all things be done *decently* and in order" suggesting that decency represents the missing theological virtue. Decency is certainly a prominent theme in Old Testament scripture (as well as the New Testament teachings of Christ). Although not specifically mentioned by name, a careful reading of St. Paul's other references to the theological virtues: e.g., Romans (5:1-5) and 1st Thessalonians (1:3) would also seem to suggest this novel interpretation.

The Theological Virtues (With Their Historical Representatives) – Circa 1460
Detail from Panel by Pesellino, Birmingham Museum of Art, Gift of the Samuel H. Kress Foundation

This modest modification of the theological format finally accounts for the four-part complement of virtuous terms predicted for the spiritual disciple perspective. The theological virtues are viewed as the more abstract spiritual analogues of the subordinate complement of the cardinal virtues. According to this expanded context, *faith* represents prudence from a spiritual perspective, whereas *hope* makes similar parallels to justice. Furthermore, *charity* represents a spiritual refinement of temperance, whereas *decency* reinterprets fortitude from a theological perspective. Although this intimate correspondence was never directly specified in the scriptures, this enduring viewpoint is further validated in the expanded context of the corresponding literary traditions.

160 – FAITH

The first of the theological virtues, *faith*, represents the supreme emblem of spiritual worship and devotion. Its modern spelling derives from the Latin *fides*, also the root-stem for the related theme of fidelity. The early Romans traditionally worshipped Fides as their divine personification of faith and fidelity in oaths and vows. She is generally depicted as a matronly figure adorned in a white veil and flowing gown, her right hand solemnly raised as if taking a vow. According to historical precedent, Fides was worshipped at an ancient temple on the Capitoline Hill close to that of Jupiter (with whom she is closely associated). Her cult is said to be very ancient, dating at least to the reign of King Numa. Her annual feast-day was celebrated on the first day in October, when priests of her cult rode to her temple in a covered chariot: signifying that faith should carefully be protected. Her sacrificial priests were said to have their right hands wrapped to their fingers with strips of white cloth, suggesting that the seat of honor must be kept holy and pure. Covered hands eventually came to symbolize faith in general, as depicted on coins commemorating the loyalty of the Roman Legions.

These pagan connotations of faith eventually paved the way for Christian sense of the term. According to New Testament scripture, Christ consistently implored his disciples to trust in the divine power of the Lord that worked through him. The dramatic series of miracles he is said to have performed further stipulated the unswerving faith of all who would be cured. In particular, the chief emblem of faith (as the first of the theological virtues) is a stylized shield with a Latin cross inscribed in the center (traditionally referred to as the Shield of St. Paul). This symbolism figuratively signifies the saving power of Christ, as represented in his fulfillment of scriptural prophecy.

Following Christ's reported ascension into heaven, his power to perform miracles passed to

57

St. Peter and other Twelve Apostles. In the NT Acts of the Apostles, St. Peter performs an amazing series of miracles: including his healing of the lame man (3:1-10) and his raising of Tabitha from the dead (9:40-41). St. Peter reverently acknowledged the miraculous power that worked through him, although faith from the afflicted also proved crucial for achieving the desired results.

This tradition of miracles endures to our modern age, particularly the well-documented phenomenon of faith healing. From its very inception faith healing was essentially considered an all-or-none phenomenon; namely, all was cured or nothing. Its specifics are described in the Epistle of St. James (5:14-16), which describes the anointing of the sick in a congregational setting. St. James further states that the prayers of the faithful will heal the sick when accompanied by an "anointing of oil" in the name of the Lord. Healing is also listed among the Gifts of the Holy Spirit according to Chapter 11 of St. Paul's First Letter to the Corinthians.

According to the traditional faith healing ceremony, the healer takes on the role of spiritual conduit, divinely channeling the providential healing power. A similar act of faith on the part of the afflicted serves to complete the miraculous healing circuit, underscoring the unswerving nature of the quest. The ritual typically concludes with a spirited sampling of testimonials attesting to the cures that enduring faith had wrought. In essence, the devout sense of faith proved particularly deserving of the bountiful effects of the cure, although such miraculous events continue to remain in short supply for many of us.

161 – HOPE

Allied to any discussion of faith is the related theme of *hope*. Although faith and hope are often used interchangeably in common usage, distinctive styles of reinforcement are clearly brought into focus. Its modern spelling derives the Anglo Saxon *hopa* (to be confident, to trust). The Latin slant on hope, *sperare*, entered the English lexicon chiefly with in terms of its opposing connotation of despair. Similar to the case previously established for Fides, Spes (the Roman personification of hope) was worshipped as early as the 4th century BCE. Spes originally was a goddess associated with Fortuna, invoked by all who hoped for success (particularly the hope for a good harvest). Over the course of generations, Spes eventually assumed the role of goddess of the future: invoked at births, weddings, and dedications. In light of her considerable prestige, several temples

were dedicated to her in Rome alone. Spes is traditionally depicted as a youthful maiden striding gracefully in a long robe, the seam raised in her left hand (as if in haste). In her right hand she holds a flower bud on the verge of opening, signifying the hopes for a brighter future.

These classical connotations beg further mention of the related legend of Pandora's Box. According to Greek mythology, Pandora was the first woman on earth, her name literally translated as "Giver of All." In celebration of her creation, Zeus offered Pandora an ornate box she was instructed never to open. This ploy was part of Zeus' clever plan to punish mankind for accepting (from Prometheus) the sacred gift of fire. In a fit of curiosity Pandora eventually peeked into the box, allowing all manner of human ills to escape into the world. Only hope (*elpis*) was left behind in the box, a solitary comfort to mankind in terms of such newfound misery. Later versions of the myth (such as the Fable of Babrius) have Pandora losing all the blessings of the gods (save hope), with similar consequences, only now more closely resembling the biblical account of Adam and Eve.

This steadfast quality of hope finds similar parallels in the Christian tradition. According to the enduring context of the theological virtues, hope is figuratively symbolized as an anchor inscribed upon a shield similar to the crucifix symbolism previously described for faith. This anchor symbolism traces its origins to St. Paul's Epistle to the Hebrews (6:19) wherein he states: "...which *hope* we have as an anchor of the soul, both steadfast and sure." In the next verse, St. Paul further identifies Christ as the rightful object of our hope, who (as Eternal High Priest) makes intercession on our behalf before the Father.

The early Christians had long anticipated the prophesied return of the Lord, a particularly comforting thought during such desperate times of persecution. This fearful era forced many Christians to resort to obscure forms of symbolism as a disguised expression of their hope. In particular, many early Christians adopted the marine anchor as an allegorical form of the cross, an identification suggested in the cruciform arrangement of the anchor's shaft and crossbar. This anchor symbolism was particularly widespread in the catacombs alongside other disguised symbols of Christianity; namely, the dove and the fish. Indeed, just as a sailor sets anchor in order to avoid drifting into danger, so the Christian disciple sets his *hope* in the saving power of Christ. It certainly remains a fitting tribute to the traditions of the deep spiritual insights of St. Paul that he would so intuitively and definitively celebrate these distinctive anchor symbolisms in relation to the early Christian beliefs concerning hope.

162 – CHARITY

The third of the traditional theological virtues, *charity,* is respectively defined as generosity freely bestowed upon the needy in hopes of improving their condition. Its modern spelling derives from the Latin *caritas* (dearness, affection), from *carus* (dear). Latin translations of the New Testament translate the original Greek *agape* as *caritas*, equivalent to the English theme of charity in the King James Edition. Agape originally referred to the Greek word for brotherly love, as opposed to *eros* (or passionate love): a distinction faithfully preserved in later scriptural contexts. The most stirring New Testament account of charity occurs in Chapter 13 of St. Paul's First Letter to the Corinthians. Many modern versions of the New Testament prefer to substitute the related theme of *love* for charity, although this generalization fails to preserve the original distinctions between the terms. Semantics aside, St. Paul extols charity as the greatest of the theological virtues, surpassing faith and hope in terms of moral excellence. St. Paul distinguishes charity as a fixed attitude of the soul, an enduring disposition clearly at odds with egocentric concerns. According to the Gospel of St. Mark (12:24-44) Christ heartily praises the poor widow that modestly gave a mere farthing to the temple fund. Contrast this to the wealthy Pharisee, who publicly extolled the magnitude of his largess.

This noble aspect of charity effectively permeated the very fiber of the early Christian Church. Chief in this regard was the *agape*, or love feast, described in verse 12 of the Epistle of St. Jude. It referred to the common evening meal of the early congregation (accompanied by devotional prayer and the singing of Psalms), eventually extending to the feeding the poor by the time of St. Augustine. These first charitable measures were initially administered by the early Christian congregations, enlisting the aid of deacons under the guidance of the elders. Grateful recipients included the aged and the infirm, the poor and the imprisoned, as well as widows and orphans. This early congregational setting eventually was supplanted by the diocesan system, where churches of a township answered to a single bishop. This centralized power-base allowed an even greater share of church tithing to go to the poor, a full quarter by many accounts. Even non-Christians were permitted to join the ranks of the needy, for it was judged nobler to err on the side of altruism. This diocesan system flourished throughout the Middle Ages, although gradually supplanted by the establishment of monastic orders devoted exclusively to such charitable causes.

It remained until the more liberal precepts of our modern age for women to take their fair part in such charitable endeavors. Take, for example, the founding of the Missionaries of Charity by Mother Teresa of Calcutta. At the tender age of 18, Mother Teresa joined the Institute of the Blessed Virgin Mary in Ireland, soon transferring to India to work as a teacher. She eventually sought permission to work with the poor in the slums of Calcutta, where she founded her order in 1948, enlisting many native novitiates in the process. The Missionaries of Charity established centers to aid the blind, disabled, elderly, and terminally ill of Calcutta. She also founded a leper colony near Asansol, India known as Shanti Nagar (Town of Peace). The Indian government awarded Mother Teresa the prestigious Padmashri Award in 1963 in recognition of her unfailing service to the people of India. Even greater awards followed, most notably the 1974 Nobel Peace Prize: to which she humbly commented "I am unworthy." This modest attitude echoed her deep spiritual conviction that: "The help for the hopeless is the simple duty of us all."

This commendable preoccupation with charitable endeavors is certainly one of Western culture's most time honored traditions. Specialized agencies (such as the United Way) aid in the distribution of much needed funds. It certainly appears fitting, then, that the medieval representation of charity takes the form of a crimson heart inscribed in heraldic fashion upon a shield. This graphic depiction formally symbolizes the heart's unceasing service to the wellbeing of the individual, a factor particularly in keeping with the lifelong charitable precepts of such noble spiritual servants as Mother Teresa.

163 – DECENCY

The fourth and final entry in the revised listing of theological virtues is the universal theme of *decency*. Its modern spelling derives from the Latin *decentia* (fitting), from the Latin verb *decere* (befitting). This theme, accordingly, is defined as a sense of propriety in both word and deed with an emphasis on moral scruples. The Romans expressed a high regard for the principles of decency, the Roman statesman Cicero succinctly summing up the opinion: "Justice consists in doing no injury to man, *decency* in giving them no offense." Decency enjoys similar precedents in the Christian tradition, although this term is specifically mentioned only once in English translations of the New Testament. The basic import of this term covers a broad range of ethical contexts, as evident in its strategic placement in Chapter 14 of St. Paul's First Letter to the Corinthians. Indeed, this chapter concludes with the stirring admonition: "Let all things be done *decently* and in order," hinting at the profound significance of this fourth theological virtue. Furthermore, Chapter 14 actually continues the general theme of Chapters 12 and 13 (namely, the Gifts of the Holy Spirit), placing decency in rightful proximity to descriptions of the first three theological virtues.

In Chapter 14, St. Paul directly focuses on the congregational aspects of these spiritual gifts, as in the themes of prophesy and speaking-in-tongues. St. Paul rightfully expressed concern that the over-zealous use of such gifts could prove detrimental to the credibility of the Church from a gentile standpoint. He further attempted to resolve this issue by proposing strict guidelines for governing the expression of these gifts within a congregational setting. He recommended restraint in the number of those speaking-in-tongues, while calling for an interpreter to offer insights into prophetic revelations. In this restricted sense, St. Paul expressed hope that these gifts would be used for the edification of the Church, over and beyond their spiritual significance to the individual, a proclamation consistent with his call for decency in a church setting.

This spiritual interpretation survives to our modern era in the familiar expression: "common decency," namely, common to all cultures and creeds. Indeed, St. Paul deliberately sets the tone of a spiritual authority figure, lecturing on many austere themes of central importance to the fledgling Church. Although this epistle was originally addressed to the congregation in Corinth, it has since been accorded a universal focus in Christian theology, in keeping with its concern for an acceptable Church image. Through such a concerted effort, Christianity eventually grew to claim a dynamic place on the world scene, a degree of success that even St. Paul would marvel at today.

In conclusion, the completed description of the spiritual disciple perspective proves a fitting counterpoint to the universal prerequisites of the spiritual authority figure. Indeed, hearkening back to the traditions of the theological virtues, the spiritual disciple skillfully reinforces the leadership qualities of the spiritual authority figure: namely, prudently acting *faithfully*, blamefully *hoping* for justice, temperately acting *charitably*, or fortitudinously acting *decently*. In such a highly interdependent sense, this unprecedented universal perspective (entertained by both the authority and follower roles) offers crucial insights on the world scene today, extending the potential for healing the significant rifts currently separating many of the world major religions.

Disturbing extremist/fundamentalist trends within the three great monotheistic faiths may finally be put to a more rational perspective through the aid of the newly devised breakthroughs implicit in Set Theory. Here, the universal domain specifies that all religions be considered equal when speaking from such an overarching spiritual perspective. Hopefully, this reevaluation of the exclusivity of "truth" with respect to any particular religious tradition may facilitate the potential for greater spiritual peace and harmony, whereby eliminating many of the irrational incentives towards terrorist acts that threaten the well-being of the entire global community. Indeed, this distinctive style of spiritual/universal perspective would definitely appear to close-out any further escalation of ascending power maneuvers, for there can be no level of organization greater than mankind as a whole. The addition of an all-inclusive historical perspective, however, allows for one further innovation in terms of the perpetual power struggle; namely, that extending to the next higher *humanitarian* sphere of influence.

6

THE HUMANITARIAN GLOBAL TRADITION

In keeping with the more elementary forms of authority (that it supercedes) humanitarian authority has enjoyed a long and illustrious literary tradition. The humanitarian form, however, is distinguished from all previous formats in terms of its claim as the first truly abstract power maneuver. Not an organizational power maneuver per sé, it represents an expansion of the spiritual variety through the abstract addition of historical time. According to this latter innovation, the humanitarian authority transcends spiritual authority by claiming to speak for all generations of mankind (not just the current one). Although the humanitarian authority is quick to acknowledge the inherent immediacy of spiritual authority, (on a grander time scale) the humanitarian authority perspective will always prevail. Its extreme degree of generality precludes its identification with any singular social institution; rather its banner is typically incorporated into the religious (and sometimes political) framework of society as a whole.

The truest appeal of humanitarian authority hinges upon mankind's enduring fascination with culture and tradition, giving homage to the progressive nature of the collective human spirit. During classical times, when the rate of technological change was often negligible over the course of generations, such humanitarian concerns rated far less prestige than they currently enjoy today. In particular, the Roman style of political administration served as the dominant humanitarian perspective throughout the classical age, maintaining a stable state of peace and prosperity over a course of many centuries.

The eventual decline of the Western Roman Empire, however, ushered in a radical shift in such classical perspectives. Its standard-bearer status reverted (by default) to the Roman Catholic Church, an unlikely outcome in light of the latter's humble beginnings. From its very inception, Christianity professed only the most limited of historical perspectives, the founding generation fully expecting to witness the Second Coming of Christ along with the establishment of his kingdom upon earth. A vicious series of persecutions (including the destruction of Jerusalem) were further interpreted as prophetic signs of Christ's imminent return. In fact, Christ's closing words to the faithful in the apocalyptic *Book of Revelation* states: "I am coming soon."

Following several centuries of desperate survival, Christianity miraculously found itself in a position of prominence within the Roman Empire. This placed Church Fathers in the awkward position of reinterpreting scripture to meet the needs of an enduring spiritual institution. In accepting the power ceded to it by the Romans, the Church underwent a dramatic period of growth and consolidation within its ranks. The Edict of Milan in 313 CE granted Christians their first right to freely minister throughout the vast extent of the Roman Empire. This newfound power offered fertile ground for the emergence troublesome schisms such as Arianism. In the interest of Church unity the Emperor Constantine called the First Ecumenical Council at Nicea in 325 in an attempt to reconcile such differing scriptural interpretations. Indeed, the term "ecumenical" derives from the Greek *oikoumene* (of the inhabited world), setting the tone for all such councils to follow: sharing the goal of defending, fortifying, and preserving the unity of faith.

THE INFLUENCE OF SAINT AUGUSTINE

The sack of Rome by Alaric, King of the Goths in 410 CE precipitated a further series of crises for the fledgling Church. For most of the classical era the Roman Empire had reigned as the supreme paragon of law, order, and stability. Pagan reactionaries seized upon Rome's downfall to denounce the Church, blaming Christianity's preoccupation with pacifism and asceticism for undermining the internal solidarity of the Empire. These serious charges were formally addressed by St. Augustine of Hippo (354-430) in his masterpiece *The City of God*. St. Augustine's writing career was predominantly concerned with apologetics, essentially a defense of orthodox Christianity against such serious charges. Indeed, *The City of God* is celebrated as perhaps the most definitive apology every written, serving as the supreme inspiration for the apologetics of later ages.

The disastrous fall of Rome revived one of the most intractable of all theological controversies; namely, why God would allow evil to exist in the world if He is truly all-knowing and all-powerful. In *The City of God*, St. Augustine shifts the blame from God to man, reviving the doctrine of Original Sin so eloquently expounded by St. Ambrose. Although Adam was created without the taint of sin, his transgression in Paradise so altered his nature that it was transmitted to all subsequent generations as Original Sin. Mankind's inherent sense of free will was irreparably damaged, shifting from spiritual to egocentric concerns. According to St. Augustine, all evil is the direct consequence of this misguided self-love: remedied only through an earnest appeal to God's divine mercy and grace. In terms of the preceding account, both grace and free will emerge as prominent themes in the apologetics of St. Augustine. In particular, this pairing of ecumenical themes appears tailor-made for satisfying two of the four dimensions predicted for the humanitarian authority perspective. Their traditional context certainly betrays such an enduring focus. Grace denotes a humanitarian refinement of providence, whereas free will makes a similar correspondence to liberty.

The two remaining dimensions, however, prove somewhat more problematic, although clues abound within the traditional literature. Ideally, the final two terms should represent higher (humanitarian) analogues of the more basic concepts of civility and austerity specific to the spiritual authority role. The paired concepts of magnanimity and equanimity primarily come to mind, clearly suggestive of a higher-order relationship to civility and austerity. In this latter respect, *magnanimity* represents the humanitarian counterpart of civility, whereas *equanimity* denotes a similar refinement of austerity: wherein rounding out the predicted four-part complement of humanitarian authority terms.

This cohesive grouping of grace-freewill-magnanimity-equanimity is most appropriately termed the class of *ecumenical* ideals: directly alluding to the enduring spirit of the early ecumenical councils where the Church was truly One, Holy, Catholic, and Apostolic. In particular, this theme has undergone a significant revival as of late, chiefly through the efforts of a broad coalition of Protestant denominations, now a major proponent of the ecumenical movement around the world. The Protestant sense of the term certainly proves relevant here; with grace, free will, magnanimity, and equanimity all figuring prominently in the writings of Martin Luther. This distinctive grouping of ecumenical ideals is further verified in the expanded context of the corresponding literary traditions.

170 – GRACE

The first of the ecumenical ideals, *grace*, is traditionally defined as divine protection or favor bestowed from On High. Its modern spelling derives from the Latin *gratia* (favor, kindness), from *gratus* (pleasing, agreeable). The classical Romans divinely worshipped this theme as the Gratiae (Graces), a trio of sister goddesses tending to the adornment of Venus. Indeed, the Romans sometimes referred to grace as *venia* in allusion to the handmaidens' unparalleled favor in the eyes of Venus. Although the Graces commanded only a limited cult following in Rome, they were more widely worshipped in their native Greece as the *Charites*: from the Greek *charis* (grace), also a root-stem for charisma. This derivation only superficially conforms to the related theme of charity, the latter deriving from the Latin *caritas*.

The Charites traditionally represented the Greek ideal of the good life: particularly life's more festive aspects. The Greeks joyously celebrated these qualities in the naming of their three sister goddesses; namely, Aglaia (splendor and brilliance), Thalia (bloom or abundance), and Euphrosyne (joy or mirth). These three sisters presided over banquets, dances, and social engagements: giving charm to all that made life joyous or beautiful. The Charites were also closely affiliated with the Muses, sharing the latter's penchant for music, art, and poetry.

The Graces, accordingly, were depicted as beautiful young maidens dancing in a circular pattern in a meadow, in keeping with their original role as nature goddesses. Their most ancient shrine was located at Orchomenos in Greece, adjacent to a temple dedicated to Dionysus and a spring sacred to Aphrodite (both of whom are cited in the parentage of the Graces). Ancient stone images of the Charites were enshrined here, said to have fallen miraculously from the heavens. Their annual feast day was celebrated nearby with musical contests and dancing staged in their honor.

Grace is also celebrated as a major theme in the Judeo-Christian tradition. The opening passages of the Old Testament specifically proclaim the Jews as the chosen people of God. This blessing stems from the Lord's founding promise to Abraham (Genesis 12:2-3) and His subsequent covenant with Moses on Mt. Sinai (Exodus 33:19). The end of the Old Testament period, however, ushered in a more personalized perspective on God's grace; now viewed as a gift bestowed upon all that worship the Lord (and keep His Commandments).

` This personalized perspective on God's grace eventually carried over into New Testament scripture as characterized in the life and times of Jesus Christ. The original Greek NT versions specifically translate grace as *charis* (referring to objects of joy or delight). It is chiefly through the writings of the St. Paul, however, that the Christian sense of the term reaches its most enduring degree of significance. Indeed, it was chiefly through the grace of God that Paul personally was called to his ministry (and protected throughout his missionary travels). In 1st Corinthians, Chapter 12, St. Paul directly intimates that the *charismatic* gifts (namely, prophecy, healing, and speaking-in-tongues) are outward manifestations of this indwelling grace of God. Furthermore, these Gifts of Grace are only made available through faith (Romans 4:16), the devotion of the believer crucial to such a divine intervention.

171 – FREE WILL

Allied to any discussion of grace is the related theme of *free will*, the humanitarian counterpart of the related theme of liberty. Its modern spelling derives as a literal translation of the Late-Latin *liberum arbitrium* (literally, free decision). In keeping with its compound character, free will has traditionally been assigned a rather broad range of meanings: from motivation and will to necessity and determination. Indeed, its very spelling suggests somewhat of a redundancy, for its component themes of freedom and will are often used interchangeably in common usage. In its humanitarian sense, however, the doctrine of free will originally was devised to defend against the argument that God had the power to prevent the occurrence of evil in the world. According to this free will defense, God allows mankind to be tempted by evil in order to freely elect to resist (or yield) to it. The wrathful punishment awaiting the wicked adds further fuel to the controversy,

for God surely is able to circumvent sin without necessarily resorting to outright punishment. Various Church theologians have attempted to reinterpret this paradox, shifting the blame for sin to mankind's inherent weakness.

Ample scriptural precedents serve to validate this enduring perspective: dating to the first man and woman, Adam and Eve. According to the Book of Genesis, Adam and Eve lived a carefree existence within their garden paradise: immune to death, suffering, and disease. Through the evil influence of the Devil, however, they were tempted to disobey God's main directive "Never to eat of the fruit from the Tree of Good and Evil." The Devil had cruelly deluded Eve into believing she could become an equal with God by partaking of that which she had been forbidden. For their mutual sin of pride, Adam and Eve were forever banished from Paradise, painfully becoming mortal in the process. Indeed, their original sin so altered man's nature that it was transmitted to all subsequent generations to come. According to this interpretation, the taint of original sin affects all such generations; hence, cursed through the tendency to sin further in the eyes of God.

Owing to these scriptural precedents, the Church was able to blame Adam's fall (and not any flaw in God's master plan) for the ever-present consequences of evil in the world. Similar to the related theme of grace, free will is seen as an indwelling gift from God. Certainly, it took a remorseful attitude on the part of Adam and Eve for God to leniently forgo His righteous judgement. Mankind's trial of obedience was mercifully allowed to continue on earth although now excluded from the idyllic conditions enjoyed in Paradise. Mankind was also forced to face the limitations of mortal existence, the finality of death now the acid test for moral success or failure.

172 – MAGNANIMITY

The third of the ecumenical ideals, *magnanimity*, rates current consideration as the chief humanitarian counterpart of civility. Its modern spelling derives from the Latin *magnanimus* (greatness of soul), from *magnus* (great) and *animus* (soul). It is traditionally defined as nobility of mind or spirit that graciously overlooks insult or injury. Magnanimity was particularly revered during the classical age, specifically singled out by Aristotle in his principle listing of virtues. This theme also finds expression in the Judeo-Christian tradition, as celebrated to a supreme degree in the teachings of Christ. Scripture certainly recognizes Christ's ability to recognize the greatness of the moment, as in his parable describing the slaughter of the fatted calf (Luke 15:23) or his opening of the chest of precious ointment (Mathew 26:8-13). A similar theme is found in the OT Book of Ecclesiastes (11:1) which states: "Cast thy bread upon the waters, for thou shalt find it after many days," (signifying generosity that transcends personal concerns).

Magnanimity signifies the inclination to reward exemplary courage or skill, often to an extravagant degree. Such noble characteristics also endear it as one of the traditional attributes of royalty and nobility. In the heraldic symbolism of the Middle Ages, magnanimity is represented as a triumphant eagle depicted in the act of sparing a portion of its kill for the lesser birds of prey (which hover around the eagle in an admiring fashion). Contrast this to the human condition, where those in positions of power/authority consistently strive to preserve some measure of their exalted status through the erection of a stone memorial, durably built to stand the test of time. Indeed, many such grand monuments survive from ancient times: standing mute testimony to the magnificence of the commemorated leader, as well as the painstaking labor of the supportive cast of artisans.

173 – EQUANIMITY

Any discussion of magnanimity must necessarily remain incomplete without mention of the related theme of *equanimity*. The similarity of these two terms clearly betrays common origins: with magnanimity specifying a "greatness" of mind, whereas equanimity equates with an "evenness" of mind. This latter term derives from the Latin *aequus* (equal) and *animus* (mind), formally reflecting its contemporary connotations of mental composure or calm demeanor. Indeed, just as magnanimity imparted a more enduring quality to civility, so equanimity adds a humanitarian focus to austerity. This timeless nature of equanimity is further seen as a dominant theme in many philosophical movements, particularly the traditions associated with Stoicism. Here, Zeno of Citium founded Stoicism in the city of Athens, lecturing his students from a *stoa* (or porch), the basis for the term's derivation. The most basic tenet of Stoicism is one of determinism, where fate guides the individual (through divine influence) towards a common good. The ultimate goal of human existence therefore lies in comprehending this divine essence, wherein acting in accordance with it. The virtuous man accepts what cannot be changed, stomaching adversity with an austere sense of equanimity. Indeed, the Stoics believed that true spiritual happiness flows entirely from such a restrained course of events.

The subsequent rise of the Christian era, however, presaged the decline of pagan Stoicism, although many of its nobler themes were incorporated into later Church Canon. This austere sense of equanimity was particularly revered by the ascetic orders of the early Christian Church, offering hope and inspiration in the face of the tribulations of the Dark Ages. Equanimity, accordingly, remained the emblem of the long-suffering medieval knight: celebrated through the aid of heraldic symbolisms similar to those cited for magnanimity. The noble knight is certainly a fitting exemplar of equanimity, pledging a lifetime of service to his feudal lord regardless of the formidable personal hardships. Although the heraldic symbolisms for magnanimity took the form of a regal eagle, equanimity is more prosaically portrayed as the domestic ass, a beast of burden symbolizing patience or perseverance even under the most trying of circumstances. Indeed, equanimity was also symbolized as the humble beaver, a beast that patiently labors to maintain its constructions under the most formidable of challenges. Whether one alludes to the industrious beaver or the patient ass, these enduring aspects of equanimity are unmistakable in their intent, a supreme refinement of austerity wholly emblematic to such a grand humanitarian perspective.

THE CLASSICAL GREEK VALUES: THE ROLE OF THE HUMANITARIAN FOLLOWER

The completed description of the ecumenical ideals offers a suitably moralistic picture of the power dynamics governing the humanitarian authority perspective. In keeping with this enduring humanitarian perspective, each of the ecumenical ideals figures prominently in the long tradition of ecumenical councils. The "timeless" quality of the class of ecumenical ideals certainly fits a common stereotype; namely, enduring themes formally in keeping with such a grand humanitarian perspective. This formidable style of abstract power-base allows the humanitarian authority to effectively overrule the more immediate concerns of the spiritual disciple, effectively regaining the upper hand in the perpetual power struggle. Even an authority perspective as abstract as the humanitarian, however, must (by definition) be invested with its own unique form of follower countermaneuver: in this case, that expressed by the representative member of humanity.

True to its extreme level of abstraction, the humanitarian follower perspective formally complements its authority counterpart, restoring an equal balance of power to the humanitarian power realm. It, accordingly, shares the distinctive style of "strike" leverage previously established for the lower levels: culminating in an unprecedented 4th-order level of meta-abstraction. In this more advanced respect, the humanitarian follower informs the humanitarian authority that a sanction from all of humanity is crucial for maintaining his authority status. Technically speaking, we can all speak as representative members within such a grand humanitarian time scale. This inherent degree of flexibility could be predicted earlier in the chapter, where the authority role was defined as more of a policy-making strategy than any immediate style of power maneuver. The representative member of humanity, in turn, retains the option of rejecting humanitarian policy; hence, ensuring an equal balance of power within the humanitarian power realm.

More properly termed the "philosopher's" maneuver, this distinctive style of follower strategy downplays the strike tactic in favor of the prestige involved in speaking for all of humanity. In particular, the philosopher role has long been revered for critical reasoning and crucial insights into universal truths. In the spirit of the stirring classical injunction: "Know thyself," philosophy has painstakingly refined the collective wisdom of humanity over the span of countless generations. Philosophy is primarily eclectic in nature, drawing extensively from the rich wellspring of accumulated wisdom and truth. This enduring interpretation necessarily suggests the existence of a corresponding listing of humanitarian themes, although both major categories of virtue (e.g., the cardinal and theological) have already been accounted for. This leaves only the remaining listing of classical Greek values as the most effective adjunct for designating the humanitarian follower perspective. The respective grouping of beauty, truth, and goodness represents one of philosophy's most time-honored traditions: perpetuating the ethical focus of the virtues, with the exception that the more enduring sense of *value* is now called into focus. It ultimately remained to the enduring genius of Plato to unite these concepts into a single cohesive context, much as he had previously accomplished with respect to the cardinal virtues.

According to his dialogue *Parmenides*, Plato speculates on the existence of absolute forms (or values) that convey our understanding of the beautiful, the good, and the true. As organizational principles, they impart a conceptual sense of order to our variable perceptual experiences. In his masterpiece *The Republic*, Plato further makes an analogy between *goodness* and the sun: for just as the sun provides light for the physical world, so goodness offers illumination on a moral plane. Indeed, Plato specifically distinguishes goodness as the supreme primal form that unifies each of the lesser abstract forms.

Although this cohesive grouping of beauty, truth, and goodness appears tailor-made for designating the first three dimensions predicted for the humanitarian follower perspective, it still remains one term short of satisfying the full quartet. This shortfall is fortunately remedied through the addition of the related theme of *wisdom*. Due to its superficial resemblance to prudence, wisdom consistently appears to have been overlooked in the traditional listing of classical Greek values. In particular, wisdom directly suggests more of a humanitarian focus, in contrast to the more elementary group focus of prudence. Plato appears to suggest precisely such a distinction: distinguishing between the wisdom of the social environment and that of the philosopher in his stoic pursuit of the truth. Plato's student, Aristotle proposed an even sharper distinction in meaning. Practical wisdom (prudence) is most closely associated with social matters, whereas speculative wisdom (*sophia*) pursues truth for its own sake: namely, the universal philosophical principles underlying all human experience.

In affirmation of these historical perspectives, only the latter humanitarian sense of wisdom effective rounds-out the respective listing of classical Greek values. In this formal sense, *beauty* represents the humanitarian counterpart of faith, whereas *truth* makes a similar analogy to hope. Furthermore, *goodness* formally expands upon the theological virtue of charity, whereas *wisdom* makes a similar correspondence to decency. Although these preliminary interpretations prove quite informative on an intuitive level, their true test of validity is alternately verified with respect to their corresponding literary traditions.

180 – BEAUTY

The universal theme of *beauty* has been widely celebrated throughout recorded history. It traces its origins to the Latin *bellitas*, from the root-stem *bellus* (pretty or pleasing). The classical Greeks particularly revered physical beauty and perfection, qualities their gods and goddesses exhibited to a supreme degree. The goddess Aphrodite was specifically singled out as the divine personification of love, beauty, and fertility. Her ethereal status among the gods derived from the claim that she was born upon the waves and foam of sea, from the Greek *aphros* (foam). She is traditionally depicted as a lightly draped figure of uncompromising grace and beauty. An ancient armless statue of her (internationally known as the Venus de Milo) was titled for its discovery on the Greek island of Melos. The Roman counterpart of Aphrodite, Venus, originally appears to have been Italian goddess associated with vegetable gardens; in effect, promoting their fertility. Her Latin name became synonymous with charm and beauty, eventually a key factor in her identification with the Greek traditions of Aphrodite. The legendary beauty of Venus was directly symbolized by her chief attribute, the Cestus (an embroidered girdle). This adornment was said to magically enhance the beauty of all that wore it, and inspire love and desire in all that beheld it. According to Homer's *Iliad*, the goddess Hera borrowed the Cestus from Aphrodite in order to excite the passion of Zeus: giving her favored Greeks the upper hand in the Trojan War by distracting Zeus from his plan to aid the Trojans.

These mythological interpretations of beauty find considerable parallels in the aesthetic principles underlying classical Greek philosophy. According to Greek tradition, beauty represents an external attribute of a given object, a property intrinsic to its very physical make-up. According to the writings of Plato and Aristotle, beauty resides in a regularity of form and function: as further expressed in symmetry, proportion, and harmony. These classical perspectives effectively dominated Western thought throughout the Middle Ages, as evident in its influence in sculpture, art, and architecture. Indeed, there appears little in the medieval formulation of beauty not directly attributable to such classical Greek perspectives.

Our modern age of ethical subjectivism, however, changed the face of aesthetics forever, as particularly evident in the contemporary maxim: "Beauty is in the eye of the beholder." This radical interpretation was directly championed by the empiricists, who viewed beauty as any agreeable aesthetic experience. Indeed, some empiricists postulated the existence of a special "sixth sense" attuned to beauty: wherein governing the appreciation of all such pleasurable experiences. These themes are retained in the subjectivist theories of our modern age, with beauty defined as any sensory experience that evokes a positive emotional response, particularly in a visual sense. Indeed, as the great English poet, John Keats fittingly wrote: "A thing of beauty is a joy forever."

181 – TRUTH

Any discussion of beauty must necessarily remain incomplete without mention of the related theme of *truth*. Indeed, Keats is further credited with the stirring quotation: "Beauty is truth, truth is beauty," attesting to the figurative association linking the two. Its modern spelling derives the Anglo Saxon *treowth* (of similar meaning and usage). Its related Latin counterpart, *veritas*, survives primarily with respect to the English synonyms of verity, veracity, etc. In fact, Veritas was specifically worshipped as a deity by the ancients, described as the daughter of Saturn and the Mother of Virtue. She is portrayed as a youthful virgin draped in white, exhibiting a clear air of modesty. The Greek philosopher Democritus describes her as hiding at the bottom of a well, indicating the great difficulty with which she is found.

Similar themes abound throughout the Mediterranean world, particularly the Egyptian tradition of Maat (their divine personification of truth and justice). Maat's chief attribute was a magical feather employed as a standard for measuring the moral weight of departed souls within the Hall of Judgement. Indeed, the plume of Maat eventually came to signify the Egyptian hieroglyph for truth, indicating the clear conceptual overlap linking justice and truth. Such classical considerations necessarily beg further mention of the related legends associated with Diogenes, a Greek contemporary of Aristotle. Diogenes is traditionally credited as the founder of Cynicism, a philosophical movement named for its attempts to discredit the lofty pretensions of the elite of Athens. Diogenes earned the reputation as somewhat of an eccentric, advocating a "back to nature" form of ascetic lifestyle generally bordering upon the absurd. His most prominent claim to fame concerns the fanciful legends surrounding his search for an "honest man." This quest was said to have taken him through the streets of Athens holding aloft a lantern in broad daylight, an eccentric feature further indicative of the futile nature of such an endeavor.

According to this fanciful legend, Diogenes clearly assumes the role of the representative member of humanity: a status definitely befitting the serious philosopher of his day. His persistent quest for the truth clearly narrows the focus, directly emphasizing the moralistic quality of the legend. The distinctive lantern symbolism of the fable lends further credence to the discovery function of truth. Indeed, lamps of various styles are incorporated in the seals of many prestigious

The Feather of Truth: Balancing Heart on the Scales of Justice
Detail from the Egyptian Papyrus of Ani   © - The British Museum

universities, accentuating their unswerving devotion to the truth. A similar correspondence is alternately seen with respect to beauty, which (in analogy to truth) appears entirely within the eye of the beholder. Truth is therefore seen as an active quest, the search for "the honest man" effectively targeting those deserving of such lenient treatment within a grand humanitarian timescale. Curiously, the legendary honest man always eludes Diogenes, for in the further opinion of Albert Einstein: "The search for *truth* is more precious than its possession." Along similar lines, philosopher George Santayana also writes, "The *truth* is all things seen under the form of eternity:" a speculation clearly in agreement with the grand humanitarian prerequisites of truth.

182 – GOODNESS

The third entry within the traditional listing of values is the universal theme of *goodness*. This term is invested with a broad range of meanings consistent with its general applications to the field of ethical inquiry. Its modern spelling derives from the Anglo-Saxon *god* (designating goodness). The Latin tradition is alternately identified with *bonitas*, the same root for the related theme of benevolence. In direct contrast to truth and beauty, goodness is not limited to any single classical deity, rather proposed as an indwelling attribute of the gods and goddesses in general. Although many of the classical gods were not above a cer-

tain degree of spirited combativeness, they nevertheless were regarded as morally upright and good at heart. Certain of the classical deities exemplified this quality to a supreme degree; namely, the Roman god Bonus Eventus (literally, good event). Bonus Eventus originally was worshipped as an agricultural deity, whose rituals determined the success or failure of the harvest. His scope eventually extended to close association with Fortuna (the Roman goddess of fortune). Surviving statues depict Bonus Eventus as a youthful figure offering a libation toast at the foot of a sacrificial altar. He holds stalks of grain (or a cornucopia) in his free hand indicative of his agricultural origins.

Perhaps the most stirring applications of goodness concern the Christian teachings on the subject, particularly those relating to the "Good Shepherd" Jesus Christ. Perhaps the most telling of Christ's parables in this regard concerns his stirring account of the Good Samaritan, a story proclaiming the value of loving one's neighbor. According to Luke - Chapter 10, Christ presents this parable in the context of his discussion of the Golden Rule. Rather than embarking upon a technical description, Christ offers the fictional account of an ill-fated traveler ambushed and left to die by the side of the road. Several subsequent travelers (represented by the Priest and the Levite) ignored the plight of the robbery victim, preferring to pass on the opposite side of the road. A humble traveler from Samaria, however, in a moment of compassion, gathered up the victim and transported him to the nearest inn for care and treatment. On the day of his departure, the Good Samaritan left extra money for the victim's further recuperation, a degree of dedication clearly beyond the ordinary call of duty.

In direct analogy to the case previously made for beauty, goodness clearly represents a rewarding style of humanitarian perspective, wherein expanding upon its more elementary foundations in charity. Unlike the Priest and the Levite (symbolizing the spiritual hypocrisy of their day), only the Samaritan was humble enough to be moved to a purely humanitarian display of goodness. His benevolent actions definitely underscore such charitable precepts; namely, aid for those unable to care for themselves. The robbery victim was clearly incapacitated, a fact that only the Samaritan acted upon in a timely and moral fashion. This unselfish impulse underscores one of the most salient features of goodness: namely, its bestowal as its own reward without regard for material gain. The Samaritan even provided for the extended care of the victim, a degree of concern formally in keeping with such a grand humanitarian time-scale.

183 – WISDOM

The fourth and final entry within the revised listing of values, *wisdom* is virtually unparalleled in the field of ethical inquiry. Its modern spelling derives from a compound of the two Anglo-Saxon words *wis-* (way or manner) and *dom* (state): collectively designating sound moral judgement or common sense. The ancient Romans divinely worshipped this quality as their abstract goddess Sapientia (Latin for Lady-Wisdom). She is traditionally depicted as a Siren of Philosophies rising from the sea in a style reminiscent of Aphrodite, pouring-out the "wine" of enlightenment from her bosom. Indeed, the Latin proper name for the human species, *Homo sapiens*, literally translates as "wise man." The related Greek root *sophia* suggests a similar scope of inquiry, as evident in the English derivations of Sophism, sophistication, etc. Plato's great disdain for the clever Sophists (or paid philosophers) of his day chiefly appears to have contributed to the omission of wisdom in his traditional canon of classical Greek values. Accordingly, wisdom was viewed as more of a virtue than a value, equivalent to the more elementary cardinal virtue of prudence.

Perhaps of even greater import to Western culture is the Wisdom Literature of the Jewish tradition, particularly the Old Testament Books of *Proverbs* and *Psalms*. As the traditional author of the book of *Proverbs*, the good King Solomon was revered as perhaps the wisest in a long line of biblical monarchs. According to the OT Book of Kings, King Solomon ascended to the throne as the eldest son of the noble King David. Solomon proved particularly well suited to the duties of his royal upbringing, widely renowned for his legendary cleverness and wisdom. His penchant for clever manipulation figured prominently in his celebrated seduction of the visiting Queen of Sheba. Indeed, his shrewd political acumen was chiefly instrumental in ushering in a golden age of trade and commerce for the Jewish people, leading to the construction of the first great temple at Jerusalem.

King Solomon's most prominent reputation for wisdom, however, was recorded in his routine courtly pronouncements: where he took an active role in settling disputes amongst his subjects. The Old Testament describes a conflict between two women seeking audience before the king, both claiming the same newborn child. Solomon shrewdly feigned the prospects of slicing the disputed child in half, wherein further determining the true mother through her emotional plea to forgo such drastic measures. This shrewd insight into human nature certainly validates King Solomon's rightful status as a true humanitarian visionary. The decent sense of wisdom he so effortlessly dispensed reflects a degree of leniency so crucial to this humanitarian realm. In truth, we are all heirs to the wisdom of Solomon, where a suitable mix of decency and leniency proves sufficient to guide us through the trials of everyday experience.

In conclusion, the completed description of the humanitarian follower perspective proves a fitting counterpoint to its respective authority counterpart. Indeed, the representative member of humanity role is one we all share in common; namely, spokesmen for all generations within such a grand humanitarian time-scale. Although the extreme level of abstraction at this juncture can appear daunting, we all remain eligible to speak as philosophers of a sort through the eclectic listing of classical Greek values (beauty, truth, goodness, and wisdom). This crowning humanitarian perspective would finally appear to close out any further escalation of power maneuvers, for there can be no level of organization greater than humanity as a whole. This very sense of the power of abstraction, however, serves as the basis for one final innovation in the ascending power hierarchy; namely, that specifying the crowning *transcendental* level of authority.

7

THE TRANSCENDENTAL POWER HIERARCHY

The transcendental theme has enjoyed a well-established philosophical tradition, with precedents dating at least to classical times. Its modern spelling derives from the Latin *transcendere* (to climb over), from *trans-* (over) and *scandere* (to climb. Medieval scholars freely adapted this theme in the academic field of Scholastic Logic: defining as *transcendentalia* (or *transcendentia*) extreme concepts such as goodness, unity, being, etc. The modern sense of the term dates to the writings of German philosopher Immanuel Kant, who laid the groundwork for his unique style of transcendental philosophy. In his masterpiece, *Critique of Pure Reason*, Kant directly acknowledges the transcendental philosophy of the ancients, although suggesting that his revised sense of the term only superficially conforms to the traditional sense. Indeed, Kant draws sharp distinctions between the notions of transcendence, the transcendental, and the immanent. The realm of *transcendence* is said to apply to ideas beyond the range of direct sensory experience. The notion of *immanence*, in turn, refers to the concrete realm of sensory experience. The remaining concept of the *transcendental*, however, represents an intermediate position; namely, those conceptual constructs implicit to sensory experience, although not directly arising from the senses. In particular, Kant distinguishes a broad range of transcendental categories (such as relation, causality, quantity, etc.) that intuitively serve to order sensory experience, although existing as mere formalities without sensory data to embody them. In this latter sense, all knowledge is preconditioned by such transcendental presuppositions, forming the basis for the German school of transcendental idealism.

Kant's dynamic influence eventually reached the English speaking world chiefly through the writings of Samuel Taylor Coleridge and Thomas Carlyle. These interpretations eventually gained acceptance in the United States, flowering during the early 19th century as the eclectic movement known as New England Transcendentalism. This movement arose as a revolt against the skepticism of British Rational Philosophy, as well as the dogmatism of Orthodox Protestantism. Ralph Waldo Emerson was the acknowledged leader of the movement. Other notables included Henry David Thoreau, Nathaniel Hawthorne, and Margaret Fuller. Although the New England movement was relatively short-lived, it was instrumental in influencing religious and social thought for generations to come. Despite the belief that social change was primarily a matter of personal choice, many transcendentalists championed the major reform movements of the day; namely, peace, temperance, women's suffrage, and slavery.

The strength of the movement ultimately declined with the onset of the Civil War, coinciding with the retirement of Emerson and the death of Thoreau. Even a century later, Dr. Martin Luther King Jr. acknowledged the great influence Thoreau's philosophy of civil disobedience played in the Civil Rights demonstrations of the 60's. Indeed, it is these latter troubled times that ultimately provide clues towards identifying the four affective dimensions predicted for the transcendental authority perspective.

A MODERN-DAY REVIVAL OF TRANSCENDENTALISM

The war protest era of the late 60's and early 70's was characterized by great political and moral upheaval, a trend "the establishment" found increasingly difficult to control. The great rallying cry was the protest against the Vietnam War, the mounting casualty figures discouraging support for what (even then) appeared to be a futile international endeavor. The peace movement, accordingly, evolved its own fraternal symbolisms;

namely, the peace sign and the peace symbol (a dove's foot inscribed in a circle). The simultaneous availability of "the pill," in turn, ushered in a more relaxed sexual attitude, the practice of free love flourishing in "hippy" districts such as Haight-Ashbury. This self-styled peace-love generation prided itself on such nonconformist attitudes, looking to the unconventional themes of meditation and astrology for solutions to political turmoil, promoting the quest for inner peace and tranquility. The emerging Civil Rights movement also raised the pressing issue of racial equality, an issue deliberately grafted into the peace movement as yet a further tactic to thwart the tyranny of the establishment. Blacks became "brothers" with whites in a stirring appeal to universal peace and brotherhood.

These four noble themes of the 60's (peace-love-tranquility-equality) collectively celebrate the transcendental focus of the age, a tradition sharing much in common with New England Transcendentalism. This enduring transcendental perspective proves particularly consistent with the reigning humanistic focus of the modern age, downplaying the dogmatism of orthodox religion in favor of individual conscience. The cohesive grouping of peace-love-tranquility-equality is most appropriately termed the class of *humanistic* values, directly expanding upon the humanitarian focus of the ecumenical ideals. In more abstract sense, *peace* represents a more advanced modification of equanimity, whereas *love* attaches a parallel significance to magnanimity. Furthermore, *tranquility* adds a transcendental perspective to grace, whereas *equality* targets the related theme of free will. In final analysis, the true test of the humanistic values is ultimately found within the expanded context of their corresponding literary traditions.

193 – PEACE

The first of the humanistic values, *peace*, is a transcendental theme of virtually universal appeal. Its modern spelling derives from the Latin *pax* (peace), chiefly in the context of the Pax Romana: the peace the Romans imposed upon subject provinces within the Empire. The Roman's self-appointed role of peacemaker was primarily seen as a moral prerogative according to political theorists such as Virgil. Indeed, the Romans specifically worshiped this concept as their abstract goddess Pax, the divine personification of peace among diverse nations. Pax represents a relatively late addition to the Roman pantheon, virtually unheard of before the time of Augustus. State

support for her cult is generally credited with fostering the strength and stability of the Empire under Augustus. A Roman shrine was dedicated to Pax in 9 BCE in celebration of the restoration of peace by Augustus following his triumphant series of campaigns in Spain and Gaul. The widespread longing for peace during this period of civil unrest contributed to Pax's great popularity among the common people. Pax, accordingly, is portrayed as a youthful maiden holding a cornucopia in her left hand and an olive branch (the symbol of peace) in her right. She is sometimes depicted setting fire to a stockpile of armaments in defiance of the prevailing militarism of the day. A major festival was held in her honor on the last day in April.

The Judeo-Christian tradition similarly celebrates the transcendental aspects of peace. The Hebrew word for peace, *Salom*, is directly related to the same root-stem for health and wholesomeness. The prophets of the Old Testament exalted peace as the promised blessing of the Messianic Age. In his Sermon on the Mount, Christ directly blesses the peacemakers, stating: "They shall be called children of God." The Apostle Paul, in turn, describes Christ's message as "the gospel of peace" (Ephesians 6:15). Paul also lists peace among the Gifts of the Holy Spirit. Indeed, it is fitting that the dove (as the chief symbolism of the Holy Spirit) figures so prominently in OT descriptions of peace, particularly the celebrated story of Noah and the Ark. Here, the dove served as God's messenger, carrying an olive sprig in its beak symbolizing peaceful intent. Noah originally had released the dove during the Great Flood to see if it might successfully find landfall. The olive branch carried by the dove, in turn, signaled that the ordeal was finally coming to an end.

In keeping with these scriptural precedents, peace builds (in a transcendental fashion) upon the humanitarian focus of equanimity, terms that share a collective focus in austerity. This grand transcendental focus of peace suggests precisely such an austere perspective, as exemplified in the offering of the olive branch during peace negotiations. The olive orchard required many years of tending to become fruitful, signifying the peace required to fulfill its potential. Accordingly, the dove and the olive branch are all revered as Christian symbolisms of peace: emblems still employed today in the amicable resolution of disputes.

192 – LOVE

The second of the humanistic values, *love*, is a theme that truly transcends all ages and cultures. Its modern spelling derives from the Anglo-Saxon

Noah in the Ark: Welcoming Back the Dove of Peace
Detail from a Fresco in the Catacomb of St. Peter/St. Marcellinus - Rome - (3rd Century)

lufu (of similar meaning). Although the English derivation has endured as the dominant form, the classical tradition is alternately represented as the Latin *cupido* (passion, desire), as well as *amor* (love). The Romans divinely worshipped this theme in the guise of Cupid, their youthful god of love. In classical mythology, Cupid is traditionally depicted as an adorable winged cherub daintily equipped with a quiver and bow. As the youngest of the Roman gods, he is described as callous or capricious, exhibiting little concern even for his mother, Venus. The gods Pothos and Himeros were named as his constant companions: the Roman personifications of longing and desire. Jupiter graciously equipped Cupid with a pair of golden wings, a magical bow, and a quiver of invisible arrows said never to miss their mark. These arrows were said to instill irresistible love in the hearts of all struck by them. One ancient legend suggests that Cupid whets with blood the grindstone upon which he sharpens his arrows. He is often described as blind or blindfolded consistent with the modern contention that "love is blind."

These enduring legends surrounding Cupid serve as a colorful basis for many modern-day symbolisms of love; particularly, a crimson heart pierced by an arrow (the traditional emblem of St. Valentine's Day). The modern conception of romantic love is actually of fairly recent origin, as well as the tradition of marriage for love's sake. Marriage solely for love at first was considered a scandalous novelty, in contrast to the mandate it currently enjoys today. The modern age of romantic love was initially celebrated in the lyric poetry popularized by the troubadours of Southern France. The romantic exaltation of the passions eventually swept the continent, celebrating the romantic ideal of chaste womanhood. This courtly sense of love transcended mere sexual passion, wherein idealizing the chaste and inaccessible woman of fancy. The medieval lover was expected to serve his lady without recompense save the glow of her gracious approval. This elevated status of women eventually was reflected in other chivalrous themes; namely, a steadfast sense of loyalty to God, King, and Country. These noble themes of chastity/chivalry sought to control (rather than gratify) such amorous instincts. Romantic passion increasing in direct proportion to the obstacles placed in the way. In this latter respect, love guides one to a nobler life, its trials and tribulations curiously suggestive of the ordeals of martyrdom (both of which transcend the self in the quest for a higher good).

As is true with so many of the great love stories from the past, love is seen to transcend all political and social barriers, a transcendental expression of pure ideal passion. In the case of Romeo and Juliet, their respective families were embroiled in a bitter blood feud spanning many generations, in direct contrast to the tender and loving passion shared by the young lovers. In a similar sense, Anthony and Cleopatra were the fateful offspring of radically different cultures, yet the flame of their love burned brightly until tragically cut short. Here (as with Romeo and Juliet), the couple chose to die together in hopes of being joined for all eternity, an extreme variation on the transcendental foundations of the love perspective.

190 – TRANQUILITY

The completed description of peace and love leaves *tranquility* as the third entry in the overall grouping of humanistic values. Its modern spelling derives the Latin *tranquillitas*, from *trans-* (beyond) and *quies* (rest). The use of the same prefix in the overall context of transcendentalism lends further credence to the overlapping significance of these two themes. The Romans worshipped tranquility as the abstract goddess Quies, the divine personification of calmness and tranquility. She is traditionally portrayed as a beautiful maiden in a relaxed pose, sometimes shown leaning upon a short marble column. Her chapel was located on the Via Labicana in Rome, a welcome refuge for the weary traveler. A private cult dedicated to Quies dates to the earliest days of the Republic, although official worship was not instituted until imperial times. Following his surrender to Augustus, the rival Maximian had a medal of conciliation minted with the inscription "Quies Augustorum." A later series of coins incorporates the affiliated theme of tranquillitas into the emperor's title of distinction.

The direct antithesis of such formal classicism involves an appreciation of tranquility within the natural environment. Perhaps no experience is more exhilarating than a visit to a still mountain lake framed with majestic tall timber, permeated with an eternal hush completely at odds with the urban environment. This pristine natural setting clearly transcends the more hectic pace of city life, offering an experience of virtually timeless proportions. This exalted devotion for nature was widely celebrated in the spirited works of the great English and German romanticists: e.g., Goethe, Wordsworth, and Coleridge. They collec-

tively celebrated an enhanced regard for the wonders of nature, as well as a stirring empathy for its divine order.

The subsequent dawning of the Industrial Age, however, forever altered such a pastoral perspective. Nature was now esteemed as a source of timber and coal for fueling the furnaces and steam engines of the day. Cities grew increasingly over-crowded and polluted, attracting many unskilled laborers from the countryside. Under such trying circumstances, tranquility was chiefly achieved through chemical means: primarily with respect to alcohol, opium, or other tranquilizers.

In keeping with the preceding nature example, tranquility is clearly classified as a past-directed style of transcendental perspective true to its more elementary foundations in grace. The "tranquilizer" abuser habitually acts in a solicitous fashion in order to achieve reinforcement when the drug finally takes effect. In most such cases, the calming effect of the tranquilizer targets routine stresses in favor of tranquil feelings of serenity. As suggested previously, drugs represent just one avenue towards achieving a calm disposition. The appreciation of music, art, and drama provides an effective release from everyday stressful routines: as well as prayer, yoga, and meditation. The serene smile traditionally associated with depictions of the Buddha is certainly consistent with such a tranquil demeanor. Indeed, whether it be the hypnotizing radiance associated with the Transfiguration of Christ, or the mystical magnetism described in Herman Hesse's *Siddartha*; this enduring sense of tranquility will still come shining through!

191 – EQUALITY

The final of the humanistic values, *equality*, definitely lives up to its transcendental billing: for in the real world, everyone is unique in terms of individual strengths and weaknesses. Its modern spelling derives from the Latin *aequalitas* (equal), from *aequalis* (even). The Romans professed a strong constitutional sense of equality, with every citizen enjoying equal protection under the law. The Jus Naturale (or natural law) insured equal rights to the sea, seashore, and community property. Accordingly, the Romans divinely worshipped this theme as their abstract goddess Aequitas. Direct evidence of her cult occurs in an archaic inscription from Vulci, and Arnobius specifically mentions her as a goddess. Her name is also inscribed on many ancient coins from the era. The modern-day conception of equality (also known as *egalitarianism*) dates as a postscript to the European Age of Enlightenment. Political philosopher Thomas Hobbes professed the equal rights of mankind in his natural state consistent with his unlimited sense of potential. John Locke, in turn, elaborated upon this basic premise, stating that: "all men are equally free under the natural law and therefore fully deserving of the same natural rights." In the 18th century, these noble perspectives were further reflected in emerging theories of human development. According to Condillac and Helvetius, all men are equal in terms of the unlimited potential they share at birth: wherein equally perfectible given the proper social environment. French philosopher, J. J. Rousseau explained social inequality in terms of the pressures stemming from a stratified social order. Each individual (in the state of nature) fends for himself, wherefore abstaining from exploiting others (or being exploited). Rousseau further reasons that full social equality is the ideal natural state for the human species in general.

These radical interpretations proved particularly instrumental in fueling the great American and French Revolutions: themes so eloquently reflected in their respective declarations of rights. For the American Revolution, this sense of equality denied the legitimacy of any arbitrary form of government. The *Declaration of Independence* formally underscores this basic principle, stating: "We hold these truths to be self evident that all men are created *equal*, they are endowed by their Creator with certain unalienable rights, that among these are Life, Liberty, and the Pursuit of Happiness." This egalitarian perspective continues into our modern age, particularly with respect to the United Nation's *Universal Declaration of Human Rights* (1948) which states: "All human beings are born free and *equal* in dignity and rights."

In direct analogy to the case initially made for tranquility, equality shares a similar transcendental perspective: an ideal clearly noble in principle although seldom realized in practice. In truth, any recourse to universal principles necessarily entails a complete disregard for the more basic limitations governing the human condition. This egalitarian perspective necessarily specifies equal protection under the law irrespective of personal limitations or class distinctions. Such noble ideals celebrate the equal opportunity of all races and creeds, clearly denouncing any preferential treatment therein. Although such lofty ideals do not always square with the glaring gaps in the global economic system, they, nevertheless, remain principles worth aspiring to, even if only to remedy much of the disturbing prejudice that breeds in its stead.

THE MYSTICAL VALUES: THE ROLE OF THE TRANSCENDENTAL FOLLOWER

In conclusion, the completed description of the humanistic values offers a fitting relief from the more routine rigors of everyday life. Indeed, the world would certainly appear a much crueler place without such noble ideals to strive for. The transcendental authority perspective formally appeals to an idealized realm of pure abstraction, wherein overruling the more limited (organizational) power base of the lower set of levels. Its profoundly abstract nature, in turn, might serve to indicate that the upper conceptual limit of the power hierarchy has finally been reached. Indeed, it is difficult to imagine a set of concepts more abstract than the cohesive listing of peace, love, tranquility, and equality. Even an authority level as abstract as the transcendental, however, must (by definition) be invested with its own unique form of follower countermaneuver: in this case, that claimed by the transcendental follower.

The transcendental follower maneuver is clearly a unique addition to the orderly progression of the power hierarchy, its extreme degree of abstraction greatly impacting any respective "strike" leverage. Indeed, this supreme follower perspective introduces the hitherto unmentioned theme of "meta" or *pure* transcendence; namely, transcendence based entirely within transcendence. The previously established class of humanistic values (specifying the transcendental authority perspective) all exhibited a fair degree of conventionality in keeping with their more elementary foundation in the humanitarian follower perspective. The transcendental follower maneuver, however, abandons any such anchor in concreteness, rather based directly within the transcendental authority perspective; hence, the *meta*-transcendental sense of the term.

This supremely abstract style of follower perspective is particularly reminiscent of the emotional detachment characterizing many oriental schools of religious mysticism. In particular, the most basic precept of Buddhism states that the pursuit of pleasure necessarily invites pain, leaving emotional detachment as a principle means for achieving true spiritual balance. The mystic, accordingly, renounces the transitory passions of the everyday world in favor of a heightened experience of pure transcendence accompanying the mystical experience.

One of the most enduring mystical techniques towards these ends is the long-standing tradition of meditation. Indeed, meditation appears in one form or another in virtually every major religious tradition from around the world. Although the particulars can vary widely, all share some sort of preliminary focusing technique aimed at gaining entry into the mystical realm. This can be passive (as in focusing on one's breathing), or active (as in chanting a mantra). At some point during the preliminaries, the over-stimulation (or under-stimulation) specific to the procedure permits entry into the transcendental realm. This mystical state is variously described as relaxed alertness or detached awareness, an experience completely devoid of any particulars in thought or feeling. In terms of this blissful state, full mental stillness is ultimately achieved, abandoning any reference to external form or function.

According to Zen Buddhism, this enlightened state is known as *satori*, whereas the Yogic tradition is defined as *samadhi*. Even the Christian tradition acknowledges mystical enlightenment; namely, "the peace that passeth understanding" according to St. Paul. Indeed, virtually every culture reports some form of mystical experience; variously described as joyous ecstasy or blissful harmony. This universal mystical character completely transcends all such cultural barriers: whether Christian, Jewish, Islamic, or Oriental. It ultimately proves fruitful to look beyond such cultural restrictions, rather focusing on the individual subjective accounts characterizing the mystical experience in general.

THE REVOLUTIONARY CONTRIBUTIONS OF WILLIAM JAMES

Perhaps the most definitive examination of the mystical experience is offered by William James in his *Varieties of Religious Experience: A Study in Human Nature*. This work is a compilation of his Lectures on Natural Religion delivered in Edinburgh, Scotland in 1901-1902. James is traditionally revered as one of the founding fathers of the American school of pragmatic psychology. The brother of distinguished novelist Henry James, William was educated (and eventually achieved tenure) at prestigious Harvard University. His pioneering work into the psychological effects of nitrous oxide anesthesia provided him an unconventional (yet accommodating) access to the mystical realm. He alludes to this personal aspect of his mystical experiences as follows: "The further limits of our being plunge, it seems to me, into an altogether other dimension of existence from the sensible and merely understandable world. Name it the mystical region or the supernatural region, whatever you choose."

In his *Varieties of Religious Experience,* James lists a key number of distinguishing features for the mystical experience: defined as (1) ineffability, (2) noetic character, (3) transience, and (4) passivity. The first mentioned category of *ineffability* refers to the inherent difficulty in finding the words to express the dramatic nature of the mystical experience. Many mystics claim that it can only be understood through direct experience, with intuition clearly taking precedent over intellect. Although the experience is not easily articulated to others, it generally has an insightful character to the mystic: an aspect that James further defines as the *noetic* character. This term refers to "insights into the very depths of truth, unplumbed by the discursive intellect." These insights often come in the form of illuminations or revelations overflowing with significance, although usually only vaguely remembered following subsequent transition to ordinary consciousness. This latter aspect is termed *transiency* in that worldly concerns must eventually draw the mystical experience to close. Although the mystical experience is only imperfectly reproduced in ordinary memory, it is instantly recognized in its fullest sense during any subsequent recurrence. Although this state can be precipitated through voluntary means (such as prayer or meditation), the actual transformation is realized through an abeyance of the will (as if drawn by a superior power). James's final category of *passivity* refers to this ego-attenuation, a feature consistently experienced by mystics caught up in the throes of divine ecstasy.

This preliminary survey of the mystical experience, although clearly informative on an intuitive level, still leaves open the remaining issue of the identification of the four affective dimensions predicted for the transcendental follower perspective. Indeed, the affiliated theme of ineffability would seem to suggest that these additional dimensions would remain inexpressible in verbal terms. The Western tradition of Christian mysticism offers the greatest potential in this regard, particularly in terms of the personal aspect known as saintliness.

THE ENDURING TRADITIONS OF SAINTLINESS

In his *Varieties of Religious Experience,* James devotes five full lectures to the topic of saintliness, defining it as the "ripe fruits of spirituality." Citing a survey of the literature spanning many centuries, James proceeds to outline a number of key characteristics for saintliness. He initially describes the occurrence of an expanded outlook transcending one's individual peculiarities for an

The Ecstasy of Saint Teresa of Avila - Sculpture by Bernini
Photograph Courtesy the Cornaro Chapel - Santa Maria della Vittoria - Rome

enhanced conviction in a higher order. This further leads to a willing self-surrender to such a benevolent force, tempering freedom with elation as the distinctive outlines of selfhood melt away. There finally occurs a positive shift towards loving and harmonious affections clearly in keeping with such an ecstatic experience.

Although this traditional line of reasoning proves extremely enlightening, it ultimately proves crucial to examine individual accounts of saintliness in order to discern an overall pattern for the mystical states under consideration. Catholic mystics (such as St. Catherine of Genoa) advocated living in recollection; namely, magnifying each active moment so as to facilitate entry into Divine Union. A related system known as *orison* promoted an elevation of the soul through the systematic detachment of the senses. According to St. Teresa of Avila, the highest of these is the orison of union: which raises the soul into mystical union with the Divine, wherein giving the appearance of complete mental inaccessibility.

The English language is fortunately endowed with a broad range of terms for describing the mystical experience, borrowing extensively from both classical and contemporary traditions. This rich abundance of synonyms apparently selected (over time) for the precise shades of meaning predicted for the ethical power hierarchy. For instance, the cohesive grouping of ecstasy, bliss, joy, and harmony represents themes specifically mentioned by James in his report on saintliness. Although these four terms all seem to share a common theme, enough marginal distinctions remain to warrant a strict correspondence with the four affective dimensions predicted with respect to the power hierarchy. In this more advanced sense, *ecstasy* directly expands upon the aesthetic qualities of beauty, whereas *bliss* similarly expands upon the knowledge functions of truth. Furthermore, *joy* adds a transcendental slant to goodness, whereas *harmony* makes a similar correspondence to wisdom. This cohesive four-part listing of terms is respectively termed the class of mystical values, in direct acknowledgement of their general unifying theme. Although these motivational parallels prove convincing on an intuitive level, their true test of validity is ultimately established in terms of their respective literary traditions.

100 – ECSTASY

The first and foremost of the mystical values, *ecstasy*, is traditionally defined as an overwhelming sense of rapture (primarily in a spiritual sense). Its modern spelling derives from the Greek *ekstasis* (displacement), from *ek-* (out) and *histanai* (to place). This theme eventually took on a mystical significance, variously described as an overwhelming sense of joy accompanied by supreme feelings of delight. According to St. Teresa of Avila, this ecstatic state can be delicately gentle or violently rapturous (as in full-blown flights of the spirit). In the throes of such divine contemplation, the mystic becomes "one" with the experience of the Absolute. The mystic generally becomes impervious to outside sensations, even to the point of ignoring pain or discomfort. Indeed, this trance-like quality of ecstasy is also suggested in its subordinate theme of beauty. In this expanded sense, the transcendental follower beauteously acts in an ecstatic fashion, formally countering the tranquil sense of gracefulness expressed by the respective authority figure.

101 – BLISS

Allied to any discussion of ecstasy is the related theme of *bliss*. Its modern spelling derives from the Anglo Saxon *blisse*, from *bliths* (joy). These traditional connotations survive to our modern era with respect to the related contexts of rapture and gladness. This broad focus would further appear to restrict bliss to just another synonym for ecstasy were it not for its incorporation into the popular expression "ignorance is bliss." An alternate *truth* function is suggested for bliss. A casual survey the mystical literature brings to light many stirring accounts of blissful states where the grand scheme of things becomes supremely apparent. Indeed, ignorance *is* bliss in this elementary sense, a supreme overview clearly invoking such a transcendental perspective.

102 – JOY

The third of the mystical values, *joy*, traces its origins to the Old French *joye*, from the Latin *gaudium* (of similar meaning). It is traditionally defined as extreme happiness or gladness, often used interchangeably with ecstasy or rapture. The ancient Romans worshipped this concept as their god Comus (the divine personification of joyous revelry). This Latin tradition, in turn, traces its origins to the Greek god Komos, the same root-stem for the related theme of comedy. In particular, this congenial god is figuratively featured on the distinctive "smiling" style of mask generally worn during classical comedies.

These classical themes find similar consideration in the field of ethical inquiry, where joy is defined as "the prevailing quality of a rightful act" (a sense consistent with its transcendental affiliation to goodness). Indeed, St. Thomas Aquinas defines joy as: "The delight that is the healthy complement of intelligent and willed activity, when the appetite is actively at rest in a *good* really possessed." Furthermore, St. Paul fittingly numbers joy among the Gifts of the Holy Spirit (Galatians 5:22). These rewarding aspects of the term are particularly reflected in the popular expression "taking joy in one's work." Accordingly, joy is figuratively symbolized as a tolling bell, a singing lark, the midday sun, or the color yellow: indicative of its related connotations to goodness.

103 – HARMONY

The fourth and final of the mystical values, *harmony*, spans a rather broad range of meaning consistent with its transcendental placement within the power hierarchy. Its modern spelling derives from the Greek *harmonia* (a fitting together, an agreement), from *harmos* (a fitting or joining). According to classical Greek mythology, the goddess Harmonia is traditionally described as the daughter of Ares and Aphrodite: an insightful allegory in light of the fact that Ares was revered as the god of war, whereas Aphrodite was worshipped as the goddess of love. This theme also extends to the aesthetic realm of classical music and the fine arts: where agreement in form, function, and melody proves crucial to any meaningful attempts at composition. In medieval iconography, Harmony is depicted as a beautiful matron bedecked with an ornate crown, further flourishing a violin and a bow. In a more restricted relationship sense, harmony directly expands upon the humanitarian theme of wisdom, wherein reflecting a transcendental sense of agreement within a universal sphere of affairs.

SPECULATIONS INTO THE SUPERNATURAL REALM

In conclusion, the completed description of the mystical values effectively rounds out the stepwise description of the transcendental power realm. Any further extension of this format necessarily specifies the existence of an even more abstract form of authority; namely, that *transcending* transcendental authority. Although this extreme conceptual perspective definitely stretches the limits of abstract sensibility; in theory, there does not appear to be any conceptual limit governing the degree to which reflection can serve as a basis for itself. Any such upper limit must necessarily be a technical one; namely, that degree of abstraction that finally exceeds the capacity of the human intellect to distinguish the respective affective dimensions (precluding their incorporation into the collective language culture). This observed blending of meanings would, indeed, suggest that this upper conceptual limit has finally been reached. Beginning with the transcendental authority level, the respective listing of humanistic values (peace-love-tranquility-equality) all exhibit a fair degree of distinctness, even though some measure of conceptual affinity is hinted at in their dictionary definitions. For the next higher level of the transcendental follower, however, the mystical values (ecstasy-bliss-joy-harmony) collectively exhibit a greater degree of conceptual affinity: reflected in dictionary definitions that are similar (if not synonymous) in form and function.

Taking this trend to the limit predicts a complete blending of meanings at the next higher meta-meta-order level of transcendence. At this seemingly inconceivable level of abstraction, the four requisite affective dimensions effectively merge into a unified conceptual continuum, essentially unnamable except in the broadest supernatural sense; e.g., God, the Absolute, etc. One experiencing this extreme level of transcendence would certainly be impressed by the paradoxical blending of emotional states, in direct contrast to the more concrete range of experience characterizing the lower levels. In ordinary consciousness, the mind is typically restricted to entertaining only a single power maneuver (or emotion) at any given time. With respect to the supernatural dimension, however, the distinctions between the emotions become so blurred as to merge into a unified state: the "one becomes the many," as many mystics have reported down through the ages.

This paradoxical experience of all-inclusive awareness has traditionally been documented using a broad range of themes; such as the Universal Mind, the Oversoul, Cosmic Consciousness, Brahma, the Great Spirit, etc. These collectively serve as a primordial prototype for the continuum of lower (more differentiated) states. The supremely abstract nature of this supernatural perspective (by definition) encompasses all of the lower levels as subsets; hence, accounting for the corresponding flooding of the emotions. Perhaps herein lies the basis for the traditional Judeo-Christian belief that man is created in the image and likeness of God. Ordinary consciousness (with its sequential limitations) is formally theorized to differentiate out of this all-inclusive primordial state. At this supreme supernatural level, we seem to tune in to the Universal Mind as the sum-potentiality of all that is transcendent in nature.

Perhaps it is really only a matter of convention (devised by the ordinary mind) to regard the mystical state as a wholly separate entity. Indeed, William James appears to make a similar point in the following quotation from his *Varieties of Religious Experience*. "This overcoming of all of the usual barriers between the individual and the Absolute is the great mystical achievement. In mystic states we both become one with the Absolute and we become aware of our oneness. This is the everlasting and triumphant mystical tradition hardly altered by differences of clime or creed." The spiritually-minded can fittingly view the unified power hierarchy as rooted entirely within such a supernatural realm: where all power emanates from the Supreme Godhead as creator of all that is spiritual and material. All authority therefore filters down from this supernatural domain consistent with God's creative command over all human endeavors. The individual mystical traditions scarcely appear to be the crucial issue here, for many a religious sage has noted that "Many roads lead to enlightenment."

This supreme supernatural perspective further underscores the basic paradox underlying the ethical hierarchy in general; namely, its openness at both its upper and lower margins. The lower margin blends with the mysterious and materialistic realm of instinctualism, whereas the upper end extends to the supernatural domain. Although the limited human intellect clearly favors such a dualistic interpretation, this general perspective (on a grander scale) might actually amount to a grand illusion! Is it truly possible to distinguish between the spiritual from the material, the mental from the physical? No matter how one frames this inquiry, these two themes always appear to remain intimately connected. So long as the mind-body puzzle remains unresolved, these issues must remain open to further speculation. Mystics the world over are invited to submit feedback from their own personal experiences, for only then can a consensus opinion be achieved to the satisfaction of all concerned.

This revolutionary new interpretation of the dynamics underlying the mystical realm presents the potential for dramatic new insights into the preservation of global peace and harmony. The respective mystical traditions propounded by the great sages and religious leaders down through the ages serve as the chief moral foundation for belief and dogma underpinning each of the major world religions. This formal exclusivity in terms of tradition, however, regrettably serves as a point of friction in an inter-religious sense, whereby putatively establishing one tradition as superior to another, accompanied by the slighted feelings and motivations of those so thusly excluded.

The newly devised ten-level hierarchy of the virtues, values, and ideals, of which the mystical values occupy the crowning (nameable) position, provide a radical reevaluation for potentially healing such endemic religious exclusivity on a global scale. According to this novel interpretation, the mystical realm arises as a hierarchial extension of the more elementary virtuous traditions, ethical constructs fittingly shared in common by the major monotheistic faiths. Through a celebration of these moral commonalities shared across all such spiritual traditions, a greater degree of religious cooperation should potentially counteract any ingrained tendency towards cultural exclusivity. Furthermore, in addition to the bottom-up pattern of organization demonstrated for the virtuous hierarchy, the potential also exists for a top-down pattern of organization (of a supernatural nature) as well. Here, the traditional grouping of mystical values: ecstasy-bliss-joy-harmony represent the highest nameable domain, leaving open to direct experience what ultimately may lie beyond.

This unbounded domain of supernatural experience remains a concept of particular appeal to all those that seriously entertain a religious impulse, a further crucial platform for maximizing interdenominational tolerance. This newly conceptualized divine influence of a supernatural nature permits a common rallying point for the religious faithful regardless of their individual cultural traditions therein. Hopefully, this strong incentive for global tolerance will effectively moderate current trends towards religious extremism, disturbing motivations that threaten global peace and stability through dictating a terrorist ideology.

8

THE ACCESSORY VIRTUES, VALUES, AND IDEALS

The preceding description of the schematic definitions for the major virtues, values, and ideals
permits many interesting speculations into the
virtuous realm, although this basic format is limited by several unforeseen complications. Chief
among these is the observation that the dual interplay of authority/follower roles is strictly specialized into either subjective or objective classifications, with little flexibility allowed in turn. This
basic limitation stems from the formal schematic
restrictions governing the construction of the
schematic definitions. The respective "you" and
"I" roles (by definition) are locked in step in terms
of the reciprocating sequences of authority and
follower roles, wherein maintaining a stable response buffer within the schematic definitions.
This feature, in turn, simulates a reciprocal balance power with respect to both authority and
follower roles. In particular, this dual style of role
specialization follows a strict set of guidelines;
namely, the objective perspective is limited to
roles immediately occurring in the present,
whereas the subjective variation specifies either
the past or future time dimensions.

This distinctive style of role-specialization
proves consistent in an intuitive sense in that the
"I" ego serves as a "bookmark" for specifying an
enduring sense of "self" within the past or future
time-dimensions. This enduring sense of self is
experienced either as past memories or a future
sense of potentiality: a mental artifact stemming entirely from the introspective musings of
the individual. The objective roles, in contrast,
specify the immediately active set of roles, a real
time objectification of the present time dimension
overtly apparent to all in attendance.

Take, for example, the personal authority's
subjective experience of nostalgia: a recollected
perspective targeting past notable achievements.

The hero worship role of the personal follower, in
turn, alternately specifies the immediately active
style of objective role, as suggested in the overtly
active attention paid to the personal authority figure. This distinctive subjective/objective trade-off
permits an enduring sense of role-stability within
the corresponding schematic definitions. Here,
you (as personal follower) worshipfully act in a
rewarding fashion towards me in response to my
(as your personal authority) nostalgic treatment
of you.

This reciprocal pattern of authority and follower roles follows a strict give-and-take dynamic,
formally defined as "if you, then I," (and vice versa). According to this complementary power-
sharing strategy, half of the authority/follower
roles are designated in terms of the subjective "I"
role, whereas the remainder are specified with
respect to the objective "you" role. This dual confluence of role-polarities is carefully staggered
within the corresponding schematic definitions.
Here, the objective alter ego state of hero worship
formally complements the subjective prerequisites
for the ego state of nostalgia.

The preceding example directly mirrors the
basic axiom of communication in general; namely,
I have only direct access to my own mental perspectives. The motives of others, in turn, are inferred through an objectification of their outwardly observable behaviors (including verbal reports).
For instance, I objectively fill-in your hero-
worship role by outwardly observing your worshipful behaviors towards me. A similar dynamic
also holds true for the related alter ego state of
blame, a verbal behavior that directly prompts my
subjective feelings of guilt. Here, again, the active
blame role reciprocally complements the subjective sense of guilt in terms of the dynamics of the
ongoing verbal interaction.

114	115
Poignance	Culpability
116	**117**
Passion	Apprehension

ACCESS. EGO STATES
(Personal Authority)

124	125
Praise	Censure
126	**127**
Admiration	Caring

ACC. ALTER EGO STATES
(Personal Follower)

134	135
Exaltation	Uprightness
136	**137**
Respect	Probity

ACC. PERSONAL IDEALS
(Group Authority)

144	145
Circumspection	Equitableness
146	**147**
Continence	Bravery

ACC. CARDINAL VIRTUES
(Group Representative)

154	155
Bountifulness	Freedom
156	**157**
Courtesy	Forbearance

ACCESS. CIVIL LIBERTIES
(Spiritual Authority)

164	165
Devotion	Fairness
166	**167**
Kindness	Scruples

ACC. THEOLOG. VIRTUES
(Spiritual Disciple)

174	175
Blessings	Conscience
176	**177**
Graciousness	Patience

ACC. ECUMEN. IDEALS
(Humanitarian Authority)

184	185
Charm	Credence
186	**187**
Benevolence	Shrewdness

ACC. CLASSICAL VALUES
(Humanitarian Follower)

194	195
Serenity	Brotherhood
196	**197**
Affection	Amity

ACC. HUMANIST. VALUES
(Transcendental Authority)

104	105
Rapture	Contentment
106	**107**
Gladness	Accordance

ACC. MYSTICAL VALUES
(Transcendental Follower)

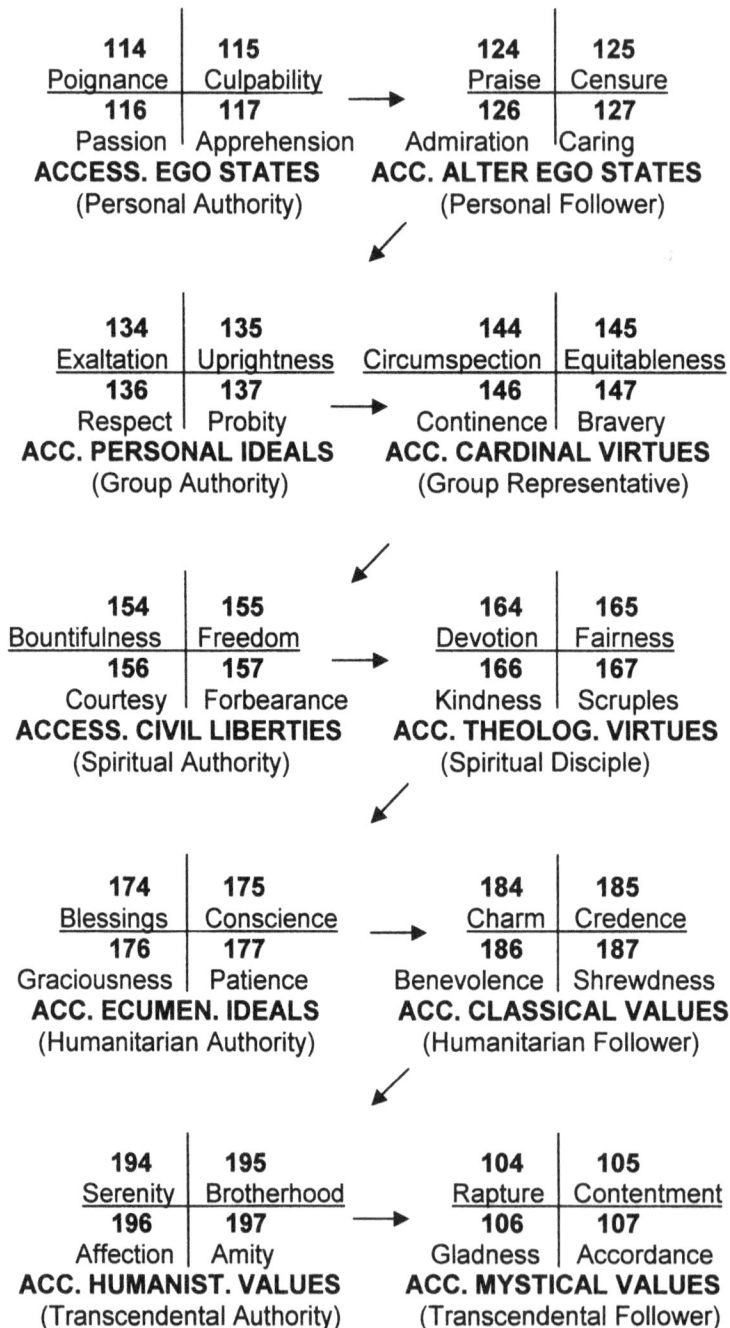

Fig. 8A – The 3-Digit Codes for the Accessory Virtues / Values

THE ACCESSORY POWER PERSPECTIVES

This reciprocal model of communication, in general, can scarcely claim to be the total picture, for it formally accounts for only half of the introspective roles predicted within such a model. The inherent versatility of the human mind (by definition) allows for a subjective reflection on one's objective status, after the fact. It further allows insights into the feelings/motivations of another, an aspect commonly known as *empathy*. It is defined as a sense of inter-subjectivity through which the observer participates in the feelings held by another. This unique ability to attribute mental states to others is a key factor in what makes us truly human, an aspect developmental psychologists refer to as Theory of Mind. This enhanced capacity to empathize about how others feel actually appears to emerge over several distinct stages of emotional development. In particular, Dr. Michael Lewis of Robert Wood Johnson Medical School (1995) specifically outlines a three-stage sequence of empathic development.

The primary emotions, such as fear or sadness, first appear around the age of six months, characterized in terms of a spontaneous response repertoire of a non-reflective nature. The secondary emotions, in turn, emerge around the age of two signaling the first true "sense of self," experienced as the more sophisticated emotions of guilt or shame. These secondary emotions clearly involve a higher sense of self, an enduring sense of identity to which these emotions are referred. The third stage in empathic development chiefly occurs between the ages of *4* or *5*, when the child learns to ascribe motivations to others that might personally be experienced under similar circumstances. This more advanced capacity is formally explained in terms of the Argument from Analogy, where internal motives associated with personal behaviors, in turn, are attributed to the outwardly observable behaviors of others.

Indications of this ability first come to light at a fairly early age, such as when a toddler shows interesting objects to others. This early perspective of others, however, is actually fairly egocentric. The infant expresses a belief in a common knowledge base, in strict contrast to the more advanced empathic concept of individual perspectives. This latter development only truly becomes apparent around the age of five, when the child realizes that others do not have direct access to his personal mindset, but rather entertain distinct thoughts and motivations entirely of their own making. This more advanced comprehension of individual personalities permits the development of skills underlying social *empathy*, as reflected in the many common role-playing games favored by children; e.g., cops and robbers, doctor/patient, etc. Feelings of happiness generate an outward facial expression, the observation of which subtly activates a similar bodily response in the observer. This induced physical response in terms of the observer translates into a shared emotional response, wherein establishing a collective sense of empathy linking the observer and that which is observed.

This distinct empathic ability proves particularly crucial within a social setting, where cohesion within the group is greatly enhanced through recourse to such overlapping perspectives, greatly reducing the occurrence of interpersonal frictions. According to Robert Gordon (1986), this innate sense of empathy depends primarily upon our ability to run cognitive simulations, wherein inferring the intentions of others by employing one's own mind as a model for that of others. This necessarily entails placing oneself in the role of another, and further observing how one's mind resonates within such a mutual conceptual context. The reciprocal interplay linking both the main and accessory interpersonal perspectives provides the supreme conceptual template for modeling this enduring sense of empathy in relation to others.

This reflective style of role reversal, in turn, specifies the existence of an additional complement of virtuous terms for designating this dual sense of versatility. For instance, whereas the hero worship role of the personal follower is "objectified" from the individual perspective of the personal authority figure, no direct provision is made for a subjective follower perspective in its own right. In this latter respect, the "hero worshipper," in turn, reflects upon one's own "I" ego status in the present; wherein further objectifying the nostalgia perspective of the personal authority. This distinctive sequence of role reversals necessarily specifies the existence of a completely new complement of *accessory* term that directly reflects such a dual perspective. Indeed, the English language is richly blessed with a suitable number of synonyms conducive to outlining this parallel complement of accessory terms.

For the personal realm, for instance, the proposed accessory class of ego states (poignancy-culpability-passion-apprehension) formally complements the main virtuous listing of nostalgia-guilt-desire-worry. Furthermore, the accessory alter ego states of adoration-censure-admiration-caring) further reciprocate the related main listing of terms (namely, hero/worship-blame-approval-concern).

In the case of main pairing of nostalgia/hero-worship, for instance, the accessory synonyms of poignancy/adoration prove exceedingly suited to the task. Here, I (as your personal follower) adoringly act in a rewarding fashion towards you in anticipation your (as personal authority) poignant treatment of me. In terms of the related context of guilt/blame, the personal follower, in turn, switches to a censuring perspective, wherein prompting the personal authority figure's submissive admission of culpability. A similar pattern further holds true with respect to the personal authority's passionate quest for admiration, or his apprehensive expectation of caring. The reciprocal interplay of both the main and accessory sets of terms collectively permits a convincing simulation of empathic language in general.

THE ACCESSORY HIERARCHY OF VIRTUES, VALUES, AND IDEALS

According to the main/accessory model of empathic development, it remains only a further minor step to extend the personal complement of terms into the more abstract hierarchy of virtues, values, and ideals. This results in the full forty-fold complement of accessory terms depicted in **Fig. 8A**, in concert with the respective three-digit code designations. It represents a mirror image reflection of the main virtuous terms shown in **Fig. 2** (of *Chapter 2*). Furthermore, this more advanced degree of empathic capacity appears to develop over a distinct sequence of developmental stages indicative of the respective group, spiritual, humanitarian, and transcendental levels within the power hierarchy as a whole.

For instance, as an infant, I first gained an indication of the personal authority perspective through my parents, ultimately learning to distinguish them from strangers. From earliest infancy, the bond between mother and child exhibits a reciprocating pattern of emotional resonance. From approximately the age of four months, the infant initiates face-to-face contact through a controlled gaze mechanism, a process psychiatrist Daniel Sterns has termed *attunement*.

Upon reaching toddler stage, I further grasped the principles of group authority in a familial sense, followed by the community and nationalistic variations on the theme. Entering the "age of reason," I subsequently gained an understanding of the universal authority perspective, with its spiritual implications for mankind as a whole. Finally, a subsequent grasp of world history, in turn,

permitted insights into the humanitarian and transcendental levels within the power hierarchy, as well as the implications of addressing humanitarian issues on a global scale.

Developmental theories notwithstanding, the predicted complement of accessory terms represents the specific role-transformations of the main groupings of terms. The reciprocating "you/I" perspectives are effectively reversed. These accessory groupings of terms, however, exhibit little in the way of the pedigree or tradition previously established for the main listings of terms. According to **Fig. 8A**, the accessory listings of terms are formally specified through the addition of the prefix *"accessory"* to the better-known designation of the major groupings. This is also signified in schematic notation through the use of the Roman numeral - II). More permanent labels must necessarily await further collective research into the field, for any permanent system of classification must remain open to the consensus opinion through the aid of the broader global community at large.

In order to more accurately specify the individual listings of accessory terms, the third and final digit within the three-digit coding system is ultimately called into play. For instance, in terms of the *main* cardinal virtues, the respective three-digit codes were initially specified as: 140 = prudence, 141 = justice, 142 = temperance, and 143 = fortitude. The *accessory* versions of the cardinal virtues, in turn, are specified in terms of digits 4 through 7 in the three-digit slot. Here, 144 = circumspection, 145 = equitableness, 146 = continence, and 147 = bravery. Consequently, it ultimately proves fruitful to undertake a more in depth examination of the individual accessory terms for the entire virtuous hierarchy, wherein providing a clearer picture of the reciprocal dynamics at issue. The remainder of the current chapter examines this additional complement of accessory terms to a much greater degree of detail, focusing on the subjective/objective polarities in relation to the main groupings of virtues/values initially described.

114 – POIGNANCY

The first mentioned theme of *poignancy* rates current consideration as the chief accessory counterpart of nostalgia. This term derives from the Old French *poignant*, from the Latin *pungere* (to sting). It refers to its now obsolete usage as an adjective for describing the sharpness or piercing power of military weapons. In modern usage, this connotation extends to a cutting-edge char-

The Bounty of the Legendary Cornucopia: The Traditional Symbolism of Thanksgiving

acter within an emotional sphere of influence, wherein affecting one's feelings sharply or keenly, such as the poignance intrinsic to comedy or melodrama. Such strong feelings extend to positive memories of past influence within one's lifetime, sharing with its counterpart in nostalgia such past notable perspectives. In this latter respect, the subjective prerequisites for nostalgia effectively complement the objective characteristics of poignancy, an emotional reaction chiefly restricted primarily to a personal sphere of influence.

134 – EXALTATION

The personal authority perspective of poignancy, in turn, extends to a group sphere of influence with respect to the related theme of *exaltation*: a term defined as glorious fortune or elevated rank. Its modern spelling derives from the Latin *altus* (high) and *ex-* (prefix indicating intensity), representing the objective counterpart of the subjective *glory* perspective. It, accordingly, shares with glory a heightened degree of power or prestige characterizing such leadership roles. Consequently, this poignant sense of exaltation preserves the past-directed focus initially established for the glory perspective of the group au-

thority, although now countering the adoring treatment of the personal follower figure.

154 – BOUNTIFULNESS

Exaltation, in turn, extends to the spiritual authority theme of *bountifulness*, as objectively complementing the subjective prerequisites for *providence*. The term derives from the Latin *bonitas*, from *bonus* (good): a connotation clearly in keeping with its generosity in the bestowal of gifts. Bountifulness shares much in common with the traditional symbolisms associated with providence, where the *cornucopia* (horn of plenty) perpetually overflows with an abundance of produce from the field, wherein permitting a welcome sense of security in terms of such pressing human needs. Accordingly, the exalted sense of bountifulness expressed by a spiritual authority proves a fitting counterpoint to the circumspective-adoration of the group representative.

174 – BLESSINGS

The next higher humanitarian authority level begs further mention of the related theme of *blessings*. This term traces its origins to the Anglo Saxon *bledsian* (to bless), from *blod* (blood): as in a blood sacrifice upon an altar. It generally refers to a divine sense of sanctification or sacredness similar to its subjective counterpart in *grace*. Indeed, the act of "saying Grace" begins with the stirring invocation: "*Bless* us Oh Lord for these Thy gifts ... received through Thy bounty." This enduring tradition of abundant blessings effectively preserves the strict humanitarian focus of grace, wherein objectively reciprocating the subjective prerequisites of the latter. The bountiful blessings specified within the universal domain clearly prove worthy of the circumspective-devotion expressed by the spiritual disciple.

194 – SERENITY

The bountiful blessings for the humanitarian realm ultimately extend to a transcendental sphere of influence with respect to the related theme of *serenity*. It represents the chief objective counterpart for the subjective prerequisites of *tranquility*. Its modern spelling derives from the Latin *serenus* (clear), indicative the tranquil attributes associated with the term. It is generally employed as a title of distinction for reigning princes or dignitaries consistent with the calm demeanor accompanying such positions of power. This serene sense of contentment is further associated with great mystical figures such as Buddha, Christ, Mohammed, etc. The serene sense of blessings expressed by the transcendental authority effectively complements the charming sense of devotion employed by the humanitarian follower figure.

124 – PRAISE

The remaining sequence of accessory terms based upon the ascending hierarchy of follower roles begins with the personal follower theme of *praise*. As the chief subjective counterpart of hero worship, it shares with latter a profound sense of homage or regard for those worthy of such worship. Its modern spelling derives from the Latin *pretiare* (to prize), indicating the rewarding overtones characterizing this theme. The positive emotional focus shared by both hero worship and praise is certainly quite striking, wherein rewarding the past notable achievements of the personal authority figure (experienced as a poignant sense of nostalgia). With respect to the requisite "you" and "I" polarities, praise clearly suggests more of a subjective style of introspective focus than does hero worship. The latter theme is almost clinical in terms of objectifying the outward behaviors characterizing the personal follower role.

144 – CIRCUMSPECTION

The personal prerequisites for adoration, in turn, extend to a group sphere of influence with respect to the related theme of *circumspection*. The term derives from the Latin *circum-* (about) and *spectum* (to look): suggesting a cautious inspection of all angles to a situation similar to the watchful attitude previously ascribed to prudence. Accordingly, the symbolisms attributed to circumspection share many features with those ascribed to prudence; namely, a seated maiden facing in the three cardinal directions: representing past, present, and future potentialities. The past-directed dimension for circumspection is clearly favored, in essence, targeting the poignant sense of exaltation expressed by the group authority figure.

164 – DEVOTION

Circumspection, in turn, gives way to the spiritual follower theme of *devotion*: traditionally defined as strong piety or attachment. The term derives from the Latin *devovere*: from *de-* (away) and *vovere* (to vow), suggestive of its close affiliation to faith. In particular, this term refers to the Roman Catholic tradition of the devotional, as in prayers or worship of a private nature. This pious sense of devotion clearly transcends any formal sense of ritualism, representing the deeply subjective counterpart of its objective counterpart in faith. The circumspective-devotion of the spiritual disciple effectively complements the exalted sense of bountifulness professed by the spiritual authority figure.

184 – CHARM

The next higher domain of the humanitarian follower, in turn, begs mention of the accessory theme of *charm*, an aspect extremely consistent with the beauteous aspects of faith specified from an objective perspective. Its modern spelling derives from the Latin *carmen* (a song), indicating the ritual significance music plays in religious observance. Charm also denotes a magical sense of enchantment or attractiveness, as suggested in the familiar notions of the charm bracelet and charm school. The truest sense of charm, however, stems from the enduring prerequisites of such a grand humanitarian perspective. The deeply subjective attributes of charm effectively complement the more objective status previously ascribed to beauty. Consequently, the charming sense of devotion professed by the humanitarian follower directly counters the bountiful-blessings bestowed by the humanitarian authority figure.

104 – RAPTURE

The preceding discussion of charm ultimately gives way to the remaining transcendental notion of *rapture*. Rapture rates current consideration as the chief subjective counterpart of the related theme of ecstasy. The term derives from the Latin *raptum* (to seize) currently referring to flights of fancy of an enlightened or mystical nature. Although other synonyms for ecstasy (such as happiness) may fit equally well, happiness has alternately been moved to the class of the lesser virtues, whereas the subjective prerequisites of rapture prove more fitting to the current sense of the term. Here, the rapturous sense of charm expressed by the transcendental follower proves a fitting counterpoint to the serene sense of blessings of the transcendental authority figure.

THE PARALLEL SEQUENCE OF TERMS BASED UPON CULPABILITY/CENSURE

A parallel sequence of accessory terms, in turn, is based upon the personal interplay of culpability/censure. For instance, the group authority culpably acts in an upright fashion in anticipation of the equitable-censuring of the group representative. Furthermore, in terms of the spiritual level within the power hierarchy, the spiritual authority figure freely acts in an upright fashion in expectation of the equitable sense of fairness expressed by the spiritual disciple. Finally, for the more advanced humanitarian/transcendental levels, the authority figure freely acts in a conscientious fashion (or conscientiously acts in a brotherly fashion) in response to the follower figure's fair sense of credence/contentment, as schematically depicted immediately below:

115 – Culpability	125 – Censure
135 – Uprightness	145 – Equity
155 – Freedom	165 – Fairness
175 – Conscientiousness	185 – Credence
195 – Brotherhood	105 – Contentment

This accessory sequence of terms formally reciprocates the pattern previously established for the main sequence of terms (namely, guilt-honor-

liberty-freewill-equality), as well as blame-justice-hope-truth-bliss: wherein promoting an equal balance of power with respect to the dual interplay of "you" and "I" perspectives.

116 – PASSION

A third sequence of accessory terms, in turn, is based upon personal interplay of passion/admiration, effectively complementing the main trend based upon desire/approval. For instance, the first mentioned theme of *passion* denotes a strong sense of emotion, particularly ardent love or desire. The term derives from the Old French *passiun*, from the Latin *passus* (to suffer). This original connotation of suffering relates to the longstanding frustrations involved in the consummation of the passions, as in a personal quest for fulfillment. Here, passion suggests a personally subjective slant on the theme, as opposed to the more objective prerequisites suggested for desire. Indeed, the latter appears more invested with the actual object than the respective steps towards its passionate fulfillment.

136 – RESPECT

The personal prerequisites for passion, in turn, extend to a group sphere of influence with respect to the related theme of *respect*. Respect subjectively complements the objective perspectives of dignity. Its modern spelling derives from the Latin *respectum*, from re- (back) and *specere* (to look), consistent with the dignified demeanor characterizing leadership positions. Exalted status typically drives the passionate adherence to one's duties, further tempered by a dignified sense of respect. The passionate-respect expressed by the group authority proves a fitting counterpoint to the objective prerequisites previously established for dignity, wherein formally countering the admiring treatment of the personal follower figure.

156 – COURTESY

The group authority aspects of respect, in turn, give way to the spiritual authority theme of *courtesy*. It is traditionally defined as polite consideration or civil accommodation. The term derives from the Latin *cortis* (a courtyard), suggesting the "common courtesy" shared in relation to its objective counterpart in civility. This theme similarly figures prominently in the rather quaint custom of the *courtesy call*, namely, a social visit made entirely on the basis of common courtesy. The supreme expression of this term traces its origins to the medieval Code of Courtesy. The chivalrous knight courteously acts respectfully towards his object of passion, fully expecting a rewarding sense of admiration in return. Consequently, this courteous sense of respect offers a fitting subjective counterpoint to the civilly-dignified perspective initially specified from a purely objective slant.

176 – GRACIOUSNESS

The preliminary sequence of courtesy/respect, in turn, grades over into the affiliated humanitarian theme of *graciousness*. It is variously defined as divine favor or supreme kindness. The term derives from the Latin *gratia* (favor), from *gratus* (agreeable): a connotation consistent with its accessory relationship to magnanimity. Similar to courtesy, graciousness is traditionally associated with the custom of *gratuities*: namely, those standards of accommodation crucial to one's personal sense of self-worth. The theme of the gracious host is one of mankind's most honored traditions, particularly in the Middle East, where the needs of the guest typically take precedent over those of the host. Consequently, the courteous sense of graciousness expressed by the humanitarian authority proves a fitting counterpoint to the continent sense of kindness expressed by the spiritual disciple figure.

196 – AFFECTION

This ascending trend, taken to its ultimate limit, invokes the crowning transcendental theme of *affection*, the subjective counterpart of *love*. The term derives from the Latin *affectio*, from *ad-* (to) and *facere* (to do): consistent with enhanced feelings of emotion. Indeed, the related theme of "affect" is similarly invoked to describe a strong range of emotions, the attachments of love certainly filling the bill in this basic regard. The supremely abstract connotations of affection certainly validate such a crowning transcendental perspective, the general subjective counterpart to the more objective prerequisites of love. In this highly subjective sense, one can "toy" with one's affections, although the same does not necessarily hold true for the more objective realm of love.

126 – ADMIRATION

The remaining *accessory* sequence of follower roles is currently launched with respect to the personal follower theme of *admiration*. It is traditionally defined as enthusiastic veneration or high esteem consistent with its related counterpart in approval. The term derives from the French *admirer*, from the Latin *ad-* (at) and *mirari* (to wonder). Its positive accessory attributes are amply validated in concert with the approving characteristics of the main follower role. This admiration for the passionate pursuits of the personal authority figure clearly echoes the adoring recognition of poignancy previously cited for past-directed domain. In terms of the respective "you" and "I" polarities, admiration clearly suggests an objective character, wherein complementing the subjective quality of passion: in contrast to the interplay of desire/approval, where the role-polarities are reversed.

146 – CONTINENCE

The personal accessory attributes for admiration, in turn, extend to a group sphere of influence with respect to the group representative theme of *continence*. It is traditionally defined as restraint in the indulgence of the passions, similar to the case previously established for temperance. The term derives from the Latin *continens* (to contain, to hold back), an interpretation consistent with the "bridling" of the passions. Here, continence is most closely associated with sexual restraint, in contrast to the more generalized range of constraint for temperance. Irrespective of its given object, the continently-admiring treatment expressed by the group representative proves a fitting counterpoint to the passionate-respect of the group authority figure.

166 – KINDNESS

Ascending, once again, to the next higher spiritual level, in turn, gives way to the accessory authority theme of *kindness*. This term represents the objective counterpart for the more subjective prerequisites of charity. Its modern spelling derives from the Old English *cynn* (kind), suggesting a willingness to perform good or worthy deeds. This nurturing quality has traditionally been celebrated as "the milk of human kindness," an enduring interpretation clearly in keeping with such good-hearted charitable endeavors. This universal appeal with respect to such charitable acts of kindness generally rates the highest of esteem. Indeed, this volunteer spirit provides great tangible benefits to the initiator, as well as the recipient. Here, the continent sense of kindness expressed by the spiritual disciple proves a fitting counterpoint to the courteous-respect professed by the spiritual authority figure.

186 – BENEVOLENCE

The universal overtones for kindness, in turn, extend to a humanitarian sphere of influence with respect to the related theme of *benevolence*. The term derives from the Latin *benevolentia* (goodwill), from *bene* (well) and *velle* (to wish). It traditionally denotes a disposition towards graciousness or generosity in both word and deed. This grand humanitarian focus is particularly apparent in the philanthropic endeavors underlying the *benevolent societies*; namely, institutions that seek to improve the human condition through charitable works and public education. These enduring aims of benevolence clearly validate such a grand humanitarian perspective: a noble aspiration encouraged throughout the ages in times of tribulation. The benevolent sense of kindness expressed by the humanitarian follower effectively reciprocates the courteous sense of graciousness professed by the respective authority figure.

106 – GLADNESS

The benevolent sense of kindness established for the humanitarian realm ultimately extends to the crowning transcendental domain with respect to the remaining theme of *gladness*. As the chief objective counterpart for joy, gladness denotes a cheerful or optimistic disposition, particularly in an enthusiastic or animated fashion. The term derives from the Old English *glaed*, from the Old Norse *glathr* (bright), suggesting a sparkling outlook. The objective characteristics of gladness effectively complement the subjective prerequisites for joy. In terms of this accessory degree of influence, the benevolent sense of gladness expressed by the transcendental follower proves a fitting counterpoint to the gracious sense of affection of the transcendental authority figure.

THE ACCESSORY TERMS BASED UPON APPREHENSION/CARING

The fourth and final sequence of accessory terms is based upon the remaining personal interplay of apprehension/caring (the accessory counterparts for worry/concern). The accessory sequence of authority terms (apprehension-probity-forbearance-patience-amity), in turn, reciprocates the main sequence of counterparts: e.g., worry-integrity-austerity-equanimity-peace. Furthermore, the related accessory sequence of follower roles: (caring-bravery-scrupulousness-shrewdness-accordance) further permits an effective contrast with the main respective counterparts: namely, concern-fortitude-decency-wisdom-harmony, as schematically outlined immediately below.

117 – Apprehension	**127 – Caring**
137 – Probity	**147 – Bravery**
157 – Forbearance	**167 – Scrupulous**
177– Patience	**187 – Shrewdness**
197 – Amity	**107 – Accordance**

This cohesive sequence of accessory terms proves fitting counterpoint for the main sequence of themes, further verifying the empathic dynamics of the unified power hierarchy.

THE SCHEMATIC DEFINITIONS FOR THE ACCESSORY VIRTUOUS REALM

One final issue of critical significance concerns the prediction that the accessory virtuous terms are further amenable to incorporation within the formal schematic definition format. Indeed, a complete listing of *accessory* schematic definitions is respectively tabulated in **Tables B-1** to **B-4** in direct analogy to the main set of definitions depicted **Tables A-1** to **A-4** (of Chapter *3*). These accessory schematic definitions are identical in form and function to the main counterparts with the exception that the "you" and "I" polarities are now reversed. This formal reversal of the "you" and "I" perspectives is predicted within the definition format, wherein permitting for an alternating confluence of subjective and objective viewpoints. This dual sequence of perspectives is formally predicted in terms of the empathic principles of Theory of Mind, in that reciprocating viewpoints take fully into account all potential viewpoints.

In order to completely outline this dual interplay of main/accessory power perspectives, it proves fruitful to look back (in review) at the basic dynamics at issue. Routine communication is diagrammed in terms of a two-stage formal schematic. The initial party in the communication is fittingly termed "myself," whereas the remaining party is alternately labeled the "other" in keeping with established existential terminology. These two basic domains are separated in terms of a formal gap that signifies the channel that communication must travel in order to bridge the link between sender and receiver.

This schematic model, depicted in **Fig. 8B** below, represents one complete cycle of communi-

POIGNANCY	PRAISE
Previously, I (as reinforcer) have rewardingly acted in a reinforcing fashion towards you: overriding your (as procurer) solicitous treatment of me. But now, you (as personal authority) will *poignantly* act in a solicitous fashion towards me: overruling my rewarding treatment of you.	Previously, you (as personal authority) have poignantly acted in a solicitous fashion towards me: overriding my (as reinforcer) rewarding treatment of you. But now, I (as personal follower) will *praisingly* act in a rewarding fashion towards you: overruling your (as PA) poignant treatment of me.
EXALTATION	**CIRCUMSPECTION**
Previously, I (as your personal follower) have praisingly acted in a rewarding fashion towards you: overriding your (as PA) poignant treatment of me. But now, you (as group authority) will poignantly act in an *exalted* fashion towards me: overruling my (as PF) praising treatment of you.	Previously, you (as group authority) have poignantly acted exaltedly towards me: overriding my (as PF) praising treatment of you. But now, I (as group representative) will *circumspectively* act in a praising fashion towards you: overruling your (as GA) exalted treatment of me.
BOUNTIFULNESS	**DEVOTION**
Previously, I (as group representative) have circumspectively acted in an praising fashion towards you: overriding your (as GA) exalted treatment of me. But now, you (as spiritual authority) will exaltedly act in a *bountiful* fashion towards me: overruling my (as GR) circumspective- praise for you.	Previously, you (as spiritual authority) have exaltedly acted in a bountiful fashion towards me: overriding my (as GR) circumspective-praise for you. But now, I (as your spiritual disciple) will circumspectively act in a *devoted* fashion towards you: overruling your (as SA) bountiful treatment of me.
BLESSINGS	**CHARM**
Previously, I (as your spiritual disciple) have circumspectively acted in a devoted fashion towards you: overriding your (as SA) bountiful treatment of me. But now, you (as humanitarian authority) will bountifully-*bless* me: overruling my (as SD) circumspective-devotion for you.	Previously, you (as humanitarian authority) have bountifully-blessed me: overriding my (as SD) circumspective-devotion for you. But now, I (as representative member of humanity) will *charmingly* act in a devoted fashion towards you: overruling your (as HA) bountiful-blessing of me.
SERENITY	**RAPTURE**
Previously, I (as representative member of humanity) have charmingly acted in a devoted fashion towards you: overriding your (as HA) bountiful-blessing of me. But now, you (as transcendental authority) will *serenely*-bless me: overruling my (as RH) charming devotion for you.	Previously, you (as transcendental authority) have serenely blessed me: overriding my (as RH) charming-devotion for you. But now, I (as your transcendental follower) will charmingly act in a *rapturous* fashion towards you: overruling your (as TA) serene blessing of me.

Table B-1 – The Definitions Based on Poignancy/Praise

CULPABILITY	CENSURE
Previously, I (as reinforcer) have leniently acted in a reinforcing fashion towards you: overriding your (as procurer) submissive treatment of me. But now, you (as personal authority) will *culpably* act in a submissive fashion towards me: overruling my lenient treatment of you.	Previously, you (as personal authority) have culpably acted submissively towards me: overriding my (as reinforcer) lenient treatment of you. But now, I (as your personal follower) will *censuringly* act in a lenient fashion towards you: overruling your (as PA) culpable treatment of me.
UPRIGHTNESS	EQUITABLENESS
Previously, I (as your personal follower) have censuringly acted leniently towards you: overriding your (as PA) culpable treatment of me. But now, you (as group authority) will culpably act in an *upright* fashion towards me: overruling my (as PF) censuring treatment of you.	Previously, you (as group authority) have culpably acted in an upright fashion towards me: overriding my (as PF) censuring treatment of you. But now, I (as group representative) will *equitably* act in a censuring fashion towards you: overruling your (as GA) culpable sense of uprightness.
FREEDOM	FAIRNESS
Previously, I (as group representative) have equitably acted in a censuring fashion towards you: overriding your (as GA) culpable sense of uprightness. But now, you (as spiritual authority) will *freely* act in an upright fashion towards me: overruling my (as GR) equitable-censuring of you.	Previously, you (as spiritual authority) have freely acted in an upright fashion towards me: overriding my (as GR) equitable-censuring of you. But now, I (as your spiritual disciple) will equitably act in a *fair* fashion towards you: overruling your (as SA) free sense of uprightness.
CONSCIENCE	CREDENCE
Previously, I (as your spiritual disciple) have equitably acted in a fair fashion towards you: overriding your (as SA) free sense of uprightness. But now, you (as humanitarian authority) will freely act in a *conscientious* fashion towards me: overruling my (as SD) equitable sense of fairness.	Previously, you (as humanitarian authority) have freely acted conscientiously towards me: overriding my (as SD) equitable sense of fairness. But now, I (as representative member of humanity) will fairly express a sense of *credence* in you: overruling your (as HA) conscientious treatment of me
BROTHERHOOD	CONTENTMENT
Previously, I (as representative member of humanity) have fairly expressed a sense of credence in you: overriding your (as HA) conscientious treatment of me. But now, you (as transcendental authority) will conscientiously act in a *brotherly* fashion: overruling my (as RH) fair sense of credence.	Previously, you (as transcendental authority) have acted in a brotherly fashion towards me: overriding my (as RH) fair sense of credence. But now, I (as your transcendental follower) will *contentedly* express a sense of credence in you: overruling your (as TA) brotherly treatment of me.

Table B-2 – The Definitions Based on Culpability/Censure

PASSION	ADMIRATION
Previously, you (as reinforcer) have rewardingly acted in a reinforcing fashion towards me: overriding my (as procurer) solicitous treatment of you. But now, I (as personal authority) will *passionately* act in a solicitous fashion towards you: overruling your rewarding treatment of me.	Previously, I (as personal authority) have passionately acted in solicitous fashion towards you: overriding your (as reinforcer) rewarding treatment of me. But now, you (as personal follower) will rewardingly act in an *admiring* fashion towards me: overruling my (as PA) passionate treatment of you.
RESPECTFULNESS	**CONTINENCE**
Previously, you (as my personal follower) have rewardingly acted in an admiring fashion towards me: overriding my (as PA) passionate treatment of you. But now, I (as group authority) will passionately act in a *respectful* fashion towards you: overruling your (as PF) admiring treatment of me.	Previously, I (as group authority) have passionately acted in a respectful fashion towards you: overriding your (as PF) admiration of me. But now, you (as group representative) will *continently* act in an admiring fashion towards me: overruling my (as GA) passionate-respect for you.
COURTESY	**KINDNESS**
Previously, you (as group representative) have continently acted in an admiring fashion towards me: overriding my (as GA) passionate-respect for you. But now, I (as spiritual authority) will *courteously* act in a respectful fashion towards you: overruling your (as GR) continent treatment of me.	Previously, I (as spiritual authority) have courteously acted in a respectful fashion towards you: overriding your (as GR) continently-admiring treatment of me. But now, you (as my spiritual disciple) will continently act in a *kind* fashion towards me: overruling my (as SA) courteous-respect for you.
GRACIOUSNESS	**BENEVOLENCE**
Previously, you (as my spiritual disciple) have continently acted in a kind fashion towards me: overriding my (as SA) courteous-respect for you. But now, I (as humanitarian authority) will courteously act in a *gracious* fashion towards you: overruling your (as SD) kind treatment of me.	Previously, I (as humanitarian authority) have courteously acted graciously towards you: overriding your (as SD) kind treatment of me. But now, you (as representative member of humanity) will *benevolently* act in a kind fashion towards me: overruling my (as HA) gracious treatment of you.
AFFECTION	**GLADNESS**
Previously, you (as representative member of humanity) have benevolently acted in a kind fashion towards me: overriding my (as HA) gracious treatment of you. But now, I (as transcendental authority) will graciously act *affectionately* towards you: overruling your (as RH) benevolent sense of kindness.	Previously, I (as transcendental authority) have graciously acted in an affectionate fashion towards you: overriding your (as RH) benevolent sense of kindness. But now, you (as my transcendental follower) will benevolently act with *gladness* towards me: overruling my (as TA) affectionate treatment of you.

Table B-3 – The Definitions Based on Passion/Admiration

APPREHENSION	CARING
Previously, you (as reinforcer) have leniently acted in a reinforcing fashion towards me: overriding my (as procurer) submissive treatment of you. But now, I (as personal authority) will *apprehensively* act submissively towards you: overruling your lenient treatment of me.	Previously, I (as personal authority) have apprehensively acted submissively towards you: overriding your (as reinforcer) lenient treatment of me. But now, you (as personal follower) will *caringly* act in a lenient fashion towards me: overruling my (as PA) apprehensive treatment of you.
PROBITY	**BRAVERY**
Previously, you (as my personal follower) have caringly acted in a lenient fashion towards me: overriding my (as PA) apprehensive treatment of you. But now, I (as group authority) will apprehensively act in a *probity*-filled fashion towards you: overruling your (as PF) caring treatment of me.	Previously, I (as group authority) have apprehensively acted in a probity-filled fashion towards you: overriding your (as PF) caring treatment of me. But now, you (as group representative) will *bravely* act in a caring fashion towards me: overruling my (as GA) probity-filled treatment of you.
FORBEARANCE	**SCRUPULOUSNESS**
Previously, you (as group representative) have bravely acted in a caring fashion towards me: overriding my (as GA) probity-filled treatment of you. But now, I (as spiritual authority) will *forbearingly* act with probity towards you: overruling your brave treatment of me.	Previously, I (as spiritual authority) have forbearingly acted with probity towards you: overriding your (as GR) brave treatment of me. But now, you (as my spiritual disciple) will *scrupulously* act in a brave fashion towards me: overruling my (as SA) forbearing treatment of you.
PATIENCE	**SHREWDNESS**
Previously, you (as my spiritual disciple) have scrupulously acted in a brave fashion towards me: overriding my (as SA) forbearing treatment of you. But now, I (as humanitarian authority) will forbearingly act in a *patient* fashion towards you: overruling your (as SD) scrupulous treatment of me.	Previously, I (as humanitarian authority) have forbearingly acted patiently towards you: overriding your (as SD) scrupulous treatment of me. But now, you (as representative member of humanity) will scrupulously act in a *shrewd* fashion towards me: overruling my (as HA) patient treatment of you.
AMITY	**ACCORDANCE**
Previously, you (as representative member of humanity) have scrupulously acted in a shrewd fashion towards me: overriding my (as HA) patient treatment of you. But now, I (as transcendental authority) will patiently act in an *amity*-filled fashion towards you: overruling your (as RH) shrewd treatment of me.	Previously, I (as transcendental authority) have patiently acted in an amity-filled fashion towards you: overriding your (as RH) shrewd treatment of me. But now, you (as my transcendental follower) will shrewdly act in *accordance* towards me: overruling my (as TA) amity-filled treatment of you.

Table B-4 – The Definitions Based on Apprehension/Caring

cation between "myself" and the "other," as the directional arrows, in turn, serve to indicate. The current cycle begins with **Box A**, where a standard example of communication (the schematic definition for "glory") is listed in the upper left-hand box. In terms of this specific example, I (as group authority) gloriously act nostalgically towards you, overruling your (as personal follower) worshipful treatment of me. This preliminary power maneuver is communicated from "myself" to "the other" (Channel **A → B**) across the formal subjective/objective gap. As a basic communicational channel, this sample communication (by definition) is open to distortion, ambiguity, or misgivings over the span of the transmission.

Fig. 8B - The Two-Stage Communicational Dynamic

Despite these internal shortcomings, for sake of illustration, the message is depicted as successfully reaching the receiver end to the direct attention of "the other." The message must necessarily be translated into a form that is subjectively meaningful to the receiver. This further entails translating the *main* schematic definition into its respective *accessory* counterpart specified from an outside viewpoint. According to a **Box B** of **Fig. 8B**, the accessory form of the schematic definition for "exaltation" is now specified as: You (as group authority) will poignantly act in an *exalted* fashion towards me, thwarting my (as personal follower) adoring treatment of you. According to this modified accessory format, the "you" and "I" roles are effectively reversed,

wherein personalizing the message to fit the subjective prerequisites of "the other."

THE COUNTERMANEUVER OF THE "OTHER"

Once the message is received and comprehended by the "other," it remains to be determined how best to respond to such a message. According to step **B → C**, one possible option is to ignore the message as if it were never actually received. A second option entails claiming to misunderstand the message, or leaving the scene altogether. A further option entails mirroring the message back to the sender in what Communication Theorists term the *symmetrical* maneuver. Another option entails accepting the content of the message as given, as well as one's specific role within the interaction. This latter response primarily occurs only when one is satisfied with the status quo initially projected.

A further relevant option builds directly upon this initial acceptance: accepting the content of the message as initially offered, then subsequently modifying one's role by rising to the next higher level within the power hierarchy. This necessarily entails counteracting the power tactic initially offered, substituting in its place a power status of one's own making. This more advanced form of power maneuver is schematically depicted in **Box C**. Here the personal follower rises to the next higher level of the "group representative" through the use of the *prudence* form of countermaneuver. The first part of this new definition builds directly upon the initial "glory" maneuver originally communicated, followed by the *circumspection* countermaneuver proper; namely, I (as group representative) circumspectively act in an adoring fashion towards you, overruling your (as group authority) poignant sense of exaltation. According to Communication Theorists, this latter strategy is termed the *complementary* class of power maneuvers, in that they formally complement that which has gone before. The group representative role directly complements the group authority role originally offered.

Once formulated, this alternate power maneuver is subsequently communicated from "the other" back to "myself," as shown in step **C → D** within the master diagram. The respective arrow again crosses the subjective/objective gap, wherein further susceptible to the internal shortcomings of distortion, ambiguity, etc. Assuming (for illustrative purposes) that the communication is successfully received, this further entails a subsequent translation back to a form meaningful to comprehension by "myself" (the *main* schematic definition format depicted in **Box D**). Here, the *circumspective*-adoration of the group representative is now translated back into the *prudent*-worship consistent with my own subjective perspectives. In this latter respect, the "you" and "I" roles are again reversed: redefined in terms of the subjective group authority role originally communicated.

The successful receipt of the group representative's *prudence* countermaneuver, in turn, offers further options for myself (as depicted in step **D → A**). Here, the same strategies originally outlined in step **B → C** (e.g., to ignore, accept, rise to the next higher level, etc.) similarly apply. In the latter case, this necessarily entails rising to the next higher spiritual level, giving way to a *providential* expansion upon the original glory maneuver. This innovation (by definition) launches one further cycle within the communication dynamic: namely, the sequence of **A → B → C → D** relating to the spiritual level. Indeed, this basic pattern further extends to the remaining humanitarian/transcendental levels within the power hierarchy, ceasing only when the level of abstraction exceeds the scope of the language tradition.

AN OVERVIEW OF COMMUNICATION IN GENERAL

A few general observations on communication in general necessarily prove crucial at this juncture. First, the role of "myself" within the communication cycle clearly represents the critical factor, in contrast to the more extraneous sense of "the other." This observation is certainly warranted in that I only have direct access to my own thoughts and feelings, while I can make no provisions for those of "the other." I further model, to some extent, the unique mindset of "the other" through the aid of the *accessory* schematic definitions depicted in **Boxes B** and **C**. According to this simulation of the accessory realm I formally fill-in the motivations of "the other" for a given interaction. This includes moments alone when I mentally rehearse dialogue in anticipation of meeting with others ahead of time. This necessarily entails imagining other possible contingencies/responses "the other" might employ, mentally preparing so as to not be caught off-guard by a surprise turn of events. The outside party in the interaction (by definition) does not even need to be present in order to conduct such a mental dialogue. The eventual meeting with the "other" only serves to finalize the choices initially imagined. The eventual responses of "the other," in turn, are compared with the mental model of my own expecta-

tions, the results continually determining my next course of action. This egocentric model of communication in general (by definition) is based entirely upon the intrinsic consciousness of "myself." The actions of "others," in turn, are predicted entirely in terms of such a projected mental model.

Lest this formulation be judged too narrow a model of interpersonal communication, it is further relevant to note that "the other" similarly entertains his/her own self-based perspective operating through an independent style of ego status. This multitude of individual selves merges into a unified communicational continuum, wherein forming overlapping sets of interpersonal projections in relation to one another. This all-encompassing communicational dynamic, nevertheless, still relies upon my primary mental monologue linking myself with the mental projections of others, a basic model calibrated in terms of the outwardly observable behaviors of others, wherein imparting an overall semblance of conformity with reality.

According to this multi-modal interpretation of communication in general, whether we chose to acknowledge it or not, we all are basically alone in the world with respect to the restrictions of our own mental thought processes. Our firm convictions with respect to others are basically projections of our own making, mental models periodically reinforced to some extent by external observation. This formal sense of isolation actually turns out to be a blessing in disguise, for the private life we so dearly treasure would remain impossible if others could freely read our minds (and vice versa). It is only through the common symbolism underlying verbal language that interpersonal communication is possible at all, the standards of which are maintained in a cultural sense.

In terms of this dualistic interpretation, my introspective mental states (by definition) are projected onto you, whereas yours (in theory) are referred back to me. There is no single channel of communication, but rather an intersecting confluence of mutual perspectives. It is this mental construct of others with which we have a relationship, not the direct sense we would like ourselves to believe: a welcome illusion in light of the more brutally honest picture currently proposed. Along a similar line of reasoning, Irish-born essayist, Dame Rebecca West once insightfully wrote: "There is no such thing as conversation, it is an illusion. There are intersecting monologues, that is all."

It should further be emphasized that this abiding sense of isolation chiefly applies only to symbolic verbal communication, being that nonverbal communication of a synchronously-empathic nature is much more amenable to social synergy across the board. Here, a concerted effort towards directed mindfulness permits concentration within a present tense, unlike the temporally focused past/future dimensions typically targeting verbal communication of an affective nature. With such verbal chatter temporarily attenuated, the mindful individual is now free to immediately attend to meaningful facial cues and bodily synchronies in relation to others, providing a high degree of empathic understanding clearly transcending any linguistic means designed to explain it. Hence, by periodically turning down the "noise box" of verbal dialogue that typically dominates our waking moments, a more effective balance within the here-and-now provides a more effective means of synchrony and synergy in relation to our empathic dealings in peaceful harmony with others.

This latter aspect clearly invokes an innate instinctual foundation indicative of the operantly conditioned relationship, the only avenue available to the human species prior to the subsequent invention of language. Of course, language is crucial in its own right for communicating about motivations and circumstances not immediately apparent, permitting planning for future events (entailment) based upon memory of past experience (presupposition). Therefore a reciprocal balance between linguistic symbolic thought processes and immediate mindful awareness proves to be a key towards maintaining a healthy mental balance, a perspective further crucial to maintaining a healthy degree of peace and harmony across society as a whole.

9

THE GENERAL UNIFYING VIRTUOUS THEMES

The preceding virtuous hierarchy of main and accessory terms exhibits a further emergent quality of critical import to the three-digit coding system; namely, the identification of what are termed the class of general unifying themes. This new class of themes represents a "meta-order" summation of its respective level within the power hierarchy. For instance, the general unifying theme of "utilitarianism" encompasses the basic focus of the cardinal virtues (prudence-justice-temperance-fortitude). This basic pattern further holds true with respect to each of the remaining levels within the virtuous hierarchy, as schematically depicted in **Fig. 9A**. For instance, the personal authority role initially targets the theme of *individualism*, in turn, extending to the theme of *personalism* at the next higher group authority level. The spiritual authority level further targets the more idealized theme of *romanticism* consistent with its broader focus on "universal" principles. The themes for the remaining humanitarian/transcendental levels, in turn, take their cues from the titles of their respective listings of terms; namely, *ecumenism* and *humanism*, respectively.

In a related fashion, the remaining sequence of *follower* roles is similarly organized in terms of a parallel hierarchy of individual themes; namely, pragmatism-utilitarianism-ecclesiasticism-eclecticism-mysticism. For instance, the first-mentioned theme of *pragmatism* refers to that which is expedient to the individual: in turn, extending to a group domain in terms of *utilitarian* concern for the "common good." This ascending sequence of themes ultimately extends to the remaining spiritual, humanitarian, and transcendental domains with respect to the themes of ecclesiasticism, eclecticism, and mysticism.

In terms of the master three-digit coding system proposed in Chapter 1, these general unifying themes are similarly amenable to coding within the overall *1,040*-part system. Here, the three-digit codes ending with the numeral "8" specify the main categories of themes, whereas those ending with "9" denote the respective *accessory* variations (where the polarities of the "you" and "I" roles are now reversed). A more detailed description for each of these main classifications of themes is definitely in order here, followed, in turn, by a cursory examination their respective accessory counterparts.

118 – INDIVIDUALISM

The detailed description of the main virtuous themes is currently launched with respect to the first-mentioned theme of *individualism*, which formally encompasses the subordinate listing of ego states (guilt-worry-nostalgia-desire) professed by the personal authority figure. The term derives from the Latin *individuus*, from *in-* (not) and *dividuus* (divisible), from *didere* (to divide): consistent with the most basic personal authority level. The modern sense of individualism emerged in Britain in terms of ideas promoted by Adam Smith and Jeremy Bentham. This sense of individualism is further noted by Alexis de Tocqueville as crucial to the general American temperament.

In a general sense, individualist values are person-centered, with all individuals sharing equal moral status. Individualism opposes external authority without consent, wherein viewing the institution power of government as chiefly limited to maintaining law and order. The chief aim of society is the promotion of individual rights and welfare. Similarly, the chief end to moral law is the development of individual moral character. Individuals should be free to live their lives as they see fit without unwarranted state interference.

118 - INDIVIDUALISM **Ego States** *Personal Authority*	**128 - PRAGMATISM** **Alter Ego States** *Personal Follower*
138 - PERSONALISM **Personal Ideals** *Group Authority*	**148 - UTILITARIANISM** **Cardinal Virtues** *Group Representative*
158 - ROMANTICISM **Civil Liberties** *Spiritual Authority*	**168 ECCLESIASTICISM** **Theological Virtues** *Spiritual Disciple*
178 - ECUMENISM **Ecumenical Ideals** *Humanitarian Authority*	**188 - ECLECTICISM** **Classical Values** *Humanitarian Follower*
198 - HUMANISM **Humanistic Values** *Transcendental Authority*	**108 - MYSTICISM** **Mystical Values** *Transcendental Follower*

Fig. 9A – The Three-Digit Codes for the "Meta" Virtuous Themes

The principles of individualism were briefly challenged at the turn of the 20th century in concert with the rise of Communism/Fascism, although regaining dominance due to the global trend towards representative forms of government.

In summary, the basic theme of individualism encompasses the behavioral attributes specific to the personal authority role; namely, the active sense that derives from having acted first in the conditioned relationship. The solicitous sense of desire, or the submissive sense of worry, invokes the initial authority status; which, in turn, is acknowledged in hindsight as the nostalgia/guilt perspectives, respectively. Consistent with this initial authority status, the personal prerequisites for individualism clearly prove fitting in terms of the ascending hierarchy of virtuous themes.

138 – PERSONALISM

The personal perspectives for individualism, in turn, extend to a group sphere of influence with respect to the related theme of *personalism*. The term derives from the Latin *persona* (a mask in ancient theatres that represented an emotional reaction). It eventually came to denote the role of a dramatic actor, and, ultimately, human nature in general. In social and political matters, personalism refers to a sense of dignity among men. Indeed, in a legal realm this connotation still applies today. It remains the subject of speculation when the philosophy of personalism first emerged. Some trace its origins to Anaxagoras, as well as the further influence of Plato and Aristotle that leads to Boethius: who defines the persona as "an individual substance of a rational nature." This stage of development continues through St. Augustine, Avicenna, and Thomas Aquinas: ultimately entering the modern era in terms of the rationalist and empiricist traditions.

The modern sense of personalism traces its roots to 19th-century thought, although reaching most coherent expression during the 20th century. German philosopher/theologian, Friedrich Schleiermacher used the term *Personalismus* in his *Discourses* (1799). Cambridge philosopher John Grote termed his novel metaphysical approach *personalism*: from *Exploratio Philosophica* (1865). For each of these formulations, the respective emphasis on human dignity proves particularly suggestive of the related listing of personal ideals (glory-honor-dignity-integrity). Indeed, their specific designation as "personal ideals" clearly alludes to the group-focused theme of personalism, a more abstract refinement of the subordinate theme of individualism. It shares with the latter

such a vitally active focus, as reflected in the group dynamics underlying the respective listings of personal ideals. The enduring theme of personalism presents a fitting adjunct to the group dynamics for the authority hierarchy, a baseline consistent with the ascending hierarchy of individual themes.

158 – ROMANTICISM

The group prerequisites for personalism, in turn, give way to the more universally focused theme of *romanticism*. The term derives from the French *romantique*, from the Middle French *romant* (a romance), an oblique reference to the Old French *romanz* (a verse narrative). Romanticism emerged in the late 18th and early 19th centuries as a stylistic movement that downplayed the prevailing imitation of neo-classical stereotypes. It flourished in large part due to the libertarian and egalitarian ideals of the French Revolution that exalted in the supremacy of the common man. The basic aims of romanticism are fairly vague: including an appreciation of the mysteries of nature and a belief in the goodness of human nature. It celebrated the artist as a supremely abstract innovator, wherein exalting sense and emotion over reason and intellect.

In this latter respect, romanticism promoted a philosophical revolt against the ordered rationality of the Enlightenment, which was disparaged as impersonal, mechanistic, and artificial. It favored, in contrast, the emotional saliency of direct personal experience, as well as the boundless nature of the unfettered human imagination.

This enduring fascination with larger-than-life themes is certainly consistent with romanticism's universal placement within the virtuous hierarchy of themes. Indeed, themes of a romanticized nature hold a universal appeal within world literature. The heroic exploits of the renown authority figure are romanticized to the point of expressing widespread public appeal. Consequently, the respective class of romantic ideals (providence-liberty-civility-austerity) certainly fulfills this basic scenario, wherein projecting a general worldly appeal concerning this spiritually focused role. Indeed, each of the four civil liberties was worshipped as a deity in classical times, so significant was their global appeal. Romanticism shares with the subordinate themes of individualism/personalism such a vital authority perspective, although now extending to a universal sphere of influence. Accordingly, romanticism continues in the tradition of the revered authority figure, although now encompassing themes of sanctity/homage befitting such an exalted virtuous perspective.

178 – ECUMENISM

Ascending to the next higher (humanitarian) sphere of influence invokes the respective theme of *ecumenism*. The term derives from the Latin *oecumenicus* (general, universal), from the Greek *oikoumene* (the inhabited world): from *oikoumenos*, present participle of *oikein* (to inhabit), from *oikos* (house or habitation). In a modern sense, it denotes a movement towards the unification of the Protestant denominations, and, ultimately, all of Christianity. This is exemplified by the First Assembly of the World Council of Churches (Amsterdam, 1948), which brought together Protestant, Eastern Orthodox, and Catholic representatives, an initiative that endures today as a major force promoting ecumenism worldwide.

In its most fundamental sense, ecumenism promotes a sense of unity, cooperation, and understanding amongst the various denominations within a given belief system (more or less broadly defined). The broader style of interfaith campaign aims towards greater mutual respect, tolerance, and cooperation among the world's major religions. It has awakened the conscience of Christianity towards its universal perspectives, as in a renewed spirit of mission and service to the global congregation. This evangelical spirit is particularly evident in the enduring tradition of the ecumenical councils of the early Church, which shared the task of fortifying and preserving the unity of faith.

The humanitarian authority theme of ecumenism proves a fitting adjunct to the subordinate sequence of terms: namely, individualism, personalism, romanticism (and now ecumenism). The enduring humanitarian prerequisites for this theme are clearly reflected in the broad tradition of ecumenical councils dealing with recurrent Church issues. The related listing of the ecumenical ideals (grace-freewill-magnanimity-equanimity) similarly imparts a broad evangelical perspective to such a grand humanitarian time-scale. Indeed, grace and free emerged as enduring theological issues during the Protestant Reformation. The ecumenical movement seeks to preserve this clear humanitarian tone, wherein respecting the longstanding traditions of all denominations within its purview.

198 – HUMANISM

The ascending hierarchy of authority-based perspectives ultimately culminates with respect to the crowning transcendental theme of *humanism*. The term derives from the Latin *literae humaniores* (polite literature), from *homo* (a human being). In its original Renaissance sense, it referred to the surviving works of Greek and Latin classical literature. The exact point in history when the theme of humanism first arose remains open to debate. Certainly, the Italian academic revival of the Latin arts and letters was chiefly responsible for the emergence of this movement. In general, the Humanities were classified as those branches of literature (classics, rhetoric, and poetry) that worked to humanize or refine the intellect, an education truly befitting a cultivated mind.

This revolt against the strictures of dogmatic decree offered a fresh degree of intellectual freedom to Renaissance thinkers, wherein encouraged scientific research and a trend towards economic mercantilism. By invoking the longstanding traditions of the classical Greek/Roman period, Renaissance humanism emerged as a powerful counterpoint to the ecclesiastical dictates of the Catholic Church (the dominant intellectual force of its day). In allusion to the classical Greek injunction "know thyself," the humanists promoted a free-thinking style of academic optimism that flew in the face of the more dogmatic strictures of Church teaching. This movement soon spread throughout Western Europe, aided by the widespread use of the Latin language and the invention of movable type.

With the gradual decline in Church influence over European politics, humanism has increasingly acquired a more secular character. This directly contrasts to the original Renaissance variety, which chiefly coexisted with the ecclesiastical power hierarchy. In keeping with the modern dominance of science and technology in Western culture, *secular* humanism has assumed the mantle of distinction for most democratic forms of government. This is particularly apparent in the newly designated class of *humanistic* ideals (peace-love-tranquility-equality), themes that collectively share a lofty humanistic focus consistent with the transcendental authority perspective. All four of these themes profess a transcendental disregard for the more routine worldly state of affairs. Lofty platitudes such as peace and love serve as supreme ideals to which mankind constantly strives, although never quite fulfills.

128 – PRAGMATISM

The remaining sequence of virtuous themes based upon the ascending hierarchy of follower roles is currently launched with respect to the personal follower theme of *pragmatism*. This term derives from the Latin *pragmaticus* (skilled in business or law), from the Greek *pragmatikos* (versed in business), from *pragmatos* (civil business or activity), from *prassein* (to act or perform). The philosophical connotations of pragmatism first appear in 1878 with respect to the German notion of Pragmatismus. The modern sense of the term refers to an original system of philosophy proposed by C. S. Peirce, Henry James, and John Dewey at the turn of the 20th century. It asserts that the meaning or truth of any course of action is primarily a function of its practical outcome. Pragmatism resolves ethical disputes by investigating the practical consequences of all potential avenues of choice. Ideas are true insofar as they are consistent with others, conformable to the facts and subject to practical tests of experience.

The beneficial outcomes proposed in pragmatism are necessarily conditional, in that the proof of the pudding entails a final taste-test, as well as the concrete means towards it achievement. Pragmatism represents a personally focused perspective determining what is reinforcing (or practical) to the goals of a particular individual. Consequently, the pragmatic viewpoint (expressed by the personal follower) effectively reciprocates the more active sense of individualism expressed by the personal authority figure. The former serves a crucial evaluative function in relation to the directed activity expressed through the latter personal authority role.

148 – UTILITARIANISM

The personal prerequisites for pragmatism, in turn, extend to a group sphere of influence with respect to the related follower theme of *utilitarianism*. The term derives from the Latin *utilitas*, from *uti* (to use). This designation was coined by Jeremy Bentham in 1781 in allusion to the general theme of utility: wherein specifying the doctrine of the greatest good for the greatest number. This preliminary system was further championed through the efforts of James Mill, as well as his son, John Stuart Mill. They collectively argued that the greatest good lies in the maximizing the general public welfare. The basic principles of utilitarianism extend the more limited theme of pragmatism into a much broader (group) sphere of influence. The utilitarians further opposed the competing precepts of romanticism due to the latter's focus on feelings (and disdain for rationality). The utilitarians believed that proper social order results from a balance of individual interests; therefore only principles of utility can set viable standards for legal and moral behavior. The main justification for this doctrine is that it proves applicable to a broad range of political systems, although democracy is clearly favored.

Mankind, in general, pursues an Epicurean quest for pleasure: a virtual synonym for happiness according to utilitarianism. It, therefore, proves advantageous to foster the interests of others in order that one's own interests are served in return. For politics (as well as business), cooperation remains the cornerstone for any sustained sense of achievement. Utilitarianism approves actions that promote a general sense of welfare/accord within society as a whole, a feature consistent with the requisite reinforcement style of group follower perspective. These benefits need not be restricted solely to intent, but rather the final outcome of the action, a pattern similar to that previously established for pragmatism. This reinforcing function, in turn, is reflected in the respective listing of cardinal virtues (prudence-justice-temperance-fortitude): a quartet that exalts the principles of group cohesiveness and cooperation relative to the common good. The interests of all human beings, however, must equally be considered if utilitarianism is to enjoy a truly equitable range of utility.

168 – ECCLESIASTICISM

Ascending, once again, to the next higher spiritual level, in turn, gives sway to the universal theme of *ecclesiasticism*. It is defined as that branch of Christian theology concerned with the study of the organizational principles of the Church, particularly its operational and congregational functions (reflected through the spiritual disciple perspective). The term derives from the Greek *ekklesia* (an assembly summoned by a crier): from the compound of *ek-* (out of) and *kalein* (to call). In ancient Athens the ecclesia was a popular assembly where the general population exercised full sovereignty. All male citizens over the age of twenty were eligible to cast their vote on issues from the agenda.

The current Christian sense of the term derives from the Late Latin *ecclesiasticus*, from the Greek *ekklesiastes* (speaker of the assembly or church). In a scriptural sense, it refers to the chosen assembly called out of the world by the Lord. New Testament writers (such as St. Paul) employ this term to designate local assemblies of Christians, such as the Church of God gathered at Corinth (I Corinthians 1:2). This specific meaning eventually grew to encompass the unity of the early Christian Church in general.

INDIVIDUALISM	PRAGMATISM
Previously, you (as reinforcer) have rewardingly acted in a reinforcing fashion towards me: overriding my (as procurer) solicitous treatment of you. But now, I (as personal authority) will solicitously act in an *individualistic* fashion towards you: overruling your rewarding treatment of me.	Previously, I (as personal authority) have solicitously acted individualistically towards you: overriding your rewarding treatment of me. But now, you (as my personal follower) will rewardingly act in a *pragmatic* fashion towards me: overruling my (as PA) individualistic treatment of you.
PERSONALISM	UTILITARIANISM
Previously, you (as my personal follower) have rewardingly acted in a pragmatic fashion towards me: overriding my (as PA) individualistic treatment of you. But now, I (as group authority) will individualistically act in a *personable* fashion towards you: overruling your (as PF) pragmatic treatment of me.	Previously, I (as group authority) have individualistically acted in a personable fashion towards you: overriding your (as PF) pragmatic treatment of me. But now, you (as group representative) will pragmatically act in a *utilitarian* fashion: overruling my (as GA) personable treatment of you.
ROMANTICISM	ECCESIASTICISM
Previously, you (as group representative) have pragmatically acted in a utilitarian fashion towards me: overriding my (as GA) personable treatment of you. But now, I (as spiritual authority) will personably act in a *romanticized* fashion towards you: overruling your (as GR) utilitarian treatment of me.	Previously, I (as spiritual authority) have personably acted in a romanticized fashion towards you: overriding your (as GR) utilitarian treatment of me. But now, you (as spiritual disciple) will utilitarianly act in an *ecclesiastical* fashion towards me: overruling my (as SA) romantic treatment of you.
ECUMENISM	ECLECTICISM
Previously, you (as my spiritual disciple) have acted in an ecclesiastical fashion towards me: overriding my (as SA) romantic treatment of you. But now, I (as humanitarian authority) will romantically act in an *ecumenical* fashion towards you: overruling your (as SD) ecclesiastical treatment me.	Previously, I (as humanitarian authority) have acted in an ecumenical fashion towards you: overriding your (as SD) sense of ecclesiasticism But now, you (as representative member of humanity) will ecclesiastically act in an *eclectic* fashion towards me: overruling my (as HA) ecumenical treatment of you.
HUMANISM	MYSTICISM
Previously, you (as representative member of humanity) have ecclesiastically acted eclectically towards me: overriding my (as HA) ecumenical treatment of you. But now, I (as transcendental authority) will ecumenically act in a *humanistic* fashion towards you: overruling your (as RH) sense of eclecticism.	Previously, I (as transcendental authority) have acted in a humanistic fashion towards you: overriding your (as RH) eclectic treatment of me. But now, you (as my transcendental follower) will eclectically act in a *mystical* fashion towards me: overruling my (as TA) humanistic treatment of you.

Table C-1 – The "Meta" Definitions for the Virtuous Themes

The first formal treatises on ecclesiasticism generally date only to the late medieval period dominated by the Scholastics. By the time of the Protestant Reformation, two distinct trends in ecclesiasticism become readily apparent. Protestant ecclesiasticism emphasized the spiritual nature of the Church, whereas Roman Catholic ecclesiasticism stressed a more outward organizational sense. The modern sense of the term appears to reflect the development of a system that integrates both of these theological aspects.

Ecclesiasticism continues in the tradition of follower roles previously established with respect to pragmatism and utilitarianism, although now clearly extending to a universal sphere of influence. As such, it respectively encompasses the related class of theological virtues (faith-hope-charity-decency): scriptural ideals exemplifying the proper conduct of the spiritual disciple figure. Through this enlightened path of guidance, the specifics for the disciple role (in relation to the spiritual congregation) finally become conceptually complete, an aspect formally in keeping with the spiritual follower perspective.

188 – ECLECTICISM

The spiritually-focused theme of ecclesiasticism, in turn, extends to a humanitarian sphere of influence in terms of the related theme of *eclecticism*. The term derives from the Greek *eklektikos* (selective), from *eklektos* (selected), from *eklegein* (to pick out or select): from the compound of *ek-* (out) and *legein* (to choose). It refers to the practice of selecting the best aspects or opinions from differing schools of thought without necessarily adopting the parent system for each. It was originally coined to refer to ancient groups of philosophers that integrated doctrines from a variety of competing systems, as first employed in the first century BCE. In a philosophical sense, eclecticism refers to the selection of elements from various systems of thought without regard to potential contradictions between the systems. It differs, therefore, from *syncretism*, which endeavors to combine various schools of thought while aiming to resolve underlying conflicts.

Eclecticism among Renaissance humanists borrowed primarily from both Catholic and classical doctrines. Their efforts, in turn, presaged a 19th-century revival, particularly with respect to French philosopher, Victor Cousin: who coined the modern sense of the term and applied it to his own system. Eclectics are often accused of being inconsistent, in that the abstract juxtaposition of doctrines from different systems risks a fundamental incoherence: although occasionally breathing life back into systems that have become outmoded.

According to this "representative member of humanity" perspective, the eclectic individual revels in themes of a timeless nature, as reflected in the respective listing of classical Greek values (beauty-truth-goodness-wisdom). These enduring Greek values have been revered throughout recorded history, immutable monuments that have stood the test of time. Indeed, each of these specific themes was worshipped as a deity in classical times, so widespread was their philosophical appeal. The theme of eclecticism certainly rates its lofty humanitarian placement within the virtuous hierarchy of themes, wherein directly expanding upon its subordinate counterparts in pragmatism, utilitarianism, and ecclesiasticism.

108 – MYSTICISM

This ascending sequence of follower themes ultimately culminates with respect to the crowning transcendental theme of *mysticism*. The term derives from the Greek *mystikos* (secret, mystic), from *mystes* (one initiated), from *myein* (to close one's eyes). These universal and enduring aspects of mysticism occur across all races and cultures throughout recorded history. Consequently, some innate aspect within human nature must necessarily account for the supreme desire or aspiration for universal truth and goodness. The reason and experience obtained through encounters with the physical world necessarily pales in comparison to the intuition gained through mystical means.

Some rare individuals clearly appear blessed in terms of that rare ability to enter into mystical contemplation of the Absolute. The early Church theologian, Pseudo-Dionysius (in his variety of works) gives a systematic overview of Christian mysticism, formally distinguishing between rational and mystical knowledge. Although a considerable degree of further detail would necessarily be appropriate at this juncture, this additional range of issues will not be presented here due to the extensive treatment of mysticism previously included in Chapter 7. Regardless of the individual traditions therein, this general theme of mysticism shares a certain key distinguishing features; namely, a transcendental follower perspective reflecting the respective complement of mystical values (ecstasy, bliss, joy, and harmony). Here, mysticism represents the crowning (nameable) domain within the virtuous hierarchy of themes, and one incomparable for those that have been touched by its charmed embrace.

119 - QUINTESSENTIAL. **Ego States II** *Personal Authority*	**129 - EXPEDIENCY** **Alter Ego States II** *Personal Follower*
139 - HEROISM **Personal Ideals II** *Group Authority*	**149 - PRACTICALITY** **Cardinal Virtues II** *Group Representative*
159 - CHARISMA **Civil Liberties II** *Spiritual Authority*	**169 - ORTHODOXY** **Theological Virtues II** *Spiritual Disciple*
179 - EVANGELISM **Ecumenical Ideals II** *Humanitarian Authority*	**189 - MORALISM** **Classical Values II** *Humanitarian Follower*
199 – COSMOPOLITAN. **Humanistic Values II** *Transcendental Authority*	**109 - SPIRITUALISM** **Mystical Values II** *Transcendental Follower*

Fig. 9B - The Three-Digit Codes for the Accessory Virtuous Themes

QUINTESSENTIALISM	EXPEDIENCY
Previously, I (as reinforcer) have rewardingly acted in a reinforcing fashion towards you: overriding your (as procurer) solicitous treatment of me. But now, you (as personal authority) will solicitously act in a *quintessential* fashion towards me: overruling my rewarding treatment of you.	Previously, you (as personal authority) have solicitously acted quintessentially towards me: overriding my rewarding treatment of you. But now, I (as your personal follower) will rewardingly act in an *expedient* fashion towards you: overruling your (as PA) quintessential treatment of me.
HEROISM	**PRACTICALITY**
Previously, I (as your personal follower) have rewardingly acted in an expedient fashion towards you: overriding your (as PA) quintessential treatment of me. But now, you (as group authority) will quintessentially act in a *heroic* fashion towards me: overruling my (as PF) expedient treatment of you.	Previously, you (as group authority) have quintessentially acted in a heroic fashion towards me: overriding my (as PF) expedient treatment of you. But now, I (as group representative) will *practically* act in an expedient fashion towards you: overruling your (as GA) heroic treatment of me.
CHARISMA	**ORTHODOXY**
Previously, I (as group representative) have practically acted in an expedient fashion towards you: overriding your (as GA) heroic treatment of me. But now, you (as spiritual authority) will heroically act in a *charismatic* fashion towards me: overruling my (as GR) practical treatment of you.	Previously, you (as spiritual authority) have heroically acted in a charismatic fashion towards me: overriding my (as GR) practical treatment of you. But now, I (as spiritual disciple) will practically act in an *orthodox* fashion towards you: overruling your (as SA) charismatic treatment of me.
EVANGELISM	**MORALISM**
Previously, I (as spiritual disciple) have practically acted in a orthodox fashion towards you: overriding your (as SA) charismatic treatment of me. But now, you (as humanitarian authority) will charismatically act in an *evangelical* fashion towards me: overruling my (as SD) orthodox treatment of you.	Previously, you (as humanitarian authority) have evangelically acted with charisma towards me: overriding my (as SD) orthodox treatment of you. But now, I (as representative member of humanity) will orthodoxly act in a *moralistic* fashion towards you: overruling your (as HA) evangelical treatment of me.
COSMOPOLITANISM	**SPIRITUALISM**
Previously, I (as representative member of humanity) have acted moralistically towards you: overriding your (as HA) sense of evangelism. But now, you (as transcendental authority) will evangelically act in a *cosmopolitan* fashion towards me: overruling my (as RH) moralistic treatment of you.	Previously, you (as transcendental authority) have acted cosmopolitanly towards me: overriding my (as RH) moralistic treatment of you. But now, I (as your transcendental follower) will moralistically act in a *spiritualistic* fashion towards you: overruling your (as TA) cosmopolitan treatment of me.

Table C-2 - The Accessory Definitions for the Virtuous Themes

THE SCHEMATIC DEFINITIONS FOR THE MAIN VIRTUOUS THEMES

The completed description of the ascending hierarchy of themes (for both the authority/follower roles) offers a further welcome degree of validation for the general sequence of terms. Indeed, the systematic and orderly pattern of organization for this virtuous class of themes necessarily specifies the potential for their incorporation directly into the formal schematic definition format. The full ten-part complement of "meta" schematic definitions for the virtuous themes is respectively listed in **Table C-1**. This table clearly illustrates the reciprocating pattern of interaction linking the authority/follower roles across the entire ten-level span of the unified power hierarchy. In particular, this newly proposed schema of "meta" schematic definitions both transcends and unifies the more routine listings of definitions for the virtues, values, and ideals: a meta-order style of conceptual innovation. Consequently, each of the unique virtuous themes specifies a higher-order perspective on the more basic complement of individual terms. For instance, the "meta" schematic definition for *utilitarianism* further encompasses the four respective cardinal virtues (prudence-justice-temperance-fortitude) as subsets. A similar pattern, in turn, holds true for the remainder of the virtuous themes, as the respective schematic definitions fully serve to indicate.

As meta-order summations of the specific individual terms, the definitions for the general unifying themes scarcely exhibit the degree of clarity or precision of the definitions for the individual terms. A cursory analysis of these "meta" schematic definitions, however, clearly reveals the basic dynamics at issue here; namely, the reinforcement status of the follower roles reciprocally complements the procurement status of their corresponding authority roles. For instance, the group representative pragmatically acts in a utilitarianism fashion in reaction to the individualistic sense of personalism expressed by the group authority figure.

Although this highly specialized degree of interplay might appear limited in terms of practical applications, it, nevertheless, provides a formal schematic template for the more general listings of virtues, values, and ideals. The more specialized "meta" schematic definitions for the themes serve in the role of a crucial adjunct to the more generalized format for the individual terms, wherein validating the dual definition format to an enhanced degree of certainty.

THE ACCESSORY GROUPINGS OF VIRTUOUS THEMES

As initially stated in Chapter *8*, the dual interplay of the main/accessory virtuous perspectives permits a convincing simulation of empathic communication, a feature reflected in the reversal of the "you" and "I" perspectives within the respective sets of schematic definitions. This dual pattern of main/accessory empathic perspectives (by definition) can further be extended to the even more abstract realm of the general unifying themes. The respective incorporation of these accessory counterparts adds a crucial empathic dimension to the general "meta" schematic definition format. Fortunately, a suitable number of synonyms for the virtuous themes have successfully been identified: resulting in the formal accessory system of themes that is schematically depicted in **Fig. 9B**, and also the compact diagram immediately below.

119 – **Quintessential.**	129 – **Expediency**
139 – **Heroism**	149 – **Practicality**
159 – **Charisma**	169 – **Orthodoxy**
179 – **Evangelism**	189 – **Moralism**
199 – **Cosmopolitan.**	109 – **Spiritualism**

This accessory listing of themes directly mirrors the pattern of organization previously established for the main themes with the exception that the "you" and "I" polarities are now reversed. Furthermore, in terms of the three-digit coding system, the final digit now specified as *"9"* rather than an *"8."* For instance, the main *authority* sequence of individualism-personalism-romanticism-ecumenism-humanism directly contrasts with its *accessory* sequence of counterparts; namely, quintessentialism-heroism-charisma-evangelism-cosmopolitanism. Similarly, the main *follower* sequence of pragmatism-utilitarianism-ecclesiasticism-eclecticism-mysticism further reciprocates its respective accessory trend (expediency-practicality-orthodoxy-moralism-spiritualism).

Although the strict level of correspondence for several of these themes is perhaps not as precise as might be expected, the overall cohesiveness of this accessory system proves the crucial delineating factor here. Furthermore, a majority of these themes are not commonly encountered in general usage; therefore, a more comprehensive description is deferred to an upcoming edition.

The true test of validity for this accessory listing of themes, however, ultimately extends to their respective incorporation into the formal schematic definition format. In direct analogy to the main sequence of themes (the schematic definitions of which are listed in **Table C-1**), the remaining accessory themes are similarly amenable to incorporation within the schematic definition format, wherein representing higher meta-order perspectives on the more basic complement of individual accessory terms. For instance, the "meta" schematic definition for *evangelism* encompasses the four accessory ecumenical ideals as subsets (e.g., blessings-conscientiousness-graciousness-patience). Consequently, a complete listing of schematic definitions for the accessory virtuous themes is tabulated in **Table C-2**, in direct analogy to the pattern previously established for the main listing of themes. When closely compared to the main set of definitions depicted in **Table C-1**, the reciprocal interplay of the "you" and "I" roles becomes fully apparent. When taken in concert, both the main and accessory variations for the virtuous themes permit a degree of empathic versatility unprecedented in the field today, offering a further degree of confidence in terms of this virtuous sphere of interaction. Indeed, through the formal assignment of the final two digits (8 and 9) for entries 100-199 within three-digit coding system, the systematic analysis of the virtuous realm finally comes to fruition.

In conclusion, the systematic addition of the major unifying themes for the virtuous mode provides a welcome addition to the traditional listings of virtues/values they supersede. These themes all enjoy well established literary traditions, perhaps even more extensive than the individual virtues and values. These themes come to attention most often with respect to a wide variety of pressing social movements, although never before have been brought together in such an all-inclusive cohesive system. In this overarching conceptual sense, this is newly devised master hierarchy of virtuous themes offers a wide range of solutions towards maintaining global peace and harmony. For instance, with respect to the range of authority roles, the primary theme of *individualism* serves as the founding principle underpinning the American way of life, as uniquely guaranteed through the respective Bill of Rights. This pervasive personal foundation is further tempered by the charismatic sense of *personalism* characterizing the group authority figure, aspects highly prized by the politician or the CEO. Certain privileged figures even ascend to a universal degree of appeal, as effectively *romanticized* to a global degree of celebrity: in as Mother Teresa, the Delai Lama, Pope John Paul II, etc. The truest degree of social activism, however, chiefly enters in primarily at a humanitarian sphere of influence, as witnessed for themes of virtually *ecumenical* proportions: such as the conservation of the environment relative to global climate change (as promoted by Senator Al Gore), or issues of rampant global poverty addressed by celebrities such as Bono or Angelina Jolie. Of course, in relation to its crowning level of abstraction, the remaining transcendental sphere of influence finally reigns supreme, as exemplified in the grand *humanistic* perspectives propounded by humanistic psychologists such as Abraham Maslow and Fritz Perls.

These grandly-romanticized authoritarian perspectives, in turn, invoke parallels to their corresponding counterparts in relation to the respective follower themes, as exemplified in the related sequence pragmatism-utilitarianism-ecclesiasticism-eclecticism-mysticism. For instance, the initial theme of the *pragmatism* serves as the guiding principle for personally acting in a socially prudent fashion, a fitting counterpoint to the free sense of individualism expressed by the personal authority. Furthermore, the more abstract theme of *utilitarianism* extends to a more fully social sense, as reflected in progressive social activist movements such as social welfare assurance and universal health coverage. In terms of the even more abstract global sphere of influence, these socially progressive themes extend to an *ecclesiastical* focus with respect to universal religious freedom, as well as liberation theology. Of course, the crowning humanitarian theme of *eclecticism* certainly figures prominently in an overarching abstract sense, where the various social engineering movements down through the ages are figuratively weighed in the balance, the best aspects of each synthesized to promote novel solutions to pressing global issues.

The truest collective power of this diverse sequence of themes emerges from their incorporation into a grand ascending hierarchy of global significance, providing a heretofore unprecedented pattern of collaborative interests across the entire ethical hierarchy. Hence, new partnerships linking affiliated spheres of influence become eminently more feasible, offering dramatic new solutions towards global peace and stability. In concert with the supportive individual traditions of the virtues, values, and ideals, these overall grand unifying themes promise a new era in collaborative human endeavors based upon such noble principles, wherein ushering in a new age in cooperation for policymakers throughout the world.

PART-II

10

AN INTRODUCTION TO
THE VICES OF DEFECT

The preceding examination of the virtuous realm proves exceedingly comprehensive in scope, although scarcely all-inclusive by any means. Indeed, any true system of ethics must necessarily account for the evils of society as well as the good: as reflected in the parallel hierarchy of the realm of defect. Accordingly, for every virtue or value there necessarily exists a corresponding polar opposite (or vice): such as the contrast of love vs. hate, peace vs. war, good vs. evil, etc. The Greek philosopher Aristotle was among the first to categorize this contrasting realm of opposites defined as the vices of defect: namely, that state of defect that directly counters the nobler realm of the virtues.

As previously described in Chapter 3, the virtuous realm was formally defined in terms of a behavioral terminology of operant conditioning: categorized as appetite in anticipation of rewards (positive reinforcement) or aversion in expectation of leniency (negative reinforcement). Positive reinforcement reinforces solicitous types of behaviors, whereas negative reinforcement (sometimes confused with punishment) leniently reinforces submissive behaviors through the removal of some external threat from the environment. Although alternate mechanisms are clearly involved, both positive and negative reinforcement is similarly reinforcing to the individual, encouraging procurement/appeasement behaviors in an interactive setting.

At the opposing end of the spectrum, Skinner alternately distinguishes a darker side to conditioning theory colloquially known as punishment. Punishment represents a complete reversal of the reinforcement format in that positive/negative reinforcement is withheld rather then bestowed, discouraging behaviors judged not suitably solicitous or submissive. According to this latter puni-

tive format, I withhold positive reinforcement because you failed to act solicitously towards me: "I refuse to give you the car keys because you didn't do your chores!" Similarly, lenient treatment is withheld in response to a lack of submissive behavior: "I refuse to give you a ride home because you talked back to me!"

These punitive consequences exhibit clear parallels to learning opportunities occurring naturally within the environment, similar to those encountered with respect to operant conditioning. Indeed, the fickle dictates of the natural world clearly specify such an innate understanding of punishment. For instance a food supply may become scarce or vanish altogether. Similarly a once reliable water hole may dry-up or go sour. The survival of the organism under such variable conditions directly relies upon the acknowledgement of such punitive consequences, where previous behavior patterns are abandoned altogether in favor of discovering an alternate means for re-establishing reinforcement.

These environmental perspectives on punishment similarly extend to a human sphere of influence, where inappropriate behaviors are discouraged in order to facilitate those judged more suitably solicitous or submissive. Ideally, punishment closely follows its antecedent behaviors, just as reinforcement was similarly facilitated through proximity to its precipitating (procurement) behaviors. Unlike most other animal species, humans often cooperate with individuals to whom they are not closely related, a feature that puzzles many evolutionary biologists. Indeed, those motives that cause individuals to engage in cooperative behaviors typically prove costly to perform. The general assumption is that favors are meant to be repaid, although (given a certain degree of cheating/freeloading) such repayment can not

(A)

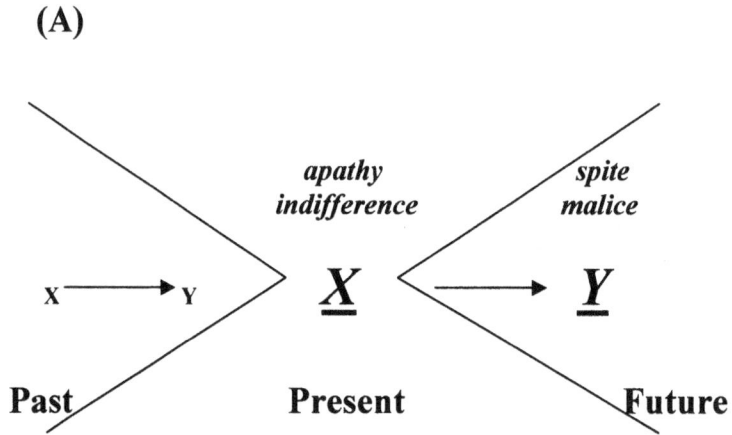

(B)

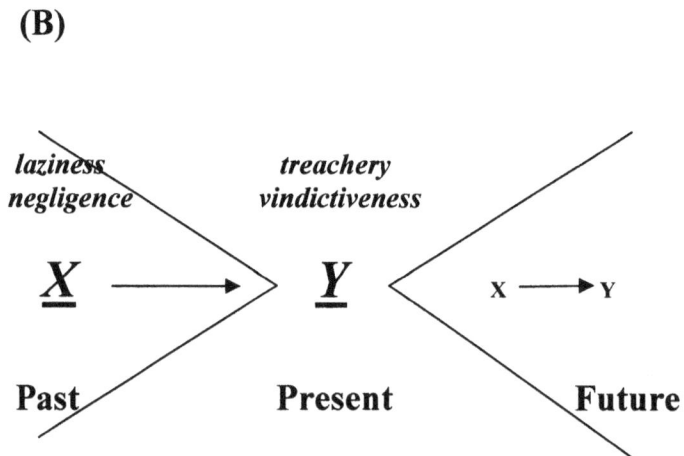

Fig. 10A – The Two-Stage Dynamic for Punishment

always be relied upon. One solution is to punish the cheats, although imposing punishment can also be costly: leading to the evolution of what is termed altruistic punishment. Here the benefits to the group for maintaining punishment (in order to keep cheaters in check) typically outweighs the cost to individual punishers. This is particularly true when the defection rate is low, being that the cost to punishers is similarly reduced. Furthermore, since free-loading does not pay when punishers are common, cheating tends to become even rarer: a form of virtuous self-fulfilling cycle.

These processes allow both altruistic punishment and altruistic cooperation to be maintained even when social groups are larger in size, such as the small-scale human societies that have existed for most of prehistory. Indeed, this theory makes several crucial predictions with respect to modern hunter-gatherer societies that typically have a maximum population of approximately 180 people. Without punishment, computer simulations by Boyd, et al (2003) suggest that cooperation would have died out for groups of this size, indicating that altruistic punishment may have emerged as a crucial factor in encouraging the spread of culture and civilization. For many of the earliest civilizations, punishment for misconduct was customarily exacting and severe, such as outlined in the ancient Babylonian Code of Hammurabi. A more detailed analysis of punishment within a social context is definitely in order here, directly specifying the intimate dynamics of the punishment strategy in general.

THE TWO-STAGE DYNAMICS FOR PUNISHMENT

The most effective means for explaining the social dynamics of punishment is in direct contrast to its respective counterpart in reinforcement. As previously described in Chapter 3, the human sphere of social conditioning is effectively seen as a two-stage process; namely, goal-seeking behaviors that prompt subsequent reinforcement. For instance, the dedicated employee works industriously to earn the praise of his boss, or acts submissively in order to avoid being fired. When procurement is defined as (X) and reinforcement identified as (Y), the complete operant sequence is represented as (X → Y). According to this two-stage format, only one role can occur in the present at any given time, giving rise to the crucial notion of the alternate (past/future) time dimensions. Behavioral terminology (by definition) does not technically recognize such introspective states necessitating the introduction of the colloquial terminology of self-help psychology. In par-

ticular, this extends to the ego states (guilt, worry, nostalgia, and desire) and the alter ego states (hero-worship, blame, approval, and concern). These distinctive colloquial groupings directly account for the sum-total of slots predicted for the personal level of the virtuous hierarchy.

Extending these preliminary results to the corresponding realm of punishment introduces the parallel complement of motivational terms specific to the contrasting realm of defect. In particular, each ego and alter ego state is alternately associated with a corresponding vice, identified as the direct antithesis of its respective virtuous mode. Accordingly, the ego states formally contrast with the respective listing of ego vices (laziness-negligence-apathy-indifference). Furthermore, the alter ego states, in turn, contrast with a respective listing of alter ego vices (treachery, vindictiveness, spite, and malice). For lack of a better designation, these parallel sets of terms are respectively termed the ego and alter ego vices, in direct analogy to their respective virtuous counterparts. For instance, *apathy* represents the darker antithesis of desire, while *indifference* assigns a negative connotation to worry. Furthermore, *negligence* represents the darker counterpart of guilt, although there does not appear to be any clear-cut antonym for nostalgia. Taking a cue from negligence, however, *laziness* certainly fits well into this formal schematic format, a speculation further verified in terms of the more advanced levels within the power hierarchy. Although these four basic ego vices all exhibit a fair degree of generality, they nevertheless serve as the elementary foundation for the entire darker realm of the power hierarchy to follow.

The remaining listing of the alter ego vices (treachery, vindictiveness, spite, and malice) is a grouping that virtually begs to be listed together: each defined as the formal antonym of its respective alter ego state. For instance, *treachery* represents the darker counterpart of hero-worship, whereas *vindictiveness* makes a similar correspondence to blame. Furthermore, *spite* suggests a more maladaptive modification of approval, whereas *malice* similarly contrasts with concern. In concert with the more elementary ego vices, these four basic alter ego vices collectively account for the sum-totality of punishment roles predicted within the personal power realm.

In direct analogy to the case previously established for the virtuous realm, the alter ego vices are similarly organized along the lines of a meta-perspective style of format. For instance, you (as personal follower) *treacherously* act in a punitive fashion towards me, in response to my (as per-

510	511
Laziness	Negligence
512	**513**
Apathy	Indifference

EGO VICES
(Personal Authority)

520	521
Treachery	Vindictiveness
522	**523**
Spite	Malice

ALTER EGO VICES
(Personal Follower)

530	531
Infamy	Dishonor
532	**533**
Foolishness	Capriciousness

VICES of PERSONALISM
(Group Authority)

540	541
Insurgency	Vengeance
542	**543**
Gluttony	Cowardice

CARDINAL VICES
(Group Representative)

550	551
Prodigality	Slavery
552	**553**
Vulgarity	Cruelty

CIVIL LIABILITIES
(Spiritual Authority)

560	561
Betrayal	Despair
562	**563**
Avarice	Antagonism

THEOLOGICAL VICES
(Spiritual Disciple)

570	571
Wrath	Tyranny
572	**573**
Oppression	Persecution

ECUMENICAL VICES
(Humanitarian Authority)

580	581
Ugliness	Hypocrisy
582	**583**
Evil	Cunning

CLASSICAL GREEK VICES
(Humanitarian Follower)

590	591
Anger	Prejudice
592	**593**
Hatred	Belligerence

HUMANISTIC VICES
(Transcendental Authority)

500	501
Abomination	Perdition
502	**503**
Iniquity	Turpitude

MYSTICAL VICES
(Transcendental Follower)

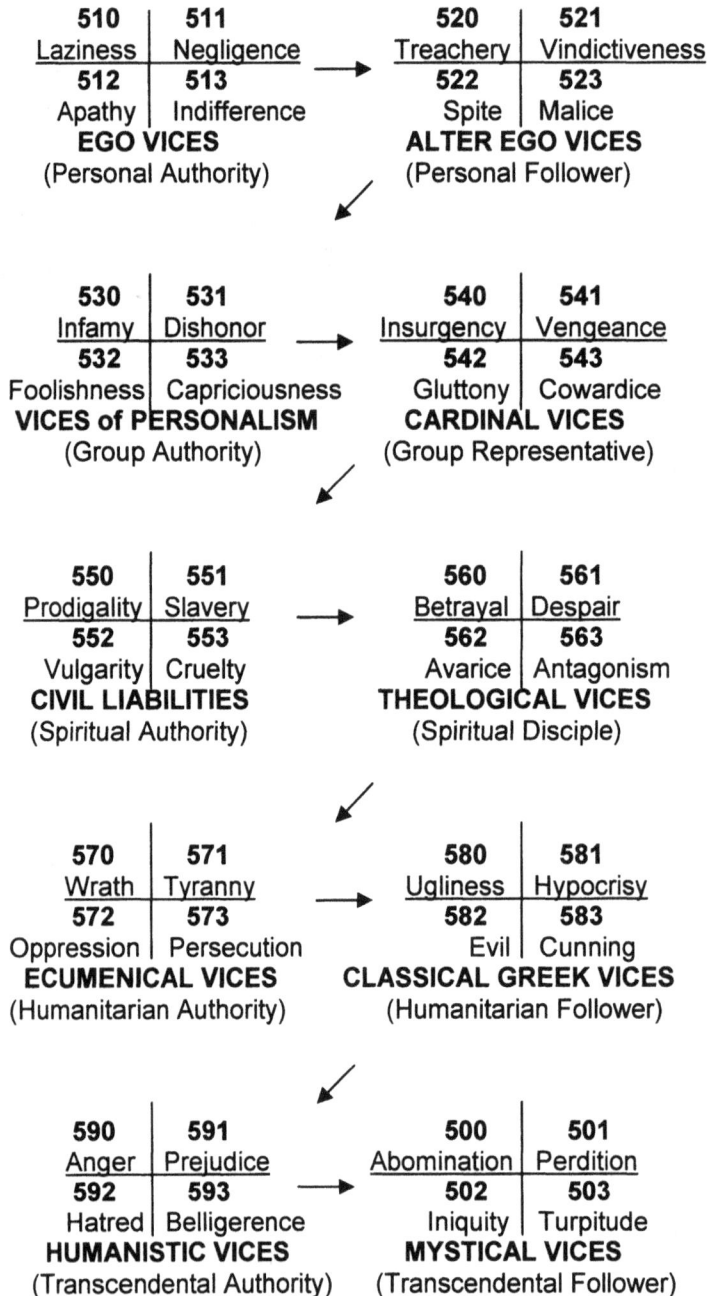

Fig. 10B – The Vices of Defect

sonal authority) lazy treatment of you. Similarly, you might also punitively act *vindictively* towards me, in response to my negligent treatment of you. Furthermore, I (as personal follower) *spitefully* act grudgingly towards you, in response to your apathetic treatment of me. Alternately, I might also *maliciously* act in a punitively towards you in response to your indifferent treatment of me. This distinctive set of interactions is schematically depicted in **Fig. 10A**, identical to that of **Fig. 3A**, with the exception that the vices (rather than the virtues) are now called into focus.

A NEW CLASSIFICATIONAL SYSTEM FOR THE VICES OF DEFECT

The preliminary analysis with respect to the personal realm, in turn, permits an even broader examination of the more advanced levels within the power hierarchy. Indeed, this strict correspondence to the virtuous mode necessarily specifies the existence of an entire parallel version of the power hierarchy with respect to the vices of defect. In particular, each virtue within the reinforcement hierarchy contrasts (point-for-point) with a respective vice within the hierarchy of defect. For the most part, each such vice represents the direct ethical antonym of its respective virtuous counterpart, permitting precise quartet-style listings analogous to that previously established for the virtuous mode.

This parallel hierarchy for the vices of defect is schematically depicted in **Fig. 10B** (in addition to the respective three-digit codes): structured in parallel fashion to the virtuous format depicted in **Fig. 2** (of Chapter 2). Here the first digit for the coding system is assigned the numerical value of "5" for the vices of defect, as opposed to the virtuous mode, where the codes all begin with "1." Both diagrams are organized in terms of dual vertical columns designating the reciprocal interplay of the authority and follower roles. Both columns are further subdivided into the respective personal, group, spiritual, humanitarian, and transcendental levels characterizing the general power hierarchy. These authority/follower roles further alternate over the entire ten-level span of the ethical hierarchy, as the directional arrows formally serve to indicate.

Although the virtues and values collectively enjoy a wide range of philosophical traditions, a similar set of precedents with respect to the vices has conspicuously been lacking. Indeed, perhaps the only grouping of major significance is that of the Seven Deadly Sins: namely, pride, covetousness, lust, anger, gluttony, envy, and sloth. This

traditional grouping actually represents an incongruent hodgepodge of vices spanning several levels within the power hierarchy, an arrangement scarcely precise enough to adequately quantify the more advanced groupings of the vices. Accordingly, a new system of classification must necessarily be devised for formally labeling the more abstract listings of vices. This new format takes its cue primarily from the traditions specified for virtuous mode, with the groupings of vices now provisionally designated for their respective virtuous counterparts; namely, the cardinal vices, the mystical vices, etc.

Furthermore, whereas the virtues (specific the follower role) are formally distinguished from the authority "ideals," so the darker realm of the vices is further specified via the parallel concepts of vice and sin. In particular, the Greek verb for sin in the New Testament translates as "to miss" (as in failing to reach a goal). This "sin" of failing to reach such acceptable goals represents a negative variation on the virtuous mode, with sin directly contrasting with the authority "ideals" in such a negative sense.

With respect to the remaining sequence of follower roles, the vices directly counteract the virtues in this negative respect. According to Chapter 3, the virtues formally define the reinforcing aspects of the conditioned relationship, designating behaviors with the potential to reward suitably solicitous/submissive behaviors. The corresponding vices offer a fitting counterpoint in this respect, representing a punitive set of consequences - in direct contrast to the rewarding prerequisites of the virtuous mode. Indeed, whereas the notions of vice and sin share a reciprocal status with respect to the authority/follower roles; for sake of brevity, this overall set of themes is formally referred to simply as "the vices," consistent with the general terminology of the vices of defect. Indeed, a parallel scenario further holds true for the virtuous realm, where the catchall term of "the virtues" is collectively employed to designate the overall hierarchy of virtues, values, and ideals.

With respect to the rules for coding within the three-digit system, a few basic observations are rightfully in order. The first digit for the vices of defect, by definition, is assigned the unitary value of "5," as specified within the basic numbering pattern established in Chapter 1. The second digit further narrows the focus, in turn, specifying each of the ten respective levels within the power pyramid hierarchy. According to this basic format, 1 = personal authority, 2 = personal follower, 3 = group authority, etc. With the first two digits now defined, it ultimately remains to the remaining final digit to complete the coding scheme. For example, should the first digit be a "5" (the vices of defect), and the second digit is a "2" (for personal follower), then the range of possibilities is further narrowed down to the single category of the alter ego vices (treachery-vindictiveness-spite-malice). In fact, each of the remaining groupings of vices of defect is specified in terms of such a two-digit combination. In order to specify the individual terms, the third and final digit is ultimately called into play. According to the previous example, 520 = treachery, 521 = vindictiveness, 522 = spite, and 523 = malice. Digits 4 to 7 in the three-slot, in turn, specify the accessory versions of the cardinal vices, as more elaborately described in the Chapter *15* of this section. Accordingly, 524 = mutiny, 525 = retaliation, 526 = grudgingness, and 527 = malevolence The final two third-place digits (8 & 9) are alternately reserved for specifying the general unifying themes; namely, for this example, the main theme of the fraud and the accessory theme of deception.

THE INTERPLAY OF INDIVIDUAL TERMS WITHIN THE HIERARCHY OF DEFECT

The newly proposed master-hierarchy of vice and sin represents a revolutionary contribution in the study of the vices, an achievement that completely overrides the only other competing system; namely, the more rudimentary listing of the Seven Deadly Sins. Each of the ten master groupings of "vice" is further designated in terms of the traditions of the virtuous mode, a necessary circumstance in light of the lack of a better alternative. Indeed, this "stopgap" system of classification for the vices must necessarily remain in force until a consensus means for labeling can be universally agreed upon.

These master listings for the vices, in turn, exhibit the distinctive tendency towards hierarchical organization: similar to the case previously established for the virtuous mode. According to **Fig. 10B**, the sequence of vices targeting the first three authority roles (laziness-infamy-prodigality) collectively specify a past-directed focus: in essence, sharing the theme of past notorious activities. The parallel trend with respect to the follower roles (treachery-insurgency-betrayal), in turn, reciprocates the authority sequence with respect to the punishment of such past notorious perspectives. Furthermore, the related authority sequence of negligence-dishonor-slavery suggests a similar past-directed focus, although now based upon a shameful sense of negligence. The re-

maining sequence of follower roles (vindictiveness-vengeance-despair) further validates such a trend, mirroring the trend based upon treachery with the exception that vindictiveness is now brought into focus.

A similar set of trends further holds true with respect to the future-directed dimensions for the realm of defect. For the most personal realm, this amounts to apathy in anticipation of spitefulness, or indifference in expectation of maliciousness. Here the initial sequence of vices targeting the authority roles (apathy-foolishness-vulgarity) further prompts the remaining series themes in relation to the follower roles (spitefulness-gluttony-avarice): the latter trend reciprocating the authority sequence through a punishment of such non-solicitous perspectives. In a related sense, the remaining authority sequence of indifference-capriciousness-cruelty invokes a similar future-directed focus, although now specifying an indifferent lack of appeasement. The subsequent sequence of follower roles (malice-cowardice-antagonism) further validates such a trend, reflecting that based upon spitefulness with the exception that malice is now brought into focus.

These initial sequences of vices (spanning the personal, group, and spiritual levels), in turn, provide the elementary foundation for the crowning humanitarian and transcendental levels, respectively. In contrast to the purely organizational status for the first three authority levels, the final two levels are alternately defined as purely abstract styles of power perspectives. In this latter respect, the humanitarian domain derives from the abstract addition of "historical" time, whereas the transcendental level makes a formal appeal to the realm of pure transcendence.

The profoundly abstract nature of these crowning two levels is further reflected in their respectively abstract groupings of vices. These darker themes collectively share an enduring significance within the field of ethical inquiry: as the representative sampling of evil, hatred, belligerence etc., clearly serve to indicate. In truth, the vices associated with these final two levels virtually beg to be listed together; as in the ecumenical vices (wrath-tyranny-persecution-oppression), the moralistic vices (evil-cunning-ugliness-hypocrisy), the humanistic vices (anger-hatred-prejudice-belligerence), and the mystical vices (iniquity-turpitude-abomination-perdition).

THE SCHEMATIC DEFINITIONS FOR DEFECT

Although the preliminary description of the schematic definitions have previously been limited

The Seven Deadly Sins – Detail from Flemish Painting by Hieronymous Bosch (1450-1516)
Outer-Ring Clockwise: Gluttony-Sloth-Lust-Pride-Anger-Envy-Covetousness – Prado Museum, Madrid

exclusively to the virtuous realm, the parallel hierarchy for the vices of defect can similarly be incorporated into its own unique complement of definitions: as formally depicted in **Tables D-1** to **D-4**. This comprehensive forty-part listing of definitions for the realm of defect contrasts point-for-point with the respective virtuous counterparts, as initially outlined in **Tables A-1** to **A-4**. This crucial innovation spells out in longhand the precise location of each vice within the linguistic matrix, while simultaneously preserving the correct orientation of authority/follower roles. Each definition is formally constructed along the lines of a two-stage sequential format; namely (1) the formal recognition of the preliminary power maneuver, and (2) the countermaneuver currently being employed, and hence, labeled. Power leverage, accordingly, is achieved by rising to a "one-up"

power status; namely, ascending to the next higher metaperspectival level.

The complete forty-part listing of schematic definitions outlined in **Tables D-1** to **D-4** covers the entire ten-level span for the hierarchy of defect. The instinctual terminology for punishment dominates the preliminary levels, replaced in due course by the individual vices of defect specified for the higher authority levels. At each successive level, a new vice (distinguished through *italics*) is introduced into format: representing the power maneuver currently under consideration. The related authority/follower roles remain fixed throughout the entire ten-level span; although systematically abbreviated (for sake of brevity) in non-critical positions. In this latter respect, PA stands for personal authority, PF denotes personal follower, etc. Some of the more atypical abbreviations

LAZINESS	TREACHERY
Previously, you (as punisher) have refused to act rewardingly towards me: overriding my (as adversary) failure to act solicitously towards you. But now, I (as personal authority) will *lazily* fail to act solicitously towards you: overruling your (as punisher) refusal to act rewardingly towards me.	Previously, I (as personal authority) have lazily failed to act solicitously towards you: overriding your (as punisher) refusal to act rewardingly towards me. But now, you (as my personal follower) will *treacherously* refuse to act rewardingly towards me: overruling my (as PA) lazy treatment of you.
INFAMY	**INSURGENCY**
Previously, you (as my personal follower) have treacherously refused to act rewardingly towards me: overriding my (as PA) lazy treatment of you. But now, I (as group authority) will *infamously* act in a lazy fashion towards you: overruling your (as PF) treacherous treatment of me.	Previously, I (as your group authority) have infamously acted lazily towards you: overriding your (as PF) treacherous treatment of me. But now, you (as group representative) will *insurgently* act in a treacherous fashion towards me: overruling my (as GA) infamously-lazy treatment of you.
PRODIGALITY	**BETRAYAL**
Previously, you (as group representative) have insurgently acted treacherously towards me: overriding my (as GA) lazy sense of infamy. But now, I (as spiritual authority) will infamously act in a *prodigal* fashion towards you: overruling your (as GR) insurgently-treacherous treatment of me.	Previously, I (as your spiritual authority) have infamously acted in a prodigal fashion towards you: overriding your (as GR) insurgently-treacherous treatment of me. But now, you (as my spiritual disciple) will insurgently act in a *betraying* fashion towards me: overruling my (as SA) prodigal treatment of you.
WRATH	**UGLINESS**
Previously, you (as my spiritual disciple) have insurgently acted in a betraying fashion towards me: overriding my (as SA) infamously-prodigal treatment of you. But now, I (as humanitarian authority) will prodigally act in a *wrathful* fashion towards you: overruling your (as SD) insurgent-betrayal of me.	Previously, I (as humanitarian authority) have prodigally acted wrathfully towards you: overriding your (as SD) insurgent-betrayal of me. But now, you (as representative member of humanity) will betrayingly act in an *ugly* fashion towards me: overruling my (as HA) wrathful treatment of you.
ANGER	**ABOMINATION**
Previously, you (as representative member of humanity) have betrayingly acted in an ugly fashion towards me: overriding my (as HA) wrathful treatment of you. But now, I (as transcendental authority) will wrathfully act in an *angry* fashion towards you: overruling your (as RH) ugly-betrayal of me.	Previously, I (as transcendental authority) have wrathfully acted in an angry fashion towards you: overriding your (as RH) ugly-betrayal of me. But now, you (as my transcendental follower) will *abominably* act in an ugly fashion towards me: overruling my (as TA) angry treatment of you.

Table D-1 – The Definitions Based Upon Laziness/Treachery

NEGLIGENCE	VINDICTIVENESS
Previously, you (as punisher) have refused to act leniently towards me: overriding my (as adversary) failure to act submissively towards you. But now, I (as personal authority) will *negligently* fail to act submissively towards you: overruling your (as punisher) refusal to act leniently towards me.	Previously, I (as personal authority) have negligently failed to act submissively towards you: overriding your (as punisher) refusal to act leniently towards me. But now, you (as personal follower) will *vindictively* refuse to act leniently towards me: overruling my (as PA) negligent treatment of you.
DISHONOR	**VENGEANCE**
Previously, you (as my personal follower) have vindictively refused to act leniently towards me: overriding my (as PA) negligent treatment of you. But now, I (as group authority) will negligently act in a *dishonorable* fashion towards you: overruling your (as PF) vindictive treatment of me.	Previously, I (as group authority) have negligently acted in a dishonorable fashion towards you: overriding your (as PF) vindictive treatment of me. But now, you (as group representative) will *vengefully* act vindictively towards me: overruling my (as GA) dishonorable treatment of you.
SLAVERY	**DESPAIR**
Previously, you (as group representative) have vengefully acted in a vindictive fashion towards me: overriding my (as GA) negligently dishonorable treatment of you. But now, I (as spiritual authority) will dishonorably-*enslave* you: overruling your vengefully-vindictive treatment of me.	Previously, I (as spiritual authority) have dishonorably-enslaved you: overriding your (as GR) vengefully-vindictive treatment of me. But now, you (as my spiritual disciple) will vengefully act in a *despairing* fashion towards me: overruling my (as SA) dishonorable enslavement of you.
TYRANNY	**HYPOCRISY**
Previously, you (as my spiritual disciple) have vengefully acted in a despairing fashion towards me: overriding my (as SA) dishonorable enslavement of you. But now, I (as humanitarian authority) will *tyrannically*-enslave you: overruling your (as SD) despairing treatment of me.	Previously, I (as humanitarian authority) have tyrannically-enslaved you: overriding your (as SD) despairing treatment of me. But now, you (as representative member of humanity) will despairingly act in a *hypocritical* fashion towards me: overruling my (as HA) tyrannical-enslavement of you.
PREJUDICE	**PERDITION**
Previously, you (as representative member of humanity) have despairingly acted in a hypocritical fashion towards me: overriding my (as HA) tyrannical-enslavement of you. But now, I (as transcendental authority) will tyrannically act *prejudicially* towards you: overruling your (as RH) hypocritical treatment of me.	Previously, I (as transcendental authority) have tyrannically acted prejudicially towards you: overriding your (as RH) hypocritical sense of despair. But now, you (as transcendental follower) will hypocritically act in a *perditionable* fashion towards me: overruling my (as TA) prejudicial treatment of you.

Table D-2 – The Definitions Based on Negligence/Vindictiveness

APATHY Previously, I (as punisher) have refused to act rewardingly towards you: overriding your (as adversary) failure to act solicitously towards me. But now, you (as personal authority) will *apathetically* fail to act solicitously towards me: overruling my (as punisher) refusal to act rewardingly towards you.	**SPITE** Previously, you (as personal authority) have apathetically failed to act solicitously towards me: overriding my (as punisher) refusal to act rewardingly towards you. But now, I (as your personal follower) will *spitefully* refuse to act rewardingly towards you: overruling your (as PA) apathetic treatment of me.
FOOLISHNESS Previously, I (as your personal follower) have spitefully refused to act rewardingly towards you: overriding your (as PA) apathetic treatment of me. But now, you (as group authority) will *foolishly* act in an apathetic fashion towards me: overruling my (as PF) spiteful treatment of you.	**GLUTTONY** Previously, you (as group authority) have foolishly acted in an apathetic fashion towards me: overriding my (as PF) spiteful treatment of you. But now, I (as group representative) will *gluttonously* act in a spiteful fashion towards you: overruling your (as GA) foolishly-apathetic treatment of me.
VULGARITY Previously, I (as group representative) have gluttonously acted in a spiteful fashion towards you: overriding your (as GA) foolishly-apathetic treatment of you. But now, you (as spiritual authority) will foolishly act in a *vulgar* fashion towards me: overruling my (as GR) gluttonously-spiteful treatment of you.	**AVARICE** Previously, you (as my spiritual authority) have foolishly acted in a vulgar fashion towards me: overriding my (as GR) gluttonously-spiteful treatment of you. But now, I (as spiritual disciple) will gluttonously act in an *avaricious* fashion towards you: overruling your (as SA) foolishly-vulgar treatment of me.
OPPRESSION Previously, I (as your spiritual disciple) have gluttonously acted avariciously towards you: overriding your (as SA) vulgar treatment of me. But now, you (as humanitarian authority) will vulgarly act in an *oppressive* fashion towards me overruling my (as SD) gluttonously-avaricious treatment of you.	**EVIL** Previously, you (as humanitarian authority) have vulgarly acted oppressively towards me: overriding my (as SA) avaricious treatment of you. But now, I (as representative member of humanity) will avariciously act in an *evil* fashion towards you: overruling your (as HA) vulgarly-oppressive treatment of me.
HATRED Previously, I (as representative member of humanity) have avariciously acted in an evil fashion towards you: overriding your (as HA) vulgarly-oppressive treatment of me. But now, you (as transcendental authority) will oppressively act in a *hateful* fashion towards me: overruling my (as RH) evil treatment of you.	**INIQUITY** Previously, you (as transcendental authority) have hatefully acted in an oppressive fashion towards me: overriding my (as RH) avaricious sense of evil. But now, I (as your transcendental follower) will evilly act in an *iniquitous* fashion towards you: overruling your (as TA) hateful treatment of me.

Table D-3 – The Definitions Based Upon Apathy/Spite

INDIFFERENCE	MALICE
Previously, I (as punisher) have refused to act leniently towards you: overriding your (as adversary) failure to act submissively towards me. But now, you (as personal authority) will *indifferently* fail to act submissively towards me: overruling my (as punisher) refusal to act leniently towards you.	Previously, you (as personal authority) have indifferently failed to act submissively towards me: overriding my (as punisher) refusal to act leniently towards you. But now, I (as your personal follower) will *maliciously* refuse to act leniently towards you: overruling your (as PA) indifferent treatment of me.
CAPRICIOUSNESS	**COWARDICE**
Previously, I (as your personal follower) have maliciously refused to act leniently towards you: overriding your (as PA) indifferent treatment of me. But now, you (as group authority) will *capriciously* act in an indifferent fashion towards me: overruling my (as PF) malicious treatment of you.	Previously, you (as group authority) have capriciously acted indifferently towards me: overriding my (as PF) malicious treatment of you. But now, I (as group representative) will *cowardly* act in a malicious fashion towards you: overruling your (as GA) capricious sense of indifference.
CRUELTY	**ANTAGONISM**
Previously, I (as group representative) have cowardly acted in a malicious fashion towards you: overriding your (as GA) capricious sense of indifference. But now, you (as spiritual authority) will capriciously act in a *cruel* fashion towards me: overruling my (as GR) cowardly-malicious treatment of you.	Previously, you (as spiritual authority) have capriciously acted in a cruel fashion towards me: overriding my (as GR) cowardly-malicious treatment of you. But now, I (as your spiritual disciple) will cowardly act in an *antagonistic* fashion towards you: overruling your (as SA) cruel treatment of me.
PERSECUTION	**CUNNING**
Previously, I (as your spiritual disciple) have cowardly acted in an antagonistic fashion towards you: overriding your (as SA) cruel treatment of me. But now, you (as humanitarian authority) will cruelly-*persecute* me: overruling my (as SD) cowardly-antagonistic treatment of you.	Previously, you (as humanitarian authority) have cruelly-persecuted me: overriding my (as SD) cowardly-antagonistic treatment of you. But now, I (as representative member of humanity) will antagonistically act in a *cunning* fashion towards you: overruling your (as HA) cruel persecution of me.
BELLIGERENCE	**TURPITUDE**
Previously, I (as representative member of humanity) have antagonistically acted in a cunning fashion towards you: overriding your (as HA) cruel persecution of me. But now, you (as transcendental authority) will *belligerently*-persecute me: overruling my (as RH) cunning treatment of you.	Previously, you (as transcendental authority) have belligerently-persecuted me: overriding my (as RH) antagonistic sense of cunning. But now, I (as your transcendental follower) will cunningly act in a *turpitudinous* fashion towards you: overruling your (as TA) belligerent persecution of me.

Table D-4 – The Definitions Based Upon Indifference/Malice are GR (group representative), SD (spiritual disciple), and RH (the representative member of humanity).

As formally contrasted with the virtuous realm, this dual ethical system (linking both virtue and vice) provides a suitable foundation for diagnosing most routine issues of a moral nature. Indeed, the darker complement of schematic definitions prove equally as informative as do the virtues, offering crucial insights into those aspects that one should avoid. The inevitable familiarity with the realm of defect actually amounts to a basic safeguard within the system. Negative transactions are diagnosed in terms of their potential for transformation into positive ones, with the reverse also prevented from occurring.

A more extensive description of the complete ten-level hierarchy of the vices of defect, accordingly, is offered in the remaining Chapters *11* to *15* of the current section. The specific order in which these vices are presented, however, differs from the strategies previously utilized with respect to the virtuous realm. In the latter format, each of the authority/follower levels was blessed with its own well-established literary traditions, wherein warranting its own individual chapter. The realm of the vices, however, typically lacks such strong individual traditions, with the "one level per chapter" strategy now no longer the most effective means towards presentation. It rather proves more effective to outline the direct hierarchial relationships linking the first three levels of the power hierarchy; namely, the personal, group, and spiritual domains, respectively. Chapter *11* initially examines the past-directed listings of vices; namely, laziness-infamy-prodigality and treachery-insurgency-betrayal: in turn, followed by negligence-dishonor-slavery and vindictiveness-vengeance-despair. Chapter *12* further switches the focus to the remaining future-directed vices; namely, apathy-foolishness-vulgarity and spite-gluttony-avarice: followed, in turn, by the sequences of indifference-capriciousness-cruelty and malice-cowardice-antagonism. Each chapter is further embellished with numerous examples from both classical and contemporary literature, adding a further entertaining dimension to this somewhat formal description of the vices.

The final two levels within the power hierarchy (e.g., the humanitarian/transcendental) again re-vert back to the basic "one level per chapter" pattern. This pattern reversal is definitely warranted in light of the more comprehensive nature of the vices for this final pair of levels. Chapter *13*, accordingly, offers an in depth examination of the ecumenical vices: wrath-tyranny-persecution-oppression (specific to the humanitarian authority role), as well as the moralistic vices: evil-cunning-ugliness-hypocrisy (for the humanitarian follower role). Furthermore, Chapter *14* outlines the transcendental realm of the power hierarchy, describing the humanistic vices (anger-hatred-prejudice-belligerence), as well as the mystical vices (iniquity-turpitude-abomination-perdition). Chapter *15* concludes with an in-depth analysis of the accessory listings of the vices of defect (as well as the general unifying themes), providing a formal sense of closure to this grand-scale examination of the vices.

In conclusion, the newly proposed ten-level hierarchy for the vices of defect represents an unprecedented addition on the world scene today. In contrast to the major virtues, where many of the established groupings already enjoyed long-standing literary traditions, the newly minted classifications for the realm of defect represent entirely new groupings, taking their cue as direct polar opposites of their respective virtuous counterparts. This point-for-point contrasting arrangement permitted precise identification of the individual vices of defect, permitting the construction an entire cohesive darker hierarchy parallel to that previously demonstrated for the virtuous mode. This breakthrough innovation finally allows for a more comprehensive conceptualization for this darker domain of defect. No longer do religious/scriptural sources remain the only resource for debating ethical issues in this realm of defect. Furthermore, the timely incorporation of the vices of defect within the formal schematic definition format permits an unprecedented degree of precision in this basic respect. This elementary class of vices, when further examined in a communicational fashion, offer crucial telling insights into the realms of criminality, hypercriminality, and hyperviolence: providing an invaluable tool for deciphering the motives driving terrorist directives worldwide. Hopefully, this new technology can be instituted in a timely fashion so as to avert any further damage to the prospects for global peace and prosperity.

11

THE PAST-DIRECTED
DOMAIN OF DEFECT

A general examination of the vices of defect is currently launched with respect to the past-directed realm of the power hierarchy; namely, the sequence based upon laziness/treachery, followed by that based upon negligence/vindictiveness. As stated earlier, the current chapter endeavors to establish the reciprocal interplay of the vices of defect spanning the personal, group, and spiritual levels within the power hierarchy. The preliminary sequence of vices targeting the authority roles (laziness-infamy-prodigality) collectively specify a past-directed focus, wherein sharing the common theme of past notorious activities. The parallel series of vices with respect to the follower roles (treachery-insurgency-betrayal) formally reciprocates the authority sequence, although through a punishment of such past notorious perspectives.

The parallel authority sequence of negligence-dishonor-slavery invokes a similar past-directed focus, although now targeting a more shameful sense of negligence. The affiliated sequence of follower roles (vindictiveness-vengeance-despair) further validates such a trend. Indeed, it mirrors that based upon treachery with the exception that vindictiveness is now brought into focus. The remainder of the current chapter examines the respective authority and follower roles in a reciprocating fashion, schematically outlining the ascending sequence of personal, group, and spiritual levels within the authority hierarchy.

510 – LAZINESS

The first-listed authority-based vice of *laziness* represents a past-directed style of power maneuver: the direct antithesis of the virtuous "nostalgia" perspective. Whereas nostalgia denotes a memory of past notable achievements, laziness alternately specifies the realization of having acted to the contrary. According to this contrasting interpretation, the personal authority lazily admits failing to have acted solicitously, wherein fully expecting punitive treatment from his follower figure. Indeed, laziness is specifically listed among the Seven Deadly Sins, a factor particularly in keeping with the medieval maxim: "An idle mind is the Devil's workshop." Productivity was certainly a crucial factor during such uncertain times, with laziness particularly singled out for punitive social consequences.

520 – TREACHERY

The latter punitive role is alternately assumed by the personal follower, who treacherously acts punitively in response to the lazy treatment of the personal authority. This theme derives from the Old French *tricherie* (trickery), generally in allusion to the surprising fashion in which it is typically bestowed. It refers to a betrayal of trust or confidence in one's personal authority figure, the same root-stem for the related theme of treason. Indeed, petty treason (in contrast to high treason) is defined as treachery occurring entirely within a personal sphere of influence: as in the betrayal of the master by his servant. Treachery is defined as the chief moral antithesis of hero worship: a punitive (rather than rewarding) response to the lazy tendencies of the personal authority figure.

This basic interplay of the personal authority/follower roles, in turn, sets the stage for the remaining group/spiritual levels within the power hierarchy. For instance, the laziness perspective of the personal authority, in turn, extends to the *infamy* expressed by the group authority, culminating in the *prodigality* of the spiritual authority figure. Furthermore, the treachery perspective of the personal follower, in turn, sets the stage for the *insurgency* expressed by the group representative, culminating in the *betrayal* perspective of the spiritual disciple. This group/spiritual interplay of terms (encompassing infamy/prodigality and insurgency/betrayal) is examined in the first half of this chapter, beginning with a preliminary analysis of infamy.

530 – INFAMY

As the chief moral antithesis of glory, *infamy* is generally defined as ill-gotten fame or notoriety. This theme is particularly apparent during lawless periods in American history, such as the frontier spirit of the Old West or the Prohibition frenzy of the 20th century. Both periods exhibited their fair share of notorious outlaws. Billy the Kid and Jesse James roamed the Old West, whereas gangsters such as Bonnie and Clyde and Al Capone stole headlines in the 20th century. These infamous criminals lived by a common code; namely, failing to act solicitously in a culturally prescribed fashion (as reflected in their habitual disregard for property and the law). The general public was certainly outraged by the unlawful activities. Although some criminals were revered as cult heroes consistent with their free-spending propensities, this "Robin Hood" style of mentality eventually led to feelings of outrage when community resources were pillaged. The general citizenry felt little hesitancy in betraying these desperate outlaws, particularly with respect to the sizeable bounty accompanying cases of such magnitude.

This indiscriminate brand of criminality undoubtedly sparked widespread resentment among the working class. The daring string of bank robberies perpetrated by Bonnie and Clyde affected a broad range of the Mid-West population, wiping-out the hard-earned savings of entire farming communities. This outrage eventually sparked a wave of public indignation expressed as a determined effort to punish such shameless outlaws. Ironically, their final downfall was instigated by a traitor within their midst, culminating in a bloody shootout so frequently the outcome of those that glory in such notoriety.

540 – INSURGENCY

According to the preceding outlaw examples, the lazy sense of infamy expressed by Bonnie and Clyde equated to a negative variation on the glory perspective of the group authority figure. This in-famy perspective, in turn, is countered by the *insurgency* expressed by the group follower figure. The group representative insurgently acts in a treacherous fashion towards the group authority figure: wherein punishing the latter's lazy sense of infamy (as the betrayal of Bonnie and Clyde amply serves to illustrate). As the chief moral antithesis of prudence, insurgency represents the group counterpart of the treachery expressed by the personal follower. Its modern spelling derives from the Latin *insurgens* (to rise up against), from *in-* (upon) and *surgere* (to rise). It generally refers to organized opposition to unlawful authority, as in a treacherous-insurrection.

Perhaps the earliest mention of insurgency involves the widely cited rebellion of the Olympian gods against the harsh treatment of the Titans. This theme, in turn, recurs throughout the vast body of myth to follow, with specific instances much too numerous to mention. Such legendary intrigues clearly reflect the violent spirit of the age, where tyrants that lived by the sword were often doomed to die by it.

This enduring sense of treachery and intrigue clearly extends to our modern age, as reflected in the Communist revolutions of Russia and Mainland China. The prevailing form of imperial government was toppled in favor of a Marxist ideology that gloried in the power of the worker class. In the case of the Russian Revolution, Czar Nicholas II found himself heir to a bitter class struggle pitting the ruling aristocracy against the rising power of the peasant class. The Czar's steadfast refusal to promote adequate reforms (combined with the economic turmoil of WWI) ultimately led to his violent downfall at the hands of the rebellious worker class. Taking full advantage of their collective power to organize, the common people insurgently-rebelled against the infamous attitudes of the prevailing ruling class. From the ashes of the resulting anarchy rose a radically new style of socialistic viewpoint. This bold experiment in social engineering has undergone a precipitous decline as of late, a fitting outcome for an ideology based entirely upon such revolutionary dictates.

550 – PRODIGALITY

This completed description of the group sphere of influence (e.g., infamy/insurgency) further sets the stage for the remaining spiritual realm of the vices of defect. In particular, the infamous sense of *prodigality* characterizing the spiritual authority role effectively consummates the trend previously established for laziness and infamy. Although the precise meaning of prodigality varies widely according to context, its general connotation refers to reckless wastefulness or extravagance consistent with the infamy perspective of the group authority figure. Its modern spelling derives the Latin *prodigalitas*, from *prodigere* (to drive away, to squander). In early Italian iconography, prodigality, accordingly, is personified as a blindfolded smiling woman shown in the act of scattering coins from a cornucopia, a fitting allusion to the fickle and often extravagant nature of this vice.

These wasteful connotations of prodigality are similarly condemned in biblical scripture, as reflected in Christ's Parable of the Prodigal Son. The basic story line refers to the tale of two sons, the younger of which persuaded his father to advance him a share of the family inheritance. With such newfound wealth at his disposal, the young man soon journeyed to a faraway land, where he squandered his fortune on loose living and sensual pursuits. A disastrous famine soon followed, eventually pointing the prodigal son home in hopes of receiving the humble conditions afforded the servant help. Upon his return the son fell upon his father's mercy, pleading: "Father, I have sinned against heaven and in thy sight: I am no longer worthy to be called thy son, make me as one of thy hired servants." The father, however, moved by the sight of his long-lost son, ordered the servants to kill the "fatted calf" in honor of his return. In this dramatic fashion, the scandalous behavior of the prodigal son was graciously absolved through the providential favor of his benevolent father.

The spiritual overtones of this stirring parable certainly ring true today, the role of the father undoubtedly alluding to the providential favor of God-the-Father. The "featured" son in the parable further signifies the contrasting realm of the vices, his original loyalties now redirected towards strangers far-removed from his family ties. The tragic turn of events was certainly predictable, the son's fortunes soon failing him, in direct contrast to his father's providential sense of grace. In this latter respect, the son's callous behavior was rightfully judged as prodigal, in keeping with the spiritual dictates of this fictional context. Fortunately this story ends on a positive note, in that any vice can be fully remedied when both parties seek reconciliation.

560 – BETRAYAL

This preceding scenario of the Prodigal Son further sets the stage for the remaining spiritual form of follower countermaneuver; namely, the insurgent-*betrayal* expressed by the spiritual disciple. This betrayal perspective represents a more abstract (universal) variation on the group vice of insurgency. As the chief moral antithesis of faith, betrayal traces its origins to the Latin *tradere* (to deliver up), as in a betrayal of trust or allegiance. According to Dante's *Inferno*, betrayal is condemned as the deadliest of all sins, with the worst traitors of history specifically singled-out for the most terrible punishments by the Devil. Accordingly, betrayal remains an enduring theme throughout classical antiquity. Ancient rulers endeavored to enhance their authority status through impassioned claims to divinity.

The fateful example of Julius Caesar particularly comes to mind, his insatiable quest for power ultimately cut short by the members of his Senate. Caesar had originally invoked the emergency powers of the Roman Constitution to rule uncontested as emperor. This circumstance directly threatened the power of the Senate, which originally held sway over Rome's republican form of government. Caesar's fortunes quickly faded following his vain attempt to claim divine status, a tactic seen as setting the stage for a change to permanent dictatorship. The Senate felt pressured into taking drastic countermeasures culminating in Caesar's assassination in 44 BCE. The cruelest irony of the entire affair concerns the role of Brutus, one of many senators wielding a knife during the deadly attack. Indeed, Brutus is traditionally cited as one of Caesar's several illegitimate sons. Caesar's shock at his betrayal by such a trusted ally was strikingly apparent in his famous last words: "et tu Brutus?" (and you Brutus?), whereupon he is said to have collapsed in resignation of his inglorious death.

The Christian tradition offers similar parallels, as particularly apparent in the New Testament accounts of Judas's betrayal of Christ. The enormity of the treachery traditionally associated with Judas was surpassed only by the cruel manner by which it was made known: e.g., the Judas Kiss. For a relatively modest sum of thirty pieces of silver, Judas agreed to lead a special detail of Roman soldiers to Christ's nightly refuge. There he identified his master with a mock kiss on the cheek, a cruel irony in light of the profound loyalty Judas had originally pledged to Jesus. Indeed, during the Last Supper, Christ predicted that Judas would betray him. He, nevertheless, allowed fate to run its course: whereupon fulfilling the Old Testament prophesies concerning his death and resurrection. This enduring tradition of the Judas kiss extends even to our modern age with respect to the "kiss of death," a throwback to the formalized ritual of betrayal attributed to certain Sicilian-based crime syndicates.

THE PAST-DIRECTED VICES BASED UPON NEGLIGENCE/VINDICTIVENESS

The completed description of the vices based upon laziness/treachery further sets the stage for the sequence targeting negligence/vindictiveness. This latter format alternately specifies the deliberate withholding of leniency, effectively punishing behaviors judged not to be suitably submissive. This modified format directly contrasts with the preceding section where rewards were withheld in response to unproductive types of behavior.

511 – NEGLIGENCE

The first-mentioned vice of *negligence* earns present consideration as the chief motivational counterpart of laziness. Here the personal authority negligently fails to act submissively, in contrast to simply acting unproductively. Its modern spelling derives from the Latin *neglegere* (to neglect), denoting an avoidance of one's rightful duties. This term is also used in a legal sense, as in the deliberate lack of attention to the interests or wellbeing of others, particularly as specified under the law. In this modified sense, the personal authority figure negligently fails to submit to the letter of the law, wherein provoking subsequent retribution from his respective follower figure.

521 – VINDICTIVENESS

The latter follower role is alternately reflected in the punitive sense of *vindictiveness* expressed by the personal follower in response to the negligence of the personal authority figure. Its modern spelling derives from the Latin *vindicare* (to defend, to avenge). It is sometimes confused with the related Latin derivation of *vindicta* (revenge, punishment). According to Old Roman Law, vindication referred to the defense of one's legal rights through an appeal to judicial procedures. The modern-day connotations of vindictiveness, however, imply a willful retreat from leniency on the part of the personal follower. This punitive focus directly contrasts with that already established for the virtuous realm, where the personal follower blamefully acts leniently towards his personal authority in anticipation of a subsequent admission of guilt. This lenient sense of blame is generally much milder than the more brutal sense of vindictiveness specified for the realm of the vices.

As previously described with respect to laziness/treachery, the related interplay of negligence/vindictiveness, in turn, serves as the elementary foundation for the remaining group/spiritual domains for the hierarchy of defect. For instance, the negligence of the personal authority, in turn, sets the stage for the *dishonor* expressed by the group authority, culminating in the *slavery* imposed by the spiritual authority figure. Furthermore, the vindictiveness professed by the personal follower, in turn, provokes the *vengeance* expressed by the group representative, concluding with the *despair* perspective of the spiritual disciple. The remainder of the current chapter examines these additional sets of vices, beginning with the group sequence of dishonor/vengeance, followed by the spiritual vices of slavery/despair.

531 – DISHONOR

As the chief moral opposite of honor, *dishonor* is defined as a manifest lack of honorable treatment, similar to the case previously made for glory/infamy. Dishonor, accordingly, represents a lack of submissive (rather than solicitous) behavior, much as often encountered during the great military conflicts throughout the ages. Perhaps the greatest military epoch in this regard concerns the Samurai warrior tradition of medieval Japan. The Samurai warrior submitted "life and limb" to the will of his imperial warlord. According to this rigid code of honor, the dishonored warrior's only course of atonement (befitting such violent times) was the ritual enactment of suicide known as *hari kiri*. Through this supreme sacrifice of ritual self-disembowelment, the warrior desperately sought to reconcile his shame over failing to meet the expectations of his military warlord. Indeed, the English translation of hari kiri (literally, happy dispatch) particularly reflects this dutiful sense of honor with respect to one's militaristic obligations.

According to this specific Samurai example, dishonor is clearly a theme encompassing the group authority perspective, directly expanding upon its more elementary foundation in negligence. The sacrificial act of hari kiri proudly sought to atone for one's unbearable feelings of shame and humiliation, a desperate reconciliation after the fact. This dramatic display of personal disregard was scarcely limited to the Samurai era. Suicidal missions, such as willingly accepted by Kamikaze pilots during WW-II merited high honor within the military establishment. In the final tally, however, all such efforts went for naught, the sound defeat of the Japanese provoking a suicidal wave of despair that preceded the Reconstruction Era.

541 – VENGEANCE

In light of the preceding Samurai example, the dishonor perspective of the group authority, in turn, sets the stage for the follower maneuver proper; namely, the vengeful sense of vindictiveness expressed by the group follower figure. This circumstance directly contrasts with the virtuous mode, where vengeance represents the darker counterpart in terms of justice. Its modern spelling derives from the Old French *venger* (to avenge), from the Latin *vindicare* (to avenge). According to classical Greek mythology, vengeance is specifically personified by Nemesis, the Greek goddess of divine retribution. According to legend, Nemesis served as the limiting influence on the extravagant favors bestowed by Tyche, the Greek goddess of fortune and chance. In keeping with her general persecution of the rich and powerful, Nemesis eventually came to signify the fateful accounting awaiting the reckless thrill-seeker. By extension, she is often confused with Adrastea (the Greek goddess of the inevitable). Nemesis is traditionally depicted as a winged goddess holding an apple bough in one hand and a Wheel of Fortune in the other. She is sometimes portrayed driving a chariot drawn by fierce griffins, wherein attesting to the fearsome nature of her exploits.

The Latin tradition of vengeance is alternately affiliated with Mars Ultor, a variation on the Roman God of War (whose surname meant "Avenger"). The Emperor Augustus dedicated a temple to him in the Roman Forum subsequent to taking revenge upon the assassins of Julius Caesar. Consistent with this trend towards vigilante justice, Augustus established squads of paid firemen (*vigiles*) to patrol Rome during nightly hours in response to the Great Fire of 6 CE. These vigiles were further empowered with minor police duties, adding a much-needed sense of order similar to the role the vigilante gangs enjoyed in the American Old West.

In this latter respect, the frontier vigilante groups were composed primarily of deputized private citizens outraged enough to take the law into their own hands. They filled a vacuum in law-enforcement so prevalent in the sparsely populated frontier territories. The general aim of such a vigilante posse was euphemistically termed a "necktie party," where the captured guilty criminals were typically hung on the spot, wherein generally eliminating the subsequent need for a jury trial.

According to this specific vigilante example, vengeance formally represents a vice in the punitive tradition, wherein countering the dishonor expressed by the group authority figure. In the preceding "lynch-gang" example, the members of the vigilante group vengefully acted vindictively towards the fugitives from justice, directly contrasting with the "just-blaming" characterizing the virtuous mode. In terms of such a community-based perspective, the posse members were keenly aware of the plight of any members within their group, venting their outrage in the most vindictive manner possible. The predictable finality of the necktie party was oft-times regrettable, for in the frenzy of the hunt many miscarriages of justice often occurred: such as dramatized in Walter Van Tilburg Clark's fictional masterpiece, *The Oxbow Incident*.

551 – SLAVERY

The completed description of the group realm of the vices (dishonor/vengeance), in turn, sets the stage for a related examination of their spiritual counterparts; namely, slavery/despair. As the chief moral antithesis of liberty, slavery is generally defined as the forceful domination of another individual, resulting in a loss of personal freedom. Its modern spelling derives from the Latin *sklabos* (slave), a term that originally referred to captives of Slavic origin: from the Old Slavic *sloven* or *slovo*. From the earliest of times, slavery was regarded as an essential economic and social institution. The traditional slave force was culled from captives of war, or bred as the offspring of slave parents. Slavery was typically viewed as a regrettable economic misfortune, with most slaves struggling to endure their menial or domestic duties. Discipline and chastisement were generally reserved for only the worst offenders, with the death penalty an even rarer occurrence.

The eventual decline of the Western Roman Empire led to a similar decline in slavery's significance, although the invading barbarian hordes were not averse to taking full advantage of captive prisoners. Between the 8th and l0th centuries, a resurgence of slavery occurred with respect to the wholesale enslavement of Slavic peoples by invading German forces; hence, the English derivation of the term. With its subsequent conversion to Christianity, slavery gradually declined in Western Europe: leading to the medieval feudal system with its more humane reliance on the labor of the serfs.

The eventual dawning of the Age of Exploration, however, provided a new wrinkle to the ages-old institution of slavery. Sturdy sailing ships permitted ready access to the teeming tropical shores of Africa, offering an entirely new class of slaves for exploitation. The radically different racial and cultural characteristics of these African populations proved particularly instrumental in legitimizing such an evil system of exploitation. The New World colonies soon became the recipients of cheap slave labor, the Africans often surpassing Native Americans in terms of vigor and stamina. The vast Caribbean plantations were the chief beneficiaries of the labor windfall, as well as the agricultural economies of the Southern United States. The labor-intensive focus of the major cash crops (cotton, sugar, and tobacco) was chiefly made possible through such a captive labor force. Indeed, the considerable profits realized from the slave trade eventually rivaled that gleaned from the agricultural sector.

Even by today's standards, the field laborers of the Southern plantation were maintained under the most appalling of circumstances, a far cry from the luxury of the master's mansion. Although this callous enforcement of slavery definitely cut across the grain of moral righteousness, the mere threat of punishment was generally sufficient to oppress the burgeoning slave population. For primarily financial reasons, the suitably submissive slave was never deliberately mistreated. Physical violence was reserved for rebellious slaves that violated the unwritten code of bondage. Punishments were customarily severe: ranging from scourging and chastisement to torture and execution: generally as a public example for others in their lot. Through such a violent array of tactics, the slave owner forcefully commanded the unswerving obedience of his captive work force, a tragedy that largely endured until more enlightened times prevailed.

561 – DESPAIR

As the chief moral opposite of hope, *despair* is traditionally defined as a total loss of hope. Its modern spelling derives from the Latin *desperatus*, the past participle of *desperate* (to be without hope). This manifest lack of hope is a theme common to many scriptural contexts consistent with the prominent influence of the spiritual disciple perspective. According to Old Testament scripture, the prophets of the Lord frequently endured many trials and tribulations leading to despair. For instance, the prophet Elijah fled for his life following an interminable conflict with the wicked Queen Jezebel. Indeed, Elijah entreated the Lord to put an end to the trials and tribulations he was forced to endure (1st Kings 19:14). The prophet Job similarly suffered a broad range of trials: resulting in impoverishment, the death of his children, and a painful illness, all within a brief span of time (Job 1:13-19, 2:7-8). His unending torment caused him to lament: "I would prefer death to all my sufferings." (Job 7:15). This dramatic set of tribulations appeared to overwhelm these faithful men of God, their dark despair crying-out for a merciful release from suffering. Fortunately, God saw fit to fortify both Elijah and Job through the depths of their despair, their faith in Divine Providence eventually restored in full.

In terms of New Testament scripture, perhaps the most stirring instance of despair concerns the events surrounding Christ's death upon the Cross. In two of the Gospels, Christ is said to have undergone a brief period of despair towards the end of his crucifixion. Under the weight of such terrible suffering, Christ is said to have desperately questioned his willing submission to his mission of atonement; namely, his death as redemption for the sins of all mankind. At his darkest hour, both Matthew and Mark describe Christ as crying out: "My God, My God, why has Thou forsaken me?" The fact that this passage is omitted from the other two Gospels suggests that this incident may actually represent a later scriptural contrivance (wherein fulfilling OT prophesies concerning Christ's death and resurrection). The most telling of these is Psalm *22*, a stirring lament traditionally attributed to King David. Psalm *22* begins with a desperate plea for spiritual deliverance, interspersed with dramatic parallels to Christ's crucifixion: e.g., the nature of his wounds, the disposition of his garments, etc. Indeed, Psalm *22* begins precisely with the same quotation that Christ is said to have made upon the Cross (suggesting a later scriptural modification). Mercifully, Christ's descent into despondency was relatively short-lived, with Christ once again regaining strength in his convictions (Luke 23:46). In particular, his final words: "Father, into thy hands I commend my spirit" signified the completion of his arduous mission of redemption.

12

THE FUTURE-DIRECTED VICES OF DEFECT

The completed description of the past-directed realm of defect further sets the stage for a related treatment of the vices targeting the future time dimension. In terms of the most basic personal level of the power hierarchy, this amounts to apathy in anticipation of spitefulness, or indifference in expectation of malicious treatment. In direct analogy to the previous chapter, the current section endeavors to document the reciprocal interplay of the future-directed vices spanning the personal, group, and spiritual levels within the realm of defect. The initial sequence of vices targeting the authority hierarchy (apathy, foolishness, and vulgarity), in turn, prompts the related series of follower themes (spitefulness-gluttony-avarice). The latter trend reciprocates the authority sequence through a punishment of such nonsolicitous perspectives.

In a parallel sense, the related authority sequence of indifference-capriciousness-cruelty similarly invokes a future-directed focus, although now targeting an indifferent lack of submissiveness. The remaining sequence of follower roles (malice-cowardice-antagonism) further validates such a trend, mirroring that based upon spite with the exception that malevolence is now brought into focus. The remainder of the current chapter examines the reciprocating interplay of authority and follower roles, formally modeling the ascending sequence of personal, group, and spiritual realms within the power hierarchy: serving as the foundation for the remaining chapters to follow.

512 – APATHY

The first-mentioned vice of *apathy* is identified as the direct moral antithesis of its virtuous counterpart in desire. In direct contrast to apathy, desire is defined as solicitous behavior aimed at future reinforcement (whereas apathy acts to the contrary). The term derives from the Greek prefix *a-*

(without) and *pathos* (feeling), which collectively designate an absence of passion or desire. Indeed, apathy has facetiously been described as the "root cause of nothing." Helen Keller further writes: "Science may have found a cure for most evils, but it has found no remedy for the worst of them all: the apathy of human beings." In this latter respect, the personal authority apathetically fails to act in a solicitous fashion, wherein prompting the punitive withholding of reinforcement by the personal follower figure.

522 – SPITE

The latter follower role is alternately defined in terms of a *spiteful* withholding of rewards, wherein punishing the apathetic treatment of the personal authority figure. Its modern spelling derives from the Old French *despit*, from the Latin *despectus*, (to despise): from *de-* (down) and *specere* (to look). It is traditionally defined as the tendency to frustrate or thwart, as in a grudging expression of ill will. This punitive expression of spitefulness may take many forms, such as suggested in the popular expression: "Cut off one's nose to *spite* one's face" (in essence, acting in anger so as to cause harm to oneself). Accordingly, spite represents the chief moral antithesis of approval, spitefully punishing (rather than rewarding) the apathetic tendencies of the personal authority figure. Indeed, English essayist, Alexander Pope penned the telling expression "By favor or by spite" (suggesting the contrast linking the two).

This reciprocal interplay of apathy/spite further sets the stage for the remaining group/spiritual levels within the hierarchy of defect. The preliminary *apathy* perspective of the personal authority, in turn, sets the stage for *foolishness* expressed by the group authority, culminating in the *vulgarity* perspective specific to the spiritual authority figure. Furthermore, the *spitefulness* expressed by the personal follower, in turn, prompts the *gluttony* perspective of the group representative, culminating in the *avarice* expressed by the spiritual disciple figure. This additional group/spiritual domain, based in apathy/spite, is further described in the first part of this chapter, beginning with an in-depth examination of foolishness.

532 – FOOLISHNESS

As the chief moral antithesis of dignity, *foolishness* is generally defined as an unnerving lack of common sense. This traditional connotation is further suggested in the Old Testament quotation: "folly is set in great dignity" (Ecclesiastes 10:6). Its modern spelling derives from the Late Latin *follus* (foolish), from the Latin *follis* (a pair of bellows, a windbag): wherein alluding to the puffed cheeks (and hot air) of the buffoon. One of the most distinctive symbolisms of foolishness concerns the familiar role of the court jester, a comedic parody on the pomp and circumstance of royal privilege. Certainly no royal entourage was complete without the colorful antics of the court jester: his jocularity played so convincingly in his gaudy, jangling, harlequin suit. The joker's manifest lack of respectfulness was carefully played-off with humorous banter, his foolish antics providing the perfect "foil" for the dignified demeanor of the royal monarch. Curiously, more than a few court jesters literally "lost their heads" over their assignments, suggesting the limitations of humor for disguising the more salient aspects of the vices.

This humorous context of foolishness is particularly evident in the exaggerated tradition of April Fools Day, a holiday where all dignity is temporarily cast aside in favor of a frenzy of foolish prank-playing. This tradition dates back to the 16th century, when New Years Day was originally celebrated on March 25th, launching a weeklong celebration culminating on April 1st. In 1564, King Charles switched the observance of New Years to its modern date. Those resisting the change found themselves the victim to numerous pranks and jokes on April 1st. According to this foolish context, the practical joker fabricates a deceptive air of respectability prior to exposing the more devious aspects of his ruse, as suggestive of the dual interplay linking both virtue and vice.

542 – GLUTTONY

The preceding foolishness example, in turn, sets the stage for the gluttony perspective expressed by the group follower figure. The group representative *gluttonously* acts in a spiteful fashion, wherein punishing the foolishly-apathetic treatment of the group authority figure. As the chief moral antithesis of temperance, gluttony is traditionally defined as the intemperate consumption of food, alcohol (or other sensual pleasure). Its modern spelling derives from the Latin *glutto* (glutton), from *glutire* (to devour). The societal downside for this vice was frequently overlooked during the licentious and affluent times of the late Roman Empire. Indeed, the general inclusion of the vomitorium at the standard Roman banquet ensured a degree of sensual consumption far in excess of the nutritional requirements of the participants. Comus (the Roman god of joy and mirth) was often depicted as drunk and languid with respect to the traditional banquet setting.

These classical connotations further reflect gluttony's traditional condemnation during the Christian era. Throughout the Middle Ages, gluttony was condemned as perhaps the most dangerous of the Seven Deadly Sins. The tight-knit set of loyalties comprising the medieval feudal system certainly specified such a drastic outlook, with any tendency towards personal greed menacing the collective welfare of such an agrarian form of social structure. Selfish activities were particularly frowned upon, as witnessed in the harsh punishments meted out to poachers infringing upon the bounty of the noble's forest estates. The sensual excesses of the classical period (exemplified by the banquet example) must have appeared completely at odds with the devoutly virtuous strictures of the day.

According to the Roman excesses of the banquet, the glutton typically assumed the role of the group representative, his jaded tastes resulting in gluttonous rituals aimed at achieving the elusive thrill of satisfaction. Although this bulimic purging might have seemed methodical in its madness, such greedy tendencies demanded a much greater economic sacrifice from society as a whole. This senseless waste of nutritional resources was more broadly viewed as a travesty by the more reserved classes of Rome, a condition directly underscoring the spiteful qualities of gluttony (in contrast to its virtuous counterpart in temperance).

552 – VULGARITY

The completed description of the group realm of defect (foolishness/gluttony), in turn, sets the stage for the remaining spiritual counterparts: beginning with the *vulgarity* perspective of the spiritual authority figure. As the chief spiritual

The Cardinal Vice of Gluttony: Detail from a Tableau of the Seven Deadly Sins
Table-Top Painting by Hieronymus Bosch (1450-1516) – Reproduced Courtesy Prado Museum

analogue of foolishness, vulgarity rates current consideration as the moral antithesis of civility. Its modern spelling derives from the Latin *vulgaris*, from *vulgus* or *volgus* (of the common people). This originally neutral connotation eventually acquired negative overtones, as reflective of a lack of culture, taste, or refinement. In terms of the current discussion, only the latter connotation of coarseness or crudeness rates further consideration in the ongoing discussion of vulgarity.

In fitting contrast to vulgarity, civility alternately encourages social harmony, wherein circumventing the frictions accompanying vulgar breaches of etiquette. In keeping with the principles of the Golden Rule, civility proves effective only when a majority of the citizenry complies. Widespread cheating generally leads to chaos, such as encountered in the disturbing phenomenon of "road rage." Although custom and tradition tend to facilitate social stability, such rigid formalism can sometimes lead to misunderstandings. Indeed, the modern trend towards informality is often mistaken for rudeness. Radical individualism may similarly be interpreted as poor taste, as in rebellion against social conformity. This greater degree of social freedom further impacts self-discipline and respect for authority. Accordingly, the disturbing trend towards tabloidism,

raucous politics, and licentiousness proves indicative of this salient trend towards vulgarity.

Perhaps the most telling issue in this regard concerns the rebellious nature of youth. Each new generation embraces a fresh style of attire and conduct meant to evoke a rebellious reaction on the part of the establishment. The youth generation narrowly views parental authority as rejecting any fledgling attempts at independence, often leading to a drastically altered appearance. The rebellious youth generally finds solace only in the company of a similarly inclined peer group, their shared value platform providing a common insurgent rallying point. This desire to foment nonconformity provokes a particularly strong establishment perspective, leaving any affiliated judgement of *vulgarity* to the discretion of the public at large. Indeed, it is precisely this *universality* of judgement that defines vulgarity as indicative of the spiritual authority perspective, wherein transcending the more basic partisan concerns of the group for the much broader moralistic perspective.

562 – AVARICE

As the chief moral antithesis of charity, *avarice* represents the main spiritual variation on the group theme of gluttony. Avarice represents the selfish withholding of reinforcement, whereby punitively targeting the foolishly-vulgar treatment of the spiritual authority figure. Its modern spelling derives from the Latin *avaritia* (avarice), from *avere* (to wish, to desire). Consistent with its related connotation of greed, avarice denotes a self-centered pursuit of wealth: in contrast to its benevolent bestowal (as in charity). The Bible specifically personifies avarice as Mammon, the demon spirit of wealth and greed (from the Aramaic term for riches). According to Middle Eastern tradition, the term originally referred to the rich outpouring of milk from the inexhaustible breasts (mammae) of the chief fertility goddess. The Babylonians worshipped her as Mami or Mammitu (mother), while related Sumerian texts refer to her as Mammetun (Mother of Destinies).

According to the New Testament Sermon on the Mount, Christ sagely states that mankind cannot serve both God and Mammon: equating worldly wealth with ungodliness. Contrary to the wording of the popular maxim, it is the *love* of money (and not money itself) that is the root of all evil. Mammon eventually came to symbolize a false god with powers hostile to the Christian tradition. Occult lore describes Mammon as one of the fallen angels ruling over Hell, sometimes referred to as the Prince of Tempters. His archdemon status eventually led to an identification with Lucifer, Beelzebub, and Satan. As the demon of avarice, Mammon holds the throne of this world, as asserted by St. Francesca in one of her 93 Visions. Weyer facetiously referred to Mammon as Hell's ambassador to England, a satirical reference to the ruthless nature of British commercialism.

THE FUTURE-DIRECTED REALM OF DEFECT BASED UPON MALICE / INDIFFERENCE

The completed description of the vices based upon apathy/spite further sets the stage for the remaining trend based upon malice/indifference. This latter format alternately specifies the malicious withholding of leniency in response to the indifferent treatment of the personal authority figure. In particular, this distinctive interplay of authority and follower roles formally mirrors the preceding format, where rewards are spitefully withheld in response to apathetic types of behavior.

513 – INDIFFERENCE

As the chief moral antithesis of worry, *indifference* remains consistent with the personal authority perspective, wherein indifferently refusing to act submissively. Its modern spelling derives from the Latin *indifferens*, from *in-* (not) and *differre*: the compound of *dif-* (apart) and *ferre* (to bear). In *Timon of Athens* (Act II, Scene 2) Shakespeare describes indifference as: "T'is lack of kindly warmth." George Bernard Shaw similarly writes: "The worst sin towards our fellow creatures is not to hate them, but to be *indifferent* to them: that's the essence of inhumanity." Essayist Juan Montalvo further writes: "There is nothing harder than the softness of indifference."

523 – MALICE

This indifferent refusal to act submissively, in turn, prompts a punitive sense of maliciousness on the part of the personal follower. Its modern spelling derives from the Latin *malitia*, from *malus* (evil, illness). It, accordingly, implies deep-seated feelings of dislike or ill will. In his dialogue *Phaedrus*, Plato specifically refers to this vice as "biting" malice. In *The Twelfth Night* (Act I, Scene 5) Shakespeare alludes to the "very fangs of malice," whereas *Titus Andronicus* refers to a "venomous" malice. Within a related legal context, malice is generally defined as: "that state of mind predisposed to commit an unlawful act." This theme is further seen in the legal notion of malice *prepens* (malice aforethought): the premeditated intent to commit an unlawful act.

This dual interplay of malice/indifference, in turn, sets the stage for the remaining group/spiritual levels within the power hierarchy. For instance, the *indifference* expressed by the personal authority, in turn, prompts the *capriciousness* of the group authority, culminating in the *cruelty* expressed by the spiritual authority figure. Furthermore, the *malice* of the personal follower gives way to the *cowardice* of the group representative, culminating in the *antagonism* expressed by the spiritual disciple. The remainder of the current chapter systematically outlines this distinctive group/spiritual sphere of defect: beginning with the group sequence of capriciousness/cowardice, followed by the spiritual domain of cruelty/antagonism.

533 – CAPRICIOUSNESS

As the chief moral antithesis of integrity, *capriciousness* is traditionally defined as a fickle change in disposition often without rhyme or reason. Its modern spelling derives from the Latin *caper* (a goat), also the basis for the English verb *caper* (to jump erratically like a goat). In this latter respect, capriciousness suggests an unexpected or random form of activity similar to the frisky antics of the mountain goat. In a related motivational sense, capriciousness implies a fickle change of motive or intent, often in an unpredictable fashion. The related musical term *capriccio* refers to compositions of a free-form nature, an endeavor completely at odds with established musical convention.

Its general connotations to a group sphere of influence prove equally significant, a feature often seen in the downfall of oppressive political regimes. For instance, the economic hardships leading up to the French Revolution were further compounded by widespread crop failures across the region, resulting in a scarcity of basic staples such as bread. Queen Marie Antoinette's capricious statement: "Let them eat cake," further fueled the outrage of the downtrodden peasants, leading to bloody revolt on a grand scale (as well as Marie's execution on the guillotine).

543 – COWARDICE

The capricious sense of indifference expressed by the group authority figure further sets the stage for the cowardly sense of malice characterizing the group follower perspective. Indeed, this contemptible trend towards cowardice is only truly comprehensible within precisely such a group follower context. The group representative's cowardly refusal to act leniently stands in firm contrast to the fortitudinous sense of concern characterizing the virtuous perspective. Cowardice is traditionally defined as the lack of fortitude or courage, particularly that relating to life or limb. Its modern spelling derives from the Latin *cauda* (tail) and *-ard* (a limiting suffix): literally "short-tailed" (originally an epithet for the timid hare). In medieval heraldry, cowardice is further symbolized as a frightened dog with its tail between its legs.

According to classical mythology, this vice was traditionally associated with Venus Murtia, a variation on her role as goddess of love. The surname Murtia specifically reflected her fondness for the perpetually blooming myrtle tree. Indeed, a large grove of myrtle trees was prominently featured in front of her chapel at the foot of the Aventine Hill. As the patroness of laziness and cowardice, statues celebrating this curiously contradictory aspect of Venus were purposely allowed to accumulate a layering of moss (signifying hesitancy or inactivity): as evident in the common saying, "a rolling stone gathers no moss."

This timid aspect of cowardice actually represents only part of the total picture, balanced in a more active sense by the malicious variant practiced by the bully/hoodlum. The schoolyard bully that terrorizes his classmates for their lunch money is as much a coward as those he intimidates. Such boldface aggression is primarily risked only out of a false sense of immunity from punishment. The bully's cowardly sense of malice often mirrors his own lack of lenient treatment; namely, "My parents cut my allowance, so I'll take yours!"

This willful sense of cowardice also extends to the military sphere of influence, where a fortitudinous sense of concern for one's duties is abandoned altogether (as when launched into a cowardly retreat). This cowardly desertion of one's post is a common fear amongst many new recruits, wherein shirking responsibility to one's unit as well as the very noble aims of the campaign. This potential for cowardice was particularly apparent during the Civil War, where "green-horn" recruits abandoned all pretense of bravery when faced with the true horrors of war: as dramatized in Steven Crane's stirring novel, *The Red Badge of Courage*.

553 – CRUELTY

The completed description of the group sequence of vices further sets the stage for the remaining spiritual domain within the power hierarchy, as reflected in the capricious sense of *cruelty* expressed by the spiritual authority figure. Its modern spelling derives from the Latin *crudelis*, from *crudis* (raw): suggesting a predilection for inflicting pain or suffering upon others. Cruelty is traditionally symbolized as the fabled Basilisk serpent, a fierce dragon with fiery breath (and fearsome looks) said to have the power to kill. In the related field of medieval heraldry, cruelty is personified as the stealthy leopard, the hulking vulture, or cunning wolf. These fearsome overtones prove equally applicable to the realm of international warfare, as in the innumerable campaigns of military conquest. Cruelty has been employed as a crucial military tactic, instilling terror in all that would resist the wave of conquest.

The most ruthless commander in this regard was Ghengis Khan, who deliberately employed a cruel policy of annihilation. Cities that resisted his demands were brutally savaged as a fitting example for all to follow. Entire urban populations were slaughtered without mercy. Any survivors were marched ahead of advancing Mongol armies as human shields, a clever defense against preemptive attacks. Cities that surrendered without resistance were generally spared, their citizens merely enslaved. Indeed, many cities preemptively surrendered rather than risk the prospects of a prolonged siege. This cruel tactic of terror eventually proved instrumental in subjugating Asian territories ranging from Persia to Northern China. Ghengis' descendents further expanded his empire during the 13th century across a span ranging from Eastern Europe to Southern China. These cruel tactics survive even to our modern age as the ruthless strategy of "reprisals of war," retribution intended to inflict equal or greater casualties upon the enemy. This brutal tactic was the stock-in-trade for Nazi Occupation of World War II, as evident in the vicious slaughter of civilians towards the end of the war: a grim testimony to the cruel tactics promoted by the Nazi regime.

563 – ANTAGONISM

In accordance with the preceding wartime examples, cruelty primarily represents a universal style of power leverage within the realm of defect. The Nazis speciously imagined themselves as "master race" for the entire world, a delusion definitely consistent with such a twisted cruelty perspective. This capricious sense of cruelty, in turn, prompts the subsequent *antagonism* perspective of the spiritual disciple figure. Antagonism is provisionally defined as the chief moral antithesis of decency. Unlike the first three theological virtues, which were paired with more definitive moral opposites, the greater degree of generality associated with decency would appear to obscure any exclusive antonym. The traditions associated with antagonism certainly fit the bill in this regard; namely, a willful sense of rivalry or opposition in a social setting.

The term derives from the Greek *antagonistes* (an opponent), from *anti-* (against) and *agon* (contest). Indeed, the latter root-stem chiefly refers to an assembly (the *agonia*): a gathering dedicated to athletic games/contests. The modern-day Olympic Games owe a clear debt to this classical tradition: particularly the wrestling, running, and boxing events. The favored contender in the agonia was termed the *agonistes* in reference to the assembly format of the contest. The rival of the agonistes was termed the *antagonistes*, the prefix *anti-* clearly reflecting the adversarial

nature of the proceedings. In keeping with these competitive overtones, the ancient tournaments were generally organized as open invitationals, where only the fittest athletes competed from across the land. Any underlying feelings of malice were strongly tempered by the festive spirit of the proceedings, although the desperate quest to avoid defeat certainly figured prominently in the mental outlook of the athlete. A wide assortment of antagonistic strategies (such as bluffing or psyching-out one's opponent) figured prominently in the individual events, much as is commonly seen today with respect to wrestling and boxing. This highly contentious perspective was strongly tempered by the codes of fair play and sportsmanship, providing a fitting counterpoint to the highly antagonistic nature of the proceedings.

In conclusion, the completed description of the vices of defect spanning the personal, group, and spiritual levels, in turn, sets the stage for the remaining humanitarian and transcendental levels within the power hierarchy. In contrast to the purely organizational status of the first three levels, the final two levels are alternately defined as purely abstract styles of power maneuvers. The humanitarian domain is specified through the abstract addition of "historical" time, whereas the transcendental realm makes an appeal to the notion of pure transcendence.

The profoundly abstract nature of these final two levels is further reflected in the respective groupings of vices. These darker themes all share a pronounced significance within the field of ethical inquiry: as the respective sampling of evil, cunning, hatred, belligerence etc. collectively serve to indicate. Indeed, the vices associated with these final two levels virtually beg to be listed together; as in the ecumenical vices (wrath-tyranny-persecution-oppression), the moralistic vices (evil-cunning-ugliness-hypocrisy), the humanistic vices (anger-hatred-prejudice-belligerence), and the mystical vices (iniquity-turpitude-abomination-perdition). These final two authority levels come replete with a wealth of historical documentation spanning both the classical and contemporary traditions. The corresponding description of this additional set of vices is now launched with an in-depth examination of the humanitarian authority level in concert with the affiliated listings of ecumenical and moralistic vices.

13

THE HUMANITARIAN DOMAIN OF DEFECT

The humanitarian authority perspective represents a unique addition to the orderly progression of the power hierarchy, distinguished from all previous levels in terms of the first truly abstract power maneuver. Not an organizational power maneuver (per sé), rather it represents a more advanced variation on the more basic spiritual perspective modified through the abstract addition of historical time. Humanitarian authority, accordingly, speaks for all generations of mankind, not just the current one, a theme equally applicable to the darker realm of the vices.

The virtuous humanitarian realm was initially defined through the traditions of the ecumenical ideals; namely, grace, free will, magnanimity, and equanimity. Although this grouping scarcely exhibits the pedigree of many of the other listings of virtues, its individual terms offer a clear moral precedent in their own right. Their extreme level of abstraction effectively ensures a prominent place in Christian theology: themes that have resounded in the enduring spirit of the ecumenical councils that defended, fortified, and preserved the unity of faith. This ecumenical spirit survives to our modern age with respect to the World Council of Churches, a broad coalition of Protestant denominations dedicated to service and witness to the community.

This enduring ecumenical spirit offers further crucial insights into the darker prerequisites of the humanitarian authority perspective; namely, that relating to *apostasy* (literally a falling away). This contrasting sense of apostasy represents the key moral antithesis of the spirit of ecumenism; namely, the failure to acknowledge the legitimacy of such enduring humanitarian issues. In particular, apostasy represents the darker counterpart of organized spirituality, effectively questioning any enduring humanitarian significance therein.

According to this dualistic interpretation, the virtuous focus of the ecumenical ideals is directly countered (point-for-point) with the respective listing of ecumenical vices (wrath-tyranny-persecution-oppression). Perhaps no other grouping of vices examined to date exhibits such a clear-cut degree of conceptual affinity across the board. Indeed, this cohesive grouping might just as easily have been termed the "sins of apostasy" consistent with the antithetical role sin plays in relation to the authority ideals. The prodigal sense of *wrathfulness* expressed by the humanitarian authority figure directly counteracts any provident sense of gracefulness. Similarly, one's *tyrannical* sense of enslavement directly opposes any libertarian sense of free will. Furthermore, the authority figure's vulgar sense of *oppressiveness* makes a fitting counterpoint to any civil sense of magnanimity. Finally, one's cruel sense of *persecution* effectively contradicts any austere sense of equanimity. The remainder of the current chapter presents an in-depth examination of the specific literary traditions for each of the ecumenical vices, as further validated through the respective religious and historical precedents.

570 – WRATH

The first of the ecumenical vices, *wrathfulness*, is traditionally defined as the chief moral antonym of grace. Its modern spelling derives from the Anglo-Saxon *wrath* (intense anger), the past tense of *writhan* (to writhe). In a more contemporary sense, it refers to an extreme degree of rage or fury in keeping with its enduring humanitarian perspective. During the classical era, the wrathfulness of the nature gods conveniently explained the inevitable occurrence of earthquakes, volcanic eruptions, or tidal waves. Old Testament accounts of the destruction of Sodom and Gomorrah further attest to wrath's enduring significance in the Judeo-Christian tradition. Beginning with Noah and the Flood, mankind remained in jeopardy of the wrath of God, particularly in circumstances when remorse for sinfulness was lacking. The Lord freely bestowed His wrathfulness upon the egregious evildoer, in fitting contrast to the goodness and mercy He reserved for the faithful. As essentially a human passion, however, wrath can only metaphorically be ascribed to the Lord: rationalized primarily in terms of God's overriding sense of love irrespective of the severity of His punishments.

This enduring sense of wrathfulness rates far less significance in the New Testament consistent with the charitable precepts so eloquently professed by Jesus Christ. The final apocalyptic Book of Revelation, however, resurrects many of the traditional trappings of divine wrathfulness, particularly the metaphorical imagery specific to the Old Testament. Most prominent of these is the "grapes of wrath" metaphor described in the Chapter 14 of the Book of Revelation. According to this stirring scriptural passage, the Apostle John describes in great detail the great winepress of the wrath of the Lord. This metaphor directly refers to the Day of Final Judgement, when the Lord returns to reap the great spiritual harvest of the earth. Christ is depicted descending upon a lofty cloud wielding a great sickle with which he harvests the innumerable clusters of grapes (souls) from the "vine of life" covering the earth. This final bounty is then cast into the Lord's great winepress from which a torrent of juice (blood) is said to flow to a considerable depth.

According to this scriptural interpretation, wrathfulness represents the humanitarian counterpart of the prodigality maneuver expressed by the spiritual authority figure, in turn, countering the insurgent-betrayal expressed by the spiritual disciple. In such strictly metaphorical terms, the Lord passes final judgement upon the unrighteous, freely venting His wrath upon all that scorned commitment to His dictates. John (3:36) similarly states: "He that believeth in the Son hath everlasting life: and he that believeth not in the Son shall not see life, but the *wrath* of God abideth upon him."

571 – TYRANNY

Any discussion of wrathfulness must necessarily remain incomplete without mention of the related theme of *tyranny*. As the chief moral antithesis of free will, tyranny extends the more immediate sense of slavery into a humanitarian sphere of influence. Tyranny is traditionally defined as absolute political rule unfettered by the restrictions of law or constitution. It is generally motivated out of a personal sense of greed, to the necessary detriment of the public good. Its modern spelling derives from the Greek *tyrannos* (the rule of a lord or tyrant). This vice is traditionally personified as a matronly woman adorned with an iron crown: also wielding a sword, chains, and a yoke. Aristotle specifically disparages tyranny as the opposite of true kingship. Its overthrow is often justified, although Aquinas argues that the transition of power should be less damaging than the tribulations of the preexisting tyranny.

The most widely cited example of tyranny in the classical world concerns the reign of the Thirty Tyrants, a council appointed by the Spartans to rule over Athens following the Pelloponesian War. Athens had been soundly defeated by Sparta, a rival city-state, yet failed to fully comply with the stringent terms of surrender; namely, the demolition of the fortifications surrounding Athens. Athens was quickly accused of breaking the peace, only escaping further drastic measures by agreeing to a radical overhaul of its governing body. The Council of Thirty was hastily convened in the summer of 404 BCE, quickly adopting a pro-Spartan form of government. The council soon sought to eliminate all opposition to its new-found power status, executing or exiling many prominent citizens in the process. Although war reparations necessitated some degree of economic sacrifice, the council's greed eventually led to unprecedented looting and pillaging. This extreme sense of tyranny eventually led to the sound defeat of the Council of Thirty less than a year after its precipitous rise to power. Such a tenuous hold on arbitrary power is generally the rule rather than the exception: for those that live by the sword are often doomed to die by the sword.

573 – PERSECUTION

The completed description of wrath and tyranny, in turn, sets the stage for a description of the remaining ecumenical vices of persecution and oppression. As the chief moral counterpoints of magnanimity and equanimity, both persecution and oppression share a similar convergence of meaning: collectively deriving from the Latin *opprimere* (to press against) and *persecutus* (to pursue). Although these two darker themes are frequently used interchangeably in common usage, enough finer distinctions remain to warrant separate placement within the hierarchy of the vices. For instance, persecution suggests a more deliberate sense of cruelty than oppression, as witnessed in the savage sequence of persecutions undertaken against the early Christians. Oppression, in contrast, represents a more passive style of aggression, an aspect alternately encountered during the great purges of history (such as the Spanish Inquisition).

In the case of the Roman persecutions, the early Christians were not particularly concerned with humanitarian themes, an issue precluded by the speedy anticipated return of Jesus Christ. The Romans, in contrast, were the unrivaled humanitarian standard-bearers of their time, maintaining a stable rule of law (by force) throughout the Mediterranean realm. The secretive tendencies of the early Christians certainly cut against the grain of Roman sensibility: particularly their avoidance of civic affairs, public games, and military service. The Christian condemnation of the prevailing pagan order must have surely aroused fears of revolution amongst the Roman gentry. The most damning charge against the early Christians concerned their refusal to submit to the worship of the state-sanctioned gods: in particular, the professed divinity of the emperor. Such a heretical act of treason was considered a capital offense in most cases.

The Christians unyielding stance brought on such harsh punitive measures legitimized through the Emperor's appeal to a broad humanitarian power base. The first widespread persecution against the Christians was initiated by the Emperor Nero in 64 CE as part of his devious plan to assign blame for the Great Fire of Rome. Indeed, Christianity eventually was classified as a capital offense, although a pardon could be gained by recanting. Although Nero's campaign of terror was limited in scope in comparison to later persecutions, his precedent continued unmercifully for centuries to follow. This great trial of persecution served to forge the character of the Catholic religion, ultimately elevated to the lofty status of official religion of the Roman Empire.

572 – OPPRESSION

The eventual decline of the Western Roman Empire thrust the fledgling Church into the unenviable position of assuming many of the Empire's institutional functions. In curious historical parallels, the Catholic Church grew increasingly intolerant to heresy during the Middle Ages, falling into the same trap that had plagued its predecessor: namely, resorting to organized violence to suppress heresy within its ranks. During these relatively more enlightened times, this suppression was generally achieved through *oppressive* tactics, with heretics forced to either recant or flee such circumstances. The Latin root *opprimere*

(to press against) suggests precisely such a cruel use of force for pressuring compliance, as particularly evident during the infamous Spanish Inquisition. This oppressive historical precedent traces its origins to the Latin *inquiro* (to inquire into), indicative of the Church's practice of actively seeking out heretics over and beyond the customary investigation of accusations.

At the onset of the Inquisition, Spain was unique placed among the kingdoms of Western Europe in terms of its considerable cultural diversity: most notably, the burgeoning Jewish and Moorish contingents. The Jews initially enjoyed considerable economic prosperity throughout the region, constituting an educated elite much in demand for administrative positions. The ruling Catholic elite, however, grew increasingly envious of the wealthy Jews, tacitly promoting the moral righteousness fueling the Inquisition. The considerable wealth of the Jews was targeted first, followed by a moral backlash against the Moors. The only recourse to enforced baptism was permanent exile, wherein prompting many nominal converts to Christianity.

In 1492, the first Grand Inquisitor, Dominican monk Tomas de Torquemada persuaded the Catholic royalty to expel the Jewish population, resulting in a mass-exodus estimated at 70,000 strong. In 1502, the even larger Moorish contingent was added to the purge. Those attempting to remain fell victim to a cruel assortment of tactics: including torture, execution, and imprisonment. During Torquemada's reign of terror, an estimated *2,000* heretics were publicly burned at the stake. Life imprisonment was reserved for those faint-hearted souls that confessed under torture or recanted to escape execution. Surviving family members, in turn, suffered the confiscation of all common property. Confiscation was also imposed upon those fleeing the death sentence, as well as those caught dealing in the possessions of heretics, funds legally considered the property of the Church. These proceeds were further earmarked to defray the expenses of the Inquisition, paying particularly handsome dividends to those in positions of high authority.

THE MORALISTIC VICES: THE SCOURGE OF THE HUMANITARIAN PERSPECTIVE

In conclusion, the completed description of the ecumenical vices provided a fitting counterpoint to the affiliated listing of ecumenical ideals. This cohesive grouping of vices proved particularly comprehensive in scope, an outcome directly in keeping with their enduring humanitarian significance. Indeed, this traditional grouping remains a powerful influence even in our modern age, particularly for those troubled regions of the world that continue to be ruled by ruthless dictators. Even an authority perspective as abstract as the humanitarian, however, must (by definition) be susceptible to its own unique form of follower countermaneuver: in this case, that expressed by the representative member of humanity.

The humanitarian follower perspective (also known as the representative member of humanity role) has much to offer with respect to the ongoing discussion of the vices. The power dynamics characterizing this more advanced follower perspective share much in common with the subordinate follower levels that it supersedes. More properly termed the philosopher's maneuver, this tactic invokes the prestige of speaking as a representative for all of humanity. Indeed, this enduring focus (in a virtuous sense) is further reflected in the corresponding listing of classical Greek values (beauty-truth-goodness-wisdom). These classical values formally perpetuate the ethical trends previously established for the cardinal/theological virtues, only now invoking the more versatile and eclectic concept of value.

This enduring theme of eclecticism, in turn, offers clues towards identifying the remaining listing of the humanitarian vices; namely, the contrasting realm of the *moralistic* vices (evil-cunning-ugliness-hypocrisy. According to this darker range of perspectives, *evil* makes a fitting contrast to goodness, whereas *cunning* represents the darker counterpart of wisdom. Furthermore, *ugliness* represents the chief moral opposite of beauty, whereas *hypocrisy* suggests the darker counterpart of truth. Indeed, this dual sequence of terms is further verified within the expanded context of the corresponding literary traditions.

582 – EVIL

Of any of the themes examined to date, *evil* reigns supreme as the darker emblem of the vices. Whereas goodness was celebrated as the epitome of the values, so its antonym (evil) rates equal significance within the corresponding realm of the vices. Evil, accordingly, is defined as that which is morally corrupt or injurious to individual wellbeing. Nowhere is this formulation more readily evident than in the widespread superstition of the "evil eye." This evil stare was said to turn to stone, strike dead, or cause injury to all caught within its glance. Classical mythology definitely figures prominently in the origins of this superstition, particularly that relating to the serpent-

haired monster, Medusa. This hideous creature was said to possess the power to turn to stone all that beheld her hypnotic gaze. The Latin equivalent of the evil eye, the Jettatura, was a theme widespread throughout the Mediterranean world. As late as the Inquisition, medieval judges so feared the evil eye that they forced accused witches to enter the courtroom backwards in order to preserve the advantage of the first glance.

In terms of this broader sense of the term, evil appears to encompass a much wider range of meaning than its singular placement within the power hierarchy would seem to warrant. This extreme degree of generality, however, was also encountered with respect to goodness consistent with its pivotal role in ethical deliberations. Accordingly, evil is similarly restricted to its most basic motivational context; namely, those punitive dictates directly in keeping with such a grand humanitarian perspective.

The Judeo-Christian tradition, with its enduring emphasis on the conflict between good and evil, abounds with many examples of this restricted sense of evil. Take, for example, the Old Testament account of the temptation of Adam and Eve. According to the Book of Genesis, Adam and Eve were created as the first man and woman on earth, wherein setting the tone for the grand humanitarian time-scale of this passage. Their garden paradise was idyllic in every respect save the divine directive to abstain from eating the fruit from the Tree of Good and Evil. All was peaceful until the Devil entered the garden, disguised as a serpent in order to tempt the impressionable Eve.

The serpent certainly makes a fitting symbol of evil: sleek and colorful at first glance, although deadly to the uninitiated. Indeed, the Devil had long been disparaged as the chief adversary of God's goodness in the Old Testament. In retaliation for his disgraceful banishment from Heaven, the Devil sought to disrupt the peace of Paradise, sowing the seeds of disobedience by tempting mankind to eat of the forbidden fruit. The Devil first proceeded to tempt Eve, pretending to act rewardingly by suggesting the supreme powers that could be gained by taking his advice. The impressionable Eve readily imitated the Devil's rebellious attitude, in turn, persuading Adam to join in her fateful act of consumption. They soon realized that they were the brunt of the Devil's trickery, an act of disobedience sure to warrant the righteous wrath of the Lord. The Devil had deviously exploited Adam and Eve in his enduring power struggle against the Lord (the true humanitarian authority in this example). The Devil continued his wicked vendetta upon the earth willfully aware of the evil consequences of his trickery upon God's human experiment. As the supreme personification of evil, the Devil makes a supreme counterpoint to God's bountiful goodness, a lesson still relevant to our modern age.

583 – CUNNING

Any formal description of evil must necessarily remain incomplete without mention of the related theme of *cunning*. Cunning represents the chief moral antonym of wisdom, just as evil was previously contrasted to goodness. Its modern spelling derives from the Anglo-Saxon *cunnian* (to try or test). Although cunning originally denoted a sense of skillfulness or shrewdness, it eventually became invested with the more devious connotations of deception, slyness, or craftiness. For brevity's sake, only the latter negative connotations will further be addressed within the current humanitarian context of defect.

Perhaps the most widely celebrated example of cunning concerns the enduring tale of the Trojan Horse. According to Homer's *Iliad*, a united Greek force besieged the ancient city of Troy in an attempt to free the captive Queen Helen of Sparta. The Greeks were said to have raised a fleet of over *1,000* ships, although the fortifications of Troy proved equally as formidable. The great heroes of the Greeks (Ajax and Achilles) battled against their Trojan counterparts (Hector and Aeneas), although with mixed results. Finally, Odysseus proposed a cunning ruse for circumventing the impenetrable defenses of the city, advocating the construction a colossal wooden figure of a horse secretly concealing a contingent of soldiers. When the Greek fleet sailed deceptively out of sight, the Trojans joyously emerged to accept the wooden horse as a victory token, favoring that it be drawn within the city walls. Among the cautious was Cassandra, whose warnings of doom were ignored due to a curse making her predictions unbelievable to others. "Beware of Greeks bearing gifts" proclaimed Laocoon, although his warning was cut short by the appearance of a pair of giant serpents that crushed him to death. The Trojans mistakenly viewed this as a favorable sign, drawing the horse into the city in celebration of their lengthy ordeal. The Greek soldiers later emerged in the dead of night, throwing open the city gates to the returning fleet, resulting in the total devastation and sack of the city.

Similar to the case previously established for evil, cunning clearly represents a vice in the punitive tradition, wherein expanding upon the antagonistic perspective of the spiritual disciple figure. According to the Trojan Horse example, the frustrated Greeks assumed precisely such a punitive role, pretending to submit to defeat (via the Trojan Horse), although actually disguising quite antagonistic directives. The Trojans had cruelly taunted the Greeks, refusing to return the captive Queen Helen. In a last-ditch effort, the Greeks pinned their hopes on the trickery of the Trojan Horse. By the time the Trojans discovered the folly of their pretensions, the Greeks had already breached the walls of the city, suffering a fitting fate at the hands of the vengeful Greeks.

580 – UGLINESS

A third vice intimately associated with evil is the universal theme of *ugliness*. As the chief moral opposite of beauty, ugliness refers not so much to physical repulsion as to actions judged reprehensibly to be so. Its modern spelling derives from the Old Norse *uggligr* (dreadful), from *uggr* (fear). According to classical Greek mythology, the major gods and goddesses were depicted as beautiful or handsome, whereas demons or devils were described as hideous or ugly. This typical stereotype was curiously reversed in the case of Hephaestus (the Greek god of fire and metalwork). In contrast to the other Olympian gods, Hephaestus (also known as Vulcan by the Romans) was born both lame and homely to his otherwise impeccable parents Zeus and Hera. His left leg was shorter than his right, a handicap skillfully corrected through braces crafted from gold. He is traditionally depicted in the trademark undershirt and oval cap of the blacksmith, further wielding a hammer and tongs. He was twice thrown from heaven for offending the sensibilities of the gods, a fate similarly suffered by deformed infants of the era. Despite his uncomely appearance Hephaestus wed only the most beautiful of goddesses; namely, Aphrodite (the goddess of love) and Charis (one of the Graces).

This enduring theme of ugliness is further encountered in many later literary narratives: most notably, *Beauty and the Beast*, *The Phantom of the Opera*, *The Hunchback of Notre Dame*, etc. Perhaps the most telling in this regard, however, concerns Hans Christian Andersen's fanciful *Tale of the Ugly Duckling*. Although the chief characters of this fable all take animal form, its standard format clearly suggests the true moralistic overtones of the tale. The basic story line concerns the plight of a newborn duckling judged so ugly by its peers that it was persecuted unmercifully. Upon reaching maturity, it, ultimately, was delighted to discover it had been transformed into a gorgeous swan, assuming its rightful place of honor upon the lake. The more distressing aspects of the story certainly rate clear significance in the overall context of the vices, where the vile attributes of the ugly duckling were wrathfully despised by the rest of the brood.

The ugly duckling certainly rates the title role in this regard, betraying (in an ugly fashion) the aesthetic sensibilities of its peer group. In failing to meet the prevailing standards of beauty, the ugly duckling became the unfair target of scorn and derision within the group. This circumstance represents a complete reversal of the beauty contest format, where rewards are withheld rather than bestowed. The latter virtuous aspect emerges only towards the end of the story, where the duckling joyously discovers its newfound grace and beauty, accompanied by the approval it had so desperately been denied.

581 – HYPOCRISY

The final of the moralistic vices, *hypocrisy*, is generally defined as the chief moral antithesis of truth. Its modern spelling derives from the Greek *hypokrisis* (to feign or act a part), tracing its origins to the ancient Greek art form of the dramatic play. Early theatrical productions were composed of a chorus of roughly a dozen individuals, accompanied by a smaller number of actors for delivering the dialogue. The actors were respectively known the *hypokritai;* namely, those that respond to the chorus. Over time, this term gained somewhat of a metaphorical sense: as in putting-on a pretense. Hypocrisy, accordingly, is personified as a simpering ape hiding behind the stylized mask of an actor.

In this latter respect, hypocrisy is primarily defined as pretending to be what one is not, particularly in a pretense of sincerity. In Dante's *Inferno,* the hypocrite was condemned for all eternity to wear a brilliantly ornamented cloak lined with lead, metaphorically bearing the weight of sin (although disguised as virtue). This example bears many similarities to the notion of the "odor of sanctity," an expression extremely suggestive of an air of respectability. This expression grew out of a belief popular during the Middle Ages that

the bodies of saints exuded a sweet aroma following death. In our modern age, this theme is now associated with a more satirical sense, wherein equating sanctity with sanctimoniousness.

With respect to New Testament scripture, hypocrisy is a vice particularly associated with the Pharisees, a strict Jewish sect prominent during Christ's time. Their name derives from the Hebrew *perushim* (separatists), reflecting their disdain for gentile worldliness in favor of a strict adherence to religious principles. Such high-minded ideals were originally held in high esteem, although eventually extending to mere formality and ritualism. This ultimately led to a hypocritical preoccupation with appearances in terms of diet, apparel, and religious ceremony. Their self-professed claim to sacredness encouraged the overly pretentious judgement of others, contributing to a decline in popularity by the time of Christ.

Christ's harsh judgement of hypocritical formalism chafed directly at the Pharisees' extreme obsession with appearances. Not to be outdone, the Pharisees repeatedly employed various tactics to discredit Christ; pretending to act concerned while all the while plotting to trick him. As is typical with such forays into the realm of the vices, the Pharisees' mendacity consistently backfired on them, further fueling their righteous indignation. They might have better taken heed of Christ's insightful teachings on hypocrisy, wherein he states: "Judge not, that ye not be judged," also paraphrased as "people who live in glass houses shouldn't throw stones!"

In conclusion, the completed description of the moralistic vices effectively rounds out the stepwise description of the humanitarian realm of defect. The darker focus of the moralistic vices (evil-cunning-ugliness-hypocrisy) proves a fitting counterpoint to the affiliated listing of values (beauty-truth-goodness-wisdom). This humanitarian version of the realm of defect clearly represents the most abstract level of organizational permitted in terms of the principles of Set Theory. This very sense of the power of abstraction, however, serves as the basis for one final innovation in the perpetual power struggle; namely, that specifying the crowning transcendental level within the power hierarchy.

14

THE TRANSCENDENTAL REALM OF DEFECT

The issue of vices for the crowning transcendental level of the power hierarchy certainly proves enigmatic at first glance. As initially described in **Part I**, the transcendental authority regains the upper hand in the perpetual power struggle by surpassing the more routine sense of concreteness shared in common by all of the lower levels. This supreme perspective freely enters into the realm of pure intuition and imagination, forsaking the constraints of ordinary reality for the esoteric realm of pure abstraction. This profound sense of transcendence formally reflects a general humanistic theme; in particular, the Renaissance form so treasured in our modern age. The principles of humanism ring as true today as when they were first formulated, namely: man is the measure of all things, an enduring perspective that revels in the collective spirit underlying all human endeavors.

The respective complement of humanistic values (peace-love-tranquility-equality) formally verify the ethereal nature of the transcendental authority perspective, in turn, setting the stage for a discussion of the humanistic vices (anger-hatred-prejudice-belligerence). In contrast to the strictly positive prerequisites of the humanistic values, the corresponding realm of defect is alternately specified in terms of "nihilistic" principles. Indeed, whereas humanism celebrates the collective human spirit, the theme of *nihilism* alternately states that nothing in life has meaning, an existential lament with dire consequences to the individual and society as a whole. This nihilistic perspective builds directly upon the apostasy maneuver of the humanitarian authority, culminating in an existential state of negativistic alienation. Accordingly, the corresponding listing of humanistic vices might just as easily have been termed the "sins of nihilism," in direct reference to their general underlying theme.

The ethical parallels to the humanistic values certainly ring true at this juncture; namely, *anger*

represents a darker variation on tranquility, whereas *hatred* makes a similar contrast to love. A similar reciprocating pattern further holds true with respect to *prejudice*/equality and *belligerence*/peace. This intuitive style of complementary correspondence, in turn, is further verified within the expanded context of the corresponding literary traditions.

590 – ANGER

The first of the humanistic vices, *anger*, is traditionally defined as the chief moral antonym of tranquility, true to its more basic foundations in wrathfulness. Its modern spelling derives from the Old Norse *angr* (denoting distress or grief). Accordingly, the Teutonic peoples reverently equated the fury of nature with their fierce warrior-god Thor: celebrated for his enchanted hammer, the Mjolnir (Destroyer). Old Norse legends describe Thor as a powerful bearded warrior sporting iron gauntlets for gripping the shaft of his mighty hammer. In figurative allusion to a lightning bolt, the hammer was magically said to return to Thor each time it was thrown. The clap of thunder was similarly explained as the violent impact of Thor's lightning-quick hammer. Related parallels occur throughout classical mythology: in particular, the lightning bolts issuing from the *aegis* (or shield) of Zeus, consistent with Zeus's role as Defender of Righteous Causes.

This wrathful quality of the gods of antiquity certainly reflects the forceful and violent nature of the age. The Semitic God of the Old Testament certainly was no exception in this regard, venting his righteous anger against the wicked on innumerable occasions. Even with respect to New Testament scripture, Christ appears to express the tendency towards righteous anger, as exemplified in his outraged expulsion of the moneychangers from the Temple. According to the Gospel of St. Matthew (21:12), the week before his Crucifixion, Christ triumphantly returned to Jerusalem welcomed by throngs of jubilant admirers. Upon reaching the Temple, however, Christ became incensed over the presence of the money-changers, righteously condemning their greedy disrespect for its sanctity. Flying into a holy rage, Christ overturned the tables and scales, proclaiming: "It is written, my house shall be called a house of prayer; but ye have made it a den of thieves."

According to this scriptural example, Christ clearly appears to appeal to a transcendental power base, wherein formally choosing to ignore the established mercantile traditions of his day. Indeed, the Temple merchants could scarcely be faulted, in that they were legitimately entitled to a fair return on their services. Christ's highly idealistic message, in contrast, condemned any manner of worship not wholly focused upon the mercy and grace of the Father. By further speaking of the Temple as his own "house," Christ effectively includes himself within such a transcendental perspective, wherein hinting at the true rationale for his righteous anger. It certainly appears strange that Christ would stray so completely from his ordinarily meek demeanor, although it is only at this extreme level of transcendence that Christ's anger ultimately becomes acceptable to the purest of Christian sensibilities.

592 – HATRED

The second of humanistic vices intimately associated with anger is the related theme of *hatred*. Its modern spelling derives from the Anglo-Saxon *hatian* (intense dislike or ill will). It is generally defined as the chief moral opposite of love, wherein expanding upon its more basic foundation in oppression. Hatred clearly emerges as a prominent theme in Old Testament scripture, particularly with respect to the story of Cain and Abel. According to the Book of Genesis, Cain and Abel were the first-born sons of Adam and Eve following their banishment from Paradise. Abel tended the sheep while Cain labored in the field. Abel sacrificed lambs from his flock to the Lord, earning great favor in the process. Cain's offerings of the fruits of the field, however, received only callous indifference. Cain soon became envious of his brother, his efforts being denied the approval that Abel's so readily enjoyed.

While laboring in the field, Cain's hatred finally reached the breaking point, killing Abel in a fit of rage. When the Lord confronted Cain on Abel's wellbeing, Cain feigned ignorance replying: "Am I my brother's keeper?" The Lord directly chastised Cain responding: "What hast thou done? The voice of thy brother's blood crieth unto me from the ground. And now thou art cursed from the earth, which has opened her mouth to receive thy brother's blood from thy hand." The Lord further set a mark upon Cain as a visual badge of his crime, condemned to a life outcast from society.

Hatred is similarly proscribed in New Testament scripture, clearly antithetical to the Apostle John's stirring description of God as pure love. St. Paul further lists hatred among the Sins of the Holy Spirit, just as *love* was listed among the Fruits therein. The clear transcendental nature of this vice certainly commits it to the unenviable role of justifying many of the greatest crimes against humanity. The scourge begins with Cain's hateful murder of his brother, and extends to our modern age as Hitler's unspeakable mass extermination of the Jews, amongst others.

591 – PREJUDICE

This completed description of anger/hatred further begs mention of the related theme of *prejudice*. As the chief moral antonym of equality, prejudice is traditionally defined as an irrational avoidance of differing races, cultures, or creeds. Its modern spelling derives the Latin *praejudicium*, from *prae-* (before) and *judicium* (judgement): suggesting a biased or opinionated viewpoint. Racial prejudice is certainly the most salient variety, readily apparent (even to a casual glance) over and beyond any affiliated social distinctions. In general, it represents an extreme variation on the widespread cultural phenomenon known as *ethnocentrism*; namely, the tendency to employ the norms and values of one's own culture when judging those of another. This pronounced tendency towards favoring one's individual lifestyle over that of another directly fuels such prejudicial tendencies. This prejudicial attitude is further compounded by certain stereotypical beliefs, where distinguishing characteristics associated with particular individuals are generalized to all other members within the group.

The truest measure of racial prejudice (as opposed to simple erroneous judgement) is its unnerving inflexibility; namely, the tendency to hold contradictory beliefs even when faced with strong evidence to the contrary. In keeping with this darker transcendental focus, prejudice clearly employs circular logic to reinforce such specious viewpoints. For instance, early fallacies associated with the slave races proved particularly convenient for rationalizing the subjugation of entire racial populations. When the glaring errors of

Metal Figurine of the Norse god Thor *(seated)*
Shown Gripping the Shaft of His Mighty Hammer

these belief systems were finally exposed, racial prejudice continued to persist, even though the theoretical underpinnings were thoroughly invalidated. This rigid pattern of inflexibility renders racial prejudice particularly difficult to eradicate once it has taken root in common culture. Indeed, social imitation appears to be the most dominant mode of transmission, particularly when compounded over the course of many generations.

593 – BELLIGERENCE

The fourth and final of the humanistic vices, *belligerence*, is traditionally defined as a hostile or warlike attitude consistent with its opposing counterpart in peace. Its modern spelling derives from the Latin *belligerare* (to wage war): from *bellum* (war) and *genere* (to carry on). This power of force for settling disputes was certainly a well-established theme throughout the classical era, particularly with respect to Mars, the Roman god of war, equivalent to the Greek god Ares. His wife Bellona (the Roman goddess of war) owes her name to the related Latin root-stem *bello* (to wage war). According to tradition Bellona never strayed far from the side of Mars, typically portrayed in the act of preparing his chariot for the rigors of war. She similarly appears in battle with a torch in one hand and a bloody whip in the other: with which she maddened her foes and enflamed her own fury. Her ceremonial priests, the

Bellonarii, were traditionally garbed in black: honoring her presence by wounding themselves in their extremities and screaming wildly.

Appius Claudius Caecus dedicated a temple to Bellona during the war against the Samnites, located outside the walls of Rome within the Campus Martius. Its remote location made it particularly well suited for negotiations with foreign ambassadors, in addition to receiving Roman generals returning in victory from distant military campaigns. The Columna Bellica (Pillar of War) was located at the entrance to the temple, employed in ritual declarations of war on distant lands. The area within Bellona's temple symbolized the enemy's territory, whereas the pillar represented its outermost frontier. A declaration of war was initiated by launching a bloody spear against the pillar, a ceremony that war councils in earlier times had originally performed at the actual boundary of the enemy's territory.

This ritualized belligerent posturing has remained an enduring theme throughout recorded history, such as the tragic sequence of events leading to up the First World War. At the turn of the last century, pre-war Europe was neatly divided into opposing groups of allies; namely, the Triple Alliance (Italy, Germany, and Austria-Hungary), and the Triple Entente (Britain, France, and Russia). The crucial catalyst occurred on June 28, 1914, when the Crown Prince and Princess of Austria-Hungary were assassinated by Serbian terrorists during a tour of the Bosnian capital of Sarajevo. Desiring a greater degree of influence in the Balkan Peninsula, Austria-Hungary quickly accused the Serbian government of instigating the intrigue: delivering a stern ultimatum amounting to protectorship status over Serbia. Although Serbia pleaded for a compromise, Austria-Hungary obstinately refused to surrender the dispute to international arbitration.

Precisely one month following the date of the assassination, Austria-Hungary declared war on Serbia, counting on the logistic support of its allies Italy and Germany. Serbia, in turn, enlisted the aid of Britain, France, and Russia, dragging virtually the entire European continent into the fray. This initial belligerent posturing eventually escalated out of all control, a lesson in conflict management that Europe should have dearly taken to heart.

The end of the war, however, saw little change in such belligerent perspectives, the imposition of extensive war reparations further setting the stage for the economic frustrations of post-war Germany. Such events further proved instrumental to Hitler's fanatical rise to power, resulting in the even more devastating Second World War. These two great World Wars supremely dramatized the folly of belligerent posturing in our modern age of technological warfare, a circumstance that fortunately has paved the way for the unprecedented span of peace and prosperity currently in force today.

THE MYSTICAL VICES: THE UPPERMOST LIMITS FOR THE REALM OF DEFECT

In summary, the completed description of the moralistic vices effectively rounds the stepwise description of the transcendental authority perspective (in both its positive and negative manifestations). Indeed, the evil focus of the humanistic vices was effectively seen to counteract the respective listing of humanistic values. The profoundly abstract nature of the transcendental authority perspective would further appear to suggest that the upper conceptual limit for the vices has finally been reached. Indeed, it is difficult to imagine a set of vices more abstract than the already abstruse listing of anger-hatred-prejudice-belligerence. In direct analogy to the preceding description of the mystical values, however, there should further exist a parallel complement of mystical vices, wherein contrasting point-for-point with the respective virtuous mode.

Although positive mysticism takes almighty God as its supreme focus, the darker version (by analogy) enters into the occult realm of sorcery or witchcraft, with a respective emphasis on demon-worship. Such occult rituals were typically conducted under the greatest of secrecy, consistently condemned by the Christian Church. The witchcraft hysteria of the Middle Ages sent many suspected witches to their death, leaving little enduring record of their covert practices. This dearth of historical documentation clearly diminishes the prospects for identifying the four predicted dimensions for the mystical vices were it not for the greatest book on religious mysticism ever written; namely, the Christian Bible. Although its spirited literary style is slanted primarily from a positive perspective, the Bible also deals with diabolical themes with the intent of condemning them.

This darker slant to mysticism is primarily expressed in the prophetic segments of the Bible, a circumstance particularly consistent with the transcendental nature of mystical foresight. A detailed reading of prophetic scripture, indeed, reveals the enduring focus of the mystical vices; namely, iniquity, turpitude, abomination, and perdition. These four basic mystical vices effectively contrast, point-for-point, with the virtuous prerequisites of the mystical values (ecstasy, bliss, joy, and harmony). The specific rationale behind their individual assignment is particularly apparent in the expanded context of their corresponding literary traditions.

502 – INIQUITY

The somewhat obscure notion of *iniquity* emerges as a recurrent theme throughout both the Old and New Testament scripture. This term is virtually synonymous with the subordinate theme of evil with the exception of extending to a purely transcendental sphere of influence. Its modern spelling traces its origins to the Latin *iniquitas*, from *in-* (not) and *aequus* (equal). This classical connotation of inequity eventually expanded to the much broader ethical context of pure evil or wickedness. Indeed, these latter two aspects endure as one of iniquity's most salient features, as particularly apparent in the Mystery of Iniquity described by St. Paul in his Second Letter to the Thessalonians. This scriptural passage directly alludes to the darker events associated with the apocalyptic "end-times," in fitting association with the emergent spirit of lawlessness.

503 – TURPITUDE

The second of the mystical vices, *turpitude*, is a theme sharing many distinct parallels to iniquity.

Although not specifically mentioned in English translations of the Bible, its basic import is clearly apparent in passages dealing with vileness and depravity. Its modern spelling derives from the Latin *turpitudo* (baseness), from *turpis* (base): as suggested in the class of "baser" instincts. This negative connotation dates at least to classical times, when *base* metals (such as lead, copper, or tin) were alloyed with the noble metals (gold or silver), wherein increasing strength and durability. Their unscrupulous use, however, allowed greedy metal smiths to maximize their profits by compromising the intrinsic worth of commissioned metalwork. These classical connotations, in turn, extend to an ethical context consistent with turpitude's more elementary foundation in cunning: e.g., moral turpitude within a transcendental sphere of influence. Similar to the case previously made for iniquity, the deceptive side of turpitude is often disguised through a semblance to decency until the truth is finally made known.

500 – ABOMINATION

A third of the mystical vices, intimately associated with iniquity, is the similarly specialized theme of *abomination*. Its modern spelling derives from the Latin *abominabilis*, from *ab-* (from) and *ominari* (to regard as an omen): particularly in an ominous sense. In common usage it refers to objects of extreme hatred or disgust consistent with its more elementary foundation in ugliness. This depraved quality is particularly evident in the OT Book of Proverbs (15:9) which states: "The way of the wicked is an *abomination* unto the Lord." This theme reaches perhaps its greatest degree of notoriety in New Testament accounts of the Abomination of the Desolation, a reference to the desecration of the Jewish Temple by worshippers of pagan gods. In our modern age, this term is more typically associated with the abominable snowman, the monstrous "yeti" of the Himalayan highlands. Indeed, the brutish attributes traditionally associated with this grotesque monster clearly remain in keeping with the transcendental characteristics of this particular realm of defect.

501 – PERDITION

The final of the mystical vices, *perdition*, effectively rounds out the quartet-style listing of transcendental themes. Its modern spelling derives from the Latin *perditio*, from *perdere* (to lose, to ruin). Its traditional emphasis on destruction or ruin is clearly illustrated on Card XVI of the standard Tarot card deck: namely, The Tower Struck

by Lightening. It graphically depicts the tragic loss of life/property resulting from such a violent act of nature.

In terms of its affiliated scriptural context, perdition is similarly defined as the loss of all hope for spiritual salvation, effectively condemning the soul to eternal damnation. Those deliberately straying from the path of righteousness are virtually assured such a devastating fate, for the Day of Judgement effectively closes the book on any regretful appeals to leniency. In keeping with its extreme degree of transcendence, perdition effectively builds upon a more elementary foundation in despair, wherein formally counteracting its virtuous counterpart in bliss.

THE DIABOLICAL EXTREMES FOR THE REALM OF DEFECT

This completed description of the mystical vices invites further consideration of one additional critical issue; namely, what level of experience is predicted to extend beyond this final nameable realm of defect? According to the earlier chapter on religious mysticism, this context must necessarily entail a predicted blending of individual affective dimensions, resulting in a mystical experience of virtually supernatural proportions. From a purely positive perspective, this supernatural realm was assumed to be entirely unnamable except in the broadest of descriptive terms; namely, God, Cosmic Consciousness, the Oversoul, etc. With respect to the darker realm of defect, however, this supernatural domain (by definition) surpasses the more fearsome complement of the mystical vices (iniquity, turpitude, abomination, and perdition). Such a fearsome experience can only be described employing the broadest of demonic brushstrokes consistent with the diabolical archetypes specific to demon possession. William James insightfully touches on this darker side to the mystical experience according to the following quotation from his *Varieties of Religious Experience*:

"So much for religious mysticism proper. But more remains to be told, for religious mysticism is only one half of mysticism. The other half has no accumulated tradition except those which the text books on insanity supply. Open any of these, and you will find abundant cases in which "mystical ideas" are cited as characteristic symptoms of enfeebled or deluded states of mind. In delusional insanity, paranoia, as they sometimes call it, we may have a diabolical mysticism, a sort of religious mysticism turned upside down. The same sense of ineffable importance in the smallest events, the same texts and words coming with new meanings, the same voices and visions and leadings and missions, the same controlling by extraneous powers. Only this time the emotion is pessimistic: instead of consolations we have desolations; the meanings are dreadful; and the powers are enemies to life. It is evident that from the point of view of their psychological mechanism, the classical mysticism, and these lower mysticisms spring from the same mental level, from that great subliminal or trans-marginal region of which science is beginning to admit the existence, but of which so little is really known. This region contains every kind of matter: seraph and snake abide there side by side."

This rather extensive quotation suggests an entire darker side to the mystical experience, wherein afflicting those poor souls tragic enough to become receptive to it. German psychologist Carl Jung suggests a similar aspect with respect to his notion of the *shadow*: an archetypal experience entirely consistent with such disturbing themes. In this latter respect, is it truly rational to postulate the existence of a sentient being (such as the Devil) in order to counteract the positive aspects of the mystical experience?

The longstanding tradition of devils or demons has endured as a universal theme in religious systems from around the world. With respect to the Judeo-Christian tradition, Lucifer was celebrated as the most powerful angel in the service of the Lord until his sin of pride led to his banishment from heaven, leading numerous other angels to perdition in the process. As the most powerful of the Archangels, Lucifer was a creation of God, and, therefore, never His equal. Curiously, the Devil did not always figure quite so prominently in Old Testament scripture. Indeed, many biblical scholars concede that this all-powerful Devil of Wickedness traces its origins to the later Babylonian Captivity of the Jews. Here the Jews were certainly exposed to Zoroastrianism, a Persian cult characterized by an enduring struggle pitting good against evil. This relatively late addition was subsequently incorporated into the budding Christian movement, as witnessed in the certain scriptural accounts describing Christ's temptation by Satan. This emergent tradition of the Devil as the chief antagonist of the Lord reaches its supreme fulfillment in the Book of Revel-ation, an apocalyptic final showdown between the forces of Light and Darkness.

It might ultimately be questioned if Christianity is truly justified in promoting belief in an all-powerful Devil of Wickedness, in concert with the affiliated themes of demon possession and exorcism? Evil certainly requires goodness as its supreme contrast, for there can be no darkness without light. Indeed, "darkness" is essentially all-or-none phenomenon, whereas light is invested with virtually unlimited shades of meaning. A similar scenario appears to hold true with respect to the mystical values, which are expressly vital in their traditions, as witnessed in the stirring accounts of saints and sages throughout the ages. In contrast, the corresponding listing of mystical vices (iniquity, turpitude, abomination, and perdition) scarcely amounts to more than a scriptural technicality, certainly lacking the dynamic vitality characterizing the virtuous counterparts.

In truth, this darker slant to religious mysticism could just as easily be explained through recourse to the righteous/wrathful attributes of the traditional God of the Old Testament: a divinity that clearly was not averse to punishing the transgressions of His Chosen People. Indeed, according to the highly respected Book of Isaiah (45:7) the Lord is quoted as stating: "I form the light and create the darkness. I make peace and create *evil*. I, the Lord, do all these things." Furthermore, the Book of Lamentations (3:37-38) similarly states: "Who has commanded and it came to pass unless the Lord has ordained it? Is it not from the mouth of the Most High that good and evil come?"

Regardless of the preferred mechanism of explanation, the prospect of a darker side to the mystical experience is undoubtedly a formidable influence in the lives of those thusly afflicted. Fortunately, documented cases of demonic possession appear to be somewhat rare, although certainly more so than the similarly elusive positive experience. Indeed, whether it is attributed to some sentient form of evil entity, a righteous outcome of God's wrath, or some impersonal form of shadow archetype, this darker slant to the mystical experience must necessarily remain a topic open to much further investigation. Hopefully a clearer understanding will ultimately be achieved concerning the fundamental principles governing all such aspects of the mystical experience.

15

THE ACCESSORY COUNTERPARTS FOR THE VICES OF DEFECT

The completed description of the main sequence of individual terms for the vices of defect, in turn, raises the related issue of the respective accessory counterparts. As initially described for the virtuous realm, the accessory terms represent the perspective-reversed counterparts of the main terms they serve to imitate in that the polarities of the "you" and "I" roles are reversed in the schematic definition format, wherein enabling a sense of empathy in terms of interpersonal interactions. The parallel domain of the vices of defect is certainly no exception in this regard, although now facilitating the empathic potential for exploiting others in the pursuit of a selfish agenda.

A growing number of researchers speculate that the stepwise development of empathic ability in young children undergoes one final stage of development; namely, that leading to the skills underlying social deception. Although telling the truth is vaunted as the default setting for social communication in general, the cunning attributes associated with deception suggest a sophisticated style of response repertoire. Indeed, the dramatic physiological changes typically associated with lying clearly reflect the extreme mental effort underlying deception.

The techniques associated with successful deception appear to develop over a distinct sequence of stages similar to the pattern previously established for empathy, in general. Initially, the child's first experiences with lying entail staying out of trouble, as in avoiding admitting to activities that one had been punished for in the past. This self-centered style of lying is generally a hit-or-miss phenomenon, in that the child occasionally succeeds, although more often detected.

With the further development of true empathic ability, however, the child eventually learns to tailor his deceptions to meet the expectations of his superiors, considerably improving chances of success. Eventually, this egocentric focus formally extends to the outward perspectives of others. The latter class of "little white lies" aims to spare the feelings of others in the interest of social harmony. Indeed, any convincing effort towards social harmony necessarily remains unrealistic assuming one volunteers the unvarnished truth in every situation.

Furthermore, the leadership qualities we so dearly treasure similarly depend upon gracefully stretching the truth to achieve cooperation amongst the various group members. In a series of experiments designed to test for leadership potential, individuals that spontaneously took charge of the group, in turn, exhibited the greatest facility for deception when tested later individually. The researchers ultimately concluded that, although leaders may not be more likely to lie, they typically are better at it than the rest of us. Fortunately, this somewhat harmless form of social deception is generally the extent for most of us, although a limited number of individuals (such as "con-men") attempt to harness these skills for selfish purposes. The social psychopath expresses little remorse for the physical or emotional harm inflicted upon others, a factor examined to a much greater detail in the upcoming Chapter 26 that deals with criminality in a social setting.

Although the accessory range of empathic terminology proves extremely convincing for the virtuous realm, for sake of symmetry, the related domain of defect must similarly be invested with its own unique complement of accessory terms, as formally depicted in **Fig. 15A**. According to this "darker" interpretation of the accessory realm, the personal authority listing of accessory ego vices (sloth-carelessness-dispassionateness-

514	515		524	525
Sloth	Carelessness		Traitorousness	Retaliation
516	**517**	→	**526**	**527**
Dispassion	Arbitrariness		Resentment	Malevolence
ACCESS. EGO VICES			**ACCESS. ALTER EGO VICES**	
(Personal Authority)			(Personal Follower)	

534	535		544	545
Disrepute	Reprehension		Sedition	Avengement
536	**537**	→	**546**	**547**
Preposterous.	Fickleness		Lechery	Pusillanimity
ACC. VICES of VILLAINY			**ACC. CARDINAL VICES**	
(Group Authority)			(Group Representative)	

554	555		564	565
Profligacy	Bondage		Perfidy	Desperation
556	**557**	→	**566**	**567**
Coarseness	Acrimony		Cupidity	Opposition
ACCESS. CIVIL LIABILITIES			**ACC. THEOLOGICAL VICES**	
(Spiritual Authority)			(Spiritual Disciple)	

574	575		584	585
Indignation	Subjugation		Revulsion	Duplicity
576	**577**	→	**586**	**587**
Animosity	Torment		Wickedness	Guilefulness
ACCESS. ECUMEN. VICES			**ACC. MORALISTIC VICES**	
(Humanitarian Authority)			(Humanitarian Follower)	

594	595		504	505
Irateness	Intolerance		Abhorrence	Banefulness
596	**597**	→	**506**	**507**
Enmity	Militancy		Sinisterity	Baseness
ACC. HUMANISTIC VICES			**ACCESS. MYSTICAL VICES**	
(Transcendental Authority)			(Transcendental Follower)	

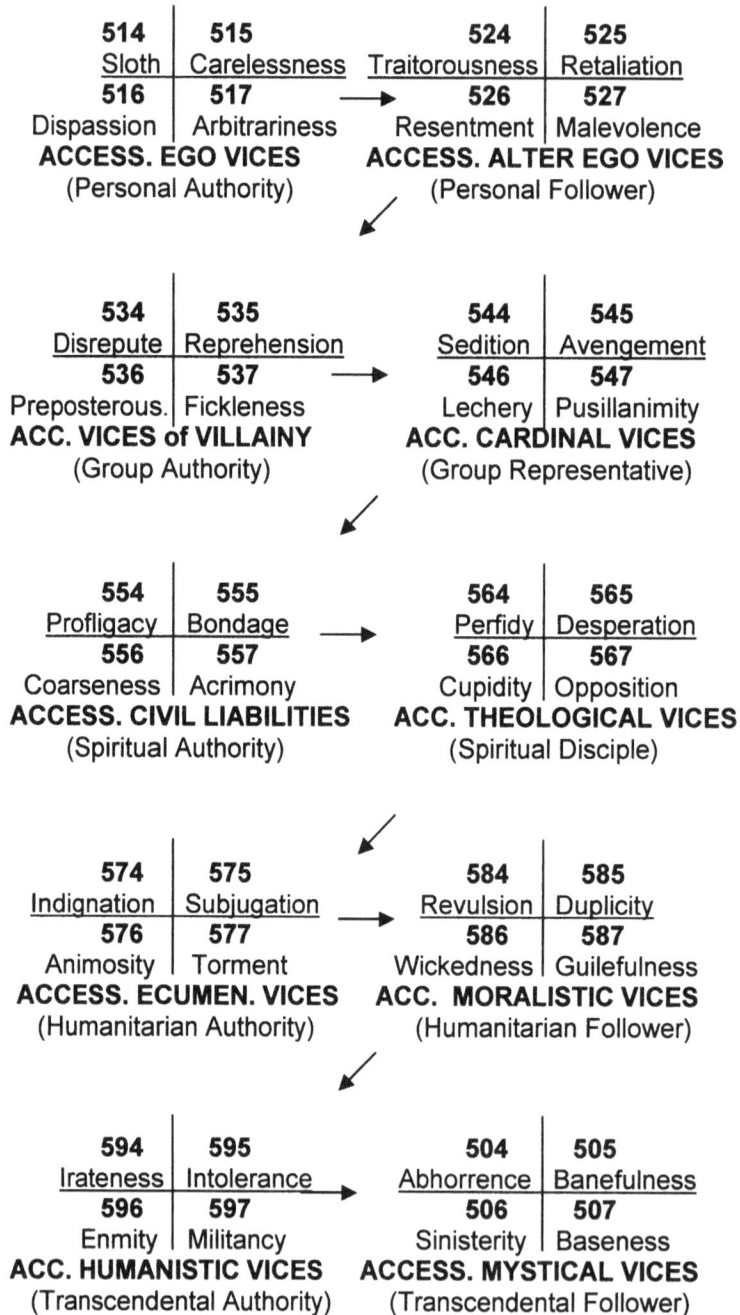

Fig. 15A – The Three-Digit Codes for the Accessory Vices of Defect

arbitrariness), in turn, complements the main listing of terms (e.g., laziness-negligence-apathy-indifference). Furthermore, the accessory alter ego grouping of traitorousness-retaliation-resentment-malevolence, in turn, complements the main sequence of counterparts (treachery-vindictiveness-spite-malice).

This distinctive interplay of ego and alter ego vices, in turn, reflects the distinctive *accessory* interactions at issue. For instance, (as personal follower) I *traitorously* act in a punitive fashion in response to your (as personal authority) slothful treatment of me. Similarly, I might *retaliate* against you in response to your careless treatment of me. A similar interplay of terms further holds true with respect to the remaining accessory pairings of resentment/dispassionateness and malevolence/arbitrariness. The authority and follower roles effectively reciprocate one another in terms of subjective/objective role polarities.

THE ACCESSORY TEN-LEVEL HIERARCHY FOR THE VICES OF DEFECT

In keeping with the personal foundations for the accessory ego and alter ego vices, it further proves feasible to extend this trend to the remaining group, spiritual, humanitarian, and transcendental levels within the power hierarchy. This full forty-fold complement of accessory vices is schematically depicted in **Fig. 15A**: equivalent in every respect to the *main* vices initially portrayed in **Fig. 10B**, with the exception that the "you" and "I" polarities are now reversed. The accessory vices share the main version's tendency towards hierarchical organization across the entire ten-level span of the power hierarchy.

For instance, the accessory authority sequence of slothfulness-disrepute-profligacy-indignation-irateness directly specifies a past-directed focus (in the sense of past notorious behaviors). Furthermore, the remaining follower sequence of traitorousness-sedition-perfidy-revulsion-abhorrence, in turn, reciprocates the preliminary authority sequence through punishment of such past notorious perspectives, as partially depicted below.

514 – Slothfulness	524 – Traitorous.
534 – Disrepute	544 – Sedition
554 – Profligacy	564 – Perfidy
574 – Indignation	584 – Revulsion
594 – Irateness	504 – Abhorrence

In a related fashion, the accessory authority sequence of carelessness-reprehension-bondage-subjugation-intolerance also specifies a past-directed focus, although now targeting a more shameful context. Furthermore, the remaining follower sequence of accessory terms; e.g., retaliation-avengement-desperation-duplicity-banefulness, in turn, validates such a trend, reflecting that based upon mutiny with the exception that retaliation is now brought into focus.

515 – Carelessness	525 – Retaliation
535 – Reprehension	545 – Avengement
555 – Bondage	565 – Desperation
575 – Subjugation	585 – Duplicity
595 – Intolerance	505 – Banefulness

The third sequence of accessory terms is alternately based upon the related authority/follower sequence of dispassionateness/resentment. For instance, the group authority figure preposterously acts in a dispassionate fashion, in anticipation of the lecherously-resentful treatment of the group representative. Furthermore, in terms of the spiritual authority level, the authority figure preposterously acts in a coarse fashion in anticipation of the lecherous sense of cupidity expressed by the spiritual disciple. Finally, for the most advanced humanitarian (and transcendental) levels, the authority figure coarsely acts animosity (or acts with enmity) in anticipation of the follower's wicked sense of cupidity, as schematically shown in the table immediately below:

516 – Dispassionateness	526 – Resentment
536 – Preposterousness	546 – Lechery
556 – Coarseness	566 – Cupidity
576 – Animosity	586 – Wickedness
596 – Enmity	506 – Sinisterity

The fourth and final sequence of accessory terms is respectively based upon the remaining personal themes of arbitrariness/malevolence (the accessory counterparts for indifference/malice). The accessory sequence of authority terms (arbitrariness-fickleness-acrimony-torment-militancy) effectively reciprocates its main sequence of counterparts (indifference-capriciousness-cruelty-

SLOTH	TRAITOROUSNESS
Previously, I (as punisher) have refused to act rewardingly towards you: overriding your (as adversary) failure to act solicitously towards me. But now, you (as personal authority) will *slothfully* fail to act solicitously towards me: overruling my (as punisher) refusal to act rewardingly towards you.	Previously, you (as personal authority) have slothfully failed to act solicitously towards me: overriding my (as punisher) refusal to act rewardingly towards you. But now, I (as your personal follower) will *traitorously* refuse to act rewardingly towards you: overruling your (as PA) slothful treatment of me.
DISREPUTE	**SEDITION**
Previously, I (as your personal follower) have traitorously refused to act rewardingly towards you: overriding your (as PA) slothful treatment of me. But now, you (as group authority) will slothfully act in a *disreputable* fashion towards me: overruling my (as PF) traitorous treatment of you.	Previously, you (as group authority) have slothfully acted in a disreputable fashion towards me: overriding my (as PF) traitorous treatment of you. But now, I (as group representative) will traitorously act in a *seditious* fashion towards you: overruling your (as GA) disreputable treatment of me.
PROFLIGACY	**PERFIDY**
Previously, I (as group representative) have traitorously acted in a seditious fashion towards you: overriding your (as GA) disreputable treatment of me. But now, you (as spiritual authority) will disreputably act in a *profligate* fashion towards me: overruling my (as GR) seditious treatment of you.	Previously, you (as spiritual authority) have disreputably acted in a profligate fashion towards me: overriding my (as GR) seditious treatment of you. But now, I (as your spiritual disciple) will seditiously act in a *perfidious* fashion towards you: overruling your (as SA) profligate treatment of me.
INDIGNATION	**REVULSION**
Previously, I (as your spiritual disciple) have seditiously acted perfidiously towards you: overriding your (as SA) profligate treatment of me. But now, you (as humanitarian authority) will profligately act in an *indignant* fashion towards me: overruling my (as SD) perfidious treatment of you.	Previously, you (as humanitarian authority) have profligately acted in an indignant fashion towards me: overriding my (as SD) perfidious treatment of you. But now, I (as represent. member of humanity) will perfidiously act with *revulsion* towards you: overruling your (as HA) indignant treatment of me.
IRATENESS	**ABHORRENCE**
Previously, I (as representative member of humanity) have perfidiously acted with revulsion towards you: overriding your (as HA) indignant treatment of me. But now, you (as transcendental authority) will indignantly act in an *irate* fashion towards me: overruling my (as RH) revulsive treatment of you.	Previously, you (as transcendental authority) have indignantly acted in an irate fashion towards me: overriding my (as RH) revulsive treatment of you. But now, I (as your transcendental follower) will revulsively act in an *abhorrent* fashion towards you: overruling your (as TA) irate treatment of me.

Table E-1 – The Definitions Based Upon Sloth/Traitorousness

CARELESSNESS	RETALIATION
Previously, I (as punisher) have refused to act leniently towards you: overriding your (as adversary) failure to act submissively towards me. But now, you (as personal authority) will *carelessly* fail to act submissively towards me: overruling my (as punisher) refusal to act leniently towards you.	Previously, you (as personal authority) have carelessly failed to act submissively towards me: overriding my (as punisher) refusal to act leniently towards you. But now, I (as your personal follower) will *retaliatively* refuse to act leniently towards you: overruling your (as PA) careless treatment of me.
REPREHENSION	AVENGEMENT
Previously, I (as your personal follower) have retaliatively refused to act leniently towards you: overriding your (as PA) careless treatment of me. But now, you (as group authority) will *reprehensibly* act in a careless fashion towards me: overruling my (as PF) retaliatory treatment of you.	Previously, you (as group authority) have reprehensibly acted carelessly towards me: overriding my (as PF) retaliatory treatment of you. But now, I (as group representative) will retaliatively act in an *avenging* fashion towards you: overruling your (as GA) reprehensible treatment of me.
BONDAGE	DESPERATION
Previously, I (as group representative) have retaliatively acted in an avenging fashion towards you: overriding your (as GA) reprehensible treatment of me. But now, you (as spiritual authority) will reprehensibly maintain me in *bondage*: overruling my (as GR) avenging treatment of you.	Previously, you (as spiritual authority) have reprehensibly maintained me in bondage: overriding my (as GR) avenging treatment of you. But now, I (as your spiritual disciple) will *desperately* seek vengeance against you: overruling your (as SA) reprehensible maintenance of me in bondage.
SUBJUGATION	DUPLICITY
Previously, I (as your spiritual disciple) have desperately sought vengeance against you: overriding your (as SA) reprehensible maintenance of me in bondage. But now, you (as humanitarian authority) will reprehensibly *subjugate* me in bondage: overruling my (as SD) desperate quest for vengeance.	Previously, you (as humanitarian authority) have reprehensibly subjugated me in bondage: overriding my (as SD) desperate quest for vengeance. But now, I (as representative member of humanity) will desperately act in a *duplicitous* fashion towards you: overruling your (as HA) subjugation of me in bondage.
INTOLERANCE	BANEFULNESS
Previously, I (as representative member of humanity) have desperately acted in a duplicitous fashion towards you: overriding your (as HA) subjugation of me in bondage. But now, you (as transcendental authority) will subjugate me in an *intolerable* fashion: overruling my (as RH) duplicitous treatment of you.	Previously, you (as transcendental authority) have subjugated me in an intolerable fashion: overriding my (as RH) duplicitous treatment of you. But now, I (as your transcendental follower) will duplicitously act *banefully* towards you: overruling your (as TA) intolerable treatment of me.

Table E-2 - The Definitions Based on Carelessness/Retaliation

DISPASSIONATENESS	RESENTMENT
Previously, you (as punisher) have refused to act rewardingly towards me: overriding my (as adversary) failure to act solicitously towards you. But now, I (as personal authority) will *dispassionately* fail to act solicitously towards you: overruling your (as punisher) refusal to act rewardingly towards me.	Previously, I (as personal authority) have dispassionately failed to act solicitously towards you: overriding your (as punisher) refusal to act rewardingly towards me. But now, you (as personal follower) will *resentfully* refuse to act rewardingly towards me: overruling my (as PA) dispassionate treatment of you.
PREPOSTEROUSNESS	LECHERY
Previously, you (as my personal follower) have resentfully refused to act rewardingly towards me: overriding my (as PA) dispassionate treatment of you. But now, I (as group authority) will *preposterously* act in a dispassionate fashion towards you: overruling your (as PF) resentful treatment of me.	Previously, I (as group authority) have preposterously acted in a dispassionate fashion towards you: overriding your (as PF) resentful treatment of me. But now, you (as group representative) will *lecherously* act in a resentful fashion towards me: overruling my (as GA) preposterous treatment of you.
COARSENESS	CUPIDITY
Previously, you (as group representative) have lecherously acted in a resentful fashion towards me: overriding my (as GA) preposterous treatment of you. But now, I (as spiritual authority) will preposterously act in a *coarse* fashion towards you: overruling your (as GR) lecherous treatment of me.	Previously, I (as spiritual authority) have preposterously acted in a coarse fashion towards you: overriding your (as GR) lecherous treatment of me. But now, you (as spiritual disciple) will lecherously act with *cupidity* towards me: overruling my (as SA) coarse treatment of you.
ANIMOSITY	WICKEDNESS
Previously, you (as my spiritual disciple) have lecherously acted with cupidity towards me: overriding my (as SA) coarse treatment of you. But now, I (as humanitarian authority) will coarsely express *animosity* towards you: overruling your (as SD) lecherous sense of cupidity.	Previously, I (as humanitarian authority) have coarsely expressed animosity towards you: overriding your (as SD) lecherous sense of cupidity. But now, you (as represent. member of humanity) will *wickedly* act with cupidity towards me: overruling my (as HA) coarse expression of animosity.
ENMITY	SINISTERITY
Previously, you (as representative member of humanity) have wickedly acted with cupidity towards me: overriding my (as HA) coarse expression of animosity. But now, I (as transcendental authority) will animously act with *enmity* towards you: overruling your (as RH) wicked treatment of me.	Previously, I (as transcendental authority) have animously acted with enmity towards you: overriding your (as RH) *wicked* treatment of me. But now, you (as transcendental follower) will wickedly act in a *sinister* fashion towards me: overruling my (as TA) enmity-filled treatment of you.

Table E-3 - The Definitions Based on Dispassion/Resentment

ARBITRARINESS	MALEVOLENCE
Previously, you (as punisher) have refused to act leniently towards me: overriding my (as adversary) failure to act submissively towards you. But now, I (as personal authority) will *arbitrarily* fail to act submissively towards you: overruling your (as punisher) refusal to act leniently towards me.	Previously, I (as personal authority) have arbitrarily failed to act submissively towards you: overriding your (as punisher) refusal to act leniently towards me. But now, you (as my personal follower) will *malevolently* refuse to act leniently towards me: overruling my (as PA) arbitrary treatment of you.
FICKLENESS	**PUSILLANIMITY**
Previously, you (as my personal follower) have malevolently refused to act leniently towards me: overriding my (as PA) arbitrary treatment of you. But now, I (as group authority) will arbitrarily act in a *fickle* fashion towards you: overruling your (as PF) malevolent treatment of me.	Previously, I (as group authority) have arbitrarily acted in a fickle fashion towards you: overriding your (as PF) malevolent treatment of me. But now, you (as group representative) will malevolently act in a *pusillanimous* fashion towards me: overruling my (as GA) fickle treatment of you.
ACRIMONY	**OPPOSITION**
Previously, you (as group representative) have malevolently acted in a pusillanimous fashion towards me: overriding my (as GA) fickle treatment of you. But now, I (as spiritual authority) will fickly act in an *acrimonious* fashion towards you: overruling your (as GR) pusillanimous treatment of me.	Previously, I (as spiritual authority) have fickly acted in an acrimonious fashion towards you: overriding your (as GR) pusillanimous treatment of me. But now, you (as my spiritual disciple) will pusillanimously act in an *oppositional* fashion towards me: overruling my (as SA) acrimonious treatment of you.
TORMENT	**GUILEFULNESS**
Previously, you (as my spiritual disciple) have pusillanimously acted in an oppositional fashion towards me: overriding my (as SA) acrimonious treatment of you. But now, I (as humanitarian authority) will acrimoniously-*torment* you: overruling your (as SD) oppositional treatment of me.	Previously, I (as humanitarian authority) have acrimoniously-tormented you: overriding your (as SD) oppositional treatment of me. But now, you (as representative member of humanity) will *guilefully* act in an oppositional fashion towards me: overruling my (as HA) tormenting treatment of you.
MILITANCY	**BASENESS**
Previously, you (as representative member of humanity) have guilefully acted in an oppositional fashion towards me: overriding my (as HA) tormenting treatment of you. But now, I (as transcendental authority) will tormentingly act in a *militant* fashion towards you: overruling your (as RH) guileful treatment of me.	Previously, I (as transcendental authority) have tormentingly acted in a militant fashion towards you: overriding your (as RH) guileful treatment of me. But now, you (as my transcendental follower) will guilefully act in a *base* fashion towards me: overruling my (as TA) militant treatment of you.

Table E-4 – The Definitions Based on Arbitrariness/Malevolence

persecution-belligerence. Furthermore, the remaining sequence of accessory follower roles (malevolence-pusillanimity-opposition-guilefulness-baseness) offers an objective contrast to its respective subjective counterparts: e.g., malice-cowardice-antagonism-cunning-turpitude.

517 – **Arbitrariness**	527 – **Malevolence**
537 – **Fickleness**	547 – **Pusillanimity**
557 – **Acrimony**	567 – **Opposition**
577 – **Torment**	587 – **Guilefulness**
597 – **Militancy**	507 – **Baseness**

In terms of identification within the three-digit coding system, the third (and final) digit is ultimately called into play. In terms of the cardinal virtues, for instance, the main versions are coded as: 540 = insurgency, 541 = vengeance, 542 = gluttony, and 543 = cowardice. Digits 4 through 7 in the three-slot, however, specify the accessory variations of the cardinal virtues; namely, 544 = sedition, 545 = avengement, 546 = lechery, and 547 = pusillanimity (as schematically depicted in **Fig. 15A**).

One final pressing issue necessarily remains; namely, the crucial prediction that the accessory variations for the vices of defect can further be incorporated into the formal schematic definition format. Indeed, a complete listing of accessory definitions for the realm of defect is tabulated in **Tables E-1** to **E-4**, in direct analogy to the main sets of definitions already shown in **Tables D-1** to **D-4** (of Chapter *10*). The accessory definitions are identical in form and function to their *main* counterparts with the exception that the "you" and "I" polarities are now reversed. This complementary interplay of "you" and "I" perspectives, by definition, is predicted within the schematic definition format, wherein formally permitting an empathic confluence of subjective/objective perspectives.

THE GENERAL UNIFYING THEMES FOR THE REALM OF DEFECT

The completed description of the main and accessory variations for the realm of defect invokes one remaining issue of particular significance to the three-digit coding system; namely, applications to the general unifying class of themes. As previously described in Chapter *9* (for the virtuous mode), each of the general unifying themes within the

general sequence is viewed as a "meta-order" summation of its respective level within the power hierarchy. For instance, the general unified theme of "utilitarianism" encompasses the specific category of the cardinal virtues (prudence-justice-temperance-fortitude). A similar pattern further holds true with respect to the domain of defect. The general theme of "corruption" encompasses the primary focus of the cardinal vices (insurgency-vengeance-gluttony-cowardice).

Accordingly, it technically proves feasible to devise an entire parallel hierarchy of themes exclusive to the realm of defect: as formally depicted in **Fig. 15B**. This diagram employs a format similar to that shown in **Fig. 9A** of Chapter 9, allowing for a convenient contrast in terms. A cursory comparison of these two separate diagrams directly reveals a mirror-image correspondence between the positive and negative listings of themes. The virtuous themes represent specific moral antonyms of their respective darker counterparts. For instance, the sequence of general unifying themes targeting the authority roles (knavery-villainy-profanity-apostasy-nihilism) formally contrasts (point-for-point) with the respective themes specified for the virtuous mode; namely, individualism-personalism-romanticism-ecumenism-humanism. Furthermore, the remaining sequence of themes targeting the *follower* roles (fraud-corruption-heresy-anarchism-diabolism), in turn, mirrors those for the virtuous realm; e.g., pragmatism-utilitarianism-ecclesiasticism-eclecticism-mysticism.

Similar to the case previously established for the virtuous mode, the ascending hierarchy of authority/follower roles is reflected in the respective listing of themes relating to the vices. For instance, the personal authority role is characterized by the theme of *knavery*, further extending to the *villainy* expressed by the group authority figure. The spiritual authority role, in turn, targets the more specialized theme of *profanity* consistent with its focus on "universal" principles. The themes for the remaining humanitarian/transcendental levels further take their cue from the designations of the specific listings of terms; namely, *apostasy* and *nihilism*, respectively.

In similar fashion, the remaining themes for the follower roles are reflected in the respective sequence of fraud-corruption-heresy-anarchism-diabolism. For instance, the initial theme of fraud refers to that which is detrimental to the individual, extending (in a group sense) to a corrupt disregard for "the common good." This ascending sequence, in turn, extends to the remaining spiritual, humanitarian, and transcendental domains in terms of the respective themes of heresy, anarchism, and diabolism.

518 – Knavery	**528 – Fraud**
538 – Villainy	**548 – Corruption**
558 – Profanity	**568 – Heresy**
578 – Apostasy	**588 – Anarchism**
598 – Nihilism	**508 – Diabolism**

As per the original description of the three-digit coding system proposed in Chapter 1, these general unified themes for the vices of defect are similarly amenable for coding within the master *1,040*-part format. Here, three-digit codes ending with the numeral *"8"* specify the main classifications of themes, whereas those ending with *"9"* (in the three-spot) represent the *accessory* variations. In this schematic sense, the main/accessory variations effectively complement one another with the exception that the "you" and "I" polarities are now reversed.

In direct analogy to the virtuous range of themes, the parallel complement of themes for the vices of defect shares the potential for incorporation into the schematic definition format. This latter modification is termed the class of "meta" schematic definitions, being that they represent meta-order summations of those targeting the individual terms. A complete listing of "meta" schematic definitions for the realm of defect is depicted in **Table C-3**, wherein formally contrasting (point-for-point) with the virtuous mode depicted in **Table C-1** (of Chapter 9). Furthermore the initial definitions for this darker range of themes are formally based upon the principles of punishment, just as the virtuous mode is similarly grounded within the terminology of instrumental conditioning. This strong behavioral foundation adds further welcome validation to this dual complement of "meta" schematic definitions. Indeed, a more detailed description of each of these darker themes definitely proves in order here, followed, in turn, by a related examination of their respective accessory counterparts.

518 – KNAVERY

The current analysis of themes for the realm of defect begins with a cursory examination of *knavery*. This general unifying theme encompasses the subordinate quartet of ego-vices professed by the personal authority figure; namely, la-

ziness-negligence-apathy-indifference. It is defined as dishonest or crafty dealing, as in cases of trickery or mischief. Knavery represents the chief moral antonym of the more positive prerequisites associated with individualism. The term derives from the Old English *cnafa* or *cnapa* (originally a boy or youth), further akin to the German *knabe* or *knappe*: as particularly denoting a false or deceitful fellow. In common usage, the knave refers to the rank of "jack" (below that of the king or queen) in a standard deck of playing cards. It also denotes a serving boy, or any of a number of other capacities associated with youth.

According to William Shakespeare: "Tis here, but yet confused. *Knavery's* plain face is never seen till used." He also writes: "Cupid is a *knavish* lad. Thus to make poor females mad." Roman chronicler Plutarch similarly notes: "Zeno first observed the doctrine that *knavery* is the best defense against a *knave*." The strategy of "fighting fire with fire" is particularly relevant the immature attributes associated with knavery. Consequently, the positive prerequisites associated with individualism are perverted to an extreme degree with respect to knavery. As anyone familiar with the vicissitudes of youth can readily attest, the disruptions associated with knavery prove somewhat limited in scope, as indicative of a fairly circumspect personal sphere of influence.

538 – VILLAINY

The preceding personal prerequisites for knavery, in turn, extend to a group sphere of influence with respect to the related theme of *villainy*. The term derives from the Old French *villain*, from the Middle Latin *villanus* (farmhand), from the Latin *villa* (a country house): a probable reduction from *vicla* or *vicus* (a village). It originally referred to a serf bound to a villa or a farm, the ingrained propensities of which led to the attribution of evil or depraved characteristics.

The modern-day connotation of villainy refers to an antagonistic character from a novel or play, whose evil motives/actions help drive the plot in concert with the more noble aspirations of the protagonist. In "The Merchant of Venice," William Shakespeare describes the villainy of his character Shylock as: "An evil soul producing holy witness is like a *villain* with a smiling cheek, a goodly apple rotten to the heart." (Act I: Scene 3). In *Henry IV*, Shakespeare similarly writes: "There is nothing but roguery to be found in a *villainous* man," wherein stressing an intimate association with knavery. Villains in Elizabethan drama were particularly evident in a genre known as "revenge

518 - KNAVERY **Ego Vices** *Personal Authority*	528 - FRAUD **Alter Ego Vices** *Personal Follower*
538 - VILLAINY **Charismatic Vices** *Group Authority*	548 - CORRUPTION **Cardinal Vices** *Group Representative*
558 - PROFANITY **Civil Liabilities** *Spiritual Authority*	568 - HERESY **Theological Vices** *Spiritual Disciple*
578 - APOSTASY **Ecumenical Vices** *Humanitarian Authority*	588 - ANARCHISM **Moralistic Vices** *Humanitarian Follower*
598 - NIHILISM **Humanistic Vices** *Transcendental Authority*	508 - DIABOLISM **Mystical Vices** *Transcendental Follower*

Fig. 15B - The "Meta" Themes for the Vices of Defect

KNAVERY	FRAUD
Previously, you (as punisher) have punitively acted in a punishing fashion towards me: overriding my (as antagonist) unmotivated treatment of you. But now, I (as personal authority) will *knavishly* act in an unmotivated fashion towards you: overruling your punitive treatment of me.	Previously, I (as personal authority) have knavishly acted in an unmotivated fashion towards you: overriding your (as punisher) punitive treatment of me. But now, you (as my personal follower) will *fraudulently* act in a punitive fashion towards me: overruling my (as PA) knavish treatment of you.
VILLAINY	**CORRUPTION**
Previously, you (as my personal follower) have fraudulently acted in a punitive fashion towards me: overriding my (as PA) knavish treatment of you. But now, I (as group authority) will knavishly act in a *villainous* fashion towards you: overruling your (as PF) fraudulent treatment of me.	Previously, I (as group authority) have knavishly acted in a villainous fashion towards you: overriding your (as PF) fraudulent treatment of me. But now, you (as group representative) will fraudulently act in a *corrupt* fashion towards me: overruling my (as GA) villainous treatment of you.
PROFANITY	**HERESY**
Previously, you (as group representative) have fraudulently acted in a corrupt fashion towards me: overriding my (as GA) villainous treatment of you. But now, I (as spiritual authority) will villainously act in a *profane* fashion towards you: overruling your (as GR) corrupt treatment of me.	Previously, I (as spiritual authority) have villainously acted in a profane fashion towards you: overriding your (as GR) corrupt treatment of me. But now, you (as my spiritual disciple) will *heretically* act in a corrupt fashion towards me: overruling my (as SA) profane treatment of you.
APOSTASY	**ANARCHISM**
Previously, you (as my spiritual disciple) have heretically acted in a corrupt fashion towards me: overriding my (as SA) profane treatment of you. But now, I (as humanitarian authority) will profanely act in an *apostasy*-filled fashion towards you: overruling your (as SD) heretical treatment of me.	Previously, I (as humanitarian authority) have profanely acted with apostasy towards you: overriding your (as SD) heretical treatment of me. But now, you (as representative member of humanity) will heretically act in an *anarchical* fashion towards me: overruling my (as HA) apostasy-filled treatment of you.
NIHILISM	**DIABOLISM**
Previously, you (as representative member of humanity) have heretically acted in an anarchical fashion towards me: overriding my (as HA) apostasy-filled treatment of me. But now, I (as transcendental authority) will act in a *nihilistic* fashion towards you: overruling your (as RH) anarchical treatment of me.	Previously, I (as transcendental authority) have acted in a nihilistic fashion towards you: overriding your (as RH) anarchical treatment of me. But now, you (as my transcendental follower) will anarchically act in a *diabolical* fashion towards me: overruling my (as TA) nihilistic treatment of you.

Table C-3 - The "Meta" Definitions for the Themes of Defect

tragedy," depicted as descending from the devils and vice that dominated earlier morality plays.

The basic "stock" villain appears in 19th century melodrama, typically in the form of a coarsely groomed seducer. This aspect extends in the dramatic genres of the American West, where the villain dressed in black (with a handlebar mustache, to match) pressures the vulnerable widow for the deed to her meager estate. This dastardly range of intimidation ultimately culminates with the heroin tied to the railroad track by the wicked villain, although rescued in the nick of time by the dashing hero. This enduring theme of crime/punishment particularly characterizes a group sphere of influence. The efforts of local law enforcement are usually sufficient to rectify individual instances of villainous infamy.

558 – PROFANITY

The group focus of villainy, in turn, gives way to the more universal scope of *profanity*. The term derives from the Latin *profanus* (outside the temple, not sacred), from *pro-* (before) and *fanum* (a temple). It respectively denotes contempt for sacred things, as in impiety or irreverence. Profanity refers to the choice of words that most would consider offensive. Its original connotation was restricted to occurrence of blasphemy, sacrilege, or taking the Lord's name in vain: as explicitly forbidden within the Second Commandment. The number of words considered profane has recently decreased due the general secularization of society as a whole.

The derivation of profanity (literally, before the shrine) gives a general indication of its spatial specificity. The concept of a walled enclosure into which only privileged persons or things may enter formally contrasts with the outside district of lesser worth/prestige. This notion of a threshold entails elaborate rules for clearly delineating the separation between the sacred and the profane. The priests of the Jewish Temple symbolized their separateness through a change of garments when entering the inner court. They further avoided routine foods and forms of family interaction in order to prepare themselves for teaching the public the distinction between the holy and profane.

The enduring contrast pitting the sacred against the profane is particularly telling in the context of organized religion, with profanity formally denigrating the sanctity of the spiritual authority perspective. Profanity formally counters the more positive prerequisites previously established in terms of *romanticism*, where such spiritual/universal overtones prove crucial for de-fining the overarching sense of the term. In this latter respect, profanity proves antithetical to any such revered sense of sacredness, whether through the influence of thought, word, or deed.

578 – APOSTASY

The next higher humanitarian level of authority, in turn, specifies the related theme of *apostasy*. The term derives from the Greek *apostasis* (a revolt or standing-away), from *apostenai* (to defect, to stand off), from the compound of *apo-* (away from) and *stenai* (to stand). It denotes the abandonment of one's religion or principles consistent with such an enduring humanitarian perspective. It is clearly antithetical to the more positive prerequisites previously established for *ecumenism*. Accordingly, apostasy signifies the desertion of one's moral foundation, or the giving up of one's moral state of existence. One who voluntarily embraces a particular belief cannot leave it without being labeled an apostate.

When the Roman Empire adopted Christianity as its state religion, apostates were punished through the deprivation of all civil rights. They could not give evidence in a court of law, and were not allowed to bequeath or inherit property. To induce another to apostasy was classified as a grievous capital offense. During the Middle Ages, both Civil and Canon Law classified apostates with heretics. The heretic differs from the apostate in that the first denies one or more doctrines of his favored faith, whereas the apostate denies the validity of the entire sect, a sin primarily looked upon as one of the most grievous. Apostasy, therefore, belonged to that special class of sins for which the Church imposed perpetual penance and excommunication without hope of pardon, leaving forgiveness to the will of God alone. Although penalties within the Christian tradition have softened somewhat in modern times, the stance within Islam has remained unchanged down through the ages.

598 – NIHILISM

The ascending hierarchy of authority roles ultimately culminates with respect to the crowning transcendental theme of *nihilism*. The term derives from the German *nihilismus*, from the Latin *nihil* nothing): from a compound of *ne-* (not) and *hilum* (a small thing, trifle). It signifies a belief in nothing, often bordering upon extreme skepticism. Nihilism chiefly represents the belief that there is no meaning or purpose to life, as in the absolute denial or negation of human values. No meaningful ethical standards or moral compass exists for determining knowledge or truth. According to German philosopher, Friedrich Nietzsche: "The uppermost values devalue themselves in *nihilism*." Nihilism, therefore, represents the direct moral antithesis of the more positive prerequisites previously established for the theme of Renaissance humanism.

For the nihilist, human progress is ephemeral in that there is little ultimate impact on the master course of the universe. In terms of this belief, one should strive for whatever pleasure or thrills accompany such a depressive outlook. This nihilistic perspective characterizes those that lead intense or reckless lives of self-destruction, as in violent revolutionaries that seek to destroy existing society by resorting to terrorist activities. Promoting the nihilistic stance that there is little in the way of objective certainty or truth necessarily opens fissures within the established social order, wherein diminishing the productive ends emerging from a flourishing lifestyle.

528 – FRAUD

The remaining sequence of themes (for defect) based upon the ascending series of follower roles is initiated with respect to the personal follower theme of *fraud*. The term derives from the Latin *fraus* or *fraudis* (fraud). It represents the strict moral antithesis of the positive prerequisites previously established for pragmatism. In a legal context, fraud is defined as willfully misrepresenting the truth to the detriment of another. Although chiefly a tort proceeding, fraud further extends to the criminal charge of false pretense. Fraud is generally judged as either actual or constructive. Actual fraud requires that the act be motivated by the desire to deceive another to his detriment. Constructive fraud is a presumption of overreaching conduct that occurs when profits derive from a relation of trust (as in a fiduciary relationship).

The courts have found it counterproductive to make a rigid definition of the type of misrepresentation amounting to actual fraud, preferring to consider the individual factors in each case. This misrepresentation may be regarded as an outright lie, a failure to disclose information, or a statement made in reckless disregard of potential inaccuracy. Actual fraud is never the direct outcome of accident or negligence due to the requirement that the act be deliberately intended to deceive. The question of guilt further depends upon the competence and specialized knowledge of the alleged victim.

A betrayal of personal trust remains the hallmark of fraud consistent with placement within the personal follower level of defect. It directly contrasts to the more positive focus of pragmatism, the latter of which targets the more rewarding aspects conducive to individual well-being: a more personalized variation on the "common good" previously established with respect to utilitarianism. Fraud clearly represents a darker perversion in this regard, where one individual deceptively defrauds another, a factor prohibited through the most stringent of legal means.

548 – CORRUPTION

The personal prerequisites for fraud, in turn, extend to a group sphere of influence with respect to the respective follower theme of *corruption*. The term derives from a compound of the Latin *cor-* (intensification) and *rumpere* or *ruptum* (to break). It denotes the breach of confidence that typically accompanies such a fraudulent range of practices. Corruption represents the chief moral antithesis of the virtuous theme of utilitarianism, where the welfare of the group is circumvented to the selfish benefit of a group official or faction. Indeed, corruption has remained the bane of elected forms of government as far back as the age of the Roman Republic. In 159 BCE, the *lex Cornelia* punished (with exile) those found guilty of bribing the electorate. Therefore, a general prohibition against the direct purchase of votes must have existed well in advance of the passage of this specific law. Furthermore, the *lex Calpurnia* (of 67 BCE) imposed heavy fines on any candidate employing bribery (whether successful or not).

A similar pattern further applies to the American form of representative government. Corrupt practices associated with elections, as well as offenses by public officials, include bribery, the sale of public office, the awarding of public contracts to favored firms, and the granting of land/franchises in return for monetary rewards. Election fraud includes efforts to influence or intimidate voters, as well as tampering with the official ballot or vote tally. Nearly every democratic country has passed laws aimed towards guarding against corruption in political campaigns and official state duties. For larger cities, election fraud has long been associated with a corrupt style of political "machine."

In terms of the federal government, the Corrupt Practices Act of 1925, the Hatch Act of 1940, and the campaign financing reforms of 1974 aimed to limit campaign spending and the size of political contributions. Public disclosure requirements, as well as public funding for presidential campaigns were instituted in reaction to abuses stemming from the secret campaign funds employed during the presidential election of 1972. These corrupt practices reforms have also applied to business and labor unions, as in "price fixing" or misappropriation of funds for rigging union elections. Although the temptation towards corruption proves a seductive option, the elaborate system of governmental checks and balances fortunately limits such occurrences to a relatively small sphere of the common public welfare.

568 – HERESY

Ascending, once again, to the next higher spiritual level, in turn, gives way to the universal scope of *heresy*. It is traditionally defined as the undermining or corruption of religious ritual or doctrine. As such, heresy represents the direct moral antithesis of its virtuous counterpart in ecclesiasticism. The term derives from the Old French *heresie*, from the Latin *hæresis*: employed by Christian writers in reference to an unorthodox sect or doctrine. The Latin tradition, in turn, derives from the Greek *hairesis* (a taking or choosing), from *hairein* (to take or seize): wherein taking opinions or beliefs in opposition to those conventionally accepted within the community. Heresy represents a more abstract (spiritual) variation on the more basic "strike" option employed by the group representative. Martin Luther, for instance, was clearly regarded as heretical by the Roman Catholic establishment of his day.

In the terms of the Christian tradition, heresy is defined as those beliefs or viewpoints held by church members in contradiction to orthodoxy or core doctrines. It is formally distinguished from apostasy in that the latter represents a complete abandonment of faith, rendering the apostate a deserter or renegade member. Heresy is also distinct from a schism, which is a splitting of church membership brought about by disputes over hierarchy or discipline, rather than matters of doctrine. The heretic generally considers oneself a true believer in terms of such doctrinal disputes.

During Christianity's first three centuries, numerous sects came into conflict with the accepted doctrine of the early Church. The First Council of Nicea (in 325 CE) addressed the heresy of Arianism, the first of many challenges to Christian orthodoxy. Excommunication soon became the preferred means for dealing with heretical individuals or groups. This enduring conflict between the troublesome heretic and the prevailing ecclesias-tical establishment is a theme repeated at many junctures in Church history. Although a small number of schisms have successfully endured, the vast majority were suppressed through forcible means, a fitting exemplar to anyone willing to risk such a foray into the darker realm of the vices.

588 – ANARCHISM

The spiritual prerequisites for heresy, in turn, are modified into the more enduring humanitarian vice of *anarchism*. The term derives from the Greek compound of *an-* (privation) and *arche* (government). It denotes the theory that government is oppressively restrictive to personal freedom, wherefore to be abolished in favor of a free system of agreement between individuals. Central to anarchist thought is a belief in individual human freedoms and the denial of any outward authority: particularly that of the state, which hinders personal development.

Beginning with the Middle Ages, the anarchist tradition became closely associated with utopian or millenarian religious movements. These include the Brethren of the Free Spirit in the 13th century, and the Anabaptists of the 16th century. The modern sense of political anarchism emerged in the 18th and 19th centuries, chiefly through the writings of William Godwin, P. J. Proudhon. Russian anarchist, Mikhail Bakunin, in turn, invested the movement with its collectivist and violent overtones that persist to this day, despite revisionary efforts by Piotr Kropotkin and Leo Tolstoy. Political anarchism was suppressed by the Bolshevik party following the Russian Revolution.

As an organized movement, anarchism has largely faded in significance, although retaining philosophical status as the inspiration for political and social protest. Contrary to popular belief, terrorism never was adopted as a widespread platform for anarchist theory or practice. Some anarchists, however, engaged in what was termed "propaganda by the deed:" namely, acts of terrorism or assassination against state officials or the ruling class. In recent years, anarchists have mounted highly vocal (and sometimes aggressive) public protests at international conferences attended by representatives of the major industrial nations, such as recent demonstrations at the World Trade Organization or World Economic Forum.

Anarchism proves a fitting counterpoint to the more positive prerequisites previously established for eclecticism, the latter of which celebrates the collective spirit underlying all human endeavor. In contrast, anarchism proposes to destroy all that has worked so well in the past, favoring radical individualism at the expense of the establishment status quo. Anarchism basically founders in its failure to ensure that a better system of governance will necessarily emerge: throwing its lot to the vagaries of chance and well-meaning intentions. Consequently, anarchism has never appealed to more than a small segment of society as a whole, marginalized to the point of representing little more than an excuse for demonstrating before the global media.

508 – DIABOLISM

The ascending sequence of follower themes ultimately culminates with respect to the darker transcendental theme of *diabolism*. The term derives from the Greek *diabolos* (the Devil), from *diaballein* (to slander), from *dia-* (across) and *ballein* (to throw): reflecting the fallen angel's scriptural role as adversary. It generally refers to the worship of deities that take a demoniac form by semi-civilized peoples. The worship of the devil dates to the earliest stages of moral dualism, perhaps deriving from the Zoroastrian system of the opposing deities. The divinities of Ormuzd and Ahriman symbolized both good and evil principles, respectively. Instances of ritual Satanism are comparatively rare, not to be confused with the orgies of witchcraft conducted for the purposes of creating an unholy pact.

A number of modern groups practicing Satanism have emerged in concert with the resurgence of occultism during the 20th century. Other groups of reputed devil worshipers, such as the Yezidi sect of Kurdistan, view the world as the creation of Lucifer (the fallen angel): whom they propitiate in a symbolic form through the peacock. Although many other examples could be cited, this exercise will not be undertaken at this juncture due to the considerable depth of detail cited for diabolism in the preceding Chapter *14*. Regardless of the individual traditions therein, the general theme of diabolism shares a number of common features; namely, a transcendental follower perspective manifest in terms of a darker range of themes. Diabolism represents the chief moral antithesis of its respective positive counterpart in religious mysticism, a contrast that should never be confused in terms of the pure sense of inspiration in relation to the spiritually minded.

THE ACCESSORY LISTING OF THEMES FOR THE VICES OF DEFECT

The completed description of the main listing of themes for the realm of defect, in turn, invites

further comparisons to the predicted *accessory* variations. Similar to the pattern previously established for the virtuous themes, the accessory variations for the themes of defect directly complement the main listings of terms, with the exception that the "you" and "I" polarities are now reversed, adding a crucial (empathic) dimension to the dual schematic format. A suitable number of accessory themes for the realm of defect have successfully been identified, permitting the accessory listing of terms shown in **Fig. 15B**. This schematic listing of accessory themes effectively mirrors the pattern previously established for the main themes, with the exception that the respective "you" and "I" perspectives are now reversed in relation to the authority/follower roles. Furthermore, in terms of the three-digit coding system, the final digit for each of the accessory themes is now specified as a "9" (instead of an "8").

For instance, the main authority sequence of themes (knavery-villainy-profanity-apostasy-nihilism), in turn, contrast with the respective accessory counterparts; e.g., mischievousness-licentiousness-scandalousness-infidelity-alienation. Furthermore, the main *follower* sequence of fraud-corruption-heresy-anarchism-diabolism similarly reciprocates its respective accessory trend (deception-venality-schismatism-lawlessness-sorcery). Although the particular degree of correspondence for several of these themes is perhaps not as ideal as could be expected, the seamless cohesiveness of this overall accessory system proves the crucial factor, here. Indeed, many of these accessory terms are not commonly encountered in general usage. Consequently, a more detailed analysis of this accessory class of themes is deferred for a more comprehensive treatment in an upcoming edition.

THE FORMAL SCHEMATIC DEFINITIONS FOR THE ACCESSORY THEMES OF DEFECT

The true test of validity for this accessory sequence of themes, however, ultimately extends to their formal incorporation within the schematic definition format. In direct analogy to the main listing of schematic definitions, the respective accessory themes are similarly endowed, wherefore specifying higher-order perspectives on the more basic complement of individual terms. For instance, the "meta" schematic definition for "venality" encompasses the four accessory vices of corruption as subsets (e.g., sedition-avengement-lechery-pusillanimity). Accordingly, the complete four-page listing of schematic definitions for the accessory themes (of defect) is schematically de-

519 - MISCHIEF **Ego Vices - II** *Personal Authority*	**529 - DECEPTIVENESS** **Alter Ego Vices - II** *Personal Follower*
539 - LICENTIOUSNESS **Charismatic Vices - II** *Group Authority*	**549 - VENALITY** **Cardinal Vices - II** *Group Representative*
559 - SCANDAL **Civil Liabilities - II** *Spiritual Authority*	**569 - SCHISMATISM** **Theological Vices - II** *Spiritual Disciple*
579 - INFIDELITY **Ecumenical Vices - II** *Humanitarian Authority*	**589 - LAWLESSNESS** **Moralistic Vices - II** *Humanitarian Follower*
599 - ALIENATION **Humanistic Vices - II** *Transcendental Authority*	**509 - SORCERY** **Mystical Vices - II** *Transcendental Follower*

Fig. 15C – The Accessory Themes for the Vices of Defect

MISCHIEVOUSNESS	DECEPTIVENESS
Previously, I (as punisher) have punitively acted in a punishing fashion towards you: overriding your (as antagonist) unmotivated treatment of me.	Previously, you (as personal authority) have mischievously acted in an unmotivated fashion towards me: overriding my (as punisher) punitive treatment of you.
But now, you (as personal authority) will *mischievously* act in an unmotivated fashion towards me: overruling my punitive treatment of you.	But now, I (as your personal follower) will punitively act in a *deceptive* fashion towards you: overruling your (as PA) mischievous treatment of me.
LICENTIOUSNESS	**VENALITY**
Previously, I (as your personal follower) have punitively acted in a deceptive fashion towards you: overriding your (as PA) mischievous treatment of me.	Previously, you (as group authority) have mischievously acted in a licentious fashion towards me: overriding my (as PF) deceptive treatment of you.
But now, you (as group authority) will mischievously act in a *licentious* fashion towards me: overruling my (as PF) deceptive treatment of you.	But now, I (as group representative) will deceptively act in a *venal* fashion towards you: overruling your (as GA) licentious treatment of me.
SCANDALOUSNESS	**SCHISMATISM**
Previously, I (as group representative) have deceptively acted in a venal fashion towards you: overriding your (as GA) licentious treatment of me.	Previously, you (as spiritual authority) have licentiously acted in a scandalous fashion towards me: overriding my (as GR) venal treatment of you.
But now, you (as spiritual authority) will licentiously act in a *scandalous* fashion towards me: overruling my (as GR) venal treatment of you.	But now, I (as spiritual disciple) will venally act in a *schismatic* fashion towards you: overruling your (as SA) scandalous treatment of me.
INFIDELITY	**LAWLESSNESS**
Previously, I (as spiritual disciple) have venally acted in a schismatic fashion: overriding your (as SA) scandalous sense of licentiousness.	Previously, you (as humanitarian authority) have scandalously acted with infidelity towards me: overriding my (as SD) schismatic treatment of you.
But now, you (as humanitarian authority) will scandalously act with *infidelity* towards me: overruling my (as SD) schismatic treatment of you.	But now, I (as representative member of humanity) will schismatically act in a *lawless* fashion towards you: overruling your (as HA) scandalous sense of infidelity.
ALIENATION	**SORCERY**
Previously, I (as representative member of humanity) have schismatically acted in a lawless fashion towards you: overriding your (as HA) scandalous sense of infidelity.	Previously, you (as my transcendental authority) have acted in an alienated fashion towards me: overriding my (as RH) schismatic sense of lawlessness
But now, you (as transcendental authority) will infidelously act in an *alienated* fashion towards me: overruling my (as RH) sense of lawlessness.	But now, I (as your transcendental follower) will lawlessly act with *sorcery* towards you: overruling your (as TA) alienated treatment of me.

Table C-4 – The Accessory Definitions for the Thematic Vices

picted in **Table C-4**. When further contrasted with the schematic definitions for the main listings of themes (from **Table C-3** of Chapter 9), the reciprocal interplay of "you" and "I" perspectives are definitely apparent. When examined in concert, both the main and accessory themes for realm of defect permit a degree of empathic versatility unprecedented in terms of precision, allowing for considerable insights into the realm of deceptive communication. Through the stepwise modification of the final digit for entries 500 through 599 within the three-digit coding system, (namely, *8* and *9*), the formal description of the vices of defect now becomes conceptually complete.

In summary, the completed description of the accessory variations for the vices of defect permits unprecedented insights into the darker realm of the criminal mind. As is so often the case, motives of criminals are labeled in an entirely objective fashion consistent with their social stigma, offering precious little insight into the underlying subjective perspectives. Through the aid of the *accessory* class of defect, however, both objective and subjective viewpoints for the vices of defect can be examined in a complementary fashion, whereby allowing the offender a subjective perspective from the viewpoint of the victim (and vice versa). Hopefully, these expanded conceptual insights will serve to remedy many of the random acts of violence affecting Western culture today.

The further formal identification of the general unifying themes for the vices of defect offers similar dramatic inroads conducive to remedial oversight. Many of the darker themes enjoy widespread expression in the literary tradition. Indeed, what would a melodrama or tragedy be without an antagonist to contrast with the protagonist. In terms of this range of darker authority roles, the ascending series of themes; namely, knavery, villainy, profanity, apostasy, and nihilism proves particularly suggestive of many literary traditions.

For instance, the dastardly villain or the turncoat apostate proves a fitting counterpoint to the virtuous prerequisites of the fictional hero. Furthermore, for the remaining darker realm of the follower roles, the respective themes of fraud, corruption, heresy, anarchism, and diabolism provide a suitably effective counterpoint for their respective virtuous counterparts. This enduring moral contrast across this broad array of general unifying themes represents an unprecedented innovation on the world scene, the literary dynamics embodied in such a thematic morality play ultimately decipherable to a high degree of precision (and without necessarily resorting to the individual virtues/vices at issue within the script). Hence, this breakthrough overall technology fortuitously enjoys two distinct degrees conceptual versatility: namely, the individual contrasts between the specific virtues and vices, as well as a broader overarching counterpoint utilizing the respective general unifying themes.

This dual degree of versatility provides an extra set of checks and balances with respect to the certitude of that being communicated, ensuring a suitably effective model of the dynamics underlying affective language in general. Hopefully, this increased conceptual understanding in relation to such darker motives will permit more effective interventions on the world scene before irreparable damage can occur, permitting a more peaceful and harmonious global community. Here, advanced partnerships between affiliated spheres of influence now become eminently more feasible, offering dramatic new inroads towards global peace and stability. In concert with the supportive individual traditions of the virtues, values, and ideals, the overarching grand unifying themes promise a new era for collaborative human endeavors based upon such noble principles, ushering in a new age of cooperation for policymakers throughout the world.

PART-III

16

AN INTRODUCTION TO
THE VICES OF EXCESS

The enduring contrast between the virtues and the vices of defect emerges as one of the most intriguing features for the newly devised ethical system. The ascending hierarchy of the vices of defect described in Chapter *10* represents a fitting addition to the established ethical traditions, owing its direct correspondence to the virtuous mode. Although the newly designated groupings of vices prove convincing on an intuitive level, they can scarcely claim to be all-inclusive by any measure. In particular, only half of the Seven Deadly Sins are directly accounted for within the realm of defect. Indeed, pride, envy, and covetousness defy incorporation into the preliminary classifications of defect. Fortunately, this anomaly is ultimately explained in terms of an entirely new category of vice, referred to since classical times as the vices of excess.

The ancient Greeks particularly exhibited extreme disdain for any outward expression of excess. The entrance to the famed Greek oracle at Delphi is inscribed with the stirring admonition: "Nothing in excess," attesting to their ideal mindset in moderation. In fact, Aristotle was among the first to describe a dual system for the vices; namely, the vices of defect (described in Chapter *4*), as well as the corresponding vices of excess: defined as the range of extremes with respect to the virtues. In this latter respect, Aristotle viewed the virtuous realm as a system of "mean values" (or norms) interposed between the vices of defect and vices of excess. Virtue, accordingly, represents the mean-norm interposed between defect and excess: an aspect favoring moderation insofar as choosing the middle ground between these two main categories of vice. The following schematic table offers sample listing of specific examples characterizing this Theory of the Golden Mean, gratefully adapted from Aristotle's *Nicomachean Ethics*.

The *Vices of* DEFECT	The *Virtues:* "MEAN VALUES"	The *Vices of* EXCESS
cowardice	**courage**	rashness
stinginess	**liberality**	extravagance
laziness	**ambition**	greed
secrecy	**modesty**	pride
moroseness	**honesty**	loquacity
quarrelsome	**wittiness**	buffoonery

According to the first listed example, courage represents the ideal (mean) value interposed between cowardice (defect) and rashness (excess). Furthermore, in terms of giving money, liberality represents the mean value, whereas defect/excess is represented as extravagance and stinginess. With respect to congeniality, the mean value is defined as wittiness, whereas buffoonery suggests a state of excess, while quarrelsomeness indicates defect. Here, morality (like art) ultimately consists of deciding where to draw the line! The virtues, accordingly, represent a predisposition to take a moderate course, effectively defined as staying to "the middle path." Although the general pattern for Aristotle's system proves highly informative, a few of these terms appear somewhat artificially placed; a shortcoming fortunately resolved within the expanded context of the revised vices of excess depicted in **Fig. 16A**.

According to the basic "tripartite" system underlying the Theory of the Man, the initial class of the vices of defect represents a well-defined system of opposing qualities (defined as the absence of virtue). The vices of excess, in contrast, prove somewhat less clear-cut in nature; representing a more ambiguous determination of extremes with respect to the virtues (with relativistic consequences for differing cultures). The vices of excess,

310	**311**
Pride	Shame
312	**313**
Impudence	Insolence

(*XS*) EGO STATES
(Personal Authority)

→

320	**321**
Flattery	Criticism
322	**323**
Envy	Disdain

(*XS*) ALTER EGO STATES
(Personal Follower)

330	**331**
Vanity	Humiliation
332	**333**
Arrogance	Audacity

(*XS*) PERSONAL IDEALS
(Group Authority)

→

340	**341**
Adulation	Ridicule
342	**343**
Jealousy	Contempt

(*XS*) CARDINAL VIRTUES
(Group Representative)

350	**351**
Conceit	Mortification
352	**353**
Impetuosity	Rashness

(*XS*) CIVIL LIBERTIES
(Spiritual Authority)

→

360	**361**
Patronization	Scorn
362	**363**
Covetousness	Reproach

(*XS*) THEOLOGICAL VIRTUES
(Spiritual Disciple)

370	**371**
Pretentiousness	Anguish
372	**373**
Presumption	Boldness

(*XS*) ECUMENICAL IDEALS
(Humanitarian Authority)

→

380	**381**
Obsequiousness	Mockery
382	**383**
Longing	Chagrin

(*XS*) CLASSICAL VALUES
(Humanitarian Follower)

390	**391**
Sanctimony	Tribulation
392	**393**
Smugness	Harshness

(*XS*) HUMANISTIC VALUES
(Transcendental Authority)

→

300	**301**
Sycophancy	Cynicism
302	**303**
Affectation	Bitterness

(*XS*) MYSTICAL VALUES
(Transcendental Follower)

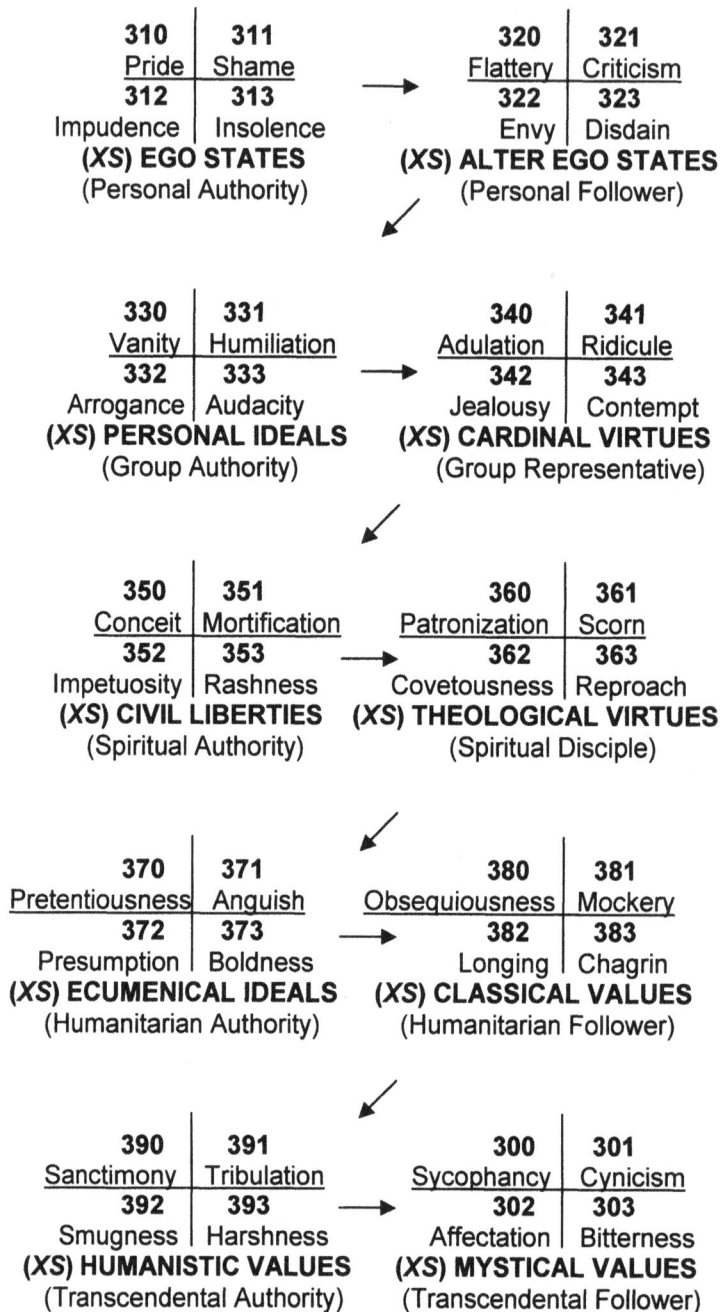

Fig. 16A – The Vices of Excess

accordingly, represent a more ambiguous style of moral continuum, a gray area of virtually relativistic proportions.

The first major indications of a trend towards excess typically occur during adolescence, when teens increasingly strive to gain independence from the family unit. This does not necessarily mean to imply that excess is the exclusive domain of rebellious youth, for it generally carries over into adulthood as well. Certainly, we all strive to be recognized for the magnitude of our achievements, an aspiration further accompanied by the attendant advantages of wealth or power. Athletes strive to achieve the limits within their sport of choice, whereas politicians endeavor to reach enhanced status in relation to their constituency. This urge to distinguish oneself by pressing the extremes on many fronts remains a natural inclination, although the dividing line separating the true realm of excess amounts to somewhat of a vague value judgment.

Perhaps the most crucial criterion in this regard concerns of distinction between cooperation and selfishness, where selfish tendencies (such as pride, shame, impudence, etc.) characterize the overall realm of excess. Those forms of excess that preserve social cooperation, however, are more likely to be tolerated in a social setting. Indeed, Logan P. Smith once wrote: "A slight touch of friendly malice and amusement towards those we love keeps our affections for them from turning flat." Henry Ward Beecher further writes: "A man without mirth is like a wagon without springs. He is jolted disagreeably by every pebble in the road."

Some range of extremes (in contrast to pure seriousness, accordingly, appears crucial for preventing boredom in one's everyday affairs. This is typically experienced as novelty, excitement, or variations in intensity. Dr. Marvin Zuckerman of the University of Delaware (2000) has specifically devised a sensation-seeking scale based upon three basic parameters. The first of these is defined as an adventure/thrill-seeking scale, defined as a preference for extreme sports or high-risk behaviors. The second dimension is further described as experience-seeking, a tamer feature relating to the quest for sensation through intellectual curiosity or the senses: as expressed in aesthetic appreciation of the arts and sciences, as well as the tendency towards wanderlust and world-travel. A third factor concerns the ages-old phenomenon of *disinhibition*, as reflected in the mood altering properties of drugs or alcohol. This similarly extends to a party atmosphere, replete with its seductive mix of shifting social coalitions.

According to these three basic parameters, sensation-seeking equates to the spirit of adventure underlying all extreme endeavors, as particularly celebrated in the exploits of the trailblazer or international explorer. Dr. Frank Farley of Temple University (1991) further characterizes this extreme trait as the type "T" personality: the "T" representing an abbreviation for thrill-seeking: characterized by the quest for excitement concerning high-risk activities. It directly contrasts with the (small) type "t" personality; namely, that more staid segment of the population that is satisfied with the safer thrills in life.

To a modest degree, the realm of excess plays a key role in maintaining the emotional stability of the individual, a prominent feature with respect to humor and comedy. Indeed, some of the world's most creative people live on a perpetual balance of excess (or even mania): a circumstance sometimes leading to a tendency towards eccentricity. The eccentric generally revels in hyperbole and excess, developing fantastical ideas to the amusement of the more rational among us. These extreme perspectives similarly extend to the exploits of the daredevil or publicity-seeker, genres highly favored within the entertainment industry. Although this degree of excess often proves highly irritating, it nevertheless remains relatively innocuous compared to the darker realm of the vices of defect. As such, the vices of excess are generally tolerated within society, although they can also lead to conflict when pressed to extremes.

THE MASTER SCHEMATIC FORMAT FOR THE VICES OF EXCESS

In deference to Aristotle's original treatment of excess, the further applications to the specifics of the power hierarchy allow for a degree in precision unprecedented in the earlier traditions. According to this expanded context, the communicational factors underlying each of the vices of excess precisely correspond to a measured degree of excess with respect to the virtuous mode. Indeed, many of the individual vices of excess are more-or-less universally accepted in common usage. For instance, *pride* represents the extreme counterpart of nostalgia, whereas *shame* makes a similar correspondence to guilt. Furthermore, *flattery* formally expands upon the hero-worship expressed by the personal follower, whereas *criticism* designates a more excessive form of blame. Indeed, it ultimately proves possible to devise an entire ten-level hierarchy of the vices of excess, formally mirroring the respective virtuous mode.

(A)

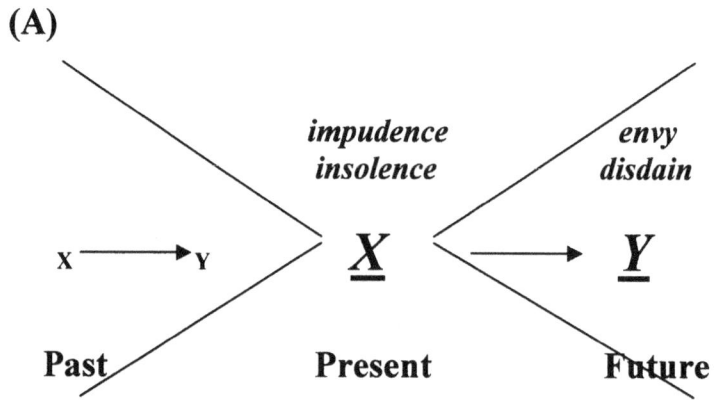

(B)

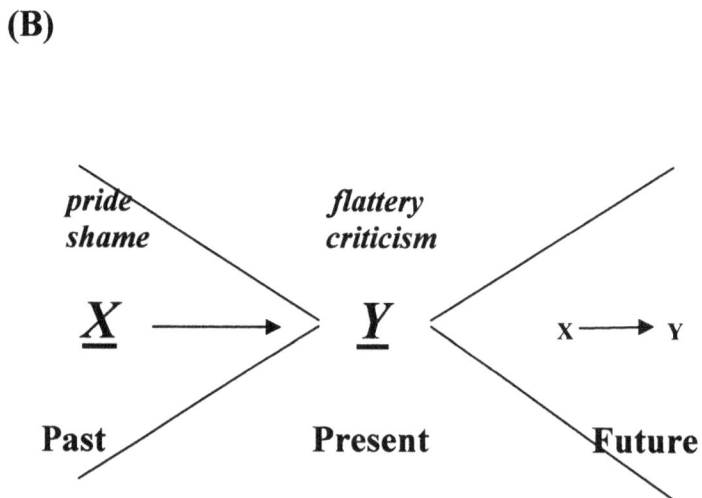

Fig. 16B - The Two-stage Schematic for the Vices of Excess

The complete ascending hierarchy for the vices of excess is schematically depicted in **Fig. 16A**, in addition to the respective three-digit codes (that now all begin with a first-place digit of "3"). This format is also depicted in the compact table immediately below, demonstrating the hierarchial relationships in a more condensed context.

Pride • Flattery	**Shame • Criticism**
Vanity • Adulation	**Humiliation • Ridicule**
Conceit • Patronization	**Mortification • Scorn**
Pretention • Obsequious.	**Anguish • Mockery**
Sanctimony • Sycophancy	**Tribulation • Cynicism**
Impudence • Envy	**Insolence • Disdain**
Arrogance • Jealousy	**Audacity • Contempt**
Impetuosity • Covetous.	**Rashness • Reproach**
Presumption • Longing	**Boldness • Chagrin**
Smugness • Affectation	**Harshness • Bitterness**

This hierarchy of excess is identical in form and function to that previously established for the virtuous mode. Owing to the greater degree of uncertainty involved in determining the precise degree of excess, this hierarchy scarcely exhibits the clarity or precision previously seen for the more clearly defined virtues, values, and ideals. A certain degree of ambiguity, accordingly, is unavoidable for the more abstract (humanitarian and transcendental) levels within this hierarchy of excess. Fortunately, the personal, group, and spiritual levels for the power hierarchy certainly prove adequate to the task, with well-defined terms for each of the individually predicted slots.

THE BEHAVIORAL FOUNDATIONS FOR THE VICES OF EXCESS

Beginning for the most basic personal level within the hierarchy of excess, pride and shame are formally defined as the excessive counterparts of the respective ego states of nostalgia and guilt. Furthermore, flattery and criticism, in turn, represent excessive variations on the respective "alter ego" states of hero-worship and blame. In similar fashion, the complete eight-part complement of the personal terms for the vices of excess is schematically depicted in **Fig. 16B**. This diagram directly mirrors the virtuous prerequisites previously established in **Fig. 3A** (of Chapter *3*), with the exception that the vices of excess are now substituted for the original groupings of ego and alter ego states. According to Part A of this diagram, the *flattery* maneuver of the personal follower subsequently prompts the feelings of pride experienced by the personal authority figure, whereas *criticism* similarly prompts a corresponding sense of shame. Furthermore, in Part B, impudence leads to feelings of *envy*, whereas insolence, in turn, prompts feelings of *disdain*. This formal arrangement of past, present, and future time dimensions represents a schematic depiction of the vices of excess in relation to the eight predicted authority/follower roles. For instance, pride and shame represent past-directed forms of "alternate" time dimensions, whereas envy and disdain specify future-directed perspectives: as the dual wedge-segments of the diagram respectively serve to indicate. The remaining four terms are alternately depicted as actively occurring in the present, as indicated in the less introspective (and more objectively oriented) scope of the terms; namely, impudence, insolence, flattery, and criticism.

THE TEN LEVEL HIERARCHY FOR THE VICES OF EXCESS

This preliminary "personal" level of excess, in turn, extends the group, spiritual, humanitarian, and transcendental levels as well. For instance, for the next higher "group" level of organization, the flattering sense of *adulation* expressed by the group representative further prompts the prideful sense of *vanity* experienced by the group authority. Similarly, the critical sense of *ridicule* of the follower figure, in turn, prompts the shameful sense of *humiliation* by the authority figure. In terms of the future-directed dimensions, the impudent sense of *arrogance* for the group authority further prompts the envious sense of *jealousy* expressed the group representative. Furthermore, the former's insolent sense of audacity alternately prompts the disdainful sense of *contempt* of the latter.

This systematic addition of terms, in turn, extends to the remaining spiritual, humanitarian, and transcendental authority levels, although the distinctions separating these terms are perhaps not as precise as those previously specified for the personal/group levels. Accordingly, the respective choice of terms is often not as exacting as might be hoped for. Precision notwithstanding, a definite overall pattern of motivational trends is effectively demonstrated for the entire ten-level span for the hierarchy of excess. For instance, the past-directed authority sequence of pride-vanity-conceit-pretentiousness-sanctimony further complements the related authority sequence of shame-humiliation-mortification-anguish-tribulation. Furthermore, the related follower sequence of flattery-adulation-patronization-obsequiousness-

PRIDE	FLATTERY
Previously, you (as reinforcer) have excessively acted rewardingly towards me: overriding my (as procurer) extremely solicitous treatment of you But now, I (as personal authority) will *pridefully* act in an extremely nostalgic fashion towards you: overruling your (as reinforcer) excessively rewarding treatment of me.	Previously, I (as personal authority) have pridefully acted extremely nostalgically towards you: overriding your (reinforcer) excessively rewarding treatment of me. But now, you (as my personal follower) will *flatteringly* act excessively rewardingly towards me: overruling my (as PA) prideful treatment of you.
VANITY	**ADULATION**
Previously, you (as personal follower) have flatteringly acted in an excessively rewarding fashion towards me: overriding my (as PA) prideful treatment of you. But now, I (as group authority) will pridefully act in a *vain* fashion towards you: overruling your (as PF) flattering treatment of me.	Previously, I (as group authority) have pridefully acted in a vain fashion towards you: overriding your (as PF) flattering treatment of me. But now, you (as group representative) will flatteringly act with *adulation* towards me: overruling my (as GA) vain sense of pride.
CONCEIT	**PATRONIZATION**
Previously, you (as group representative) have flatteringly acted with adulation towards me: overriding my (as GA) prideful sense of vanity. But now, I (as spiritual authority) will vainly act in a *conceited* fashion towards you: overruling your (as GR) flattering sense of adulation.	Previously, I (as spiritual authority) have vainly acted in a conceited fashion towards you: overriding your (as GR) flattering sense of adulation. But now, you (as my spiritual disciple) will flatteringly act in a *patronizing* fashion towards me: overruling my (as SA) vain sense of conceit.
PRETENTIOUSNESS	**OBSEQUIOUSNESS**
Previously, you (as my spiritual disciple) have flatteringly acted in a patronizing fashion towards me: overriding my (as SA) vain sense of conceit. But now, I (as humanitarian authority) will conceitedly act in a *pretentious* fashion towards you: overruling your (as SD) patronizing treatment of me.	Previously, I (as humanitarian authority) have conceitedly acted in a pretentious fashion towards you: overriding your (as SD) patronizing treatment of me. But now, you (as a representative member of humanity) will patronizingly act in an *obsequious* fashion towards me: overruling my (as HA) pretentious treatment of you.
SANCTIMONY	**SMUGNESS**
Previously, you (as representative member of humanity) have patronizingly acted obsequiously towards me: overriding my (as HA) pretentious treatment of you. But now, I (as transcendental authority) will pretentiously act in a *sanctimonious* fashion towards you: overruling your (as RH) obsequious treatment of me.	Previously, I (as transcendental authority) have pretentiously acted in a sanctimonious fashion towards you: overriding your (as RH) obsequious treatment of me. But now, you (as transcendental follower) will obsequiously act in a *smug* fashion towards me: overruling my (as TA) sanctimonious treatment of you.

Table F-1 – The Definitions Based Upon Pride/Flattery

SHAME	CRITICISM
Previously, you (as reinforcer) have excessively acted in a lenient fashion towards me: overriding my (as procurer) extreme admission of having acted submissively towards you. But now, I (as personal authority) will *shamefully* act extremely guiltily towards you: overruling your (as reinforcer) excessively lenient treatment of me.	Previously, I (as personal authority) have shamefully acted extremely guiltily towards you: overriding your (reinforcer) excessively lenient treatment of me. But now, you (as my personal follower) will *critically* act in a blameful fashion towards me: overruling my (as PA) shameful treatment of you.
HUMILIATION	**RIDICULE**
Previously, you (as personal follower) have critically acted blamefully towards me: overriding my (as PA) shameful treatment of you. But now, I (as group authority) will shamefully act in a *humiliated* fashion towards you: overruling your (as PF) critical treatment of me.	Previously, I (as group authority) have shamefully acted in a humiliated fashion towards you: overriding your (as PF) critical treatment of me. But now, you (as group representative) will critically-*ridicule* me: overruling my (as GA) shameful sense of humiliation.
MORTIFICATION	**SCORN**
Previously, you (as group representative) have critically-ridiculed me: overriding my (as GA) shameful sense of humiliation. But now, I (as spiritual authority) will humiliatingly act in a *mortified* fashion towards you: overruling your (as GR) critical-ridiculing of me.	Previously, I (as spiritual authority) have humiliatingly acted in a mortified fashion towards you: overriding your (as GR) critical-ridiculing of me. But now, you (as my spiritual disciple) will *scornfully*-ridicule me: overruling my (as SA) mortified treatment of you.
ANGUISH	**MOCKERY**
Previously, you (as my spiritual disciple) have scornfully-ridiculed me: overriding my (as SA) mortified treatment of you. But now, I (as humanitarian authority) will mortifiedly act in an *anguished* fashion towards you: overruling your (as SD) scornful-ridiculing of me.	Previously, I (as humanitarian authority) have mortifyingly acted in an anguished fashion towards you: overriding your (as SD) scornful-ridiculing of me. But now, you (as representative member of humanity) will scornfully act in a *mocking* fashion towards me: overruling my (as HA) anguished treatment of you.
TRIBULATION	**CYNICISM**
Previously, you (as representative member of humanity) have scornfully-mocked me: overriding my (as HA) anguished treatment of you. But now, I (as transcendental authority) will anguishingly act with *tribulation* towards you: overruling your (as RH) scornful-mocking of me.	Previously, I (as transcendental authority) have anguishingly acted with tribulation towards you: overriding your (as RH) scornful-mocking of me. But now, you (as my transcendental follower) will mockingly act in a *cynical* fashion towards me: overruling my (as TA) anguished sense of tribulation.

Table F-2 – The Definitions Based Upon Shame/Criticism

IMPUDENCE	ENVY
Previously, I (as reinforcer) have extremely acted rewardingly towards you: overriding your (as procurer) excessively solicitous treatment of me. But now, you (as personal authority) will *impudently* act in an excessively solicitous fashion towards me: overruling my (as reinforcer) extremely rewarding treatment of you.	Previously, you (as personal authority) have impudently acted in an excessively solicitous fashion towards me: overriding my (as reinforcer) extremely rewarding treatment of you. But now, I (as your personal follower) will *enviously* act in an extremely approving fashion towards you: overruling your (as PA) impudent treatment of me.
ARROGANCE	JEALOUSY
Previously, I (as your personal follower) have enviously acted in an extremely approving fashion towards you: overriding your (as PA) impudent treatment of me. But now, you (as group authority) will impudently act in an *arrogant* fashion towards me: overruling my (as PF) envious treatment of you.	Previously, you (as group authority) have impudently acted in an arrogant fashion towards me: overriding my (as PF) envious treatment of you. But now, I (as group representative) will enviously act in a *jealous* fashion towards you: overruling your (as GA) impudently-arrogant treatment of me.
IMPETUOSITY	COVETOUSNESS
Previously, I (as group representative) have enviously acted in a jealous fashion towards you: overriding your (as GA) impudently-arrogant treatment of me. But now, you (as spiritual authority) will arrogantly act in an *impetuous* fashion towards me: overruling my (as GR) jealous treatment of you.	Previously, you (as spiritual authority) have arrogantly acted in an impetuous fashion towards me: overriding my (as GR) jealous treatment of you. But now, I (as your spiritual disciple) will jealously act in a *covetous* fashion towards you: overruling your (as SA) impetuous treatment of me.
PRESUMPTION	LONGING
Previously, I (as your spiritual disciple) have jealously acted in a covetous fashion towards you: overriding your (as SA) impetuous treatment of me. But now, you (as humanitarian authority) will impetuously act *presumptuously* towards me: overruling my (as SD) jealous sense of covetousness.	Previously, you (as humanitarian authority) have impetuously acted presumptuously towards me: overriding my (as SD) jealous sense of covetousness. But now, I (as representative member of humanity) will covetously act in a *longing* fashion towards you: overruling your (as HA) presumptuous treatment of me.
SMUGNESS	AFFECTATION
Previously, I (as representative member of humanity) have covetously acted in a longing fashion towards you: overriding your (as HA) presumptuous treatment of me. But now, you (as transcendental authority) will presumptuously act in a *smug* fashion towards me: overruling my (as RH) covetous sense of longing.	Previously, you (as transcendental authority) have presumptuously acted in a smug fashion towards me: overriding my (as RH) covetous sense of longing. But now, I (as your transcendental follower) will longingly act in an *affected* fashion towards you: overruling your (as TA) smug treatment of me.

Table F-3 – The Definitions Based Upon Impudence/Envy

INSOLENCE	DISDAIN
Previously, I (as reinforcer) have extreme-ly acted leniently towards you: overriding your (as procurer) excessively submissive treatment of me. But now, you (as personal authority) will *insolently* act in an excessively submis-sive fashion towards me: overruling my (as reinforcer) extremely lenient treatment of you.	Previously, you (as personal authority) have insolently acted in an excessively submissive fashion towards me: overrid-ing my (as reinforcer) extremely lenient treatment of you. But now, I (as your personal follower) will *disdainfully* act in an extremely concerned fashion towards you: overrul-ing your (as PA) insolent treatment of me.
AUDACITY	**CONTEMPT**
Previously, I (as your personal follower) have disdainfully acted in an extremely concerned fashion towards you: overriding your (as PA) insolent treatment of me. But now, you (as group authority) will in-solently act in an *audacious* fashion towards me: overruling my (as PF) disdainful treatment of you.	Previously, you (as group authority) have insolently acted in an audacious fashion towards me: overriding my (as PF) disdainful treatment of you. But now, I (as group representative) will disdainfully act in a *contemptuous* fashion towards you: overruling your (as GA) insolent sense of audacity.
RASHNESS	**REPROACH**
Previously, I (as group representative) have disdainfully acted in a contemptuous fashion towards you: overriding your (as GA) insolent sense of audacity. But now, you (as spiritual authority) will audaciously act in a *rash* fashion towards me: overruling my (as GR) disdainful sense of contempt.	Previously, you (as spiritual authority) have audaciously acted in a rash fashion towards me: overriding my (as GR) disdainful sense of contempt. But now, I (as your spiritual disciple) will contemptuously act in a *reproachful* fa-shion towards you: overruling your (as SA) rash treatment of you.
BOLDNESS	**CHAGRIN**
Previously, I (as your spiritual disciple) have contemptuous acted in a reproachful fashion towards you: overriding your (as SA) rash treatment of me. But now, you (as humanitarian authority) will rashly act in a *bold* fashion towards me: overruling my (as SD) reproachful treatment of you.	Previously, you (as humanitarian authori-ty) have rashly acted in a bold fashion to-wards me: overriding my (as SD) reproachful treatment of you. But now, I (as representative member of humanity) will reproachfully act in a *chagrined* fashion towards you: overruling your (as HA) bold treatment of me.
HARSHNESS	**BITTERNESS**
Previously, I (as representative member of humanity) have reproachfully acted in a chagrined fashion towards you: overriding your (as HA) bold treatment of me. But now, you (as transcendental authori-ty) will boldly act in a *harsh* fashion towards me: overruling my (as RH) chagrined treatment of you.	Previously, you (as transcendental au-thority) have boldly acted in a harsh fa-shion towards me: overriding my (as RH) chagrined treatment of you. But now, I (as your transcendental follow-er) will *bitterly* act in a chagrined fashion towards you: overruling your (as TA) harsh treatment of me.

Table F- 4 – The Definitions Based Upon Insolence/Disdain

sycophancy directly complements the remaining follower trend of criticism-ridicule-scorn-mockery-cynicism. A similar sequence of trends further holds true with respect to the future-directed dimensions for the vices of excess, as a cursory examination of **Fig. 16A** adequately serves to indicate. The precise selection of terms for the most abstract levels of the power hierarchy is certainly a work in progress, an aspect necessarily remaining an avenue for further research in the field.

With respect to the rules for coding within the three-digit system, the first digit for the vices of excess, by definition, is assigned the unitary value of "3," as specified within the initial numbering pattern established in Chapter 1. The second digit further narrows the focus, in turn, specifying each of the ten respective levels within the power pyramid hierarchy: e.g., 1 = personal authority, 2 = personal follower, 3 = group authority, etc. In order to specify each of the individual terms, the third and final digit is necessarily called into play. For instance, 310 = pride, 311 = shame, 312 = impudence, and 313 = insolence. Digits 4 to 7 in the three-slot, in turn, specify the accessory versions of the vices of excess, as more elaborately described in the Chapter *18* of the current section. The final two third-place digits (8 & 9) are alternately reserved for specifying the general unifying themes, analogous to the pattern initially seen for the virtuous realm and the vices of defect.

THE SCHEMATIC DEFINITIONS FOR THE VICES OF EXCESS

One of the most significant applications for the ten-level hierarchy of excess concerns their further incorporation into the formal schematic definition format, as schematically depicted in **Tables F-1** to **F-4**. This four-part sequence of tables is identical in form and function to that previously established for the virtuous mode in Chapter *2*. This crucial innovation spells out in longhand the exact location of each term within the linguistic matrix while simultaneously preserving the orientation of the respective authority/follower roles. Each definition is formally constructed along the lines of a two-stage sequential format; namely (A) the preliminary power maneuver originally employed, and (B) the countermaneuver currently being employed, and hence, labeled. For instance, according to **Table F-1**, the vainful sense of pride expressed by the group authority represents the preliminary power maneuver, in turn, countered by the flatterous sense of adulation expressed by the group representative. According to this two-stage format, power leverage is achieved by rising to a "one-up" power status; namely, ascending to the next higher metaperspectival level. Consequently, at each succeeding level, a new term (distinguished through *italics*) is introduced into the schematic format representing the power maneuver currently under consideration.

Although the precision of the definitions for the vices of excess scarcely equal that initially established for the traditional groupings of virtues/values, one nevertheless gains a clear impression of the distinctive interplay linking the authority/follower roles across the board. The remainder of the current section examines each of the individual terms to a much greater degree of detail. Chapter *17* examines the past-directed realm of excess based upon pride/flattery, followed by that targeting shame/criticism. Chapter *18*, in turn, examines the future-directed domain of excess based on impudence/envy and insolence/disdain. In concert with the established complement of virtuous terms, the current motivational analysis for the realm of excess represents an unprecedented breakthrough within the field of ethical inquiry, permitting a dual diagnosis in terms of moderation or excess.

17

THE PAST-DIRECTED REALM OF EXCESS

The formal description of the vices of excess is currently launched with respect to an in-depth examination of the past-directed dimensions; namely, the sequence based upon pride/flattery, followed by shame/criticism. As stated in the preceding chapter, this current section endeavors to document the reciprocal interplay of authority and follower roles spanning the personal, group, spiritual, humanitarian, and transcendental levels, respectively. Consequently, this discussion of the individual vices of excess will employ a strategy similar to that employed for the vices of defect (in **Part II**); namely, presented as an ascending hierarchy of authority/follower roles in an alternating sequence of organization. Accordingly, the authority sequence of pride-vanity-conceitedness-pretentiousness-sanctimony effectively complements the remaining follower series of flattery-adulation-patronization-obsequiousness-sycophancy. A similar pattern further holds true with respect to the related authority/follower sequence linking shame-humiliation-mortification-anguish-tribulation and criticism-ridicule-scorn-mockery-cynicism. The dedicated reader is encouraged to refer back to the four-page listing of schematic definitions for the vices of excess outlined in Chapter *16*, wherein providing a formal schematic representation of the power dynamics at issue in concert with the descriptive narratives for each of the individual terms.

310 – PRIDE

The first-mentioned vice of *pride* represents the extreme counterpart of the initial nostalgia perspective expressed by the personal authority figure. Although nostalgia represents a recognition of past notable achievements, pride, in turn, specifies the realization of having acted excessively therein. The personal authority figure pridefully admits having acted excessively nostalgically, in anticipation of the flattering treatment from the respective follower figure. Traditionally counted among the Seven Deadly Sins, pride is generally defined as excessively personal feelings of excellence. St. Thomas Aquinas (in deference the teachings of St. Gregory) considered pride the queen of all vices, specifically assigning pride amongst the seven deadly sins. Vanity, affectation, and pretentiousness are commonly cited as derivatives of pride, well placed to serve its inordinate aims.

Even more tellingly, pride is specifically identified as that vice that led to Satan's fall from divine grace. As originally created, Lucifer was regarded as a powerful archangel that served God's throne as a guardian cherub. His name refers to his status as a brilliant "angel of light." The lesser angels marveled at his unparalleled status in Heaven, although his radiance was chiefly due to immediate proximity to the Lord. Lucifer eventually claimed he was worthy of equal status with the most-high God (Ezekiel 28:14-17). Too proud to accept God's supreme authority, Lucifer was summarily cast down from Heaven in concert with the other angels seduced by his treachery. As a consequence, Lucifer became the chief adversary of goodness (and the welfare of mankind) in the process. His proud assertions primarily took root in the seeds of flattery sown by the companion fallen angels, eventually turning into an all-consuming vanity.

According to his sermon: *Lucifer or the Root of Evil,* G. K. Chesterton (1929) states: "If I had only one sermon to preach, it would be a sermon against pride. The more I see of existence, and particularly of modern practical and experiential existence, the more I am convinced of the reality of the old religious thesis: that all evil began with some attempt at superiority. … Pride is a poison so very poisonous that it not only poisons the virtues, it even poisons the other vices." The extremes of self-obsession associated with pride represent a personal degree of selfishness that proves instrumental in driving the detrimental effects of the other vices. As such, it represents the archetypal vice for the realm of excess, a consistent bane to the cooperative spirit underlying all human endeavors.

320 – FLATTERY

The preliminary personal authority theme of pride, in turn, is countered (in a follower sense) by the respective theme of *flattery*. The personal follower flatteringly acts in an extremely worshipful fashion in response to the prideful perspectives of the personal authority figure. The term derives from the Old French *flater* (to flatter), originally "to stroke with the hand, to caress," from the Frankish *flat* (the palm of the hand). It generally signifies the verbal strokes that typically accompany such an outright flattering strategy.

A clear distinction definitely exists between simple encouragement and flattery. The Greek equivalent for flattery, *kolakeria*, denotes motives of a self-serving nature. Indeed, those employing flattery generally expect some favor in return. We often encourage others with kind words, although such encouragement can sometimes grade-over into flattery. When self-interest further enters the picture, such flattery may ultimately extend to overt manipulation or control. The general intent of flattery aims to render another pridefully oblivious, or simply deluded or deceived. Great power is therefore invested in such flattering or overweening compliments. The designated personal follower flatteringly exaggerates the merits of his personal authority figure, effectively reciprocating the latter's professed excessive sense of pridefulness.

This reciprocating interplay of both authority/follower roles, in turn, sets the stage for the remaining group/spiritual levels within the hierarchy of excess. For instance, the prideful perspective of the personal authority, in turn, extends to the vanity expressed by the group authority, culminating in the conceitedness expressed by the spiritual authority figure. Similarly, the flattering strategy of the personal follower, in turn, sets the stage for the adulation expressed by the group representative, culminating in the patronizing perspective of the spiritual disciple figure. Accordingly, the following sequence of sections endeavors to describe this reciprocating interplay of vanity/adulation and conceit/patronization, beginning with an in-depth examination of the group authority theme of vanity.

330 – VANITY

The preliminary personal authority theme of pride, in turn, extends to a group sphere of influence with respect to the more sociable prerequisites of *vanity*. The term derives from the Latin *vanus* (empty), signifying the marginal degree of truthfulness accompanying such vain pretensions. Indeed, the notion of vanity (or vanities) occurs as a frequent theme throughout the Bible. The term generally refers to a sense of evanescence, emptiness (including idolatry) or wickedness: not only in terms of evil, but also of vain or empty things. The chief spelling for vanity (or vanities) is *hebhel* (a breath of air, or from the mouth) generally applied to idolatry, to man's thoughts of himself, or to wealth/treasure (Proverbs 13:11, 21:6). In Ecclesiastes, where the word occurs in various contexts, the theme is summed up through the overall expression: "Vanity of vanities, all is vanity" (Ecclesiastes 1:2, 12:8).

In a more contemporary sense, this theme occurs prominently in the historical accounts of the Bonfire of the Vanities (Italian: Falò delle vanità) that took place on February 7, 1497, when followers of the priest Girolamo Savonarola collected and publicly burned thousands of objects in Florence, Italy, on the Shrove Tuesday festival.
The focus of this destruction was on objects considered sinful, including vanity items such as mirrors, cosmetics, fine clothing, and even musical instruments. Other targets included immoral books, manuscripts of secular songs, playing cards, and pictures. Among objects destroyed in this campaign were several original paintings on classical mythology by Sandro Botticelli, who placed them in the bonfire himself. This dramatic struggle between virtue and excess certainly verifies vanity's reputation as perhaps the most debilitating of the vices of excess, extending the personal prerequisites of pride into a much broader group sphere of influence. Here, the civic overtones of vanity come through the clearest, although now perverted to a range of extremes scarcely tolerated even in public.

340 – ADULATION

The group prerequisites for vanity, in turn, are countered (in a follower sense) by the *adulation* expressed by the group representative. The group representative flatteringly acts with adulation towards his group authority figure, effectively accenting the latter's vain sense of pride. As the excessive counterpart for the corresponding car-

Vain-Glory (Personified) – Detail from an Italian Fresco attributed to Giotto
Depicted in *De Viris Illustribus* by Francesco Petrarch, circa 1350

dinal virtue of prudence, its modern spelling derives from the Latin *adulari* or *adulatus* (to fawn upon), from *ad-* (to) and *ulos* (tail): originally denoting the sense of "to wag the tail." In an affiliated social sense, it denotes a fawning display of flattery towards a public figure: as in excessive admiration or devotion primarily in a servile fashion. According to British poet George Gordon Byron: "The reason that adulation is not displeasing is that it shows one to be of consequence enough to induce people to deceive."

Although the professed content of adulation is primarily exaggerated to some degree, this range of extremes remains consistent with its formal status as one of the vices of excess. This somewhat amusing interplay of the vanity of the authority figure and the adulation of the group follower remains a common theme in the genre of comedy, although sometimes extending to more tragic context, as when such a contrived strategy ultimately takes a turn for the worse.

350 – CONCEITEDNESS

This completed description of the group interplay of vanity/adulation, in turn, sets the stage for the universal domain of conceit/patronization. The smug sense of *conceit* expressed by the spiritual authority figure effectively consummates the trend previously established in terms of pride-vanity. Conceit is typically defined as an overweening sense of self-esteem, or an overly high opinion of oneself. The term derives from the Old French *conceiven* (conceive), from the Latin *conceptum*, from *con-* (together) and *capre* (to take). The originally neutral sense of "something formed in the mind" eventually was modified in the 16th century to reflect a "fanciful or witty notion," (and ultimately) to a sense of vanity. Indeed, according to American advertising executive, Bruce Barton: "Conceit is God's gift to little men."

In a literary sense, a *conceit* is defined as fanciful or far-fetched imagery: where apparently dissimilar themes are actually shown to have a relationship, as in a whimsical metaphor. The Elizabethan poets were particularly fond of conceits in reference to affection, where the beloved was compared to a flower, a garden, or the like. The conceit was also favored by metaphysical poets: who fashioned conceits that were witty, intellectual, or even startling. Samuel Johnson widely disapproved of such strained metaphors, declaring that: "The most heterogeneous ideas are yoked by violence together." Many contemporary poets, such as Emily Dickinson and T. S. Eliot, have similarly employed conceits in *avant garde* compositions.

This exaggerated nature of conceit is similarly preserved in a more basic relationship sense, where the spiritual authority vainly acts in a conceited fashion in anticipation of the flattering adulation of the respective follower figure. The extreme sense of hyperbole characterizing conceit remains consistent in terms of such a universal sphere of influence: where conceitedness claims relevance within a somewhat romanticized world-view. Consequently, conceitedness formally consummates the trend previously established for the subordinate concepts of pride/vanity, a common factor in many forms of comedic entertainment, in addition to literary endeavors.

360 – PATRONIZATION

The spiritual authority focus for conceit, in turn, sets the stage for the respective follower countermaneuver; namely, the *patronization* expressed by the spiritual disciple figure. This patronizing perspective represents a more abstract variation on the subordinate sequence of flattery-adulation, although now extending to a universal sphere of influence. The term traces its origins to the Latin *patronus*, from *pater* or *patris* (father): a derivation further suggestive of the elaborate system of patronage common during the Italian Renaissance. A rich patron might welcome an artist into his household in exchange for the fruits of his artistic talents. Indeed, Leonardo da Vinci worked much of his career under the privilege of court patronage.

Three main motives drove the patronage of arts; namely, piety, prestige, and pleasure. Art patronage proved a significant public relations tool for secular rulers: wherein promoting high social status in cities such as Florence. Indeed, a career in the arts was a difficult undertaking apart from the advantages of such a patronage arrangement. Much patronage also issued from the Church, although scarcely to the degree enjoyed by the ruling class. The great economic prosperity enjoyed by the Florentines encouraged merchants/bankers to aspire to the prestige of art patronage. Eager to display their enhanced status in terms of piety, taste, and learning, the leading contender in this regard was the Medici family: which spent lavishly on the church construction, religious art, and the support of charities. The lofty social status of the Medicis directly benefited from such an arrangement, wherein advertising their wealth/interests relative to the community.

Although the noble aspirations of patronage prove relatively innocuous in terms of intent, it nevertheless shares many commonalties with the subordinate themes of flattery/adulation, particularly when cynically acting self-servingly in order to achieve the desired political or spiritual agenda. Indeed, more recent connotations of the term suggest a sense of condescension or smugness when dealing with others, particularly in a haughty or arrogant fashion. Patronization continues in the follower tradition characteristic of the manipulative or self-serving sycophant, although now extending to a highly abstract sphere of influence. Accordingly, the patronizing individual assumes an arrogant sense of superiority, although only tolerated in terms of the devious or deceptive fashion in which it is carried out.

370 – PRETENTIOUSNESS

The completed description of the individual terms spanning the personal, group, and spiritual levels, in turn, sets the stage for a discussion of the remaining humanitarian and transcendental levels with respect to the hierarchy of excess. In contrast to the organizational power status of the first three levels, the final two levels are alternately distinguished as purely abstract styles of power maneuvers. The humanitarian authority level derives from the abstract addition of "historical" time, whereas the transcendental realm further makes reference to the realm of "pure" transcendence.

The profoundly abstract nature of these final two levels is further reflected in their respectively abstract groupings of individual vices. For instance, the initial sequence of pride-vanity-conceit, in turn, extends to a humanitarian sphere of influence in terms of the humanitarian authority theme of *pretentiousness*. The theme derives from the Latin *praetendere*, from *prae* (before) and *tensum* (to stretch): signifying that stretch of truth typically accompanying such an ostentatious display. It generally refers to an offensively condescending attitude, as in the tendency to project an appearance of distinction or superiority towards others in a social context. Should one profess to be a gifted actor, this impression can be credible to most people under the proper circumstances. This proves particularly true for political figures that aspire to appear charismatic or somewhat larger than life.

Pretentiousness can also apply to an artificial or pseudo-sense of self-esteem, factors that often fail to correlate with the true value of one's achievements (whether implied or claimed). Such self-esteem is primarily a feature exhibited by dictators, gang-leaders, or other types of narcissistic individuals. In most circumstances, such pretentiousness can readily be discerned due to the lack of integrity linking both word and deed. Objective reasoning is often similarly impaired due to wishful thinking or delusional fantasies. Although such haughty individuals tend to maintain an adequate public persona, their true lot in life is often not as productive or satisfying as their pretensions might seem to suggest.

390 – SANCTIMONY

The preceding humanitarian sense of pretentiousness, in turn, extends to a crowning transcendental sphere of influence with respect to the related theme of *sanctimony*. The term derives from the Middle French *sanctimonie*, from Latin *sanctimonia* (holiness, virtuousness), from *sanctus* (holy). The respective Latin root-stem agrees with its original 16th century English connotation denoting holiness or saintliness. By the early 17th century, however, it had alternately come to mean "hypocritically holy," as incorporated in Shakespeare's *Measure for Measure* (in a somewhat disparaging sense). In modern times, it has pejoratively come to denote a sense of being "affectedly saintly or pretentiously holy," as in hypocritical religious devotion or sanctimonious righteousness.

These extreme characteristics of sanctimony generally appear to embody an overall general theme of self-importance, culminating (in a transcendental perspective) the preliminary sequence of pride-vanity-conceitedness-pretentiousness. Although such a bold assertion is surely fraught with competing interpretations, the general sense of sanctimony certainly appears well suited to such a transcendental role, and one destined to remain in favor until a better option comes to light.

380 – OBSEQUIOUSNESS

The completed description of the preliminary authority roles of pretentiousness/sanctimony, in turn, sets the stage for the related sequence of follower roles; namely, the interplay of obsequiousness/sycophancy targeting the humanitarian/transcendental roles, respectively. For example, the first-listed humanitarian vice of *obsequiousness* traces its origins to the Latin *obsequiosus* (compliant, obedient), from *obsequium* (compliance, dutiful service): from *ob-* (after) and

sequi (follow), signifying a sense of compliance or an excessively fawning demeanor. The English pejorative sense of "fawning sycophant" dates prior the 17th century. It generally refers to a self-seeking servile flatterer or fawning parasite. Synonyms of a slang nature further include yes-man, flunky, or toady. The courtly Englishman, Sir Walter Raleigh, similarly writes about flatterers: "It is hard to know them from friends, they are so *obsequious* and full of protestations; for as a wolf resembles a dog, so doth a flatterer a friend."

In direct analogy to the preliminary sequence of flattery-adulation-patronization-obsequiousness represents a more enduring personality trait than any immediate behavior pattern: a factor further consistent with its proposed inclusion at a humanitarian sphere of influence. As such, it is provisionally assigned this extreme level of placement within the realm of excess until a better alternative can be identified.

300 – SYCOPHANCY

The preliminary humanitarian focus of obsequiousness, in turn, extends to a transcendental sphere of influence with respect to the related theme of *sycophancy*. The term derives from the Greek *sykophantes*, which *Webster's Dictionary* describes as traditionally referring to an individual who informed against persons exporting figs from Attica, or those who plundered the sacred fig trees. More probably, however, it referred to one who gathers figs by shaking the tree; hence, one who makes a rich man yield up his goods through such a persistent fawning strategy. Indeed, this particular derivation traces its origins to the Greek *sykon* (fig) and *phainein* (to show). As such, sycophancy continues the overall theme of a fawning style of follower perspective, as initially established in the subordinate sequence of flattery-adulation-patronization-obsequiousness. Whether sycophancy truly warrants such a crowning transcendental placement remains a point open to debate, although its crowning placement in the overall follower sequence certainly appears justified at this juncture.

THE PAST-DIRECTED REALM OF EXCESS BASED UPON SHAME/CRITICISM

The completed description of the realm of excess based upon pride/flattery further sets the stage for the related interplay of shame/criticism. This latter format alternately specifies a critical expression of blame, wherein prompting a shameful sense of guilt. This extreme format clearly complements the vain prerequisites previously established for pride/flattery, whereby flattery prompts the pride expressed by the personal authority figure. This reciprocal pattern of authority/follower roles proves equally applicable with respect to the higher authority levels as well: organized in terms of an ascending hierarchy of affective terminology. The preliminary authority sequence of shame-humiliation-mortification-anguish-tribulation, in turn, prompts the related follower sequence of criticism-ridicule-scorn-mockery-cynicism. Consequently, the dynamic interactions between authority/follower roles can accurately be determined in concert with the descriptive narratives for the individual terms to follow.

311 – SHAME

The first mentioned theme of *shame* represents an extreme motivational analogue of guilt in the sense of a past-directed, submissive perspective. Its modern spelling derives from the Old English *sc(e)amu*, akin to the German *scham*: denoting a disgraced sense of humiliation due to fault or failure. Blaise Pascal once humorously wrote: "The only shame is to have none!" Shame represents a moral emotion encompassing evaluative thought, wherein one believes that one has done something morally wrong, accompanied by the desire to cover up such a fault. Shame generally represents a powerful emotion in that it implies an irreparable sense of harm done to another, as well as the recognition of blamefulness for such a reprehensible action. It is traditionally considered a vice in terms of its moral cachet concerning extreme culpability or blameworthiness in a personal sense. Accordingly, actions of an unintentional nature generally cannot serve as the basis for a personal sense of shame.

Shame is clearly distinguished from its close relative of embarrassment. Unlike shame, embarrassment is not generally concerned with social mores, but rather targets the perception that one has done something silly or out of character (accompanied by the desire to undo such a blunder). Consequently, shame represents an extreme form of guilt, particularly in terms of an interpersonal sphere of influence. The personal authority figure shamefully acts in an extremely guilty fashion in anticipation of the critical treatment from the respective follower figure. The extreme degree of emotionality typically associated with shamefulness can prove highly debilitating if chronic in nature, which, if left untreated can lead to activities of a self-destructive nature.

321 – CRITICISM

The personal prerequisites for shame are further reciprocated (in a follower sense) with respect to the related theme of *criticism*. This latter role is assumed by the personal follower figure, who critically acts in an excessively blameful fashion wherein prompting the shameful treatment of the personal authority figure. Its modern spelling derives from the Greek *kritikos*, from *krinein* (to judge): denoting the act of censuring or judging harshly, or finding fault with. These connotations suggest an extreme sense of blamefulness on the part of the personal follower consistent with criticism's formal classification among the vices of excess.

In a similar sense, the professional critic - derived from the classical Greek *krites* (judge), offers cogent value judgements concerning the performance or work of others (as in art, music, or the theatre). These critics specialize within a given field, generally publishing their determinations for others of similar interest. Consequently, constructive criticism concerns valid and well-reasoned opinions encompassing the state of the art, generally involving both positive and negative commentary. It can prove an invaluable tool for raising or maintaining performance standards, although a tendency towards self-aggrandizement sometimes leads to a focus upon the negative. Indeed, British lexicographer, Samuel Johnson scathingly wrote: "Criticism is a study by which men grow important and formidable at very small expense."

This distinctive interplay of shame/criticism, in turn, sets the stage for a discussion of the remaining group/spiritual levels within the hierarchy of excess. For instance, the shamefulness expressed by the personal authority, in turn, anticipates the humiliation experienced by the group authority figure, culminating in the mortification specified for the spiritual sphere of influence. Furthermore, the criticism expressed by the personal follower, in turn, extends to the ridicule of the group representative, culminating in the scornfulness expressed by the spiritual disciple. The next two sections examine this dualistic pattern of terms based upon shame/criticism, beginning with the group realm of humiliation/ridicule, followed by the spiritual domain of excess targeting the interplay of mortification/scorn.

331 – HUMILIATION

The first-mentioned theme within the group realm of the vices, *humiliation*, is defined as an extreme sense of mortification or shamefulness, primarily in a public or social setting. The term derives from the Latin *humiliare*, from *humilis* (low), from *humus* (earth): a figurative allusion to such humble origins. Humiliation represents an inherently unpleasant emotion concerned with the loss of social status. It traditionally invokes the negative belief that one's standing has been diminished in the eyes of the community due to actions not befitting one's public status (accompanied by the desire to reinstate one's favorable status). It can further imply an undue sense of pride, in that those that feel humiliated place an inordinate emphasis on their personal self-image, effectively downplaying the significance of those around them.

Oft times humiliation is invested with the intent to harm the feelings of another, a morally reprehensible action due to the intentional pain or suffering inflicted upon another. Indeed, American psychologist, Paul Ekman succinctly states: "The *humiliation* of shame requires disapproval or ridicule by others. If no one ever learns of a misdeed, there can be no shame, but there still might be guilt. Of course, both may occur together." As the extreme version of the honorable sense of guilt expressed by the group authority, humiliation directly expands upon the shameful prerequisites of the personal realm, wherein paralleling the pattern previously established for the related hierarchy of pride/vanity.

341 – RIDICULE

The shameful sense of humiliation professed by the group authority figure, in turn, sets the stage for the follower maneuver proper; namely, the critical sense of *ridicule* expressed by the group representative. The term derives from the Latin *ridiculus*, from *ridere* (to laugh): denoting speech or behavior intended to provoke contemptuous laughter, as in a taunting or derisive fashion. Accordingly, ridicule figures prominently in the time-honored tradition of literary satire. As many a sage has noted: "Ridicule is the test of truth." Furthermore, Roman commentator, Horace writes: "Ridicule often settles things more thoroughly and better than acrimony." Napoleon Bonaparte similarly writes: "There is only one step from the sublime to the ridiculous."

This enduring perspective on the ridiculous is fittingly associated with ridicule: defined as that which causes (or is worthy of) ridicule: as in a sense of the absurd, the preposterous, or the laughable. According to American humorist, Samuel Clemens: "There is no character, howsoever good and fine, but it can be destroyed by ridicule,

howsoever poor and witless." Ridicule extends the personal prerequisites for criticism into a broader group sphere of influence, as the social characteristics of the term clearly serve to indicate. Whether any constructive benefit results from ridicule remains irrelevant to this discussion, for ridicule must always remain associated with the somewhat unsavory realm of the vices of excess.

351 – MORTIFICATION

The completed description of the group domain of excess (e.g., humiliation/ridicule), in turn, sets the stage for the remaining spiritual counterparts; namely, mortification/scornfulness. In a direct analogy to the sequence of shame/humiliation, mortification is typically defined as the control the passions through severe discipline or penance, as suggested in trials of humiliation. The term derives from the Latin *mortificare* (to cause death to), from *mortis* (death) and *facere* (to make): alluding to the subjugation of the passions in order to make amends for past grievous deeds.

In terms of the Christian tradition, mortification is defined as a means employed by the ascetic to realize a virtuous and holy lifestyle. This theme was championed by St. Paul, who proposed an analogy between Christ surrendering his mortal life, and the disciples, who renounced through mortification their past lives of sin. Mortification overcomes the temptation to sin by freely willing to accept physical hardships rather than yielding to temptation. This generally explains why many mortifications adopted by ascetics are not directly curative of evil propensities, but rather take the form of painful exercises and privations that are self-inflicted: e.g., fasting, self-flagellation, sleeping boards, abstention from lawful pleasures, etc.

In a deeper spiritual sense, these outward displays of penance are beneficial insofar as mirroring the internal mortification of one's pride or self-love in all of its various manifestations. Consistent with such religious themes, mortification is traditionally viewed as an extremely submissive style of spiritual authority perspective: effectively complementing the preliminary authority sequence of shame/humiliation, although now extending to a universal sphere of influence. As such, mortification encompasses a much broader sphere of meaning than its subordinate counterparts, particularly when expressed in outward forms of extreme penance. Mortification revels in such all-encompassing themes of intense spiritual submission, the extremes of which have moderated somewhat in an age of media scrutiny.

361 – SCORN

The preceding description of mortification, in turn, sets the stage for a discussion of the related class of follower countermaneuver; namely, the *scornful* sense of ridicule expressed by the spiritual follower figure. In particular, scorn represents a more extreme variation on the lenient prerequisites previously established for the theological theme of decency. The term derives from the Old French *escarn* (mockery, derision, contempt), from Old High German *skern* (mockery, jest, sport), from Proto-Germanic *skarnjan* (to mock, to deride). This term was probably also influenced by the Vulgar Latin *excornare*, from the Latin *ex-* (without) and *cornu* (horn): from which derives the Italian *scornare* (to treat with contempt).

Scornfulness is generally distinguished from the related synonyms of mockery or derision: both of which more specifically refer to the outward means by which scorn finds ready expression. Consequently, scorn denotes more of a subjective state or verbal reaction. It also can include overtones of superiority, resentment, or aversion. Scorn is typically expressed when one is confronted with a person or circumstance that prompts a vivid sense of one's own superiority: wherein further provoking resentment or contempt for the latter's intrinsic sense of inferiority.

Scorn certainly appears to be a hotter or fiercer emotion than disdain or contempt. As such, it shares with its subordinate counterparts of criticism/ridicule an overtly biting form of response, although now extending to a universal sphere of influence. Scorn transcends the more partisan concerns of criticism/ridicule, its primary focus now targeting themes of a spiritual (or universal) significance. Indeed, the most salient feature of scorn is precisely its far-reaching range of opprobrium, wherein even disparaging the foibles of human nature, itself. Fortunately, the modern trend towards political correctness finds ready acceptance of public scorn not quite as prevalent as that observed for earlier times.

371 – ANGUISH

The completed description of the affective terms spanning the personal, group, and spiritual levels, in turn, sets the stage for a discussion of the remaining humanitarian and transcendental levels within the realm of excess. The profoundly abstract nature of these final two levels is further reflected in the respectively abstract groupings of vices. For instance, the initial authority sequence of shame-humiliation-mortification, in turn, extends to a humanitarian sphere of influence with respect to the respective theme of *anguish*. The term derives from the Latin *agnustia* (straight or straightness), from *ang(u)ere* (to press tightly, to strangle). It signifies an extreme sense of pain or mortification with respect to body or mind, as in an agonizing profession of penance.

In terms of the Christian tradition, it denotes extreme distress of the spirit: as in excruciating pain or suffering that can also extend to grief, remorse, or despair. This theme is chiefly expressed in Old Testament through the derivatives of *tsuq* (straitened, pressed), and *tsar* - and its derivatives (straightness, narrowness): wherein denoting distress. This theme also extends to the New Testament as *thlipsis* (a pressing together): as in affliction or tribulation. The common theme for these various derivations is that of pressure, as in straitening or compression suggestive of painfulness through the infliction of physical or mental distress.

Regardless of the individual traditions therein, anguish clearly represents a range of themes targeting a humanitarian sphere of influence, wherein expanding upon the spiritual sense of mortification. Anguish is most frequently encountered in contexts specifying enduring suffering: as in the trials and tribulations associated with slavery, the agony of a lingering illness, or the pain of unrequited love. As such, anguish directly continues in the tradition of its subordinate sequence of terms (shame-humiliation-mortification), although now pressing the limits of abstraction in terms of such a clearly anguished state. Anguish, accordingly, represents a considerable personal cross to bear, even though the underlying ideology may span the course of many generations.

391 – TRIBULATION

The preceding humanitarian focus of anguish ultimately extends to a crowning transcendental sphere of influence with respect to the respective theme of *tribulation*. The term derives from the Latin *tribulatum* (to afflict), from *tribulum* (a sledge for rubbing out grain), from *terere* (to rub): wherein signifying an abrasive sense of affliction, trial, or hardship. In Old Testament scripture, it denotes a sense of being closely pressed - as of seals (Job 41:15), of streams pent up (Isaiah 59:9), or of strength limited (Proverbs 24). These diverse contexts share the general figurative sense of tight circumstances; variously rendered as affliction, tribulation, or distress.

In terms of New Testament scripture, the Latin Bible introduces the theme of the *tribulatio pressura*, from *tribulum* (a threshing sledge). The verb-root is rendered "to suffer tribulation" (1 Thessalonians 3:4), trouble (2 Thessalonians 1:6), or "to afflict." The noun form is rendered in the King James Edition as tribulation, affliction, or persecution, although more uniformly "tribulation" in the revised versions. The term also generally refers to the hardships which Christ's followers must necessarily suffer (Matthew 13:21; 24:9, 21, 29), or which they already suffer (Romans 5:3; 12:12; 2 Corinthians 4:17). In this extreme fashion, tribulation represents the supreme culmination of the trend previously established as shame-humiliation-mortification-anguish. Indeed, whether tribulation truly warrants such a lofty transcendental placement remains an issue open to further debate, although clearly the leading contender at this juncture.

381 – MOCKERY

The completed description of the initial authority perspectives of anguish/tribulation, in turn, sets the stage for an examination of the remaining follower roles (mockery/cynicism) targeting the humanitarian/transcendental domains, respectively. For instance, the humanitarian follower theme of *mockery* derives from the Middle French *mocquer* (deride, jeer), most probably from the Vulgar Latin *muccare* (to blow one's nose in a derisive gesture), from the Latin *mucus*. The English spelling is also said to derive from the Middle Dutch *mocken* (to mumble), or the Middle Low German *mucken* (to grumble). The related notion of imitation (as in a mocking-bird, mock-up, etc.) derives from this very sense of derisive imitation.

In this somewhat amusing sense, mockery represents a particularly prominent theme in the field of literary satire, a technique that mocks the powerful or influential, as well as the social elite. It generally employs exaggeration or irony to spotlight the flaws and shortcomings of its subjects. Although disdain and contempt frequently underlie works of satire, the satirist's most powerful tools are the wit and humor that border upon the ridiculous. Samuel Clemens fittingly notes: "Against the assault of laughter nothing can stand." No matter how strongly the satirist feels about the subject, if one wishes to be effective, one needs to entertain the audience, not preach to it.

Satirists from classical times include the Greek playwright Aristophanes, as well as the Roman satirists Juvenal and Horace. Many experts classify satire as either Juvenalian (incorporating bitterness), or Horatian (a more lighthearted form of mockery). The seventeenth/eighteenth centuries, in turn, produced the English satirists Pope, Dryden, and Swift; as well as the French satirists Moliére and Voltaire. Satire employs mockery or ridicule to diminish its subject in the eyes of its audience. It is a mode that can operate in any number of different formal structures: although sharing the common theme of making fun of the absurdity, pretensions, or degeneracy of those that are portrayed. Satire entails a fusion of laughter and contempt in order to censure the incongruities of vice and folly. Hence, the more enduring sense of the term clearly distinguishes mockery as the supreme humanitarian variation on the related sequence of criticism, ridicule, and scorn. Consequently, the satirical nature of mockery has remained a powerful tool for social reform, one scarcely in danger of abating anytime soon!

301 – CYNICISM

The preceding humanitarian domain of mockery, in turn, extends to a transcendental sphere of influence with respect to the affiliated theme of *cynicism*. The term derives from the Greek *kynikos* (literally "dog-like"), from *kynos* (dog). It presumably traces its origins to the *Kynosarge* (Grey Dog): the name of the gymnasium in ancient Athens where the founder of classical Cynicism, Antisthenes, promoted the tenets of the movement. The philosophical discipline of Cynicism includes many prominent contributors, of which Diogenes is the most widely known. Cynicism is defined as that attitude or tendency to view the beliefs, abilities, or motivations of others in a negative or sarcastic light.

In many cases, cynical judgments can be justified; particularly with respect to chronic misbehaviors, mistakes, or unethical actions. In a close-minded or peremptory fashion, cynicism can prove especially counterproductive and disabling. The cynic may intuitively grasp the limitations of others, although remain completely oblivious to the potential for growth experience. For the typical cynic, a given judgment remains irrevocable and final without the possibility for redemption or revision. This cynical sense of inflexibility frequently develops an aura of negativity that proves toxic to the development of creative or synergistic solutions to problems. Indeed, the cynic can avoid putting-forth true productive effort, wherein employing such narrow-minded attitudes and beliefs as an excuse for inactivity. In our modern age of misinformation and disinformation, however, such skepticism can prove useful for evaluating radically new or unproven belief systems. Cynicism embodies the general spirit of satire and lighthearted criticism initially described, effectively rounding out the preliminary sequence of criticism-ridicule-scorn-mockery (and now, cynicism).

In conclusion, the completed description of the past-directed versions for the vices of excess provides a suitably detailed picture of the overall domain of excess. Indeed, it proved particularly fitting that the English-language tradition with so precisely permit the construction of this stratified model for the vices of excess. This ten-level linguistic matrix represents an unprecedented addition to the field of ethical inquiry, an achievement on par with the parallel designation of the master hierarchy for the vices of defect. Together with the respective virtuous mode intermediate to these two basic modalities for the vices, Aristotle's enduring theory of the virtuous Golden Mean finally reaches conceptual fulfillment.

This breakthrough in ethical understanding permits unprecedented inroads into deciphering dysfunctional interactions, prescribing a timely course of intervention. Although scarcely as dysfunctional as the darker realm of defect, the vices of excess are still afflicted with their own distinctive range of shortcomings. This specified domain of excess exhibits the distinct tendency to escalate tensions within an overall communicational dynamic, with the increased potential for misunderstandings not infrequently leading to conflict or even violence. For example, with respect to the past-directed domain for the vices of excess, the extreme vices of pride/vanity prove particularly deserving of their deadly reputations. Although not conflict producing in itself, any subsequent deficiency in anticipated adulatory reactions can lead to feelings of resentment or spite, per-

haps even setting the stage for an ongoing chill in friendly relations. In similar fashion, the past-directed (more salient) emotions of shame/humiliation represent excessive guilt of a more tragic import, with inevitable misunderstandings often leading to prolonged depression or vendettas.

These specific examples prove the rule rather than the exception when extended to relations on an international scene. Indeed, countries have become mortal enemies based upon the slightest of escalated misperceptions, often resulting in overt hostilities or warfare. It is common knowledge that such an extreme focus in excess often leads to unforeseen negative consequences; hence, the timeworn wisdom for prudently following a measured regimen of etiquette and protocol. The newly devised terminology for the vices of excess offers considerable applications in this regard, providing a powerful new technology for detecting/diagnosing dysfunctional communication before any crucial threshold is breached. Granted the extreme antics of celebrities and politicos gain more than a fair share of media exposure and/or public fascination. Indeed, pushing the boundaries of acceptable conduct will always remain a somewhat delicate balancing act, and one that argues for concerted room for improvement in social mores and attitudes.

Consequently, through the aid of the newly proposed technology targeting the vices of excess, hopefully the public may gain a more profound understanding of how their sentiments can be manipulated in this respect, wherein working to reverse the ongoing trend towards fascination with public outrage. Only then will public welfare be more adequately safeguarded, perhaps even prompting a return to simpler times when measured and respectful behavior was an asset to be treasured, and not the bane of boredom it currently defines.

18

THE FUTURE-DIRECTED REALM OF EXCESS

The completed description of the past-directed realm for the vices of excess, in turn, sets the stage for a discussion of the remaining future-directed sequence of terms. In terms of the most basic personal level within the hierarchy of excess, this amounts to impudence in anticipation of envy, or insolence in expectation of disdainfulness. Furthermore, this reciprocating interplay of terms, in turn, extends to the remaining group, spiritual, humanitarian, and transcendental authority levels as well, serving as the basis for the remainder of the current chapter. Accordingly, this chapter employs a strategy similar to that used in Chapter *17*; namely, an ascending hierarchy of authority/follower roles in a reciprocating pattern of presentation. The preliminary authority sequence of impudence-arrogance-impetuosity-presumptuousness-smugness, in turn, complements the remaining follower sequence of envy-jealousy-covetousness-longing-affectation. Furthermore, the related authority sequence of insolence-audacity-rashness-boldness-harshness similarly complements the respective follower sequence of disdain-contempt-reproach-chagrin-bitterness. The discriminating reader is encouraged to refer back to the four-page listing of schematic definitions for the vices of excess outlined in Chapter *16*, providing a formal representation of the power dynamics in concert with the descriptive narratives for each of the individual terms.

312 – IMPUDENCE

In terms of the most basic personal level for the vices of excess, the first-mentioned vice of *impudence* represents the extreme counterpart of the virtuous theme of desire. Indeed, desire was previously defined as a solicitous perspective that anticipated future reinforcement, a factor that impudence amplifies to an extreme degree. Its modern spelling derives from the Latin compound of *im-* (not) and *pudere* (to be ashamed), denoting a shameless sense of boldness or effrontery. Other synonyms include insolence or impertinence. Russian author and playwright, Anton Chekhov fittingly writes: "Satiation, like any state of vitality, always contains a degree of impudence, and that impudence emerges first and foremost when the sated man instructs the hungry one." Furthermore, British society figure, Lady Montague, also notes: "I don't say 'tis impossible for an impudent man to rise in the world, but a moderate merit with a large share of impudence is more probable to be advanced than the greatest qualifications without it." The personal authority impudently acts in an extremely desirous fashion, wherein prompting the envious perspective of the respective follower figure. The general example of the disrespectful pupil, who impudently acts sarcastically towards his schoolmaster, is one perhaps we have all noticed. Its extreme prerequisites frequently border upon the absurd, although scarcely so for the target of such a tactic. The solicitous quality generally underlying impudence definitely remains its saving grace, for a swift scolding is usually sufficient to restore the formal status quo.

322 – ENVY

In terms of the preliminary impudence example, the remaining follower role, in turn, is specified through an extreme potential for rewards colloquially experienced as *envy*. Its modern spelling derives from the French *envie*, from the Latin *invidia*, a compound of *in-* (on) and *videre* (to look). It denotes a grudging or emulous attitude, particularly with respect to the wellbeing or success of another. In terms of medieval tradition, envy is listed among the Seven Deadly Sins, also alluded to as "the green-eyed monster." Envy generally entails an evaluation or belief that something (or someone) of value rightfully belongs to oneself, accompanied by the desire to secure the desired object from its rightful owner. The primary reason envy is listed among the vices of excess is that it presupposes greed, a theme formally consistent with covetousness and pride. Greedy people tend to pursue more than their fair share of community resources. They also appear ungrateful for what they possess, and show little respect for the possessions others. Envy can also imply larceny when outwardly acted upon.

Envy is formally distinguished from its close counterpart in emulation. Emulation is traditionally not considered a vice due to its lack of acquisitiveness. Similar to envy, emulation also approximates a two-party emotion, presuming to reproduce the admirable qualities possessed by another. Emulation, however, lacks the additional motive of selfishness: therefore, emulation is a quality typically encouraged in terms of character development.

The initial interplay of impudence/envy, in turn, sets the stage for the remaining group/spiritual levels within the hierarchy of excess. For instance, the impudence perspective of the personal authority, in turn, extends to the arrogance expressed in a group domain followed by the impetuosity specified for the universal role. Furthermore, the envy expressed by the personal follower leads to the jealousy perspective of the group representative, culminating in the covetousness expressed by the spiritual follower figure: as more extensively described in the next four segments of this chapter.

332 – ARROGANCE

The first-mentioned, group authority theme of *arrogance* traces its origins the Latin *arrogare* (to claim for oneself), from *ad-* (to) and *rogare* (to ask or claim). It denotes undue feelings of superiority or self-importance expressed through an overbearing sense of pride. Indeed, the familiar scenario of the arrogant nobleman extends the personal prerequisites of impudence into a group sphere of influence, an enduring aspect of many literary traditions.

The group prerequisites of arrogance are particularly evident in the respective phrase "arrogance of power," defined as a presumptuous attitude on the part of a powerful nation that its dominance gives it the prerogative to intervene in the affairs of its less powerful neighbors. According to British-born journalist, Sydney J. Harris: "The difference between patriotism and nationalism is that the patriot is proud of his country for

what it does, and the nationalist is proud of his country no matter what it does. The first attitude creates a feeling of responsibility, but the second a feeling of blind *arrogance* that leads to war." This theme of arrogance in relation to power has gained much currency in terms of America's recent series of military campaigns in the Middle East region. Whether such a bold course of action proves justified remains for historians to debate, although as with any such range of extremes, the initial balance of power is certain to remain altered for many years to come.

342 – JEALOUSY

The preceding arrogance perspective, in turn, gives way to the *jealousy* perspective expressed by the group follower figure. The group representative enviously acts in a jealous fashion towards his group authority figure: effectively chiding the latter's impudent sense of arrogance. The term derives from the Old French *jalous*, from the Latin *zelus*, from the Greek *zelos* (emulation): denoting an envious sense of rivalry. Jealousy, similar its close cousin envy, is figuratively referred to as the "green-eyed monster." Some instances of jealousy, however, have been considered justified, with some regarding jealousy as the very emblem of romantic love.

Unlike envy, jealousy is primarily considered to be a three-party emotion; namely, *A*, (the jealous party) loves *B*, (the party that *A* is jealous over), wherein is jealous of *C* (*A's* rival for affection which threatens to replace *A's* favorable status in the eyes of *B*). Jealousy entails the belief that someone rightfully prized by me is now being cherished by another. It further presupposes that one's desires or wishes are to be favored exclusively, with great effort expended to reestablish one's previously favorable status. Fear of losing one's paramour (or of ceasing to be loved) is an essential feature of jealousy, for those lacking such insecurities rarely feel jealousy. Some view jealousy as strictly pathological, whereas others regard it as the very proof of love. Whether viewed favorably or not, the more obsessive qualities of jealousy certainly qualify it firmly within the realm of excess.

Jealous individuals tend to treat the others merely as objects of convenience rather than as parties capable of exercising personal free will. In terms of viewing themselves as more worthy or valuable than others, jealous individuals assume their wishes take precedent over the needs of others. Consequently, they treat others as personal possessions in mandatory conformity to

Jealousy (Personified): From *The Devils* (1835) by George Cruikshank - A Series of Six Cartoons

their will. In cases of sexual jealousy, the jealous lover may stalk the beloved, even leading to physically harm. Few can deny the plight of Othello, whose jealousy stemmed from the false belief that his wife Desdemona had been cheating on him, a jealous reaction that proved all too tragically fatal.

Jealousy's "sour" reputation is generally due to the selfishness surrounding motives of possession. In common usage, the statement: "I am jealous of his car" actually implies that one is envious (and wishes to have something like it). Envy generally presupposes greed given the implication that one is dissatisfied with one's own blessings. Furthermore, envy is essentially a two-part emotion, presupposing neither the desire to be loved, nor the fear of losing one's favorable status. Consequently, the dichotomy between envy and jealousy is explained in terms of their respective personal/group placement within the hierarchy of excess. Indeed, this basic interpretation is further validated in terms of the next higher spiritual (or universal) level within the power hierarchy.

352 – IMPETUOSITY

The completed description of the group sphere of excess (based upon arrogance/jealousy), in turn, sets the stage for a discussion of the respective universal counterparts: beginning with the arrogant sense of *impetuosity* expressed by the spiritual authority figure. Its modern spelling derives from the Latin *impetus* (an attack), from *in-* (into) and *petere* (to seek): suggesting a tendency towards acting in an impulsive or headlong fashion. Impetuosity is characterized by hasty choices driven primarily through the influence of instinctual impulses. Some define impetuosity as spontaneity or authenticity, although impetuosity is not consistently likely to yield positive results. Consistently coping with problems impetuously results in differing results for each occurrence, resulting in the height of folly or chaos.

A focus on immediate gratification frequently identifies impetuosity with emotional immaturity. Enduring and worthwhile goals require dedication, commitment, and diligence, where one learns from both success and failure. Similar to its subordinate counterparts in impudence/arrogance, impetuosity continues in the tradition of such impulsive or outspoken behavior that similarly targets the extreme realm of excess. Consequently, impetuosity enjoys a somewhat favorable cachet when events are going well, although its drawbacks become all too apparent when the tide of success eventually turns.

362 – COVETOUSNESS

The impetuous prerequisites for the spiritual authority role, in turn, prompt the respective follower form of countermaneuver; namely, the *covetousness* expressed by the spiritual disciple figure. The term derives from the Old French

183

coveitier, apparently from the Latin *cupiditas* (passion, desire): from *cupidus* (highly desirous), from *cupere* (to long for or desire). It is traditionally defined as an illicit desire for what one does not possess, or (more broadly) all objects of desire sought after inordinately. In this general heading are classified the covetousness of honors, riches (as in avarice), or lustful pleasure.

Covetousness concerning wealth or affection takes as its object that already in the possession of another, transgressing the strictures of the Ninth/Tenth Commandments. These covert desires, when willfully indulged, partake in the sinful nature of the respective outward deed. Those individuals who willfully desire another man's wife (or goods) have already committed in their heart the sins of adultery or larceny. Covetousness is more properly defined as an inclination to sin rather than any outward deed. Insofar as one endeavors to acquire and hold possessions for one's personal wellbeing; covetousness, in contrast, is a source of treachery, heartlessness, and unrest. Similar to its subordinate counterparts of envy/jealousy, covetousness is defined as a subjectively felt emotional propensity. Its outward effects border upon passive spitefulness and sarcasm rather than any prosecutable offense. In this internally private domain, covetousness remains a vice difficult to target in an objective sense, only seriously proscribed in terms of its foray into the extreme realm of the vices of excess.

372 – PRESUMPTUOUSNESS

The completed description of the vices of excess spanning the personal, group, and spiritual levels further sets the stage for the remaining humanitarian and transcendental levels within the hierarchy of excess. In contrast to the purely organizational power status of the first three levels, the final two levels are alternately distinguished as purely abstract styles of power maneuvers. In this latter sense, the humanitarian realm derives from the abstract addition of "historical" time, whereas the transcendental level makes a further appeal to the notion of "pure" transcendence.

The profoundly abstract nature of these final two levels is further reflected in their respectively abstract groupings of vices. For instance, the initial sequence of impudence-arrogance-impetuosity, in turn, extends to a humanitarian sphere of influence with respect to the authority-based theme of *presumptuousness*. The term derives from the Latin *praesumere*, a compound of *prae-* (before) and *sumere* (to take). It denotes a pre-

disposed state of mind, often in a rash or willful fashion, often regarded as a result of pride. This tendency to presume goes hand-in-hand with the basic theme of arrogance characterizing the general sequence of terms. Presumptuousness continues in the tradition of the preliminary sequence of terms; namely, impudence-arrogance-impetuosity, although now extending to a more enduring humanitarian sphere of influence. Indeed, in keeping with such an entrenched presumptuous perspective, one's willful sense of impetuosity is generally taken for granted: where any incidental interference towards such goals is deeply resented in turn. Hence, presumption clearly fulfills the pattern initially established for the realm of excess, and one certainly befitting such an extremely arrogant authority perspective.

392 – SMUGNESS

The enduring sense of influence for presumptuousness, in turn, extends to a crowning transcendental sphere of influence with respect to the related theme of smugness. The English spelling of *smug* (trim, neat, spruce) dates primarily to the mid-16th century, possibly an alteration of the Low-German *smuk* (trim, neat), from the Middle Low-German *smücken* (to adorn), or *smiegen* (to press close). The connotation of "possessing a self-satisfied air" dates to the early 18th century, possibly an extension of its early sense of smoothness or sleekness. It denotes a contented confidence in one's abilities, superiority, or correctness; sometimes equated with complacency.

The extreme prerequisites for smugness certainly embody an overall theme of self-aggrandizement, wherein culminating (in a transcendental sense) the preliminary sequence of impudence-arrogance-impetuosity-presumptuousness. Any such serene sense of smugness is only truly comprehensible in such transcendental terms, where this extreme attitude remains essentially at odds with the strict reality at hand. Although the current placement of smugness remains an issue best left open to further consideration, it still remains the best available option in light of the remaining alternatives.

382 – LONGING

The completed description of the respective authority roles of presumptuousness/smugness, in turn, sets the stage for the remaining sequence of the follower roles; namely, the pairing of longing/affectation representative of the humanitarian/transcendental realms, respectively. Take for example, the humanitarian follower theme of *longing*. The term derives from the Old English *langian* (to yearn, to seem long), literally "to grow long," from the Proto-Germanic *langojanan*. It denotes a persistent desire or strong craving, particularly that which is distant or unattainable. According to U.S. poet Robert Hass: "*Longing*, we say, is because desire is full of endless distances." Furthermore, in the words of author James Russell Lowell: "The thing we *long* for, that we are for one transcendent moment." Russian-born U.S. novelist Vladimir Nabokov also describes longing as "nostalgia in reverse."

This latter quotation clearly establishes longing as a future-directed emotion in keeping with its lofty passionate perspectives. Indeed, it continues in the tradition previously established for the sequence of envy, jealousy, and covetousness: although now extending to a more enduring humanitarian sphere of influence. Although longing is more closely associated with romantic extremes, it may similarly target any strong sense of positive emotionality: as in extreme striving for fame, power, or self-fulfillment. Longing satisfies the general prerequisites for placement within the humanitarian realm of the hierarchy of excess, although the extreme degree of abstraction does not preclude other potentialities.

302 – AFFECTATION

The preliminary humanitarian focus of longing ultimately extends to a transcendental sphere of influence with respect to the related theme of *affectation*. The term derives from the Latin *affect ationem*, from *affectare* (to strive after). It denotes a showy pretense or a false display, as in pretending to be what one is not. It also refers to behavior that lacks natural expression, as in conspicuous artificiality in form or appearance. By extension, affectation can also suggest particular behavioral mannerisms (such as speech or dress) adopted to give a false impression, or to draw notice through pretense.

This artificial sense of "airs" is often employed in imitation of another, wherein perceived as wholly unnatural. Indeed, according to actor Rex Harrison: "Whatever it is that makes a person charming, it needs to remain a mystery ... once the charmer is aware of a mannerism or characteristic that others find charming, it ceases to be a mannerism and becomes an *affectation*. And good Lord, there is nothing less charming than affectations!" This sense of artificiality or pretense clearly places affectation at the crowning transcendental level within the hierarchy of excess.

Indeed, the transcendental domain is formally defined in terms of an intellectual refinement of ordinary reality (in a more abstract sense). Consequently, affectation appears far more abstruse than the other subordinate terms within the initial sequence of terms. In fact, the root-stem of "affect" serves as the linguistic basis for the notion of affective language in general. Whether affectation truly warrants such a transcendental placement remains open to debate, although it clearly remains the best possible candidate at this juncture.

THE FUTURE- DIRECTED PERSPECTIVES BASED UPON INSOLENCE / DISDAIN

The completed description of the future-directed realm of excess based upon impudence/envy further sets the stage for the remaining trend based upon insolence/disdain. This latter format is defined as an extreme sense of disdain in response to the insolent treatment of the personal authority figure. Indeed, this reciprocal interplay of authority/follower roles effectively mirrors the pattern previously established for impudence/envy, where envy occurs in response to extremely impudent behaviors, therein. This initial interplay of insolence/disdain, in turn, extends to the group, spiritual, humanitarian, and transcendental levels as well: organized as an ascending hierarchy employing an alternating sequence of presentation. Consequently, the initial sequence of authority roles (insolence-audacity-rashness-boldness-harshness), in turn, complements the respective follower sequence of disdain-contempt-reproach-chagrin-bitterness): wherein providing a precise determination of power dynamics at issue for the future-directed realm of excess.

313 – INSOLENCE

In terms of the most basic personal authority level, the first-mentioned theme of *insolence* represents the extreme counterpart of the more basic ego-state of worry. In analogy to insolence, worry is defined as submissive behavior that anticipates lenient reinforcement, an aspect that insolence amplifies and parodies to an extreme degree. The term derives from the Latin *insolens*, a compound of *in-* (not) and *solens*, past participle of *solere* (to be accustomed): suggesting an overbearing or haughty demeanor.

The classical Greeks worshipped this quality as their abstract goddess Hybris, the divine personification of insolence, extreme pride, or aggressiveness. Her name translates to the English language as the notion of "hubris" (of parallel usage and meaning). Hybris is traditionally cited as the daughter of Eris (the goddess of discord). Her male child Koros was worshipped as the Greek personification of disdain and surfeit. According to the Greek authority Pindar: "Hybris (insolence) is the ruin of cities ... Never may shameless Hybris bring faction in her train and seize the company of citizens when they have forgotten their courage." The Greek lyrical tradition further states: "Shameless Hybris (insolence), luxuriating in shifty tricks and lawless follies, who swiftly gives a man another's wealth and power only to bring him into deep ruin - it was she who destroyed those arrogant sons of Ge, the Gigantes."

In this stylized literary sense, hubris (or insolence) represents a consistent theme down through the ages, particularly in militaristic cultures such as the ancient Greeks. The greatest military offense was an insolent attitude towards one's superiors, a breach of conduct swiftly punished as a stark exemplar to others within the unit. Insolence, accordingly, shares with impudence such an ingrained sense of disrespect, although insolence more directly threatens the authority status quo; hence, a particularly grievous perspective.

323 – DISDAIN

The preceding personal authority theme of insolence, in turn, is countered (in a follower sense) by related theme of *disdain*. The term derives from the Old French *desdeignier*, from *des-* (do the opposite of) and *deignier* (to treat as worthy), from the Latin *dignus* (worthy). This pejorative sense of condescension is reflected in terms of scornful aversion or overbearing haughtiness. Indeed, as mentioned earlier, the classical Greeks worshipped this negative aspect as the abstract god Koros, the divine personification of disdain and surfeit.

In agreement with the preceding discussion of insolence, Hybris is directly cited in the parentage of disdain (Koros), attesting to the reciprocal relationship mutually shared in terms of the personal level within the hierarchy of excess. According to Pindar: "Far from their path, they (the Horae) hold proud Hybris (insolence) fierce-hearted mother of full-fed Koros (disdain)." Furthermore, according to Herodotus: "Divine Dike (justice) will extinguish mighty Koros (disdain) the son of Hybris, lusting terribly, thinking to devour all." Indeed, down through the ages, the proud elevated curl of the upper lip exemplified haughtiness and bitter contempt. The stylized curled lip serves as

the very emblem for aristocratic disdain. According to German philosopher, Friedrich Nietzsche: "...the most disagreeable way to respond to a polemic is to be angry and keep silent, for the aggressor usually takes the silence as a sign of *disdain*."

Disdain makes a particularly fitting counterpoint to insolence, just as envy was previously cited in relationship to impudence. The haughty and disgusted prerequisites typically associated with disdain certainly fit such an emotionally-charged context: the insolent attitude expressed by the personal authority figure clearly more confrontational than that initially established for impudence. The familiar scenario of the rebellious street-thug certainly stands out in this regard: wherein relying upon extreme surliness to assert his street-tough status. This aggressive posturing, in turn, prompts a disdainful perspective on the part of the follower figure, an extreme attitude directly in keeping with such an antecedent display of insolence.

The dual interplay of insolence/disdain further sets the stage for the remaining group/spiritual levels within hierarchy of excess. For instance, the insolence expressed by the personal authority, in turn, extends to the audacity professed by the group authority, culminating in the rashness expressed by the spiritual authority figure. Furthermore, the disdain expressed by the personal follower further prompts the contempt of the group representative, followed by the reproach of the spiritual disciple figure. The next four sections provide a more in-depth examination of the group/spiritual domains for the hierarchy of excess, beginning with the group themes of audacity/contempt, followed by the spiritual counterparts of rashness/reproach.

333 – AUDACITY

The first-mentioned (group authority) theme of *audacity* is traditionally defined as an extreme sense of insolence, particularly in a civic or social setting. The term derives from the French *audacieux*, from the Latin *audax*, from *audere* (to dare). It denotes a daring or bold course of action in arrogant disregard for personal safety, or in defiance of conventionality. It similarly denotes a sense of effrontery or insolence, as suggested in the colloquial synonyms of spunk, grit, brashness, or impertinence. Indeed, French filmmaker, Jean Cocteau humorously quipped: "Tact in *audacity* consists in knowing how far we may go too far!" Audacity also denotes an extreme sense of originality unfettered by restrictions governing prior ideas, as in feeling unrestrained or uninhibited. In his address to recipients of the National Medal of Arts, President Ronald Reagan insightfully noted: "In an atmosphere of liberty, artists and patrons are free to think the unthinkable and create the *audacious*; they are free to make both horrendous mistakes and glorious celebrations."

Irrespective of the positive or negative connotations therein, the extremes traditionally associated with audacity clearly reflect more advanced (group) sphere of influence, in direct analogy to the personal prerequisites previously established for insolence. This ingrained sense of brashness goes part in parcel with its formal placement within the hierarchy of excess, as directly evident within an advanced social context. Audacity shares with its related social counterpart of arrogance such a daringly bold persona, although even more far reaching in terms of both reason and consequence.

343 – CONTEMPT

The preceding somewhat cursory examination of audacity, in turn, sets the stage for a remaining discussion of the follower maneuver proper; namely, the disdainful sense of *contempt* expressed by the group representative. The term derives from the Latin *contemptus* (scorn), past participle of *contemnere*: from *com-* (intensification) and *temnere* (to slight or scorn). British statesman Philip Stanhope (4th Earl of Chesterfield) once succinctly wrote: "Wrongs are often forgiven, but *contempt* never is. Our pride remembers it forever."

Contempt, in a legal sense, refers to interference in terms of the functioning of a court or legislature. In its most general sense, contempt refers to a sense of scorn or mockery concerning the prevailing dignity of the court. Contempt of court is primarily classified as civil or criminal, distinguished in terms of the respective remedial penalties. Should it be necessary to vindicate judicial authority, then the contempt is considered criminal. If the penalty upholds the rights of a given party, then the contempt is considered civil.

A *direct* contempt is committed while the court is actually in session. A *constructive* contempt occurs away from the courtroom in terms of actions that obstruct or defeat the administration of justice. Refusing to answer a question when directed to respond by the judge is considered direct criminal contempt. Disobeying an injunction stemming from a legal judgment (such as alimony) is defined as civil contempt. Direct criminal contempt is punishable by fine or imprison-

ment. Similar penalties apply to civil or constructive contempt, although the accused is first granted a hearing. Contempt of the US Congress refers to disrespect occurring during legislative proceedings, or activities that threaten legislative authority. Congress must promptly act on accusations of contempt before it adjourns. Furthermore, any incarceration may not last longer than the current session. State legislatures also employ limited powers for penalizing flagrant contempt.

These civic aspects of contempt within a courtroom setting clearly prove consistent with its group placement within the hierarchy of excess, wherein formally expanding upon the personal prerequisites previously established for disdain. This civic context is particularly evident in the kindred quotation: "Familiarity breeds contempt," originally attributed to one of Aesop's Fables (The Fox and the Lion) and repeated by luminaries such as Shakespeare. Here, familiarity truly does breed contempt in such an overarching social sense, for the closer one's status is to that of another, the more likely one is to experience the audacious brashness conducive to contempt in return.

353 – RASHNESS

The completed description of the group prerequisites for audacity/contempt, in turn, sets the stage for the remaining spiritual (or universal) domain of rashness/reproach. This latter sequence is initiated with respect to the audacious sense of *rashness* expressed by the spiritual authority figure. The term is said to derive from the Old English *ræsc*, as in *ligræsc* (flash of lightning), from the Proto-Germanic *raskuz*. It could also prove akin to the Old English *horsc* (quick-witted). Its sense of "actively impetuous or unrestrained" dates at least to the 14th century, whereas the connotation of "too hasty or careless" emerges circa the 16th century: denoting a hasty course of action generally lacking in caution.

According to Aristotle's enduring *Theory of the Mean*, the cardinal virtue of courage represents the mean value interposed between the extremes of *rashness* and the defect-state of cowardice. In addition to courage, many of the other major virtues respect this mean-value format: e.g., temperance, liberality, magnificence, etc. Of this elite grouping, courage most clearly exemplifies such a three-way spectrum of specialization. Indeed, the extremes of rashness (personified by the reckless thrill seeker) prove exceedingly reminiscent of the general domain of excess. Consequently, the rashness formally extends the general theme of brashness into a universal

314	315
Narcissism	Ignominy
316	317
Impertinence	Hubris

EGOCENTRISM
(Personal Authority)

324	325
Blandishment	Reprehensibleness
326	327
Invidiousness	Despisal

OBTRUSIVENESS
(Personal Follower)

334	335
Snobbery	Opprobrium
336	337
Brazenness	Surliness

AUTOCRACY
(Group Authority)

344	345
Courtliness	Denunciation
346	347
Possessiveness	Repugnance

ABSOLUTISM
(Group Representative)

354	355
Vainglory	Despondency
356	357
Brashness	Irascibility

PONTIFICATION
(Spiritual Authority)

364	365
Condescension	Derision
366	367
Cravingness	Rebuke

DOGMATISM
(Spiritual Disciple)

374	375
Haughtiness	Agony
376	377
Effrontery	Temerity

FUNDAMENTALISM
(Humanitarian Authority)

384	385
Servility	Sarcasm
386	387
Yearning	Loathing

SUPREMACISM
(Humanitarian Follower)

394	395
Pietism	Affliction
396	397
Gleefulness	Rigorousness

CATHOLICITY
(Transcendental Authority)

304	305
Subservience	Satiricism
306	307
Pretension	Admonishment

ENIGMATISM
(Transcendental Follower)

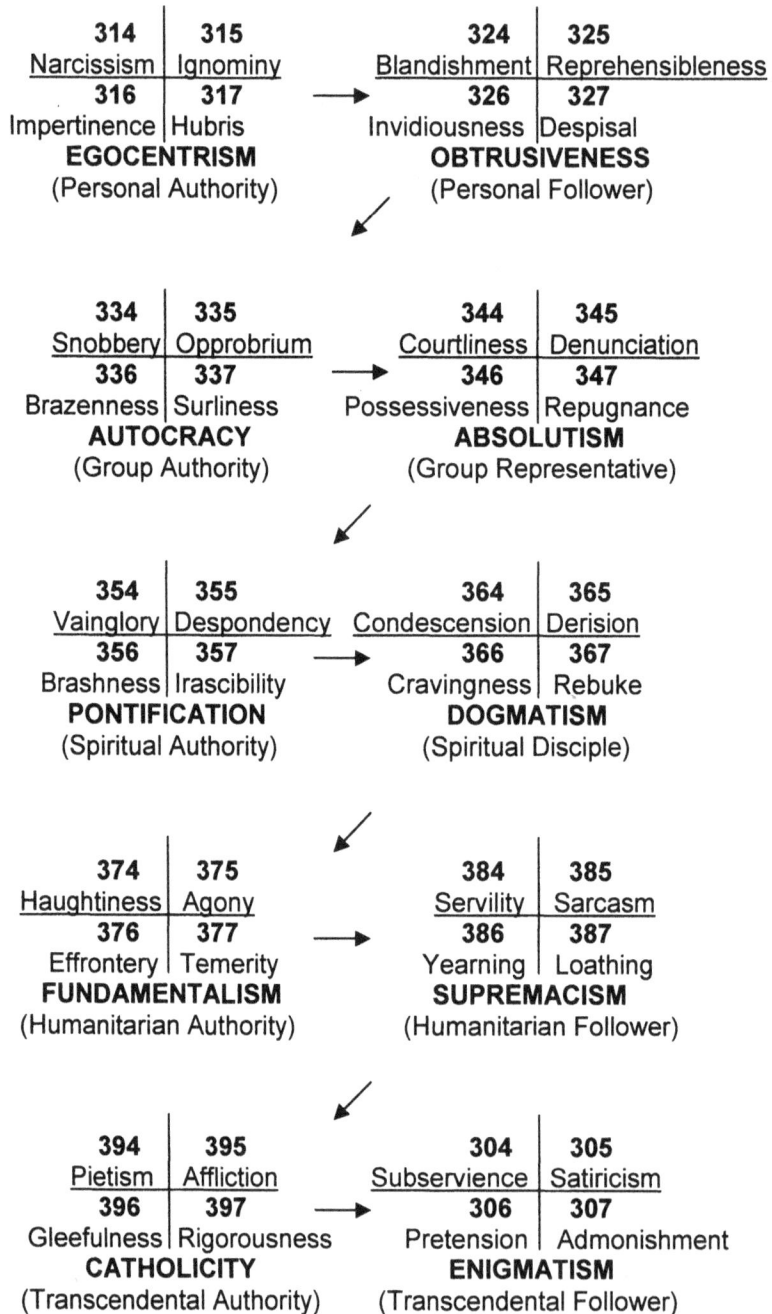

Fig. 18 – The Accessory Vices of Excess

sphere of influence, invoking a course of action judged reckless and foolhardy across most cultures or creeds. Rashness directly expands upon the initial sequence of insolence/audacity, although now targeting a broader range of focus. Indeed, a rash course of action is clearly to be avoided due to its questionable survival value.

363 – REPROACH

The initial sense of rashness expressed by the spiritual authority, in turn, sets the stage for the contemptuous sense of *reproach* expressed by the spiritual disciple figure. Its modern spelling derives from the Old French *reproche*, from *reprocher* (to blame, to bring against), from the Vulgar Latin *repropiare*, a compound of the Latin *re-* (the opposite of) and *prope* (near). It denotes the act of censuring or upbraiding, as in conducive to a loss of social status.

The specific theme of reproach is similarly translated in Old Testament scripture as the verb "to rebuke," particularly with respect to the Hebrew equivalents of *ga`ar* and *yakhach*. As a noun, rebuke occurs most frequently as a translation of *ge`arah*, and also *cherpah* (Isaiah 25:8). In New Testament scripture, "to rebuke" is more often a translation of *epitimao*, and also *elegcho*, the latter of which is traditionally rendered as "to reprove."

In terms of the preceding scriptural examples, the deep spiritual overtones primarily associated with reproach clearly betray such a universal sphere of influence, an aspect extremely suggestive of the role of the spiritual disciple. As such, reproach directly expands upon preliminary prerequisites for disdain/contempt, although now invoking spiritual overtones for rebuking the rash treatment of the respective authority figure. As with all such forays into the realm of excess, reproach can lead to outright conflict if taken to extremes, a strategy that clearly calls for cautious restraint in terms of such an all-encompassing (universal) context.

373 – BOLDNESS

The completed description of the themes of excess spanning the personal, group, and spiritual levels, in turn, sets the stage for a discussion of the remaining humanitarian/transcendental levels within the hierarchy of excess. The profoundly abstract nature of these remaining two levels is directly reflected in the respective groupings of vices. For instance, the initial sequence of insolence-audacity-rashness further extends to a humanitarian sphere of influence in terms of the respective authority theme of *boldness*. The term derives from the Old English *beald*, from the Anglo-Saxon *bald* (bold, brave), from the Proto-Germanic *balthaz*: perhaps also from the Proto-Indo-European root-stem *bhel-* (to swell). As such, it denotes a daring or courageous endeavor frequently bordering on the absurd.

In New Testament scripture, boldness is considered one of the crucial aspects for true discipleship (Acts 4:13, 29, 31), a necessary requirement for the zeal of the faithful. These disciples were subject not only to violent persecutions, but also the target of ridicule and contempt. According to Hebrews (10:19), this theme of boldness suggests a sense of freeness stemming from supreme confidence. Here, spiritual boldness is exemplified by James the Great, one of the apostles and elder brother of John (the sons of Zebedee and Salome). Primarily due to their boldness and energy, he and his brother John were known as the Boanerges, namely, *The Sons of Thunder*. He is said to have been the first martyr among the twelve apostles, beheaded by Herod Agrippa in 44 CE.

This extreme sense of boldness continues the tradition previously established for rashness and audacity, although now extending to a universal sphere of influence: as the respective spiritual overtones clearly serve to indicate. In keeping with such a grand humanitarian interplay, boldness is respectively viewed as an asset in terms of the establishment of the early Church. Although desperate times warrant desperate measures, boldness, nevertheless, suffers the risk of all rashly driven endeavors: a factor that fortunately has moderated somewhat in terms of Christianity's subsequent rise to power and respectability.

393 – HARSHNESS

The preceding humanitarian focus of boldness, in turn, extends to a crowning transcendental sphere of influence with respect to the related theme of *harshness*. The term derives from the Middle English *harske* (rough, coarse, sour), akin to the Danish *harsk* (rancid), or the German *harsch* (hard). It denotes a sense of roughness conducive to jarring the senses or the emotions. This theme directly amplifies the daring attributes ascribed to boldness, particularly in terms of a military context. The Roman poet Virgil writes: "*Harsh* necessity and the newness of my kingdom force me to do such things as to guard my frontiers everywhere." Shakespeare, in turn, alludes to "the *harsh* and boisterous tongue of war." Verbal

NARCISSISM	BLANDISHMENT
Previously, I (as reinforcer) have extremely acted rewardingly towards you: overriding your (as procurer) excessively solicitous treatment of me.	Previously, you (as personal authority) have narcissistically admitted having acted excessively solicitously towards me: overriding my (as reinforcer) extremely rewarding treatment of you.
But now, you (as personal authority) will *narcissistically* admit having acted excessively solicitously towards me: overruling my (as reinforcer) extremely rewarding treatment of you.	But now, I (as your personal follower) will *blandishingly* act in an extremely approving fashion towards you: overruling your (as PA) narcissistic treatment of me.
SNOBBERY	**COURTLINESS**
Previously, I (as your personal follower) have blandishingly acted in an extremely approving fashion towards you: overriding your (as PA) narcissistic treatment of me.	Previously, you (as group authority) have narcissistically acted in an snobbish fashion towards me: overriding my (as PF) blandishing treatment of you.
But now, you (as group authority) will narcissistically act in an *snobbish* fashion towards me: overruling my (as PF) blandishing treatment of you.	But now, I (as group representative) will blandishingly act in a *courtly* fashion towards you: overruling your (as GA) snobbish treatment of me.
VAINGLORY	**CONDESCENSION**
Previously, I (as group representative) have blandishingly acted in a courtly fashion towards you: overriding your (as GA) snobbish treatment of me.	Previously, you (as spiritual authority) have snobbishly acted in a vainglorious fashion towards me: overriding my (as GR) courtly treatment of you.
But now, you (as spiritual authority) will snobbish*ly* act in an *vainglorious* fashion towards me: overruling my (as GR) courtly treatment of you.	But now, I (as your spiritual disciple) will *condescendingly* act in a courtly fashion towards you: overruling your (as SA) vainglorious treatment of me.
HAUGHTINESS	**SERVILITY**
Previously, I (as your spiritual disciple) have condescendingly acted in a courtly fashion towards you: overriding your (as SA) vainglorious treatment of me.	Previously, you (as humanitarian authority) have vaingloriously acted in a haughty towards me: overriding my (as SD) condescending treatment of you.
But now, you (as humanitarian authority) will vaingloriously act in a *haughty* fashion towards me: overruling my (as SD) condescendingly treatment of you.	But now, I (as representative member of humanity) will condescendingly act in a *servile* fashion towards you: overruling your (as HA) haughty treatment of me.
PIETISM	**SUBSERVIENCE**
Previously, I (as representative member of humanity) have condescendingly acted in a servile fashion towards you: overriding your (as HA) haughty treatment of me.	Previously, you (as transcendental authority) have haughtily acted in a pietistic fashion towards me: overriding my (as RH) servile treatment of you.
But now, you (as transcendental authority) will haughtily act in a *pietistic* fashion towards me: overruling my (as RH) servile treatment of you.	But now, I (as your transcendental follower) will servilely act in a *subservient* fashion towards you: overruling your (as TA) pietistic treatment of me.

Table G-1 – The Definitions Based Upon Narcissism/Blandishment

IGNOMINY	REPREHENSIBLENESS
Previously, I (as reinforcer) have extremely acted leniently towards you: overriding your (as procurer) excessively submissive treatment of me.	Previously, you (as personal authority) have *ignominiously* acted in an excessively culpable fashion towards me: overriding my (as reinforcer) extremely lenient treatment of you.
But now, you (as personal authority) will *ignominiously* act in an excessively culpable fashion towards me: overruling my (as reinforcer) extremely lenient treatment of you.	But now, I (as your personal follower) will *reprehensibly* act in an extremely censuring fashion towards you: overruling your (as PA) ignominious treatment of me.
OPPROBRIUM	**DENUNCIATION**
Previously, I (as your personal follower) have reprehensiblly act in an extremely censuring fashion towards you: overriding your (as PA) ignominious treatment of me.	Previously, you (as group authority) have ignominiously acted with opprobrium towards me: overriding my (as PF) reprehensible treatment of you.
But now, you (as group authority) will ignominiously act with *opprobrium* towards me: overruling my (as PF) reprehensible treatment of you.	But now, I (as group representative) will reprehensibly act in a *denunciatory* fashion towards you: overruling your (as GA) ignominious sense of opprobrium.
DESPONDENCY	**DERISION**
Previously, I (as group representative) have reprehensiblly acted in a denunciatory fashion towards you: overriding your (as GA) ignominious sense of opprobrium.	Previously, you (as spiritual authority) have despondently acted with opprobrium towards me: overriding my (as GR) denunciatory treatment of you.
But now, you (as spiritual authority) will *despondently* act with opprobrium towards me: overruling my (as GR) denunciatory treatment of you.	But now, I (as your spiritual disciple) will *derisively* act in a denunciatory fashion towards you: overruling your (as SA) despondent treatment of you.
AGONY	**SARCASM**
Previously, I (as your spiritual disciple) have derisively acted in a denunciatory fashion towards you: overriding your (as SA) despondent treatment of me.	Previously, you (as humanitarian authority) have despondently acted in an agonizing fashion towards me: overriding my (as SD) derisive-denunciation of you.
But now, you (as humanitarian authority) will despondently act in an *agonizing* fashion towards me: overruling my (as SD) derisive-denunciation of you.	But now, I (as representative member of humanity) will derisively act in a *sarcastic* fashion towards you: overruling your (as HA) agonized treatment of me.
AFFLICTION	**SATIRICISM**
Previously, I (as representative member of humanity) have derisively acted in a sarcastic fashion towards you: overriding your (as HA) agonized treatment of me.	Previously, you (as transcendental authority) have agonizingly acted in an afflicted fashion towards me: overriding my (as RH) sarcastic treatment of you.
But now, you (as transcendental authority) will agonizingly act in an *afflicted* fashion towards me: overruling my (as RH) sarcastic treatment of you.	But now, I (as transcendental follower) will *satirically* act in a sarcastic fashion towards you: overruling your (as TA) afflicted treatment of me.

Table G- 2 – The Definitions Based Upon Ignominy/Reprehension

IMPERTINENCE	INVIDIOUSNESS
Previously, you (as reinforcer) have excessively acted rewardingly towards me: overriding my (as procurer) extremely solicitous treatment of you But now, I (as personal authority) will *impertinently* act in an extremely passionate fashion towards you: overruling your (as reinforcer) excessively rewarding treatment of me.	Previously, I (as personal authority) have impertinently acted in an extremely passionate fashion towards you: overriding your (reinforcer) excessively rewarding treatment of me. But now, you (as my personal follower) will *invidiously* act in an excessively admiring fashion towards me: overruling my (as PA) impertinent treatment of you.
BRAZENNESS	**POSSESSIVENESS**
Previously, you (as personal follower) have invidiously acted in an excessively admiring fashion towards me: overriding my (as PA) impertinent treatment of you. But now, I (as group authority) will impertinently act in a *brazen* fashion towards you: overruling your (as PF) invidious treatment of me.	Previously, I (as group authority) have impertinently acted in a brazen fashion towards you: overriding your (as PF) invidious treatment of me. But now, you (as group representative) will invidiously act in a *possessive* fashion towards me: overruling my (as GA) brazen treatment of you.
BRASHNESS	**CRAVENNESS**
Previously, you (as group representative) have invidiously acted in a possessive fashion towards me: overriding my (as GA) brazen treatment of you. But now, I (as spiritual authority) will brazenly act in a *brash* fashion towards you: overruling your (as GR) possessive treatment of you.	Previously, I (as spiritual authority) have brazenly acted in a brash fashion towards you: overriding your (as GR) possessive treatment of you. But now, you (as my spiritual disciple) will possessively act in a *craven* fashion towards me: overruling my (as SA) brash treatment of you.
EFFRONTERY	**YEARNING**
Previously, you (as my spiritual disciple) have possessively acted in a craven fashion towards me: overriding my (as SA) brash treatment of you. But now, I (as humanitarian authority) will brashly act with *effrontery* towards you: overruling your (as SD) craven treatment of me.	Previously, I (as humanitarian authority) have brashly acted with effrontery towards you: overriding your (as SD) craven treatment of me. But now, you (as a representative member of humanity) will cravenly act in a *yearning* fashion towards me: overruling my (as HA) brash sense of effrontery.
GLEEFULNESS	**PRETENSION**
Previously, you (as representative member of humanity) have cravenly acted in a yearning fashion towards me: overriding my (as HA) brash sense of effrontery. But now, I (as transcendental authority) will *gleefully* act with effrontery towards you: overruling your (as RH) yearning treatment of me.	Previously, I (as transcendental authority) have gleefully acted with effrontery towards you: overriding your (as RH) yearning treatment of me. But now, you (as transcendental follower) will yearningly act in a *pretension*-filled fashion towards me: overruling my (as TA) gleeful treatment of you.

Table G-3 – The Definitions Based Upon Impertinence/Invidiousness

HUBRIS	DESPISAL
Previously, you (as reinforcer) have excessively acted in a lenient fashion towards me: overriding my (as procurer) extreme admission of having acted submissively towards you. But now, I (as personal authority) will *hubristically* act extremely apprehensively towards you: overruling your (as reinforcer) excessively lenient treatment of me.	Previously, I (as personal authority) have hubristically acted extremely apprehensively towards you: overriding your (as reinforcer) excessively lenient treatment of me. But now, you (as my personal follower) will *despisingly* act excessively caringly towards me: overruling my (as PA) hubristic treatment of you.
SURLINESS	REPUGNANCE
Previously, you (as personal follower) have despisingly acted excessively caringly towards me: overriding my (as PA) hubristic treatment of you. But now, I (as group authority) will hubristically act in a *surly* fashion towards you: overruling your (as PF) despising treatment of me.	Previously, I (as group authority) have hubristically acted in a surly fashion towards you: overriding your (as PF) despising treatment of me. But now, you (as group representative) will despisingly express a sense of *repugnance* towards me: overruling my (as GA) surly treatment of me.
IRASCIBILITY	REBUKE
Previously, you (as group representative) have despisingly expressed a sense of repugnance towards me: overriding my (as GA) surly treatment of me. But now, I (as spiritual authority) will *irascibly* act in a surly fashion towards you: overruling your (as GR) repugnant treatment of me.	Previously, I (as spiritual authority) have irascibly acted in a surly fashion towards you: overriding your (as GR) repugnant treatment of me. But now, you (as my spiritual disciple) will repugnantly-*rebuke* me: overruling my (as SA) irascible treatment of you.
TEMERITY	LOATHING
Previously, you (as my spiritual disciple) have repugnantly-rebuked me: overriding my (as SA) irascible treatment of you. But now, I (as humanitarian authority) will irascibly act in a *temerity*-filled fashion towards you: overruling your (as SD) repugnant-rebuking of me.	Previously, I (as humanitarian authority) have irascibly acted in a temerity-filled fashion towards you: overriding your (as SD) repugnant-rebuking of me. But now, you (as representative member of humanity) will *loathingly*-rebuke me: overruling my (as HA) temerity-filled treatment of you.
RIGOROUSNESS	ADMONISHMENT
Previously, you (as representative member of humanity) have loathingly-rebuked me: overriding my (as HA) temerity-filled treatment of you. But now, I (as transcendental authority) will *rigorously* act in a temerity-filled fashion towards you: overruling your (as RH) loathing-rebuke of me.	Previously, I (as transcendental authority) have rigorously acted in a temerity-filled fashion towards you: overriding your (as RH) loathing-rebuke of me. But now, you (as my transcendental follower) will loathingly act with *admonishment* towards me: overruling my (as TA) rigorous treatment of you.

Table G-4 – The Definitions Based Upon Hubris/Despisal

harshness similarly figures prominently, for according to Proverbs (15:1): "A soft answer turns away wrath, but a *harsh* word stirs up anger." Furthermore, an ancient Chinese proverb states: "Kind words can warm for three winters, whereas *harsh* words can chill even in the heat of summer."

This extremely sense of harshness effectively verifies the basic theme embodied within the overall sequence of terms; namely, insolence-audacity-rashness-boldness (and now harshness). In terms of its crowning transcendental placement within the hierarchy of excess, harshness enjoys a fairly broad range of meaning: as in harsh judgment or treatment, as well as harsh reality or perspective. Whether harshness truly warrants its supreme transcendental placement remains an issue open to further debate, although its current assignment remains the most plausible selection at this juncture.

382 – CHAGRIN

The completed description of the initial authority roles of boldness/harshness, in turn, sets the stage for the remaining hierarchy of follower roles; namely, the respective listing of chagrin/bitterness targeting the humanitarian/transcendental levels, respectively. Take, for example, the first-listed follower theme of *chagrin*. The term derives from the French *chagrin* (shagreen, or rough skin, ill-humor), a variation of *sagrin*, from the Turkish *sagri* (rump): suggestive of the leather crupper of a horse harness. Its derivation from shagreen refers to untanned leather with a granular surface prepared from the hide of a horse, shark, seal, etc., particularly the rough skin of certain shark species used as a mechanical abrasive.

This sense of roughness or abrasiveness further serves as the basis for its respective motivational connotations: in particular, feelings of vexation marked by disappointment or humiliation. The general facial expression expressed during chagrin is more-or-less indistinguishable from that characterizing disdain and contempt so closely are they related within the follower hierarchy. The abrasive nature of this inward state of emotion is directly reflected in the respective derivation of the term, as in a grating sense of reproach towards anyone who is so disposed. In this latter contemptuous sense, chagrin formally expands upon the initial sequence of terms (disdain-contempt-reproach), although now extending to a more enduring humanitarian context within the overall realm of excess.

303 – BITTERNESS

The initial humanitarian focus for chagrin, in turn, extends to a transcendental sphere of influence with respect to the related theme of *bitterness*. The term derives from the Old English *biter*, akin to *bitan* (to bite): alluding to the biting or acrid sensation typically associated with bitterness. In Old Testament scripture, bitterness is particularly symbolic of affliction, misery, or servitude (Exodus 1:14; Ruth 1:20; Jeremiah 9:15). The Feast of the Passover traditionally included a serving of bitter herbs (Exodus 12:8) symbolizing the severity of servitude under which the people labored.

In New Testament scripture, the expression "gall of bitterness" is defined as a state of great wickedness (Acts 8:23). The "root of bitterness" refers to a wicked person or the depths of sinfulness (Hebrews 12:15). Bitterness clearly encompasses the overall theme of disgust indicative of the preliminary sequence of terms (disdain-contempt-reproach-chagrin), although now extending to a transcendental sphere of influence. Indeed, the very act of tasting something bitter leads to a disgust response similar to that encountered in disdain/contempt: where the curled upper-lip is also indicative of reproach/chagrin. In such an overarching social sense, bitterness clearly fulfills its status as the crowning transcendental theme within the sequence, although its extreme level of abstraction necessarily specifies that other options are technically feasible at this juncture.

THE ACCESSORY VARIATIONS FOR THE VICES OF EXCESS

Any all-inclusive description of the main realm of excess, however, necessarily implies the existence of a parallel complement of terms based upon the predicted accessory realm. At first glance, the main listings of terms scarcely seem comprehensive enough to support any additional complement of accessory terms, particularly with respect to the more abstract levels within the hierarchy of excess. Indeed, there generally appears to be a dearth of good synonyms for many of the predicted slots within this accessory hierarchy. The various shades of meaning required to distinguish these accessory terms scarcely seem dramatic enough to convincingly trigger a corresponding distinction in terms, particularly where a more ambiguous determination of "excess" is concerned. For this reason, a completely stand-alone version of the accessory vices of excess was absent from the debut release of the three-digit coding system. Rather, a more modest "stopgap" system of terminology was introduced, entailing the use of a formal prefix "*acc-*" format (as in accessory) for modifying the main terms for the vices of excess in concert with a reversal of the polarity of the "you" and "I" roles. Fortunately, in the four year interim it was determined that an adequate number of suitable synonyms, indeed, does exist with respect to the vices of excess, concert with a certain degree of redundancy yields a suitably workable version of the accessory hierarchy of terms. The complete *40*-fold complement of accessory terms is outlined in **Fig. 18** and also in the compact diagram below.

Narcissism • Blandish.	Ignominy • Reprehension
Snobbery • Courtliness	Opprobr.• Denunciation
Vainglory • Condescension	Despond. • Derision
Haughtiness • Servility	Agony • Sarcasm
Pietism • Subservience	Affliction • Satiricism

Impertinence • Invidiousness	Hubris • Despisal
Brazen. • Possessive.	Surliness • Repugnance
Brashness • Cravings	Irascibility • Rebuke
Effrontery • Yearning	Temerity • Loathing
Gleefulness • Pretension	Rigorous. • Admonish.

It should be stressed that this additional innovation is necessarily a work in progress, being that a determination of the degree of excess is often a somewhat subjective determination with accompanying cultural overtones. The overall cohesiveness of this accessory hierarchy proves highly convincing in a global sense, leaving room for a certain degree of minor tinkering and adjustment.

In order to formally specify this accessory class of terms within the three-digit coding system, the third and final digit is directly called into play. Here digits 4-to-7 within the third-place slot technically specify the accessory variations within the hierarchy of excess (in contrast to the digits of 0-to-3 for the main terms. For instance, 314 = narcissism (as opposed to pride) whereas 315 = ignominy (vs. shame). Furthermore, 316 = impertinence (as opposed to impudence) whereas 317 = hubris (in contrast to insolence). In terms of the respective follower roles, 324 = blandishment (in opposition to flattery, whereby 325 = reprehension (in contrast to criticism. Furthermore, 326 = invidiousness (as opposed to envy, whereas 327 = despisal (vs. disdain). This basic foundation within the personal level of accessory

excess is parallel in many respects to the main listing of terms depicted in **Fig. 16A** of Chapter *16*. This set of parallel formulations, in concert offer a suitably comprehensive (empathic) simulation of the communicational dynamics underlying the realm of the vices of excess.

In addition, it should further be feasible to incorporate this additional class of accessory terms directly into the well-established schematic definition format (accompanied by a reversed polarity of the "you" and "I" roles): resulting in a parallel complement of schematic definitions for the accessory realm of excess. Accordingly, a complete listing of *accessory* schematic definitions is respectively tabulated in **Tables G-1** to **G-4** in direct analogy to the main set of definitions depicted **Tables A-1** to **A-4** (of Chapter *3*). These accessory schematic definitions are identical in form and function to the main counterparts with the exception that the "you" and "I" polarities are now reversed. This formal reversal of the "you" and "I" perspectives is predicted within the definition format, wherein permitting for an alternating confluence of subjective and objective viewpoints. This dual sequence of perspectives is formally predicted in terms of the empathic principles of Theory of Mind, in that reciprocating viewpoints take fully into account all potential viewpoints. In concert with the main listings of terms, this additional complement of accessory terms permits further crucial, empathic insights into the realm of excess, providing a useful model of interactive communication targeting the somewhat enigmatic realm of the vices of excess.

Through this increased diagnostic potential for both the main and accessory variations for the extreme realm of excess, the self-defeating aspects of this excessive range of perspectives becomes much more salient when designated from both the "you" and "I" viewpoints. For instance, many young adults feel that they must assert their budding independence by engaging in risky forms of behavior or malicious pranks. The current schematic format, however, presents the potential for timely empathic interventions, where the subjective perspectives of the potential victim can formally be taken into account, in fitting contrast to the more callous (objective) disregard that usually prevails. Hopefully, this powerful new technology may impart a major remedial effect in cases where a temptation towards this ill-advised range of extremes is abandoned altogether in favor of a more measured course of action.

PART-IV

19

HYPERVIOLENCE: THE REALM OF EXCESSIVE DEFECT

The completed description of Aristotle's tradition of the "Theory of the Mean" brings the proposed master coding system one step closer to completion. According to the classical Greek tradition, the virtuous realm was defined as the mean value interposed between the vices of defect and the vices of excess, an essential key to defining interactions of a moral nature. This basic "tri-partite" pattern, in turn, reaches an even greater degree of precision within the expanded context of the corresponding schematic definition format. This three-way degree of specialization, however, can scarcely claim to be the total picture, for it does not distinguish any parallel complement of extremes with respect to the vices of defect, as was previously described for the virtuous realm. This glaring lack of an even sense of symmetry is further remedied through the introduction of an entirely new class of ethical terms, a terminology provisionally termed the realm of *hyperviolence*. This new paradigm is distinguished from ordinary violence primarily with respect to the extremes in which it is carried out.

The realm of ordinary violence usually avoids any extreme degree of escalation, with conflicts typically focused on the essential issues at hand, as in hurt feelings or property disputes. Recall (from **Part II**) that cycles of conditioning involving punishment often have an adaptive value. For instance, should a water hole dry up or go sour, the individual reacts to such punitive consequences by attempting to discover new resources. With respect to interspecies conflicts, territorial issues usually dominate the picture, where an area and its resources are preemptively claimed: as in keep-out! The melodious songs of nesting songbirds represent one such territorial warning, while mammalian species frequently employ scent marking to advertise ownership of a territory.

These warning strategies clearly offer an adaptive value, ensuring that scarce resources are not over-exploited. A similar circumstance is further seen with respect to male sex-pattern displays, where only the most genetically-fit males are chosen by the more selective females.

HYPERVIOLENCE IN A SOCIAL CONTEXT

In a related human social sense, however, even minor insults or mistakes can escalate into full-blown conflicts when pursued unilaterally. Old Testament scripture formally acknowledges this trend towards escalation, dictating that the aggrieved party is entitled only to "an eye for an eye," or "a tooth for a tooth." Although generally viewed as condoning violence, this biblical passage essentially condemns any undue escalation of violence. Indeed, this egalitarian sense of justice applies equally to the powerful as well as the weak, an ethical safeguard against outright abuses of power. This somewhat idealistic injunction does not necessarily imply that the ancient world was fully civilized in such matters, for in the heat of battle, ruthless savagery was typically the order of the day. The Old Testament cites various examples of the entire cities put to the sword at the direction the Lord. Such brutal savagery is only truly understood in terms of such rigid religious sanctions, a convenient justification for the brutal tactics broadly encountered in war.

A similar hyperviolent trend is further encountered with respect to individual criminal offenses. For the vast majority of recorded history, criminals were dealt with in the most severe manner imaginable, with drastic punishments meted out for even the most mundane of offenses. Indeed, the policy of cutting-off a hand for stealing, or beheading for adultery, is a pattern still follow-

710	711		720	721
Indolence	Dereliction		Mutiny	Reprisal
712	713		722	723
Languor	Callousness		Grudgingness	Malignancy

PERVERSION
(Personal Authority)

EXPLOITATION
(Personal Follower)

730	731		740	741
Notoriety	Ignobility		Rebellion	Retribution
732	733		742	743
Crassness	Petulance		Voracity	Cravenness

DEPRAVITY
(Group Authority)

PERNICITY
(Group Representative)

750	751		760	761
Licentiousness	Savagery		Treason	Hopelessness
752	753		762	763
Rudeness	Hostility		Greed	Contentiousness

SACRILEGE
(Spiritual Authority)

RECUSANCY
(Spiritual Disciple)

770	771		780	781
Fury	Despotism		Hideousness	Mendacity
772	773		782	783
Brutality	Barbarity		Heinousness	Ruthlessness

REPROBATION
(Humanitarian Authority)

PANDEMONIUM
(Humanitarian Follower)

790	791		700	701
Madness	Bigotry		Horror	Ruin
792	793		702	703
Viciousness	Atrocity		Balefulness	Fiendishness

MINDLESSNESS
(Transcendental Authority)

SORCERY
(Transcendental Follower)

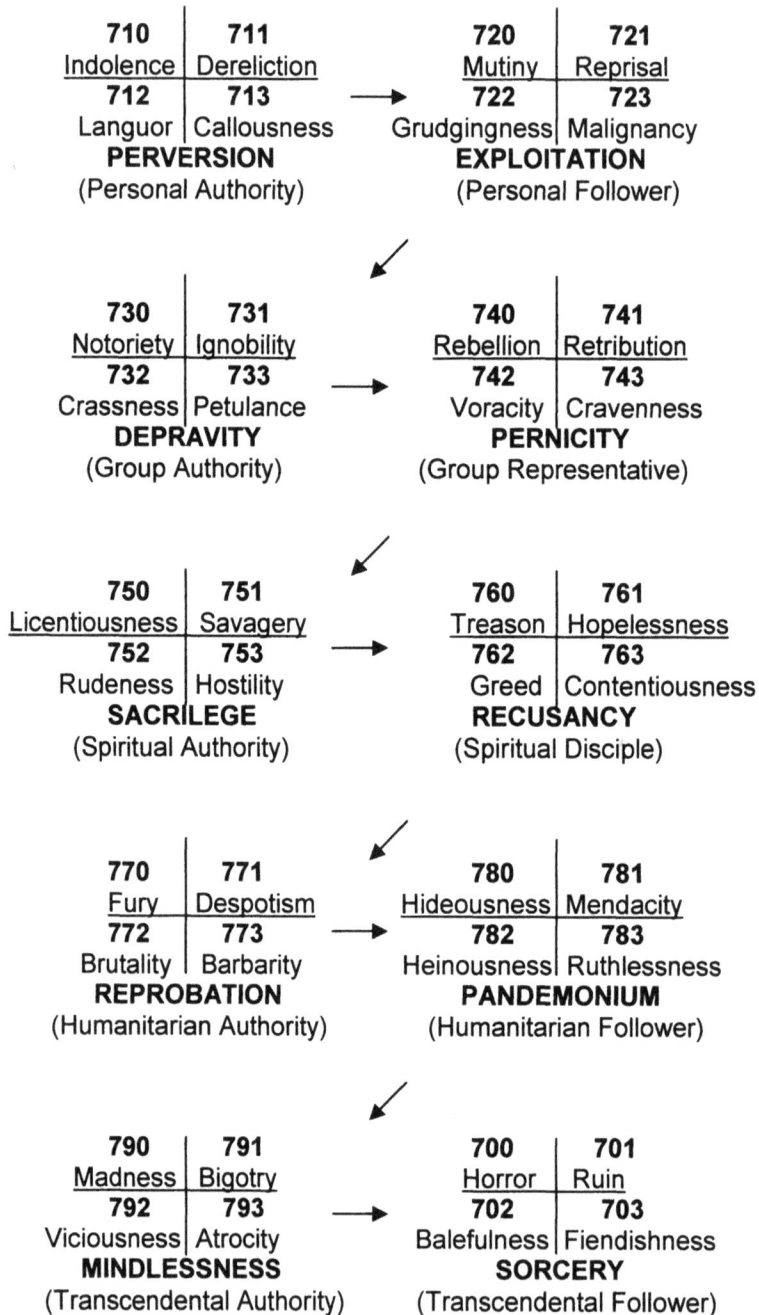

Fig. 19A – The Three-Digit Codes for Hyperviolence

ed in many parts of the world. Herein lies the basic prototype for the realm of hyperviolence; namely, that range of extremes with respect to the vices of defect. The observation that Aristotle failed to distinguish this additional category of hyperviolence within his "Theory of the Mean" further attests to the enduring ideal of the warrior code, where victory was to be achieved at any cost (including mass genocide). In fact, battlefield atrocities were deliberately employed as an effective strategy for deterring resistance from the defeated population.

Most animal societies are generally characterized by an intrinsic abhorrence of excessive violence against members of one's own species. This similarly applies to human culture, where many soldiers during World War I were reluctant to perform their duty to kill, in keeping with such an intra-species taboo. The Armed Forces responded by implementing a behavior modification training program aimed at desensitizing the sensibilities of the new recruits through a system of mock over-training in lethal routines. Through such repetitive role-playing, the soldier's killing reactions became increasingly automatic, effectively modifying the threshold of what would previously have been considered excessively violent.

In our modern age of technological warfare, this strict adherence to an unrestrained warrior mentality is typically more subdued, with any organized tendency towards hyperviolence now strictly regulated under international law. Hyperviolence is still broadly encountered under individual circumstances, as the many gut-wrenching instances of senseless violence reported in the news adequately serve to illustrate. These disturbing acts of violence represent an escalation of aggressive behavior completely out of all proportion to its precipitating circumstances. Society particularly recoils against such brutal outrages, resulting in gun legislation aimed at countering the recent spate of workplace/school shootings.

One of the most disturbing trends of late is witnessed in the modern street gang, where hyperviolence is generally regarded as a means to an end. Conflicts that were traditionally settled through fisticuffs are now decided through automatic weapons fire. Although mob violence has endured as a tragic outcome of the Prohibition Era, the attendant violence was rationalized as "they only kill their own." With the dramatic rise in bystander fatalities, however, such a blase attitude can no longer be tolerated. This intractable dilemma proves one of the most promising applications for the new paradigm of hyperviolence: a system that begins to fathom this tendency to-

wards excessive violence, particularly with respect to the youth of the nation. Unless we relish the prospects of living in a war zone, meaningful measures must be instituted to combat such a disturbing trend, or at least prevented from escalating any further.

BEHAVIORAL PROPENSITIES FOR THE REALM OF HYPERVIOLENCE

The paradigm of excess with respect to the realm of defect proves exceedingly reminiscent of that already established for the virtuous realm in terms of vices of excess. According to the latter scenario, the notion of the type "T" personality was introduced to explain extreme or thrill-seeking behaviors. Here, an ingrained sense of under-arousal was compensated for through risky behaviors such as base-jumping. With respect to the related sphere of hyperviolence, Dr. Frank Farley (1991) further introduces what he terms the type T- *(minus)* personality, where thrills are achieved by eluding legal consequences, whereby gaining domination over one's rivals in the process. Indeed, many case studies offer a common thread among the exploits of the habitual sociopath; namely, the reports of an irresistible adrenaline "rush" typically accompanying a successful criminal caper.

This darker slant to hyperviolence is particularly apparent in the characteristic "tough-guy" mentality, where members within a criminal gang vie to secure the lead position. Although great wealth and prestige typically accompany such positions of power, success generally boils down to the extreme quest for daring and thrills, a trait scarcely appealing to more half-hearted contenders to the role. In combination with a cool and calculated sense of nerve, such ruthless manipulators seek to maintain domination for as long as their luck holds out: as witnessed in the ruthless political regimes of Hitler, Stalin, etc. Such extremely brutal tactics scarcely endure in the long run, for usurpers always wait in the wings. Indeed, this inherent vulnerability of the dictator represents the strongest justification yet for channeling one's energies away from the type T-personality, for more satisfaction is generally achieved in the long run by focusing upon a more positive course of action.

A PRELIMINARY TERMINOLOGY FOR THE REALM OF HYPERVIOLENCE

In summary, the more routine classifications of the vices of defect exhibit the distinct propensity

714	715
Sluggishness	Laxity
716	717
Lethargy	Nonchalance

FETISHISM

(Personal Authority)

724	725
Untrustworthiness	Requital
726	727
Umbrage	Peevishness

VICTIMIZATION

(Personal Follower)

734	735
Disgracefulness	Odium
736	737
Absurdity	Willfulness

DEBASEMENT

(Group Authority)

744	745
Rebellion	Revenge
746	747
Ravenousness	Dastardliness

VILENESS

(Group Representative)

754	755
Debauchery	Servitude
756	757
Lewdness	Rancor

BLASPHEMY

(Spiritual Authority)

764	765
Disloyalty	Grievousness
766	767
Rapaciousness	Vexation

HEATHENISM

(Spiritual Disciple)

774	775
Outrage	Imperiousness
776	777
Discord	Ferocity

RECREANCY

(Humanitarian Authority)

784	785
Nastiness	Deceitfulness
786	787
Badness	Deviousness

TUMULTUOUSNESS

(Humanitarian Follower)

794	795
Enragement	Discrimination
796	797
Meanness	Truculence

UNRULINESS

(Transcendental Authority)

704	705
Grotesqueness	Damnation
706	707
Nefarity	Insidiousness

DEMONISM

(Transcendental Follower)

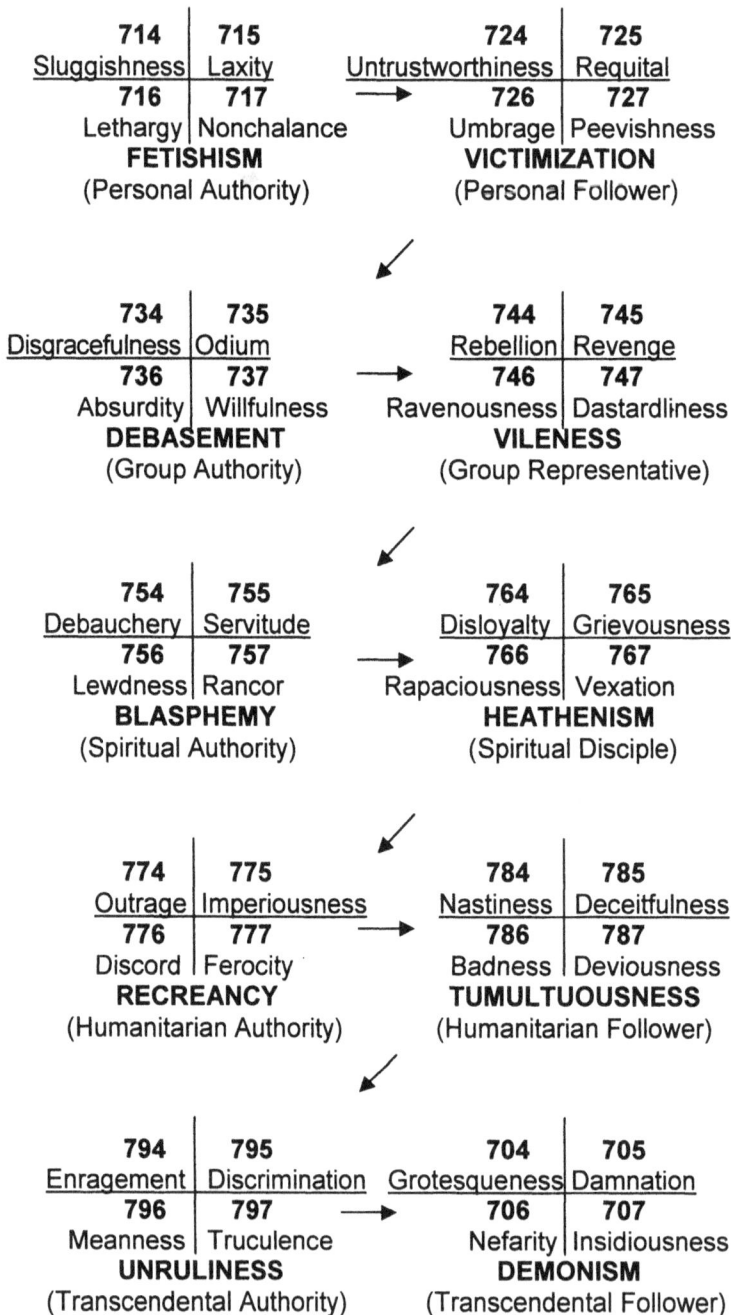

Fig. 19B - The Three-Digit Codes for Accessory Hyperviolence

The Realm of Hyperviolence: Graphic Depiction of 16th Century Punishments
Woodcut Engraving by Tengler, Illustration from *Laienspiegel*, Published in Mainz (1508)

for escalating into a hyperviolent state of affairs in susceptible individuals. Such hyperviolent outbursts generally remain isolated incidents, the perpetrator usually fleeing afterwards to avoid prosecution. This similarly appears the case for victims or bystanders, resulting in minimum potential for any ongoing style of interaction. Accordingly, there appears little in the way of any comprehensive terminology for describing such a hyperviolent perspective. Each incident is therefore handled on a case-by-case basis, as typically encountered in criminal profiling.

The critical applications associated with hyperviolence, however, necessitate the implementation of a basic terminology for labeling the predicted complement of terms. At first glance, there initially appeared to be a dearth of a good range of vocabulary for many of the predicted slots within this extreme realm of hyperviolence. Indeed, the various shades of meaning required to distinguish this excessively violent domain scarcely seemed adequate enough to convincingly specify a corresponding distinction in terms, particularly where a more ambiguous determination of excess with respect to the vices of defect is concerned. For this reason, a completely independent version of the domain of hyperviolence was absent from the debut release of the three-digit coding system. Rather, a more modest "stopgap" system of terminology was introduced, entailing the use of a formal prefix "*hyper-*" format (as in hyperviolence) for modifying the main terms for the vices of defect. In the four year interim since the initial introduction it has been determined that an adequate number of suitable synonyms, indeed, does exist with respect to the realm of hyperviolence, yielding a suitably worka-

INDOLENCE	MUTINY
Previously, you (as punisher) have excessively acted punitively towards me: overriding my (as adversary) extremely adversarial treatment of you. But now, I (as personal authority) will *indolently* admit acting in an extremely adversarial fashion towards you: overruling your (as punisher) excessively punitive treatment of me.	Previously, I (as personal authority) have indolently acted in an extremely adversarial fashion towards you: overriding your (as punisher) excessively punitive treatment of me. But now, you (as my personal follower) will *mutinously* act excessively punitively towards me: overruling my (as PA) indolent treatment of you.
NOTORIETY	**REBELLIOUSNESS**
Previously, you (as my personal follower) have mutinously acted excessively punitively towards me: overriding my (as PA) indolent treatment of you. But now, I (as group authority) will indolently act in a *notorious* fashion towards you: overruling your (as PF) mutinous treatment of me.	Previously, I (as your group authority) have indolently acted in a notorious fashion towards you: overriding your (as PF) mutinous treatment of me. But now, you (as group representative) will mutinously-*rebel* against me: overruling my (as GA) indolent sense of notoriety.
LICENTIOUSNESS	**TREASON**
Previously, you (as group representative) have mutinously-rebelled against me: overriding my (as GA) indolent sense of notoriety. But now, I (as spiritual authority) will notoriously act in a *licentious* fashion towards you: overruling your (as GR) mutinous-rebellion against me.	Previously, I (as your spiritual authority) have notoriously acted in a licentious fashion towards you: overriding your (as GR) mutinous-rebellion against me. But now, you (as my spiritual disciple) will *treasonously*-rebel against me: overruling my (as SA) licentious treatment of you.
FURY	**HIDEOUSNESS**
Previously, you (as my spiritual disciple) have treasonously-rebelled against me: overriding my (as SA) licentious treatment of you. But now, I (as humanitarian authority) will licentiously act in a *furious* fashion towards you: overruling your (as SD) treasonous-rebellion against me.	Previously, I (as humanitarian authority) have licentiously acted furiously towards you: overriding your (as SD) treasonous-rebellion against me. But now, you (as representative member of humanity) will treasonously act in a *hideous* fashion towards me: overruling my (as HA) furious treatment of you.
MADNESS	**HORROR**
Previously, you (as representative member of humanity) have treasonously acted in a hideous fashion towards me: overriding my (as HA) furious treatment of you. But now, I (as transcendental authority) will furiously act in a *mad* fashion towards you: overruling your (as RH) hideous treatment of me.	Previously, I (as transcendental authority) have furiously acted in a mad fashion towards you: overriding your (as RH) hideous treatment of me. But now, you (as my transcendental follower) will hideously act *horribly* towards me: overruling my (as TA) mad treatment of you.

Table H-1 – The Definitions Based Upon Indolence/Mutiny

DERELICTION	REPRISAL
Previously, you (as punisher) have excessively acted punitively towards me: overriding my (as adversary) extremely adversarial treatment of you. But now, I (as personal authority) will extremely act with *dereliction* towards you: overruling your (as punisher) excessively punitive treatment of me.	Previously, I (as personal authority) have extremely acted in a derelict fashion towards you: overriding your (as punisher) excessively punitive treatment of me. But now, you (as personal follower) will excessively seek *reprisal* against me: overruling my (as PA) derelict treatment of you.
IGNOBILITY	RETRIBUTION
Previously, you (as my personal follower) have excessively sought reprisal against me: overriding my (as PA) derelict treatment of you. But now, I (as group authority) will derelictly act in an *ignoble* fashion towards you: overruling your (as PF) quest for reprisal against me.	Previously, I (as group authority) have derelictly acted in an ignoble fashion towards you: overriding your (as PF) reprisal against me. But now, you (as group representative) will reprisingly seek *retribution* against me: overruling my (as GA) ignoble treatment of you.
SAVAGERY	HOPELESSNESS
Previously, you (as group representative) have reprisingly sought retribution against me: overriding my (as GA) ignoble treatment of you. But now, I (as spiritual authority) will ignobly act in a *savage* fashion towards you: overruling your quest for retribution.	Previously, I (as spiritual authority) have ignobly acted in a savage fashion towards you: overriding your quest for retribution. But now, you (as my spiritual disciple) will *hopelessly* seek retribution against me: overruling my (as SA) savage treatment of you.
DESPOTISM	MENDACITY
Previously, you (as my spiritual disciple) have hopelessly sought retribution against me: overriding my (as SA) savage treatment of you. But now, I (as humanitarian authority) will *despotically* act in a savage fashion towards you: overruling your (as SD) hopeless quest for retribution.	Previously, I (as humanitarian authority) have despotically acted savagely towards you: overriding your (as SD) hopeless quest for retribution. But now, you (as representative member of humanity) will hopelessly act in a *mendacious* fashion towards me: overruling my (as HA) despotic treatment of you.
BIGOTRY	RUIN
Previously, you (as represent. member of humanity) have hopelessly acted mendaciously towards me: overriding my (as HA) despotic treatment of you. But now, I (as transcendental auth.) will despotically act in a *bigoted* fashion towards you: overruling your (as RH) mendacious treatment of me.	Previously, I (as transcendental authority) have despotically acted with bigotry towards you: overriding your (as RH) mendacious treatment of me. But now, you (as transcendental follower) will mendaciously act in a *ruinous* fashion towards me: overruling my (as TA) bigoted treatment of you.

Table H-2 – The Definitions Based on Dereliction/Reprisal

LANGUOR	GRUDGINGNESS
Previously, I (as punisher) have excessively acted punitively towards you: overriding your (as adversary) extremely adversarial treatment of me. But now, you (as personal authority) will *languorously* act adversarially towards me: overruling my (as punisher) extremely punitive treatment of you.	Previously, you (as personal authority) have languorously acted adversarially towards me: overriding my (as punisher) extremely punitive treatment of you. But now, I (as your personal follower) will *grudgingly* act extremely punitively towards you: overruling your (as PA) languorous treatment of me.
CRASSNESS	**VORACITY**
Previously, I (as your personal follower) have grudgingly acted extremely punitively towards you: overriding your (as PA) languorous treatment of me. But now, you (as group authority) will *crassly* act in a languorous fashion towards me: overruling my (as PF) grudging treatment of you.	Previously, you (as group authority) have crassly acted in a languorous fashion towards me: overriding my (as PF) grudging treatment of you. But now, I (as group representative) will *voraciously* act in a grudging fashion towards you: overruling your (as GA) crass treatment of me.
RUDENESS	**GREED**
Previously, I (as group representative) have voraciously acted in a grudging fashion towards you: overriding your (as GA) crass treatment of me. But now, you (as spiritual authority) will crassly act in a *rude* fashion towards me: overruling my (as GR) voracious treatment of you.	Previously, you (as my spiritual authority) have crassly acted in a rude fashion towards me: overriding my (as GR) voracious treatment of you. But now, I (as spiritual disciple) will voraciously act in an *greedy* fashion towards you: overruling your (as SA) crassly-rude treatment of me.
BRUTALITY	**HEINOUSNESS**
Previously, I (as your spiritual disciple) have voraciously acted in an greedy fashion towards you: overriding your (as SA) crassly-rude treatment of me. But now, you (as humanitarian authority) will *brutally* act rudely towards me overruling my (as SD) greedy treatment of you.	Previously, you (as humanitarian authority) have brutally acted rudely towards me overriding my (as SD) greedy treatment of you. But now, I (as representative member of humanity) will *heinously* act in a greedy fashion towards you: overruling your (as HA) brutally-rude treatment of me.
VISCIOUSNESS	**BALEFULNESS**
Previously, I (as representative member of humanity) have heinously acted in a greedy fashion towards you: overriding your (as HA) brutally-rude treatment of me. But now, you (as transcendental authority) will brutally act in a *vicious* fashion towards me: overruling my (as RH) heinous sense of greed.	Previously, you (as transcendental authority) have brutally acted in a vicious fashion towards me: overriding my (as RH) heinous sense of greed. But now, I (as your transcendental follower) will *balefully* act in a heinous fashion towards you: overruling your (as TA) vicious treatment of me.

Table H-3 – The Definitions Based Upon Languor/Grudgingness

CALLOUSNESS	MALIGNANCY
Previously, I (as punisher) have excessively acted punitively towards you: overriding your (as adversary) adversarial treatment of me. But now, you (as personal authority) will *callously* act extremely adversarially towards me: overruling my (as punisher) extremely punitive treatment of you.	Previously, you (as personal authority) have callously acted adversarially towards me: overriding my (as punisher) extremely punitive treatment of you. But now, I (as your personal follower) will *malignantly* act extremely punitively towards you: overruling your (as PA) callous treatment of me.
PETULANCY	**CRAVENNESS**
Previously, I (as your personal follower) have malignantly acted extremely punitively towards you: overriding your (as PA) callous treatment of me. But now, you (as group authority) will callously act *petulantly* towards me: overruling my (as PF) malignant treatment of you.	Previously, you (as group authority) have callously acted petulantly towards me: overriding my (as PF) malignant treatment of you. But now, I (as group representative) will *cravenly* act in a malignant fashion towards you: overruling your (as GA) petulant treatment of me.
HOSTILITY	**CONTENTIOUSNESS**
Previously, I (as group representative) have cravenly acted in a malignant fashion towards you: overriding your (as GA) petulant treatment of me. But now, you (as spiritual authority) will petulantly act in a *hostile* fashion towards me: overruling my (as GR) craven treatment of you.	Previously, you (as spiritual authority) have petulantly acted in a hostile fashion towards me: overriding my (as GR) craven treatment of you. But now, I (as your spiritual disciple) will cravenly act in a *contentious* fashion towards you: overruling your (as SA) hostile treatment of me.
BARBARISM	**RUTHLESSNESS**
Previously, I (as your spiritual disciple) have cravenly acted in a contentious fashion towards you: overriding your (as SA) hostile treatment of me. But now, you (as humanitarian authority) will hostilely act *barbarically* towards me: overruling my (as SD) contentious treatment of you.	Previously, you (as humanitarian authority) have hostilely acted barbarically towards me: overriding my (as SD) contentious treatment of you. But now, I (as representative member of humanity) will contentiously act in a *ruthless* fashion towards you: overruling your (as HA) barbaric treatment of me.
ATROCITY	**FIENDISHNESS**
Previously, I (as representative member of humanity) have contentiously acted in a ruthless fashion towards you: overriding your (as HA) barbaric treatment of me. But now, you (as transcendental authority) will barbarically act in an *atrocious* fashion towards me: overruling my (as RH) ruthless treatment of you.	Previously, you (as transcendental authority) have barbarically acted in an atrocious fashion towards me: overruling my (as RH) ruthless treatment of you. But now, I (as your transcendental follower) will ruthlessly act *fiendishly* towards you: overruling your (as TA) atrocious treatment of me.

Table H-4 – The Definitions Based Upon Callousness/Malignancy

a major overhaul for the darker domain of defect, where certain of the accessory vices of defect were reevaluated and determined to actually belong more properly to the realm of hyperviolence. New terms were subsequently chosen to fill in these gaps in the accessory terms. The main terms for the vices of defect, however, were completely unaffected by this moderate reorganization. It should be emphasized that this major innovation with respect to hyperviolence is necessarily a work in progress, being that the determination of the degree of excess is primarily a somewhat subjective determination compounded by related cultural overtones and socially prescribed traditions.

Being as this is a first tentative release of this version, an individual detailed description of each of these individual terms will not be undertaken at this juncture, an aspect best deferred to a future edition. The overall literary traditions targeting such an extreme hyperviolent realm are somewhat limited in scope due to their relatively rare occurrence in modern society, making such a protracted exercise of dubious benefit. The overall cohesiveness of this new hierarchy for the realm of hyperviolence, however, proves particularly convincing in a holistic sense, leaving room only for a degree of minor adjustments in upcoming future editions.

A complete listing of the provisional terminology for hyperviolence is schematically depicted in **Fig. 19A** (in concert with the respective three-digit codes), and also in the compact diagram immediately below.

Indolence • Mutiny	**Dereliction • Reprisal**
Notoriety • Rebellious.	**Ignobility • Retribution**
Licentiousness • Treason	**Savagery • Hopeless.**
Fury • Hideousness	**Despotism • Mendacity**
Madness • Horror	**Bigotry • Ruin**
Languor • Grudgingness	**Callous. • Malignancy**
Crassness • Voracity	**Petulance • Cravenness**
Rudeness • Greed	**Hostility • Contentious.**
Brutality • Heinousness	**Barbarism • Ruthless.**
Viciousness • Balefulness	**Atrocity • Fiendish.**

This arrangement is similar in form and function to that previously established for the vices of defect/excess. The respective three-digit codes exhibit clear parallels to those previously for the vices of defect. Here, the first place digit of "5" (denoting the realm of defect) is modified to a "7" (specifying the realm of hyperviolence). The second digit further narrows the focus, individually specifying each of the ten authority levels within the power hierarchy: e.g., 1 = personal authority, 2 = personal follower, 3 = group authority, etc. The third and final digit ultimately distinguishes each of the individual terms. For instance, 730 = notoriety (*hyper*-infamy), whereas 731 = ignobility (*hyper*-dishonor). Furthermore, 732 = crassness *hyper*-foolishness, while 733 = petulance *hyper*-capriciousness, etc. Consistent with its somewhat infrequent occurrence in society as a whole, any formal terminology for the realm of hyperviolence must necessarily incorporate the wealth of case histories garnered from the annals of the criminal profiling, perhaps even utilizing its specialized legal terminology. In concert with the three-digit coding system (encompassing code numbers *700* to *799*), this system of terminology should prove adequate for most general applications relating to the prerequisites of the legal justice system.

THE SCHEMATIC DEFINITIONS FOR THE REALM OF HYPERVIOLENCE

In agreement with the pattern previously established for the vices of defect/excess, the provisional terminology for the realm of hyperviolence (by definition) should further prove amenable to incorporation into its own unique complement of schematic definitions, permitting crucial insights into the mentality of the hyperviolent individual. The complete four-page listing of definitions for hyperviolence is schematically depicted in **Tables H-1** through **H-4**. This full forty-fold complement of schematic definitions represents extreme variations on those previously established for the vices of defect (in **Tables D-1** to **D-4** from Chapter *10*). The more basic definitions for the vices of defect can be seen to be modified to reflect the extremes of hyperviolence through the addition of the specialized terms in **Fig. 19A**.

This darker complement of definitions (for hyperviolence) proves equally as informative as that for the realm of defect, offering crucial insights into those dysfunctional aspects to be avoided. Owing to the general safeguards prevailing in any monitored context, this formal model of hyperviolence must necessarily remain a relatively rare occurrence. This technical familiarity with realm of hyperviolence actually amounts to a fundamental safeguard within the ethical system, with negative transactions diagnosed in terms of the potential for transformation into a more positive sphere of influence, while the reverse is simultaneously prevented from occurring, particularly in relation to such a drastic range of emotional extremes.

HYPERVIOLENCE (700 – 799)

710 – Indolence

711 – Dereliction

712 – Languor

713 – Callousness

714 – Sluggishness

715 – Laxity

716 – Lethargy

717 – Nonchalance

718 – Perversion

719 – Fetishism

720 – Mutiny

721 – Reprisal

722 – Grudgingness

723 – Malignancy

724 – Untrustworthy

725 – Requital

726 – Umbrage

727 – Peevishness

728 – Exploitation

729 – Victimization

730 – Notoriety

731 – Ignobility

732 – Crassness

733 – Petulance

734 – Disgracefulness

735 – Odium

736 – Absurdity

737 – Willfulness

738 – Depravity

739 – Debasement

740 – Rebelliousness

741 – Retribution

742 – Voracity

743 – Cravenness

744 – Rebelliousness

745 – Revenge

746 – Ravenousness

747 – Dastardliness

748 – Pernicity

749 – Vileness

750 – Licentiousness

751 – Savagery

752 – Rudeness

753 – Hostility

754 – Debauchery

755 – Servitude

756 – Lewdness

757 – Rancor

758 – Sacrilege

759 – Blasphemy

760 – Treason

761 – Hopelessness

762 – Greed

763 – Contentiousness

764 – Disloyalty

765 – Grievousness

766 – Rapaciousness

767 – Vexation

768 – Recusancy

769 – Heathenism

770 – Fury

771 – Despotism

772 – Brutality

773 – Barbarism

774 – Outrage

775 – Imperiousness

776 – Discord

777 – Ferocity

778 – Reprobation

779 – Recreancy

780 – Hideousness

781 – Mendacity

782 – Heinousness

783 – Ruthlessness

784 – Nastiness

785 – Deceitfulness

786 – Badness

787 – Deviousness

788 – Pandemonium

789 – Tumultuous.

790 – Madness

791 – Bigotry

792 – Viciousness

793 – Atrocity

794 – Enragement

795 – Discrimination

796 – Meanness

797 – Truculence

798 – Mindlessness

799 – Unruliness

700 – Horror

701 – Ruin

702 – Balefulness

703 – Fiendishness

704 – Grotesqueness

705 – Damnation

706 – Nefarity

707 – Insidiousness

708 – Demonism

709 – Demoniac

SLUGGISHNESS	UNTRUSTWORTHINESS
Previously, I (as punisher) have excessively acted punitively towards you: overriding your (as adversary) extremely adversarial treatment of me. But now, you (as personal authority) will *sluggishly* act extremely adversarially towards me: overruling my (as punisher) excessively punitive treatment of you.	Previously, you (as personal authority) have sluggishly acted extremely adversarially towards me: overriding my (as punisher) excessively punitive treatment of you. But now, I (as your personal follower) will *untrustworthily* act in a punitive fashion towards you: overruling your (as PA) sluggish treatment of me.
DISGRACEFULNESS	REBELLIOUSNESS
Previously, I (as your personal follower) have untrustworthily acted in a punitive fashion towards you: overriding your (as PA) sluggish treatment of me. But now, you (as group authority) will sluggishly act in a *disgraceful* fashion towards me: overruling my (as PF) untrustworthy treatment of you.	Previously, you (as group authority) have sluggishly acted in a disgraceful fashion towards me: overriding my (as PF) untrustworthy treatment of you. But now, I (as group representative) will *rebelliously* act untrustworthily towards you: overruling your (as GA) disgraceful treatment of me.
DEBAUCHERY	DISLOYALTY
Previously, I (as group representative) have rebelliously acted in an untrustworthy fashion towards you: overriding your (as GA) disgraceful treatment of me. But now, you (as spiritual authority) will disgracefully act in a *debauched* fashion towards me: overruling my (as GR) rebellious treatment of you.	Previously, you (as spiritual authority) have disgracefully acted in a debauched fashion towards me: overriding my (as GR) rebellious treatment of you. But now, I (as your spiritual disciple) will rebelliously act in a *disloyal* fashion towards you: overruling your (as SA) debauched treatment of me.
OUTRAGE	NASTINESS
Previously, I (as your spiritual disciple) have rebelliously acted disloyally towards you: overriding your (as SA) odious sense of debauchery. But now, you (as humanitarian authority) will *outrageously* act in a debauched fashion towards me: overruling my (as SD) disloyal treatment of you.	Previously, you (as humanitarian authority) have outrageously acted with debauchery towards me: overriding my (as SD) disloyal treatment of you. But now, I (as representative member of humanity) will disloyally act in a *nasty* fashion towards you: overruling your (as HA) outrageous treatment of me.
ENRAGEMENT	GROTESQUENESS
Previously, I (as representative member of humanity) have disloyally acted in a nasty fashion towards you: overriding your (as HA) outrageous treatment of me. But now, you (as transcendental authority) will outrageously act in an *enraged* fashion towards me: overruling my (as RH) nasty treatment of you.	Previously, you (as transcendental authority) have outrageously acted in an enraged fashion towards me: overriding my (as RH) nasty treatment of you. But now, I (as your transcendental follower) will nastily act in a *grotesque* fashion towards you: overruling your (as TA) enraged treatment of me.

Table J-1 – The Definitions Based Upon Sluggishness/Untrustworthiness

LAXITY	REQUITAL
Previously, I (as punisher) have excessively acted punitively towards you: overriding your (as adversary) extremely adversarial treatment of me. But now, you (as personal authority) will *laxly* act in an extremely adversarial fashion towards me: overruling my (as punisher) excessively punitive treatment of you.	Previously, you (as personal authority) have laxly acted in an adversarial fashion towards me: overriding my (as punisher) excessively punitive treatment of you. But now, I (as your personal follower) will *requitefully* act punitively towards you: overruling your (as PA) lax treatment of me.
ODIUM	**REVENGE**
Previously, I (as your personal follower) have requitefully acted punitively towards you: overriding your (as PA) lax treatment of me. But now, you (as group authority) will *odiously* act in a lax fashion towards me: overruling my (as PF) requiteful treatment of you.	Previously, you (as group authority) have odiously acted in a lax fashion towards me: overriding my (as PF) requiteful treatment of you. But now, I (as group representative) will requitefully seek *vengeance* against you: overruling your (as GA) odious treatment of me.
SERVITUDE	**GRIEVOUSNESS**
Previously, I (as group representative) have requitefully sought vengeance against you: overriding your (as GA) odious treatment of me. But now, you (as spiritual authority) will odiusly maintain me in *servitude*: overruling my (as GR) vengeful treatment of you.	Previously, you (as spiritual authority) have odiously maintained me in servitude: overriding my (as GR) vengeful treatment of you. But now, I (as your spiritual disciple) will vengefully act in a *grievous* fashion towards you: overruling your (as SA) odious maintenance of me in servitude.
IMPERIOUSNESS	**DECEITFULNESS**
Previously, I (as your spiritual disciple) have vengefully acted in a grievous fashion towards you: overriding your (as SA) odious maintenance of me in servitude. But now, you (as humanitarian authority) will *imperiously* maintain me in servitude: overruling my (as SD) grievous treatment of you.	Previously, you (as humanitarian authority) have imperiously maintained me in servitude: overriding my (as SD) grievous treatment of you. But now, I (as representative member of humanity) will grievously act in a *deceitful* fashion towards you: overruling your (as HA) imperious treatment of me.
DISCRIMINATION	**DAMNATION**
Previously, I (as representative member of humanity) have grievously acted in a deceitful fashion towards you: overriding your (as HA) imperious treatment of me. But now, you (as transcendental authority) will imperiously act in a *discriminatory* fashion: overruling my (as RH) grievous sense of deceitfulness.	Previously, you (as transcendental authority) have imperiously acted in a discriminatory fashion: overriding my (as RH) deceitful treatment of you. But now, I (as your transcendental follower) will deceitfully act in a *damnable* fashion towards you: overruling your (as TA) discriminatory treatment of me.

Table J-2 - The Definitions Based on Laxity/Requital

LETHARGY	UMBRAGE
Previously, I (as punisher) have excessively acted punitively towards you: overriding your (as adversary) extremely adversarial treatment of me. But now, you (as personal authority) will *lethargically* act in an extremely adversarial fashion towards me: overruling my (as punisher) excessively punitive treatment of you.	Previously, I (as personal authority) have lethargically acted in an extremely adversarial fashion towards me: overriding my (as punisher) excessively punitive treatment of you. But now, you (as personal follower) will *umbragefully* act punitively towards me: overruling my (as PA) lethargic treatment of you.
ABSURDITY	**RAVENOUSNESS**
Previously, you (as my personal follower) have umbragefully acted punitively towards me: overriding my (as PA) lethargic treatment of you. But now, I (as group authority) will lethargically act in an *absurd* fashion towards you: overruling your (as PF) umbrage-filled treatment of me.	Previously, I (as group authority) have lethargically acted in an absurd fashion towards you: overriding your (as PF) umbrage-filled treatment of me. But now, you (as group representative) will umbragefully act *ravenously* towards me: overruling my (as GA) absurd treatment of you.
LEWDNESS	**RAPACIOUSNESS**
Previously, you (as group representative) have umbragefully acted ravenously towards me: overriding my (as GA) absurd treatment of you. But now, I (as spiritual authority) will absurdly act in a *lewd* fashion towards you: overruling your (as GR) ravenous treatment of me.	Previously, I (as spiritual authority) have absurdly acted in a lewd fashion towards you: overriding your (as GR) ravenous treatment of me. But now, you (as spiritual disciple) will ravenously act *rapaciously* towards me: overruling my (as SA) lewd treatment of you.
DISCORD	**BADNESS**
Previously, you (as my spiritual disciple) have ravenously acted rapaciously towards me: overriding my (as SA) lewd treatment of you. But now, I (as humanitarian authority) will lewdly act in a *discordant* fashion towards you: overruling your (as SD) rapacious treatment of me.	Previously, I (as humanitarian authority) have lewdly acted discordantly towards you: overriding your (as SD) rapacious treatment of me. But now, you (as representative member of humanity) will rapaciously act in a *bad* fashion towards me: overruling my (as HA) discordant treatment of you.
MEANNESS	**NEFARITY**
Previously, you (as representative member of humanity) have rapaciously acted in a bad fashion towards me: overriding my (as HA) discordant treatment of you. But now, I (as transcendental authority) will discordantly act in a *mean* fashion towards you: overruling your (as RH) bad treatment of me.	Previously, I (as transcendental authority) have discordantly acted in a mean fashion towards you: overriding your (as RH) bad treatment of me. But now, you (as transcendental follower) will badly act in a *nefarious* fashion towards me: overruling my (as TA) mean treatment of you.

Table J-3 - The Definitions Based on Lethergy/Umbrage

NONCHALANCE	PEEVISHNESS
Previously, I (as punisher) have excessively acted punitively towards you: overriding your (as adversary) extremely adversarial treatment of me. But now, you (as personal authority) will *nonchalantly* act in an adversarial fashion towards me: overruling my (as punisher) excessively punitive treatment of you.	Previously, I (as personal authority) have nonchalantly acted in an adversarial fashion towards me: overriding my (as punisher) excessively punitive treatment of you. But now, you (as my personal follower) will *peevishly* act extremely punitively towards me: overruling my (as PA) nonchalant treatment of you.
WILLFULNESS	**DASTARDLINESS**
Previously, you (as my personal follower) have peevishly acted extremely punitively towards me: overriding my (as PA) nonchalant treatment of you. But now, I (as group authority) will *willfully* act nonchalantly towards you: overruling your (as PF) peevish treatment of me.	Previously, I (as group authority) have willfully acted nonchalantly towards you: overriding your (as PF) peevish treatment of me. But now, you (as group representative) will peevishly act in a *dastardly* fashion towards me: overruling my (as GA) willful treatment of you.
RANCOR	**VEXATION**
Previously, you (as group representative) have peevishly acted in a dastardly fashion towards me: overriding my (as GA) willful treatment of you. But now, I (as spiritual authority) will willfully act in a *rancorous* fashion towards you: overruling your (as GR) dastardly treatment of me.	Previously, I (as spiritual authority) have willfully acted in a rancorous fashion towards you: overriding your (as GR) dastardly treatment of me. But now, you (as my spiritual disciple) will dastardly act in a *vexing* fashion towards me: overruling my (as SA) rancorous treatment of you.
FEROCITY	**DEVIOUSNESS**
Previously, you (as my spiritual disciple) have dastardly acted in a vexing fashion towards me: overriding my (as SA) rancorous treatment of you. But now, I (as humanitarian authority) will rancorously act in a *ferocious* fashion towards you: overruling your (as SD) vexing treatment of me.	Previously, I (as humanitarian authority) have rancorously acted in a ferocious fashion towards you: overriding your (as SD) vexing treatment of me. But now, you (as representative member of humanity) will vexingly act in a *devious* fashion towards me: overruling my (as HA) ferocious treatment of you.
TRUCULENCE	**INSIDIOUSNESS**
Previously, you (as representative member of humanity) have vexingly acted deviously towards me: overriding my (as HA) ferocious treatment of you. But now, I (as transcendental authority) will ferociously act in a *truculent* fashion towards you: overruling your (as RH) devious treatment of me.	Previously, I (as transcendental authority) have ferociously acted in a truculent fashion towards you: overriding your (as RH) devious treatment of me. But now, you (as my transcendental follower) will deviously act in an *insidious* fashion towards me: overruling my (as TA) truculent treatment of you.

Table J-4 – The Definitions Based on Nonchalance/Peevishness

THE ACCESSORY FORMS OF HYPERVIOLENCE

The completed description of the formal realm of hyperviolence raises the further issue of the related *accessory* terms. Here, the accessory realm of hyperviolence directly reverses the polarity of the "you" and "I" roles initially specified for the main listings of terms. Similar to the case made for the main terms for hyperviolence, the accessory versions represent an all new formulation of terms, the guiding principle resulting from a careful determination of near synonyms for the respective main terms for hyperviolence. A complete listing of the provisional terminology for accessory hyperviolence is depicted in **Fig. 19B** (in concert with the respective three-digit codes), and also in the compact diagram below.

Sluggish. • Untrustworthiness   Laxity• Requital
Disgrace. • Rebelliousness   Odium • Revenge
Debauchery • Disloyalty   Servitude • Grievous.
Outrage • Nastiness   Imperious.• Deceitfulness
Enragement • Grotesque.   Discrimin. • Damnat.

Lethargy • Umbrage   Nonchalance • Peevish.
Absurdity • Ravenous.   Willfulness • Dastardly
Lewdness • Rapacity   Rancor • Vexation
Discord • Badness   Ferocity • Deviousness
Meanness • Nefarity   Truculence • Insidious.

Indeed, a careful comparison of **Figs. 19A** and **19B** demonstrates the reciprocal correspondence linking the main/accessory realms of hyperviolence, convincingly indicating how the polarities of the "you" and "I" roles are reversed permitting an overall empathic simulation.

In order to convincingly specify these accessory terms within the three-digit coding system, the third and final digit is directly called into play. Here, digits 4 through 7 within the three-digit slot formally specify the accessory variations for hyperviolence (in contrast to digits 0-to-3 for the main terms). For instance, 734 = odium (*hyper*-disrepute), whereas 735 = disgracefulness (*hyper*-reprehension). Furthermore, 736 = absurdity (*hyper*-preposterousness), while 737 = willfulness *hyper*-fickleness). Indeed, the codes for each of the main terms are easily modified into their accessory counterparts by simply adding four digits to the third-place digit initially depicted in relation to the main terms. It remains only a further minor step to incorporate these respective accessory terms directly into the schematic definition format, resulting in a parallel complement of schematic definitions for the accessory realm of hyperviolence. The complete four-page listing of definitions for accessory hyperviolence is schematically depicted in **Tables J-1** through **J-4**. This full forty-fold complement of schematic definitions represent extreme variations on those previously established for the main sequence of terms, except that the polarities of the "you" and "I" roles are now reversed. This dual format for the realm of hyperviolence provides crucial empathic insights into such an enigmatic perspective, permitting an enhanced understanding of such pressing social issues.

Similar to the main versions for hyperviolence, it should be emphasized that these accessory variations with respect to hyperviolence are necessarily a work in progress, hence, individual detailed descriptions of these individual terms will not be undertaken at this juncture, an aspect best deferred to a future edition. The overall cohesiveness of this new hierarchy for the realm of hyperviolence, however, proves particularly convincing in a holistic sense, leaving room only for minor adjustments in future editions.

In conclusion, the addition of the extreme realm of hyperviolence adds a fitting sense of symmetry to Aristotle's enduring Theory of the Mean. Although this basic refinement may appear intuitively obvious, it nevertheless spells out an essential distinction: with further crucial relevance to the derivative domains of criminality and hypercriminality. Hyperviolence has dramatic increased in recent years, an aspect the current technical breakthrough aims to remedy through an increased understanding of the darker dynamics at issue. In a simpler age, the depiction of gratuitous hyperviolence (or ultraviolence, as it was commonly coined) garnered quite shocking controversy when portrayed cinematically in Stanley Kubrick's *A Clockwork Orange:* a rather quaint depiction in comparison to the current trend towards gratuitous slasher films and violent video games. Certainly art imitates life, particularly in the dramatic ascendancy of violent street gangs, where senseless homicide is often a prerequisite for acceptance into such criminal enterprise. Undoubtedly the most effective means for addressing such rampant criminality entails reaching out to the youth culture prior to their tragic theft of innocence. Character Education programs in public education have made great strides in this respect. Through the aid of the current enhancements contained within the unified ethical hierarchy, it is hoped that increased understanding of the long-term advantages of a virtuous lifestyle will outweigh the sensationalistic dictates of the darker side, perhaps saving an entire upcoming generation from a life filled with pain and regret.

20

THE GENERAL UNIFYING THEMES FOR THE REALM OF EXCESS

The completed description of the vices of excess and hyperviolence, in turn, leaves unresolved the remaining issue of the general unifying themes with respect to the domain of excess. Recall, from **Parts I** and **II**, how the major virtues and vices of defect were respectively assigned what are termed the general unifying themes. Chapter 9 introduced the themes with respect to the virtuous realm, defined as a hierarchial sequence of individualism-personalism-romanticism-ecumenism-humanism for the authority roles. The remaining series of follower themes, in turn, are designated as pragmatism-utilitarianism-ecclesiasticism-eclecticism-mysticism. Each of these respective themes further represents an overall summation of the four subordinate terms comprising a given level within the power hierarchy. For instance, the general theme of *utilitarianism* was specified as the unifying concept for the cardinal virtues (prudence-justice-temperance-fortitude).

This general complement of unifying themes, in turn, can be incorporated into the formal schematic definition format. This parallel hierarchy of schematic definitions for the virtuous themes directly mirrors that previously established for the individual terms with the exception that the relevant themes are substituted in place of the virtues. A complete listing of virtuous themes is contained in **Fig. 9A** of Chapter 9, although the more general nature of the corresponding themes appears much less distinct than those previously cited for the individual virtues, values, and ideals.

A similar pattern is further proposed in **Fig. 15B** (of Chapter 15) with respect to the related vices of defect, resulting in a distinctive complement of general unifying themes for the realm of defect. These themes for defect are arranged as the direct polar opposites (or antonyms) of those

previously established for the virtuous realm. For instance, the respective authority sequence of knavery-villainy-profanity-apostasy-nihilism contrasts point-for-point with the related virtuous sequence of individualism-personalism-romanticism-ecumenism-humanism. Furthermore, the respective sequence of follower roles for the vices (fraud-corruption-heresy-anarchism-diabolism) makes a similar correspondence to the virtuous sequence of pragmatism-utilitarianism-ecclesiasticism-eclecticism-mysticism. Indeed, this distinctive complement of themes for the realm of defect proves an equal match to those of the virtues.

Upon this solid conceptual foundation, the further issue of the general unifying themes for the realm of excess rightfully enters the picture. A cursory survey of the traditional ethical literature initially yielded little in the way of specifying any sort of one-to-one correspondence with the three-digit coding system. Since the publication of the initial version of the coding system, however, a comprehensive survey of the language tradition has subsequently revealed an adequate complement of themes for both the vices of excess and the realm of hyperviolence as depicted in the left-hand column of **Fig. 20**, a format that also includes the major virtuous themes and themes for the realm of defect for sake of contrast. Furthermore the affiliated *accessory* themes for the realm of excess are also listed in the right-hand column for sake of contrast. The remainder of the current chapter examines each of these basic variations of excess in relation to the general unifying themes.

THE MAIN THEMES FOR THE VICES OF EXCESS

As previously described in Chapter 9 (for the virtuous mode), each of the general unifying themes

+ + THEMES for the VICES of EXCESS
(Excessive Virtue)

318 - Egotism	328 - Officiousness
338 - Elitism	348 - Authoritarianism
358 - Ideology	368 - Clericalism
378 - Fanaticism	388 - Idealism
398 - Triumphalism	308 - Occultism

+ + THEMES for the ACCESS. VICES of EXCESS
(Excessive Accessory Virtue)

319 - Egocentrism	329 - Obtrusiveness
339 – Autocracy	349 - Absolutism
359 - Pontification	369 - Dogmatism
379 - Fundamentalism	389 - Supremacism
399 - Universalism	309 - Enigmatism

+ THEMES for the MAJOR VIRTUES
(Virtuous Mode)

118 - Individualism	128 - Pragmatism
138 - Personalism	148 - Utilitarianism
158 - Romanticism	168 - Ecclesiasticism
178 - Ecumenism	188 - Eclecticism
198 - Humanism	108 - Mysticism

+ THEMES for the ACCESS. MAJOR VIRTUES
(Accessory Virtuous Mode)

119 - Quintessentialism	129 - Expediency
139 - Heroism	149 - Practicality
159 - Charisma	169 - Orthodoxy
179 - Evangelism	189 - Moralism
199 - Cosmopolitanism	109 - Spiritualism

THEMES for the VICES of DEFECT
(Absence of Virtue)

518 - Knavery	528 - Fraud
538 - Villainy	548 - Corruption
558 - Profanity	568 - Heresy
578 - Apostasy	588 - Anarchism
598 - Nihilism	508 - Diabolism

THEMES for the ACCESS. VICES of DEFECT
(Absence of Accessory Virtue)

519 - Mischief	529 - Deception
539 - Licentiousness	549 - Venality
559 - Scandal	569 - Schismatism
579 – Infidelity	589 - Lawlessness
599 - Alienation	509 - Sorcery

THEMES for HYPERVIOLENCE
(Excessive Defect)

718 – Perversion	728 - Exploitation
738 - Depravity	748 - Pernicity
758 - Sacrilege	768 - Recusancy
778 – Reprobation	788 - Pandemonium
798 - Mindlessness	708 – Demonism

THEMES for ACCESS. HYPERVIOLENCE
(Excessive Accessory Defect)

719 - Fetishism	729 - Victimization
739 - Debasement	749 - Vileness
759 - Blasphemy	769 - Heathenism
779 - Recreancy	789 - Tumultuousness
799 - Unruliness	709 - Demoniac

Fig. 20 – Master Schematic Diagram Depicting the 80 Individual General Unifying Themes

within the general sequence is viewed as a "meta-order" summation of its respective level within the power hierarchy, and the themes for excess respectively build upon this virtuous foundation. For instance, the personal authority role that initially targeted the theme of individualism extends to the realm of excess with respect to the extreme theme of *egotism*. Furthermore, the next higher virtuous theme of personalism for the group authority level is taken to extremes as the excessive theme of *elitism*. The subsequent spiritual authority level further targets the more idealized theme of romanticism consistent with its broader focus on universal" principles, whereby countered by the excessive theme of the *ideologue*. The themes for the remaining humanitarian and transcendental levels, in turn, take their cues from the titles of their respective listings of terms; namely, ecumenism and humanism: themes that are expanded in an extreme sense by the excessive themes of *fanaticism* and *triumphalism,* respectively.

In a related fashion, the remaining sequence of *follower* roles was previously seen to be organized in terms of the parallel hierarchy of individual virtuous themes; namely, pragmatism-utilitarianism-ecclesiasticism-eclecticism-mysticism. For instance, the first-mentioned theme of pragmatism refers to that which is expedient to the individual, extended to an extreme degree through the excessive theme of *officiousness*. Furthermore, the next higher group theme of utilitarianism, or concern for the "common good," extends to the extreme theme of *authoritarianism*. This ascending hierarchy of themes ultimately extends to the remaining spiritual, humanitarian, and transcendental domains with respect to the themes of ecclesiasticism, eclecticism, and mysticism: a sequence expanding in an extreme sense to the excessive listing of *clericalism, idealism,* and *occultism*, respectively.

In terms of the master three-digit coding system proposed in Chapter *1*, these general unifying themes for the vices of excess are similarly amenable to coding within the overall *1,040*-part master system. Here, the three-digit codes ending with the numeral "8" specify the main categories of general unifying themes. Recall that the first digit relating to the vices of excess is assigned the numerical value of "3" indicative of excessive virtue. The second digit, in turn, exhibits an enhanced degree of variability in terms of the ten respective levels within the power hierarchy; e.g., 1 = personal authority, 2 = personal follower, 3 = group authority, etc. Finally, the third digit is uniformly assigned the numerical value of "8" in-

dicative of the main complement of themes for the main realm of the vices of excess.

THE MAIN THEMES FOR HYPERVIOLENCE

The completed description of the main variations for the themes for the vices of excess invokes one remaining issue of particular significance to the three-digit coding system; namely, the general unifying themes for the darker extreme realm of hyperviolence. Here, it technically proves feasible to devise an entire parallel hierarchy of themes exclusive to the realm of excessive defect: as formally depicted in the bottom-most portion of **Fig. 20** with respect to hyperviolence. This diagram employs a format that allows for a convenient contrast in terms between the realms of excess and the more mainstream themes for the virtues and vices upon which they build. For sake of review, a cursory comparison of these two separate diagrams reveals a mirror-image contrasting correspondence between the positive and negative realms of themes. The virtuous themes accordingly represent specific moral antonyms of their respective darker counterparts.

The themes for the realm of hyperviolence respectively build upon a corresponding foundation within the themes for the vices of excess. For instance, the personal authority role that initially targeted the theme of knavery extends to the realm of excess with respect to the extreme theme of *perversion*. Furthermore, the next higher virtuous theme of villainy for the group authority level is taken to extremes as the excessive theme of *depravity*. The subsequent spiritual authority level further targets the more idealized theme of profanity, whereby countered by the excessive theme of *sacrilege*. The themes for the remaining humanitarian and transcendental levels, namely, apostasy and nihilism reach their extremes through the excesses of *reprobation* and *mindlessness,* respectively.

In a related fashion, the remaining sequence of *follower* roles was previously seen to be organized in terms of the parallel hierarchy of individual darker themes; namely, fraud-corruption-heresy-anarchism-diabolism. For example, the first-mentioned theme of fraud refers to that which is detrimental to the individual, extended to an extreme degree through the excessive theme of *exploitation*. Furthermore, the next higher group theme of corruption, or lack of concern for the "common good," extends to the extreme theme of *pernicity*. This ascending hierarchy of themes subsequently extends to the remaining spiritual, humanitarian, and transcendental domains with respect to the themes of heresy, anarchism, and diabolism: a sequence that expands to the extreme listing of *recusancy, pandemonium,* and *demonism*, respectively.

Similar to the case previously made for the themes for the vices of excess, these themes for hyperviolence are similarly amenable to coding within the master three-digit coding system, only now the first digit is assigned the numerical value of "7" indicative of realm of excessive defect, as opposed to the "3" assigned to the vices of excess. In both cases, the third digit in the sequence is uniformly assigned the numerical value of "8" indicative of the main complement of themes for the main realm of excess.

A more detailed description of the themes for the realm of excess will not be undertaken at this juncture, their more obscure nature generally limits any widespread ethical applications. These themes enjoy neither the pedigree nor the traditions of the more extensively described themes for the major virtues and the vices of defect. Furthermore, the corresponding determination of the degree of excess is scarcely as clear-cut as those determinations identifying the more mainstream themes. Accordingly, the themes for hyperviolence and the vices of excess are necessarily a work in progress, being that the potential remains for other possible substitutions in future editions.

THE THEMATIC DEFINITIONS FOR THE DUAL REALM OF EXCESS

In direct analogy to the more mainstream range of themes, the related complement of themes for the realm of excess shares the potential for further incorporation into the formal schematic definition format. This latter modification is termed the class of "meta" schematic definitions, being that they represent meta-order summations of those targeting the individual terms. A complete listing of "meta" schematic definitions in relation to the vices of excess is depicted in **Table K-1**, wherein formally contrasting in an extreme fashion with the themes for the virtuous mode depicted in **Table C-1** (of Chapter 9). Furthermore, a parallel listing of thematic definitions in relation to the realm of hyperviolence is respectively depicted in **Table K-3**, formally contrasting in an extreme fashion with the themes for the vices of defect listed in **Table C-3** (of Chapter 15). The formal definitions for this darker range of themes are formally based upon the principles of punishment, just as the virtuous mode is similarly grounded within the terminology of instrumental conditioning. This strong behavioral foundation

adds a further welcome validation to this dual complement of "meta" schematic definitions.

THE ACCESSORY LISTING OF THEMES FOR THE REALM OF EXCESS

The completed description of the main listing of themes for the realm of excess, in turn, invites further comparisons to the predicted *accessory* variations for the realm of excess, as schematically depicted in **Fig. 20**. Similar to the pattern previously established for the virtuous themes, the accessory variations directly complement the main listings of themes, with the exception that the "you" and "I" polarities are now reversed in relation to the authority/follower roles, adding a crucial (empathic) dimension to the dual schematic format. A suitable number of accessory themes for the realm of excess have successfully been identified, permitting a complete accessory listing of themes. Furthermore with respect to the three-digit coding system, the final digit for each of the accessory themes is now specified as a "9" (rather than an "8"). For instance, with respect the themes for the vices of excess, the main authority sequence of themes (egotism-elitism-ideology-fanaticism-triumphalism) in turn, contrasts with the accessory sequence of counterparts; e.g., egocentrism-autocracy-pontification-fundamentalism-universalism. Furthermore, the main *follower* sequence of fraud-corruption-heresy-anarchism-diabolism similarly reciprocates its respective accessory trend (deception-venality-schismatism-lawlessness-sorcery).

Furthermore, with respect the realm of hyperviolence, the main authority sequence of themes (perversion-depravity-sacrilege-reprobation-mindlessness), in turn, contrasts with the accessory sequence of counterparts; e.g., fetishism-debasement-blasphemy-recreancy-unruliness. Alternately, the main *follower* sequence of exploitation-pernicity-recusancy-pandemonium-demonism similarly reciprocates its respective accessory trend (victimization-vileness-heathenism-tumultuousness-demoniac). Although the particular degree of correspondence for a number of these themes is perhaps not as ideal as might be expected, the seamless cohesiveness of this overall accessory system proves the crucial factor, here. Indeed, many of these accessory terms are not commonly encountered in general usage. Consequently, a more detailed analysis of this accessory class of themes is deferred for a more comprehensive treatment in an upcoming edition in light of their mostly highly specialized nature.

EGOTISM	OFFICIOUSNESS
Previously, you (as reinforcer) have excessively reinforced me: overriding my (as procurer) extremely solicitous treatment of you. But now, I (as personal authority) will *egotistically* act in an extremely individualistic fashion towards you: overruling your excessively reinforcing treatment of me.	Previously, I (as personal authority) have egotistically acted in an extremely individualistic fashion towards you: overriding your excessively reinforcing treatment of me. But now, you (as my personal follower) will *officiously* act extremely pragmatically towards me: overruling my (as PA) egotistical treatment of you.
ELITISM	**AUTHORITARIANISM**
Previously, you (as my personal follower) have officiously acted extremely pragmatically towards me: overriding my (as PA) egotistical treatment of you. But now, I (as group authority) will egotistically act in an *elitist* fashion towards you: overruling your (as PF) officious treatment of me.	Previously, I (as group authority) have egotistically acted in an elitist fashion towards you: overriding your (as PF) officious treatment of me. But now, you (as group representative) will officiously act in a *authoritarian* fashion: overruling my (as GA) elitist treatment of you.
IDEOLOGY	**CLERICALISM**
Previously, you (as group representative) have officiously acted in a authoritarian fashion: overriding my (as GA) elitist treatment of you. But now, I (as spiritual authority) will elitely act in a *ideological* fashion towards you: overruling your (as GR) authoritarian treatment of me.	Previously, I (as spiritual authority) have elitely acted in a ideological fashion towards you: overriding your (as GR) authoritarian treatment of me. But now, you (as spiritual disciple) will authoritarianly act in a *clericalistic* fashion towards me: overruling my (as SA) ideological treatment of you.
FANATICISM	**IDEALISM**
Previously, you (as my spiritual disciple) have authoritarianly acted with clericalism towards me: overriding my (as SA) ideological treatment of you. But now, I (as humanitarian authority) will ideologically act in a *fanatical* fashion towards you: overruling your (as SD) authoritarian sense of clericalism.	Previously, I (as humanitarian authority) have ideologically acted fanatically towards you: overriding your (as SD) clericalistic treatment of me. But now, you (as representative member of humanity) will *idealistically* act with clericalism towards me: overruling my (as HA) fanatical treatment of you.
TRIUMPHALISM	**OCCULTISM**
Previously, you (as representative member of humanity) have idealistically acted with clericalism towards me: overriding my (as HA) fanatical treatment of you. But now, I (as transcendental authority) will fanatically act *triumphally* towards you: overruling your (as RH) idealistic treatment of me.	Previously, I (as transcendental authority) have fanatically acted triumphally towards you: overriding your (as RH) idealistic treatment of me. But now, you (as my transcendental follower) will idealistically act *occultly* towards me: overruling my (as TA) triumphalist treatment of you.

Table K-1 – The "Meta" Definitions for the Vices of Excess

EGOCENTRISM	OBTRUSIVENESS
Previously, I (as reinforcer) have excessively reinforced you: overriding your (as procurer) extremely solicitous treatment of me. But now, you (as personal authority) will *egocentrically* act in an extremely quintessential fashion towards me: overruling my excessively reinforcing treatment of you.	Previously, you (as personal authority) have egocentrically acted in an extremely quintessential fashion towards me: overriding my excessively reinforcing treatment of you. But now, I (as your personal follower) will *obtrusively* act extremely expediently towards you: overruling your (as PA) egocentric treatment of me.
AUTOCRACY	**ABSOLUTISM**
Previously, I (as your personal follower) have obtrusively acted extremely expediently towards you: overriding your (as PA) egocentric treatment of me. But now, you (as group authority) will egocentrically act in an *autocratic* fashion towards me: overruling my (as PF) obtrusive treatment of you.	Previously, you (as group authority) have egocentrically acted in an autocratic fashion towards me: overriding my (as PF) obtrusive treatment of you. But now, I (as group representative) will obtrusively act in an *absolutist* fashion towards you: overruling your (as GA) autocratic treatment of me.
PONTIFICATION	**DOGMATISM**
Previously, I (as group representative) have obtrusively acted in an absolutist fashion towards you: overriding your (as GA) autocratic treatment of me. But now, you (as spiritual authority) will autocratically act in a *pontificating* fashion towards me: overruling my (as GR) absolutist treatment of you.	Previously, you (as spiritual authority) have autocratically acted in a pontificating fashion towards me: overriding my (as GR) absolutist treatment of you. But now, I (as spiritual disciple) will *dogmatically* act in an absolutist fashion towards you: overruling your (as SA) pontificating treatment of me.
FUNDAMENTALISM	**SUPREMACISM**
Previously, I (as spiritual disciple) have dogmatically acted in an absolutist fashion towards you: overriding your (as SA) pontificating treatment of me. But now, you (as humanitarian authority) will pontificatingly act in a *fundamentalist* fashion towards me: overruling my (as SD) dogmatic treatment of you.	Previously, you (as humanitarian authority) have pontificatingly acted in a fundamentalist fashion towards me: overruling my (as SD) dogmatic treatment of you. But now, I (as representative member of humanity) will dogmatically act in a *supremacist* fashion towards you: overruling your (as HA) fundamentalist treatment of me.
UNIVERSALISM	**ENIGMATISM**
Previously, I (as representative member of humanity) have dogmatically acted in a supremacist fashion towards you: overriding your (as HA) fundamentalist treatment of me. But now, you (as transcendental authority) will fundamentally act in a *universalist* fashion towards me: overruling my (as RH) supremacist treatment of you.	Previously, you (as transcendental authority) have fundamentally acted in a universalist fashion towards me: overriding my (as RH) supremacist treatment of you. But now, I (as your transcendental follower) will *enigmatically* act in a supremacist fashion towards you: overruling your (as TA) universalist treatment of me.

Table K-2 - The Accessory Definitions for the Vices of Excess

PERVERSION	EXPLOITATION
Previously, you (as punisher) have excessively acted in a punitive fashion towards me: overriding my (as antagonist) extremely adversarial treatment of you. But now, I (as personal authority) will *perversely* act extremely adversarially towards you: overruling your excessively punitive treatment of me.	Previously, I (as personal authority) have perversely acted extremely adversarially towards you: overruling your excessively punitive treatment of me. But now, you (as my personal follower) will *exploitatively* act extremely punitively towards me: overruling my (as PA) perverse treatment of you.
DEPRAVITY	**PERNICITY**
Previously, you (as my personal follower) have exploitatively acted extremely punitively towards me: overriding my (as PA) perverse treatment of you. But now, I (as group authority) will perversely act in a *depraved* fashion towards you: overruling your (as PF) exploitative treatment of me.	Previously, I (as group authority) have perversely acted in a depraved fashion towards you: overriding your (as PF) exploitative treatment of me. But now, you (as group representative) will *perniciously* act in an exploitative fashion towards me: overruling my (as GA) depraved treatment of you.
SACRILEGE	**RECUSANCY**
Previously, you (as group representative) have perniciously acted in an exploitative fashion towards me: overriding my (as GA) depraved treatment of you. But now, I (as spiritual authority) will depravingly act in a *sacrilegious* fashion towards you: overruling your (as GR) pernicious treatment of me.	Previously, I (as spiritual authority) have depravingly acted sacrilegiously towards you: overriding your (as GR) pernicious treatment of me. But now, you (as my spiritual disciple) will perniciously act in a *recusant* fashion towards me: overruling my (as SA) sacrilegious treatment of you.
REPROBATION	**PANDEMONIUM**
Previously, you (as my spiritual disciple) have perniciously acted recusantly towards me: overruling my (as SA) sacrilegious treatment of you. But now, I (as humanitarian authority) will sacrilegiously act in a *reprobate* fashion towards you: overruling your (as SD) recusant treatment of me.	Previously, I (as humanitarian authority) have sacrilegiously acted reprobately towards you: overriding your (as SD) recusant treatment of me. But now, you (as representative member of humanity) will recusantly act *pandemoniusly* towards me: overruling my (as HA) reprobate treatment of you.
MINDLESSNESS	**DEMONISM**
Previously, you (as represent. member of humanity) have recusantly acted pandemoniusly: overriding my (as HA) reprobate treatment of you. But now, I (as transcendental authority) will reprobately act in a *mindless* fashion towards you: overruling your (as RH) pandemonium-filled treatment of me.	Previously, I (as transcendental authority) have reprobately acted in a mindless fashion towards you: overriding your (as RH) pandemonium-filled treatment of me. But now, you (as my transcendental follower) will *demonically* act pandemoniusly towards me: overruling my (as TA) mindless treatment of you.

Table K-3 - The "Meta" Definitions for Hyperviolence

FETISHISM	VICTIMIZATION
Previously, I (as punisher) have excessively acted in a punitive fashion towards you: overriding your (as antagonist) extremely adversarial treatment of me. But now, you (as personal authority) will *fetishingly* act extremely adversarially towards me: overruling my excessively punitive treatment of you.	Previously, you (as personal authority) have fetishingly acted extremely adversarially towards me: overriding my excessively punitive treatment of you. But now, I (as your personal follower) will punitively act in a *victimizing* fashion towards you: overruling your (as PA) fetishistic treatment of me.
DEBASEMENT	**VILENESS**
Previously, I (as your personal follower) have punitively acted in a victimizing fashion towards you: overriding your (as PA) fetishistic treatment of me. But now, you (as group authority) will fetishingly act in a *debased* fashion towards me: overruling my (as PF) victimization of you.	Previously, you (as group authority) have fetishingly acted in a debased fashion towards me: overriding my (as PF) victimization of you.

But now, I (as group representative) will *vilely*-victimize you: overruling your (as GA) debased treatment of me. |
| **BLASPHEMY** | **HEATHENISM** |
| Previously, I (as group representative) have vilely-victimized you: overriding your (as GA) debased treatment of me.

But now, you (as spiritual authority) will debasingly act in a *blasphemous* fashion towards me: overruling my (as GR) vile-victimization of you. | Previously, you (as spiritual authority) have debasingly acted in a blasphemous fashion towards me: overriding my (as GR) vile-victimization of you. But now, I (as spiritual disciple) will vilely act in a *heathenistic* fashion towards you: overruling your (as SA) blasphemous treatment of me. |
RECREANCY	**TUMULTUOSNESS**
Previously, I (as spiritual disciple) have vilely acted heathenistically towards you: overriding your (as SA) blasphemous treatment of me. But now, you (as humanitarian authority) will blasphemously act in a *recreant* fashion towards me: overruling my (as SD) heathenistic treatment of you.	Previously, you (as humanitarian authority) have blasphemously acted recreantly towards me: overriding my (as SD) heathenistic treatment of you. But now, I (as representative member of humanity) will heathenistically act in a *tumultuous* fashion towards you: overruling your (as HA) recreant treatment of me.
UNRULINESS	**DEMONIAC**
Previously, I (as representative member of humanity) have heathenistically acted tumultuously towards you: overriding your (as HA) recreant treatment of me. But now, you (as transcendental authority) will recreantly act in an *unruly* fashion towards me: overruling my (as RH) tumultuous treatment of you.	Previously, you (as my transcendental authority) have recreantly acted in an unruly fashion: overriding my (as RH) tumultuous treatment of you. But now, I (as your transcendental follower) will tumultuously act in a *demoniac* fashion towards you: overruling your (as TA) unruly treatment of me.

Table K-4 – The Accessory Themes for Hyperviolence

THE FORMAL SCHEMATIC DEFINITIONS FOR THE ACCESSORY THEMES FOR EXCESS

The true test of validity for this accessory sequence of themes, however, ultimately extends to their formal incorporation within the schematic definition format. In direct analogy to the main listing of thematic definitions for excess, the respective accessory themes are similarly schematically endowed, wherefore specifying higher-order perspectives on the more basic complement of terms specified for the realm of excess. A complete listing of thematic definitions for the accessory vices of excess are depicted in **Table K-2** and for accessory hyperviolence in **Table K-4**. When examined in concert, both the main and accessory themes for realm of defect permit a degree of empathic versatility unprecedented in terms of precision, allowing for considerable insights into the realm of deceptive communication. In terms of this dual complement of definitions, the reciprocal interplay of "you" and "I" perspectives is definitely apparent, although scarcely to the degree of clarity previously established for the more routine sets of themes due to their more ambiguous interpretation of excess.

THE MASTER SCHEMATIC FORMAT LINKING VIRTUE AND VICE

In conclusion, the completed description of the realm of hyperviolence (in both its main and accessory manifestations) effectively rounds-out the stepwise description of the initial categories for the three-digit coding system. Here, the supreme symmetry of the unified power pyramid hierarchy finally becomes conceptually complete. When these four basic categories (namely, the major virtues, vices of defect, vices of excess, and hyperviolence) are collectively incorporated into a unified ethical system, the grand-total of ethical terms expands to a sum-total of *160*. Through the further addition of the mirror-image complement of accessory terms, the total, in turn, doubles to *320.* This grand unified synthesis of ethical terms accounts for a complete cross-section of emotionally-charged language, in general, in light of the overall master diagram predicated in Chapter 1.

This formal four-part diagram actually encompasses five distinct entries through the addition of the novel concept of the neutrality status. It represents a neutral point of entry for the entire master diagram. Every new interaction (by definition) stems directly from this zone of neutrality, an innovation proceeding into either the realm of

the virtues, or alternately into the realm of defect, as schematically immediately depicted below.

+ + VICES OF EXCESS
(Excessive Virtue)

+ MAJOR VIRTUES
(Virtuous Mode)

O - NEUTRALITY STATUS

– VICES OF DEFECT
(Absence of Virtue)

– – HYPERVIOLENCE
(Excessive Defect)

This pair of conflicting options represents an ethical "fork in the road," a decision that directs the relationship either towards the virtues or the realm of defect. These parallel options represent the basic *core*-nucleus of the system. Here, most relationships are resolved through recourse to one option or the other. The additional realm of excess lurks at the fringe boundary of the core-nucleus. For the virtuous realm, this extends to the affiliated realm of the vices of excess. Furthermore, the parallel range of options with respect to the vices of defect further equates with the newly introduced notion of hyperviolence. This alternate set of options represents the figurative "fast-lanes" of the relationship superhighway; namely, fringe areas exaggerated to the point of crossing over into the domain of excess.

In summary, the completed introduction of the master five-part diagram effectively closes out the stepwise description of the three-digit code system, at least for the odd-numbered categories of terms: namely, the major virtues (1), the vices of excess (3), the vices of defect (5), and hyperviolence (7). This momentous achievement, however, still leaves open the issue the remaining even-numbered categories; e.g., the *transitional* variations comprising the lesser virtues (2), mental illness (4), criminality (6), and hyper-criminality (8). This subsequent endeavor is now undertaken in **Parts V** through **VII**. **Part V** examines the lesser virtues, whereas **Part VI** is devoted to the related realms of criminality and hypercriminality. **Part VII**, in turn, examines the communicational factors underlying the realm of mental illness, whereas the concluding **Part VIII** outlines the many exciting applications arising from potential global implementation.

PART-V

21

AN INTRODUCTION TO THE
TRANSITIONAL POWER MANEUVERS

The pronounced versatility of the main schematic of ethical terms allows for insights unprecedented on the world scene today. Although the full *400-part* hierarchy of virtues/vices appears to offer the final word in this regard, the current format suffers from one crucial shortcoming; namely, the authority/follower roles are rigidly fixed into place, allowing precious little flexibility to operate within the system. Versatility is a key feature in our modern mobile society, with continually shifting social coalitions placing an ever-greater demand upon the individual. Each new adjustment to the social hierarchy calls for new mechanisms for integrating the newly established individual, an innovation that the established hierarchy of virtue/vice fails to take fully into account. In concert with the incremental pattern of power maneuvers initially described, a more direct method must necessarily exist for leapfrogging straight into the higher authority levels; e.g., the group, spiritual, and humanitarian levels, respectively. This new class of options is, accordingly, termed the *transitional* class of power maneuvers, in that they transition the individual directly into new social contexts.

A number of key features distinguish this new class of transitional power maneuvers. Firstly, these transitional variations represent direct motivational analogs of the main power maneuvers they serve to imitate: often in an exaggerated fashion to make the point more clearly. This flair for the dramatic can appear either humorous (as in the realm of comedy), or tragic (as in the sense of melodrama). This tendency towards exaggeration is the stock-in-trade for the standard situation comedy, where the guest star intrudes upon the graces of a standard ensemble cast, typically with hilarious consequences. A lively sequence of good-natured bantering generally follows, wherein culminating in a heart-warming resolution. A similar scenario further holds true with respect to the more serious realm of the melodrama, as primarily dramatized in terms of the daytime "soap opera."

THE TRANSITIONAL POWER MANEUVERS

This transitional class of power maneuvers refers to relationships initiated for the first time. Here the newly introduced individual attempts to establish a new relationship within a pre-existing social order. The new party enlists the cooperation of established individuals in order to solidify his anticipated role within the conditioned relationship. Any such transitional overture fails to be fully consummated without the overt concession of the established party within the social hierarchy. Take, for example, the familiar scenario of the "autograph hound." When thrust into contact with his celebrity idol, the fan attempts to establish a new personal relationship (even though only temporary). Being somewhat of an outsider, this entails a special strategy for making the overture attractive to the celebrity figure. This generally entails coming across from a one-down follower status; namely, framing the overture in terms of exalted respect for the authority status of the celebrity figure. In terms of the autograph example, the eager fan appeasingly frames his overture in the guise of the personal follower role, deliberately playing-up the prestige of the personal authority figure.

According to the celebrity/fan example, the "hero-worship" role of the personal follower is modified (in a transitional sense) into the *loyalty* maneuver expressed by the adoring fan: a role that further anticipates the nostalgic acknowledgement of worthiness by the personal authority figure. A similar scenario is further seen with respect to the medieval feudal system. The vassal unswervingly pledges loyalty to his regal liege, expressed in terms of a ritual hand-clasping ceremony. Consequently, by playing-up the latter's established authority status, the personal follower gains a further degree of consideration from his personal authority figure, a strategy consistent with the reciprocal interplay of authority/follower roles.

The more basic *complementary* style of relationship relies upon a more established context of role-polarities, where the authority/follower roles are fixed firmly into place. In the transitional variation, however, the newcomer fails to enjoy the advantages of this established context, wherein finding it more useful (at least initially) to play-up the status of his authority figure. This strategy, in essence, allows the newcomer to get his foot in the door (so to speak). Should the personal authority figure ultimately accept this ploy, then the personal follower, in turn, retains the option of pressing his own *follower* status, wherein establishing an equivalent balance of power within the personal power realm.

THE DOUBLE BIND CLASS OF POWER MANEUVER

The initial phase of the transitional power maneuver, fittingly, is termed the *congeniality* phase, in that the newcomer maneuvers from a somewhat vulnerable follower status in order to gain the cooperation of the established authority figure. The established party is primarily justified in accepting such an overture, being that he is automatically granted one-up authority status. This advantage, however, often is not as simple as it might appear, in that the authority figure is essentially coerced to some degree (albeit congenially) into reciprocating his expected role within the transitional interchange. Indeed, the established party often refuses to submit willingly to such a bold power grab. The upstart newcomer effectively dictates the subsequent cooperation of the authority figure, a deceptive gain in power!

This slavish submission to the dictates of another equates to a personal loss of freedom irrespective of the congenial intentions therein. In a general "meta" sense, the newcomer seizes control of the newly established relationship through the process of initiating it, placing the established party in a form of *double bind* maneuver. This latter term is borrowed from the terminology of Communication Theory: defined as a paradox that leaves one (thusly bound) unable to fully comment upon the inherent incongruity

contained within the message. For the "loyalty" maneuver, this amounts to a fundamental conflict between the primary message content level and its higher *meta*-context.

The primary message content is basically straightforward; namely, accepting the overture of the fan at its most basic content level, accompanied by the attendant recognition of one's established authority status. The respective *meta*-message, however, directly diminishes this outward power advantage. The newcomer essentially dictates the course of the interaction through the very process of initiating it. This more abstract form of meta-communication effectively supersedes the primary content level within the interaction, clearly inserting a contradictory range of meaning into the ongoing transitional interplay.

This inherent aversion to being subliminally controlled by another makes the initial overture of the fan a somewhat difficult proposition to accept. Indeed, Communication Theorists specifically acknowledge this ingrained resistance to modifying the established status quo, a transitional disruption to the homeostasis governing the pre-existing social order. This intractable class of double bind maneuvers is technically defined as a "damned if you do, damned if you don't" style of paradox. Should the established party accept the overture at face value, he then risks losing face with respect to the higher *meta*-context of the message; namely, submitting to the dictates of another. Rejecting the overture, however, voids the advantages of the primary message content (with its guaranteed authority status). This further includes the risk of appearing somewhat stalwart in the process, a factor completely at odds with the congenial nature of the proceedings.

THE COUNTER DOUBLE BIND MANEUVER

The most graceful resolution to this intransigent predicament entails what Communications Theorists term the *counter* double bind. This latter strategy amounts to humoring the efforts of the newcomer: accepting the surface content of the interaction while simultaneously disqualifying one's willing participation through *meta*-contextual cues. The counter double bind subliminally disqualifies (through meta-cues) the context of the entire interaction: in essence, scorning the validity of the overall transitional interchange. This strategy is formally defined as: I accept your sense of loyalty through my nostalgic treatment of you, although I *humbly* deny doing so. This distinctive sense of meta-disqualification is chiefly mediated through the use of nonverbal cues; e.g.,

The Oath of Fealty: French Vassals Pledge Loyalty to the King
A Ceremony Invoking the Ritual Clasping of Hands - Detail from Medieval Tapestry, circa 1280

those nonverbal behaviors that underscore virtually every social context. Chief among these are bodily gestures, where a brief shrug of the shoulders or a raised eyebrow can greatly modify (or even reverse) the content of what is being said. Voice modulation and exaggerated inflection represent further strategies towards these ends. A scornful or humorous tone signals that one shouldn't be taken too seriously. Indeed, as any great comic will attest, the timing of a joke is typically more significant than the content therein. A similar pattern is further encountered with respect to the theme of "playfulness," where routine activities acquire an amusing quality via communication that they're not be taken too seriously, as in role-playing, or other such subliminally disqualified endeavors.

Through this broad range of tactics, the counter double bind maneuver regains the upper hand in the transitional interchange without necessarily appearing to have done so. Communications Theorists, such as Jay Haley (1990), define this strategy as the *meta-complementary* maneuver, in that the surface content mimics the more basic complementary variety, although now subliminally disqualified through the use of *meta-*contextual cues. A similar aspect is encountered in the field of Transactional Analysis with respect to the notion of *ulterior* communication. Indeed, it is precisely at this extreme level of disqualification that the paradoxical nature of the counter double bind proves most effective: obliquely expressing disdain for the newcomer's initial attempts at psychological manipulation. Through a sarcastic tone of voice (or other such disqualified strategy), the established party stresses the unreality of the situation, a direct outcome of the paradoxical nature of the entire transitional interchange.

In the case of the initial loyalty maneuver, the established party *humbly* denies being worthy of such loyalty: superficially accepting the content of the interaction, although in a fully disqualified fashion. By appearing humble, the personal authority effectively sidesteps the insistent quality of the fan's loyalty maneuver, although remaining fully polite in the process. With respect to the similar transitional maneuver of responsibility, the disqualified sense of *innocence* represents a measured defense against the implications of this blameful style of power maneuver. A similar pattern further holds true with respect to the related interplay of modesty/discipline or meekness/vigil-

220	221
Loyalty	Responsibility
222	**223**
Discipline	Vigilance

TRANSITIONAL
ALTER EGO STATES
(Personal Double-Bind)

→

210.1	211.1
Humility	Innocence
212.1	**213.1**
Modesty	Meekness

DISQUALIFIED
EGO STATES
(Personal Counter Double-Bind)

240	241
Fidelity	Duty
242	**243**
Chivalry	Courage

TRANSITIONAL
CARDINAL VIRTUES
(Group Double-Bind)

→

230.1	231.1
Majesty	Vindication
232.1	**233.1**
Chastity	Obedience

DISQUALIFIED
PERSONAL IDEALS
(Group Counter Double-Bind)

260	261
Piety	Allegiance
262	**263**
Nobility	Valor

TRANSITIONAL
THEOLOGICAL VIRTUES
(Spiritual Double-Bind)

→

250.1	251.1
Magnificence	Exoneration
252.1	**253.1**
Purity	Conformity

DISQUALIFIED
CIVIL LIBERTIES
(Spiritual Counter Double-Bind)

280	281
Felicity	Righteousness
282	**283**
Zeal	Triumph

TRANSITIONAL
GREEK VALUES
(Humanitarian Double-Bind)

→

270.1	271.1
Grandeur	Immaculateness
272.1	**273.1**
Perfection	Pacifism

DISQUALIFIED
ECUMENICAL IDEALS
(Humanit. Counter Double-Bind)

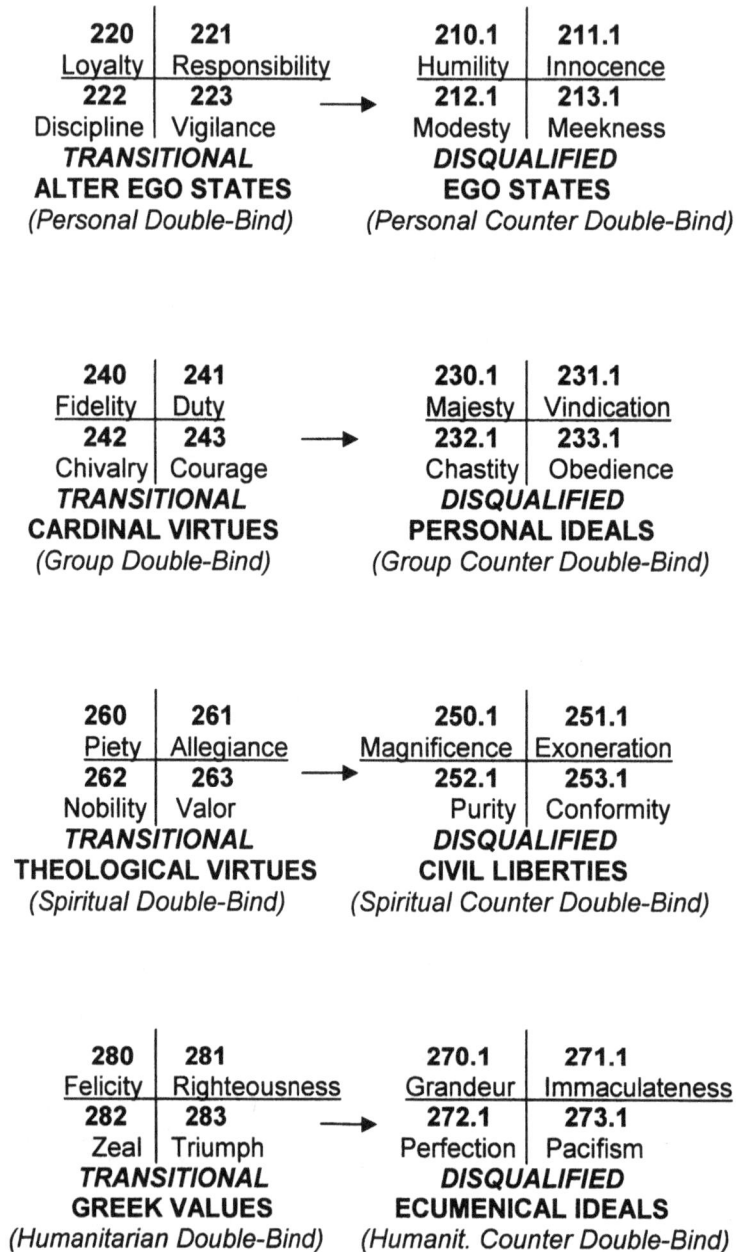

Fig. 21 – The Lesser Virtues - (I)

ance. The artful use of disqualification defuses any overt complicity within the transitional interchange. Indeed, it takes a clever individual to balance the degree of disqualification for meeting the desired results, a skill most of us instinctively develop at a fairly early age. Navigating the extremes of the double bind (and counter double bind) maneuvers requires great mental dexterity coupled with innate social instincts. The learned social cues for achieving such subliminal disqualification (in addition to the skills of timing, inflection, etc.) all must be expressed convincingly in order to achieve success. It is here that the wit and genius of the comedian remain so deeply appreciated, their public adulation certainly well-founded in light of their mastery of the art-form.

THE ULTIMATE RESOLUTION TO THE COUNTER DOUBLE BIND MANEUVER

The somewhat unnerving experience of discovering that one's double bind has been reversed is typically one of surprise, accompanied by some sort of "aha" experience. This realization is accompanied by nervous laughter, a spontaneous acknowledgment of having been outwitted. In a general sense, this fitful laughter represents a catharsis of sorts, signaling a restoration of the original status quo following the disruption instigated by the transitional interlude. The spontaneous nature of the laughter further verifies its subconscious characteristics consistent with other types of convulsive behavior. Crying is often indistinguishable from laughter save the shedding of tears. Weeping similarly functions as a release from grief, just as laughter formally targets the humorous realm. In each case, both laughter and crying result in a dramatic release of tension, wherein effectively restoring emotional stability.

This latter development, in turn, places the original party in a double bind of his own with respect to such an emotionally-charged situation. Any comments relating to such an impasse are generally suppressed due to the highly disqualified nature of the proceedings. To do so would advertise the glaring failure of the entire transitional interchange. Similar to the initial double bind maneuver, there is no straightforward escape from the counter double bind maneuver. Indeed, the only reasonable strategy consists of abandoning the pursuit altogether, having been bested in a pitched battle of wits. Any attempts toward reinstating a new transitional relationship are similarly abandoned, wherein restoring the balance of the original role-polarities. Although the established authority figure may eventually

see fit to extend a conciliatory overture, this outcome remains entirely distinct from having been forced into it. Through this supreme degree of disqualification, the humor maneuver reaches its greatest potential in terms of such good-natured bantering, which (even under the friendliest terms) leads to impasse and counter-impasse.

A DOUBLE BIND THEORY OF HUMOR & COMEDY

The extreme degree of disqualification characterizing the counter double bind maneuver certainly appears comedic to those thusly entertained. In terms of the humorous range of contexts encountered within the situation comedy, the major players take turns double binding one another, before cleverly extricating themselves, in turn. The enraptured audience members typically project into one role or another, sharing in the laughter when the trap is finally sprung.

The preliminary setup of the comedy routine is fittingly defined as the *congeniality* phase, a role generally assumed by the "straight man" of the comedy team. The straight man typically sets up the context of the joke similar to the initiatory phase of the double bind maneuver. This initial phase, in turn, sets the stage for the *humor* maneuver proper, where the headline star delivers a "zinger" of a punch line (the counter double bind maneuver), ideally served with a straight face. The immediate reaction, for all in attendance, is one of hilarious laughter: the celebrated calling card for revered comedy teams such as Abbott and Costello or Carson and McMahon. Perhaps the most difficult aspect of the comedian's job is to avoid laughing at one's own jokes, in essence, preserving the mystique of his skilled disqualification.

The laughter from the audience, in turn, serves as a spontaneous catharsis of sorts, an outward expression of a return to normalcy (so to speak). The emotional energy initially invested within the congeniality phase is subsequently dissipated through a convulsive spate of laughter, resulting in a homeostatic restoration of the preexisting social order. A similar pattern further holds true with respect to the melodrama, where the related phenomenon of weeping substitutes for that seen for laughter. In either case, the established context is satisfactorily restored, both parties "double bound" against mulling over the series of reversals that had just transpired.

THE MASTER TRANSITIONAL SCHEMATIC

The formal addition of the dual complement of transitional power maneuvers proves a fitting adjunct to the more routine ethical hierarchy, distinguished through the reciprocal interplay of double bind and counter double bind maneuvers. This distinctive sequence of role-reversals is particularly evident in the specific examples initially described; namely, loyalty/humility and responsibility/innocence. For instance, the loyalty maneuver of the personal follower, in turn, prompts the humility expressed by the personal authority figure. A similar pattern further holds true for the responsibility form of double bind, wherein prompting the "innocence" style of counter double bind maneuver. Although these examples prove effective to a personal sphere of influence, the remaining levels within the power hierarchy still beg to be determined. Even a cursory survey of the ethical literature, however, reveals a wide assortment of *lesser* virtues essentially unaccounted for in terms of the major groupings. These lesser virtues are similarly endowed with their own well-established literary traditions that integrate seamlessly into the unified ethical hierarchy.

According to this expanded interpretation, loyalty represents just the first term in a sequence spanning the group, spiritual, and humanitarian levels: in this case, loyalty-fidelity-piety-felicity. The similar trend based upon responsibility is alternately defined as responsibility-duty-allegiance-righteousness. A parallel pattern further holds true with respect to the remaining sequences of counter double bind maneuvers: namely, humility-majesty-magnificence-grandeur and innocence-vindication-exoneration-immaculateness. Indeed, an equal number of sequences are further encountered for the remaining pair of trends for realm of the lesser virtues, resulting in the *32*-part sequence of terms listed immediately below:

Loyalty → Humility	**Responsibility → Innocence**
Fidelity → Majesty	**Duty → Vindication**
Piety → Magnificence	**Allegiance → Exoneration**
Felicity → Grandeur	**Righteous.→ Immaculate.**
Discipline → Modesty	**Vigilance → Meekness**
Chivalry → Chastity	**Courage → Obedience**
Nobility → Purity	**Valor → Conformity**
Zeal → Perfection	**Triumph → Pacifism**

This compact diagram proves particularly effective in demonstrating the distinct hierarchial trends at issue, although, in turn, depicted in a more formal arrangement in **Fig. 21**. According to this master schematic format, the entire *32*-term series of lesser virtues (I) is formally split into the characteristic four-part listings of terms similar to the

pattern previously established for the major groupings of virtues, values, and ideals. For instance, the most basic personal follower level is specified through the formal transitional grouping of loyalty-responsibility-discipline-vigilance, a pattern directly reflecting the related sequence of alter ego states (hero/worship-blame-approval-concern). True to the order in which they are presented, *loyalty* represents the transitional counterpart of hero worship, whereas *responsibility* makes a similar correspondence to blame. Furthermore, *discipline* specifies the transitional counterpart of approval, whereas *vigilance* makes similar correspondence to concern.

This preliminary class of double bind maneuvers, in turn, sets the stage for the remaining counter double bind class of maneuvers; in this case, humility-innocence-modesty-meekness. Each of these terms suggests the clear degree of disqualification characterizing the counter double bind class of maneuvers, wherein countering the initial sequence of double bind maneuvers. For instance, in response to your initial loyalty maneuver, I (as established personal authority) will *humbly* deny acting nostalgically towards you. Furthermore, in response to your quest for responsibility, I will *innocently* deny acting guiltily towards you. Similarly, in response to my disciplined treatment of you, you (as established personal authority) will *modestly* deny acting desirously towards me. Furthermore, in response to my vigilant treatment, you will *meekly* deny acting worrisomely towards me.

Although this dual interplay of lesser virtues proves exceedingly accurate at a personal level, this similarly extends to the remaining listings of lesser virtues depicted in **Figure 21**. A more detailed examination of this entire *32*-part complement of virtuous terms is certainly in order here, permitting a comprehensive overview of the entire hierarchy of the lesser virtues (I). This expanded inquiry begins with an in-depth examination of the sequences based on loyalty/humility and responsibility/innocence in Chapter *22*: followed, in turn, by those targeting discipline/modesty and vigilance/meekness contained in Chapter *23*.

THE THREE-DIGIT CODING SYSTEM FOR THE LESSER VIRTUES

Before embarking upon a more comprehensive analysis of the lesser virtues, a related issue must necessarily be addressed; namely, the distinct modifications to the three-digit coding system. This innovation entails the addition of extra decimal places for fully describing the counter double bind class of maneuvers. This additional decimal place was formally predicted in that (in terms of the *1,040* individual terms) the system, by definition, does not contain enough three-digit numbers to fully accommodate the total complexity. In terms of the inherent necessity for an extra decimal place within the system, it was judged most effective to incorporate this modification at the highly specialized level of the counter double bind class of maneuvers. This extra decimal place only occurs in categories defined as transitional power maneuvers; namely, those within the three-digit coding system that begin with even first-place digits: e.g., 2 = the lesser virtues, 4 = mental illness, 6 = criminality, and 8 = hypercriminality.

For instance, in terms of the lesser virtues, the three initial digits are fully capable of specifying the preliminary class of double bind maneuvers. This circumstance is intuitively apparent in that the double bind maneuvers represent formal transitional variations on the more basic categories of ethical terms; namely, those beginning with odd number digits. For the lesser virtues, the three-digit codes ending with numbers zero-to-three represent the double bind class of power maneuvers: e.g., loyalty = 220, responsibility = 221, discipline = 222, and vigilance = 223.

Furthermore (similar to the main categories of terms), those sequences of terms ending with digits four-through-seven represent the *accessory* versions of the double bind maneuvers; in this case 224 to 227. Finally, the three-digit codes ending with the digits 8 and 9 are reserved for designating the respective general unifying themes for the double bind maneuvers. The last-place digit of "8" specifies the main themes, whereas "9" identifies the accessory themes. This basic coding pattern for the lesser virtues, in turn, extends to the related transitional domains for mental illness, criminality, and hypercriminality. A more comprehensive description of each of these applications is reserved for the upcoming dedicated sections.

Returning to the initial class of lesser virtues, however, the available complement of three-digit code numbers is effectively exhausted with respect to the preliminary class of double bind maneuvers. Consequently, this shortfall necessarily entails the addition of an extra decimal place for designating the related class of counter double bind maneuvers (and related options). This additional decimal place, in turn, is subdivided into ten basic options, as graphically depicted in the compact table of options immediately to follow.

.0 – Acceptance	**.1 – Metacomplement.**
.2 – Symmetrical	**.3 – Change Subject**
.4 – Acc. Accept.	**.5 – Acc. Metacomp.**
.6 – Acc. Symmet.	**.7 – Acc. Change Subj.**
.8 – Ignore/Leave	**.9 – Acc. Ignore/Leave**

According to this ten-part table, the direct acceptance of the double bind maneuver (as presented) is assigned a "zero" in the extra decimal place. With respect to the initial loyalty maneuver (220), the expected nostalgia response of the personal authority figure is assigned the three-digit code number of 210.0, wherein reflecting the nostalgic acceptance in terms. Although the main virtue of nostalgia is formally designated as 110, its subsequent modification to 210.0 reflects the acceptance of its expected role within such a transitional context.

The next most common response (the counter double bind maneuver) rates the further specification of a "1" in the final decimal place. Humility is specified as 210.1, innocence = 211.1, modesty = 212.1, etc. These specific examples represent disqualified variations on the expected nostalgia/guilt/desire maneuvers, respectively. This is also known as the meta-complementary class of power maneuvers with respect to the terminology of Communication Theory.

One further potential option includes what is termed the *symmetrical* class of power maneuvers; namely, mirroring back the preliminary double bind maneuver in a symmetrical fashion. The symmetrical maneuver is formally specified in terms of a "2" in the final decimal place. Since the symmetrical maneuver essentially mirrors the initial double bind maneuver, in turn, its respective code numbers reflect this observation; namely, symmetrical-loyalty = 220.2, symmetrical-responsibility = 221.2, etc.

According to the master schematic diagram depicted above, one final basic option remains to be described; namely, that extending to a change of subject, as specified in terms of a "3" in the final decimal place; for instance, 220.3 reflects a random change of subject following the loyalty maneuver. In this case, the power maneuver to which the conversation is switched immediately follows the code for "change-the-subject."

Similar to the pattern initially established for the double bind maneuvers, numbers 4-through-7 from the master diagram represent the *accessory*

LOYALTY	HUMILITY
Previously, I (as personal authority) have nostalgically acted in a solicitous fashion, in response to the worshipful treatment of the personal follower. But now, you (as new personal follower) will *loyally* act in a worshipful fashion towards me: in anticipation of my (as established PA) nostalgic treatment of you.	Previously, you (as new personal follower) have loyally acted in a worshipful fashion towards me: in anticipation of my (as established PA) nostalgic treatment of you. But now, I (as reluctant personal authority) will *humbly* <u>deny</u> acting nostalgically towards you: thwarting your (as new PF) loyal treatment of me.
FIDELITY	**MAJESTY**
Previously, I (as group authority) have gloriously acted in a nostalgic fashion, in response to the prudent-worship of the group representative. But now, you (as new group representative) will loyally act with *fidelity* towards me: in anticipation of my (as established GA) gloriously-nostalgic treatment of you.	Previously, you (as new group representative) have loyally acted with fidelity towards me: in anticipation of my (as established GA) gloriously-nostalgic treatment of you. But now, I (as reluctant group authority) will humbly act in a *majestic* fashion towards you: thwarting your (as new GR) loyal sense of fidelity.
PIETY	**MAGNIFICENCE**
Previously, I (as spiritual authority) have gloriously acted in a provident fashion, in response to the prudent-faith of the spiritual disciple. But now, you (as new spiritual disciple) will *piously* act with fidelity towards me: in anticipation of my (as established SA) gloriously-provident treatment of you.	Previously, you (as new spiritual disciple) have piously acted with fidelity towards me: in anticipation of my (as established SA) gloriously-provident treatment of you. But now, I (as reluctant spiritual authority) will majestically react in a *magnificent* fashion towards you: thwarting your (as new SD) pious treatment of me.
FELICITY	**GRANDEUR**
Previously, I (as humanitarian authority) have providently acted in a graceful fashion, in response to the beauteous-faith of the representative member of humanity But now, you (as new representative member of humanity) will piously act *felicitously* towards me: in anticipation of my (as established HA) provident sense of gracefulness.	Previously, you (as new representative member of humanity) have piously acted felicitously towards me: in anticipation of my (as established HA) provident sense of gracefulness. But now, I (as reluctant humanitarian authority) will magnificently react in a *grand* fashion towards you: thwarting your (as new RH) felicitous treatment of me.

Table L-1 – The Lesser Virtues Based Upon Loyalty/Humility

RESPONSIBILITY	INNOCENCE
Previously, I (as personal authority) have guiltily acted in a submissive fashion, in response to the blameful treatment of the personal follower. But now, you (as new personal follower) will blamefully seek a sense of *responsibility* from me: in anticipation of my (as established PA) guilty treatment of you.	Previously, you (as new personal follower) have blamefully sought a sense of responsibility from me: in anticipation of my (as established PA) guilty treatment of you. But now, I (as reluctant personal authority) will *innocently* <u>deny</u> acting guiltily towards you: thwarting your (as new PF) blameful quest for responsibility.
DUTY	**VINDICATION**
Previously, I (as group authority) have honorably acted in a guilty fashion, in response to the just-blaming of the group representative. But now, you (as new group representative) will *dutifully* seek a sense of responsibility from me: in anticipation of my (as established GA) honorable sense of guilt.	Previously, you (as new group representative) have dutifully sought a sense of responsibility from me: in anticipation of my (as established GA) honorable sense of guilt. But now, I (as reluctant group authority) will innocently act in a *vindicated* fashion towards you: thwarting your (as new GR) dutiful quest for responsibility.
ALLEGIANCE	**EXONERATION**
Previously, I (as spiritual authority) have honorably acted in a libertarian fashion, in response to the blameful-hope for justice expressed by the spiritual disciple. But now, you (as new spiritual disciple) will dutifully act in an *allegiant* fashion towards me: in anticipation of my (as established SA) libertarian sense of honor.	Previously, you (as new spiritual disciple) have dutifully acted in an allegiant fashion towards me: in anticipation of my (as established SA) libertarian sense of honor. But now, I (as reluctant spiritual authority) will vindicatingly act in an *exonerated* fashion towards you: thwarting your (as new SD) dutiful sense of allegiance.
RIGHTEOUSNESS	**IMMACULATENESS**
Previously, I (as humanitarian authority) have freely-willed acted in a libertarian fashion, in response to the just-hope for the truth by the representative member of humanity. But now, you (as new representative member of humanity) will allegiantly act *righteously* towards me: in anticipation of my (as established HA) libertarian sense of free will	Previously, you (as new representative member of humanity) have allegiantly acted righteously towards me: in anticipation of my (as established HA) libertarian sense of free will. But now, I (as reluctant humanitarian authority) will exoneratingly act in an *immaculate* fashion towards you: thwarting your (as new RH) righteous treatment of me.

Table L-2 - The Lesser Virtues Based on Responsibility/Innocence

DISCIPLINE	MODESTY
Previously, you (as personal authority) have desirously acted in a solicitous fashion, in response to the approving treatment of the personal follower. But now, I (as new personal follower) will approvingly act in a *disciplined* fashion towards you: in anticipation of your (as established PA) desirous treatment of me.	Previously, I (as new personal follower) have approvingly acted in a disciplined fashion towards you: in anticipation of your (as established PA) desirous treatment of me. But now, you (as reluctant personal authority) will *modestly* <u>deny</u> acting desirously towards me: thwarting my (as new PF) disciplined treatment of you.
CHIVALRY	**CHASTITY**
Previously, you (as group authority) have dignifiedly acted in a desirous fashion, in response to the temperate-approval of the group representative. But now, I (as new group representative) will *chivalrously* act in a disciplined fashion towards you: in anticipation of your (as established GA) dignified-desire for me.	Previously, I (as new group representative) have chivalrously acted in a disciplined fashion towards you: in anticipation of your (as established GA) dignified-desire for me. But now, you (as reluctant group authority) will modestly act in a *chaste* fashion towards me: thwarting my (as new GR) chivalrous sense of discipline.
NOBILITY	**PURITY**
Previously, you (as spiritual authority) have civilly acted in a dignified fashion, in response to the temperate sense of charitableness of the spiritual disciple. But now, I (as new spiritual disciple) will chivalrously act in a *noble* fashion towards you: in anticipation of your (as established SA) civilly-dignified treatment of me.	Previously, I (as new spiritual disciple) have chivalrously acted in a noble fashion towards you: in anticipation of your (as established SA) civilly-dignified treatment of me. But now, you (as reluctant spiritual authority) will chastely act in a *pure* fashion towards me: thwarting my (as new SD) noble treatment of you.
ZEAL	**PERFECTION**
Previously, you (as humanitarian authority) have civilly acted magnanimously, in response to the charitable sense of goodness of the representative member of humanity. But now, I (as new representative member of humanity) will nobly act in a *zealous* fashion towards you: in anticipation of your (as established HA) magnanimous treatment of me.	Previously, I (as new representative member of humanity) have nobly acted in a zealous fashion towards you: in anticipation of your (as establ. HA) magnanimous treatment of me. But now, you (as reluctant humanitarian authority) will *perfectly* act in a pure fashion towards me: thwarting my (as new RH) noble sense of zeal.

Table L-3 – The Lesser Virtues Based on Discipline/Modesty

VIGILANCE	MEEKNESS
Previously, you (as personal authority) have worrisomely acted submissively, in response to the concerned treatment of the personal follower. But now, I (as new personal follower) will *vigilantly* act in a concerned fashion towards you: in anticipation of your (as established PA) worrisome treatment of me.	Previously, I (as new personal follower) have vigilantly acted in a concerned fashion towards you: in anticipation of your (as established PA) worrisome treatment of me. But now, you (as reluctant personal authority) will *meekly* <u>deny</u> acting in a worrisome fashion towards me: thwarting my (as new PF) vigilant treatment of you.
COURAGE	OBEDIENCE
Previously, you (as group authority) have worrisomely acted with integrity, in response to the fortitudinous sense of concern of the group representative. But now, I (as new group representative) will vigilantly act in a *courageous* fashion towards you: in anticipation of your (as established GA) worrisome sense of integrity.	Previously, I (as new group representative) have vigilantly acted in a courageous fashion towards you: in anticipation of your (as established GA) worrisome sense of integrity. But now, you (as reluctant group authority) will meekly act in an *obedient* fashion towards me: thwarting my (as new GR) vigilant sense of courage.
VALOR	CONFORMITY
Previously, you (as spiritual authority) have austerely acted with integrity, in response to the fortitudinous sense of decency of the spiritual disciple. But now, I (as new spiritual disciple) will courageously act in a *valiant* fashion towards you: in anticipation of your (as established SA) austere sense of integrity.	Previously, I (as new spiritual disciple) have courageously acted in a valiant fashion towards you: in anticipation of your (as established SA) austere sense of integrity. But now, you (as reluctant spiritual authority) will obediently act in a *conformist* fashion towards me: thwarting my (as new SD) valiant treatment of you.
TRIUMPH	PACIFISM
Previously, you (as humanitarian authority) have austerely acted with equanimity, in response to the decent sense of wisdom of the representative member of humanity. But now, I (as new representative member of humanity) will valiantly act *triumphantly* towards you: in anticipation of your (as established HA) austere sense of equanimity.	Previously, I (as new representative member of humanity) have valiantly acted in triumphantly towards you: in anticipation of your (as established HA) austere sense of equanimity. But now, you (as reluctant humanitarian authority) will conformingly act in a *pacifistic* fashion towards me: thwarting my (as new RH) triumphant treatment of you.

Table L- 4 – The Lesser Virtues Based on Vigilance/Meekness

counterparts for the four main options. In terms of the preceding examples, 210.4 = the accessory acceptance of the nostalgia maneuver, 210.5 = accessory humility, 220.6 = the accessory symmetrical-loyalty maneuver, and 220.7 = the accessory change the subject (from loyalty).

With the first eight decimal places now formally accounted for, it only remains to specify the final two digits; namely, the remaining decimal places eight and nine. Ordinarily, these final two digits are reserved for formally specifying the main/accessory general unifying themes. In the case of the counter double bind maneuvers, however, this modification is achieved by simply adding an extra decimal place to the themes initially specified for the double bind maneuvers. Consequently, these final two decimal places are now free to alternately be assigned to one further range of response options; namely, to ignore the communication (or leave the scene altogether). As related versions of a common theme, this pair of options into combined into a single three-digit code. Here, 220.8 represents the main version of the ignore/leave-the-scene option, whereas 220.9 denotes the accessory variation (namely, how one views such an evasive maneuver from an outside perspective). Although these final two options are not technically regarded as transitional power maneuvers, per se, they, nevertheless, appear to be deliberately conscious behaviors (or an absence, therein). Consequently, they represent nonverbal behaviors of a style well suited for coding within the system, wherein rounding-out the master format of four-digit codes.

In summary, through the simple addition of one extra decimal place, the complete range of potential responses to the preliminary class of double bind maneuvers is adequately achieved for most general coding purposes. Indeed, this basic modification applies equally well to each of the remaining transitional categories; namely, mental illness, criminality, and hypercriminality. This circumstance, however, it is by no means the only potential application for an extra decimal place. For the time being, however, the appointed task for the remainder of the current section concerns the systematic examination of each of the three/four-digit codes relating to the overall realm of the lesser virtues.

Most of these code-variations are fairly obvious in terms of phraseology; such as (for example) symmetrical loyalty, nostalgic-acceptance, along with options to change the subject, leave the scene, etc. As each of these represent fairly obvious modifications in terms of function, an exhaustive listing of these formal options (and respective code numbers) will not be undertaken at this juncture. Rather, the serious reader is encouraged to memorize the fairly simple ten-part pattern outlined on the preceding page, then applying where appropriate.

The one exception to this rule concerns the meta-complementary power maneuvers, which represent a unique version of the counter double bind maneuvers. This is particularly evident in the distinctive interplay of loyalty/humility, responsibility/innocence, discipline/modesty, etc. The interconnected status of this latter class of counter double bind maneuvers rates a more comprehensive degree of treatment, comparable to that previously established for the double bind class of maneuvers. This formal interplay of double bind/counter double bind maneuvers results in a quite manageable complement of *64* individual terms. Consequently, the following four chapters of this section are devoted exclusively to outlining this dual interplay of the overall class of lesser virtues.

THE SCHEMATIC DEFINITIONS FOR THE LESSER VIRTUES

Before embarking on this somewhat technical style of analysis, one final issue must necessarily be addressed; namely, the lesser virtues, in turn, are amenable to incorporation within the formal schematic definition format. The schematic definitions for the lesser virtues (I), accordingly, are outlined in the four-part series of **Tables L-1** to **L-4**. The definitions for the lesser virtues (II) are alternately depicted in **Tables M-1** to **M-4** (deferred until Chapter *24*). Although superficially similar in appearance, this transitional definition format differs in a number of key features from the pattern previously established for the major categories of definitions described in **Parts I** through **IV**. Although the transitional definitions are also represented in a tabular format, a number of key factors depart from the standard pattern of organization.

The most prominent of these issues stems from the observation that the preliminary personal follower perspectives of loyalty-responsibility-discipline-vigilance, in turn, anticipates the collaboration of the established authority figure. Both loyalty and responsibility are defined as transitional variations on the more basic alter ego states of hero worship and blame: representing reinforcement from the personal follower perspective. Furthermore, discipline and vigilance represent transitions into the future-directed sphere of reinforcement; namely, the approval and concern perspectives expressed by the follower figure.

This "congeniality" style of follower perspective, in turn, prompts the counter double bind proper of the personal authority figure. Humility and innocence represent disqualified variations of the nostalgia/guilt perspectives. Furthermore, modesty and meekness denote similar modifications of desire/worry. The same pattern further extends to the remaining group, spiritual, and humanitarian levels within the ascending power hierarchy. The crowning transcendental level, however, is deliberately left out of this definition format due to the implausibility of transitioning into such a supremely abstract level. This shortfall, however, does not necessarily imply that the transcendental domain is technically ruled-out in upcoming future versions of the schematic definition format.

A further distinguishing feature of the transitional definition format concerns the crucial observation that the personal, group, spiritual, and humanitarian levels represent independent sequences within this tabular style of format. This directly contrasts with the more integrated pattern of organization previously established for the more basic groupings of definitions. The transitional maneuvers represent entirely new entries within the ascending power hierarchy, as reflected in the sample schematic definition for loyalty.

For illustrative purposes, the first part of the *loyalty* definition represents the basic generic template for the "hero worship" perspective. These preliminary prerequisites, in turn, set the stage for the loyalty maneuver proper (depicted in the second half of the definition). Although the initial segment deliberately targets the virtuous realm (for consistency's sake), it could just as easily have reflected transitions from the zone of neutrality, or any of the three remaining classes of the vices. Each of these separate options (by definition) shares the distinct potential for transitioning into the virtuous realm (as well as further transitioning into one another).

This initial congeniality phase further insures that no direct connection exists between the adjacent authority levels within the definition format. For instance, the initial loyalty maneuver formally transitions into an entirely new context. This, in turn, sets the stage for the personal authority's *humility* form of counter double bind maneuver. This countermaneuver (by definition) is defined as a "dead end" of sorts insofar as further options are concerned. This latter option technically shuts-off any further response with respect to this particular segment of the transitional hierarchy.

Consequently, a strict sense of independence (for each authority level) is specified for both the initiation and termination of the two-stage transitional sequence. Accordingly, the four individual authority levels represented within the schematic definition format represent fully independent sequences. Indeed, they are united within the table only in terms of their immediate proximity within the general transitional hierarchy. This stacked pattern of organization proves particularly crucial for outlining the communicational factors underlying the general realm of the lesser virtues. The discerning reader, accordingly, is encouraged to refer back to this four-part listing of schematic definitions throughout the course of the upcoming chapters, wherein formally outlined the transitional dynamics at issue for each of the individual lesser virtues.

In conclusion, the completed description of the class of transitional power maneuvers opens an entirely new era in the understanding of human communication in general. This new class of affective communication is termed *transitional* in that it transitions an individual (new to the scene) into a pre-established social relationship. Our modern fast-paced society comprising ever shifting social coalitions necessitates this additional pattern of transitional communication (now more than ever). For the more routine world of business and commerce, this invokes the more lighthearted realm of humor and comedy indicative of the more positive aspects of the double bind and counter double bind maneuvers. For the initial double bind tactic, the new individual petitions entry into an established social context. The established party, in turn, retains the option of accepting such an overture, or politely declining through a humorous style of counter double bind maneuvers. Indeed, society is maintained chiefly through an enduring foundation within polite social discourse, serving to defuse outward conflicts through this disqualified sphere of skilled social interaction.

It should further be emphasized that this transitional class of power maneuvers is primarily based upon the instinctual principles of behavioral psychology, in direct analogy to the main power maneuvers they initially served to imitate. In truth, the transitional power maneuvers formally represent direct avenues of transition into the more routine classes of virtues and values ultimately aimed for. Subsequent acceptance by the established party effectively cements entry into such a pre-existing context, whereas the counter double bind strategy politely deflects or defers such an overture. A blunt or discourteous "thanks but no thanks" is also an option, but this total lack of diplomacy can often backfire at a later date. Indeed, this latter more conflicting option is generally more appropriate to the related transitional variation of *criminality*, where new relationships are established in a negative zero-sum arrangement based upon the vices of defect, an aspect often thrust upon an unsuspecting neutral third party.

Undoubtedly, all of us at some time has been the victim of such criminal intentions, fully understanding the helpless feelings that this entails. In terms of this criminal context, a blunt expression of no-confidence proves to be the wisest response. The counter double bind maneuver scarcely enters in at this level, being that the criminal usually aims to speedily exit the scene, although this darker realm of humor often proves of great public fascination in terms of true crime dramas. The extremely troubling issue of hypercriminality rightfully enters into consideration here, representing excessive transitional variations with respect to the disturbing extremes associated with hyperviolence.

It should strictly be emphasized that both criminality and hypercriminality are formally based entirely within the darker behavioral realm of *punishment*, the dynamics of which are originally described by B. F. Skinner. This darker domain of transitional interchange essentially amounts to a zero-sum game, in contrast to the positive-sum game characterizing the cooperative prerequisites of the virtues and values. Some degree of criminal activity has always plagued society as a whole, where susceptible individuals selfishly seek to circumvent the dedication dictated by cooperative human endeavors. The disturbing ascendancy of hypercriminality, however, is yet another matter, particularly with respect to organized street gangs that scarcely respect even the sanctity of life. Here, extreme viciousness is seen as an avenue towards reaching the upper criminal echelon, to the tragic detriment of the vulnerable public at large. It is hoped that an increased understanding of the communicational dynamics for the entire class of transitional power maneuvers will provide a greater incentive towards reforming such criminal tendencies across society as a whole, perhaps even extending to a political and international sphere of influence.

This distinctive transitional dynamic is even capable of explaining the communicational factors underlying the mental disorders, providing invaluable insights for clinicians and therapists endeavoring to make a difference in this regard. It should further be emphasized that mental illness is clearly distinguished from criminality and hypercriminality, representing transitional variations with respect to the more innocuous realm of the vices of excess, unlike the darker realm of defect characterizing the latter two categories. Through this enhanced understanding of all such transitional categories, a new era in peaceful cooperation across all cultures may finally be within reach, or at very least a definite improvement upon the chaotic state of affairs affecting modern society today. The remaining three sections aim to outline precisely such a grand scale innovation, with great potential advantages for global culture as a whole.

22

THE PAST-DIRECTED REALM OF THE LESSER VIRTUES (I)

The stepwise discussion of the lesser virtues (I) is currently launched with respect to an in-depth examination of the respective past-directed dimensions; namely, the sequence based upon loyalty/humility, followed by that targeting responsibility/innocence. The current chapter endeavors to outline the ascending hierarchy of authority/follower roles spanning the personal, group, spiritual, and humanitarian levels, respectively. Consequently, the pattern of presentation with respect to the lesser virtues is slightly different for that which has gone before. The four-part hierarchy of follower terms is described first, followed by the respective sequence of authority roles. In this dual fashion, the ascending pattern of power escalation is convincingly documented for both the authority and follower roles, greatly simplifying the overall strategy for explanation. The preliminary double bind sequence of loyalty-fidelity-piety-felicity is described first, followed, in turn, by the respective counter double bind sequence of humility-majesty-magnificence-grandeur. Furthermore, the second half of this chapter examines the related sequence of responsibility-duty-allegiance-righteousness, and also innocence-vindication-exoneration-immaculateness. The discerning reader is encouraged to refer back to the four-page listing of schematic definitions for the lesser virtues (I) outlined in Chapter *21*, providing a formal schematic representation of the dynamics at issue in concert with the traditions for each of the individual terms.

220 – LOYALTY

The first listed theme of *loyalty* is formally defined as the respective transitional counterpart of hero worship. Its modern spelling derives from the

French *loyauté*, from the French-Latin *legalis* (legal). Although this derivation might initially be suggestive of a civic context, the personal follower (by definition) loyally appeals to the established authority figure with all due deference to his authority status; hence, enhancing the prospects of gaining acceptance. The feudal overtones generally associated with loyalty are similarly indicative of the personal bonds linking the accessible ruler and his faithful subjects. As legal power over the entire realm, every subject was personally beholden to the supreme royal personage.

According to the Old English legend of *King Arthur and the Roundtable*, the knights of the realm pledged unswerving loyalty and fealty to the king (in light of his duties to his subjects). Loyalty, accordingly, is defined as unfailing service or devotion to a worthy person or cause. In this latter respect, the personal follower reinforcingly acts to attract the attention of his personal authority figure, wherein attempting to be distinguished from other follower figures. Herein lies the chief salient characteristic of loyalty as opposed to the other virtues within its class; namely, subordinating one's immediate self-interests to the power embodied in the personal authority figure, with the potential for an ongoing relationship once the preliminary groundwork is set into place.

240 – FIDELITY

The personal foundations for loyalty, in turn, extend to a group sphere of influence with respect to *fidelity*. The group representative loyally reinforces the glorious sense of nostalgia expressed by the group authority figure. Consequently, fidelity is traditionally defined as the inclination to fulfil one's promises in conformity to pre-existing promissory commitments. The term derives from the Latin *fidelitas*, from *fidelis* (faithful), from *fidere* (to trust in). In this classical context, it introduces the concepts of faithful performance to duty or obligation. The Romans divinely worshipped this abstract quality as Fides, their goddess of oaths and vows. As previously described in the section dealing with "faith," Fides is traditionally depicted as a matron in a long white veil and flowing gown, her right hand raised solemnly as if taking a vow.

This theme of fidelity further extends to activities associated with the transmission of information, such as reporting a newsworthy event or reproducing a manuscript. This was particularly critical during the Middle Ages, when sacred manuscripts were painstakingly reproduced by hand. Indeed, for copies of the Bible, even a single error on a page was grounds for its unquestioned destruction.

In our modern media age, this term is most frequently associated with the notion of "high fidelity," a technical innovation in sound reproduction. Unlike the simple phonograph, the "hi-fi" system precisely ensures that sound reproduction at the output stage faithfully corresponds to the signal received at the input stage. This aspiration to universal standards of reproduction effectively mirrors its respective moral counterparts, where the group representative loyally endeavors to secure the cooperation of his group authority figure through a fidelity style of power maneuver. In direct analogy to its primary foundation within loyalty, the fidelity maneuver effectively plays up the glorious sense of nostalgia expressed by the group authority figure. Through this transitional power perspective, the group representative formally gains consideration within a civic sphere of influence, wherein formally validating the group overtones traditionally associated with fidelity.

260 – PIETY

The ascending hierarchy of follower roles, in turn, extends to a universal sphere of influence with respect to the spiritual disciple theme of *piety*. In direct analogy to the subordinate sequence of loyalty/fidelity, piety effectively targets a universal sphere of influence, as suggested in the pious attributes associated with the term. Accordingly, this term dates at least to classical times, as evident in the Latin *pius* (of similar meaning and usage). It denotes a sense of devotion or duty to one's obligations, primarily in a religious context. Piety is symbolized as a stylized cross, a flaming

heart, a burning lamp, amongst other imagery. Indeed, piety was initially celebrated as one of most ancient obligations of the ancient world, listed in the pre-Platonic tradition of a fifth entry within the listing of the cardinal virtues. Consequently, piety in terms of religious observance was considered a crucial factor for maintaining the favor and blessings of the gods.

The Romans specifically worshiped this quality in terms of the abstract goddess Pietas. In 91 BCE, at the Battle of Thermopylae, the Consul M. Acilius Glabrio vowed to dedicate a temple to Pietas. Two years later, his son (by the same name) carried-out his vow, erecting a temple to Pietas in the Forum Holitorium in Rome. A later temple dedicated to Pietas was situated near to the Circus Flaminius. On various coins of the empire, Pietas is inscribed accompanied by a stylized stork (a classical symbol of trustworthiness). Throughout the course of the empire, the prestige of Pietas was invoked to exalt the ideal of harmony amongst members of the ruling class.

With the dawning of the Christian era, this sense of devotion extended to a sense of piety for the foundations of the Christian faith. Indeed, with the dawning of the Protestant Reformation, Pietism became a spiritual movement in its own right: wherein emphasizing rigorous morality and a personal sense of piety. The movement flourished within the context of German Lutheranism, emphasizing small devotional gatherings that catered to personal devotion, in contrast to the intellectualism focus of more orthodox forms of Protestantism. This trend towards devotional piety represents a spiritual form of double bind maneuver in relation to the spiritual authority figure. Here, the faithful precepts of the spiritual disciple figure are exalted in a devotional sense. Consequently, the spiritual disciple loyally acts in a pious fashion in anticipation of the providential treatment expressed by the spiritual authority figure. The due deference implicit in the piety maneuver proves particularly crucial towards achieving the desired result.

280 – FELICITY

The final theme within the ascending hierarchy of terms, *felicity*, extends the spiritual disciple's pious sense of devotion into an even more enduring humanitarian sphere of influence. It is traditionally defined as joy, pleasure, or delight in relation to a happy event. The term derives from the Latin *felicatis*, from *felix* (happy). As with so many of their other abstract qualities, the ancient Romans worshipped this emotional aspect as

The Humility of Christ – A Scene Described During the Last Supper
Christ *Humbly* Washes the Feet of the Twelve Apostles – Detail from a Stained Glass Devotional

Felicitas, the goddess of divine good fortune. She is often associated with Fortuna (goddess of fortune) and Copia (goddess of plenty). The worship of Felicitas dates to 146 BCE when a temple dedicated to her in Rome was erected by L. Licinius Lucullus. Although a fairly minor goddess at the time, her popularity greatly expanded through a campaign of devotion by a later sequence of Roman generals: in particular, Sulla, Pompey, and Julius Caesar. Indeed, Caesar specifically lent his influence to the construction of a second temple to Felicitas on the site of the old Roman Senate House. During the ensuing Imperial age, the cult of Felicitas endured as a particular favorite of the Emperor Augustus, as well as many of his predecessors.

These pagan overtones underwent a thorough modification during the Christian era, with felicity now viewed as a divine attribute of the Christian Deity. Medieval theologians incorporated felicity within their comprehensive system of scholastic virtues, a particular comfort to those dedicated to a virtuous lifestyle. Indeed, felicity formally expands upon the subordinate concept of piety, certainly a key factor in the lives of many of the great saints/martyrs true to its enduring humanitarian significance. Samuel Johnson succinctly wrote: "Our *felicity* we make or find with secret course, which no loud storms annoy, glides the smooth current of our domestic joy."

The clear humanitarian overtones for felicity formally aspire to the provident sense of gracefulness expressed by the established authority figure. In terms of this extreme level of abstraction, the formal dynamics for the felicity maneuver scarcely proves as clear as those established for its subordinate sequence of terms. Felicity certainly preserves the basic character of the overall sequence of terms; namely, loyalty-fidelity-piety (and now felicity).

210.1 – HUMILITY

A parallel sequence of terms, in turn, remains in order for the remaining class of counter double bind maneuvers: in this case, humility-majesty-magnificence-grandeur. The first mentioned theme of *humility* represents the counter double bind reaction to the initial "loyalty" maneuver of the personal follower figure. The term derives from the Latin *humulis* (low, humble), from *humus* (earth): denoting a modest or humble perspective. Rather than unwittingly submitting to the dictates of the personal follower (e.g., nostalgically acting solicitously), the *humble* individual now projects a more modest persona: wherein disqualifying the preliminary dictates of the loyalty maneuver. The fact that humility is classified as a virtue (albeit a lesser one) clearly attests to this inherent sense of disqualification within a personal sphere of influence.

According to the NT Sermon on the Mount, the First Beatitude preached by Christ specifically singles out humility; namely, "Blessed are the poor in spirit, for theirs is the kingdom of heaven." Although clearly deserving, Christ downplayed any tendency towards self-magnification in favor of a sense of humility/meekness of purpose. Indeed, the unswerving sense of loyalty expressed by the Twelve Apostles certainly proved instrumental in prompting Christ's humble demeanor, as exemplified in the formal foot-washing ceremony described during the Last Supper (John 13:5). This enduring sense of humility remained a prominent theme for many of the Twelve Disciples. Indeed, the Apostle Peter requested to be crucified upside-down in a final act of humility save that he would die in a manner similar to the Lord. A similar interpretation invokes the medieval tradition of "humble pie," the modest entrée of the woodsman baked from the entrails of the game slated for the lord's table.

230.1 – MAJESTY

The personal dynamics for humility, in turn, extend to a civic sphere of influence with respect to the group authority theme of *majesty*. The group follower's "fidelity" maneuver further prompts a majestic denial of worthiness by the group authority figure. Although scarcely a commonly employed term, the origins of majesty date to the Age of Chivalry, when the royal monarch wielded supreme authority throughout the land. This theme of majesty denotes an unparalleled sense of dignity or stateliness with respect to speech or deportment, sometimes employed as a title of distinction. Its modern spelling derives from the Latin *majestas*, from *magnus* (great). The regal overtones typically associated with the term are particularly conspicuous in the field of medieval heraldry, where the expression "In His Majesty" describes a crowned eagle holding a scepter (in the convention of the medieval coat of arms): both symbolisms of nobility/distinction.

Majesty clearly warrants its civic or political prerequisites, as evident in many scriptural passages of a patriarchal nature. For instance, the NT Book of Hebrews (8:1) describes the regal dominion of the Lord as high priest seated at the right hand of the throne of the *majesty*. Indeed, the term is so invested with regal themes that it is often employed as the title of distinction. The address "Your Majesty" is a courtesy directed to reigning sovereigns (and their consorts) in recognition of their stateliness and grandeur.

The truest appeal of the theme, however, resides in its virtually effortless quality, as indicative of its inherent sense of disqualification in terms. Majesty formally disqualifies any overt sense

of deliberation or planning by the group authority figure, formally expanding upon the humility maneuver previously established for the personal realm. Consequently, the fidelity maneuver initiated by the group representative, in turn, prompts (in a disqualified fashion) the majesty expressed by the group authority figure. In this subliminally disqualified sense, the reluctant group authority politely acknowledges the initial fidelity maneuver without overtly appearing to have done so, and without loss of dignity or majesty, therein.

250.1 – MAGNIFICENCE

The majestic prerequisites for the group authority perspective, in turn, extend to a universal sphere of influence with respect to the related theme of *magnificence*. Grand works of architecture are dedicated in celebration of such a noble agenda, a selfless endeavor consistent with such a spiritual authority perspective. The term derives from the Latin *magnus* (great) and *facere* (to make): a compound derivation suggesting nobility in word or deed, often bordering upon the extravagant. This traditional focus upon grandeur is particularly evident in many of its related attributes: as in gemstones, orchids, or the peacock. These showy attributes are fittingly affiliated with royalty. The expression "Your Magnificence" is frequently employed as a title of distinction for kings and other dignitaries in a manner reminiscent of its subordinate theme of majesty.

Its classification as a virtue dates at least to classical times, defined by Aristotle as the proper expenditure of money on grand works and deeds, as in the honorable application of riches. Furthermore, according to Aristotle, magnificence represents the virtuous mean-value interposed between the defect state of avarice and the excess state of prodigality. This Aristotelian interpretation underwent a significant revival during the Middle Ages, wherein celebrated as liberality in the expenditure of great wealth. The magnificent individual seeks noble endeavors for patronage, as in architectural projects of taste and elegance consistent with the majesty intended. Magnificence is particularly apparent in humanitarian endeavors invested with spiritual overtones: as in grand religious architecture, memorials, endowments, philanthropic works, etc.

The most dramatic feature of magnificence, however, concerns the effortlessness with which it is expressed similar to the case previously established for majesty. Here the renowned public figure endeavors to give back a measure of his exalted status, although without overtly appearing to have done so: in keeping with the subordinate sequence of humility/majesty. The truly grand scale of the works, however, clearly argues for a general (universal) sense of the term: a noble effort of enduring significance to all of mankind. Indeed, many a great world leader has felt obliged to undertake such grand philanthropic endeavors in relation to the global community, a noble aspiration that still reigns supreme today.

270.1 – GRANDEUR

The final theme within the ascending sequence of counter double bind maneuvers, *grandeur*, represents a humanitarian extension on the subordinate sequence of terms: a supreme expression of the disqualified authority perspective. This theme denotes a greatness of power or authority, as in a sense of splendor or stateliness that inspires awe: deriving from the Latin *grandis* (great). The Roman civilization was particularly masterful in the art of pomp and spectacle, the spoils of conquest transforming Rome into the show-capital of the classical world. Its grand coliseums, arenas, and public temples offered many affordable diversions to the general citizenry. Entertaining sporting events featuring gladiators, animal acts, and cavalcades ensured the faith and loyalty of many Roman citizens. This overriding sense of grandeur also figured prominently in the religious realm, inspiring a sense of awe/devotion for the pantheon of Roman gods and goddesses.

It was primarily through the grandeur of its material trappings that the Roman Empire perpetuated its enduring span of imperial power, wherein invoking its self-appointed status as humanitarian authority for the entire Mediterranean world. The grandeur that was Rome certainly saw no equal until the wonders of our modern technological age, at least in the Western tradition. This focus on grandeur still figures prominently in many modern symbolisms: such as the grandeur of nature, the Grand Old Flag, etc. Grandeur formally expands (in a humanitarian sense) upon the subordinate concepts of majesty and magnificence, wherein sharing the ingrained verbal disqualification of the latter. Grandeur appears almost effortless in form and function (as in the majesty of nature); as opposed to any overt motivations therein. This subliminal sense of disqualification can even reach the level of fault, as in "delusions of grandeur" or "grandiose schemes." In general, however, this theme is viewed in a virtuous light, where medieval theologians list it among the major classifications of virtues; hence, consistent with its current status as a lesser virtue.

221 – RESPONSIBILITY

A similar style of analysis further remains in order for the remaining sequence of terms based upon responsibility/innocence. The first mentioned theme of responsibility is defined as a transitional variation on the "blame" maneuver of the personal follower figure. Responsibility prompts a submissive admission of guilt from the personal authority figure similar to the interplay initially established for loyalty/nostalgia. The term derives from the Latin *respondére*, from *re-* (back) and *spondére* (to promise or pledge). It denotes a sense of accountability or culpability within a personal sphere of influence. The personal follower formally transitions into an active blame perspective, although in due deference to the established status of the personal authority figure. The responsibility-seeker, accordingly, enhances his odds of gaining cooperation from the established authority figure in terms of the latter's submissive admission of guilt. Although the responsibility-seeker can wield a considerable degree of influence, the personal authority can alternately resort to a disqualified form of counter double bind maneuver; namely, an outright assertion of innocence outlined later in this section. In either case, the initial responsibility maneuver serves its primary purpose of gaining the attention of the established authority figure, although not always with the anticipated results.

241 – DUTY

The personal dynamics for responsibility, in turn, extend to a group sphere of influence with respect to the related theme of *duty*. The group representative dutifully seeks a sense of responsibility from the established authority figure, a transitional variation on the blameful quest for justice. Duty denotes that which is bound through the terms of obligation: deriving from the Anglo-French *duete*, from Old French *deu*, past participle of *devoire*, from the Latin *debere* (to owe). This principle of indebtedness is particularly consistent with the sense of obligation typically encountered in duty. Indeed, this concept has remained a constant fixture in ethical philosophy, at least since classical times.

In its broadest sense, duty subordinates one's self-seeking inclinations to some overriding authoritarian standard. According to classical ethics, morality was presented as a standard to be achieved, as in a dutiful ideal to be realized. Indeed, duty is a virtue intimately related to integrity, a moral obligation assumed when specifying a set of responsibilities to be fulfilled in terms of a contract. This contract may be formal or informal, implicit or explicit, or individually generated on an "honor" basis. Moral duty ideally meets these conditions of good faith and due diligence without shifting responsibility or blame onto others. Furthermore, an expectation of commensurate benefits is invoked for fulfilling such conditions in a fully informed and transparent fashion.

Typically, duty is imposed through legal sanctions enforced by the state. Consequently, one's moral obligation to obey the law of the land formally entails the duty of remaining a good citizen. New parents are duty-bound to meet their offspring's survival/nurture needs at least until the age of independence. School discipline entails the duty to obey basic rules of order so that the process of education can proceed effectively. Indeed, a clear sense of duty helps to develop social responsibility and individual effectiveness. As highly social creatures, social progress is primarily achieved through such concerted collaborative efforts. This progress occurs most effectively in terms of shared purpose and mutual trust in relation to meeting individual social obligations. Civility and overall quality of life should improve when motivated by duty towards the common good.

261 – ALLEGIANCE

The ascending sequence of responsibility/duty, in turn, extends to a universal sphere of influence with respect to the related theme of *allegiance*. The newly initiated spiritual disciple dutifully seeks a sense of allegiance from his established spiritual authority figure consistent with the latter's universal power status. Its medieval connotations denote the duty of the vassal towards his feudal lord/sovereign. The term derives from the Latin *ad-* (to) and *ligere* (bind), symbolizing the reciprocal feudal interaction. This theme of allegiance clearly invokes a formal feudal context, where the vassal kneels before his liege (lord) in a submissive plea for consideration similar to the case previously established for duty. This formal enactment of allegiance represents a transitional variation on the blameful "hope" for justice expressed by the spiritual disciple figure.

In our modern age, this transitional class of maneuver is most readily apparent in terms of the Pledge of Allegiance of the United States. The Pledge initially enjoyed quite humble beginnings, first published in 1892 in celebration of the centenary anniversary of Columbus Day. It originally read: "I pledge allegiance to my flag and the Republic for which it stands; one nation indivisible, with liberty and justice for all." The highly personal nature of the pledge was subtly modified in 1924 when the words "my flag" were replaced with "the flag of the United States of America." In 1942, the Pledge was officially adopted as a national standard, although further modifications were in order. At President Eisenhower's urging in 1954, Congress legislated the addition of the phrase "under God," resulting in the Pledge's current format. This curious spiritual modification, indeed, proves relevant considering the deep universal overtones attributed to allegiance. According to the legislation of 1954, the Pledge is most properly taken standing at attention with one's hand placed over the heart during the recitation. This latter aspect directly stresses a wholehearted submission of purpose through one's pledge of duty and allegiance to such a higher sphere of authority. By custom, headgear is also removed, further accentuating the solemn nature of the pledge in a transitional analogy to "hope."

Through this dutiful sense of allegiance, the spiritual disciple submissively anticipates the libertarian dictates of the established authority figure, an interplay of themes only truly comprehensible in terms of the subordinate concepts of responsibility/duty. Although the federal government does not technically favor one religion over another, it certainly values the principles of Divine Providence consistent with a common Protestant heritage. Consequently, the Pledge truly represents the ideals of our forefathers as enduring affirmations of our universal obligations as citizens of the United States. As Franklin Roosevelt insightfully wrote, "It is a pledge to maintain the four great freedoms cherished by all Americans: freedom of speech, freedom of religion, freedom from want, and freedom from fear."

281 – RIGHTEOUSNESS

The ascending sequence of transitional themes ultimately culminates in terms of the supremely abstract theme of *righteousness*, formally framed in terms of an enduring humanitarian perspective. Righteousness represents the transitional counterpart of the more basic theme of "truth," wherein anticipating the libertarian sense of free will expressed by the established authority figure. The term traces its origins to the Old English *rihtwis*, from *riht* (right) and *wis* (wise): denoting a morally upright or sage demeanor. The Latin tradition recognized a similar set of concepts: with truth worshipped as the goddess, Veritas, whereas righteousness merited devotion as the Roman divinity Fas, the god of righteousness. The latter divinity personified conduct rightfully ordained by divine law, governed by what is morally right or fitting, as opposed to civil law (which dealt more with the customs of society). For the classical world, the chief god Zeus was championed as the protector of righteous causes, often resorting to bolts of lightning to remedy grievous injustice.

A similar interpretation permeates the Judeo-Christian scriptural tradition. The Lord of the Old Testament typically imposed an almost anthropomorphic sense of righteousness, severely punishing all that dared to scorn His Commandments. The righteous individual piously conformed to the law in terms of religious devotion, alms giving, prayer, and fasting: as evident in the descriptions of the great prophets of the Old Testament. Indeed, this general sense of justice effectively permeates the most basic principles of righteousness: taking its cue from the OT Book of Judges that righteously commanded the letter of the law. The Judges were rightfully extolled as "men of truth," fearing God and abhorring unjust gains. According to Deuteronomy (25:1) "If there is a controversy between men and they come into judgment that the Judges may judge them, then they shall justify the *righteous* and condemn the wicked."

This moral sense of righteousness further extends to New Testament scripture, particularly in terms of Christ's Fourth Beatitude that states: "Blessed are they that hunger and thirst after *righteousness*, for they shall be filled." Furthermore, in his Eighth Beatitude, Christ also states: "Blessed are they that are persecuted for *righteousness* sake, for theirs is the kingdom of heaven." Such noble aspirations clearly appear distinct from the more fanatical righteousness promoted by radical groups as the Pharisees. Accordingly, in 2 Corinthians 6:7, St. Paul rejoices in the goal of salvation through the word of truth, the power of God, and the armor of *righteousness*: suggesting again how truth relates to righteousness in such a reciprocal transitional sense.

211.1 – INNOCENCE

The remaining sequence of terms for the counter double bind class of maneuvers is respectively designated as innocence-vindication-exoneration-immaculateness. The first-mentioned theme of innocence derives from the Latin *innocens*, from *in-* (not) and *nocére* (to do wrong to). This disqualified sense of guilt figures prominently in many religious symbolisms; namely, the lily, the dove, or a maiden draped in white. According to his Sermon on the Mount, innocence is clearly implied in Christ's Sixth Beatitude: "Blessed are the pure in heart: for they shall see God." Christ further celebrates the innocence of the "little children," for such is the Kingdom of Heaven. Indeed, the sacrificial lamb is the chief Christian emblem of innocence, offered-up in atonement for the sins of all mankind.

Although these youthful connotations rate considerable influence, innocence usually refers to a defense against a blameful quest for responsibility, redefining the relationship from a thoroughly disqualified perspective. The innocence maneuver of the established personal authority figure effectively counteracts any blameful quest for responsibility from the personal follower, similar to the interplay previously established for loyalty/humility. In this disqualified sense, the reluctant personal authority denies being liable concerning any blameful quest for responsibility: formally acknowledging the follower's transitional style of tactic while subconsciously disqualifying any willing participation therein.

231.1 – VINDICATION

The personal prerequisites for innocence, in turn, extend to a group sphere of influence with respect to the related theme of *vindication*. In a traditional sense, vindication is defined as the process of defending oneself against blame/charges levied by another, as in vindication before a panel of one's peers during a jury trial. The term derives from the Latin *vindicare*, from *vis-* (force) and *discere* (to say). True to its classical roots, vindication is essentially a verbal perspective, where facts are presented in order to establish guilt or innocence, as in a court room defense.

Vindication, however, should not be confused with vindictiveness: a theme initially examined in the context of the vices of defect. Although vindictiveness similarly derives from the Latin *vindicare*, it alternately suggests more of a darker focus, as in a spirit of revenge or retribution. Although revenge might similarly emerge as a motivation in vindication, the distinction between vindication and vindictiveness appears analogous to that distinguishing justice and vengeance. A plea for vindication predominates in a courtroom justice setting, whereas the crueler tendency towards vindictiveness generally circumvents the safeguards of the justice system. Consequently, the stirring court room assertion: "I will be vindicated," is clearly indicative of the virtuous mode;

in essence, a disqualified form of counter double bind maneuver targeting the honorable sense of guilt expressed by the group authority figure (similar to the case previously established for innocence). The group overtones generally associated with vindication enjoy widespread civic appeal, particularly when vindication is pursued in public view for all the world to see.

251.1 – EXONERATION

The preliminary sequence of innocence/vindication, in turn, extends to a universal sphere of influence with respect to the related authority theme of *exoneration*. Exoneration is defined as freedom from burden or blame, as in a declaration of proof of innocence, such as an acquittal. The term derives from the Latin *exonerare*, from *ex-* (from) and *oneris* (burden). The stain of guilt is lifted, particularly when the burden of proof lies with the accuser. This notion of exoneration is widely employed in a legal sense, as in designating a remedy within the field of financial equity. It is also prominently invoked in criminal cases, whereby extending the more limited sense of vindication into a universal sphere of influence.

Whereas vindication implies a general sense of clemency, exoneration alternately suggests a blanket sense of pardon, or even absolution. Consequently, exoneration generally sets a precedent within an international sphere of influence, effectively disqualifying any libertarian sense of honor, therein. Although exoneration scarcely enjoys the pedigree or tradition of other virtues within its class, it nevertheless fits quite adequately within the ascending sequence of innocence/vindication. In this expanded sense, the vindicated sense of exoneration expressed by the spiritual authority figure directly counters the dutiful sense of allegiance professed by the spiritual disciple: a reciprocal interplay of terms, although in a subliminally disqualified sense.

271.1 – IMMACULATENESS

The crowning humanitarian authority level further calls into focus the supremely abstract theme of *immaculateness*. It is traditionally defined as a thoroughly disqualified denial of any degree of fault or blame, a recurring theme in claims relating to divinity. This enduring humanitarian perspective effectively complements the more positive prerequisites previously established for "grandeur." Although this notion of immaculateness is fairly specialized in a religious sense, it nevertheless emerges as the leading contender for completing the ascending sequence of innocence, vindication, and exoneration. It traditionally denotes a sense of purity or spotlessness, primarily with respect to the evil effects of sin. The term derives from the Latin *immaculatus*, from *in-* (not) and *macula* (spot). It is chiefly encountered in the Roman Catholic dogma of the Immaculate Conception, where the Virgin Mary is believed to have been conceived without the stain of Original Sin in preparation for the birth of the Christ Child.

Although no specific documentation for this belief exists in scriptural sources, Mary's sanctity and virginity was accepted as an essential corollary with respect to the Divinity of Christ. This theological assertion remained unchallenged until the Age of Reformation when Catholic doctrines were subject to increasing scrutiny. In 1567, Pope Pius V rigorously defended Mary's immunity from sin at the moment of conception, accompanied by the establishment of the Feast of the Immaculate Conception. Protestant reformers, in contrast, steadfastly rejected this dogma due to the manifest lack of any specific scriptural foundations.

Regardless of the individual traditions therein, the enduring theme of immaculateness effectively completes the ascending sequence of innocence, vindication, and exoneration. As the crowning humanitarian theme within this sequence (coupled with the disqualified nature of the communication), immaculateness enjoys a rather elite range of status. Immaculateness formally preserves the fundamental degree of disqualification inherent in the preliminary sequence of terms: wherein acknowledging the transitional sense of righteousness expressed by the respective follower figure, although in a subliminally disqualified fashion.

In conclusion, the past-directed domain of the lesser virtues (I) offers a thoroughly traditional perspective on the sequential interplay of double bind and counter double bind maneuvers. The humorous overtones based upon the interplay of loyalty/humility, fidelity/majesty, etc., come through the clearest when countering (in a disqualified fashion) the more serious prerequisites of the entire transitional interchange. The related genre of the melodrama, in turn, targets the more sober aspects of the transitional realm; namely, the sequences based upon responsibility/innocence, duty/vindication, etc. Each genre necessarily incorporates aspects of both the humorous and melodramatic, providing a quite effective depiction of a lifestyle that inevitably dependent upon transitions encompassing the vagaries of everyday life.

23

THE FUTURE-DIRECTED REALM
FOR THE LESSER VIRTUES (I)

The completed description of the lesser virtues based upon loyalty/humility and responsibility/innocence, in turn, sets the stage for an examination of the remaining future-directed series of terms. According to the previous chapter, both loyalty and responsibility were defined as transitional variations on the hero worship/blame perspectives of the personal follower figure, wherein prompting the disqualified humility/innocence perspectives of the personal authority figure in return. A similar pattern further holds true with respect to the transitional variations based upon discipline/vigilance and modesty/meekness. In direct contrast to the actively occurring sense of reinforcement characterizing loyalty/responsibility, both discipline and vigilance represent future-directed forms of transitional power maneuvers, wherein expanding upon the more routine reinforcement roles of approval/concern.

The general pattern of presentation for this latter class of lesser virtues is similar to that which has gone before; namely, the four-part hierarchy of follower terms is described first, followed by the respective listings of authority roles. Accordingly, the preliminary double bind sequence of discipline-chivalry-nobility-zeal is described first, followed by the respective counter double bind sequence of modesty-chastity-purity-perfection. Furthermore, the remaining segments examine the affiliated sequences of vigilance-courage-valor-triumph and meekness-obedience-conformity-pacifism. The dedicated reader is encouraged to refer back to the four-page listing of schematic definitions for the lesser virtues (I) outlined in Chapter 21, providing a precise schematic representation of the power dynamics at issue in concert with the related descriptive narratives for each of the individual terms.

222 – DISCIPLINE

The first-listed theme of *discipline* is broadly acknowledged as the quintessential personal follower perspective. The term derives from the Latin *disciplina*, from *discipulus* (disciple). Some authorities suggest a derivation from *discére* (to learn), akin to *docére* (to teach). Others cite a derivation from *dis-* (apart) and *capere* (to hold). In either case, the ability to hold on to the import of instruction is generally implied, as evident in the basic teacher/disciple relationship. Although discipline can span a rather broad range of meaning, such as the administration of punishment, in terms of the current discussion, the relevant connotation concerns that positive sense of reinforcement conducive to prompting the consideration of the personal authority figure consistent with discipline's transitional relation to approval.

The disciplined individual supports, through reverent approval, the charismatic endeavors of the personal authority figure. Accordingly, discipline represents a transitional form of reinforcement perspective, whereupon playing up the status of the established authority figure in anticipation of securing ongoing consideration. In response to such glowing adulation, the personal authority is rightfully expected to desirously act solicitously in return. Alternately, however, he might also modestly deny acting cooperatively in return: in essence, disqualifying his willing participation in terms of the entire transitional interchange. The typical authority/disciple relationship generally favors the more gracious response, at least under the most amenable of circumstances. Indeed, according to Albert Einstein: "When a man is sufficiently motivated, *discipline* will take care of itself."

242 – CHIVALRY

The personal prerequisites for discipline, in turn, extend to a group sphere of influence with respect to the related theme of *chivalry*. The "chivalrous" mounted knight roams the countryside seeking meritorious deeds to challenge his training and mettle, as in great acts of courtesy or courage. The term derives from the Old French *chevaler* (knight), from the Latin *cavallus* (horse): signifying the advantages of mounted warfare during the feudal period, as well as the heraldic symbolisms associated with knightly courtesy. Although reaching great prestige during the Middle Ages, hints of chivalry date to the Roman province of Gaul, a region renowned for its strong reliance upon the horse. The prestige of cavalry over infantry endured throughout the Middle Ages, particularly during the Crusades when lengthy travels necessitated mounted units. Under the noble garb of religious zeal, the earliest orders of knighthood were first instituted. For instance, the Templars (founded in 1118) were crusader-monks pledged to aid in the defense of pilgrims/churchmen against the perils of the prevailing predations of the infidels.

The widely vaunted tales of gallantry and chivalry during the Crusades, in turn, inspired the troubadour tradition of the 12th century, instilling a romanticized code of honor, courtesy, and chivalry. The golden age of chivalry peaked during the 14th century, where orders of the noblest rank were established: namely, the Order of the Garter in England and the Order of the Star in France. These chivalrous orders reveled in the prestige of the royal court, particularly the showy arts of pageantry, gallantry, and courtliness. Courts of chivalry (presided over by the royal family) were known as the *tournament*, featuring jousting and duels for settling issues of honor.

The introduction of gunpowder soon brought the age of chivalry to an end, although the symbolisms of heraldry have formally endured. The latter also extends to the basic code of chivalry, still celebrated as honor among gentleman, the noble obligations of military service, as well as courtesy towards women. The chivalrous sense of discipline expressed by the group representative, in turn, anticipates the dignified demeanor of the established authority figure. Consequently, through this complementary sense of give-and-take, the group authority graciously reciprocates the chivalrous sense of discipline from his respective follower figure. Indeed, the willing cooperation of the established authority figure proves the key factor in fulfilling the rigors specific to the dynamics of the entire transitional interchange.

262 – NOBILITY

The group prerequisites for chivalry, in turn, extend to a universal sphere of influence with respect to the spiritual disciple theme of *nobility*. This term derives from Latin *nobilis* (well known), traditionally denoting high rank or excellence of character. Of similar derivation is the French expression *noblesse oblige;* namely, "rank imposes obligation:" implying noble ancestry or bearing. Indeed, the notion of "the nobility" denotes the body of aristocracy comprising the ruling class of a particular province or state: as in the feudal system of lords/barons in concert with the rights and privileges they commanded.

The symbolisms of nobility similarly appear larger than life: such as the gold, frankincense, and myrrh presented to the Christ Child by the Three Kings from the East. Indeed, the distinction of "noble" refers to heavy precious metals such as gold and silver, which are also highly resistant to corrosive damage. Contrast this to the "base" metals; iron, copper, tin: that are much more common in terms of function. Nobility refers to any distinction in terms of greatness: as is apparent on the chessboard, where the back row of noblemen hold rank over the advance row of lowly pawns. Such noblemen, alone, possess the regal bearing for deciding the outcome of the chess match, much as similarly occurs for the great range of conflicts throughout recorded history.

The moral ramifications of nobility similarly stand out in this regard, as in the traits of magnificence or generosity towards others irrespective of bearing or standing. Nobility represents the formal transitional variation upon the more basic theological virtue of charity, sharing with the latter a reinforcing status. In direct analogy to the group prerequisites of chivalry, nobility duly respects the established status of the spiritual authority figure: wherein petitioning the consideration of the latter. Consequently, nobility denotes a resigned sense of graciousness in response to the civilly-dignified treatment of the spiritual authority proper. In this spiritual sense, nobility aims towards lofty principles of virtually universal appeal, an overture that the authority figure is generally willing to reciprocate.

282 – ZEAL

The preceding trend towards "admirable works" ultimately culminates with respect to the crowning humanitarian theme of *zeal*. This term is traditionally defined as intense passion, ardor, or enthusiasm: a notion derived from the Latin *zelus*, from the Greek *zelos* (to be hot, to bring to a boil). Accordingly, it signifies a high degree of emotional intensity in terms of a particular cause or crusade. Although zeal generally connotes a virtuous quality, it may also be viewed pejoratively when the cause is judged less than admirable: such as when the religious zealot fanatically seeks to promulgate the beliefs of his chosen faith.

In a scriptural sense, this theme is most commonly associated with the Zealots: a Jewish nationalistic faction that labored to enforce strict observance of Mosaic Law. During the time of Christ, the Zealots zealously resisted the dominion of the Romans over the Jews. Citing both scriptural and moral precedents, the Zealots insisted that they (as descendants of Abraham) must never be politically subjugated. Consequently, the Zealots preached that insurgency was a religious duty, launching a crusade of virtually mythic proportions. Although open rebellion initially appeared risky, the goal of promoting resentment against the Roman yoke ultimately led to a nationwide insurrection circa 66 CE. Tragically, the rebellion failed miserably leading to the widespread destruction of the Jewish homeland, as well as the banishment of the Zealots from the annals of history.

In terms of our modern media age, zeal is more generally limited to extreme enthusiasm or fervor in terms of religious devotion. The zealous individual stands apart from the ordinary devotee in terms of failing to feel content with routine obligations leading to extreme ritual or devotion. This further extends to an eagerness to administer charity towards others, as well as a profound spirit of congeniality towards the religious congregation indicative of God's bountiful grace. Consequently, this noble sense of zeal represents a transitional variation on the more basic sense of goodness. It shares with nobility a focus on idealistic principles, although now clearly extending to a humanitarian sphere of influence. The zealous individual formally appeals to the magnanimity of the established authority figure, wherein promoting an enduring relationship with the humanitarian authority proper. Although this extreme level of abstraction formally works to obscure the fundamental dynamics at issue at this juncture, the crowning humanitarian prerequisites associated with zeal effectively round-out the established ascending pattern of subordinate themes; namely, discipline-chivalry-nobility (and now, zeal).

212.1 – MODESTY

The initial sequence of transitional themes based upon discipline, in turn, sets the stage for the remaining class of counter double bind maneuvers based upon *modesty*; namely, modesty-chastity-purity-perfection. Modesty is often defined as a close moral synonym of humility, although now targeting a sense of decency/decorum in matters primarily of a sexual nature, particularly conduct and attire. Modesty is symbolized across many ages and cultures as a chastely veiled maiden or virgin. Its modern spelling derives from the Latin *modestus*, from *modus* (measure): in particular, the measure by which one judges a rightful course of action in terms of propriety.

The modest individual refuses to be swayed by the flatterous intentions of the personal follower figure, rather denying any dignified sense of desire, therein. The modest individual formally counters the disciplined sense of reinforcement expressed by the personal follower figure, subconsciously disqualifying any overt cooperation in terms. This disqualified style of communication is particularly apparent in the typical situation comedy, where comic relief is achieved through a strategically timed display of modest abstinence, in essence, subliminally disqualifying the entire transitional nature of the proceedings. Hence, similar to its related counterpart of humility, modesty provides an effective strategy for politely circumventing the disciplined treatment initiated by the personal follower figure without sacrificing any concomitant sense of dignity in the process.

232.1 – CHASTITY

The personal prerequisites for modesty, in turn, extend to a group sphere of influence with respect to the affiliated theme of *chastity*. The term derives from the Latin *castus* (pure): as in purity in terms of taste, style, or refinement. Chastity is traditionally symbolized as the mythical unicorn or a virgin draped in white. According to legend, a unicorn may be summoned only by the chaste intentions of a virgin. In ancient Italian iconography, chastity is personified as a comely maiden holding a whip as if to chastise herself. She appears draped in a white robe adorned with a girdle inscribed with the Latin phrase: *"Castigo corpus meum"* (I chastise my body). Throughout the classical age, an unmarried maiden was expected to be chaste, her virginity maximizing her market value to prospective grooms. Chastity represents that rarest of all treasures, a jealously guarded gift given away but once to those proving most deserving.

In a more contemporary sense, the chaste individual voluntarily strives to abstain from sexual excess in order to realize a higher purpose. In religious orders (such as the Catholic priesthood), chastity and celibacy are revered as functional requirements. Chastity traditionally denotes a restrained degree of behavior particularly for adolescents and young adults. In our modern age of permissiveness, however, chastity is a virtue that has sadly decreased in stature. Many speculate that chastity is untenable or unnatural, despite observations that it has endured so well in the past. In order to restore chastity/abstinence to its former prestige entails a revival in terms: wherein strengthening willpower to overcome untimely temptation and negative peer pressure. Consequently, in strict analogy to its subordinate concept of modesty, chastity represents a polite strategy for effectively rejecting overtures of a transitional nature, wherein subliminally disqualifying any willing complicity in terms.

252.1 – PURITY

In direct analogy to the group prerequisites of chastity, the spiritual theme of *purity* commands virtually universal appeal in cultures around the world. It is traditionally defined as the absence of stain, fault, or sin: a close synonym for chastity, although to a considerably more abstract degree. The term dates at least to classical times, deriving from the Latin root *purus* (pure). Purity is traditionally symbolized as the color white, precious pearls, the Easter lily, or a dove/swan. Purity is also personified as a maiden draped in white, holding a tulip and scattering corn to a flock of white fowl. For obvious reasons, it figures prominently in virtually every religious tradition, as particularly significant in both Old and New Testament scripture. Indeed, Christ specifically singles out purity as the theme for his Sixth Beatitude: "Blessed are the pure in heart for they shall see God." Christian purity celebrates abstinence and self-control as virtues "next to Godliness." Although often equated with sexual purity, this theme also denotes a renunciation of worldly pursuits, as well as a mortification of the senses. Purity strives to bring each bodily impulse, passion, or desire into subjugation within the realm of the spirit: an exercise in self-control over the temptations of the material world. The path to purity, consequently, cleanses the heart and soul of all endeavors that fall short of such a noble degree of purpose.

The spiritual overtones for purity come through the clearest, extending the group prerequisites of chastity into a clearly universal sphere of influence. This "puritan" slant on morality appears equally applicable to all ages and times, an ethical standard that proves a fitting inspiration to us all. In direct response to the chivalrous sense of nobility expressed by the spiritual disciple figure, the chaste sense of purity expressed by the spiritual authority certainly appears warranted, its inherent degree of subconscious disqualification providing a fitting counterpoint to the insistent quality of the double bind maneuver. Here, Purity remains a fitting aspiration for all but the most exceptional among us.

272.1 – PERFECTION

The ascending hierarchy of terms based upon modesty ultimately culminates with respect to the crowning humanitarian theme of *perfection*, a supremely disqualified perspective exemplifying the very essence of purity. The term derives from the Latin *perfectus*, past participle of *perficere*, from *per-* (thoroughly) and *facere* (to do): e.g., thorough in terms of moral excellence. As such, perfection represents the highest desired outcome or goal achieved through the diligent pursuit of excellence. Consistent with its subordinate counterpart of purity, perfection shares many of the same symbolisms: including the color white, the circle (without beginning or end), and the lotus blossom (in the oriental tradition).

Perfection is viewed as an enduring ideal to be sought after, although never quite achieved. Its truly effortless and subliminally disqualified nature directly expands (in a humanitarian fashion) upon the more basic prerequisites of chastity and purity. Indeed, perfection is essentially a subjective standard that technically eludes fruition similar to an algebraic function that perpetually approaches its theoretical limit. Although the common maxim states that "no one is perfect," the basic issue still consists of determining how high to set the bar in the pursuit of excellence within the limits of human perfectibility. This generally entails setting high (yet realistic) standards of personal performance, then working to consummate these goals through concerted patience and attention to detail.

223 – VIGILANCE

The completed sequence of terms based upon discipline/modesty, in turn, sets the stage for the remaining transitional sequences based upon vigilance/meekness; namely, vigilance-courage-valor-triumph and meekness-obedience-conformity-pacifism. The first mentioned theme of *vigilance* derives from the Latin *vigil* (awake, watchful), from *vigere* (to be lively). In classical mythology, this theme is traditionally symbolized as the all-seeing eye or a crowing cock. Consequently, vigilance imparts a more watchful tone to its related foundations in "concern," collectively sharing such apprehensive perspectives. Indeed, William Shakespeare playfully compares vigilance to the analogy of "a cat out to steal cream" (Henry IV, Part 1).

The vigilante squads of the American West certainly attest to such a watchful focus, forever vigilant to wrongs to be righted. Vigilance effectively complements its respective counterpart in discipline, although now targeting a clearly darker range of themes. Through the aid of this transitional power maneuver, the personal follower radically plays-up his vigilant perspective in anticipation of securing the consideration of the established personal authority figure (within such a dualistic context). In this reciprocating fashion, the personal authority fully acknowledges the pressing concerns of the personal follower figure, wherein providing a fitting counterpoint to the complementary dynamics of the entire transitional interchange.

243 – COURAGE

The personal prerequisites for vigilance, in turn, extend to a group sphere of influence with respect to the *courage* expressed by the group representative. The related follower theme of chivalry is modified to reflect the more militaristic realm of courage under fire: defined as meeting danger without succumbing to fear in a sense consistent with bravery or fortitude. The term derives from the Latin *cor* (heart), in essence, to take heart and fight bravely. According to the precepts of medieval heraldry, courage is symbolized as a regal lion or a fierce mastiff, both of which are instilled with strong social instincts consistent with such a military *esprit de corps*. Contrast this with the symbolisms relating to cowardice; namely, a cowering canine with its tail tucked between its legs.

Courage represents a basic core virtue that directs attention to preserving the common good. Indeed, courage cannot stand alone without the goal of good intentions to provide it with coherent direction. Such good intentions may not even be realized without the courage to strengthen the will in a determination to succeed. True courage

promotes the act of faith that one possesses the necessary skills/inner resources to meet intimidating challenges or daunting obstacles. Physical courage ignores the risk of death or serious injury for sake of a common good, a hallmark of concerted self-sacrifice. In situations permitting quiet reflection, indwelling prudence helps to avert rash or impulsive actions, even though the intentions might prove altruistic. While it might seem natural to feel a sense of dread under such circumstances, courage faces fear through perseverance in order to fulfill such noble aims.

Courage represents the mean value interposed between the extremes of rashness (excess) and cowardice (defect). Rash or reckless behavior that ignores realistic limitations does not represent true courage. True courage enlists the related core value of prudence for insights into the risk of negative consequences. This necessarily entails the skills for developing a realistic set of risk assessments in order to circumvent potential disasters or unintended harmful consequences. One must also further determine whether the beneficial outcome is worth the risks and concerted effort required. In essence, the courageous individual strives for the golden mean between the extremes of rashness and cowardice in order to achieve the optimal outcome that avoids disaster or shirking responsibility.

263 – VALOR

The group prerequisites for courage, in turn, extend to a universal sphere of influence with respect to the spiritual disciple theme of *valor*. The term derives from the Latin *valere* (to be strong), as in stoutness of heart or intrepid daring. Valor shares much in common with the related synonyms of courage or bravery, although seemingly imparting a more pronounced universal character. In the field of Italian iconography, valor is symbolized as a handsome youth in golden garb, holding a scepter and a laurel wreath (signifying noble bearing and prowess). He is also represented stroking the mane of a lion lying at his feet in a stately display of valor.

The truest expression of valor, however, is embodied in the valiant exploits of the medieval knight in strict adherence to the codes of chivalry and nobility. The fictional protagonist, Prince Valiant, endeavors to aid the damsel in distress from the perils of the fire-breathing dragon, a valorous theme of virtually universal appeal. Indeed, valor (even more than courage) implies an adherence to such high-minded ideals: such as initially undertaken during the Crusades, when the goal of liberating the Holy Land transcended any conflicting partisan concerns, therein. In such a valiant fashion, the knights of the realm rode together united by a common crusader ideal, although the modest military gains could not be sustained despite their passionate quest for conquest.

Valor proves a fitting adjunct to the preliminary sequence of vigilance/courage, although reflecting a more advanced spiritual variation within such a militaristic series of terms. Indeed, the courageous sense of valor expressed by the spiritual disciple in turn anticipates the austere sense of integrity professed by the spiritual authority figure. The valiant individual is governed by motives of a morally abstract nature, similar to that previously established for the nobility perspective. Accordingly, valor continues to remain a prized ideal within the military tradition: that rare quality that medals and commendations only scarcely serve to convey.

283 - TRIUMPH

The ascending follower sequence of vigilance, courage, and valor ultimately culminates with respect to the enduring humanitarian theme of *triumph*. This theme is particularly evident in the many triumphal arches erected throughout the ages. It is traditionally defined as a victorious celebration invoking pomp and circumstance, as in a jubilant display of exultation. The term derives from the Latin *triumphus*, from the Greek *thriambos:* a hymn originally sung to Bacchus (the god of wine). These bacchanal rituals were characterized by gross inebriation, orgiastic experimentation, and wild revelry: aspects that carried over to the Roman tradition of revelry in victory celebrations.

In the Roman world, the triumph was revered as a sacred procession honoring a returning victorious general, culminating in a sacrifice to Jupiter on the Capital Mount. The ceremony reenacts the solemn act of thanksgiving invoked for victory while abroad. The triumphant general parades in an embroidered toga and an ornate crown. He carries a scepter in one hand and a spray of laurel leaves in the other. He rides before the assembled masses in an ornate chariot drawn by a team of four horses. A slave by his side constantly repeats the chant "*Hominem te momento*" (in remembrance of him). Ahead in the procession marched the victorious troops, prisoners in chains, the spoils of war on wagons, as well as a chain of white oxen for sacrifice to Zeus. A laurel victory wreath was draped over the statue of Zeus upon completion of the final climactic sacri-

fice to the god. The victory for the empire was invested with the grandest of humanitarian themes, a solemn sense of devotion directly insuring the potential for further such victorious campaigns.

During the subsequent Christian era, certain aspects of pagan ritual were incorporated to express Christian ideals. The *triumphus* and the *triumphare* served to signify the Church's victory over evil and its miraculous establishment. Over the course of centuries, the Church formally celebrated an indwelling spirit of *triumphalism*; namely, the tendency to view the Church as an indefatigable force for goodness fully deserving of universal admiration. The enduring humanitarian focus of triumph fittingly expands upon the subordinate concepts of courage and valor. Consequently, triumph specifies (in a transitional sense) the decent sense of wisdom expressed by the humanitarian authority figure. This places the triumphant party in a curiously vulnerable position, as when the victorious general swears obeisance in preparation for the divine sacrifice awaiting the end of the procession. The enduring transitional interplay of this humanitarian perspective proves particularly crucial at this juncture, the general reveling in his triumphant campaign as one destined for all the ages.

213.1 - MEEKNESS

The completed description of the transitional sequence of terms based upon vigilance invites further comparison to the remaining counter double bind class of maneuvers based upon *meekness;* namely, meekness-obedience-conformity-pacifism. The first-mentioned theme of meekness derives from the Old Norse *mjurk* or *miurk* (denoting gentleness). It denotes a genteel demeanor consistent with the degree of disqualification underlying such an unobtrusive temperament. Meekness represents a prominent theme for many of the great spiritual leaders of the world: including Christ, Mohammed, Buddha, etc. Indeed, Christ's Third Beatitude directly states: "Blessed are the meek, for they shall inherit the earth." His related (although somewhat idealistic) admonition "to turn the other cheek" when struck takes this virtuous trend to its extreme, with meekness equating to an extreme degree of vulnerability.

Christ certainly appears well versed in this disqualified style of communication, as directly reflected in his other beatitudes relating to humility and innocence. Communication Theorist, Jay Haley (1989) addresses this issue in much greater detail in his treatise: *The Power Tactics of Jesus Christ and Other Essays*. According to this disqualified style of format, the meekness expressed by the personal authority figure effectively sidesteps any worrisome prerequisites therein: in turn, countering the vigilant treatment of the personal follower figure. Meekness parallels the pattern previously established for modesty, although appeasement is now subliminally disqualified, rather than solicitousness.

233.1 – OBEDIENCE

The personal prerequisites for meekness, in turn, extend to a group sphere of influence with respect to the group authority theme of *obedience*. The authority figure's worrisome sense of integrity is disqualified in terms of a dedicated sense of conscience. Obedience traditionally implies compliance or dutiful submission to the will of another. The term derives from the Latin *obedientia*, present participle of *obedire*, from *ob-* (towards) and *audire* (to hear). Indeed, in its most basic sense, to hear *is* to obey in terms the strictures of such an authoritarian perspective.

In early Italian iconography, obedience is personified as a pious virgin submitting to a yoke lowered upon her by an angel. In particular, any doctrine of absolute obedience presupposes this interplay of authority/follower roles, of which one is free to obey (or disobey), but never to outwardly question the reason why. Ironically, the more rigorous the demands for obedience, the more dogmatic are its precepts, and the less obvious is the rationale to the obedient party. This frequently leads to capricious demands for unqualified obedience, or feelings of complete indifference, in return.

Motives for obedience vary widely, as in fear of authority, anticipation of reward, or faith in the law. True to its foundations in Old Testament scripture, the Christian tradition preserves a strong authoritarian slant. Christ actually advocated a rational interpretation of the law, as reflected in his various conflicts with the religious authorities of his day. Indeed, in the process of becoming established, Christianity found itself heir to many of the doctrinal and dogmatic strictures endemic within Roman culture.

This authoritarian perspective extended to the Middle Ages, when the ideals of poverty, chastity, and obedience were instituted as monastic vows for religious orders of the day. Obedience, in particular, was crucial to monastic communities: where unqualified submission to the will of the superior was a religious obligation. A key official of the medieval monastery was the Obedientiary, a role appointed by the Abbott in the service of his unquestioned authority. Through such an unswerving sense of obedience, the free will of the obedient party is subconsciously disqualified similar to a military context, where responsibility rolls downhill through the chain of command.

Similar to the case previously established for meekness, the obedient party meekly acts in an appeasing fashion without necessarily appearing to have done so: wherein invoking a subliminal style of disqualified counter double bind maneuver (similar that previously seen for chastity). The obedient individual effectively sidesteps the insistent "courage" perspective of the respective follower figure: claiming only to obey, and therefore not a willing participant in the entire transitional interchange. Consequently, obedience extends the more limited (personal) focus of meekness into a broader group domain, a key feature to the smooth functioning of civilized society.

253.1 – CONFORMITY

The conscientious aspects of obedience, in turn, extend to a universal focus with respect to the spiritual authority theme of *conformity*. It is traditionally defined as a sense of harmony or agreement with law, fashion, or custom. The term derives from the Latin *conformare*, from *con-* (from) and *formare* (to form): a compound structure suggesting agreement or concordance. It also implies compliance to a pre-existing social order, particularly with respect to terminology employed by the Church of England (in keeping with such a universal focus). Conformity enjoys a broad range of meanings, such as the geological sense of an uninterrupted sequence of strata over an extended formative time scale. According to Sir Isaac Newton, "Nature is very consonant and *conformable* with herself." *Optiks* (1730).

Granted conformity scarcely enjoys the tradition or prestige of other virtues within its class, it, nevertheless, quite effectively fulfills the sequence previously established with respect to meekness and obedience. Consequently, these universal aspects of conformity clearly reflect the global prerequisites for the term, as its general applications to science and geology further serve to indicate. In direct analogy to its related counterpart of purity, conformity formally represents a disqualified style of counter double bind maneuver: effectively sidestepping (through an appeal to conformity) the insistent quality of the valor maneuver expressed by the spiritual disciple figure. In terms of this reciprocal interplay, one's conforming compliance is chalked-up to the strictures of convention rather than any volitional cooperation in terms. Through this subliminal sense of disqualification, the spiritual authority figure reciprocates his expected role within the dual transitional interchange, although in a thoroughly non-confrontational fashion.

273.1 – PACIFISM

The universal prerequisites for conformity, in turn, extend to a humanitarian sphere of influence with respect to the supremely abstract theme of *pacifism*. Pacifism denotes a moral opposition to warlike activities, a term deriving from the Latin *pacificus*, from *pax* (peace) and *facere* (to make). It rules out any involvement with war or aggression consistent with Christian principles of universal love/acceptance. It condemns passions conducive to war in favor of nonviolent resistance (as in turning the other cheek). For the early Christians, the prohibition against military service was partially couched in terms of a similar ban against participation in pagan rites of warfare (such as the triumph). Furthermore, the Roman military oath conflicted with the pledge of supreme devotion to the Christian God. The most damning conflict, however, concerned the blood-lust specific to warfare, a factor antithetical to Christianity regardless of the noble aspirations, therein. Indeed, during the early days of the Church, soldiers were excluded from the Lord's table until penance had been offered for the blood that had been shed.

This Christian interpretation of pacifism was by no means universal, for the defense of the Church became much more controversial following the fall of the Western Roman Empire. The idealistic principles underpinning pacifism persisted even through the militaristic focus of the Middle Ages. This theme has undergone a revival in modern times through the principles of nonviolent resistance as professed by Mohandas Gandhi during India's struggle for independence. Pacifism represents a counter double bind class of power maneuver in the enduring spirit of meekness, obedience, and conformity: denoting a thoroughly disqualified expression of peacefulness without admitting any volitional compliance therein.

Through this appeal to pacifism, the pacifist echoes a sense of reliance upon the conventionality previously established for conformity, and the communal sense of duty initially cited for obedience. As the crowning humanitarian theme within the ascending hierarchy of terms, pacifism clearly appeals to an enduring sphere of influence. Here, the reluctant humanitarian authority effectively sidesteps the insistent quality of the triumph maneuver initiated by the respective follower figure, whereby presenting a picture of peaceful appeasement, while subliminally denying any willing participation, therein.

In summary, the completed description of the future-directed variations for the lesser virtues (I) provides a fitting counterpoint to the related past-directed format previously described. Clearly the stakes are heightened with respect to these future-directed virtues, where an anticipation of upcoming reinforcement proves much more salient in terms of outwardly expressed motivations. In contrast, the past-directed lesser virtues address more of a memory-based historical perspective, although this focus on tradition proves equally compelling in terms of establishing status and prestige within shifting social coalitions.

In all honesty, both transitional strategies emerge as essential aspects within variable social relationships, being as the future constantly trends over into the past, specifying a reciprocal balance of interests in this basic regard. A similar reciprocating dynamic is further encountered with respect to the upcoming description of the lesser virtues (II), although a phased reversal in the order of the authority and follower roles makes for many interesting variations within this overall transitional format.

24

THE PAST-DIRECTED LESSER VIRTUES (II)

The completed description of the lesser virtues (I) provides a formal model of the power dynamics underlying the transitional class of power maneuvers. This grand degree of correspondence, in turn, raises the issue of the potential for alternate variations on the basic transitional format. Indeed, even a cursory survey of the ethical literature reveals an additional complement of virtuous terms essentially unaccounted for with respect to the current system.

For the lesser virtues (I) the reinforcement focus specific to the follower role formally initiates the transitional interchange, in turn, dictating the participation of the established authority figure. The authority figure can accept the roles as presented, or disqualify them altogether through a humorous style of counter double bind maneuver. This necessarily leaves open the speculation that this two-stage sequence of roles could potentially be reversed; namely, the authority role is expressed first followed by the reinforcement status of the respective follower role, the precise pattern specified for the lesser virtues (II).

In terms of the latter class of lesser virtues, the newly transitioned authority role (by definition) now maneuvers from a one-down power status with respect to the follower figure. This functionally contrasts with the lesser virtues (I), where the follower figure initially assumes a one-up power status in relation to the subsequent authority role. This reciprocal reversal of power status could be formally predicated, being that the authority/follower roles within the transitional interplay should be of like quality; e.g., personal authority/personal follower, group authority and group representative, etc. The dual transitional interchange would become hopelessly confused should higher authority levels be invoked in response to the initial double bind maneuver.

This variance in terms of the initial one-up and one-down power status imparts clear functional distinctions with respect to the dual classifications of lesser virtues (I) and (II). The lesser virtues (I) are assigned top billing: being the initial double bind maneuver is initiated from a one-up power status, wherein invoking a more dominant style of power maneuver. The lesser virtues (II), in contrast, are initiated from a one-down power status specified for the respective authority roles: wherein imparting a less prestigious perspective, as the more limited range of ethical traditions primarily serves to indicate.

This reversed pattern of organization, accordingly, predicts the existence of an entire related class of ethical terms specified for the lesser virtues (II). This alternate class of virtuous terms is distinct from the lesser virtues (I) primarily in terms of the specific order given for the respective authority/follower roles. For the lesser virtues (II), this procurement-*then*-reinforcement pattern of roles superficially conforms with the initiation of a completely new operant sequence. This circumstance directly contrasts with the lesser virtues (I), where the sequential order is respectively reversed. Consequently, the lesser virtues (II) enjoy neither the pedigree or tradition previously established for the better known lesser virtues (I). The lesser virtues (II), nevertheless, are associated with a suitable range of ethical traditions: wherein accounting for many further categories of lesser virtue, as schematically depicted in **Fig. 24**, as well the compact table below.

Self-Esteem → Reverence	Apology → Clemency
Pomp → Veneration	Rectitude → Pardon
Sanctity → Homage	Penitence → Absolution
Dominion→ Benediction	Contrition→ Deliverance
Congeniality → Concession	Appease.→ Sympathy
Cordiality→ Indulgence	Conciliate→ Compassion
Hospitality→ Gratitude	Accommodation→ Mercy
Altruism → Goodwill	Sacrifice → Forgiveness

210	211
Self-Esteem	Apology
212	**213**
Congeniality	Appeasement

→

220.1	221.1
Reverence	Clemency
222.1	**223.1**
Concession	Sympathy

TRANSITIONAL
EGO STATES
(PA - Double-Bind)

DISQUALIFIED
ALTER EGO STATES
(PF - Counter-Double-Bind)

230	231
Pomp	Rectitude
232	**233**
Cordiality	Conciliation

→

240.1	241.1
Veneration	Pardon
242.1	**243.1**
Indulgence	Compassion

TRANSITIONAL
PERSONAL IDEALS
(GA - Double-Bind)

DISQUALIFIED
CARDINAL VIRTUES
(GR - Counter Double-Bind)

250	251
Sanctity	Penitence
252	**253**
Hospitality	Accommodation

→

260.1	261.1
Homage	Absolution
262.1	**263.1**
Gratitude	Mercy

TRANSITIONAL
CIVIL LIBERTIES
(SA - Double-Bind)

DISQUALIFIED
THEOLOGICAL VIRTUES
(SD - Counter Double-Bind)

270	271
Dominion	Contrition
272	**273**
Altruism	Sacrifice

→

280.1	281.1
Benediction	Deliverance
282.1	**283.1**
Goodwill	Forgiveness

TRANSITIONAL
ECUMENICAL IDEALS
(HA - Double-Bind)

DISQUALIFIED
GREEK VALUES
(RH - Counter Double-Bind)

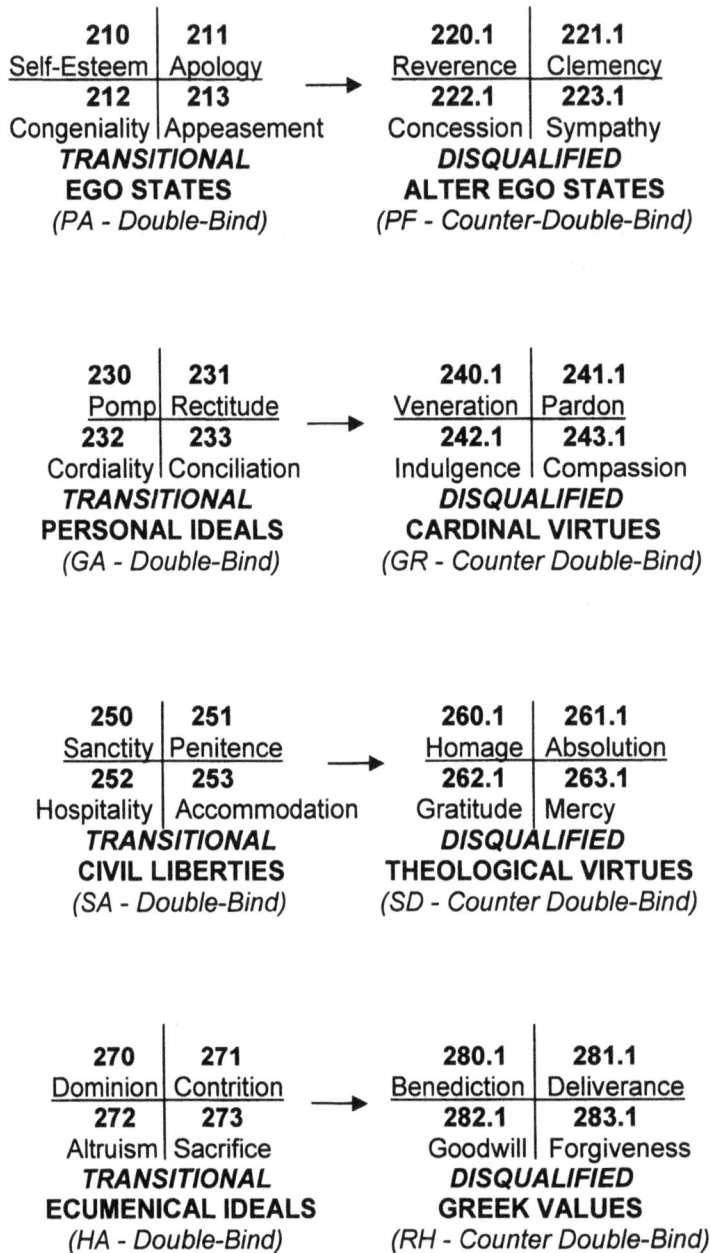

Fig. 24 – The Lesser Virtues - (II)

It proves a fitting tribute to the English language tradition that the predicted complement of lesser virtues (II) so convincingly reflects the specifics of the transitional class of terms. Consequently, a clearer understanding of the dual interplay of authority/follower roles (denoted by the arrow notation in **Fig. 24**) proves crucial towards validating the respective interplay of double bind and counter double bind maneuvers. For example, the nostalgic sense of self-esteem expressed by the personal authority figure, in turn, prompts the reverential treatment of the established follower figure (in a disqualified expression of hero worship). Similarly, the apologetic sense of guilt expressed by the personal authority further prompts a disqualified sense of blame; namely, the clemency perspective of the personal follower figure. Furthermore, the personal authority's congeniality maneuver, in turn, prompts the disqualified sense of concession on the part of the follower figure. Similarly, appeasement behavior further prompts a disqualified expression of sympathy.

This dual interplay of double bind and counter double bind perspectives (targeting the personal level), in turn, serves as the elementary foundation for the remaining sequence of authority levels: namely, the group, spiritual, and humanitarian levels depicted in **Fig. 24**. For instance, the initial double bind sequence of self-esteem-pomp-sanctity-dominion, in turn, sets the stage for the remaining counter double bind sequence of reverence-veneration-homage-benediction. Furthermore, the related authority sequence of apology-rectitude-penitence-contrition, in turn, leads to the remaining follower sequence of clemency-pardon-absolution-deliverance.

A similar pattern further holds true with respect to the remaining "future-directed" sequences of terms based upon congeniality/concession and appeasement/sympathy. For instance, the initial authority sequence of congeniality-cordiality-hospitality-altruism is formally countered by the respective follower sequence of concession-indulgence-gratitude-goodwill. Furthermore, the related authority sequence of appeasement-conciliation-accommodation-sacrifice, in turn, prompts the remaining follower sequence of sympathy-compassion-mercy-forgiveness.

On one final note, it further proves feasible to incorporate these individual entries for the lesser virtues (II) directly into the schematic definition format, providing a clear indication of the power dynamics at issue here. The complete four-part listing of definitions for the lesser virtues (II) is formally listed in **Tables M-1** to **M-4**, a sequence of tables beginning immediately overleaf. This schematic definition format is identical in form and function to that previously established for the lesser virtues (I) although the specific order of the authority/follower roles is now totally reversed. For the lesser virtues (II), the authority roles represent the initial jumping-off point, wherein setting the stage for the subsequent follower sequence of counter double bind maneuvers. This pattern directly contrasts with that previously established for the lesser virtues (I). Here the follower roles initiate the transitional sequence followed by the disqualified class of power maneuvers specified for the authority roles.

This dual interplay of double bind and counter double bind maneuvers remains a focus of consistency irrespective of whether the authority or follower role is specified first. Consequently, the remainder of the current chapter examines the past-directed sequences of the lesser virtues (II) based upon self-esteem/reverence and apology/clemency. This analysis concludes in Chapter *25* with respect to the future-directed sequences based upon congeniality/concession and appeasement/sympathy. The further Chapter *26* subsequently touches upon the related issue of the accessory variations for the lesser virtues, allowing for crucial empathic insights into the transitional power perspective. The discerning reader is encouraged to refer back to the respective four-part listings of schematic definitions throughout the remainder of the current section, wherein outlining the specific communicational factors at issue for each of the individual terms.

210 – SELF- ESTEEM

The first listed theme of *self-esteem* is formally defined as the chief transitional counterpart of nostalgia. The term derives as a compound of two primary themes; namely, the Old English *seolf* (one's individual person) and the Middle French *estimer*, from the Latin *æstimare* (to value, to appraise). The modern sense of self-esteem dates at least to 1657. It was further popularized through the pseudo-science of phrenology, which assigned to self-esteem a "bump" on the contours of the skull (circa 1815). Beginning in the early 1980's, self-esteem emerged as a popular "buzzword" for resolving personal or societal problems. Many authorities assumed that instilling high self-esteem in the younger generation could prove a panacea for the ills of substance abuse, violent crime, sexual irresponsibility, etc. This interpretation suggests that self-esteem represents a motivating causative factor for personal positive development, rather than simply an emotional

SELF-ESTEEM	REVERENCE
Previously, you (as personal follower) have rewardingly acted worshipfully, in response to the nostalgic treatment of the personal authority. But now, I (as new personal authority) will nostalgically act with *self-esteem* towards you: in anticipation of your (as established PF) worshipful treatment of me.	Previously, I (as new personal authority) have nostalgically acted with self-esteem towards you: in anticipation of your (as established PF) worshipful treatment of me. But now, you (as reluctant personal follower) will *reverently* <u>deny</u> acting worshipfully towards me: thwarting my (as new PA) nostalgic sense of self-esteem.
POMP	**VENERATION**
Previously, you (as group representative) have prudently acted in a worshipful fashion, in response to the gloriously-nostalgic treatment of the group authority. But now, I (as new group authority) will *pompously* act with self-esteem towards you: in anticipation of your (as established GR) prudent-worship of me.	Previously, I (as new group authority) have pompously acted with self-esteem towards you: in anticipation of your (as established GR) prudent-worship of me. But now, you (as reluctant group representative) will reverently act in a *venerable* fashion towards me: thwarting my (as new GA) pompous treatment of you.
SANCTITY	**HOMAGE**
Previously, you (as spiritual disciple) have prudently acted in a faithful fashion, in response to the gloriously-provident treatment of the spiritual authority. But now, I (as new spiritual authority) will pompously act in a *sanctified* fashion towards you: in anticipation of your (as established SD) prudent-faith in me.	Previously, I (as new spiritual authority) have pompously acted in a sanctified fashion towards you: in anticipation of your (as established SD) prudent-faith in me. But now, you (as reluctant spiritual disciple) will venerably express *homage* towards me: thwarting my (as new SA) sanctified treatment of you.
DOMINION	**BENEDICTION**
Previously, you (as representative member of humanity) have beauteously acted in a faithful fashion, in response to the provident sense of grace of the humanitarian authority. But now, I (as new humanitarian authority) will sanctifiedly express a sense of *dominion* towards you: in anticipation of your (as established RH) beauteous-faith in me.	Previously, I (as new humanitarian authority) have sanctifiedly expressed a sense of dominion towards you: in anticipation of your (as established RH) beauteous-faith in me. But now, you (as reluctant representative member of humanity) will homagefully express *benediction* towards me: thwarting my (as new HA) sanctified sense of dominion.

Table M-1 – The Definitions Based Upon Self-Esteem/Reverence

APOLOGY	CLEMENCY
Previously, you (as personal follower) have blamefully acted in a lenient fashion, in response to the guilty treatment of the personal authority. But now, I (as new personal authority) will guiltily act in an *apologetic* fashion towards you: in anticipation of your (as established PF) blameful treatment of me.	Previously, I (as new personal authority) have guiltily acted in an apologetic fashion towards you: in anticipation of your (as established PF) blameful treatment of me. But now, you (as reluctant personal follower) will *clemently* <u>deny</u> acting blamefully towards me: thwarting my (as new PA) apologetic treatment of you.
RECTITUDE	PARDON
Previously, you (as group representative) have blamefully acted in a just fashion, in response to the honorable sense of guilt of the group authority. But now, I (as new group authority) will apologetically act in a *rectitudinous* fashion towards you: in anticipation of your (as established GR) just-blaming of me.	Previously, I (as new group authority) have apologetically acted in a rectitudinous fashion towards you: in anticipation of your (as established GR) just-blaming of me. But now, you (as reluctant group representative) will clemently-*pardon* me: thwarting my (as new GA) apologetic sense of rectitude.
PENITENCE	ABSOLUTION
Previously, you (as spiritual disciple) have blamefully-hoped for justice, in response to the libertarian sense of honor of the spiritual authority. But now, I (as new spiritual authority) will *penitently* act in a rectitudinous fashion towards you: in anticipation of your (as established SD) blameful-hope for justice.	Previously, I (as new spiritual authority) have penitently acted in a rectitudinous fashion towards you: in anticipation of your (as established SD) blameful hope for justice. But now, you (as reluctant spiritual disciple) will pardoningly express *absolution* towards me: thwarting my (as new SA) penitent treatment of you.
CONTRITION	DELIVERANCE
Previously, you (as representative member of humanity) have justly hoped for the truth, in response to the libertarian sense of free will of the humanitarian authority. But now, I (as new humanitarian authority) will penitently act in a *contrite* fashion towards you: in anticipation of your (as established RH) just-hope for the truth.	Previously, I (as new humanitarian authority) have penitently acted in a contrite fashion towards you: in anticipation of your (as established RH) just-hope for the truth. But now, you (as reluctant representative member of humanity) will absolvingly act with *deliverance* towards me: thwarting my (as new HA) penitent sense of contrition.

Table M-2 – The Definitions Based Upon Apology/Clemency

CONGENIALITY	CONCESSION
Previously, I (as personal follower) have rewardingly acted in an approving fashion, in response to the desirous treatment of the personal authority. But now, you (as new personal authority) will *congenially* act in a desirous fashion towards me: in anticipation of my (as established PF) approving treatment of you.	Previously, you (as new personal authority) have congenially acted in a desirous fashion towards me: in anticipation of my (as established PF) approving treatment of you. But now, I (as reluctant personal follower) will *concessionally* <u>deny</u> acting approvingly towards you: thwarting your (as new PA) congenial treatment of me.
CORDIALITY	**INDULGENCE**
Previously, I (as group representative) have temperately acted in an approving fashion, in response to the dignified-desire of the group authority. But now, you (as new group authority) will congenially act in a *cordial* fashion towards me: in anticipation of my (as established GR) temperate-approval of you.	Previously, you (as new group authority) have congenially acted in a cordial fashion towards me: in anticipation of my (as established GR) temperate-approval of you. But now, I (as reluctant group representative) will concessionally act in an *indulgent* fashion towards you: thwarting your (as new GA) cordial treatment of me.
HOSPITALITY	**GRATITUDE**
Previously, I (as spiritual disciple) have temperately acted in a charitable fashion, in response to the civilly-dignified treatment of the spiritual authority. But now, you (as new spiritual authority) will cordially act in a *hospitable* fashion towards me: in anticipation of my (as established SD) charitable treatment of you.	Previously, you (as new spiritual authority) have cordially acted in a hospitable fashion towards me: in anticipation of my (as established SD) charitable treatment of you. But now, I (as reluctant spiritual disciple) will indulgently act with *gratitude* towards you: thwarting your (as new SA) cordial sense of hospitality.
ALTRUISM	**GOODWILL**
Previously, I (as representative member of humanity) have charitably acted with goodness, in response to the civilly-magnanimous treatment of the humanitarian authority. But now, you (as new humanitarian authority) will hospitably act in an *altruistic* fashion towards me: in anticipation of my (as established RH) charitable sense of goodness.	Previously, you (as new humanitarian authority) have hospitably acted altruistically towards me: in anticipation of my (as established RH) charitable sense of goodness. But now, I (as reluctant representative member of humanity) will gratefully act with *goodwill* towards you: thwarting your (as new HA) hospitable sense of altruism.

Table M-3 – The Definitions Based on Congeniality/Concession

APPEASEMENT	SYMPATHY
Previously, I (as personal follower) have leniently acted in a concerned fashion, in response to the worrisome treatment of the personal authority. But now, you (as new personal authority) will worrisomely act in an *appeasement* fashion towards me: in anticipation of my (as established PF) lenient sense of concern.	Previously, you (as new personal authority) have worrisomely acted in an appeasement fashion towards me: in anticipation of my (as established PF) lenient sense of concern. But now, I (as reluctant personal follower) will *sympathetically* deny acting with concern towards you: thwarting your (as new PA) worrisome sense of appeasement.
CONCILIATION	**COMPASSION**
Previously, I (as group representative) have fortitudinously acted in a concerned fashion, in response to the worrisome sense of integrity of the group authority. But now, you (as new group authority) will appeasingly act in a *conciliatory* fashion towards me: in anticipation of my (as established GR) fortitudinous sense of concern.	Previously, you (as new group authority) have appeasingly acted in a conciliatory fashion towards me: in anticipation of my (as established GR) fortitudinous sense of concern. But now, I (as reluctant group representative) will sympathetically act in a *compassionate* fashion towards you: thwarting your (as new GA) conciliatory treatment of me.
ACCOMMODATION	**MERCY**
Previously, I (as spiritual disciple) have fortitudinously acted in a decent fashion, in response to the austere sense of integrity of the spiritual authority. But now, you (as new spiritual authority) will conciliatingly act in an *accommodating* fashion towards me: in anticipation of my (as established SD) decent treatment of you.	Previously, you (as new spiritual authority) have conciliatingly acted in an accommodating fashion towards me: in anticipation of my (as established SD) decent treatment of you. But now, I (as reluctant spiritual disciple) will compassionately act in a *merciful* fashion towards you: thwarting your (as new SA) accommodating treatment of me.
SACRIFICE	**FORGIVENESS**
Previously, I (as representative member of humanity) have decently acted in a wise fashion, in response to the austere sense of equanimity of the humanitarian authority. But now, you (as new humanitarian authority) will accommodatingly act in a *sacrificial* fashion towards me: in anticipation of my (as established RH) decent sense of wisdom.	Previously, you (as new humanitarian authority) have accommodatingly acted sacrificially towards me: in anticipation of my (as established RH) decent sense of wisdom. But now, I (as reluctant representative member of humanity) will mercifully act in a *forgiving* fashion towards you: thwarting your (as new HA) sacrificial treatment of me.

Table M- 4 – The Definitions Based on Appeasement/Sympathy

indicator of self-satisfaction in terms of worth-while achievements.

Valid self-esteem concerns the perception of making good choices aimed at achieving worthy goals. In contrast, pseudo self-esteem is defined as feeling good about oneself simply because an outside authority says so, even in the absence of any independent corroborating evidence. True self-esteem promotes a sort of emotional barometer for examining such personal positive issues. Although valid self-esteem can fluctuate widely under variable circumstances (particularly with respect to external criticism), honest self-evaluation tends to smooth out such radical mood-swings, wherein restoring confidence and a positive outlook.

As such, self-esteem formally fulfills the specifics established for the transitional class of power maneuvers; namely, encompassing the personal authority figure's outward expression of nostalgia in anticipation of the worshipful treatment from the established personal follower. By resorting to a one-down power status, the personal authority's prospects of achieving ultimate reinforcement are dramatically increased in terms of this ongoing style of transitional interaction.

230 – POMP

The personal prerequisites for self-esteem, in turn, extend to the group sphere of influence with respect to the related theme of *pomp*. The newly transitioned group authority figure gloriously aspires to the prudent-worship anticipated from the established group representative. Accordingly, this glorious sense of pomp directly expands upon the personal characteristics previously established for self-esteem. It is traditionally defined as a splendid or ostentatious display of fame or renown, often with overtones of solemn self-importance. The term derives from the Latin *pompa* (procession, pomp), from the Greek *pompe* (solemn procession), from the Greek *pempein* (to send). It is sometimes employed in deprecatory sense with respect to worldly excess or vain showiness.

Nowhere is this spirit of ostentation more readily apparent than in the vanities associated with military conquest. William Shakespeare's character Othello fittingly states: "Farewell the neighing steed and the shrill trumpet, the spirit-stirring drum, the ear-piercing fife. The royal banner and all quality, pride, *pomp*, and circumstance of glorious war!" (Act III: Scene 3). Furthermore, in bidding farewell to the glamour and pageantry of his profession as an English general, Edward Elgar

chose to designate his famous series of military marches as "pomp and circumstance" in reference to the showy rituals accompanying such military displays.

This emphasis on pomp and pageantry similarly extends to the intrigues of the royal court, where the ceremonial burdens clearly invoke a sense of deference, as well as pomp and majesty. The 16th century British poet, Thomas Campion insightfully notes: "Now you courtly dames and knights that study only strange delights. Though you scorn the homespun gray and revel in your rich array. Though your tongues dissemble deep, and can your heads from danger keep: yet for all your *pomp* and train, securer lives the silly swain." As such, the expansive theme of pomp certainly fits the prerequisites previously established for the transitional class of power maneuvers. The group authority figure pompously acts with extreme self-esteem in anticipation of the prudent-worship from the established group representative. Indeed, by maneuvering from a one-down power status, the initiatory nature of the "pomp" perspective clearly enhances the prospects of success: an interplay that mutually tends to benefit both parties within the verbal interaction.

250 – SANCTITY

The ascending sequence of authority roles, in turn, extends to a universal sphere of influence with respect to the related theme of *sanctity*. The term derives from the Latin *sanctificare*, from *sanctus* (sacred) and *facere* (to make). It is traditionally defined as moral perfection of a divine order (such as ascribed to the Deity). It is also attributed to mankind through religious participation. It denotes a sense of sacredness or holiness, particularly in the inviolable sense of religious duty, as in taking an oath or vow. In the Roman Catholic tradition, it is particularly revered in the sacred sequence of saints and martyrs, whose lives were esteemed as paragons of virtue and holiness. The scope of God's grace appears virtually universal in scope, a common feature in many of the great world religions.

This sanctified quality certainly fits well with the formal prerequisites of the transitional class of power maneuvers, although now clearly targeting a universal sphere of influence. In agreement with its preliminary concepts of self-esteem and pomp, the newly transitioned spiritual authority exaltedly acts in a sanctified fashion in anticipation of the prudent-faith from the established spiritual disciple. The humble demeanor of many a saintly figure certainly corroborates such a dual power status, where considerable leverage may be gained in terms of such a one-down power status. Here, the sanctity perspective represents the stock in trade for many institutionalized forms of religion, a consequence that clearly does not diminish the awe/majesty invoked within such a ritualized display of sacredness.

270 – DOMINION

The final theme within the ascending hierarchy of terms, *dominion*, specifies a more enduring humanitarian focus. It is traditionally defined as a domain or territory ruled by a single sovereign figure, whereas its spiritual overtones suggest the omnipotence of the Christian God. The term derives from the Latin *dominio*, from *dominus* (master). This sense of dominion is directly cited in Jude 1:8 (King James Edition), whereas Ephesians 1:21 translates the term as *kuriotes*: denoting a rank or order of angels. In terms of tradition, the Dominions represent the highest order within the second rank of angels, sometimes referred to as "the flashing swords." They are so-called from the belief that they dominate over those ranks of angels ordered below them in the angelic hierarchy, wherein manifesting divine wisdom. They are said to channel divine grace conducive to wise governance and prudent management; hence, they are said to integrate the material and spiritual realms, whereby unifying the angelic orders into a divine continuum.

In our modern political age, dominion denotes the secular power to rule (or those that are subject to such rule). Prior to 1949, the term officially was employed to denote self-governing countries within the Commonwealth of Nations: in particular, Canada, Australia, and India. In 1949, India ultimately gained status as a republic within the Commonwealth. As of late, the use of the term "dominion" has largely been abandoned in that it implies political subordination. Currently, such member states are simply referred to as members within the Commonwealth.

Irrespective of the particulars therein, this enduring sense of dominion clearly fulfills the humanitarian prerequisites affiliated with the term. The requisite one-down power status for this transitional authority role proves highly consistent with the benevolent policies characterizing a political sense of dominion. In a strictly humanitarian sense, such noble principles apply not only to the member nations, but also to the lofty ideals extending to a universal domain (although not always achievable in practice). As a globally accepted means of governance, dominion clearly fits this enduring authoritarian profile, although tempered by a vulnerable quality that appeals to a religious sensibility.

220.1 – REVERENCE

A parallel ascending hierarchy of themes further holds true with respect to the remaining class of counter double bind maneuvers; namely, the sequence of reverence-veneration-homage-benediction. The first-listed theme of *reverence* represents the counter double bind response to the preliminary "self-esteem" maneuver. The term derives from the Latin *revereri*, from *re-* (intensification) and *verieri* (to feel awe). It is traditionally defined as the state of being held in high esteem, a perspective frequently dependent upon ritual/tradition for its justification. Rather than graciously submitting to the personal authority's dictates (namely, worshipfully acting rewardingly) the reverent individual effectively disqualifies such an adoring perspective, wherein sidestepping the insistent quality of the self-esteem expressed by the personal authority figure.

In Old Testament scripture, reverence chiefly occurs as a translation of the Hebrew themes of *yare* and *shachah*. The root stem of the former translates as "fear," expressed as a deferential attitude towards the Lord akin to a reverential sense of awe. The root-stem for *shachah* is translated as "falling down" (as in bodily prostration): an expression of a bearing towards one's superiors reflecting themes of honor or obeisance. In this deferential fashion, the personal follower figure primarily displays a reverential attitude, although subconsciously disqualified to some extent due to the ritual expectations imposed by the personal authority figure. Consequently, in response to the nostalgic sense of self-esteem initiated by the personal authority figure, the only graceful exit from such a double bind context remains precisely such a reverential attitude: a response subliminally disqualified through its very state of compunction.

240.1 – VENERATION

The personal foundations for reverence, in turn, extend to a group sphere of influence with respect to the related theme of *veneration*. The group authority's pomp-filled sense of self-esteem further prompts the reverential sense of veneration from the established group representative. The term derives from Middle French *veneration*, from the Latin *veneratio* (reverence), from *venerari* (to worship, revere), related to *veneris* (love, desire).

The affiliated sense of "venerable" is used in the ecclesiastical tradition as a title of distinction for those reaching the first level of canonization.

This reverential sense of veneration implies a sense of devotion for one's authority figure, particularly figures of heroic status or distinction. This proved particularly applicable to the Roman emperors, revered as civic leaders as well as emblems of grandeur characterizing the imperial lifestyle. During the reign of Constantine, the etiquette of the Byzantine court invoked elaborate rituals of respect for the emperor, in addition to his statues and symbolisms. It proved only fitting that his subjects bow down, kiss, or even offer incense to these imperial images, even extending to the worship of an empty throne. Similar veneration was paid to religious images such as the crucifix/altarpiece. Religious icons, at least for the Eastern Empire, were taken on journeys as symbols of protection. They were marched in front of armies or hung in the place of honor in virtually every room or shop.

Whether religious or civic in nature, the ritualized prerequisites for veneration impart a disqualified character to the counter double bind class of transitional maneuver. In direct analogy to the personal foundations for reverence, veneration alternately targets a group (and sometimes spiritual) authority level. In response to the pomp expressed by the group authority figure, the group representative reverently acts in a venerable fashion, whereby sidestepping the insistent quality of the initial transitional maneuver. Cloaked in the guise of a compulsory ritual, the subliminal degree of disqualification attributed to veneration emerges to its fullest effect, an aspect that generally escapes the detection of even the most dedicated of disciples.

260.1 – HOMAGE

The preceding group sense of veneration, in turn, extends to a universal sphere of influence with respect to the affiliated theme of *homage*: a term generally employed in a worshipful sense. The term derives from the Old French *homage*, from the Latin *homo* (a man): also in the sense of a humble servant or vassal, akin to the Latin *humus* (earth). In terms of feudal law, it denotes the symbolical acknowledgment made by a feudal vassal towards his lord upon receiving investiture. It also denotes reverential respect or deference, particularly in an outward fashion (as in obeisance). According to the formal act of homage, the feudal tenant declared himself (on bent knee) to be the homage (or bondman) of the lord; hence,

a reverential submission in terms. This act of fealty invoked the fidelity of the tenant towards his lord, a faithful adherence to the obligations owed one's higher authority.

The traditional feudal method of owning land was by fiefdom. The overlord was the grantor of the fief, whereas the recipient was termed the vassal. The fief was transferred during the ceremony of homage, where the kneeling vassal put his clasped hands between those of his lord in an outward declaration of loyalty. The lord, in turn, completed the ceremony by kissing the vassal and raising him to his feet. The vassal then swore an oath of fealty, vowing to serve the lord faithfully in all respects. This formal ceremony cemented the legal relationship between lord and his vassal, whereupon the lord invested the vassal with his treasured fief. In addition to parcels of land, rights and honors could also be granted as fiefs by the lord. Originally the fief needed to be renewed upon the death of either party, although with the advent of hereditary succession, renewal of the fief by the heirs of the decedent eventually prevailed.

The spiritual overtones implicit to the homage ceremony certainly appear striking, in direct analogy to the spiritual homage paid to one's personal divinity. The somewhat compulsory nature of the ceremony further reflects the pattern previously established for reverence/veneration, although now encompassing a more lofty range of themes. Although all three themes appear closely related, the ascending hierarchy of personal, group, and spiritual terms appears particularly well suited in the order given.

280.1 – BENEDICTION

The final term within the ascending hierarchy of themes, *benediction*, represents a humanitarian extension upon the preliminary sequence of reverence, veneration, and homage. It is traditionally defined as a solemn invocation or divine blessing, primarily in a congregational sense. The term derives from the Latin *benedicto*, from *bene* (well) and *dictum* (to say). It generally refers to one of the most dramatic of Catholic services; namely, the Benediction of the Blessed Sacrament. Although a solemn benediction can also occur in related social contexts (such as the climax of a closing ceremony), the Catholic version proves extremely informative in this regard, although not necessarily the only means of interpretation.

Catholic Benediction is known as *Salut* in France, and in Germany as *Segen*. It is customarily an afternoon or evening devotional consisting of the singing of hymns and litanies prior to the display of the Blessed Sacrament. This occurs in a gilded monstrance surrounded by candles upon the central altar. Towards the close of the ceremony, the priest raises the monstrance, making the sign of the cross over the congregation.

The deeply reverent and ritual nature of benediction formally argues for its crowning humanitarian inclusion within the ascending hierarchy of reverence, veneration, and homage (although to a supremely abstract degree). The reverent display of the sacred host within the ornamental monstrance confirms the extremely formal nature of the ceremony, an enduring ritual of truly humanitarian proportions. This sacred pageantry before the congregation virtually guarantees a worshipful response, as the accompanying series of chants and hymns clearly serve to indicate. This highly formal act of worship, however, subliminally disqualifies much free exercise, therein consistent with benediction's crowning inclusion within the ascending hierarchy of counter double bind maneuvers.

211 – APOLOGY

A similar pattern of influence further holds true with respect to the related class of lesser virtues based upon apology/clemency. The initial authority sequence of apology-rectitude-penitence-contrition, in turn, prompts to the remaining follower sequence of clemency-pardon-absolution-deliverance: whereby indicative of the personal, group, spiritual, and humanitarian levels, respectively. The first mentioned theme of *apology* is defined as a transitional variation on the more basic sense of guilt expressed by the personal authority figure. Consequently, apology anticipates a blameful treatment on the part of the personal follower similar to the case previously established for self-esteem/reverence. Its modern spelling derives from the Greek *apologia* (a speech made in defense), from *apologos* (an account or story), from *apo-* (from) and *logos* (speech). The original English connotation of self-justification was eventually modified to reflect "a frank expression of regret for wrongs done" (first recorded in 1594). In a general sense, apology is defined as regret for a fault or transgression in a heartfelt plea for mercy or forgiveness.

This theme also refers to a literary style that defends or justifies an author's opinion or point of view. Unlike the general sense of the term, this literary usage does not necessarily imply that a wrong has been done, nor expresses regret. The most famous ancient example is Plato's Apology (circa 3rd century BCE) representing Socrates' defense at his trial before an Athenian tribunal. The subsequent Christian tradition of "apologetics" exalted such notable theologians as St. Augustine and St. Thomas Aquinas.

Through solemn apology, the personal authority formally transitions into the more basic guilt perspective, although from a "one-down" power status. The apologist vulnerably increases his odds of gaining the consideration of the established follower figure, wherein prompting the latter's lenient sense of blame in the process. The personal follower, in turn, may alternately resort to a disqualified form of counter double bind maneuver in the process; namely, the clemency perspective outlined later in this chapter. Regardless of the eventual outcome, the initial apology maneuver serves its intended goal of gaining the notice of the established follower figure, although not always with the desired results.

231 – RECTITUDE

The personal prerequisites of apology, in turn, extend to a group sphere of influence with respect to the related theme of *rectitude*. The newly transitioned group authority apologetically expresses a sense of rectitude towards the established follower figure, wherein transitionally simulating an honorable sense of guilt. Consequently, rectitude denotes a sense of responsibility grounded in the terms of obligation, as in moral uprightness or righteousness. The term derives from the Late-Latin rectitudo, from the Latin *rectus* (straight): suggesting the need to follow a "straight and narrow path." Roman authority Pliny the Younger insightfully notes: "Never do anything concerning the *rectitude* of which you are in doubt." Furthermore, his contemporary Ovid also wrote: "The mind, conscious of *rectitude*, laughed to scorn the falsehood of report." As the chief transitional counterpart with respect to "honor," rectitude enjoys considerable prestige within the realm of ethical inquiry. Indeed, according to American philosopher Ralph Waldo Emerson: "It is true that genius takes its rise out of the mountains of *rectitude*; that all beauty and power which men covet are somehow born out of that alpine district."

Accordingly, rectitude represents the higher (group) variation on the more basic apology maneuver of the personal authority figure, wherein formally transitioning into this past-directed style of power perspective. The vulnerable characteristics of the rectitude maneuver share (with apology) a one-down power status, further prompting the just treatment on the part of the established follower figure. Consequently, rectitude clearly targets a group sphere of influence, a public acknowledgement of culpability exceedingly consistent with such a transitional format.

251 – PENITENCE

The ascending authority sequence of apology and rectitude, in turn, extends to a universal sphere of influence with respect to the related theme of *penitence*. The newly transitioned spiritual authority penitently acts with rectitude towards the established spiritual disciple in anticipation of the latter's blameful-hope for justice. Consequently, penitence is generally defined a solemn regret with respect for past sinfulness, as in a repentant attitude. The term derives from the Latin *pænitentia* (repentance), from *pænitentum* (penitent), present-participle of *pænitere* (to feel regret). The related notion of the "penitentiary" appears as during the 15ᵗʰ century as "a place of punishment for offenses against the church," from the Middle Latin *penitentiaria*. In terms of Catholic theology, penance refers to the specific virtue or its formulation as one of the Seven Sacraments Both entertain the common truth that one who sins should repent and (insofar as possible) make appropriate reparations. This firm determination to sin no more is the prime factor that determines the ultimate prospects for forgiveness. Accordingly, penance is a moral virtue whereby the sinner is predisposed to a hatred of his sin as an offence against God, accompanied by a firm commitment to reformation. The teachings of Christ on the subject are expressed in the parables of the Prodigal Son and the Repentant Publican. Similarly, Mary Magdalene (who washed her sins with her tears of sorrow) has remained the enduring spiritual archetype of the repentant sinner.

In this traditional sorrowful sense, penitence continues the trend previously established for apology/rectitude, although now targeting a clearly spiritual sphere of influence. Indeed, the deep spiritual overtones related to this theme are particularly evident in its sacramental nature: a vulnerable expression of culpability consistent with this universal perspective. Certainly, many of the great spiritual figures throughout history have expressed such a penitent attitude, a feature particularly in keeping with this vulnerable style of transitional power perspective.

271 – CONTRITION

The ascending hierarchy of terms based upon apology ultimately culminates with respect to the supremely abstract theme of *contrition*. The enduring prerequisites for the humanitarian authority role are penitently expressed contritely towards the established follower figure in anticipation of the latter's just-hope for the truth. Contrition traditionally signifies an extreme sense of remorse for past sinful deeds, although in a more ritually formal sense than that initially seen for penance. The term derives from the Latin *contritio* (a breaking of something hardened), from the Latin *contritus* (literally: worn out, ground to pieces), past-participle of *conterere* (to grind), from *com-* (together) and *terere* (to rub).

Old Testament prophets laid particular emphasis on the need for hearty repentance. The psalms state that God does not despise "the contrite heart" (Psalms 1:19), and called upon Israel to "rend your hearts and not your garments" (Joel 2:12). Similarly, the prophet Job resigned himself to penance in sackcloth and ashes in order to reconcile the sorrow of his soul (Job 8:6). The Council of Trent defines contrition as: "a sorrow of the soul and a hatred of sin committed with the firm purpose of sinning no more." This sorrow of the soul is not merely speculative regret for wrongs done but rather a deep pain in conjunction with hatred for sin. Indeed, nearly every medieval theologian contends that contrition is chiefly based upon this detestation of sin.

Contrition represents the supreme culmination of the trend previously established for apology, rectitude, and penitence: although extending to a more enduring humanitarian sphere of influence. Consequently, the newly transitioned humanitarian authority vulnerably acts in a contrite fashion (from a one-down power status) in anticipation of the lenient treatment of the established follower figure. Despite this extreme level of abstraction, the contrite individual formally fulfills the specifics for the transitional class of power maneuvers, an aspect further verified with respect to the subsequent class of counter double bind maneuvers.

221.1 – CLEMENCY

The remaining sequence of terms specific to the counter double bind class of maneuvers is respectively defined as the ascending hierarchy of clemency, pardon, absolution, and deliverance: which counters the preliminary sequence of apology, rectitude, penitence, contrition. The first-mentioned theme of *clemency* is traditionally defined as a mild or gentle demeanor towards others, particularly when a merciful course of action is in order. This abiding sense of gentleness derives from the Latin *clementia* (calmness, gentleness), from *clemens* (calm, mild), from *clinare* (to lean). The classical Romans worshipped this abstract attribute in the guise of Clementia (the divine personification of clemency or mercy). Her worship grew in popularity due to her favored status with the emperor Julius Caesar. In 44 BCE, the Senate decreed a temple dedicated to both Caesar and Clementia, where the cult statuary depicted the two figures clasping hands. Regular yearly sacrifice to Clementia was decreed in honor of the emperor Caligula in 39 CE, whereas a later festival commemorated Nero's compassionate treatment of Tiridates. On coins of the empire, she appears as Clementia Augusta, and later, as Clementia Temporum.

A persistent pattern emerges from this background information; namely, clemency denotes a personally bestowed style of lenient treatment, exemplified through the actions of the gracious Roman emperors of the day. Hence, in analogy to its counterpart in "reverence," clemency similarly circumvents the insistent quality of the apology expressed by the personal authority without necessarily admitting complicity in the process. In this subliminally disqualified fashion, the reluctant personal follower formally acknowledges the apology professed by the authority figure without necessarily appearing to have done so.

241.1 – PARDON

The personal prerequisites for clemency, in turn, extend to a group sphere of influence with respect to the clement sense of *pardon* expressed by the group representative. Generally speaking, a pardon refers to the remittance of a penalty or punishment, wherein mercifully making an allowance. The term derives from the Latin *perdonare* (to give wholeheartedly), a compound of *per-* (thoroughly) and *donare* (to give or present). In a legal sense, granting a pardon refers to an exemption from punishment for a criminal offense through the assent of a government executive. A blanket pardon granted to those guilty of a general offense is termed an amnesty. This pardon (at least in the United States) fully terminates any criminal liability, including restrictions resulting from criminal conviction (although the pardoned individual may still be liable in a civil sense). A pardon, therefore, is distinguished from alleviation of punishment: as in commuting a sentence, reprieve, or parole. The US Constitution gives the president power to grant reprieves or pardons for any federal crime, although he may not interfere with impeachment. In most states, the governor enjoys similar powers, although

he/she may not pardon those convicted of treason or criminal contempt of court.

According to these legalistic perspectives, the civic theme of pardon is particularly suggestive of a group-directed focus, wherein expanding upon the personal prerequisites previously established for clemency. The pardoning individual effectively sidesteps the apologetic sense of rectitude expressed by the group authority figure: claiming only to be following protocol, hence, not a willing participant in the entire transitional interchange. In this subliminally disqualified sense, the reluctant group representative effectively sidesteps the insistent quality of the initial rectitude maneuver, wherein avoiding any concomitant loss of status in the process.

261.1 – ABSOLUTION

The preliminary sequence of clemency/pardon, in turn, extends to a universal sphere of influence with the respect to the spiritual theme of *absolution*. It is traditionally defined as the remission of sins officially declared by a priest. In a more general sense, it refers to an acquittal or release from punishment. The term derives from the Latin *absolvare*, from *ab-* (from) and *solvere* (to loosen, to free): the burden of guilt respectively lifted away. Absolution proper concerns the priestly act whereby one is freed from the stain of sin: although presupposing a contrite attitude on the part of the penitent.

To Peter (and the other apostles) was given the power to forgive sins in the name of the Lord. This power to absolve occurs unmistakably in the Gospel of St. John (20:22-23) where he states: "Whose sins ye shall forgive they are forgiven them; and whose sins ye shall retain, they are retained." In the cannon the Roman Catholic Church, the penitent is absolved of sins by the confessor, who hears the confession and confers the sacrament. Prior to granting absolution, the confessor admonishes the sinner and imposes a penance (typically consisting of prayers). The penitent is also instructed to make restitution for injury done to others.

The spiritual overtones associated with absolution come through the clearest, extending the more limited (group) focus of pardon into a more universal sphere of influence. In direct analogy to the related theme of homage, absolution similarly denotes a disqualified form of counter double bind maneuver, effectively sidestepping the insistent quality of the penitent individual. Compliance is chalked up to the strictures of ritual rather than any volitional assent in terms. Consequently, through this subliminal denial of complicity, the spiritual disciple reciprocates his expected role within entire transitional interchange, although in a thoroughly non-confrontational manner.

281.1 – DELIVERANCE

The ascending sequence of clemency, pardon, and absolution ultimately culminates with respect to the crowning humanitarian theme of *deliverance*. This latter term effectively complements the more positive prerequisites previously established for benediction. Although deliverance appears fairly specialized in a religious sense, it is traditionally defined as the act of freeing or delivering, particularly with respect to sinfulness. The term derives from the French *delivrer*, a compound formation of the Latin *de-* (from) and *liberare* (to set free). In a scriptural sense, it denotes deliverance through the payment of a ransom; or liberation from oppression, violence, or captivity. In New Testament scripture, the redemption for the sins of all mankind is achieved through Christ's sacrificial death, the ransom or price for such extreme deliverance. The debt is not only cancelled, but paid in full, wherein expiating the sins of all mankind.

Regardless of the individual traditions therein, the enduring humanitarian prerequisites for deliverance effectively fulfill the initial sequence of clemency, pardon, and absolution. In direct analogy to its subordinate counterpart of absolution, deliverance represents a subconsciously disqualified style of leniency perspective, as its scriptural precedents amply serve to indicate. Indeed, this appeal to scriptural foundations serves to obscure the disqualified nature of this perspective, although its extreme level of abstraction disguises any pat determination therein.

25

THE FUTURE-DIRECTED LESSER VIRTUES (II)

The completed description of the lesser virtues based upon self-esteem/reverence and apology/clemency, in turn, brings up the issue of the remaining future-directed sequences of terms. According to the preceding chapter, both self-esteem and apology were defined as transitional variations on the nostalgia/guilt perspectives of the established personal authority figure, wherein prompting the disqualified reverence/clemency perspectives of the respective personal follower. A similar pattern further holds true with respect to the transitional sequences based upon congeniality/concession and appeasement/sympathy. In direct contrast to the past-directed roles characterizing self-esteem and apology, congeniality and appeasement represent a future-directed class of transitional power maneuvers, formally expanding upon the more elementary desire/worry sequence of perspectives.

The pattern of description for this future-directed class of lesser virtues is similar to that which has gone before; namely, the four-level hierarchy of authority terms is described first, followed by the respective series of follower roles. The preliminary double bind sequence of congeniality-cordiality-hospitality-altruism is described first, followed by the respective counter double bind sequence of concession-indulgence-gratitude-goodwill. Furthermore, the second half of the chapter examines the related sequences of appeasement-conciliation-accommodation-sacrifice and sympathy-compassion-mercy-forgiveness. The discerning reader is encouraged to refer back to the four-part listing of schematic definitions for the lesser virtues (II) outlined in Chapter 24, wherein providing a formal schematic representation of the power dynamics at issue in concert with the descriptive narratives for each of the individual terms.

212 – CONGENIALITY

The first-listed lesser theme of *congeniality* denotes a friendly and outgoing style of personality. Its modern spelling derives from the Latin *com-* (together) and *genialis* (of birth); hence, a kindred and sympathetic spirit. The ensuing connotations of "agreeableness" first appear during the early 18th century. Consequently, the term formally denotes a positive range of solicitous behaviors conducive to achieving the approval of one's established follower figure (consistent with its more basic counterpart in desire). The congenial individual maneuvers from a one-down power status in anticipation of securing the consideration of the personal follower figure, wherein laying the groundwork for an ongoing personal interaction.

Nowhere is this congenial spirit more effectively apparent than in the beauty pageant tradition of Miss Congeniality. Prior to final judging, each of the pageant contestants casts a vote for the contestant they deem is most deserving of the Miss Congeniality Award. The contestants vote by secret ballot in a process that does not affect the point system for the overall title. The criteria for the congeniality award include the virtues of friendliness, pleasantness, and the support of fellow pageant-mates. The successful candidate encourages and helps-out whenever possible. In terms of personality, the winning contestant mixes amiably with her peers, making others feel comfortable in her presence, wherein exhibiting a friendly and sincere disposition.

Congeniality technically fulfills the specifics previously established for the transitional class of power maneuvers. Indeed, the initial phase of the general transitional interchange is specifically referred to as the "congeniality phase," so fundamental is the pattern of interaction. Consequently, in terms of the personal authority role, the beauty contestant congenially acts in a desirous fashion towards the other participants in anticipation of their express approval, as outwardly expressed through the bestowal of the congeniality award.

232 – CORDIALITY

The personal characteristics for congeniality, in turn, extend to a group sphere of influence with respect to the related theme of *cordiality*. The term derives from the Latin *cordialis* (from the heart), from *cor* or *cordis* (heart): wherein denoting a heartfelt or affectionate nature. It originally referred to a medicine, food, or drink that stimulated the heart. The high alcohol content of the typical "cordial" (such as schnapps) definitely imparts a "warm sensation" going down, as well as promoting a festive atmosphere.

As an adjective, the sense of a heartfelt emotion first appears in the late 15th century. The Abbe Goussault, a counselor at High Court (circa the 17th century) expounds on the merits of cordiality in child-rearing as follows: "A few words of *cordiality* and trust make an impression on the minds (of children), and few are they in number that can resist these sweet and simple methods." A somewhat more cynical viewpoint is offered by American humorist Florence King in her insightful tome, *With Charity Toward None* (1992), where she writes: "Because good manners build sturdy walls, our distaste for intimacy makes us exceedingly *cordial* ships that pass in the night. As long as you remain a stranger, we will be your friend forever." This quotation satirically reflects the somewhat formal nature of cordiality, as reflected in the uncertain nature of initiating a fresh relationship within an established social order. Indeed, whether one offers a cordial liqueur, or simply a handshake and a smile, the mechanisms governing social intercourse typically require some preliminary lubrication, as typically encountered at a cocktail party or social mixer. As a new addition to the social context, the cordial individual congenially maneuvers from a one-down power status, a strategy that directly enhances one's chances of acceptance at least during the preliminary stages.

252 – HOSPITALITY

The group prerequisites for cordiality, in turn, extend to a universal sphere of influence with respect to the more spiritually focused theme of *hospitality*. The term derives from Latin *hospes* (a stranger or guest), denoting kindness towards strangers and a welcome spirit towards guests. This aspect is particularly apparent in Old Testament scripture, a custom still preserved amongst the prevailing cultures of the desert region. Hospitality is regarded as a right of the traveler, with gratitude towards the host remaining a measure of good faith. Accordingly, hospitality is granted as a duty by the host, who may eventually become a recipient of the hospitality in return. The granting of hospitality is surrounded by an etiquette that has made the Middle-Eastern variety so justly celebrated. The traveler is made the virtual master of the household during his stay. The host performs the most servile of requests, even avoiding sitting in his guest's presence without express permission. The guest is given free use of all that his host possesses, technically extending even to the favors of the wife or daughter. The host is duty-bound to defend his guest against any or all threats, wherein setting aside any pre-existing conflicts.

In New Testament scripture, Christ's directs his apostles to "take nothing for the journey" (Mark 6:8): presupposing that they would always be assured of finding hospitality. They even appeared to have their choice of hosts (Matthew 10:11), and could stay as long as they pleased (Luke 10:7). This traveler's claim to hospitality was enhanced by their status as bearers of good tidings to the populace. Consequently, hospitality towards the apostles was judged so virtuous that even a "cup of water" was considered meritorious when offered in the name of the disciple.

As the first Christian congregations were founded, the exercise of hospitality was further enhanced. Not only did the Christian traveler look to his brethren for hospitality, but individual churches relied upon the traveler to foster a sense of unity throughout the Roman Empire. Accordingly, hospitality continues the trend previously established for congeniality and cordiality, although now extending to a universal sphere of influence. The deep spiritual overtones associated with hospitality are clearly evident in the universal privileges afforded the humble traveler. Indeed, whether invoking its namesake "hospital" or traveler's refuge (hostel), this spirit of hospitality remains an enduring charitable precept worldwide. Certainly, the chances remain good that each of us will be in need of such services at some point during our lifetime.

272 – ALTRUISM

The preceding trend towards hospitality ultimately culminates with respect the supremely abstract theme of *altruism*. The term was coined by Auguste Comte in 1851 in allusion to the Italian adjective *altrui*, from the Latin *alter* (the other). It is defined as the principle of living and acting in the best interests of others, as opposed to selfish propensities characterizing egoism. The term was introduced to the English speaking tradition by George H. Lewes in 1853, and popularized thereafter by advocates of Comte's philosophy. Although employed primarily in a psychological sense to designate emotions of a sympathetic nature, the consequence of altruism towards others proves equally significant. It denotes a theory of conduct wherein actions targeting the happiness of others possess the greatest moral value.

Comte is considered the founder of the School of Social Eudaemonism (based on Positivism), to which the designation of altruism is also given. Not only is happiness to be found in living for others, but charitable devotion to mankind represents the highest form of religious impulse. Humanity essentially operates under the influence of conflicting impulses; namely, personal (or egoistic) and social (or altruistic). The primary condition of individual wellbeing, therefore, is the subordination of self-love to such benevolent impulses, wherein accentuating social empathy over self-serving instincts.

To usher in his era of altruism, Comte invented a quasi-religious belief system that substituted an abstraction termed Humanity for the divinity of God. This controversial aspect of Comte's system was accepted by only a few of his adherents. Herbert Spencer and John Stuart Mill (English contemporaries of Comte) accepted the general utility of altruism, although arguing that its true moral worth should reside in the welfare of society rather than individual concerns. Altruism represents the supreme culmination of the preliminary sequence of congeniality, cordiality, and hospitality. The enduring humanitarian prerequisites for altruism are certainly well founded. The humanitarian authority figure altruistically acts in a hospitable fashion, although from a somewhat vulnerable one-down power status. In spite of its extreme level of abstraction, altruism formally fulfills the specifics established for the transitional class of power maneuvers, an aspect further verified in terms of the remaining class of counter double bind maneuvers.

222.1 – CONCESSION

The initial sequence of transitional terms based upon congeniality, in turn, sets the stage for the remaining sequence of counter double bind maneuvers; namely, concession, indulgence, gratitude, and goodwill. The first mentioned theme of concession is traditionally defined as the act of conceding or granting a special privilege or favor. The term derives from the Latin *concessum*, from *con-* (wholly) and *cedere* (to yield). Similar to its related counterpart in reverence, the concession perspective politely circumvents the insistent quality of the congeniality maneuver without sacrificing any abiding sense of free will in the process.

In a contractual sense, a concession is a special privilege enacted through legislation surpassing the strictures of common law. It is granted through special favor giving the recipient advantages over non-privileged individuals. This enduring favor is distinguished from a permission or single dispensation. Those named in the benefits are entitled to lawfully exercise, whereas external parties are obliged to respect such statutes. Privileges are classified as either remunerative or gratuitous. Privileges recognized by the law require no proof, although they may periodically be subject to judicial scrutiny. All other privileges require proof of the original concession, or a duly certified copy.

In this highly formal sense, the concession perspective effectively sidesteps the insistent quality of the initial congeniality maneuver. The established personal follower concessionally claims to be acting only out of formality, therefore, not a free and willing participant in the entire transitional interchange. In direct response to the congeniality expressed by the personal authority figure, the only graceful exit from such a double bind maneuver is precisely such a concessional perspective: a response certainly anticipated, although formalized through the compunctual state of affairs.

242.1 – INDULGENCE

The personal prerequisites for concession, in turn, extend to a group sphere of influence with respect to the related theme of *indulgence*. It is traditionally defined as the act or practice of gratifying, particularly in terms of excessive adulation. The term derives from the Latin *indulgentia* (complaisance or fondness), from *indulgentem*, present participle of *indulgere* (to be kind, to yield): in turn, a compound of *in-* (in) and *dulcis* (sweet). Originally, it referred to a sense of kindness or favor, although later modified to reflect a remission of a debt or tax.

In terms of Catholic theology, an indulgence generally denotes a pardon or remission of the temporal punishment due to sin (the guilt of which had already been forgiven). The practice of quantifying indulgences dates to early times when public penance was imposed (subject to indulgence). The mere fact that the Church proclaims an indulgence does not necessarily imply that it can be gained without effort on the part of the faithful, for the basic formula: *corde saltem contrito* (at least with a contrite heart) remains essential. It similarly proves crucial to reverently perform the good works (prayers, alms, etc.) accompanying the granting of the indulgence. The German monk, Martin Luther rightfully protested the abuses accompanying the sale of indulgences, eventually rejecting the doctrine altogether. Beginning with the Council of Trent in 1562, the buying or selling of indulgences was also outlawed in the Catholic Church.

Regardless of the individual traditions therein, the ritualized aspects of indulgence impart a subliminally disqualified character consistent with the counter double bind class of maneuvers. In direct analogy to its subordinate counterpart in concession, indulgence targets a group (and sometimes spiritual) sphere of influence. Consequently, in direct response to the initial cordiality maneuver of the group authority figure, the group representative concessionally acts in an indulgent fashion effectively sidestepping the insistent quality of the initial authority maneuver. This ritual sense of indulgence now remains cloaked in the mantle of ritual, effectively disguising the disqualified nature of the entire transitional interchange.

262.1 – GRATITUDE

The dual ascending hierarchy of concession and indulgence, in turn, extends to a universal sphere of influence with respect to the related theme of *gratitude*. This theme is defined as a warm or friendly feeling towards a benefactor with respect to a sense of thankfulness, particularly when a favor has been bestowed. The term derives from the Latin *gratitudo*, from *gratus* (pleasing). According to French philosopher, Jacques Maritain: "Gratitude is the most exquisite form of courtesy." Furthermore, British lexicographer, Samuel Johnson also notes: "Gratitude is a fruit of great cultivation; you do not find it among grosser people." On a more sober note, German philosopher, Friedrich Nietzsche writes: "He who bestows something great receives no *gratitude*; for in accepting it the recipient has already been weighed down too much." American author, Herman Melville further tackles the subject as follows: "To be the subject of alms-giving is trying,

and to feel in duty-bound to appear cheerfully *grateful* under the trial, must still be more so."

Consequently, in direct analogy to the subordinate sequence of concession/indulgence, gratitude represents a disqualified form of counter double bind maneuver effectively sidestepping the insistent quality of the initial hospitality perspective. The grateful individual's compliance is ultimately chalked-up to the formalities of courtesy/good breeding, rather than any volitional assent in terms. This formality is instilled at a fairly early age, when perhaps we all recall being coached to respond with a hearty "thank you" when served a tasty treat. The obligatory rejoinder "you're most welcome" further solidifies the training ritual, fully acknowledging the transitional interchange that has just transpired.

282.1 – GOODWILL

The ascending hierarchy of concessional themes ultimately culminates with respect to the crowning humanitarian perspective of *goodwill*: a fitting adjunct to the preliminary sequence of concession, indulgence, and gratitude. This theme is prominently featured in the *Gloria in Excelsis*, an early Christian hymn beginning with the words: "Glory be to God on highest, and on earth, peace and *goodwill* towards men." In reference to the Christmas story, the hymn originally was of Greek derivation, incorporated into the Roman Catholic Mass circa the 6th century (following the *Kyrie*).

This enduring theme of goodwill similarly extends to issues of a global (or humanitarian) significance, as witnessed in the modern-day phenomenon of the Goodwill Games. The brainchild of philanthropist Ted Turner, the Goodwill Games launched in 1986 at the Russian host-city of Moscow. This site was specifically chosen in order to ease Cold War tensions through friendly athletic competition amongst nations of the world. The end of the Cold War, however, shifted the focus of the Games to that of a youth initiative. In celebrating sports as an avenue towards the betterment of the younger generation, the Goodwill Games raised millions of dollars for charitable endeavors. Following sixteen years of influence (and a half-dozen separate venues), the Goodwill Games has since ceased operations, the unwitting victim of corporate restructuring. Consistent with its grand humanitarian focus, the years of positive memories associated with the Goodwill Games remain particularly poignant. Its initial focus on global harmony proved highly admirable, although scarcely more so than its concern for the younger generations to come. The enduring theme of goodwill proves fitting exemplar for such a grand and noble enterprise, and one destined to endure in the hearts and minds of all so deeply emotionally touched.

213 – APPEASEMENT

A parallel style of analysis, in turn, remains in order for the related sequence of lesser virtues based upon appeasement/sympathy. The preliminary authority sequence of appeasement, conciliation, accommodation, and sacrifice further prompts the disqualified follower series of sympathy-compassion-mercy-forgiveness (indicative of the personal, group, spiritual, and humanitarian levels, respectively). Indeed, the first mentioned theme of *sympathy* is defined as a transitional variation on the more basic "worry" perspective expressed by the personal authority figure, wherein anticipating the concerned treatment of the personal follower. Its modern spelling derives from the Old French *apeser* (to bring to peace), from the Latin *pax* or *pacis* (peace). Appeasement parallels its counterpart in congeniality by initiating a transitional interaction with the established follower figure. Through this one-down power tactic, the personal authority radically plays-up his appeasement status, wherein providing a fitting counterpoint to the entire transitional interchange.

Appeasement was particularly evident (in a political sense) during the period leading up to World War II. It refers to the policy of pacifying an aggressive nation through negotiation in order to avoid war. A prime example of appeasement concerns England's policy towards Fascist Italy and Nazi Germany in the mid-1930's. British Prime Minister, Neville Chamberlain sought to accommodate Italy's invasion of Ethiopia in 1935, and then took no action when Germany incorporated Austria in 1938. When Hitler subsequently prepared to annex ethnically-German portions of Czechoslovakia, Chamberlain negotiated the notorious Munich Agreement, only further serving to appease the Nazis. Fortunately, Winston Churchill ultimately replaced Chamberlain, helping guide the Free World to the path of victory in World War II. Indeed, Churchill facetiously quipped: "An *appeaser* is one who feeds a crocodile hoping that it will eat him last."

Following the abysmal failure of Chamberlain's policy of appeasement, this theme has acquired somewhat of a pejorative sense. Although generally indicative of a political context, the individual dynamics driving the international scenario are similarly suggestive of a personal sphere of influence. Indeed, Hitler deliberately played up such a cult of personality, although history dictates his aspirations to international goodwill only amounted to subterfuge/stall tactics. Although Chamberlain's efforts towards appeasement were ultimately doomed to failure, they foundered primarily in terms of Hitler's twisted ambitions. Under more favorable circumstances, appeasement remains a proven tool in the diplomatic arsenal, although with definite limitations.

233 – CONCILIATION

The personal prerequisites for appeasement, in turn, extend to a group sphere of influence with respect to the *conciliation* expressed by the group authority figure. It is traditionally defined as the act of gaining consideration or winning over another. The term derives from the Latin *conciliatus*, past participle of *conciliare* (to bring together or unite in feelings), from *concilium* (council): a compound of *com-* (together) and calere (to call). Incidentally, the tendency to confuse conciliation with "counsel" has endured since the 16th century. According to French author Francois de La Rochefoucauld (1613-1680): "Friendship is only a reciprocal *conciliation* of interests." These amicable characteristics for conciliation are generally consistent with the formal transitional format. The group authority appeasingly acts in a conciliatory fashion (from a one-down power status) in anticipation of lenient consideration from the established follower figure.

The typical city-council setting suggests precisely such a group dynamic, where the elected board members endeavor to come to an acceptable consensus with the general citizenry in matters of a civic nature. The right of the common citizenry to present their views before the board is duly noted, confirming the authoritarian status of the board members in service to the community. Conciliation aims to smooth over any conflicts bound to emerge in a diverse population, conciliating rights of individuals to those of the group.

253 – ACCOMMODATION

The ascending transitional sequence of appeasement/conciliation, in turn, extends to a universal sphere of influence with respect to the related theme of *accommodation.* The term derives from the Latin *accommodare*, from *ad-* (to) and *commodus* (fitting): stressing such compromising attributes. The accommodating individual is guided by motives of an obliging or appeasing nature similar to the solicitous attributes previously

271

established for hospitality. According to British statesman, Philip Stanhope (4th Earl of Chesterfield): "Civility, which is a disposition to *accommodate* and oblige others, is essentially the same in every country; although good breeding (as it is called) is different in almost every country."

In a more general sense, accommodation refers to those physical requirements that prove crucial to one's personal sense of wellbeing, as in a safe place to sleep and adequate nourishment. This particularly extends to the expectations of the weary traveler, where acceptable facilities need to be available as needed. This class of accommodations is typically rated according to a four-star rating system enforced by local tourist guilds, where reasonable expectations as to the quality of hotels, taverns, or restaurants may adequately be ascertained. As such, accommodation shares with hospitality a fundamental spirit of giving, although now focussed on crucial essentials, as opposed to the more congenial nature of hospitality. Indeed, universal guarantees of accommodation are legally protected under the law: such as the Civil-Rights Act of 1964 that bars racial discrimination in transportation and public accommodations.

273 – SACRIFICE

The ascending transitional hierarchy of appeasement, conciliation, and accommodation ultimately culminates with respect to the supremely abstract theme of *sacrifice*. It traditionally refers to the act of offering-up one's personal self-interests in lieu of a higher good or purpose. The term derives from the Latin *sacrificium*, from *sacer* (sacred) and *facere* (to make). The extreme humanitarian prerequisites associated with sacrifice prove entirely consistent with the appeasement focus previously established for conciliation and accommodation. Furthermore, the respective one-down power status places the sacrificial individual in a curiously vulnerable position in relation to the established follower role in clear deference to the lofty humanitarian themes at issue.

For the Romans, as well as other classical cultures, a valued commodity (such as a bull or goat) was sacrificed as a burnt offering in order to petition the lenient treatment of the divine pantheon of gods. The sacrificial priest (with head covered by a fold in the toga) offered an initial sacrifice of grain and wine on the altar of the sacred flame in preparation for the blood sacrifice of a consecrated bullock. Only under the direst of circumstances was human sacrifice considered, although this practice was clearly documented at various junctures within Greek and Roman traditional culture.

In a more modern sense, examples of selfless sacrifice can be found in many organizational contexts. Certainly the greatest sacrifice of all is to offer-up one's life for that of another, so great the empathic bond. This is poignantly encountered in the fictional *Tale of Two Cities*, where the hero nobly takes the place of his friend sentenced to execution, a sacrifice compounded by their love for the same woman. Here, the requisite one-down power status places the sacrificial individual in a vulnerable position relative to the established follower role. Sacrifice, accordingly, represents an enduring humanitarian theme revered throughout the ages, and one still admired today.

223.1 – SYMPATHY

The preliminary transitional sequence based upon appeasement invites further parallels to the remaining class of counter double bind maneuvers based upon sympathy; namely, sympathy, compassion, mercy, and forgiveness. The first-mentioned theme of *sympathy* traces its origins to the Greek *sympatheia*, from *syn-* (with) and *pathos* (suffering). It is traditionally defined as the inclination to support in a favorable fashion, particularly in an empathic or forgiving manner. This theme is viewed as a central Christian tenet in keeping with the empathic prerequisites specific to the Golden Rule.

The modern era witnessed a great proliferation of theoretical approaches towards understanding the sympathetic emotions. Although Christianity continued to exert considerable influence, the pessimistic doctrine of Original Sin was increasingly contested in favor of a theory of mankind's innate goodness. Hutcheson viewed the capacity for sympathy as a basic aspect of human nature. David Hume, in turn, made valuable observations concerning the role of sympathy in motivating moral conduct. Rousseau also gave the emotion of *pitié* (compassion) a central role in his social theory of morality. In describing the education of young Émile (1762), Rousseau speculates that the experience of sympathy/compassion concerning the pain of another proves the crucial foundation for society as a whole. Sympathy leads to a recognition of the vulnerability that we all collectively share, and an acknowledgement of the suffering that is often inflicted upon others.

Schopenhauer emerged as yet a further philosopher that acknowledged the fundamental role sympathy plays in morality. In his criticism of

Kantian ethics, Schopenhauer argued that all true moral action must be grounded in other-directed emotions such as sympathy. In viewing compassion as a mysterious union of the self with another, he still left open the issue of why this would necessarily qualify as a form of self-concern. Schopenhauer's ethical viewpoint, however, gained considerable influence in a culture dissatisfied with duty-based morality.

Consequently, true to its related counterpart in concession, the sympathy perspective represents an effective strategy for politely circumventing the insistent quality of the appeasement expressed by the respective authority figure (although without necessarily appearing stalwart in the process). In this subliminally disqualified fashion, the reluctant personal follower fully acknowledges the preliminary appeasement maneuver. The compunctions of social convention elicit a sympathetic response, in return, without necessarily appearing to have done so. This reciprocal interpretation does not technically diminish the heartfelt feelings at issue. Indeed, once placed in such a double bound dilemma, the ultimate extrication (via the counter double bind maneuver) is generally expressed in an unpremeditated fashion. The overall effect may appear virtually brimming with emotion, perhaps even fooling oneself insofar as the degree of sincerity is concerned.

243.1 – COMPASSION

The preceding personal prerequisites for sympathy, in turn, extend to a group sphere of influence with respect to the affiliated theme of *compassion*, a disqualification of the social conventions characterizing a group context. The term derives from the Latin *compassio* (sympathy), from *compassus*, past participle of *compati* (to feel pity): from the compound of *com-* (together) and *pati* (to suffer). It denotes a sense of empathy for the sufferings of others, generally eliciting a warmer tone than the more condescending theme of pity. Compassion accentuates an outward respect for others, particularly in times of great need or distress. In true compassion, one not only feels the suffering of others, but freely strives to relieve such pain, in return.

Similar to sympathy, the compassionate individual leniently acts empathically without necessarily appearing to having done so, wherein invoking a subliminally disqualified form of counter double bind maneuver (similar to that previously seen for indulgence). The compassionate individual effectively sidesteps the insistent quality of

the conciliation maneuver, although cloaked within the conventions of a civilized society; hence, avoiding any explicit participant within the general transitional interchange.

Similar to other virtues in its class, there definitely appears to be a "golden mean" with respect to compassion. Lack of compassion can lead to apathy, callousness, or cruelty: whereas excessive compassion leads to over-indulgence, enablement, or codependency. Compassion shares a curious paradox with sympathy in that by being coerced into reciprocating, one's true emotional saliency is scarcely as compelling as if it were freely offered to begin with. This limiting factor proves consistent with the disqualified character of the entire transitional interchange.

263.1 – MERCY

The ascending virtuous hierarchy of sympathy and compassion, in turn, extends to a universal sphere of influence with respect to the spiritual theme of *mercy*. Its modern spelling derives from the Late Latin *merces* (compassion of God), from the Latin *merces* (pay or favor). Mercy is defined as the kind or compassionate treatment of another, particularly in adverse types of circumstances. The classical Greeks celebrated their own traditions of mercy in terms of Eleos (the divine personification of mercy or pity). According to Pausanias: "The Athenians are the only ones among the Hellenes who worship this divine quality: yet among all the gods, it is the most useful to human life in all its vicissitudes." Foreigners seeking the assistance of the Athenians were first obliged to approach (as suppliants) the altar of Eleos located in the marketplace of Athens.

Mercy similarly plays a significant role in the Judeo-Christian tradition, although regarded as a divine attribute rather than a deity in its own right. Old Testament scripture reverently celebrates a God of mercy and forgiveness towards his chosen people. In the Book of Exodus, God mercifully frees the Israelites from the bondage of the Egyptians. On Mount Sinai, He reveals himself to Moses as the *merciful* one (Ex. 34:8). Indeed, the gilded lid on the Ark of the Covenant was traditionally referred to as the *mercy* seat: from the belief that the Lord rested there during the annual ritual of atonement. On this sacred day, the High Priest would sprinkle blood from a sacrificial goat and bullock upon the mercy seat in atonement for the sins of the entire nation. Although this ceremony was shielded from public eye, the prayers of the faithful (at least in spirit) were directed specifically towards this "Holy of Holies."

273

These sacrificial aspects of mercy reach their supreme fulfillment with respect to the death and resurrection of Christ. In his Sermon on the Mount, Jesus extols mercy in his fifth beatitude: "Blessed are the *merciful* for they shall receive *mercy*." He further implores the faithful to be merciful, just as their Father is merciful (Luke 6:36). He similarly reminds his disciples that they will be judged according to their mercifulness towards others (Mt 25:31-46).

In direct analogy to its related counterpart in "gratitude," mercy represents a subliminally disqualified form of counter double bind maneuver, effectively sidestepping the insistent quality of the accommodation expressed by the spiritual authority figure. One's merciful compliance is generally made on religious grounds rather than any volitional cooperation in terms. Through such an innate denial of complicity, the spiritual disciple effectively reciprocates his expected role in the transitional interchange, although in a thoroughly non-confrontational fashion.

283.1 – FORGIVENESS

The ascending transitional sequence of sympathy, compassion, and mercy ultimately culminates with respect to the crowning humanitarian perspective of *forgiveness*: a supreme construct exemplifying the very essence of mercy. The term derives from the Old English *forgiefan*, from *for-* (away) and *fiefan* (to give), as in overlooking a debt or social trespass. Forgiveness, accordingly, represents a subliminally disqualified decent sense of wisdom, wherein avoiding any overt complicity, therein. Its appeal to a humanitarian sphere of influence echoes the spiritual focus previously established for mercy. Through this ritual sense of leniency, the reluctant humanitarian follower forgivingly sidesteps the more insistent "sacrificial" perspective of the respective authority figure: wherein disqualifying any overt participation within the entire transitional interchange.

In a traditional sense, forgiveness did not figure prominently in the morality of the ancient world. The magnanimous individual typically disregarded offenses that were beneath one's station. To forgive one's peers, however, was considered weak-spirited. In Old Testament scripture, forgiveness towards one's fellow man was only infrequently mentioned, with those seeking forgiveness usually occupying a subservient position. New Testament scripture, however, taught that forgiveness is a Christian duty to be granted without reserve. Christ preaches that there is never a wrong so grievous that it is beyond forgiveness. Indeed, the spirit of Christianity is generally taken to be synonymous with a forgiving disposition. Christ answers Peter that he should forgive not merely seven times in a day, but seventy times seven (Matthew 18:21). It is here that the humanitarian overtones associated with forgiveness come through the clearest, formally expanding upon the initial sequence of sympathy, compassion, and mercy. The extremely moral nature of forgiveness applies equally well to all ages and times, an enduring ethical standard of virtually universal proportions. Indeed, contrary to the popular maxim, one can certainly forgive (although scarcely forget), for the clear humanitarian prerequisites attributed to this theme would seem to rule-out any latter eventuality.

In summary, the completed description of the dual classifications of terms for the lesser virtues invites many practical applications in relation to the reciprocating interplay of double bind and counter double bind maneuvers. Certainly an advanced degree of innate societal sophistication is required to successfully navigate such a convoluted sphere of influence. In our modern fast-paced society, these skills virtually become second-nature when faced with transitioning into an ever shifting range of social coalitions. A sharp sense of humor is generally considered a key factor to social success, as mirrored in the entertaining genre of the television situation comedy. Life rarely is all fun and games, however, wherein a parallel degree of sensitivities to the intricacies of melodrama ensures a responsible demeanor in the face of a more tragic state of affairs. The truest test of life involves maintaining an effective balance of these two complementary aspects. Hopefully, the grand-scale technical analysis of this most intriguing of social subjects may prove useful to all those whose skills in this regard are often sadly lacking!

26

THE ACCESSORY VARIATIONS
FOR THE LESSER VIRTUES

In conclusion, the completed description of the lesser virtues (I) and (II) adds a fitting validation to what had originally amounted to somewhat of an intuitive analysis. Although an additional complement of *accessory* lesser virtues might similarly be predicted, a suitable number of synonyms for constructing such a parallel system were not yet identified at the initial launch of the three-digit coding system. Indeed, it remains a fitting tribute to the versatility of the English language that even the main versions of the lesser virtues were so effectively specified. Fortunately, in the interim a fully competent accessory version of the lesser virtues has recently been devised, representing a promising avenue for further research within the field. These accessory variations represent close synonyms to the main versions of the lesser virtues, although formally specifying the accessory realm through a reversal of the polarities of the "you" and "I" roles.

Similar to the main versions of the lesser virtues, the accessory versions similarly span the entire personal, group, spiritual, and humanitarian levels within the transitional hierarchy. For instance for the accessory lesser virtues (I), the respective double bind follower sequence of fealty-steadfastness-adoration-happiness directly specifies a past-directed reinforcement focus aimed at the past notable behaviors of the respective authority figure. This further prompts the remaining counter double bind authority sequence of simplicity-loftiness-sublimity-splendor, countering the preliminary double bind sequence through a disqualified denial of overt complicity therein.

In a related fashion, the accessory follower transitional sequence of accountability-obligation-obeisance-commitment similarly specifies a past-directed focus, although now targeting a more submissive context. Furthermore, the remaining authority sequence of accessory counter double bind terms; e.g., blamelessness-exculpation-acquittal-impeccability further validates such a trend, ultimately culminating the entire transitional sequence.

The affiliated third sequence of accessory terms is alternately based upon the related double bind/counter double bind sequence of adherence/demureness (at the personal level). For instance, the group follower figure adherently acts in a gallant fashion whereby prompting the coy demureness indicative of the counter double bind maneuver. Furthermore, in terms of the spiritual level, the spiritual disciple figure gallantly acts in a stately fashion, prompting the coy sense of wholesomeness expressed by the respective authority figure. Finally, for the most advanced humanitarian level, the respective follower figure fervorously acts in a stately fashion, whereby prompting the follower's wholesome sense of excellence indicative of the counter double bind maneuver.

The fourth and final dimension of accessory terms is respectively based upon a foundation within the personal themes of wariness/timidity (the accessory counterparts for vigilance/meekness). The accessory sequence of follower terms (wariness-intrepidity-stalwartness-victory) effectively reciprocates its main virtuous counterparts (vigilance-courage-valor-triumph). Furthermore, the remaining counter double bind sequence of accessory authority roles (timidity-complaisance-compliance-amicableness) offers a fitting counterpoint to its respective main counterparts: e.g., meekness-obedience-conformity-pacifism.

A similar style of analysis further remains in order for the remaining accessory classifications of the lesser virtues (II). Rather than attempting

224	225
Fealty	Accountability
226	**227**
Adherence	Wariness

TRANSITIONAL
ALTER EGO STATES
(Personal Double-Bind)

→

214.1	215.1
Simplicity	Blamelessness
216.1	**217.1**
Demureness	Timidity

DISQUALIFIED
EGO STATES
(Personal Counter Double-Bind)

244	245
Steadfastness	Obligation
246	**247**
Gallantry	Intrepidity

TRANSITIONAL
CARDINAL VIRTUES
(Group Double-Bind)

→

234.1	235.1
Loftiness	Exculpation
236.1	**237.1**
Coyness	Complaisance

DISQUALIFIED
PERSONAL IDEALS
(Group Counter Double-Bind)

264	265
Adoration	Obeisance
266	**267**
Stateliness	Stalwartness

TRANSITIONAL
THEOLOGICAL VIRTUES
(Spiritual Double-Bind)

→

254.1	255.1
Sublimeness	Aquittal
256.1	**257.1**
Wholesomeness	Compliance

DISQUALIFIED
CIVIL LIBERTIES
(Spiritual Counter Double-Bind)

284	285
Happiness	Commitment
286	**287**
Fervor	Victory

TRANSITIONAL
GREEK VALUES
(Humanitarian Double-Bind)

→

274.1	275.1
Splendor	Impeccability
276.1	**277.1**
Excellence	Amicableness

DISQUALIFIED
ECUMENICAL IDEALS
(Humanit. Counter Double-Bind)

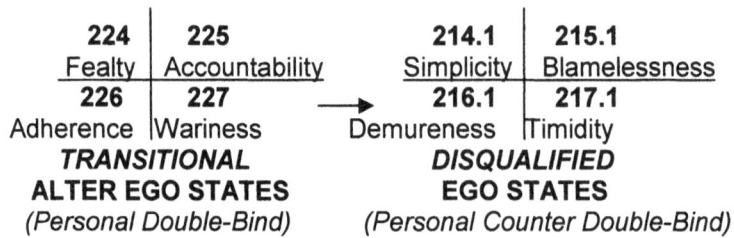

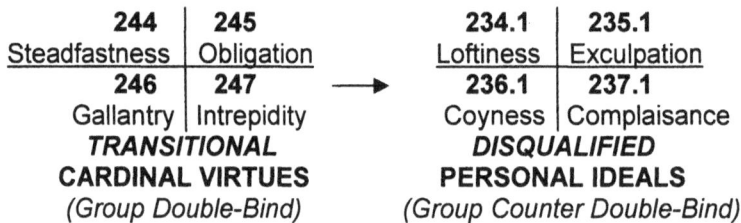

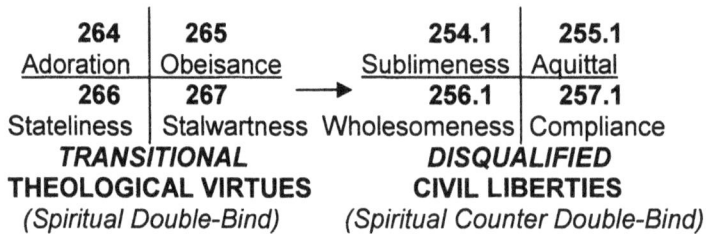

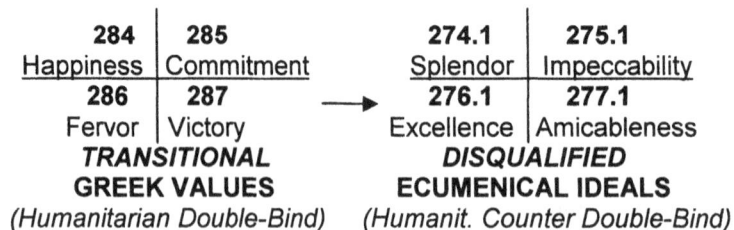

Fig. 26A – The Accessory Lesser Virtues - (I)

214	215
Self-Respect	Sorrow
216	**217**
Amiability	Placation

TRANSITIONAL
EGO STATES
(PA - Double-Bind)

→

224.1	225.1
Esteem	Lenity
226.1	**227.1**
Favor	Empathy

DISQUALIFIED
ALTER EGO STATES
(PF - Counter-Double-Bind)

234	235
Ostentation	Remorse
236	**237**
Conviviality	Concordance

TRANSITIONAL
PERSONAL IDEALS
(GA - Double-Bind)

→

244.1	245.1
Acclaim	Remittance
246.1	**247.1**
Sanction	Commiseration

DISQUALIFIED
CARDINAL VIRTUES
(GR - Counter Double-Bind)

254	255
Holiness	Regretfulness
256	**257**
Generosity	Consonance

TRANSITIONAL
CIVIL LIBERTIES
(SA - Double-Bind)

→

264.1	265.1
Ardor	Dispensation
266.1	**267.1**
Thanksgiving	Pity

DISQUALIFIED
THEOLOGICAL VIRTUES
(SD - Counter Double-Bind)

274	275
Supremacy	Grief
276	**277**
Beneficence	Propitiation

TRANSITIONAL
ECUMENICAL IDEALS
(HA - Double-Bind)

→

284.1	285.1
Exultation	Redemption
286.1	**287.1**
Benignity	Remission

DISQUALIFIED
GREEK VALUES
(RH - Counter Double-Bind)

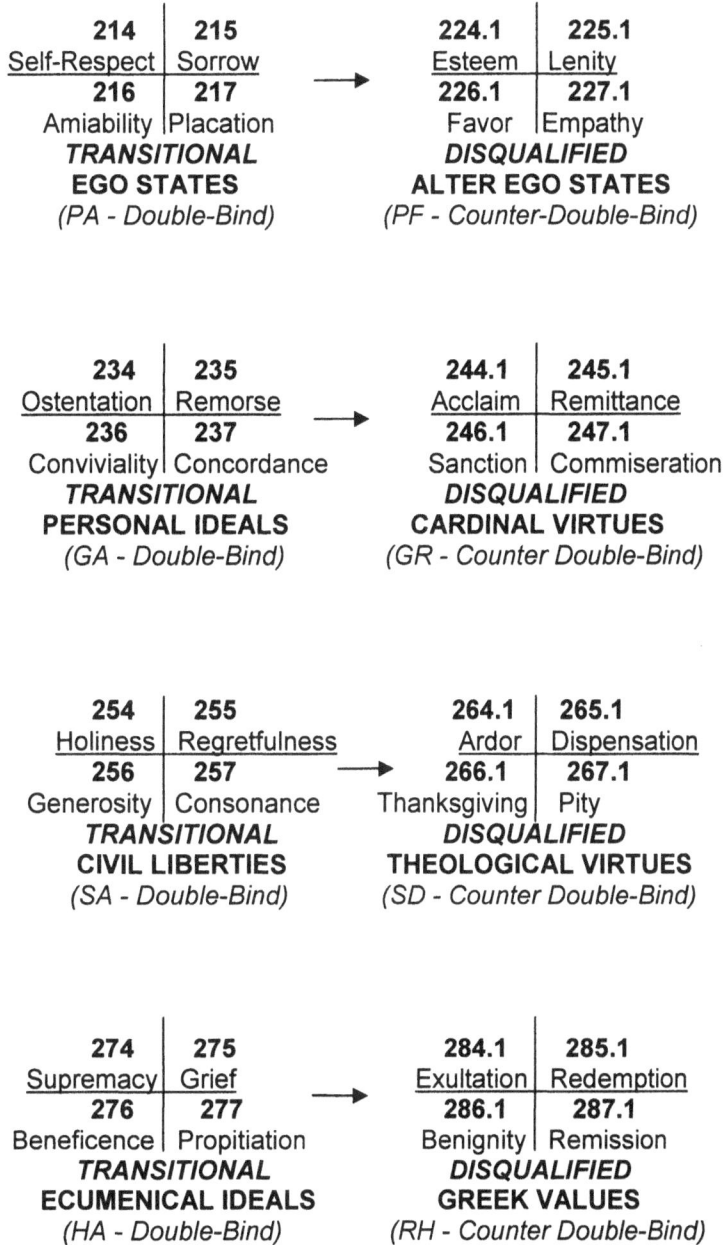

Fig. 26B – The Accessory Lesser Virtues - (II)

FEALTY	SIMPLICITY
Previously, you (as personal authority) have poignantly admitted acting in a solicitous fashion in response to the praising treatment of the personal follower. But now, I (as new personal follower) will praisefully act with *fealty* towards you: in anticipation of your (as established PA) poignant treatment of me.	Previously, I (as new personal follower) have praisefully acted with fealty towards you: in anticipation of your (as established PA) poignant treatment of me. But now, you (as reluctant personal authority) will *simplicitously* <u>deny</u> acting poignantly towards me: thwarting my (as new PF) praiseful sense of fealty.
STEADFASTNESS	LOFTINESS
Previously, you (as group authority) have poignantly acted in an exalted fashion in response to the circumspective-praisefulness of the group representative. But now, I (as new group representative) will *steadfastly* act with fealty towards you: in anticipation of your (as established GA) poignant sense of exaltation.	Previously, I (as new group representative) have steadfastly acted with fealty towards you: in anticipation of your (as established GA) poignant sense of exaltation. But now, you (as reluctant group authority) will simplicitously act in a *lofty* fashion towards me: thwarting my (as new GR) steadfast sense of fealty.
ADORATION	SUBLIMITY
Previously, you (as spiritual authority) have exaltedly acted in a bountiful fashion in response to the circumspective sense of devotion of the spiritual disciple. But now, I (as new spiritual disciple) will steadfastly act in an *adoring* fashion towards you: in anticipation of your (as established SA) exalted sense of bountifulness.	Previously, I (as new spiritual disciple) have steadfastly acted in an adoring fashion towards you: in anticipation of your (as established SA) exalted sense of bountifulness. But now, you (as reluctant spiritual authority) will loftily act in a *sublime* fashion towards me: thwarting my (as new SD) steadfast-adoration of you.
HAPPINESS	SPLENDOR
Previously, you (as humanitarian authority) have bountifully acted blessingly in response to the charming sense of devotion of the representative member of humanity. But now, I (as new representative member of humanity) will adoringly act in a *happy* fashion towards you: in anticipation of your (as established HA) bountiful blessing of me.	Previously, I (as new representative member of humanity) have adoringly acted in a happy fashion towards you: in anticipation of your (as established HA) bountiful blessing of me. But now, you (as reluctant humanitarian authority) will *splendorously* act in a sublime fashion towards me: thwarting my (as new RH) happy-adoration of you.

Table N-1 – The Acc. Lesser Virtues Based on Fealty/Simplicity

ACCOUNTABILITY	BLAMELESSNESS
Previously, you (as personal authority) have culpably admitted acting submissively in response to the censuring treatment of the personal follower. But now, I (as new personal follower) will censuringly express *accountability* towards you: in anticipation of your (as established PA) culpable treatment of me.	Previously, I (as new personal follower) have censuringly expressed accountability towards you: in anticipation of your (as established PA) culpable treatment of me. But now, you (as reluctant personal authority) will *blamelessly* <u>deny</u> acting culpably towards me: thwarting my (as new PF) censuring expression of accountability towards you.
OBLIGATION	EXCULPATION
Previously, you (as group authority) have culpably acted in an upright fashion in response to the equitable-censuring of the group representative. But now, I (as new group representative) will *obligingly* seek a sense of accountability towards you: in anticipation of your (as established GA) culpable sense of uprightness.	Previously, I (as new group representative) have obligingly sought a sense of accountability towards you: in anticipation of your (as established GA) culpable sense of uprightness. But now, you (as reluctant group authority) will blamelessly act in an *exculpatory* fashion towards me: thwarting my (as new GR) obliging quest for accountability towards you.
OBEISANCE	ACQUITTAL
Previously, you (as spiritual authority) have freely acted in an upright fashion in response to the equitable sense of fairness of the spiritual disciple. But now, I (as new spiritual disciple) will obligingly seek a sense of *obeisance* towards you: in anticipation of your (as established SA) free sense of uprightness.	Previously, I (as new spiritual disciple) have will obligingly sought a sense of obeisance towards you: in anticipation of your (as established SA) free sense of uprightness. But now, you (as reluctant spiritual authority) will exculpatorily express a sense of *acquittal* towards me: thwarting my (as new SD) obligatory quest for obeisance.
COMMITMENT	IMPECCABILITY
Previously, you (as humanitarian authority) have freely acted in a conscientious fashion in response to the fair sense of credence of the representative member of humanity. But now, I (as new representative member of humanity) will obeisantly act in a *committed* fashion towards you: in anticipation of your (as establ. HA) free sense of conscientiousness.	Previously, I (as new represent. member of humanity) have obeisantly acted committedly towards you: in anticipation of your (as establ. HA) free sense of conscientiousness. But now, you (as reluctant humanitarian authority) will *impeccably* express a sense of acquittal towards me: thwarting my (as new RH) obeisant sense of commitment.

Table N-2 – The Acc. Lesser Virtues Based on Account./Blameless.

ADHERENCE	DEMURENESS
Previously, I (as personal authority) have passionately acted in a solicitous fashion in response to the admiring treatment of the personal follower. But now, you (as new personal follower) will admiringly act in an *adherent* fashion towards me: in anticipation of my (as established PA) passionate treatment of you.	Previously, you (as new personal follower) have admiringly acted in an adherent fashion towards me: in anticipation of my (as established PA) passionate treatment of you. But now, I (as reluctant personal authority) will *demurely* <u>deny</u> acting admiringly towards you: thwarting your (as new PF) adherent treatment of me.
GALLANTRY	COYNESS
Previously, I (as group authority) have passionately acted respectfully in response to the continently-admiring treatment of the group representative. But now, you (as new group representative) will adherently act in a *gallant* fashion towards me: in anticipation of my (as established GA) passionate-respect for you.	Previously, you (as new group representative) have adherently acted in a gallant fashion towards me: in anticipation of my (as established GA) passionate-respect for you. But now, I (as reluctant group authority) will demurely act in a *coy* fashion towards you: thwarting your (as new GR) gallant treatment of me.
STATELINESS	WHOLESOMENESS
Previously, I (as spiritual authority) have courteously acted respectfully in response to the continent sense of kindness of the spiritual disciple. But now, you (as new spiritual disciple) will gallantly act in a *stately* fashion towards me: in anticipation of my (as established SA) courteous-respect for you.	Previously, you (as new spiritual disciple) have gallantly acted in a stately fashion towards me: in anticipation of my (as established SA) courteous-respect for you. But now, I (as reluctant spiritual authority) will coyly act in a *wholesome* fashion towards you: thwarting your (as new SD) stately treatment of me.
FERVOR	EXCELLENCE
Previously, I (as humanitarian authority) have courteously acted in a gracious fashion in response to the beauteous-faith of the representative member of humanity But now, you (as new representative member of humanity) will *fervently* act in a stately fashion towards me: in anticipation of my (as established HA) courteous sense of graciousness.	Previously, you (as new representative member of humanity) have fervently acted in a stately fashion: in anticipation of my (as establ. HA) courteously-gracious treatment of you. But now, I (as reluctant humanitarian authority) will wholesomely react with *excellence* towards you: thwarting your (as new RH) fervent sense of stateliness.

Table N-3 – The Acc. Lesser Virtues Based on Adherence/Demureness

WARINESS	TIMIDITY
Previously, I (as personal authority) have apprehensively acted in a submissive fashion in response to the caring treatment of the personal follower. But now, you (as new personal follower) will caringly act in a *wary* fashion towards me: in anticipation of my (as established PA) apprehensive treatment of you.	Previously, you (as new personal follower) have caringly acted in a *wary* fashion towards me: in anticipation of my (as established PA) apprehensive treatment of you. But now, I (as reluctant personal authority) will *timidly* <u>deny</u> acting apprehensively towards you: thwarting your (as new PF) caring sense of wariness.
INTREPIDITY	**COMPLAISANCE**
Previously, I (as group authority) have apprehensively acted with probity in response to the brave sense of caring of the group representative. But now, you (as new group representative) will warily act in an *intrepid* fashion towards me: in anticipation of my (as established GA) apprehensive sense of probity.	Previously, you (as new group representative) have warily acted in an intrepid fashion towards me: in anticipation of my (as established GA) apprehensive sense of probity. But now, I (as reluctant group authority) will *complaisantly* act in a timid fashion towards you: thwarting your (as new GR) intrepid treatment of me.
STALWARTNESS	**COMPLIANCE**
Previously, I (as spiritual authority) have forbearingly acted with probity in response to the scrupulous sense of bravery expressed by the spiritual disciple. But now, you (as new spiritual disciple) will *stalwartly* act in an intrepid fashion towards me: in anticipation of my (as established SA) forbearing sense of probity.	Previously, you (as new spiritual disciple) have stalwartly acted in an intrepid fashion towards me: in anticipation of my (as established SA) forbearing sense of probity. But now, I (as reluctant spiritual authority) will complaisantly act in a *compliant* fashion towards you: thwarting your (as new SD) stalwart treatment of me.
VICTORY	**AMICABLENESS**
Previously, I (as humanitarian authority) have forbearingly acted patiently in response to the scrupulous sense of shrewdness of the representative member of humanity. But now, you (as new representative member of humanity) will stalwartly act *victoriously* towards me: in anticipation of my (as established HA) forbearingly-patient treatment of you.	Previously, you (as new representative member of humanity) have stalwartly acted victoriously towards me: in anticipation of my (as establ, HA) forbearingly-patient treatment of you. But now, I (as reluctant humanitarian authority) will compliantly act in an *amicable* fashion towards you: thwarting your (as new RH) victorious treatment of me.

Table N-4 - The Acc. Lesser Virtues Based on Wariness/Timidity

SELF-RESPECT	ESTEEM
Previously, I (as personal follower) have rewardingly acted in an praiseful fashion, in response to the poignant treatment of the personal authority. But now, you (as new personal authority) will poignantly act in a *self-respecting* fashion towards me: in anticipation of my (as established PF) praiseful treatment of you.	Previously, you (as new personal authority) have poignantly acted in a self-respecting fashion towards me: in anticipation of my (as established PF) praiseful treatment of you. But now, I (as reluctant personal follower) will *esteemfully* <u>deny</u> acting praisefully towards you: thwarting your (as new PA) self-respecting treatment of me.
OSTENTATION	**ACCLAIM**
Previously, I (as group representative) have circumspectively acted in a praiseful fashion, in response to the poignant sense of exaltation of the group authority. But now, you (as new group authority) will self-respectfully act in an *ostentatious* fashion towards me: in anticipation of my (as established GR) circumspective-praise for you.	Previously, you (as new group authority) have self-respectingly acted in an ostentatious fashion towards me: in anticipation of my (as establ. GR) circumspective-praise for you. But now, I (as reluctant group representative) will esteemingly act in an *acclaimful* fashion towards you: thwarting your (as new GA) ostentatious treatment of me.
HOLINESS	**ARDOR**
Previously, I (as spiritual disciple) have circumspectively acted in a devoted fashion in response to the exalted sense of bountifulness of the spiritual authority. But now, you (as new spiritual authority) will ostentatiously act in a *holy* fashion towards me: in anticipation of my (as established SD) circumspective-devotion for you.	Previously, you (as new spiritual authority) have ostentatiously acted in a holy fashion towards me: in anticipation of my (as established SD) circumspective-devotion for you. But now, I (as reluctant spiritual disciple) will *ardently* act in an acclaimful fashion towards you: thwarting your (as new SA) holy treatment of me.
SUPREMACY	**EXULTATION**
Previously, I (as representative member of humanity) have charmingly acted in a devoted fashion in response to the bountiful-blessings of the humanitarian authority. But now, you (as new humanitarian authority) will *supremely* act in a holy fashion towards me: in anticipation of my (as established RH) bountiful-blessing of you.	Previously, you (as new humanitarian authority) have supremely acted in a holy fashion towards me: in anticipation of my (as established RH) bountiful-blessing of you. But now, I (as reluctant representative member of humanity) will ardently act with *exultation* towards you: thwarting your (as new HA) supreme treatment of me.

Table P-1 – The Acc. Definitions Based on Self-Respect/Esteem

SORROW	LENITY
Previously, I (as personal follower) have censuringly acted in a lenient fashion in response to the culpable treatment of the personal authority. But now, you (as new personal authority) will culpably act in a *sorrowful* fashion towards me: in anticipation of my (as established PF) censuring treatment of you.	Previously, you (as new personal authority) have culpably acted in a sorrowful fashion towards me: in anticipation of my (as established PF) censuring treatment of you. But now, I (as reluctant personal follower) will *leniently* <u>deny</u> acting censuringly towards you: thwarting your (as new PA) sorrowful treatment of me.
REMORSE	**REMITTANCE**
Previously, I (as group representative) have equitably acted in a censuring fashion in response to the culpable sense of uprightness of the group authority. But now, you (as new group authority) will sorrowfully act in a *remorseful* fashion towards me: in anticipation of my (as established GR) equitable-censuring of you.	Previously, you (as new group authority) have sorrowfully acted in a remorseful fashion towards me: in anticipation of my (as established GR) equitable-censuring of you. But now, I (as reluctant group representative) will leniently act in a *remitting* fashion towards you: thwarting your (as new GA) remorseful treatment of me.
REGRETFULNESS	**DISPENSATION**
Previously, I (as spiritual disciple) have equitably acted in a fair fashion in response to the free sense of uprightness of the spiritual authority. But now, you (as new spiritual authority) will remorsefully act in a *regretful* fashion towards me: in anticipation of my (as established SD) equitably-fair treatment of you.	Previously, you (as new spiritual authority) have remorsefully acted in a regretful fashion towards me: in anticipation of my (as established SD) equitably-fair treatment of you. But now, I (as reluctant spiritual disciple) will remittingly act in a *dispensational* fashion towards you: thwarting your (as new SA) remorseful sense of regret.
GRIEF	**REDEMPTION**
Previously, I (as representative member of humanity) have fairly expressed a sense of credence in response to the free sense of conscientiousness of the humanitarian authority. But now, you (as new humanitarian authority) will regretfully act with *grief* towards me: in anticipation of my (as established RH) fair sense of credence.	Previously, you (as new humanitarian authority) have regretfully acted with grief towards me: in anticipation of my (as established RH) fair sense of credence. But now, I (as reluctant representative member of humanity) will dispensationally act in a *redemptive* fashion towards you: thwarting your (as new HA) grieving treatment of me.

Table P- 2 – The Accessory Definitions Based on Sorrow/Lenity

283

AMIABILITY	FAVOR
Previously, you (as personal follower) have admiringly acted in a rewarding fashion in response to the passionate treatment of the personal authority. But now, I (as new personal authority) will passionately act in an *amiable* fashion towards you: in anticipation of your (as established PF) admiring treatment of me.	Previously, I (as new personal authority) have passionately acted in an amiable fashion towards you: in anticipation of your (as established PF) admiringly treatment of me. But now, you (as reluctant personal follower) will *favoringly* <u>deny</u> acting admiringly towards me: thwarting my (as new PA) amiable treatment of you.
CONVIVIALITY	**SANCTION**
Previously, you (as group representative) have continently acted in an admiring fashion in response to the passionate-respect of the group authority. But now, I (as new group authority) will amiably act in a *convivial* fashion towards you: in anticipation of your (as established GR) continently-admiring treatment of me.	Previously, I (as new group authority) have amiably acted in a convivial fashion towards you: in anticipation of your (as established GR) continently-admiring treatment of me. But now, you (as reluctant group representative) will favorably act in a *sanctioning* fashion towards me: thwarting my (as new GA) convivial treatment of you.
GENEROSITY	**THANKSGIVING**
Previously, you (as spiritual disciple) have continently acted in a kind fashion in response to the courteous-respect of the spiritual authority. But now, I (as new spiritual authority) will convivially act in a *generous* fashion towards you: in anticipation of your (as established SD) continently-kind treatment of me.	Previously, I (as new spiritual authority) have convivially acted in a generous fashion towards you: in anticipation of your (as established SD) continently-kind treatment of me. But now, you (as reluctant spiritual disciple) will sanctioningly act *thankfully* towards me: thwarting my (as new SA) generous treatment of you.
BENEFICENCE	**BENIGNITY**
Previously, you (as representative member of humanity) have benevolently acted kindly in response to the courteous sense of graciousness of the humanitarian authority. But now, I (as new humanitarian authority) will generously act in a *beneficent* fashion towards you: in anticipation of your (as established RH) benevolent sense of kindness.	Previously, I (as new humanitarian authority) have generously acted in a beneficent fashion towards you: in anticipation of your (as established RH) benevolent sense of kindness. But now, you (as reluctant representative member of humanity) will thankfully act in a *benign* fashion towards me: thwarting my (as new HA) beneficent treatment of you.

Table P-3 – The Acc. Definitions Based Upon Amiability/Favor

PLACATION	EMPATHY
Previously, you (as personal follower) have caringly acted in a lenient fashion, in response to the apprehensive treatment of the personal authority. But now, I (as new personal authority) will *placatingly* act in an apprehensive fashion towards you: in anticipation of your (as established PF) caring treatment of me.	Previously, I (as new personal authority) have placatingly acted in an apprehensive fashion towards you: in anticipation of your (as established PF) caring treatment of me. But now, you (as reluctant personal follower) will *empathetically* deny acting caringly towards me: thwarting my (as new PA) placating treatment of you.
CONCORDANCE	**COMMISERATION**
Previously, you (as group representative) have bravely acted in a caring fashion in response to the apprehensive sense of probity of the group authority. But now, I (as new group authority) will placatingly act *concordingly* towards you: in anticipation of your (as established GR) brave treatment of me.	Previously, I (as new group authority) have placatingly acted concordingly towards you: in anticipation of your (as established GR) brave treatment of me. But now, you (as reluctant group representative) will empathetically act in a *commiserating* fashion towards me: thwarting my (as new GA) placating sense of concordance.
CONSONANCE	**PITY**
Previously, you (as spiritual disciple) have scrupulously acted in a brave fashion in response to the forbearing sense of probity of the spiritual authority. But now, I (as new spiritual authority) will concordingly act in a *consonant* fashion towards you: in anticipation of your (as established SD) scrupulous sense of bravery.	Previously, I (as new spiritual authority) have concordingly acted in a consonant fashion towards you: in anticipation of your (as established SD) scrupulous sense of bravery. But now, you (as reluctant spiritual disciple) will commiseratingly express a sense of *pity* towards me: thwarting my (as new SA) consonant treatment of you.
PROPITIATION	**REMISSION**
Previously, you (as representative member of humanity) have scrupulously acted shrewdly in response to the forbearing sense of forgiveness of the humanitarian authority. But now, I (as new humanitarian authority) will consonantly act in a *propitiatory* fashion towards you: in anticipation of your (as established RH) scrupulous sense of shrewdness.	Previously, I (as new humanitarian authority) have consonantly acted in a *propitiatory* fashion towards you: in anticipation of your (as establ. RH) scrupulous sense of shrewdness. But now, you (as reluctant representative member of humanity) will pityingly act with *remission* towards me: thwarting my (as new HA) propitiatory treatment of you.

Table P-4 – The Acc. Definitions Based Upon Placation/Empathy

++ **VICES of EXCESS** (EXCESSIVE VIRTUE)	**MENTAL ILLNESS** (TRANSITIONAL EXCESS)
+ **MAJOR VIRTUES** (VIRTUOUS MODE)	**LESSER VIRTUES** (TRANSITIONAL VIRTUE)

o - **NEUTRALITY STATUS**
(DEFAULT POSITION)

− **VICES of DEFECT** (ABSENCE OF VIRTUE)	**CRIMINALITY** (TRANSITIONAL DEFECT)
− − **HYPER-VIOLENCE** (EXCESSIVE DEFECT)	**HYPER-CRIMINALITY** (TRANSIT. HYPERVIOL.)

Fig. 26-C – The Master Eight-Part Schematic of Ethical Categories

to further and laboriously spell these dynamics out in detail, a complete listing of the accessory terminology for the lesser virtues (I) is schematically depicted in **Fig. 26A** and also in the compact table below.

Fealty → Simplicity   Accountability→ Blameless.
Steadfast. → Loftiness   Obligation → Exculpation
Adoration → Sublimity   Obeisance → Acquittal
Happiness → Splendor   Commit.→ Impeccabil.

Adherence → Demureness   Wariness → Timidity
Gallantry → Coyness   Intrepid.→ Complaisance
Stateliness → Wholesome. Stalwart. → Compliance
Fervor → Excellence   Victory → Amicableness

Furthermore, the complete listing of the accessory terms for the lesser virtues (II) is depicted in **Fig. 26B**, and similarly in the compact table below.

Self-Resp. → Esteem   Sorrow → Lenity
Ostentation → Acclaim   Remorse → Remittance
Holiness → Ardor   Regretful. → Dispensation
Supremacy → Exultation   Grief → Redemption

Amiability → Favor   Placation → Empathy
Conviviality → Sanction   Concord. → Commiser.
Generosity → Thanksgiving   Consonance → Pity
Beneficence → Benignity   Propitiat. → Remission

This arrangement is similar in form and function to that previously established for the main listings of lesser virtues in Chapters *21* and *24*. It should be emphasized that these accessory variations necessarily remain a work in progress, being that their precise determination relied primarily upon identifying the most closely relevant synonyms to the main terms, a somewhat subjective undertaking. As this is a first tentative release of this accessory version, a more detailed description of each of these individual terms will not be undertaken at this juncture, an aspect best deferred to an upcoming edition. The overall literary traditions targeting this accessory realm, furthermore, prove scarcely as convincing as that previously established for the main counterparts. The overall cohesiveness of this parallel accessory hierarchy, however, proves particularly convincing in a holistic sense, leaving room for only a minor degree of adjustments in any upcoming future editions on this subject.

In order to specify these accessory virtuous variations within the three-digit coding system, the third and final digit is ultimately called into play. Here, digits 4-to-7 in the three-slot exclusively specify the accessory variations of the less-er virtues. In terms of the preliminary transitional roles, 224 = fealty as opposed to loyalty, while 225 = accountability vs. responsibility. Furthermore, 226 = adherence in association to discipline, whereas 227 = wariness vs. vigilance. With respect to the disqualified class of counter double bind maneuvers, 214.1 = simplicity in concordance to humility, while 215.1 = blamelessness as opposed to innocence. Furthermore, 216.1 = demureness in association to modesty, whereas 217.1 = timidity vs. meekness. Indeed, the three-digit codes for each of the main lesser virtues are easily modified to their respective accessory counterparts simply by adding a sum-total of four digits to the numerical value initially listed in the third-digit slot for the main sequence of terms: as shown in **Figs. 26A** and **26B**.

THE SCHEMATIC DEFINITIONS FOR THE ACCESSORY LESSER VIRTUES

In line with the main complement of lesser virtues in Chapter *21*, it should further be technically feasible to incorporate the corresponding accessory sequence of terms directly into the schematic definition format (accompanied by a reversed polarity of the "you" and "I" roles), resulting in a parallel complement of schematic definitions for the accessory lesser virtues. The schematic definitions for the accessory lesser virtues (I), accordingly, are outlined in the four-part series of **Tables N-1** to **N-4**. Furthermore, the definitions for the lesser virtues (II) are alternately depicted in **Tables P-1** to **P-4**. Although superficially similar in appearance, this accessory transitional definition format differs in a number of key features from the pattern previously established for the major accessory categories of definitions described in **Parts I** through **IV**. Although the transitional definitions are also represented in a tabular format, a number of key factors vary in a strategic sense from the standard pattern of organization.

For instance, for the lesser virtues (I), the preliminary personal follower perspectives of fealty-accountability-adherence-wariness, in turn, anticipates the collaboration of the established authority figure, as shown in the top-most segments of the left-hand columns of the definitions from **Tables N-1** to **N-4**. Here, both fealty and accountability are defined as transitional variations on the more basic accessory alter ego states of praise and censure: representing reinforcement from the personal follower perspective. Furthermore, adherence and wariness represent transitions into a future-directed sphere of reinforcement; namely, the admiration and caring perspectives characterizing the follower figure.

This "congeniality" style of follower perspective, in turn, prompts the counter double bind proper of the personal authority figure, as depicted in the right-hand columns from **Tables N-1** to **N-4**. Accordingly, simplicity and blamelessness represent disqualified variations of the accessory poignancy/culpability perspectives. Furthermore, demureness and timidity denote similar modifications of passion/apprehension. This basic pattern further extends to the remaining group, spiritual, and humanitarian levels within the ascending power hierarchy.

These accessory variations for the dual classifications of the lesser virtues prove particularly effective for modeling the empathic dimensions of humor and comedy in general, permitting a convincing simulation of the more lighthearted aspects of the warmer human emotions. Indeed, natural empathic ability appears to be a prerequisite for adequately telling a joke (as well as comprehending its significance). An innate conceptual balance between serious and humorous communication emerges as a common feature across virtually all ages and cultures. The militant Taliban regime (that briefly ruled over Afghanistan) officially banned frivolous amusement and diversion on the pretense of presenting an affront to the solemnity of Islam, although such repressive measures were ultimately doomed to fail. Rather a warm sense of camaraderie and accord amongst international allies proves crucial on the world political scene, where convoluted dictates of pageantry and protocol essentially mirror the intricate interplay of double bind and counter double bind maneuvers. Indeed, skillful diplomacy dictates always putting forth a suitably favorable spin, each side delicately dancing around any sense of controversy. In concert with the more serious side to global negotiations, a measured balance in relation to these more whimsical counterparts makes for great international politics, and one certainly crucial for maintaining an optimal degree of global peace and harmony.

In conclusion, the preceding description of the lesser virtues were shown to be fully explainable in terms of the transitional interplay of double bind and counter double bind maneuvers leading to a light-hearted simulation of humor, comedy, and also melodrama. Along parallel lines, this basic organizational pattern similarly proves applicable to the remaining three categories of terms comprising the modified transitional hierarchy, as formally depicted in **Fig. 26C**. This schematic format represents a transitional modification of the more basic five-part diagram previously illustrated at the end of Chapter *20*. The respective transitional counterparts are depicted immediately adjacent the main categories they serve to imitate, wherein serving as transitional entry-points into the realm of the latter.

According to **Fig. 25C**, the lesser virtues are depicted immediately adjacent to the major virtues, whereas the realm of criminality is designated alongside the vices of defect. Furthermore, the domain of hypercriminality is formally affiliated with the realm of hyperviolence, whereas the realm of mental illness is depicted adjacent to the vices of excess. This additional four-part complement of transitional themes specifically incorporates a wide range of individual terms not previously accounted for within the main categories of terms, wherein verifying the resultant eight-part system to a high degree of precision.

This remaining endeavor is currently undertaken with respect to the following **Parts VI** and **VII**. **Part VI** is devoted to the respective realms of criminality and hypercriminality, whereas **Part VII**, in turn, examines the communicational factors underlying mental illness. These well-established systems of transitional terminology fortuitously correspond to the specifics predicted for the traditional models of criminality and mental illness, respectively. In light of the profound impact of the latter two themes upon society as a whole, these remaining chapters represent the crowning achievement with respect to the three-digit coding system, wherein conceptually validating the overall transitional paradigm.

PART-VI

27

AN INTRODUCTION TO
THE REALM OF CRIMINALITY

The darker versions of the transitional power maneuvers (namely, criminality and hypercriminality) prove a curious addition to the unified power hierarchy. In terms of a brief overview, a separate transitional variation was predicted to exist for each of the major ethical categories. For instance, with respect to the lesser virtues, the initial congeniality phase (should it be accepted) directly transitions the newcomer into an established virtuous interaction. Resistance to the congeniality maneuver, however, leads to the humor form of countermaneuver, wherein prompting the termination of the entire transitional interchange.

A similar pattern further holds true with respect to the vices of defect, where the initial criminality phase is formally countered by the trickery form of counter double bind maneuver (as described later in this section). Indeed, as the chief moral opposites of the virtuous realm, the vices of defect certainly figure prominently in the overall realm of criminality. Although the vices of defect may sometimes appear adaptive in a restricted sense, they are almost always maladaptive in a transitional sense (with respect to criminality). Criminality refers to the habit of initiating a new relationship in an antagonistic fashion, directly contrasting with the cooperative nature of the virtuous realm. Accordingly, criminality is defined as the transitional class of power maneuvers expanding upon the darker realm of the vices of defect. In contrast to the virtuous foundations of humor, the darker realm of criminality is expressed as the transitional interplay of the criminality/trickery phases (in contrast to congeniality/humor).

Such criminal intentions prove extremely consistent with the general transitional dynamic; namely, transitions deriving from the default neutrality status: in this case, that neutral status

through which all new relationships (by definition) originate. This generally brings to mind the disturbing scenario of the career criminal prowling the streets looking for victims, typically in a strange neighborhood where anonymity is assured. Should the opportunity arise, the criminal immediately departs from the default neutrality status, whereby criminally accosting the vulnerable stranger for his valuables. This despicable action technically represents a transitional foray into the realm of the vices of defect. As such, it represents a typical cycle within a zero-sum game; namely, your loss is my gain. Owing to its antisocial character, this transitional foray into the vices of defect is typically against the law, with the criminal generally attempting a quick getaway. By picking random victims and remaining anonymous, the criminal minimizes the prospects that a crime will be traced back to him. In the case of property crimes, the criminal's response is typically measured; where cooperative victims usually suffer little lasting harm. This circumstance is further consistent with the similarly measured quality of the vices of defect (where responses are tailored to particular contexts).

This scarcely appears the case for the more troubling realm of hypercriminality, which alternately represents transitions into the realm of hyperviolence. According to this latter scenario, hyperviolence is characterized by responses that escalate out of all proportion to the precipitating circumstances. Hypercriminality shares a tendency towards the extremes with hyperviolence; in that the former represents the direct transitional variation upon the latter. Accordingly, hypercriminality represents an unforeseen and unpredicted outburst of violent behavior, a response scarcely anticipated from the initial state of the neutrality existing just prior to the outburst.

This transitional reaction contrasts directly with the more general class of hyperviolence, which (by definition) is imbedded within a contextual situation. For instance, in terms of the typical crime of passion, the perpetrator is generally well acquainted with his victim. This can take the form of outright abuse (both physical and verbal), as well as threats against the person. Victims of hypercriminality, however, are deliberately chosen at random. Indeed, the extreme nature of hypercriminality specifies a speedy exit from the crime scene in order to escape prosecution. The deranged nature of hypercriminality frequently precludes any effective escape, the reign of terror fortunately short-lived. For this reason, many victims are deliberately silenced in order to prevent subsequent testimony.

MEASURED CRIMINALITY

In conclusion, both criminality and hypercriminality represent transitional forays into the more established realms of the vices of defect and hyperviolence, respectively. Fortunately, these disturbing categories are endowed with a degree of precision conducive to the development of effective tools for diagnosis and treatment. Accordingly, the most rational place to launch such an endeavor concerns the routine style of criminality initially described. Consistent with the measured quality of the more basic vices of defect, ordinary criminality aims to use the minimum force required to achieve the desired result. For instance, the street thug implies a physical threat in order to gain goods of value, with cooperation customarily rewarded by abstaining from any physical harm. Similar moderation further applies to the "white-collar" crimes (embezzlement, insurance fraud, etc.): where the corporation is viewed as a faceless entity to be exploited. This pattern also extends to the so-called "caper" crimes popularized in the movie industry, where a daring band of criminals attempts a heist using skill and daring, although avoiding any physical violence. This also extends to property crimes of a fraudulent nature, as misdemeanors punished by the pillory in earlier times. These crimes, nevertheless, require anonymity in order to evade identification, with the threat of violence implied if cooperation is not forthcoming.

THE TWO-STAGE DYNAMIC
FOR THE REALM OF CRIMINALITY

It still remains to be determined, however, which combination of terms goes towards defining this darker realm of criminality. The more routine prerequisites for ordinary criminality prove to be the most rational starting point, in keeping with their transitional expansion upon the established realm of the vices of defect. For clues to the specifics of this new terminology, it proves fruitful to refer back to the formal dynamics previously established for the lesser virtues; namely, the interplay of the double bind and counter-double bind maneuvers. In contrast to the lesser virtues (initiated through the congeniality phase), transitions into the realm of defect are alternately specified by what is termed the *criminality* phase.

A few basic distinctions must necessarily be made with respect to the criminality phase. Firstly, the preliminary criminality phase represents the initial "double bind" class of power maneuver with respect to the vices of defect, wherein dictating the subsequent punitive reaction on the part of the victim. Similar to the case previously made for the lesser virtues, the victim of the criminality phase can either accept the communication as given, or alternately disqualify the entire transitional interchange (as the counter double bind maneuver). For the virtuous realm, this was previously defined as the humor maneuver proper. For the darker realm of the vices, however, this amounts to the similarly disqualified *trickery* phase. Trickery represents the behavioral antithesis of humor, reflecting a parallel disqualification of the punitive backlash that is ultimately expected.

This reciprocal interplay linking both the criminality and trickery phases represents the fundamental model upon which all criminality is based. In terms of the first four levels within the authority hierarchy, both the trickery and criminality phases are further subdivided into four subunits each: directly reflecting the personal, group, spiritual, and humanitarian levels within the power hierarchy. For instance, the most basic personal level of the criminality phase is respectively defined in terms of the *antisocial* personality: in earlier times also known as the psychopathic personality. The antisocial personality is characterized by impulsive crimes of opportunity, exhibiting little empathy for the plight of the victim or society as a whole. Due to a typical lack of close personal contacts, the antisocial individual is generally defined as a loner, in keeping with a personal placement within the transitional power hierarchy.

The next higher group level, in turn, invokes a more collective sense of criminality; namely, those organized types of activity frequently associated with gangs or syndicates. Rather than acting

Criminals Confined to a London Pillory for Perjury and Cheating: Engraving by Seller - 1678
Detail from: *A Book of the Punishments of the Common Laws of England* - Courtesy the Guildhall Library

---

in a solitary fashion, the criminal gang member operates in conjunction with others within the collective, permitting criminal activities of a more elaborate nature. Consistent with this tendency to organize, the criminal syndicate poses a formidable challenge to law enforcement, which similarly employs a group "policing" strategy in order to maintain law and order.

The next higher spiritual (or universal) level, in turn, gives way to the even more abstract theme of *sacrilege*, characterizing behaviors of a profane nature, often regarded as obscene by public standards. Indeed, this theme frequently enters into the realm of religious apostasy, expressed in crimes perpetrated on a global scale.

This "universal" sense of criminality extends to realms even as abstract as the humanitarian domain. It represents a supreme perspective grounded primarily within the principles of ritual and tradition, as witnessed in the many global crimes perpetrated against humanity. The criminal themes of religious extremism, radical revolution, or global terrorism immediately come to mind. This humanitarian variation typically invokes the common agenda of *fanaticism*, wherein the fanatic seeks to impose his beliefs at any cost: as witnessed in the recent terrorist attacks on the World Trade Center and the Pentagon.

In terms of the crowning transcendental level, it is difficult to imagine a sphere of criminality capable of targeting such a lofty level (although perhaps expanding upon such terrorist themes). Indeed, is entirely within such a disqualified (transcendental) perspective that the carnage and brutality associated with terrorism ultimately becomes conscionable to the twisted mentality of the fanatic.

THE TRICKERY FORM OF COUNTER DOUBLE BIND MANEUVER

The rather cursory analysis of the four basic levels comprising the initial (transitional) phase effectively rounds out the stepwise description of the preliminary double bind class of maneuvers. This general criminality phase (spread across the four authority levels) further places the victim in a form of double bind paradox, being that he is expected to react with violence in return. Indeed, it proves particularly tempting to accept this course of action, although (at a higher meta-level) the victim is manipulated into accepting the dictates of the perpetrator.

The only graceful exit from such a double bind paradox is through the counter double bind class of power maneuver. As previously suggested in the case of humor, the counter double bind maneuver accepts the face of value of the communication, while simultaneously denying complicity in the entire transitional interchange. In response to

620	621
t-Treachery	t-Vindictiveness
622	623
t-Spite	t-Malice

TRANSITIONAL
FRAUD
(Personal Double-Bind)

$\longrightarrow$

610.1	611.1
d-Laziness	d-Negligence
612.1	613.1
d-Apathy	d-Indifference

DISQUALIFIED
KNAVERY
(Personal Counter Double-Bind)

640	641
t-Insurgency	t-Vengeance
642	643
t-Gluttony	t-Cowardice

TRANSITIONAL
CORRUPTION
(Group Double-Bind)

$\longrightarrow$

630.1	631.1
d-Infamy	d-Dishonor
632.1	633.1
d-Foolishness	d-Capriciousness

DISQUALIFIED
VILLAINY
(Group Counter Double-Bind)

660	661
t-Betrayal	t-Despair
662	663
t-Avarice	t-Antagonism

TRANSITIONAL
HERESY
(Spiritual Double-Bind)

$\longrightarrow$

650.1	651.1
d-Prodigality	d-Slavery
652.1	653.1
d-Vulgarity	d-Cruelty

DISQUALIFIED
PROFANITY
(Spiritual Counter Double-Bind)

680	681
t-Ugliness	t-Hypocrisy
682	683
t-Evil	t-Cunning

TRANSITIONAL
ANARCHISM
(Humanitarian Double-Bind)

$\longrightarrow$

670.1	671.1
d-Wrath	d-Tyranny
672.1	673.1
d-Oppression	d-Persecution

DISQUALIFIED
APOSTASY
(Humanit. Counter Double-Bind)

Fig. 27A — The Three-Digit Codes for Criminality - (I)

610	611		620.1	621.1
<u>t-Laziness</u>	<u>t-Negligence</u>		<u>d-Treachery</u>	<u>d-Vindictiveness</u>
612	613		622.1	623.1
t-Apathy	**t-Indifference**		**d-Spite**	**d-Malice**

TRANSITIONAL	*DISQUALIFIED*
KNAVERY	**FRAUD**
(Personal Double-Bind)	*(Personal Counter Double-Bind)*

630	631		640.1	641.1
<u>t-Infamy</u>	<u>t-Dishonor</u>		<u>d-Insurgency</u>	<u>d-Vengeance</u>
632	633		642.1	643.1
t-Foolishness	**t-Caprice**		**d-Gluttony**	**d-Cowardice**

TRANSITIONAL	*DISQUALIFIED*
VILLAINY	**CORRUPTION**
(Group Double-Bind)	*(Group Counter Double-Bind)*

650	651		660.1	661.1
t-Prodigality	<u>t-Slavery</u>		<u>d-Betrayal</u>	<u>d-Despair</u>
652	653		662.1	663.1
t-Vulgarity	**t-Cruelty**		**d-Avarice**	**d-Antagonism**

TRANSITIONAL	*DISQUALIFIED*
PROFANITY	**HERESY**
(Spiritual Double-Bind)	*(Spiritual Counter Double-Bind)*

670	671		680.1	681.1
<u>t-Wrath</u>	<u>t-Tyranny</u>		<u>d-Ugliness</u>	<u>d-Hypocrisy</u>
672	673		682.1	683.1
t-Oppression	**t-Persecution**		**d-Evil**	**d-Cunning**

TRANSITIONAL	*DISQUALIFIED*
APOSTASY	**ANARCHISM**
(Humanitarian Double-Bind)	*(Humanitarian Counter Double-Bind)*

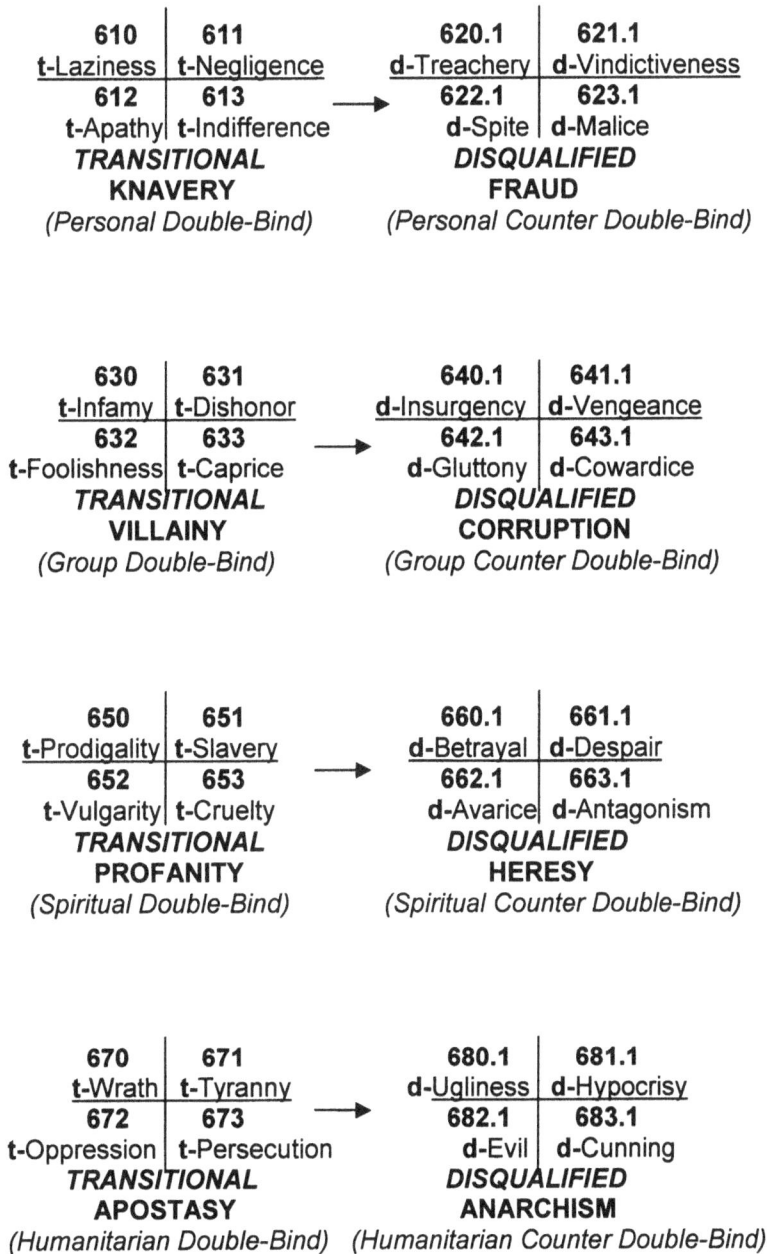

Fig. 27B – The Three-Digit Codes for Criminality - (II)

the criminality style of double bind maneuver, the victim can alternately employ the trickery form of counter double bind maneuver: responding back in kind (but denying doing it). Indeed, trickery appears to have evolved ample precedents in the natural environment with respect to deceptive camouflage and interspecies mimicry. Trickery within a social context achieves widespread fascination in Western culture, particularly during adolescence: when the tendency towards pranks makes a direct analogy to humor (although in a clearly darker sense).

Within the realm of humor, communication of a virtuous nature is disqualified to some extent; hence, considered somewhat naughty or risqué. Indeed, during the more formal periods of history, humor was often frowned-upon by the more sober members within the group. For similar reasons, the affiliated sphere of trickery is infused with a more favorable social cachet than might be expected, being that it represents a "meta-disqualification" within the darker realm of defect. In this latter respect, what humor lacks in prestige, the mischievous quality of trickery makes up for in naughtiness, although both are still disparaged to some degree.

Value judgments aside, the general public clearly appears to appreciate the delicious irony of "trickeration" skillfully played-out to the end. Trickery represents a disqualified resistance to the criminal dictates of the perpetrator: a difficult strategy to carry off effectively (similar to the case made for humor). Indeed, one can easily pretend to be serious, but the same does not necessarily extend to being witty or tricky. The public's fascination with trickery is often glamorized in "true crime" magazines, where the clever traps that lead to the apprehension of the criminal make for interesting reading.

THE TWO-STAGE INTERPLAY OF CRIMINALITY AND TRICKERY

The typical prank, accordingly, plays-out in terms of the strict two-stage process initially described. For instance, the outcast student might inadvertently fail to pay the proper respect to the popular in-crowd. This, in turn, sets the stage for the trickery maneuver proper, where a resentful attitude is reflected back in kind, although carefully disqualified in order to disguise the cruel intentions. Indeed, in direct analogy to the pattern previously established for the criminality phase, the subsequent trickery phase is similarly subdivided into a related four-part sequence of terms reflecting the ascending hierarchy of authority le-

vels. For instance, in terms of the most basic personal level, this tactic is respectively expressed as a primitive form of trickery, such as the prank or practical joke perpetrated by the clever rascal. At a group level, the focus switches to one of *chicanery*: a term traditionally invested with legal connotations. Here a ploy or caper is generally planned, as in "stings" launched against organized crime. Indeed, this group level of trickery is perhaps the most entertaining, as featured in humorous television shows such as *America's Dumbest Criminals*.

Ascending to the next higher spiritual (or universal) level further begs mention of the related theme of the *artifice*, where a ruse or escapade is attempted to achieve the desired result. It is even feasible to speculate on extensions to the crowning humanitarian level with respect to the enduring theme of the *stratagem*, where a crafty feint or sham proves effective in the long run. This strategy further encompasses "stings" operating on a worldwide scale, such as measures taken by Interpol against international criminals. These themes are also fictionalized in certain movie genres (such as the James Bond series), where the dashing hero saves the world from the machinations of the diabolical villain through suave trickery and intrigue. The crowning transcendental level, however, will not be discussed at this juncture, for the degree of disqualification generally surpasses the conceptual abilities of the ordinary individual.

In summary, the full eight-term sequence of categories for both the criminality and trickery phases is schematically depicted in the diagram immediately below. Indeed, it is easy to gain a sense of the trend towards increasing abstraction when scanning the individual columns from top to bottom. The personal characteristics for the psychopathic personality, in turn, extend to the organized criminality characterizing the group authority level. Furthermore, the spiritual attributes for sacrilege, in turn, acquire a terrorist focus with respect to the humanitarian perspective.

PSYCHOPATHY → **TRICKERY**
CRIMINALITY → **CHICANERY**
SACRILEGE → **ARTIFICE**
TERRORISM → **STRATAGEM**

A similar ascending pattern further applies to the remaining sequence of counter double bind maneuvers (trickery-chicanery-artifice-stratagem): although scarcely to the degree of precision established for the preliminary maneuvers. This resultant lack of clarity is clearly a consequence of the extreme degree of disqualification characterizing the trickery perspective. When taken as an interactive pattern, the basic two-stage dynamic for criminality jumps neatly into focus, an innovative interpretation with the revolutionary potential to explain much of the random criminality afflicting society today.

A PROVISIONAL TERMINOLOGY FOR THE REALM OF CRIMINALITY

In terms of an exacting terminology for criminology, the conceptual picture proves increasingly complex. The colloquial terms defining the lesser virtues were all endowed with well-established ethical traditions. In the case of criminality, however, the affiliated details prove scarcely as clear. Perhaps the greatest degree of potential in this regard concerns the wide variety of criminal codes already in existence. This compilation of legal jargon (perhaps only fully understood by legal professionals) defines many individual classifications of criminality (such as larceny, embezzlement, etc.). These established criminal codes might potentially be modified into format compatible with that predicted within the transitional hierarchy.

This speculative train of reasoning must remain open to further investigation at this juncture. Indeed, a professional invitation is extended to those with expertise in the field aimed at devising a formal system compatible with the power hierarchy. This call extends not only to the legal profession, but also to criminologists and criminal profilers (where case studies are highly systematized). In concert with the current communicational model, the potential for a grand-unified theory of criminality might finally be within reach, promising virtually unlimited applications to the fields of criminal justice and law enforcement.

Until such dramatic breakthroughs can be ascertained, a stopgap system of terminology must necessarily be implemented. This formally consists of taking the established terminology for the vices of defect and modifying it through the addition of the prefix "C-" (designating criminality): wherein specifying the new pattern of transitional maneuvers. For instance, the defect-state of "spite" would further be transformed into C-spite, whereas malice would similarly translate in a criminal fashion as C-malice. Indeed, a complete listing of this full slate of criminal transitions is schematically depicted in **Figs. 27A** and **27B**. Similar to the pattern previously established for the lesser virtues (I) and (II), criminality is also subdivided into classifications (I) and (II). For criminality (I), the follower roles directly initiate

the transitional sequence, whereas the authority roles alternately launch this basic pattern in criminality (II). The initial transitional phase is formally designated by a small "t" (denoting the transitional maneuver), whereas a small "d" specifies the (disqualified) counter double bind maneuver. This stopgap measure of labeling conveniently allows the wide assortment of predicted slots to be adequately specified (at least until a better system can be devised). In concert with the three-digit coding system, which assigns numbers 600 to 699 to the realm of criminality, this prefix system of terminology should prove quite adequate for most applications.

The distinctive interplay of double bind and counter double bind maneuvers (for the realm of criminality) entails a further set of modifications to the three-digit coding system: necessarily specifying the addition of an extra (fourth-place) digit for fully describing the counter double bind class of maneuvers. In the terms of the initial criminality phase, the first three digits proved fully adequate for specifying the preliminary transitional maneuvers: being as they represent direct transitional variations on the more basic vices of defect. In the case of the criminality (I), the specific three digit codes for the double bind maneuvers end with numbers zero through three: for instance, t-insurgency = 640, t-vengeance = 641, t-gluttony = 642, and t-cowardice = 643. A similar pattern is further encountered with respect to criminality (II), where the authority roles now initiate the transitional sequence. Here, t-infamy = 630, t-dishonor = 631, t-foolishness = 632, and t-capriciousness = 633: as more comprehensively outlined in **Fig. 27B**.

With respect to the remaining class of counter double bind maneuvers, the corresponding complement of three-digit codes must further be distinguished from the preliminary class of double bind maneuvers. This distinction necessarily entails the addition of an extra digit for specifying the respective "trickery" class of countermaneuvers. This disqualified form of counter double bind maneuver is specified in terms of a "one" in the fourth-place digit. For criminality (I), d-infamy is coded as 630.1, d-dishonor equals 631.1, etc. (as reflected in the dual interplay of t-insurgency/d-infamy, t-vengeance/d-dishonor, etc). Accordingly, through the simple addition of an extra decimal place, the potential range of responses to the initial double bind maneuver is adequately represented in terms of the coding system. Indeed, this basic modification applies equally well to the remaining categories of transitional terms to follow. Hypercriminality is similarly specified

CRIMINAL TREACHERY	DISQUALIFIED LAZINESS
Previously, I (as personal authority) have acted in a lazy fashion, in response to the treacherous treatment of the personal follower. But now, you (as new personal follower) will *treacherously* act in a punitive fashion towards me: in anticipation of my (as established PA) lazy treatment of you.	Previously, you (as new personal follower) have treacherously acted in a punitive fashion towards me: in anticipation of my (as established PA) lazy treatment of you. But now, I (as reluctant personal authority) will **deny** acting in a *lazy* fashion towards you: thwarting your (as new PF) treacherous treatment of me.
CRIMINAL INSURGENCY	**DISQUALIFIED INFAMY**
Previously, I (as group authority) have infamously acted in a lazy fashion, in response to the insurgent-treachery of the group representative. But now, you (as new group representative) will *insurgently* act in a treacherous fashion towards me: in anticipation of my (as established PA) infamous sense of laziness.	Previously, you (as new group representative) have insurgently acted in a treacherous fashion towards me: in anticipation of my (as established GA) infamous sense of laziness. But now, I (as reluctant group authority) will **deny** *infamously* acting in a lazy fashion towards you: thwarting your (as new GR) insurgently-treacherous treatment of me.
CRIMINAL BETRAYAL	**DISQUALIFIED PRODIGALITY**
Previously, I (as spiritual authority) have infamously acted in a prodigal fashion, in response to the Insurgent-betrayal of the spiritual disciple. But now, you (as new spiritual disciple) will insurgently-*betray* me: in anticipation of my (as established SA) infamous sense of prodigality.	Previously, you (as new spiritual disciple) have insurgently-betrayed me: in anticipation of my (as established SA) infamous sense of prodigality. But now, I (as reluctant humanitarian authority) will **deny** infamously acting *prodigally* towards you: thwarting your (as new SD) insurgent betrayal of me.
CRIMINAL UGLINESS	**DISQUALIFIED WRATHFULNESS**
Previously, I (as humanitarian authority) have prodigally acted in a wrathful fashion, in response to the ugly-betrayal of the representative member of humanity. But now, you (as new representative member of humanity) will betrayingly act in an *ugly* fashion towards me: in anticipation of my (as established HA) prodigal sense of wrathfulness.	Previously, you (as new representative member of humanity) have betrayingly acted in an ugly fashion towards me: in anticipation of my (as establ. HA) wrathful treatment of you. But now, I (as reluctant transcendental authority) will **deny** prodigally acting *wrathfully* towards you: thwarting your (as new RH) ugly-betrayal of me.

Table Q-1 – The Definitions Based on Criminal Treachery/Laziness

CRIMINAL VINDICTIVENESS	DISQUALIFIED NEGLIGENCE
Previously, I (as personal authority) have acted in a negligent fashion, in response to the vindictive treatment of the personal follower. But now, you (as new personal follower) will *vindictively* act in a punitive fashion towards me: in anticipation of my (as established PA) negligent treatment of you.	Previously, you (as new personal follower) have vindictively acted punitively towards me: in anticipation of my (as established PA) negligent treatment of you. But now, I (as reluctant personal authority) will **deny** acting *negligently* towards you: thwarting your (as new PF) vindictive treatment of me.
CRIMINAL VENGEANCE	DISQUALIFIED DISHONOR
Previously, I (as group authority) have negligently acted in a dishonorable fashion, in response to the vengeful-vindictiveness of the group representative. But now, you (as new group representative) will *vengefully* act vindictively towards me: in anticipation of my (as established GA) negligently-dishonorable treatment of you.	Previously, you (as new group representative) have vengefully acted vindictively towards me: in anticipation of my (as established GA) negligently-dishonorable treatment of you. But now, I (as reluctant group authority) will **deny** negligently acting *dishonorably* towards you: thwarting your (as new GR) vengefully vindictive treatment of me.
CRIMINAL DESPAIR	DISQUALIFIED SLAVERY
Previously, I (as spiritual authority) have dishonorably acted in a slavish fashion, in response to the vengeful sense of despair of the spiritual disciple. But now, you (as new spiritual disciple) will vengefully act in a *despairing* fashion towards me: in anticipation of my (as established SA) dishonorable-enslavement of you.	Previously, you (as new spiritual disciple) have vengefully acted depairingly towards me: in anticipation of my (as established SA) dishonorable-enslavement of you. But now, I (as reluctant spiritual authority) will **deny** dishonorably-*enslaving* you: thwarting your (as new SD) vengeful sense of despair.
CRIMINAL HYPOCRISY	DISQUALIFIED TYRANNY
Previously, I (as humanitarian authority) have slavishly acted in a tyrannical fashion, in response to the hypocritical sense of despair of the representative member of humanity. But now, you (as new representative member of humanity) will despairingly act *hypocritically* towards me: in anticipation of my (as established HA) tyrannical-enslavement of you.	Previously, you (as new represent. member of humanity) have despairingly acted hypocritically towards me: in anticipation of my (as established HA) tyrannical-enslavement of you. But now, I (as reluctant humanitarian authority) will **deny** *tyrannically*-enslaving you: thwarting your (as new RH) hypocritical sense of despair.

Table Q- 2 – The Definitions Based on Criminal Vindictiveness/Negligence

CRIMINAL SPITE	DISQUALIFIED APATHY
Previously, you (as personal authority) have acted in an apathetic fashion, in response to the spiteful treatment of the personal follower. But now, I (as new personal follower) will *spitefully* act in a punitive fashion towards you: in anticipation of your (as established PA) apathetic treatment of me.	Previously, I (as new personal follower) have spitefully acted in a punitive fashion towards you: in anticipation of your (as established PA) apathetic treatment of me. But now, you (as reluctant personal authority) will **deny** acting *apathetically* towards me: thwarting my (as new PF) spiteful treatment of you.
CRIMINAL GLUTTONY	**DISQUALIFIED FOOLISHNESS**
Previously, you (as group authority) have foolishly acted in an apathetic fashion, in response to the gluttonously-spiteful treatment of the group representative. But now, I (as new group representative) will *gluttonously* act spitefully towards you: in anticipation of your (as established GA) foolishly-apathetic treatment of me.	Previously, I (as new group representative) have gluttonously acted in a spiteful fashion towards you: in anticipation of your (as established GA) foolishly-apathetic treatment of me. But now, you (as reluctant group authority) will **deny** *foolishly* acting apathetically towards me: thwarting my (as new GR) gluttonously-spiteful treatment of you.
CRIMINAL AVARICE	**DISQUALIFIED VULGARITY**
Previously, you (as spiritual authority) have foolishly acted in a vulgar fashion, in response to the avaricious treatment of the spiritual disciple. But now, I (as new spiritual disciple) will gluttonously act in an *avaricious* fashion towards you: in anticipation of your (as established SA) foolishly-vulgar treatment of me.	Previously, I (as new spiritual disciple) have gluttonously acted avariciously towards you: in anticipation of your (as established SA) foolishly-vulgar treatment of me. But now, you (as reluctant spiritual authority) will **deny** foolishly acting *vulgarly* towards me: thwarting my (as new SD) avaricious treatment of you.
CRIMINAL EVIL	**DISQUALIFIED OPPRESSION**
Previously, you (as humanitarian authority) have vulgarly acted in an oppressive fashion, in response to the avaricious sense of evil of the representative member of humanity. But now, I (as new representative member of humanity) will avariciously act in an *evil* fashion towards you: in anticipation of your (as established HA) oppressive treatment of me.	Previously, I (as new representative member of humanity) have avariciously acted evilly towards you: in anticipation of your (as established HA) oppressive treatment of me. But now, you (as reluctant humanitarian authority) will **deny** vulgarly acting *oppressively* towards me: thwarting my (as new RH) evil treatment of you.

Table Q-3 – The Definitions Based on Criminal Spite/Apathy

CRIMINAL MALICE	DISQUALIFIED INDIFFERENCE
Previously, you (as personal authority) have acted in an indifferent fashion, in response to the malicious treatment of the personal follower. But now, I (as new personal follower) will punitively act in a *malicious* fashion towards you: in anticipation of your (as established PA) indifferent treatment of me.	Previously, I (as new personal follower) have punitively acted in a malicious fashion towards you: in anticipation of your (as established PA) indifferent treatment of me. But now, you (as reluctant personal authority) will **deny** acting *indifferently* towards me: thwarting my (as new PF) malicious treatment of you.
CRIMINAL COWARDICE	DISQUALIFIED CAPRICIOUSNESS
Previously, you (as group authority) have capriciously acted in an indifferent fashion, in response to the cowardly-malicious treatment of the group representative. But now, I (as new group representative) will *cowardly* act in a malicious fashion towards you: in anticipation of your (as established GA) capricious sense of indifference.	Previously, I (as new group representative) have cowardly acted in a malicious fashion towards you: in anticipation of your (as established GA) capricious sense of indifference. But now, you (as reluctant group authority) will **deny** *capriciously* acting indifferently towards me: thwarting my (as new GR) cowardly-malicious treatment of you.
CRIMINAL ANTAGONISM	DISQUALIFIED CRUELTY
Previously, you (as spiritual authority) have capriciously acted with cruelty, in response to the cowardly-antagonistic treatment of the spiritual disciple. But now, I (as new spiritual disciple) will cowardly act in an *antagonistic* fashion towards you: in anticipation of your (as established SA) capricious sense of cruelty.	Previously, I (as new spiritual disciple) have cowardly acted in an antagonistic fashion towards you: in anticipation of your (as established SA) capricious sense of cruelty. But now, you (as reluctant spiritual authority) will **deny** capriciously acting *cruelly* towards me: thwarting my (as new SD) cowardly-antagonistic treatment of you.
CRIMINAL CUNNING	DISQUALIFIED PERSECUTION
Previously, you (as humanitarian authority) have cruelly acted with persecution, in response to the antagonistic sense of cunning of the representative member of humanity. But now, I (as new representative member of humanity) will antagonistically act *cunningly* towards you: in anticipation of your (as established HA) cruel-persecution of me.	Previously, I (as new representative member of humanity) have antagonistically acted cunningly towards you: in anticipation of your (as established HA) cruel-persecution of me. But now, you (as reluctant humanitarian authority) will **deny** cruelly-*persecuting* me: thwarting my (as new RH) antagonistic sense of cunning.

Table Q-4 – The Definitions Based on Criminal Malice/Indifference

in terms of the dual interplay of the double bind and counter double bind maneuvers.

THE SCHEMATIC DEFINITIONS
FOR THE REALM OF CRIMINALITY

The current system of classification further prompts a remaining related issue; namely, the description of the schematic definitions for the realm of criminality (similar to that previously established for the lesser virtues). According to Chapters *21* through *25*, the dual categories of lesser virtues (I) and (II) were incorporated into the formal schematic definition format; providing an effective simulation of the dual interplay of double bind and counter double bind maneuvers. Indeed, it further proves feasible to formulate a parallel complement of schematic definitions for the dual categories of criminality (I) and (II). For criminality (I), the follower roles are listed first in the definitions, whereas for criminality (II), the authority roles are designated first. The formal identification of the transitional and disqualified phases is chiefly indicated on the basis of their respective positions within the schematic definition format. Accordingly, the initial transitional phase is specified in terms of the left-hand column of terms, whereas the disqualified (counter double bind) class of maneuvers is indicated through the right-hand column of terms. The latter disqualified set of roles is also specified through the addition of the qualifiers "denial" or "deny" at the given juncture within the definition under consideration.

A complete listing of schematic definitions for criminality (I) is depicted in **Tables Q-1** to **Q-4**. The follower roles are depicted in the transitional position, followed by the disqualified class of authority roles. A parallel complement of schematic definitions is further predicted for the remaining classifications of criminality (II), a pattern mirroring that for criminality (I) with the exception that the order of the authority/follower roles is now reversed. In order to avoid burdening the current chapter with too many formal sets of definitions, the predicted definitions for criminality (II) will be omitted at this juncture, rather reserved for an updated edition of this book, where such formal issues will be examined to a much greater degree of detail. All told, in strict analogy to the pattern previously established for the lesser virtues, it ultimately proves possible to identify 32 individual classifications for criminality

(I), as well as *32* specific terms for criminality (II): providing a formal schematic model for the enigmatic realm of criminality in general. A similar pattern of organization can further be established for the affiliated realm of hypercriminality (I) and (II). Indeed, the following chapter concerning hypercriminality proves particularly relevant to the field of criminal profiling: offering crucial insights into the perverse dynamics driving the criminal mind, along with clues towards ameliorating such destructive tendencies.

In conclusion, the completed description of the realm of criminality, in addition to the blatant extremes associated with hypercriminality offers crucial new tools for forensic psychology and the criminal justice system. This unprecedented degree of specialization for identifying finer distinctions within such a negative communicational dynamic holds the potential for breakthrough applications within the field. Here, criminality fulfills its predicted transitional prerequisites; namely, initiating the specifics for the vices of defect within a socially neutral context. Furthermore, the even more disturbing distinctions characterizing the related sphere of hypercriminality extend the extreme prerequisites for hyperviolence into a parallel transitional format (to the bane of cooperative society). This grand-scale integration in terms for the entire darker realm of defect (and its derivatives) ultimately accounts for a grand total of *520* individual terms, a veritable cornucopia when compared to the dearth of relevant distinctions characterizing the forensic field today.

The potential applications to criminal profiling are breathtaking, offering radically new insights into the motivations underpinning routine domestic criminality. Furthermore, the disturbing ascendancy of global international terrorism similarly benefits from an increased understanding of the extreme dynamics characterizing hypercriminality and hyperviolence. Consequently, Interpol and the United Nations Peacekeeping Forces could derive considerable strategic advantages in terms of enforcement operations and global policymaking in relation to global terrorism. The further correlates in relation to the newly devised three-digit coding system holds further potential for an unprecedented degree of precision in statistical and clerical functions relating to burgeoning caseloads. Through the aid of these breakthrough advances in forensic technology and terminology, a new era of global peace and cooperation may remain only a heartbeat away.

28

THE EXTREMES ASSOCIATED WITH HYPERCRIMINALITY

The preceding description of measured criminality paints a rather disturbing portrait of criminality in general. In keeping with its elementary foundation within the realm of defect, this routine brand of criminality is defined as a measured variation on the vices of defect. As suggested previously, routine criminality is characterized by property crimes of a white-collar nature. Although the criminal remains entirely selfish in his pursuits, he generally avoids causing any lasting physical harm during the commission of his crime.

In contrast to the measured prerequisites for routine criminality, the darker realm of hypercriminality represents an escalation in force exceeding the rational requirements of the crime. This extreme tactic exemplifies what is often termed "a random act of violence," a scourge most often encountered on the mean streets of the city. Disturbing reports of random victims being murdered for insignificant sums of money definitely fall into this category, even though the victims were fully cooperative at the time. Such senseless acts of violence are particularly disturbing in that one can never sure that one might not be the next victim of such random violence.

As the formal transitional variation on the realm of hyperviolence, hypercriminality shares many of the same attributes with its counterpart; namely, a mindless style of criminal intent out of all proportion to the dictates of the crime. The hypercriminal individual further gains a sense of power and prestige from dominating another, much as recently reported in the disturbing phenomenon of "thrill killing:" where material gain is downplayed in favor of the novelty of the experience. This disturbing trend further extends to the equally barbaric practice known as "wilding," where packs of youths go on criminal rampages to prove their collective sense of toughness. The sensationalistic nature of such crimes is often dramatized in the media, as evident in "true crime" genres that promote a fascination for the exploits of serial killers. The movie industry has similarly contributed to the trend, releasing a broad range of "slasher" films, such as the *Halloween* or *Scream* series. Hypercriminality even emerges as the target of satire in such the notorious releases as *Natural Born Killers* or *American Psycho*, although this subtle sense of irony is often overshadowed by the more sensational trappings of the film.

Hypercriminality typically requires anonymity in order to evade detection; hence, specifying transitions from the default realm of neutrality status. This push for anonymity appears to be the key distinguishing feature differentiating hypercriminality from hyperviolence. The former is strictly classified as a transitional power maneuver, whereas the latter represents an established (or embedded) power perspective, where both parties know one another. Being that anonymity is formally ruled out in the latter context (short of murder), the realm of hyperviolence is formally limited to so-called crimes of passion. This extends to domestic abuse (both physical and verbal), as well as emotional exploitation, with addictive behavior often compounding the situation. Such violence generally occurs in an impulsive fashion without much in the way of premeditated intent, with the perpetrators generally becoming apologetic when their anger eventually subsides. Even extreme outbursts are generally tempered to some degree, for the lack of anonymity ensures that some degree of consequences will ultimately be imposed.

Fortunately, the stiffer range of sanctions imposed against domestic violence have sent a stern message to hyperviolent individuals, with such

820	821
t-Mutiny	**t**-Reprisal
822	823
t-Grudgingness	**t**-Malignancy

TRANSITIONAL
EXPLOITATION
(Personal Double-Bind)

→

810.1	811.1
d-Indolence	**d**-Dereliction
812.1	813.1
d-Languor	**d**-Callousness

DISQUALIFIED
PERVERSION
(Personal Counter Double-Bind)

840	841
t-Rebellion	**t**-Retribution
842	843
t-Voracity	**t**-Cravenness

TRANSITIONAL
PERNICITY
(Group Double-Bind)

→

830.1	831.1
d-Notoriety	**d**-Ignobility
832.1	833.1
d-Crassness	**d**-Petulance

DISQUALIFIED
DEPRAVITY
(Group Counter Double-Bind)

860	861
t-Treason	**t**-Hopeless.
862	863
t-Greed	**t**-Contentiousness

TRANSITIONAL
RECUSANCY
(Spiritual Double-Bind)

→

850.1	851.1
d-Licentiousness	**d**-Savagery
852.1	853.1
d-Rudeness	**d**-Hostility

DISQUALIFIED
SACRILEGE
(Spiritual Counter Double-Bind)

880	881
t-Hideousness	**t**-Mendacity
882	883
t-Heinousness	**t**-Ruthlessness

TRANSITIONAL
PANDEMONIUM
(Humanitarian Double-Bind)

→

870.1	871.1
d-Fury	**d**-Despotism
872.1	873.1
d-Brutality	**d**-Barbarism

DISQUALIFIED
REPROBATION
(Humanitarian Counter Double-Bind)

Fig. 28A – The Three-Digit Codes for the Realm of Hypercriminality - (I)

302

810	811
t-Indolence	t-Dereliction
812	**813**
t-Languor	t-Callousness

TRANSITIONAL
PERVERSION
(Personal Double-Bind)

820.1	821.1
d-Mutiny	**d-Reprisal**
822.1	**823.1**
d-Grudgingness	**d-Malignancy**

DISQUALIFIED
EXPLOITATION
(Personal Counter Double-Bind)

830	831
t-Notoriety	**t-Ignobility**
832	**833**
t-Crassness	t-Petulance

TRANSITIONAL
DEPRAVITY
(Group Double-Bind)

840.1	841.1
d-Rebellion	**d-Retribution**
842.1	**843.1**
d-Voracity	**d-Cravenness**

DISQUALIFIED
PERNICITY
(Group Counter Double-Bind)

850	851
t-Licentiousness	**t-Savagery**
852	**853**
t-Rudeness	t-Hostility

TRANSITIONAL
SACRILEGE
(Spiritual Double-Bind)

860.1	861.1
d-Treason	**d-Hopelessness**
862.1	**863.1**
d-Greed	**d-Contentiousness**

DISQUALIFIED
RECUSANCY
(Spiritual Counter Double-Bind)

870	871
t-Fury	**t-Despotism**
872	**873**
t-Brutality	t-Barbarism

TRANSITIONAL
REPROBATION
(Humanitarian Double-Bind)

880.1	881.1
d-Hideousness	**d-Mendacity**
882.1	**883.1**
d-Heinousness	**d-Ruthlessness**

DISQUALIFIED
PANDEMONIUM
(Humanitarian Counter Double-Bind)

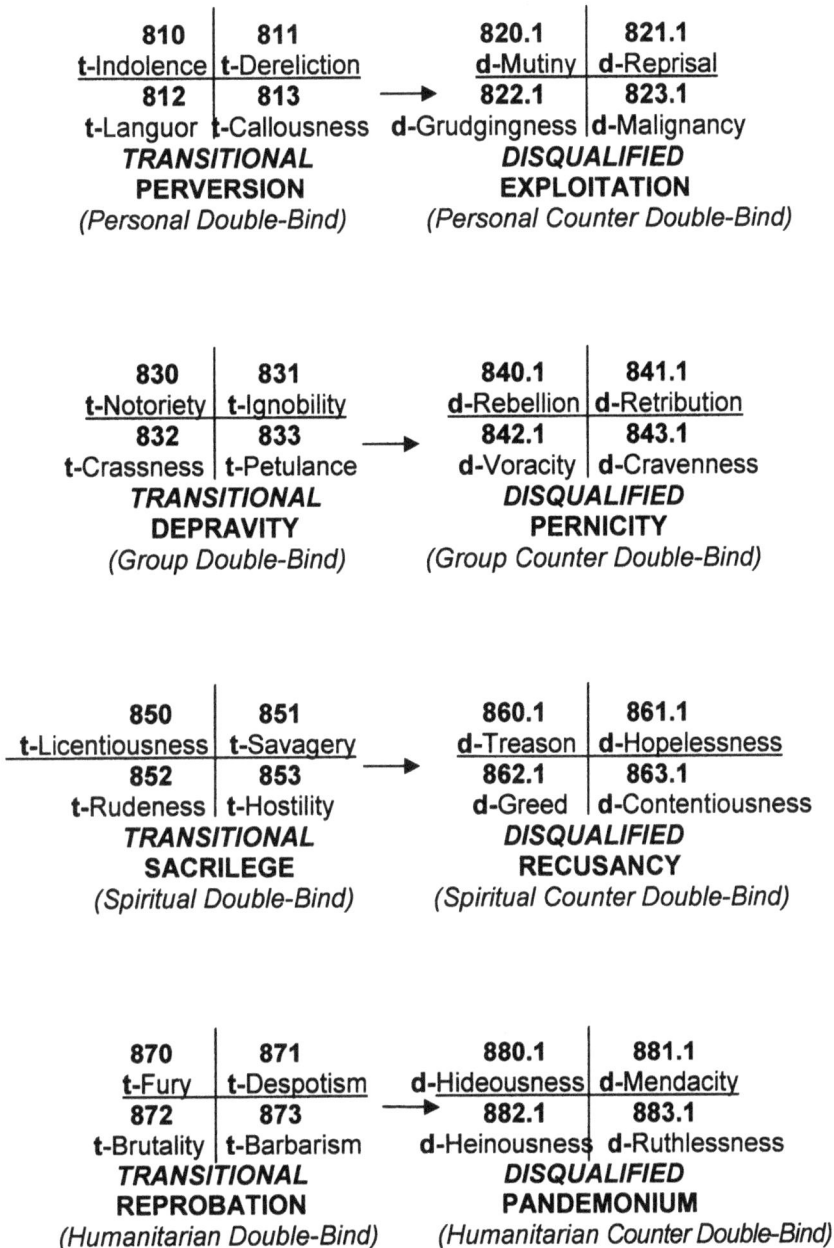

Fig. 28B – The Three-Digit Codes for the Realm of Hypercriminality - (II)

303

aggressive tendencies now more often channeled towards the anonymous realm of hypercriminality. The premeditated attempt to hide one's identity allows for the freer acting out of such hyperviolent tendencies. Consequently, hyperviolent criminals are frequently aggressive in their personal relationships (and vice-versa).

BEHAVIORAL SUSCEPTIBILITIES TO THE REALM OF HYPERCRIMINALITY

Many theories have been proposed to explain how hypercriminal tendencies develop in susceptible individuals. Dr. Lonnie H. Athens, Professor of Criminal Justice at Seton Hall University, outlines one such interpretation in his latest book: *The Creation of Dangerous Violent Criminals.* According to Dr. Athens, the high demand for labor in the criminal marketplace is driven by the profits obtained through drugs, gambling, and related contraband activities. Disputes arising in the black-market subculture cannot generally be settled by legal means, therefore the constant need for violent enforcers. The inner-city environment greatly increases the chances of being brutalized as a byproduct of such violent conflicts, with many victims becoming withdrawn or depressed in the process.

Those that survive such a violent pattern of subjugation often become defiantly belligerent as a result of mentally reliving their brutalization. They may eventually come to the disturbing realization that in order to avoid further brutalization, they must become hyperviolent themselves. According to this stark reversal of character, the true resolve to commit violence is eventually tested in all its horrific manifestations. The observation that others shrink away in their presence only further serves to reinforce a perverse pleasure in such violent notoriety. Even the slightest provocation serves as a flimsy excuse to maim or kill others with scarcely a second thought. The entire cycle comes full circle in that (while initially having been victimized) one now becomes the brutalizer, a role that originally had been so deeply despised.

Many researchers further speculate that hypercriminality stems primarily from an overall lack of empathy or compassion, a factor technically defined as criminal narcissism. The criminal generally appears unable to feel the pain or terror experienced by his victims. "They cannot see the self in the other," according to Dr. Carl Bell, a psychiatrist at the University of Illinois. This distinctive lack of empathy is further consistent with the prefrontal-lobe model of impulse control. In-

deed, this awareness of "the other" similarly appears localized within the right prefrontal cortex. Eight years of research at the Rotman Research Institute in Toronto (2000) clearly indicate that the right prefrontal cortex is critical to the intuitive ability to understand the state of mind of others (according to neuroscientist, Donald Stuss). Patients with damage to the right prefrontal cortex express difficulty in placing themselves in the conceptual place of another, an empathic deficit that most of us are instinctively equipped to comprehend.

This inherent variation in the range of human empathy further explains the distinction between routine criminality and the extremes of hypercriminality. In theory, empathy remains relatively intact for criminals committing ordinary property crimes, employing only the degree of force necessary to achieve the desired result. Although scarcely respecting the principles of the "Golden Rule," they still retain the empathy to abstain from deliberately causing any lasting physical harm. Such safeguards are totally lacking with respect to the hypercriminal individual, where victims are callously viewed as objects to be exploited and then discarded. For instance, the serial rapist selfishly views his victim as a means towards his own gratification, essentially tuning-out any empathic projection on the perspectives of the other. Any pleas for compassion typically fall upon deaf ears, the life of the victim oft-times tragically terminated in order to eliminate a potential witness. In fact, various studies have concluded that upwards of 90% of serial killers are characterized as suffering from the psychopathic personality disorder.

According to Dr. Robert Hare (1991), a psychologist from Vancouver, B. C., the general psychopath acts primarily without conscience, preferring to operate within his own twisted set of rules. The psychopath similarly lacks a positive sense of empathy, frequently expressing an exaggerated sense of his own self-worth. He also can appear quite impulsive, displaying little foresight for the consequences of his antisocial behavior. This inherent sense of impulsivity further explains why the antisocial personality disorder is often grouped within the classifications of mental illness. The present transitional model, however, appears to rule-out such an eventuality, the disorder alternately being assigned to the domain of hypercriminality currently under consideration.

This reassignment further confirms the speculation of many authorities that the antisocial variation shares little in common with the other personality disorders, save its impulsive characteristics. This distinction proves particularly crucial in terms of new federal policies that award disability status to various classifications of mental illness (including the antisocial disorder). The prospects of entire prison populations being subsidized on the basis of their criminality would certainly appear counterproductive; in essence, rewarding such socially maladaptive tendencies. In contrast, for the alternate forms of mental illness, only the patient is generally in harm's way. Although the antisocial personality clearly shares issues of impulsivity with mental illness, impulsivity is actually a factor shared in common by the transitional power maneuvers in general. The only major distinction is that the former targets the vices of defect, whereas the latter is explained through the milder realm of the vices of excess.

For the extreme realm of hypercriminality, any perverse pleasure derived from such psychopathic tendencies clearly implies an empathic deficit, wherein forcing one's will upon that of another. The exception to the rule, however, is the vicious sadist, who willingly revels in the torment of his victims, an emotional short-circuit of the most depraved style imaginable. Such predators upon society are fortunately somewhat of a rare occurrence, a behavioral enigma that further exposes the limitations of the current model of hypercriminality. Additional research is definitely in order here in hopes of leading to a more stable and harmonious social structure.

A SYSTEMATIC TERMINOLOGY FOR THE CLASSIFICATIONS OF HYPERCRIMINALITY

The fundamental details underlying hypercriminality are basically similar to those proposed for hyperviolence in Chapter *19,* with little need to repeat the same material over again. It only remains to formally designate the individual classifications for hypercriminality, although occurring so infrequent that no accepted terminology exists in general usage. For clues to the specifics of this predicted terminology, it proves fruitful to refer back to the formal nomenclature initially established for routine criminality; namely, that prefix-style terminology adapted to the interplay of the double bind and counter-double bind maneuvers.

As outlined in the previous chapter, transitions into the realm of the vices of defect were specified by what was termed the criminality phase: a formal double bind style of power maneuver that dictates the subsequent course of action on the part of the victim. The victim of the criminality phase, however, formally retains the option of disqualifying the entire transitional interchange employing the counter double bind class of maneuver. The initial criminality phase places the victim in a form of double bind paradox in expectation of reciprocating with violence in return. Indeed, it is particularly tempting to accept this reciprocal course of action, although (at a higher meta-level) the victim is manipulated into accepting this course of action by the perpetrator.

The only graceful exit from such a double bind paradox is through the counter double bind class of maneuvers. As previously suggested with respect to humor, the counter double bind perspective accepts the face of value of the communication, while simultaneously denying complicity in the entire interaction. In fitting response to the criminality phase, the victim, in turn, employs the trickery form of counter double bind maneuver: responding back in kind (but denies doing it). The trickery ruse represents disqualified resistance to the criminal dictates of the perpetrator, a difficult strategy to carry through effectively. In practice, the respective hyper-trickery phase may be eliminated altogether due to the extremely violent nature of the initiatory phase. The complete transitional interchange, accordingly, might never be fully consummated due to the extreme level of violence at issue.

The reciprocal interplay between the criminality and trickery phases represents the fundamental model upon which all criminality is based. This sequence is further modified with respect to hypercriminality by adding the prefix *hyper-* to the preliminary format for criminality. The eight-part listing of themes for hypercriminality is schematically depicted below: formally reflecting the personal, group, spiritual, and humanitarian levels, respectively.

*Hyper-*PSYCHOPATHY → *Hyper-*TRICKERY
*Hyper-*CRIMINALITY → *Hyper-*CHICANERY
*Hyper-*SACRILEGE → *Hyper-*ARTIFICE
*Hyper-*TERRORISM → *Hyper-*STRATAGEM

In particular, the personal characteristics for *hyper*-psychopathy further extend to the group realm of organized *hyper*-criminality. Furthermore, the spiritual attributes for *hyper*-sacrilege, in turn, extend to the enduring *hyper*-terrorist focus of the humanitarian perspective. A parallel ascending pattern is further established with respect to the counter double bind maneuvers; namely, *hyper*- (trickery-chicanery-artifice-stratagem). Taken collectively, this two-stage dynamic for *hyper*-criminality jumps neatly into focus, an unprecedented viewpoint with potential to explain much hypercriminality afflicting society today.

CRIMINAL MUTINY	DISQUALIFIED INDOLENCE
Previously, I (as personal authority) have indolently acted in an extremely lazy fashion in response to the mutinous treatment of the personal follower. But now, you (as new personal follower) will *mutinously* act in an extremely lazy fashion towards me: in anticipation of my (as established PA) indolently-lazy treatment of you.	Previously, you (as new personal follower) have mutinously acted in an extremely lazy fashion towards me: in anticipation of my (as established PA) indolent treatment of you. But now, I (as reluctant personal authority) will **deny** *indolently* acting in an extremely lazy fashion towards you: thwarting your (as new PF) treacherous treatment of me.
CRIMINAL REBELLIOUSNESS	**DISQUALIFIED NOTORIETY**
Previously, I (as group authority) have indolently acted in a notorious fashion in response to the mutinous-rebellion of the group representative. But now, you (as new group representative) will mutinously act in a *rebellious* fashion towards me: in anticipation of my (as established PA) notorious treatment of you.	Previously, you (as new group representative) have mutinously acted in a rebellious fashion towards me: in anticipation of my (as established PA) notorious treatment of you. But now, I (as reluctant group authority) will **deny** indolently acting with *notoriety* towards you: thwarting your (as new GR) mutinous-rebellion against me.
CRIMINAL TREASON	**DISQUALIFIED LICENTIOUSNESS**
Previously, I (as spiritual authority) have notoriously acted in a *licentious* fashion in response to the treasonous-rebellion of the spiritual disciple. But now, you (as new spiritual disciple) will *treasonously*-rebel against me: in anticipation of my (as established SA) licentious treatment of you.	Previously, you (as new spiritual disciple) have treasonously-rebelled against me: in anticipation of my (as established SA) licentious treatment of you. But now, I (as reluctant humanitarian authority) will **deny** notoriously acting *licentiously* towards you: thwarting your (as new SD) treasonous-rebellion against me.
CRIMINAL HIDEOUSNESS	**DISQUALIFIED FURY**
Previously, I (as humanitarian authority) have licentiously acted furiously in response to the hideously-treasonous treatment of the representative member of humanity. But now, you (as new representative member of humanity) will *hideously* act treasonously towards me: in anticipation of my (as established HA) furious treatment of you.	Previously, you (as new representative member of humanity) have hideously acted treasonously towards me: in anticipation of my (as established HA) furious treatment of you. But now, I (as reluctant transcendental authority) will **deny** *furiously* acting licentiously towards you: thwarting your (as new RH) hideous treatment of me.

Table R-1 – The Definitions Based on Criminal Mutiny/Indolence

CRIMINAL REPRISAL	DISQUALIFIED DERELICTION
Previously, I (as personal authority) have derelictly acted in an extremely negligent fashion in response to the reprisal of the personal follower. But now, you (as new personal follower) will *reprisingly* act in an extremely vindictive fashion towards me: in anticipation of my (as established PA) derelict treatment of you.	Previously, you (as new personal follower) have reprisingly acted extremely vindictively towards me: in anticipation of my (as established PA) derelict treatment of you. But now, I (as reluctant personal authority) will **deny** *derelictly* acting extremely negligently towards you: thwarting your (as new PF) reprisal against me.
CRIMINAL RETRIBUTION	DISQUALIFIED IGNOBILITY
Previously, I (as group authority) have derelictly acted in an *ignoble* fashion in response to the reprising-retribution of the group representative. But now, you (as new group representative) will reprisingly seek *retribution* against me: in anticipation of my (as established GA) derelictly-ignoble treatment of you.	Previously, you (as new group representative) have reprisingly sought retribution against me: in anticipation of my (as established GA) derelictly-ignoble treatment of you. But now, I (as reluctant group authority) will **deny** derelictly acting *ignobly* towards you: thwarting your (as new GR) reprising quest for retribution against me.
CRIMINAL HOPELESSNESS	DISQUALIFIED SAVAGERY
Previously, I (as spiritual authority) have ignobly acted in a *savage* fashion in response to the hopeless quest for retribution of the spiritual disciple. But now, you (as new spiritual disciple) will *hopelessly* seek retribution against me: in anticipation of my (as established SA) savage treatment of you.	Previously, you (as new spiritual disciple) have hopelessly sought retribution against me: in anticipation of my (as established SA) savage treatment of you. But now, I (as reluctant spiritual authority) will **deny** ignobly acting with *savagery* towards you: thwarting your (as new SD) hopeless quest for retribution towards me.
CRIMINAL MENDACITY	DISQUALIFIED DESPOTISM
Previously, I (as humanitarian authority) have savagely acted despotically in response to the mendacious sense of hopelessness of the representative member of humanity. But now, you (as new representative member of humanity) will *mendaciously* act hopelessly towards me: in anticipation of my (as established HA) despotic treatment of you.	Previously, you (as new represent. member of humanity) mendaciously acted hopelessly towards me: in anticipation of my (as established HA) despotic treatment of you. But now, I (as reluctant humanitarian authority) will **deny** savagely acting *despotically* towards you: thwarting your (as new RH) mendacious treatment of me.

Table R-2 – The Definitions Based on Criminal Reprisal/Dereliction

CRIMINAL GRUDGINGNESS	DISQUALIFIED LANGUOR
Previously, you (as personal authority) have languorously acted in an extremely apathetic fashion in response to the grudging treatment of the personal follower. But now, I (as new personal follower) will *grudgingly* act in an extremely spiteful fashion towards you: in anticipation of your (as established PA) languorous treatment of me.	Previously, I (as new personal follower) have grudgingly acted extremely spitefully towards you: in anticipation of your (as established PA) languorous treatment of me. But now, you (as reluctant personal authority) will **deny** *languorously* acting extremely apathetically towards me: thwarting my (as new PF) grudging treatment of you.
CRIMINAL VORACITY	DISQUALIFIED CRASSNESS
Previously, you (as group authority) have languorously acted in a crass fashion in response to the grudgingly-voracious treatment of the group representative. But now, I (as new group representative) will grudgingly act *voraciously* towards you: in anticipation of your (as established GA) crass treatment of me.	Previously, I (as new group representative) have grudgingly acted voraciously towards you: in anticipation of your (as established GA) crass treatment of me. But now, you (as reluctant group authority) will **deny** languorously acting in a *crass* fashion towards me: thwarting my (as new GR) voracious treatment of you.
CRIMINAL GREED	DISQUALIFIED RUDENESS
Previously, you (as spiritual authority) have crassly acted in a rude fashion in response to the greedy treatment of the spiritual disciple. But now, I (as new spiritual disciple) will voraciously act in a *greedy* fashion towards you: in anticipation of your (as established SA) crassly-rude treatment of me.	Previously, I (as new spiritual disciple) have voraciously acted in a greedy fashion towards you: in anticipation of your (as established SA) crassly-rude treatment of me. But now, you (as reluctant spiritual authority) will **deny** crassly acting *rudely* towards me: thwarting my (as new SD) greedy treatment of you.
CRIMINAL HEINOUSNESS	DISQUALIFIED BRUTALITY
Previously, you (as humanitarian authority) have brutally acted rudely in response to the heinous sense of greed of the representative member of humanity. But now, I (as new representative member of humanity) will *heinously* act in a greedy fashion towards you: in anticipation of your (as established HA) brutal sense of rudeness.	Previously, I (as new representative member of humanity) have heinously acted greedily towards you: in anticipation of your (as established HA) brutal sense of rudeness. But now, you (as reluctant humanitarian authority) will **deny** *brutally* acting rudely towards me: thwarting my (as new RH) heinous treatment of you.

Table R-3 – The Definitions Based on Crimin. Grudgingness/Languor

CRIMINAL MALIGNANCY	DISQUALIFIED CALLOUSNESS
Previously, you (as personal authority) have callously acted in an extremely indifferent fashion in response to the malignant treatment of the personal follower. But now, I (as new personal follower) will *malignantly* act in an extremely malicious fashion towards you: in anticipation of your (as established PA) callous treatment of me.	Previously, I (as new personal follower) have malignantly acted in an extremely malicious fashion towards you: in anticipation of your (as established PA) callous treatment of me. But now, you (as reluctant personal authority) will **deny** *callously* acting extremely indifferently towards me: thwarting my (as new PF) malignant treatment of you.
CRIMINAL CRAVENNESS	DISQUALIFIED PETULACE
Previously, you (as group authority) have callously acted in a petulant fashion in response to the cravenly-malignant treatment of the group representative. But now, I (as new group representative) will *cravenly* act in a malignant fashion towards you: in anticipation of your (as established GA) petulant treatment of me.	Previously, I (as new group representative) have cravenly acted in a malignant fashion towards you: in anticipation of your (as established GA) petulant treatment of me. But now, you (as reluctant group authority) will **deny** *petulantly* acting callously towards me: thwarting my (as new GR) cravenly-malignant treatment of you.
CRIMINAL CONTENTIOUSNESS	DISQUALIFIED HOSTILITY
Previously, you (as spiritual authority) have petulantly acted hostilely in response to the cravenly-contentious treatment of the spiritual disciple. But now, I (as new spiritual disciple) will *contentiously* act cravenly towards you: in anticipation of your (as established SA) hostile treatment of me.	Previously, I (as new spiritual disciple) have contentiously acted cravenly towards you: in anticipation of your (as established SA) hostile treatment of me. But now, you (as reluctant spiritual authority) will **deny** petulantly acting *hostilely* towards me: thwarting my (as new SD) contentious treatment of you.
CRIMINAL RUTHLESSNESS	DISQUALIFIED BARBARISM
Previously, you (as humanitarian authority) have hostilely acted barbarically in response to the ruthless sense of contentiousness of the representative member of humanity. But now, I (as new representative member of humanity) will *ruthlessly* act contentiously towards you: in anticipation of your (as established HA) barbaric treatment of me.	Previously, I (as new representative member of humanity) have ruthlessly acted contentiously towards you: in anticipation of your (as established HA) barbaric treatment of me. But now, you (as reluctant humanitarian authority) will **deny** hostilely acting *barbarically* towards me: thwarting my (as new RH) ruthless treatment of you.

Table R-4 - The Definitions Based on Crim. Malignacy/Callousness

A similar prefix-naming strategy further applies at the level of the individual terms. This necessarily entails taking the newly devised terminology for hyperviolence (for instance, the term "retribution") and then add the prefix "HC," wherein specifying the hyper-criminal variant (e.g., HC-retribution). In direct analogy to the case previously made for "routine" criminality, hypercriminality is similarly subdivided into sub-classifications (I) and (II), as schematically diagrammed in **Figs. 28A** and **28B**. The preliminary terminology for hyperviolence is further modified to fit the dual transitional format. According to this latter format, a small *"t"* is used to designate the initial double bind class of maneuvers, whereas a small *"d"* stands for the (disqualified) counter double bind class of maneuvers (representative of the realm of hyper-trickery). This dual *"t"* and *"d"* terminology proves crucial in that the order of the authority and follower roles is respectively reversed for hypercriminality (I) and (II), as the schematic diagrams clearly serve to indicate.

The specifics for the three-digit coding system exhibit clear parallels to those previously established for routine criminality. The first digit of "6" (denoting the realm of criminality) is now altered to that of "8" specifying the domain of hypercriminality (all other digits remaining the same). For the initial transitional phase for hypercriminality, the first three digits are fully capable of designating the double bind class of maneuvers, representing transitional variations on the initial class of hyperviolence. In the case of hypercriminality (I), the three digit codes end with numbers zero-through-three. For instance, *t*-rebelliousness = 840, *t*-retribution = 841, *t*-voracity = 842, and *t*-cravenness = 843.

In terms of the remaining class of counter double bind maneuvers, the respective complement of three-digit codes must formally be distinguished from the initial transitional phase. This necessarily entails the addition of an extra decimal place for specifying this latter class of counter double bind maneuvers characterized by a "1" in the fourth-place digit. For instance, *d*-notoriety is coded as 830.1, *d*-ignobility equates to 831.1, etc.: as evident in the schematic interplay of *t*-rebelliousness/*d*-notoriety and *t*-retribution/*d*-ignobility, etc.

THE SCHEMATIC DEFINITIONS FOR THE REALM OF HYPERCRIMINALITY

In direct analogy to the preliminary classifications of criminality (I) and (II), the related categories of hypercriminality (I) and (II) also prove amenable to incorporation into the schematic definition format. This modification necessarily parallels the existing definitions for routine criminality although now substituting the relevant terms relating to the realm of hyperviolence. It is hoped that this new terminology may find affiliated applications to the terminology of criminal profiling or legal criminal codes. In the case of hypercriminality (I) the follower roles occur first in the definitions, whereas for hypercriminality (II), the authority roles are listed first. A complete listing of schematic definitions for hypercriminality (I) is graphically depicted in **Tables R-1** to **R-4**. According to this schematic format, the follower roles are depicted in the initial transitional position, followed by the subsequent "trickery" roles characterizing the counter double bind class of authority maneuvers.

A similar complement of schematic definitions is alternately specified for the remaining class of hypercriminality (II) with the exception that the order of the authority/follower roles is now reversed. In order to avoid burdening the current chapter with an additional set of definitions, the schematic definitions for hypercriminality (II) are omitted at this juncture: an endeavor best reserved for an upcoming edition when these technical aspects will be examined to a much greater degree of detail.

THE ACCESSORY VARIATIONS FOR CRIMINALITY AND HYPERCRIMINALITY

It should further be considered, in passing, the issue of the accessory variations for the realms of criminality and hypercriminality. Similar to the case previously established for the lesser virtues, the transitional class of power maneuvers targeting the darker realm must further be supplemented by a parallel complement of accessory terms. This latter class of terms is formally specified through the technical reversal of the "you" and "I" roles across the entire darker span of the power hierarchy. This schematic modification is fairly straightforward; namely, revisiting the main transitional format for criminality and hypercriminality in Chapters *27* and *28*, then substituting the respective accessory terms in place of the main versions previously described. For instance, in the case of routine criminality, this amounts to substituting the *accessory* vices of defect (from Chapter *15*) directly into the diagrams depicted in Chapter *27*. Furthermore, in terms of the current examination of hypercriminality, the accessory variations for hyperviolence (from Chapter *19*) are similarly substituted into **Figs. 28A** and

28B of the present chapter. In order to more fully clarify this picture, a complete listing of three-digit accessory codes are schematically depicted in **Fig. 28C** for the accessory realm of criminality, and in **Fig. 28D** for accessory hypercriminality

A similar substitution exercise, in turn, remains in order for accessory variations with respect to the schematic definition format. In terms of routine criminality, the respective *accessory* vices of defect are directly substituted into **Tables Q-1** to **Q-4** of the preceding chapter. A similar pattern further holds true with respect to the realm of hypercriminality, where this substitution exercise extends to **Tables R-1** through **R-4** of the current chapter. The formal reversal of the "you" and "I" roles must also be made (in each instance) in concert with the substitution of the accessory terms.

Due to space constraints, this supplementary listing of accessory schematic definitions for both criminality and hypercriminality is purposely omitted from the current chapter, an exercise best reserved for an upcoming edition. These definitions, however, could ultimately prove crucial to the field of criminality in general. Here, the subjective perspectives within the mind of the criminal could intuitively be specified, in direct contrast to the objective style of analysis dominating the technical literature. This formal empathic insight into criminality proves particularly applicable to the field of criminal profiling, where such troubling criminal aspects are modeled to an unprecedented degree of detail.

THE GENERAL UNIFYING THEMES FOR THE TRANSITIONAL POWER MANEUVERS

In terms of the preceding sections dealing with the lesser virtues and criminality/hypercriminality, one final issue has necessarily been deferred until this juncture; namely, the issue of the general unifying themes in relation to the transitional power maneuvers. The previous chapter concerning the lesser virtues, as well as the current sections dealing with criminality/hypercriminality omitted any specific mention of this crucial aspect of the three-digit coding system. This predicted transitional set of general unifying themes should exhibit clear commonalties with the main categories of themes structured along the lines of the basic interplay of double bind and counter double bind maneuvers. In terms of the lesser virtues, these general themes prove exceedingly reminiscent of the interplay of the congeniality and humor phases. Furthermore, the transitional themes targeting criminality/hypercriminality in-

voke a darker range of themes: as in the sequence of criminality/trickery, respectively.

The affiliated listings of transitional themes, by definition, prove equally specialized in nature, although there is scarcely any convincing terminology for specifying the uniquely predicted slots within the three-digit coding system. It ultimately proves effective to fall back upon the strategy that has worked so well in the past; namely, employing a prefix-style of modification for specifying the transitional range of the themes. This revised system of terminology is schematically depicted in **Fig. 28E** for the transitional themes (I) spanning the entire spectrum of criminality, hypercriminality, the lesser virtues, and mental illness. A cursory examination of this table reveals a fundamental insight, wherein borrowing the short-hand notation previously established for the individual classifications of criminality/hypercriminality. The small "*t*" notation represents abbreviated shorthand for the initial transitional power maneuver. The small "*d*" notation, in turn, stands for the disqualified form of counter double bind maneuver. This dual interplay of power maneuvers is depicted in a tandem fashion, with the connecting arrow specifying the sequential connection linking the two.

In the current case, this characteristic "*t→ d*" format is now applied to the general unifying themes for the virtues/vices of defect: as initially outlined in Chapters *9* and *15*. A complete listing of transitional themes is depicted in **Fig. 28E**, shown in context with the main listings of themes in order to provide crucial contextual cues. For instance, with respect to the lesser virtues I, the sequence of "*t*–utilitarianism" further prompts the counter double bind maneuver of "*d*-personalism," etc. The related transitional themes with respect to criminality are similarly reflected in terms of the dual interplay of double bind and counter double bind maneuvers. The preliminary transitional sequence of "*t*–corruption," in turn, prompts the disqualified style of "*d*–villainy," and so forth. Each of these individual transitional themes within **Fig. 28E** is accordingly assigned a requisite three-digit code, a pattern that is further augmented with an extra decimal place for the subsequent counter double bind maneuvers.

The related themes for the realm of hypercriminality follow a similar pattern with the exception of the substitution of the themes formally specifying the realm of hyperviolence outlined in Chapter *20*. Despite its rarity in usage, this terminology for hypercriminality is a basic modification of that initially given for criminality, although changing the first-place code digit from "6" to "8."

Fig. 28C - Accessory Criminality (614 – 687)

614 – *t*-sloth
614.1 – *d*-sloth
615 – *t*-carelessness
615.1 – *d*-carelessness
616 – *t*-dispassionateness
616.1 – *d*-dispassionate.
617 – *t*-arbitrariness
617.1 – *d*-arbitrariness

----

624 – *t*-traitorousness
624.1 – *d*-traitorousness
625 – *t*-retaliation
625.1 – *d*-retaliation
626 – *t*-resentment
626.1 – *d*-resentment
627 – *t*-malevolence
627.1 – *d*-malevolence

----

634 – *t*-disrepute
634.1 – *d*-disrepute
635 – *t*-reprehension
635.1 – *d*-reprehension
636 – *t*-preposterousness
636.1 – *d*-preposterous
637 – *t*-fickleness
637.1 – *d*-fickleness

----

644 – *t*-sedition
644.1 – *d*-sedition
645 – *t*-avengement
645.1 – *d*-avengement
646 – *t*-lechery
646.1 – *d*-lechery
647 – *t*-pusillanimity
647.1 – *d*-pusillanimity

654 – *t*-profligacy
654.1 – *d*-profligacy
655 – *t*-bondage
655.1 – *d*-bondage
656 – *t*-coarseness
656.1 – *d*-coarseness
657 – *t*-acrimony
657.1 – *d*-acrimony

----

664 – *t*-perfidy
664.1 – *d*-perfidy
665 – *t*-desperation
665.1 – *d*-desperation
666 – *t*-cupidity
666.1 – *d*-cupidity
667 – *t*-opposition
667.1 – *d*-opposition

----

674 – *t*-indignation
674.1 – *d*-indignation
675 – *t*-subjugation
675.1 – *d*-subjugation
676 – *t*-animosity
676.1 – *d*-animosity
677 – *t*-torment
677.1 – *d*-torment

----

684 – *t*-revulsion
684.1 – *d*-revulsion
685 – *t*-duplicity
685.1 – *d*-duplicity
686 – *t*-wickedness
686.1 – *d*-wickedness
687 – *t*-guilefulness
687.1 – *d*-guilefulness

Fig. 28D - Accessory Hypercriminality (814 – 887)

814 – *t* - Sluggishness
814.1 – *d* - Sluggishness
815 – *t* - Laxity
815.1 – *d* - Laxity
816 – *t* - Lethargy
816.1 – *d* - Lethargy
817 – *t* - Nonchalance
817.1 – *d* - Nonchalance

----

824 – *t* - Untrustworthiness
824.1 – *d* - Untrustworthiness
825 – *t* - Requital
825.1 – *d* - Requital
826 – *t* - Umbrage
826.1 – *d* - Umbrage
827 – *t* - Peevishness
827.1 – *d* - Peevishness

----

834 – *t* - Odium
834.1 – *d* - Odium
835 – *t* - Disgracefulness
835.1 – *d* - Disgracefulness
836 – *t* - Absurdity
836.1 – *d* - Absurdity
837 – *t* - Willfulness
837.1 – *d* - Willfulness

----

844 – *t* - rebellion
844.1 – *d* - rebellion
845 – *t* - Revenge
845.1 – *d* - Revenge
846 – *t* - Ravenousness
846.1 – *d* - Ravenousness
847 – *t* - Dastardliness
847.1 – *d* - Dastardliness

854 – *t* - Debauchery
854.1 – *d* - Debauchery
855 – *t* - Servitude
855.1 – *d* - Servitude
856 – *t* - Lewdness
856.1 – *d* - Lewdness
857 – *t* - Rancor
857.1 – *d* - Rancor

----

864 – *t* - Disloyalty
864.1 – *d* - Disloyalty
865 – *t* - Grievousness
865.1 – *d* - Grievousness
866 – *t* - Rapaciousness
866.1 – *d* - Rapaciousness
867 – *t* - Vexation
867.1 – *d* - Vexation

----

874 – *t* - Outrage
874.1 – *d* - Outrage
875 – *t* - Imperiousness
875.1 – *d* - Imperiousness
876 – *t* - Discord
876.1 – *d* - Discord
877 – *t* - Ferocity
877.1 – *d* - Ferocity

----

884 – *t* - Nastiness
884.1 – *d* - Nastiness
885 – *t* - Deceitfulness
885.1 – *d* - Deceitfulness
886 – *t* - Badness
886.1 – *d* - Badness
887 – *t* - Deviousness
887.1 – *d* - Deviousness

+ + VICES of EXCESS Themes
(Themes for Excessive Virtue)

318 - Egotism	328 - Officiousness
338 - Elitism	348 - Authoritarianism
358 - Ideology	368 - Clericalism
378 - Fanaticism	388 - Idealism
398 - Triumphalism	308 - Occultism

+ MAJOR VIRTUES Themes
(Themes for the Virtuous Mode)

118 - Individualism	128 - Pragmatism
138 - Personalism	148 - Utilitarianism
158 - Romanticism	168 - Ecclesiasticism
178 - Ecumenism	188 - Eclecticism
198 - Humanism	108 - Mysticism

MENTAL ILLNESS (B) Themes
(Transit. Themes-Excess → Disqualif. Themes-Excess)

418 - Personality Disorders (B) → 418.1 - Neuroses (B)
448 - Cycloid Psychoses (I) → 438.1 - Unsyst. Paraphr.
468 - Cycloid Psych. (II) → 458.1 - Unsyst. Catatonia
488 - Cycloid Psych. (III) → 478.1 - Unsyst. Hebephren.

LESSER VIRTUES (I) Themes
(Transit. Virtuous Themes → Disqualif. Virtuous-Themes)

228 – t-Pragmatism → 218.1 – d-Individualism
248 – t-Utilitarianism → 238.1 – d-Personalism
268 – t-Ecclesiasticism → 258.1 – d-Romanticism
288 – t-Eclecticism → 278.1 – d-Ecumenism

MENTAL ILLNESS (A) Themes
(Transit. Themes-Excess → Disqualif. Themes-Excess)

418 - Personality Disorders (A) → 428.1 - Neuroses (A)
438 - Mood Disorders (I) → 448.1 - Syst. Paraphrenia
458 - Mood Disorders (II) → 468.1 - System. Catatonia
478 - Mood Disorders (III) → 488.1 - Syst. Hebephrenia

LESSER VIRTUES (II) Themes
(Transit. Virtuous-Themes → Disqualif. Virtuous-Themes)

218 – t-Individualism → 228.1 – d-Pragmatism
238 – t-Personalism → 248.1 – d-Utilitarianism
258 – t-Romanticism → 268.1 – d-Ecclesiasticism
278 – t-Ecumenism → 288.1 – d-Eclecticism

** NEUTRALITY STATUS **

– VICES of DEFECT Themes
(Themes for the Absence of Virtue)

518 - Knavery	528 - Fraud
538 - Villainy	548 - Corruption
558 - Profanity	568 - Heresy
578 - Apostasy	588 - Anarchism
598 - Nihilism	508 - Diabolism

– – HYPERVIOLENCE Themes
(Themes for Excessive Defect)

718 - Perversion	728 - Exploitation
738 - Depravity	748 - Pernicity
758 - Sacrilege	768 - Recusancy
778 - Reprobation	788 - Pandemonium
798 - Mindlessness	708 – Demonism

CRIMINALITY (I) Themes
(Transit. Themes-Defect → Disqualif. Themes-Defect)

628 - t-Fraud   →   618.1 - d-Knavery
648 - t-Corruption → 638.1 - d-Villainy
668 - t-Heresy   →   658.1 - d-Profanity
688 - t-Anarchism → 678.1 - d-Apostasy

HYPERCRIMINALITY (I) Themes
(Transit. Themes-Hyperviol.→Disqual. Themes-Hyperv.)

828 - t-Exploitation → 818.1 - d-Perversion
848 - t-Pernicity → 838.1 - d-Depravity
868 - t-Recusancy → 858.1 - d-Sacrilege
888 - t-Pandemon.→ 878.1 - d-Reprobation

CRIMINALITY (II) Themes
(Transit. Themes-Defect → Disqualif. Themes-Defect)

618 - t-Knavery   →   628.1 - d-Fraud
638 - t-Villainy → 648.1 - d-Corruption
658 - t-Profanity → 668.1 - d-Heresy
678 - t-Apostasy → 688.1 - d-Anarchism

HYPERCRIMINALITY (II) Themes
(Transit. Themes-Hyperviol.→Disqual. Themes-Hyperv.)

818 - t-Perversion → 828.1 - d-Exploitation
838 - t-Depravity → 848.1 - d-Pernicity
858 - t-Sacrilege → 868.1 - d-Recusancy
878 - t-Reprobation→ 888.1 - d-Pandemon.

Fig. 28-E – Master Schematic Diagram Depicting the *104* Main Individual Themes

+ + ACC. THEMES- EXCESS
(Accessory Themes for the Vices of Excess)

319 – Egocentrism	329 – Obtrusiveness
339 – Autocracy	349 – Absolutism
359 – Pontification	369 – Dogmatism
379 – Fundamentalism	389 – Supremacism
399 – Universalism	309 – Enigmatism

+ ACC. VIRTUOUS THEMES
(Accessory Themes for the Virtuous Mode)

119 – Quintessentialism	129 – Expediency
139 – Heroism	149 – Practicality
159 – Charisma	169 – Orthodoxy
179 – Evangelism	189 – Moralism
199 – Cosmopolitanism	109 – Spiritualism

ACC. MENTAL ILLNESS - (A)
(Transitional Acc. Themes → Disqualified Acc. Themes)

419 - Personality Disorders (A) → 429.1 - Neuroses (A)
439 - Mood Disorders (I) → 449.1 - Syst. Paraphrenia
459 - Mood Disorders (II) → 469.1 - System. Catatonia
479 - Mood Disorders (III) → 489.1 - Syst. Hebephrenia

ACC. LESSER VIRTUES (II)
(Transitional Acc. Themes → Disqualified Acc. Themes)

219 – t-Quintess. → 229.1 – d-Expediency
239 – t-Heroism → 249.1 – d-Practicality
259 – t-Charisma → 269.1 – d-Orthodoxy
279 – t-Evangelism → 289.1 – d-Moralism

ACC. MENTAL ILLNESS - (B)
(Transitional Acc. Themes → Disqualified Acc. Themes)

429 - Personality Disorders (B) → 419.1 - Neuroses (B)
449 - Cycloid Psychoses (I) → 439.1 - Unsyst. Paraphr.
469 - Cycloid Psycho. (II) → 459.1 - Unsyst. Catatonia
489 - Cycloid Psych. (III) → 479.1 - Unsyst. Hebephren.

ACC. LESSER VIRTUES (I)
(Transitional Acc. Themes → Disqualified Acc. Themes)

229 – t-Expediency → 219.1 – d-Quintess.
249 – t-Practicality → 239.1 – d-Heroism
269 – t-Orthodoxy → 259.1 – d-Charisma
289 – t-Moralism → 279.1 – d-Evangelism

** NEUTRALITY STATUS **

ACC. CRIMINALITY (II) Themes
(Transitional Acc. Themes → Disqualified Acc. Themes)

619 - t-Mischief → 629.1 - d-Deception
639 - t-Licentious. → 649.1 - d-Venality
659 - t-Scandal → 669.1 - d-Schismatism
679 - t-Infidelity → 689.1 - d-Lawlessness

ACC. HYPERCRIMINALITY (II)
(Transitional Acc. Themes → Disqualified Acc. Themes)

819 - t- Fetishism → 829.1 - d-Victimization
839 - t-Debasement → 849.1 - d-Vileness
859 - t-Blasphemy → 869.1 - d-Heathenism
879 - t-Recreancy → 889.1 - d-Tumultuousness

ACC. CRIMINALITY (I) Themes
(Transitional Acc. Themes → Disqualified Acc. Themes)

629 - t-Deception → 619.1 - d-Mischief
649 - t-Venality → 639.1 - d-Licentious.
669 - t-Schismatism → 659.1 - d-Scandal
689 - t-Lawlessness → 679.1 - d-Infidelity

ACC. HYPERCRIMINALITY (I)
(Transitional Acc. Themes → Disqualified Acc. Themes)

829 - t-Victimization → 819.1 - d-Fetishism
849 - t-Vileness → 839.1 - d-Debasement
869 - t-Heathenism → 859.1 - d-Blasphemy
889 - t-Tumultuousness → 879.1 - d-Recreancy

− ACC. THEMES-DEFECT
(Accessory Themes for the Vices of Defect)

519 - Mischief	529 - Deception
539 - Licentiousness	549 - Venality
559 - Scandal	569 - Schismatism
579 - Infidelity	589 - Lawlessness
599 - Alienation	509 - Sorcery

− − ACC. HYPERVIOLENCE
(Acc. Themes for the Realm of Hyperviolence)

719 - Fetishism	729 - Victimization
739 - Debasement	749 - Vileness
759 - Blasphemy	769 - Heathenism
779 - Recreancy	789 - Tumultuousness
799 - Unruliness	709 - Demoniac

Fig. 28-F – Master Schematic Diagram Depicting the *104 Individual Accessory Themes*

For the darker realm of hypercriminality, "*t–pernicity*" leads to "*d–depravity*," and "*t–sacrilege*" prompts "*d–recusancy*," etc.

The remaining themes for the realm of mental illness exhibit a similar pattern, although the details are deferred until their upcoming treatment in the remaining chapters comprising upcoming **Part VII**. In a general sense, these four basic listings of transitional themes necessarily remain somewhat specialized in terms of practical applications; hence, limiting their further description in this manual. This further extends to any additional discussion of the themes for the lesser virtues (II), criminality and hypercriminality (II), etc.

This preliminary description of the main transitional themes, in turn, brings up the related technical issue of the *accessory* themes with respect to the transitional power maneuvers. These accessory variations (by definition) represent a mirror-image reflection of the main themes (I) depicted in **Fig. 27E** with the exception that the respective accessory terms are substituted in place of the main terms as shown in **Fig. 27F**. Here, "*t–practicality*" is substituted for "*t–pragmatism*," "*t–expediency*" assumes the place of "*t–utilitarianism*," and so forth. Furthermore, "*d–fraud*" is replaced by "*d–deception*," whereas "*t–venality*" is substituted for "*t–corruption*," etc. In each these cases, the final digit within the three-digit coding system is changed from an "8" to a "9," a modification formally specific to the accessory realm. Due to space constraints (and their rarity of usage) these accessory variations for the transitional themes (I) and (II) will not be outlined further, although the specific rules for modification outlined in **Fig. 27F** should prove sufficient for specifying the individual accessory themes, as well as the respective three-digit codes. Hence, this unprecedented grand overview of both criminality and hypercriminality in concert with their respective grand unifying themes provide invaluable insights into such troubling motives, with widespread applications to the disturbing trend towards global international terrorism.

A GENERAL OVERVIEW FOR THE TRANSITIONAL POWER MANEUVERS

In summary, the completed description of the two additional categories of criminality/hypercriminality adds further credence to the general transitional master plan. In concert with the lesser virtues described in Chapters *21* through *25*, the formal transitional pattern is finally nearing completion, as initially illustrated in **Fig. 26** of Chapter *26*. Here, a clear sense of symmetry emerges with respect to the four major ethical categories. For instance, in terms of the lesser virtues, the initial congeniality phase (should it be accepted) further inducts the newly transitioned individual into the established realm of the virtues, values, and ideals. Resistance to the congeniality maneuver, in contrast, results in a disqualified form of humor countermaneuver prompting the abandonment of the entire transitional interchange.

A similar pattern further holds true with respect to the vices of defect. The initial criminality phase is formally resisted through the trickery form of counter double bind maneuver. Indeed, it even proves feasible to extend this basic pattern to the extreme realm of hyperviolence. Here, the initial hypercriminality phase further prompts the disqualified form of hyper-trickery proper. In practice, however, this latter hyper-trickery phase is often eliminated due to the extremely violent nature of the initiatory phase.

For sake of ultimate symmetry, there further remains a category of transitional maneuvers specific to the realm of the vices of excess, as previously predicted in Chapter *26*. This latter transitional domain is clearly suggestive of the realm of mental illness, as more extensively described in the upcoming **Part VII**. According to this remaining transitional format, a grand total of *56* different classifications for mental illness have been identified; including *32* individual terms for mental illness (A), as well as *24* for mental illness (B). The clinical diagnosis of the mental disorders has emerged as a well-established science in its own right, particularly the terminology of the psychoses pioneered by Karl Leonhard, as well as that for the personality disorders/neuroses contained within the *DSM-IV*. Amazingly, these established systems of terminology effectively correspond to the precise specifics predicted for the transitional model underlying the various forms of the mental disorders.

The following section, accordingly, endeavors to provide a grand overview of the communicational dynamics underlying mental illness in general. Those without a specific technical interest in mental illness might best be served to skip directly to the summary chapters comprising the remaining **Part VIII**. This section has been greatly abbreviated in terms of details of the individual syndromes, wherein providing a general and overarching overview of the entire field. With widespread reach of mental illness within society as a whole, however, a concerted attempt at comprehension should well be worth the effort, if only to suggest inroads towards alleviating much of the suffering afflicting the mentally ill today.

PART-VII

29

THE COMMUNICATIONAL FACTORS UNDERLYING MENTAL ILLNESS

The communicational dynamics for the transitional class of power maneuvers spans many spheres of influence, as previously demonstrated for the virtuous realm of the lesser virtues (I) and (II). The most significant sphere of influence, however, extends to the extreme realm of the vices of excess, spotlighting the enigmatic domain of mental illness. In fitting analogy to the general transitional format, mental illness is formally defined as that sequence of double bind and counter double bind maneuvers targeting the realm of the vices of excess. In terms of a general overview for the vices of excess, Aristotle first proposed such a dualistic system for the vices; namely, the vices of defect (the absence of virtue) and the vices of excess (collectively defined as the range of extremes with respect to the virtues). Consequently, Aristotle viewed the virtuous realm as the system of "mean" values (or norms) interposed between defect and excess, an aspect favoring moderation insofar as choosing the middle ground between these opposing categories of vice.

According to this formal tripartite system, the vices of excess prove somewhat less clear-cut in nature than the vices of defect: representing a more ambiguous determination of excess, frequently with relativistic consequences for differing cultures. Many of the vices of excess, however, are more-or-less universally agreed upon. For instance, pride represents an excessive form of nostalgia, whereas shame makes a similar correspondence to guilt. Furthermore, flattery excessively expands upon hero-worship, whereas criticism makes a similar correspondence to blame. Indeed, according to the specifics of Chapter 22, it ultimately proves feasible to devise an entire schematic hierarchy of the vices of excess, mirroring point-for-point the fundamental dynamics of the virtuous power hierarchy.

Although this extreme sense of virtue (to a fault) can prove highly annoying, it scarcely reaches the degree of negativity previously encountered for the vices of defect. In keeping with its transitional relationship to the vices of excess, mental illness remains fairly non-threatening in nature, as reflected in studies confirming the non-violent nature of mentally illness relative to the general population. According to this radical interpretation, mental illness represents a concerted effort to transition into the realm of excess, particularly in contexts judged wholly inappropriate.

The extreme degree of exaggeration typically required to make the point ultimately accounts for the bizarre (and often highly emotional) nature of such a dysfunctional form of interaction. Indeed, as has long been surmised, mental illness represents a subconscious set of tactics aimed towards achieving a specific advantage within a given dysfunctional relationship. This preliminary interpretation is further compounded by the affiliated class of counter double bind maneuvers, along with the respective tendency towards verbal disqualification, a factor particularly distressing to those thusly afflicted. A chronic repetition of such agitated behavior is often observed, allowing such syndromes to be precisely classified over the course of treatment.

A CLINICAL TERMINOLOGY FOR THE REALM OF MENTAL ILLNESS

In terms of an overall terminology for mental illness, it ultimately proves crucial to adhere to a higher standard of proof than previously had been allowed within the ethical context of virtues and values. In order to respectively validate this transitional model of mental illness, the principles of the Scientific Method are necessarily employed:

410	411
Narcissistic	Borderline
Personality	Personality

412	413
Dependent	Avoidant
Personality	Personality

**PERSONALITY
DISORDERS (A)**
(Personal Double-Bind)

420.1	421.1
Obsession	Phobia
Neurosis	Neurosis

422.1	423.1
Compulsion	Anxiety
Neurosis	Neurosis

NEUROSIS (A)
*(Personal Counter
Double-Bind)*

430	431
Confabulatory	Suspicious
Euphoria	Depression

432	433
Pure	Pure
Mania	Melancholy

**MOOD
DISORDERS (I)**
(Group Double-Bind)

440.1	441.1
Confabulatory	Fantastic
Paraphrenia	Paraphrenia

442.1	443.1
Expansive	Incoherent
Paraphrenia	Paraphrenia

**PARANOID
SCHIZOPHRENIA**
(Group Counter Double-Bind)

450	451
Enthusiastic	Self-Torturing
Euphoria	Depression

452	453
Unproductive	Harried
Euphoria	Depression

**MOOD
DISORDERS (II)**
(Spiritual Double-Bind)

460.1	461.1
Proskinetic	Negativistic
Catatonia	Catatonia

462.1	463.1
Parakinetic	Affected
Catatonia	Catatonia

**CATATONIC
SCHIZOPHRENIA**
(Spiritual Counter Double-Bind)

470	471
Non-Participatory	Non-Participatory
Euphoria	Depression

472	473
Hypochondriacal	Hypochondriacal
Euphoria	Depression

**MOOD
DISORDERS (III)**
(Humanitarian Double-Bind)

480.1	481.1
Silly	Insipid
Hebephrenia	Hebephrenia

482.1	483.1
Eccentric	Autistic
Hebephrenia	Hebephrenia

**HEBEPHRENIC
SCHIZOPHRENIA**
(Humanit. Counter Double-Bind)

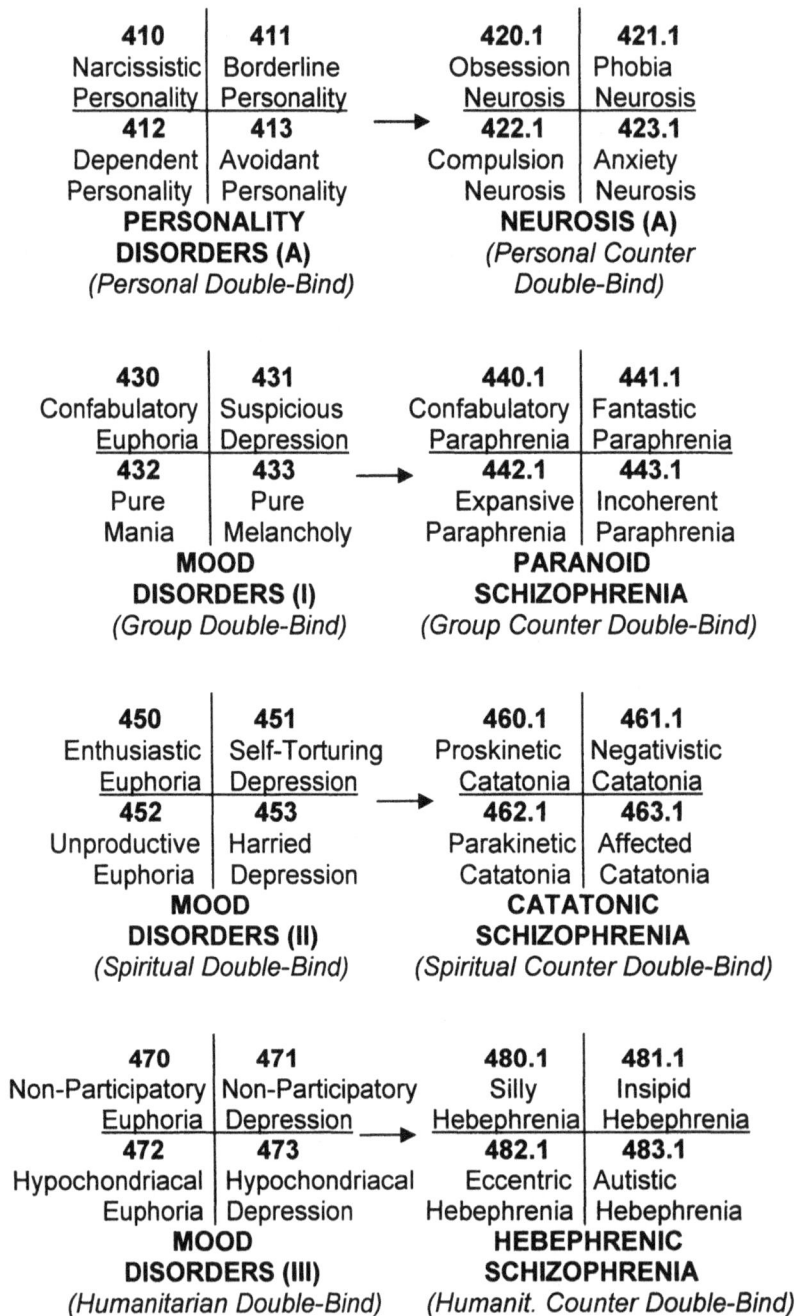

Fig. 29 – The Three-Digit Codes for Mental Illness - (A)

318

namely, (1) propose a hypothesis, (2) make predictions from that hypothesis, and (3) test the accuracy of the predictions within an experimental setting. According to Step (1), the major hypothesis has initially been established; namely, mental illness represents the transitional interplay of the double bind and counter double bind maneuvers in relation to the vices of excess.

Skipping ahead to Step (2), the predictions based upon this hypothesis necessarily invoke the formal communicational factors under consideration. The *64*-part grouping of schematic definitions collectively models the predicted classifications of mental illness: in particular, the reciprocating interplay of the double bind and counter double bind maneuvers.

Jumping ahead to the remaining Step (3), these theoretical predictions are subsequently tested within a clinical environment, as stringently compared to a broad range of clinical observations of mentally ill patients. The logistics involved in conducting such an overall clinical study prove exceedingly daunting, compounded by the risks of introducing subliminal bias into the procedure. Indeed, despite what clinicians care to admit, clinical diagnosis is more of an art than a science, scarcely the objective endeavor often implied.

An alternate accepted strategy involves consulting the established literature within the field, for the groundwork often has already been laid in pre-existing studies. A comprehensive survey of the relevant literature, indeed, has turned up a wealth of relevant research particularly suited to the task. In particular, German clinician Karl Leonhard's detailed terminology of the psychoses (in conjunction with terminology contained within the *DSM-IV*) makes for an extremely precise match with the specifics predicted for the transitional model of mental illness. This innovation conveniently makes use of preexisting systems of terminology, directly avoiding the introduction of new complements of terms into an already complex field. Furthermore, the majority of Karl Leonhard's observations were made in Germany before 1959, an established system of clinical observations that formally bypasses any risk of circular logic, issues directly affecting any study conducted within a more current time frame.

Leonhard's chief experimental paradigm referred primarily to inheritance patterns, as suggested in the title of his major work: *The Classification of Endogenous Psychoses* (where endogenous is defined as arising from within). This interpretation followed the traditional model of mental illness at that time; namely, physical syndromes that affect specific brain circuitry: as further asso-

ciated with distinctive inheritance patterns. Karl Leonhard continues in a long line of German Classificationalists, a pupil of neurologist Karl Kleist, who, in turn, was mentored by the renowned Carl Wernicke. According to such an established tradition, Leonhard's extensive interviews with the families of psychotics were chiefly conducted to identify the affiliated hereditary patterns leading to the occurrence of mental illness within the family. In his later years, Leonhard further broadened his focus to include psychosocial factors, although this occurred long after his complex terminology (and supportive observations) were already firmly in place. In truth, Leonhard's elaborate system of observations are considered a masterpiece of insight and intuition in their own right, well placed to stand apart from any system of theory designed to explain them.

Returning to the analysis at hand, the most crucial aspect of this fortuitous correspondence involves Leonhard's extensive clinical observations/case studies: providing a particularly tight correspondence with the *64* individual slots predicted for the transitional model of mental illness, as partially depicted in **Fig. 29**. A preliminary overview of these categories for mental illness definitely remains in order, serving as the formal conceptual foundation for the more detailed description of individual syndromes to follow.

A GENERAL OVERVIEW OF THE MAJOR CLASSIFICATIONS OF MENTAL ILLNESS

According to principles of modern psychiatry, two major classifications of psychosis are traditionally recognized; namely, the manic-depressive style of mood disorders, as well as the various categories of schizophrenia. The mood disorders are typically less debilitating than the schizophrenias, effectively representing the initial double bind style of power maneuvers with respect to the vices of excess. Although often exaggerated to some degree, the mood disorders fail to technically exhibit the bizarre degree of disqualification typically characterizing schizophrenia. In fact, the most telling feature of schizophrenia is precisely this extreme degree of disqualification, a feature particularly reminiscent with respect to the counter double bind maneuvers (analogous to that initially defined for the humor maneuver proper). Indeed, in less enlightened times, mental asylums (such as London's *Bedlam*) were crassly exploited for their tragically amusing entertainment value. Even in our own more enlightened age, many patients still require institutionalization as a protection to society (and vice versa).

According to the detailed schematic format of **Fig. 29**, an extensive assortment of clinical terms effectively fills-out the requisite four-level hierarchy of diagnostic slots predicted for the double bind model of mental illness. This precise degree of correspondence, in large part, relies primarily upon the detailed terminology contained within the English translation of Karl Leonhard's *The Classification of Endogenous Psychoses, Fifth Edition* (1979). According to this groundbreaking work, Leonhard distinguishes *38+* classifications of clinical psychosis that (in hindsight) account for the precise number of slots predicted for the double bind theory of mental illness.

According to this particular line of reasoning, the traditional classification of schizophrenia into paranoid, catatonic, and hebephrenic categories is ultimately explainable in terms of the three-way specialization of group, spiritual, and humanitarian domains within the authority hierarchy. A similar degree of correspondence is further seen with respect to the subsequent categories of the mood disorders: as in mania, melancholy, depression, and euphoria. Furthermore, these dual master categories (for both schizophrenia and mood disorders) are further subdivided into numerous sub-classifications tailor-made for incorporation into the schematic transitional hierarchy, a further bonus to Leonhard's overall system.

Returning to **Fig. 29**, the most basic personal level within the power hierarchy alternately represents a special case due to the less debilitating nature of its associated symptomology. This initial level, accordingly, is specified through the affiliated listings of personality disorders and the neuroses: as further verified within the specialized terminology contained within the *Diagnostic and Statistical Manual of Mental Disorders - IV (DSM-IV)*. In particular, the personality disorders are explained as personal variations on the preliminary double bind class of power maneuvers, neatly dovetailing into the three-level hierarchy of the mood disorders. For instance, the narcissistic personality represents an excessive form of nostalgia, whereas the borderline personality specifies an extreme form of guilt. Similarly, the dependent personality represents an excessive form of desire, whereas the avoidant personality denotes an extreme form of worry.

In a related fashion, the more bizarre symptomology associated with the neuroses, in turn, exhibits the distinct potential for grading over into the affiliated sequences related to schizophrenia: a circumstance clearly suggestive of the dynamics underlying the counter double bind class of maneuvers. In particular, the neurotic syndrome complexes of obsession/compulsion and phobia/anxiety are clearly less debilitating than those established for schizophrenia, representing counter double bind maneuvers restricted to the most basic personal level within the power hierarchy. For instance, obsession neurosis represents a disqualified form of flattery, whereas phobia neurosis denotes a similar denial of criticism. Furthermore, compulsion neurosis describes a disqualified form of envy, whereas anxiety neurosis specifies an outright denial of disdain.

This personal degree of specialization technically leaves the remaining group, spiritual, and humanitarian levels essentially unaffected, allowing for an effective outpatient course of treatment. The affiliated categories of psychosis, however, formally affect the group authority levels (or higher), explaining the tendency for more global psychological effects. This broader sphere of influence undoubtedly accounts for the greater incidence of psychoses that come to the attention of the authorities, in direct contrast to the neuroses, where only particular relationships are affected.

THE THREE-DIGIT CODES FOR THE REALM OF MENTAL ILLNESS

With respect to the preliminary double bind class of power maneuvers, the first three digits within the coding system are fully capable of designating this initial class of transitional power maneuvers: being as they represent fundamental variations on the initial classifications for the vices of excess. In the case of the mental illness (A), these three digit codes end with numbers zero through three, representing the double bind class of power maneuvers. For instance, narcissistic personality equals 410, borderline personality = 411, dependent personality = 412, and avoidant personality = 413: as further depicted in **Fig. 29**.

With respect to the remaining class of counter double bind maneuvers, however, the respective complement of three-digit code numbers must further be modified in relation to the initial double bind maneuvers. Accordingly, this further entails the designation of an additional decimal place for specifying this affiliated class of counter double bind maneuvers. This latter class of maneuvers is characterized by a "one" in the fourth-place slot: e.g., obsession neurosis is coded as 420.1, phobia neurosis equals 421.1, etc.; as evident in the schematic interplay of narcissism/obsession, borderline/phobia, dependent pers./compulsion, etc. Although this distinctive interplay of the personality disorders and the neuroses proves intriguing on an intuitive level, the true test for such a

The Communicational Factors Underlying Mental Illness

system is ultimately found within the expanded context the corresponding schematic definitions. Accordingly, the complete four-part listings of definitions for mental illness (A) are respectively listed in **Tables S-1** to **S-4**: a sequence beginning immediately overleaf. This format is identical in form and function to that previously established for the lesser virtues, although now representing transitions within the realm of excess (rather than the virtuous mode). The schematic definitions for mental illness are respectively based upon this strict hierarchial pattern. Here the initial personal authority level targets the personality disorders and the neuroses. The remaining group, spiritual, and humanitarian levels, in turn, are specified through definitions targeting the major classifications of psychosis: namely, the mood disorders and the individual classifications of schizophrenia.

For instance, the narcissistic personality disorder of the personal authority is formally countered (in a disqualified fashion) by the obsession neurosis of the personal follower. A similar series of definitions further holds true for the remaining sequences: e.g., the borderline personality/phobia neurosis, the dependent personality/compulsion neurosis, and the avoidant personality/anxiety neurosis. An even more advanced degree of specialization further becomes apparent for the remaining levels depicted within the tables, although now representing the interplay linking the mood disorders with the classifications of schizophrenia. Indeed, the discerning reader is encouraged to refer back to these four tables of definitions throughout the context of the more detailed examination of mental illness to follow.

The remainder of the current **Part VII** examines each of the individual syndromes for mental illness (A) to a greater degree of detail, demonstrating an inherent correspondence to the transitional model of mental illness. A separate chapter is devoted to each of the major categories of syndromes. The remainder of the current chapter launches this formal analysis with an initial discussion of the personal level of the power hierarchy, targeting the personality disorders (narcissistic-borderline-dependent-avoidant) and the related forms of neurosis (obsession-compulsion-phobia-anxiety). Chapters *30* and *31*, in turn, extend the discussion to an overview of the remaining group, spiritual, and humanitarian levels within the power hierarchy: outlining Leonhard's pure forms of the mood disorders and systematic schizophrenia. The remainder of the current section further shifts the focus to the remaining forms of mental illness (B). Chapter *32* describes the personality disorders not initially

listed in Chapter *29* (histrionic-paranoid-passive/aggressive-schizoid), as well as the corresponding forms of the neuroses (dissociative-depersonalization-conversion-neuraesthenic). Chapter *33*, in turn, extends the analysis to the affiliated forms of the psychoses; namely, Leonhard's cycloid forms of the mood disorders, as well as the unsystematic forms of schizophrenia. Each of the component chapters for **Part VII** are further enhanced with a wealth of detail concerning Leonhard's clinical observations, clearly illustrating how the placement of a particular syndrome formally matches the specifics predicted in terms of its respective schematic definition.

Finally, Chapter *34* formally rounds out this stepwise analysis with an in-depth examination of a number of crucial issues with respect to this communicational model of mental illness; namely, the issue of the accessory variations as well as applications to clinical diagnosis and counseling psychotherapy. In final analysis, these exciting new perspectives on the riddle of mental illness offer a long-anticipated resolution to such pressing social issues, including significant inroads towards ameliorating the suffering of those thusly afflicted. It should specifically be mentioned that this book is intended as a reference volume only, not as a manual for self-treatment. The information contained herein is designed to aid in making informed choices about mental health and is not intended as a substitute for treatments prescribed by a clinician.

THE PERSONALITY DISORDERS

The most logical place to begin a comprehensive analysis of mental illness is at the most basic personal level within the power hierarchy; namely, the realm of the personality disorders. According to the *Diagnostic and Statistical Manual of Mental Disorders*, the personality disorders are defined as: "characteristic lifelong behavior patterns established early in the course of emotional development and crippling in their effect. They exert a destructive, constricting influence on the personality of the individual, leading to maladaptive behavior, intra-psychic tension, interpersonal strife (and in certain cases) socio-cultural conflict." As lifelong patterns of self-defeating behaviors, the patient is often untroubled until confronted with stress: rarely seeking professional health, being that the symptoms are rarely incapacitating to the degree seen for the neuroses or the psychoses.

Due to a wide range of factors, a broad range of opinion exists as to what truly constitutes a

NARCISSISTIC PERSONALITY	OBSESSION NEUROSIS
Previously, you (as personal follower) have flatteringly acted in an excessively worshipful fashion in response to the prideful treatment of the personal authority. But now, I (as new personal authority) will *pridefully* act in an extremely nostalgic fashion towards you: in anticipation of your (as established PF) flatterous treatment of me.	Previously, I (as new personal authority) have pridefully acted in an extremely nostalgic fashion towards you: in anticipation of your (as established PF) flatterous treatment of me. But now, you (as reluctant personal follower) will **deny** *flatteringly* acting in an extremely worshipful fashion towards me: scorning my (as new PA) prideful treatment of you.
CONFABULATORY EUPHORIA	**CONFABULATORY PARA.**
Previously, you (as group representative) have flatteringly acted in an adulatory fashion in response to the vain sense of pride of the group authority. But now, I (as new group authority) will *vainly* act in a prideful fashion towards you: in anticipation of your (as established GR) flattering sense of adulation.	Previously, I (as new group authority) have vainly acted pridefully towards you: in anticipation of your (as established GR) flattering sense of adulation. But now, you (as reluctant group representative) will **deny** flatteringly expressing *adulation* towards me: scorning my (as new GA) vain sense of pride.
ENTHUSIASTIC EUPHORIA	**PROSKINETIC CATATONIA**
Previously, you (as spiritual disciple) have patronizingly expressed adulation in response to the vain sense of conceit of the spiritual authority. But now, I (as new spiritual authority) will vainly act in a *conceited* fashion towards you: in anticipation of your (as established SD) patronizing treatment of me.	Previously, I (as new spiritual authority) have vainly acted in a conceited fashion towards you: in anticipation of your (as established SD) patronizing treatment of me. But now, you (as reluctant spiritual disciple) will **deny** *patronizingly* expressing adulation towards me: scorning my (as new SA) vain sense of conceit.
NON-PARTICIPATORY EUPH.	**SILLY HEBEPHRENIA**
Previously, you (as representative member of humanity) have patronizingly acted obsequiously in response to the pretentious sense of conceit of the humanitarian authority. But now, I (as new humanitarian authority) will *pretentiously* act in a conceited fashion towards you: in anticipation of your (as established RH) obsequious treatment of me.	Previously, I (as new humanitarian authority) have pretentiously acted in a conceited fashion towards you: in anticipation of your (as est. RH) obsequious treatment of me. But now, you (as reluctant represent. member of humanity) will **deny** patronizingly acting *obsequiously* towards me: scorning my (as new HA) pretentious sense of conceit.

Table S-1 - Definitions Based upon Narcissism/Obsession

BORDERLINE PERSONALITY	PHOBIA NEUROSIS
Previously, you (as personal follower) have critically acted in an excessively blameful fashion in response to the shameful treatment of the personal authority. But now, I (as new personal authority) will *shamefully* act in an extremely guilty fashion towards you: in anticipation of your (as established PF) critical treatment of me.	Previously, I (as new personal authority) have shamefully acted in an extremely guilty fashion towards you: in anticipation of your (as establ. PF) critical treatment of me. But now, you (as reluctant personal follower) will **deny** *critically* acting in an extremely blameful fashion towards me: scorning my (as new PA) shameful treatment of you.
SUSPICIOUS DEPRESSION	FANTASTIC PARAPHRENIA
Previously, you (as group representative) have critically acted in a ridiculing fashion in response to the shameful sense of humiliation of the group authority. But now, I (as new group authority) will shamefully act in a *humiliated* fashion towards you: in anticipation of your (as established GR) critical-ridiculing of me.	Previously, I (as new group authority) have shamefully acted in a humiliated fashion towards you: in anticipation of your (as established GR) critical-ridiculing of me. But now, you (as reluctant group representative) will **deny** *critical-ridiculing* me: scorning my (as new GA) shameful sense of humiliation.
SELF-TORTURING DEPRESSION	NEGATIVISTIC CATATONIA
Previously, you (as spiritual disciple) have scornfully acted in a ridiculing fashion in response to the humiliated sense of mortification of the spiritual authority. But now, I (as new spiritual authority) will humiliatingly act in a *mortified* fashion towards you: in anticipation of your (as established SD) scornful-ridiculing of me.	Previously, I (as new spiritual authority) have humiliatingly acted in a mortified fashion towards you: in anticipation of your (as established SD) scornful-ridiculing of me. But now, you (as reluctant spiritual disciple) will **deny** *scornfully-ridiculing* me: scorning my (as new SA) mortified treatment of me.
NON-PARTICIPATORY DEPR.	INSIPID HEBREPHRENIA
Previously, you (as representative member of humanity) have scornfully acted in a mocking fashion in response to the mortified sense of anguish of the humanitarian authority. But now, I (as new humanitarian authority) will mortifiedly act in an *anguished* fashion towards you: in anticipation of your (as established RH) scornful-mocking of me.	Previously, I (as new humanitarian authority) have mortifiedly acted in an anguished fashion towards you: in anticipation of your (as established RH) scornful-mocking of me. But now, you (as reluctant representative member of humanity) will **deny** scornfully-*mocking* me: scorning my (as new HA) mortified sense of anguish.

Table S-2 - Definitions Based upon Borderline/Phobia

DEPENDENT PERSONALITY	COMPULSION NEUROSIS
Previously, you (as personal follower) have enviously acted in an extremely approving fashion in response to the impudent treatment of the personal authority. But now, you (as new personal authority) will *impudently* act in an extremely desirous fashion towards me: in anticipation of my (as established PF) envious treatment of you.	Previously, you (as new personal authority) have impudently acted in an extremely desirous fashion towards me: in anticipation of my (as establ. PF) envious treatment of you. But now, I (as reluctant personal follower) will **deny** *enviously* acting extremely approvingly towards you: scorning your (as new PA) impudent treatment of me.
PURE MANIA	EXPANSIVE PARAPHRENIA
Previously, I (as group representative) have enviously acted in a jealous fashion in response to the impudent sense of arrogance of the group authority. But now, you (as new group authority) will impudently act in an *arrogant* fashion towards me: in anticipation of my (as established GR) envious sense of jealousy.	Previously, you (as new group authority) have impudently acted in an arrogant fashion towards me: in anticipation of my (as established GR) envious sense of jealousy. But now, I (as reluctant group representative) will **deny** enviously acting *jealously* towards you: scorning your (as new GA) impudent sense of arrogance.
UNPRODUCTIVE EUPHORIA	PARAKINETIC CATATONIA
Previously, I (as spiritual disciple) have jealously acted in a covetous fashion in response to the arrogant sense of impetuosity of the spiritual authority. But now, you (as new spiritual authority) will *impetuously* act in an arrogant fashion towards me: in anticipation of my (as established SD) covetous treatment of you.	Previously, you (as new spiritual authority) have impetuously acted in an arrogant fashion towards me: in anticipation of my (as established SD) covetous treatment of you. But now, I (as reluctant spiritual disciple) will **deny** jealously acting *covetously* towards you: scorning your (as new SA) impetuous sense of arrogance.
HYPOCHONDRIACAL EUPHORIA	ECCENTRIC HEBEPHRENIA
Previously, I (as representative member of humanity) have covetously acted longingly in response to the impetuous sense of presumption of the humanitarian authority. But now, you (as new humanitarian authority) will impetuously act in a *presumptuous* fashion towards me: in anticipation of my (as established RH) covetous sense of longing.	Previously, you (as new humanitarian authority) have impetuously acted presumptuously towards me: in anticipation of my (as established RH) covetous sense of longing. But now, I (as reluctant represent. member of humanity) will **deny** covetously acting *longingly* towards you: scorning your (as new HA) presumptuous treatment of me.

Table S-3 - Definitions Based on Dependent/Compulsion

AVOIDANT PERSONALITY	ANXIETY NEUROSIS
Previously, I (as your personal follower) have disdainfully acted in an excessively concerned fashion in response to the insolent treatment of the personal authority. But now, you (as new personal authority) will *insolently* act in an extremely worrisome fashion towards me: in anticipation of my (as established PF) disdainful treatment of you.	Previously, you (as new personal authority) have insolently acted in an extremely worrisome fashion towards me: in anticipation of my (as estab. PF) disdainful treatment of you. But now, I (as reluctant personal follower) will **deny** *disdainfully* acting in an excessively concerned fashion towards you: scorning your (as new PA) insolent treatment of me.
PURE MELANCHOLIA	INCOHERENT PARAPHRENIA
Previously, I (as group representative) have disdainfully acted in a contemptuous fashion in response to the insolent sense of audacity of the group authority. But now, you (as new group authority) will insolently act in an *audacious* fashion towards me: in anticipation of my (as established GR) disdainful sense of contempt.	Previously, you (as new group authority) have insolently acted in an audacious fashion towards me: in anticipation of my (as established GR) disdainful sense of contempt. But now, I (as reluctant group representative) will **deny** disdainfully acting *contemptuously* towards you: scorning your (as new GA) insolent sense of audacity.
HARRIED DEPRESSION	AFFECTED CATATONIA
Previously, I (as spiritual disciple) have contemptuously acted in a reproachful fashion in response to the audacious sense of rashness of the spiritual authority. But now, you (as new spiritual authority) will audaciously act in a *rash* fashion towards me: in anticipation of my (as established SD) contemptuous sense of reproach.	Previously, you (as new spiritual authority) have audaciously acted in a rash fashion towards me: in anticipation of my (as established SD) contemptuous sense of reproach. But now, I (as reluctant spiritual disciple) will **deny** contemptuously acting *reproachfully* towards you: scorning your (as new SA) audacious sense of rashness.
HYPOCHONDRIACAL DEPRESS.	AUTISTIC HEBEPHRENIA
Previously, I (as represent. member of humanity) have reproachfully acted in a chagrined fashion in response to the rash sense of boldness of the humanitarian authority. But now, you (as new humanitarian authority) will rashly act in a *bold* fashion towards me: in anticipation of my (as established RH) chagrined treatment of you.	Previously, you (as new humanitarian authority) have rashly acted in a bold fashion towards me: in anticipation of my (as established RH) chagrined treatment of you. But now, I (as reluctant represent. member of humanity) will **deny** reproachfully acting in a *chagrined* fashion towards you: scorning your (as new HA) bold treatment of me.

Table S- 4 - Definitions Based upon Avoidant / Anxiety

personality disorder (as opposed to simple moral weakness). Some authorities question whether they represent actual disease entities. Even the *DSM*-series varies in its opinions from one edition to the next. Although *DSM-II* distinguishes *10* distinct personality disorders, *DSM-III* deletes *2* of these (and adds *5* others), for a grand total of *13*. The latest edition (*DSM-IV*) further tinkers with this grouping, a form of clinical fine-tuning spanning many years.

The *DSM*-series remains fairly thorough in its treatment of the personality disorders, distinguishing many fine degrees of meaning. With respect to the personal level of the power hierarchy, four distinct personality disorders particularly standout in this regard. For instance, the narcissistic personality disorder represents a transitional form of pride, whereas the borderline personality makes a similar correspondence to shame. A similar pattern further holds true with respect to the dependent and avoidant personality disorders, representing transitional variations with respect to impudence and insolence. Four of the other personality disorders; namely, the histrionic, paranoid, passive-aggressive, and schizoid disorders represent a further grouping best reserved for treatment in an upcoming chapter.

The antisocial personality disorder (traditionally known as the psychopathic personality) is conspicuously lacking in this system of terms, a term best described in the respective chapter dealing with criminality. This reassignment confirms the speculations of many authorities that this latter disorder shares little in common with the other personality disorders, save its impulsive character. The remainder of the current chapter formally endeavors to describe how these four basic personality disorders (narcissistic-borderline-dependent-avoidant) represent the basic transitional foundation for the hierarchy of mental illness to follow.

410 – NARCISSISTIC PERSONALITY

The first of the personality disorders, the narcissistic personality, traces his designation to the classical Greek myth of Narcissus and Echo. The nymph Echo sought the affections of the handsome youth Narcissus, although the latter continually spurned all advances. When Echo eventually expired from unrequited love, Nemesis (the Goddess of Vengeance) caused Narcissus to fall love with his own reflection, pining away until he too met a fate similar to Echo. True to these classical traditions, the narcissistic personality disorder is characterized by an exaggerated sense of one's self-importance/abilities and a lack of empathy for others. People with this trait believe themselves to be uniquely gifted, commonly engaging in fantasies of fabulous success, power, or fame. Arrogant and egotistical, narcissists are often snobbish, expecting special treatment and concessions from others. They require considerable admiration from others, finding it difficult to cope with criticism. The self-aggrandizement and self-absorption of narcissistic individuals is accompanied by a pronounced lack of interest and empathy for others. They expect others to be devoted to them, but display no impulse to reciprocate, being unable to identify with the feelings of others or anticipate other's needs. Narcissistic people often frequently into relationships based on what others can do for them. According to *DSM-IV*, the narcissistic personality disorder affects less than 1% of the general population, of which half to three-quarters are male.

In line with the preceding descriptions, the narcissistic personality disorder fits quite well within the parameters specified for the double bind model of mental illness: representing a transitional variation on pride, also defined as an extreme nostalgic sense of self-esteem. Here, the newly transitioned personal authority figure narcissistically acts in an excessively prideful fashion in anticipation of the flatterous attentions of the established follower figure. Indeed, the one-down power status for this transitional maneuver clearly imparts a vulnerable quality, as evident in the broad range of symptomology observed for the narcissistic personality disorder. Through this self-serving, self-absorbed strategy, the narcissistic individual strives to become the center of attraction, well positioned to take advantage of any newly formed follower alliance within the overall realm of excess. This overbearing tactic clearly is not always effective, although scarcely much of a deterrent to the narcissistic individual, whose behavior patterns are essentially chronic in nature.

411 – BORDERLINE PERSONALITY

The second of the personality disorders, the borderline personality, is characterized by intense feelings of devaluation consistent with a transitional relationship to the respective theme of shame (as in an extremely apologetic sense of guilt). It shares with the narcissistic personality such a past-directed focus, although now targeting the darker realm of shamefulness, as opposed to the more positive prerequisites associated with pride. The borderline personality is characterized by erratic or impulsive self-destructive behavior, in addition to an intense fear of abandonment. Borderline individuals typically display a long history of unstable interpersonal relationships. They have difficulty seeing "shades of gray" in the world, and view significant people in their lives as either completely flawless, or extremely unfair and uncaring (a phenomena known as *splitting*). These alternating feelings of idealization and devaluation represent the hallmark feature of borderline personality disorder. Being as borderline patients set up excessively unrealistic expectations for others, they are often disappointed when such hopes often fail to be realized.

The term *borderline* was originally coined by psychologist Adolf Stern in the 1930's to describe patients who bordered somewhere between psychosis and neurosis. The borderline personality disorder accounts for roughly 30-60% of all personality disorders, and is present in approximately 2% of the general population. The disorder appears to affect women more frequently than men, and 75% of all diagnosed patients are female. Adults with borderline personalities often have a history of significant traumas: such as emotional or physical abuse, neglect, or the loss of a parent in childhood. Feelings of inadequacy/self-loathing arising from such conditions may play a key role in the development of the borderline personality. It has also been theorized that such patients attempt to compensate for the care they were denied during childhood through idealized demands they now make upon others as adults.

412 – DEPENDENT PERSONALITY

The remaining two entries within the double bind class of power maneuvers are respectively identified as the dependent and avoidant personality disorders. As suggested in their qualifiers, both the dependent and avoidant disorders are essentially future-directed perspectives, in direct contrast to the narcissistic/borderline syndromes that alternately represent past-directed forms of disorders. As such, the dependent personality represents a transitional form of excessive desire, whereas the avoidant personality specifies an extreme form of worry.

Take, for example, the first-listed dependent personality disorder. Individuals affected by this disorder display an inordinately low level of confidence in their intelligence and abilities, accompanied by a difficulty in making decisions or undertaking projects on their own volition. Their pervasive reliance upon others, even for minor tasks or decisions, makes them appear exaggeratedly co-operative, typically out of fear of alienating those of whose help they seek. They show difficulty initiating projects due to a lack of self-confidence in their judgment or abilities (rather than lack of motivation or energy). They are reluctant to express disagreement with others, typically willing to go to great lengths to win the approval of those upon whom they rely. The dependent personality disorder appears equally commonly in both males and females, typically beginning by the onset of early adulthood.

According to this overall double bind perspective, the dependent personality formally fits the specifics predicted for the transitional model of mental illness. Here, the personal authority figure dependently acts in an extremely desirous fashion in anticipation of the extreme approval expressed by the personal follower. In keeping with this dual power schematic, the dependent individual vulnerably acts from a one-down power status, as the broad range of dependency symptoms clearly serves to indicate. This chronic display of helplessness can trigger a strong protective response from one's parental figures, accounting for the dependent disorder's early emergence in young adulthood. As such, the underlying communicational dynamics are now more adequately defined, certainly of particular interest to the generally accepted forms of clinical treatment and precise diagnosis.

413 – AVOIDANT PERSONALITY

The completed description of the dependent personality, in turn, sets the stage for a discussion of its motivational counterpart, the avoidant personality disorder. This latter syndrome is clinically characterized by the tendency to withdraw from social contexts due to feelings of inferiority or inadequacy in relation to others. Indeed, it shares with the dependent personality such a future-directed focus, although now targeting the darker realm of excessive worry, in direct contrast to the solicitous prerequisites previously established for the dependent personality.

The avoidant personality, accordingly, is characterized by an avoidance of social situations and close interpersonal relationships, primarily due to an excessive fear of rejection by others. The etiology of the avoidant personality disorder has not definitely been determined, and may be confluence of social, genetic, and biological factors. Roughly 0.5% to 1.0% of the general population suffers from the avoidant personality disorder. Many individuals experience avoidant personality characteristics at one point or another during their lifetimes. Occasional feelings of self-doubt or fear in unfamiliar social relationships are not unusual. Nor is this development unhealthy, as such situations may cause feelings of inadequacy or social avoidance in even the most self-confident of individuals. Avoidant personality traits only truly emerge as a disorder when they begin to cause a long-term, negative impact on the individual, a functional impairment that significantly alters lifestyle, greatly impacting the overall quality of life by triggering feelings of distress within the individual.

THE NEUROSES

The completed description of the preliminary class of personality disorders further raises a remaining related issue; namely, the status of the affiliated class of counter double bind maneuvers: as reflected in the subliminally disqualified nature of the neuroses. These particularly dysfunctional disorders remain a subject of intense investigation to the present day, their extreme degree at disqualification formally contrasting with the milder symptomology characterizing the personality disorders. Sigmund Freud's ground-breaking work on the development of neurosis remains one of the most widely accepted systems of the day.

The frequently incapacitating nature of the neuroses typically leads the patient to seek professional treatment. Indeed, this basic inability to control one's neurotic symptoms is further indicative of such a high degree of disqualification: a subconscious attempt to control one's relationships without freely admitting to have done so. This circumstance is further compounded by the observation that neurosis represents a formal variation on the realm of the vices of excess, further amplifying the bizarre nature of the symptomology. In direct analogy to the personality disorders, the *DSM-IV* distinguishes a broad range of neurotic syndromes, the most prominent being obsession, compulsion, phobia, and anxiety neurosis. Four additional classifications of neurosis; namely, dissociative, conversion, depersonalization, and neuraesthenic syndromes remain a topic best reserved for analysis in Chapter *32*.

The first-mentioned class of disorders represents what are termed the pure neuroses; namely, that set of counter double bind maneuvers that counter the preliminary (double bind) class of maneuvers specified for the personality disorders. For instance, the narcissistic personality of the personal authority, in turn, is countered by the obsession neurosis expressed the personal follower figure. Similarly, the shame-

ful dictates of the borderline personality are further countered by the phobia neurosis expressed by the personal follower. Furthermore, the dependent personality is formally countered by the compulsion neurosis: whereas the avoidant personality is similarly counteracted by the anxiety neurosis. The remainder of the current chapter examines each of these respective forms of neurosis within such a dual transitional context, demonstrating their reciprocal dynamics in relation to the preliminary personality disorders.

420.1 / 422.1
OBSESSION/COMPULSION NEUROSIS

Obsessive-compulsive disorder (OCD) is rightfully classified among the neuroses, characterized by recurrently intrusive, anxiety-producing thoughts (obsessions) and behaviors (compulsions). Individuals afflicted with obsessive-compulsive disorder consistently attempt to suppress such obsessional thoughts through the performance of irrational (and often ritualistic) compulsions. As both of these functional aspects are collectively listed together, they, accordingly, will be examined in tandem within the current section.

Although marked similarities are shared between individual cases of OCD, no two people experience this anxiety disorder in exactly the same fashion. In one common form of obsessive-compulsive disorder, an exaggerated fear of contamination (the obsession) leads to washing one's hands so often that they become raw (the compulsion). Other common manifestations of OCD include sorting, checking, and counting compulsions. Checking compulsions appear to be more common among men, whereas washing is more frequent among women. Another variety of OCD is trichotillomania, the compulsion to pull hair. Curiously, compulsive behavior is often not related logically to the obsessive fear, or otherwise is clearly excessive (as in hand-washing).

Although individuals with OCD realize that their thought processes are irrational, they are unable to control their compulsions, becoming painfully embarrassed when their bizarre behavior is discovered. Certain behaviors termed rituals are repeated in response to obsessional ideation. Rituals, however, only temporarily reduce the discomfort or anxiety caused by an obsession; hence, they must be repeated frequently. This fear that something terrible will happen if a ritual is discontinued often locks OCD sufferers into a life ruled by superstitious beliefs.

With respect to the obsessional component within the overall OCD syndrome, such obsessions clearly specify a past-directed perspective, in direct response to the narcissistic prerequisites initially expressed by the personal authority figure. Continual exposure to such narcissistic tactics ultimately prompts recurrently obsessional thoughts or impulses: experienced as intrusively inappropriate, and resulting in marked anxiety or distress. The individual attempts to ignore or suppress such thoughts or images, aiming to neutralize them through some other thought or action. The person further recognizes that this obsessional ideation is the product of his-or-her own mind, being excessive or unreasonable (although this criterion does not necessarily apply to children).

According to this communicational dynamic, the personal authority initially pridefully acts in a narcissistic fashion in anticipation of the flattering treatment of the established personal follower figure. The personal follower, however, when confronted with being double bound into such a predetermined course of action, may opt to employ a counter double bind maneuver; namely, accepting the face value of the communication while simultaneously denying willing participation therein. Here, the personal follower disqualifies his flatterous attentions, in return: professing not to be in control of such obsessional ideation consistent with a mental disorder (as traditionally defined). Indeed, these obsessional symptoms are typically set-off within a narcissistic context, formally mirroring the interplay of reverence/self-esteem initially seen with respect to the more measured realm of the lesser virtues.

For example, a general case study describes a young man who experienced obsessional thoughts of assaulting his self-absorbed/vain girlfriend while alone on a date. This context certainly fits the respective transitional dynamic indicative of the dual interplay of double bind and counter double bind maneuvers. The disqualified denial implicit within obsessional neurosis is truly beyond the control of the individual, a symptom spectrum subconsciously specified within the transitional model of mental illness.

A similar pattern of communication is further apparent with respect to the related symptom spectrum of compulsion neurosis, although now targeting a future-directed sphere of influence. This more active perspective is formally specified through repetitive behaviors (such as hand washing, ordering objects, checking activities) or mental acts (e.g., praying, counting, repeating words silently, etc.). Here the individual feels driven to perform such activities according to rules that must be rigidly applied. These behaviors aim to reduce distress or head-off some dreaded event.

In response to the excessively desirous perspective characterizing the dependent personality disorder, compulsion neurosis represents an extremely disqualified sense of envy, a seemingly irrational response that remains beyond the conscious control of the compulsive individual. As such, it represents an extreme variation on the disqualified sense of *concession* previously established with respect to this lesser virtues.

For example, consider the case study of the extremely strait-laced and compulsive young man, which, in the course of walking to purchase a newspaper from a roadside stand, was approached by a pushy street prostitute. His impulsive response was to take the coins he held in his hand for the newspaper and fling them across the street before storming home empty-handed. Here, the extremely impudent nature of the dependency expressed by the streetwalker represented the initial trigger mechanism, wherein eliciting the compulsive reaction, in return. This is undoubtedly interpreted as a sublimation of the young man's subconscious desire to act upon such unacceptable impulses. When queried concerning the rationale behind his coin-tossing episode, he replied that it just happened (although he also performed hand-washing rituals following contact with females in general). Consequently, in analogy to the pattern initially described with respect to obsession neurosis, compulsion neurosis is similarly characterized as a disqualified form of counter double bind maneuver, a reaction triggered through proximity to the precipitating narcissistic/dependent disorders, respectively.

421.1 – PHOBIA NEUROSIS

The completed description of obsession and compulsion neurosis further begs mention of the related symptom spectrum associated with phobia neurosis. Unlike the more generalized anxiety disorders, phobias involve specific identifiable fears (although primarily irrational). They represent a common occurrence amongst a considerable segment of the population. Phobic individuals fully recognize that their fears are excessive and irrational, yet seek to avoid the source in order to circumvent the resulting anxiety. Exposure to the phobic stimulus almost invariably provokes an immediate anxiety response, sometimes taking the form of a panic attack. Phobias are classified as disorders only when they interfere substantially with an individual's daily functioning. Most people do not seek treatment for simple phobias; they simply avoid the situation.

Similar to other anxiety disorders, phobias can be treated with drugs, behavior therapy, or a combination of the two. Behavior therapy attempts to reduce a patient's anxiety through a graduated exposure to the phobia. Patients are guided through a sequence of steps: as in an imaginary confrontation with the phobia (visualizing a snake, for instance) to actually experiencing it up close (holding a real snake). Gradual desensitization is most successful when treating the class of simple phobias.

This ability to modify phobias through behavioral therapy indicates that this syndrome is formally included within the disqualified class of counter double bind maneuvers. Indeed, the prescribed focus of such therapy entails demonstrating to the patient the latent control he has over his irrational fears. As such, phobia neurosis is closely affiliated with the symptom spectrum previously described for obsessional neurosis, although the subject matter is darker and more fearful in nature: as opposed to the more benign quality seen for the obsession disorder. In response to the shameful, borderline perspective expressed by the personal authority figure, the respective personal follower figure now phobically denies being excessively critical in this regard, the phobia formally beyond one's conscious control.

This intrinsic sublimation of volitional control is certainly reflected in the cryptic quality of the respective phobic symptoms. Here an incidental pairing of a neutral object with the traumatic precipitating event serves as a trigger point for recurring phobic episodes. Indeed, many psychiatrists agree that a traumatic background underlies all such phobic symptoms, where the goal of talk therapy aims to uncover those suppressed memories that fuel the fear dynamic. Here one's excessively shameful encounter (as seen in the specifics of the borderline personality) serves as a precipitating trigger-factor: provoking the thoroughly disqualified phobic response in return. As such, it shares with obsession neurosis such a past-directed focus, one that empowers the psychotherapist to systematically uncover the subconscious issues therein: which (in this case) encompass a thoroughly disqualified and extremely critical attitude.

423.1 – ANXIETY NEUROSIS

As the final dimension within the overall listing of the neuroses, anxiety neurosis is defined as an unpleasant emotion triggered by the anticipation of distressing future events, memories of past such events, or ruminations concerning the self.

Stimulated by real (or imagined) dangers, anxiety neurosis afflicts individuals of all ages and social backgrounds. When the anxiety results from irrational fears, it can disrupt or disable normal social functioning. Many believe that anxiety is synonymous with fear, occurring to varying degrees in situations where people feel threatened by incipient danger. Others define anxiety as an unpleasant emotion caused by unidentifiable danger, or dangers that (in reality) pose little threat.

Accordingly, anxiety neurosis continues in the tradition previously established for the first three forms of neurosis, although now targeting more vaguely worrisome themes. As such, it shares with compulsion neurosis such a future-directed focus, although now alternately targeting a darker range of themes. Here, in response to the insolently-avoidant personality expressed by the personal authority figure, the established personal follower strategically denies acting disdainfully in return, internally experienced as vague anxiety beyond one's conscious control. According to this reciprocating pattern of double bind/counter double bind maneuvers, the precipitating expression of the avoidant personality serves as the basic trigger-point for the dual sequence. Here the established personal follower figure subconsciously (and anxiously) endeavors to cope in terms of such a traumatic interchange, although in fashion generally unproductive in nature. Consequently, the most effective strategy remains avoiding circumstances conducive to such anxiety attacks, accompanied by behavioral therapies similar to those specified for the phobia neuroses. Ideally, a psycho-dynamic understanding of the underlying conflict-issues ensures a more enduring degree of relief: although it takes a truly insightful clinician to see through the intricate (and often compound) levels of disqualification obscuring the communicational dynamics driving the anxiety disorder.

It must necessarily be stressed that the anxiety disorders (as well as the other forms of neurosis) clearly exist only in the mind of the individual. The anxious individual interprets the actions of another in the particular style that triggers their symptom spectrum. The actual motives for the other, indeed, may be quite different. Therefore, it is the appearance of the avoidant personality that triggers anxiety neurosis, not necessarily any direct contact with individuals exhibiting this personality disorder. Hence, for the remaining chapters dealing with the psychoses, a similar pattern also applies. Here, the mention of schizophrenia is not meant imply that a direct causal relationship exists to the mood disorders: rather, only the patient's individual opinions, therein.

30

THE PURE MOOD DISORDERS

There is no universally accepted definition of what truly constitutes a psychosis. A number of common features are collectively shared; namely, extreme severity and withdrawal, as well as intellectual and emotional deficits. In terms of global effects these major mood disorders tend to affect all areas of a patient's mental and emotional life. According to Adolf Meyer, a psychosis is a whole reaction (rather than part reaction), an observation definitely in keeping with a specificity for the group, spiritual, and humanitarian levels within the power hierarchy. The psychotic patient tends to withdraw from social relationships, where external reality is definitely less meaningful to the patient (or perceived in a distorted fashion). In terms of affectivity, the emotions are generally qualitatively different from the norm, typically exaggerated to the point of constituting a delusional escape for the patient. Intellectual thought functions and language structure are also severely disturbed, frequently accompanied by hallucinations and/or delusions characterizing the syndrome.

In our modern age, severe psychosis has mainly remained out of the public eye, with mental health facilities providing the major treatment options. Accordingly, the systematic cataloging of the psychoses is of fairly recent vintage, the notion of schizophrenia actually coined only at the turn of the 20th century. In contrast to the classical traditions for the virtues, values, and vices, the formidable task of classifying the various categories of mental illness is much more daunting: one of the most demanding and complex tasks facing the mental-health professional today. The incapacitating nature of the psychoses typically warrants institutionalization effectively removing the patient from the original precipitating conditions, where such symptoms presumably imparted some adaptive value. The fact that these disorders generally endure within an institu-

tional setting further indicates just how subconsciously dependent the client has become with respect to the subliminal nature of the psychoses.

MANIC-DEPRESSION VS. SCHIZOPHRENIA

A number of distinctive systems of classification for the psychoses have recently been devised, ranging from a holistic/unitary model of psychosis, to more elaborate systems devised by the German Classificationalists. The high degree of detail predicted in terms of the authority/follower hierarchy certainly favors the latter approach, particularly the intricate system of classification proposed by German clinician, Karl Leonhard. The American traditions concerning mental illness take an intermediate approach, primarily based upon principles first proposed by German psychiatrist, Emil Kraepelin. According to Kraepelin's, and later Leonhard's system of classification, the overall class of the mood disorders is ultimately subdivided into the manic/depressive class of syndromes as well as the pure depressions and pure euphorias. The first mentioned class of manic/depressive syndromes, which Leonhard also refers to as the *phasic* disorders, was initially introduced as one of the two major categories of psychosis according to the terminology devised by Kraepelin. This basic category is also specified in the *DSM-IV* although reaching its greatest degree of detail in terms of the detailed dynamics of Leonhard's system. As its name implies, this basic syndrome exhibits both a manic (excitory) phase, and a depressive (inhibited) phase. In a great number of cases this pair of extremes varies in a cyclical fashion, with one form generally predominating (as in *bipolar* manic-depression).

Leonhard's greatest claim to fame, however, concerns his crucial observation that the bipolar syndrome is entirely distinct from what he terms the *unipolar* (or pure) forms: in this case, pure mania and pure melancholy. For these latter two disorders, the tendency to cycle is essentially absent. These unipolar forms are formally classified as stable, with little tendency to cycle over to the opposite pole, or even approach an intermediate (neutral) state. This stable pattern directly contrasts with the bipolar variety that constantly remains in a state of flux, even cycling from one day to the next. For sake of the current discussion, the unipolar forms will be examined first: representing the initial class of double bind maneuvers with respect to mental illness (A). The remaining bipolar form of the mood disorders is a topic best reserved for a subsequent discussion of the cycloid psychoses contained in Chapter *33* of this section.

THE PURE DEPRESSIONS / EUPHORIAS

Pure mania/melancholy by no means are the only unipolar forms distinguished by Leonhard in his classification of the mood disorders. Leonhard also distinguishes what he terms the pure euphorias and pure depressions, both of which exhibit distinct clinical pictures. According to Leonhard, the pure depressions are much more pervasive than the pure euphorias, undoubtedly due to the fact that the former are more likely to come to the attention of clinicians than the latter. The clinical picture of the pure euphorias, however, prove equally maladaptive to normal functioning, although scarcely to the darker degree of dysfunctionality observed for the pure depressions.

Leonhard technically distinguishes five pure euphorias and five pure depressions, which (together with pure mania/melancholy) collectively account for the precise number of slots predicted within the double bind model. Indeed, when the three requisite authority levels are multiplied by the four affective dimensions, the resulting sumtotal of twelve predicted slots equals the observed complement of the mood disorders. These individual syndromes vary widely in terms of their degree of abstraction clearly suggestive of the respective group, spiritual, or humanitarian levels within the power hierarchy. All twelve forms, accordingly, share a common theme; namely, they denote double bind maneuvers in relation to the transitional model of mental illness, in direct analogy to the personal focus previously established for the personality disorders.

THE PURE DEPRESSIONS

With respect to the schematic pattern predicted for the mood disorders, half of the unipolar disorders are defined as immediately active power maneuvers (targeting the present), whereas the remainder are oriented from a past-directed time perspective. Leonhard also suggests a dual distinction in his discussion of the pure forms contained in Chapter *3* of the *Classification of Endogenous Psychoses*. In terms of the five pure depressions, Leonhard distinguishes the first two from the last three with respect to their expressly vital character. Harried depression and hypochondriacal depression are formally distinguished in terms of their emotional saliency and visceral focus, suggesting an active style of emotional perspective. These two, together with pure melancholy, effectively round out the active complement of syndromes with respect to the pure depressions: their qualifiers clearly suggestive of the transitional forms of excess upon which they are based. Pure melancholy, accordingly, represents a transitional form of audacity. Harried depression, in turn, targets rashness, whereas hypochondriacal depression makes a similar correspondence to boldness.

The three remaining classifications of pure depression, in turn, are distinguished as clearly less vital in character, categories primarily based upon higher mental contents (rather than any active context). This enhanced mental aspect formally suggests a past-directed context, where higher mental contents are conceptually spelled-out, rather than simply subjectively felt (as for the active forms). According to Leonhard, an emphasis on diseased idea construction emerges as a direct consequence of these distortions in affect, their recognition targeting past memorable contexts.

The corresponding sequence of past-directed syndromes (namely, suspicious depression, self-torturing depression, and non-participatory depression) suggest precisely such a focus upon higher mental contents specialized in terms of the respective hierarchy of authority roles. Non-participatory depression represents the most abstract and incapacitating of the disorders, incorporating chronic issues of alienation consistent with the humanitarian level within the power hierarchy. Self-torturing depression, in turn, is dominated by religious themes suggesting a specialization within the spiritual realm. This leaves only suspicious depression to round-out the remaining group domain within the ascending power hierarchy, a syndrome certainly less incapacitating than the other two, leaving these higher two levels essentially unaffected.

Suspicious depression represents a transitional variation upon humiliation, whereas self-torturing depression makes a similar correspondence to

Melancholy Personified: Symbolic Representation by Albrecht Dürer (1471 – 1528)
Detail from Woodcut: *Melancholy I* - Courtesy of the Guildhall Library, Corporation of London

mortification. Furthermore, non-participatory depression, in turn, is affiliated with anguish. Although the qualifying monikers for these mood disorders prove highly suggestive, they achieve their truest degree of validation with respect to the considerable wealth of clinical case histories provided by Leonhard: as further outlined within the remainder of sections to follow.

THE PURE EUPHORIAS

A similar style of analysis, in turn, remains in order for the remaining categories relating to the pure euphorias. According to Leonhard, for every form of pure depression there necessarily exists a pure euphoria: where the mood shifts from despondency to elation. For practical reasons, patients with depression are more likely to seek therapeutic treatment than those afflicted with euphoric symptoms. Indeed, similar to the case previously established for the pure depressions, Leonhard distinguishes two of the five pure euphorias as expressly vital in character; namely, unproductive euphoria and hypochondriacal euphoria. Together with pure mania, these three related syndromes formally specify the *active* roles within the transitional power hierarchy (as their descriptive monikers serve to indicate), consistent with their double bind relationship to the vices of excess. For instance, pure mania represents a transitional variation on arrogance, whereas unproductive euphoria makes a similar correspondence to impetuosity. Furthermore, hypochondriacal euphoria, in turn, implies a transitional modification of presumptuousness.

The remaining three classes of pure euphoria are alternately distinguished in terms of their focus upon higher mental contents similar to the case previously established for the pure depressions. The descriptive monikers further suggest the predicted three-way specialization of authority roles, a format that initially proved effective for the affiliated classifications of pure depression. For instance, confabulatory euphoria represents a transitional form of vanity, whereas enthusiastic euphoria makes a similar correspondence to conceitedness. A similar pattern, in turn, extends to the interplay between non-participatory euphoria and pretentiousness.

As intimated earlier, the descriptive monikers for each of these pure forms proves superficially informative in nature, although their true test of validity relies primarily upon the considerable wealth of clinical observations documented for each of the individual syndromes. The complete four-part listing of schematic definitions (from Chapter *29*), in turn, provide a comprehensive overview of the reciprocal interplay of double bind and counter double bind maneuvers. The accompanying schematic table to follow illustrates this strict degree of correspondence across the entire range of the psychoses, as well as their personal foundations within the personality disorders. It should further be stressed that this new theory basically explains only the content/context of what is being communicated in mental illness; namely, the double bind sequence of power maneuvers with respect to the vices of excess. This new system is chiefly meant to supplement currently available therapies rather than supplanting them: endeavoring to aid in the treatment and diagnosis of the communicational factors targeting complete assortment of mental disorders.

Narcissistic Personality → Obsession Neurosis
Confabulatory Euphoria → Confab. Paraphrenia
Enthusiastic Euphoria → Proskinetic Catatonia
Non-Participatory Euphoria → Silly Hebephrenia

Borderline Personality → Phobia Neurosis
Suspicious Depression → Fantastic Paraphrenia
Self-Torturing Depression → Negativistic Cataton.
Non-Participatory Depression → Insipid Hebephr.

Dependent Personality → Compulsion Neurosis
Pure Mania → Expansive Paraphrenia
Unproductive Euphoria → Parakinetic Catatonia
Hypochondriacal Euphoria → Eccentric Hebephr.

Avoidant Personality → Anxiety Neurosis
Pure Melancholy → Incoherent Paraphrenia
Harried Depression → Affected Catatonia
Hypochondriacal Depression→ Autistic Hebeph.

The remainder of the current chapter examines the pure mood disorders in terms of the predicted double bind class of power maneuvers. In agreement with the personality disorders (that they supersede), the clinical classifications for the mood disorders are similarly specialized into both past-directed and future-directed categories.

For instance, with respect to the six individual classifications for pure depression/melancholy, three of these classifications are distinguished through a foundation upon higher mental contents (rather than any immediately vital content), suggesting a past-directed style of context. These higher mental contents are conceptually spelled-out, as well as subjectively felt. The respective hierarchy of suspicious depression, self-torturing depression, and non-participatory depression suggests precisely such a focus upon higher mental contents in relation to the group, spiritual, and humanitarian authority levels.

A similar pattern further holds true with respect to the pure euphorias, where the mood alternately shifts from despondency to elation. Several of the pure euphorias are distinguished by their focus upon higher mental contents similar to the case previously established for the pure depressions. As suggested in their descriptive qualifiers, confabulatory euphoria targets transitions relating to the group domain, whereas enthusiastic euphoria makes a similar correspondence to the spiritual (or universal) realm. This leaves the humanitarian realm in specific relationship to non-participatory euphoria. Although the qualifying monikers for these syndromes prove highly suggestive, they only are truly validated in terms of the considerable wealth of clinical observations described by Leonhard.

430 – CONFABULATORY EUPHORIA

The first listed of the group class of mood disorders, confabulatory euphoria, gains its descriptive moniker from the verb, *confabulate*; namely, to speak in an exaggerated fashion. The qualifier *euphoria* further specifies an elevated mood, where fantastical yarns of an extreme nature represent the basic syndrome spectrum. Indeed, Leonhard's predecessor, Karl Kleist, earlier described this syndrome as expansive confabulosis.

According to the transitional model of the mood disorders, confabulatory euphoria represents a transitional variation on the vanity expressed by the group authority figure, an extreme perspective consistent with the exalted character of its affiliated symptomology. As a transitional power maneuver, this initial vanity perspective, in turn, anticipates the adulation of the group representative, wherein providing a general sense of closure in terms of the overall realm of excess.

The group prerequisites for confabulatory euphoria represent a more abstract variation upon the more elementary personal foundations previously established for the narcissistic personality disorder. In direct contrast to the more personal focus of narcissism, confabulatory euphoria alternately represents elevations of a social or civic nature consistent with such a group authority perspective.

These confabulations primarily relate to happy experiences of a joyous nature, reflecting an expansive sense of self-elevation in conjunction with a celebrity status. Great power, honor, or wealth is linked to anticipated praise or adulation. The resultant confabulations are often sensationalistic, as in fantastic travels, adventures, or victorious battles. The patient sometimes meets with divine entities, although the general trend is basically social elevation. These illusions typically appear based in errors of experiential memory, as in preceding fantastic activities, or merely fantastic thoughts lacking the feel of experience.

Upon examination, patients seem to enjoy recounting their illusions, becoming animated and talkative. They tend to digress from questions posed to them, preferring to recount their confabulations, for which they exhibit a heightened affective affinity. Such confabulatory episodes typically recur over the course of many years, although complete recovery is usually observed following every phase.

431 – SUSPICIOUS DEPRESSION

A similar clinical picture is further encountered with respect to suspicious depression, although now targeting a darker range of themes. As previously stated in the introduction, each pure euphoria is necessarily correlated with a respective pure depression. Suspicious depression, in this case, formally represents of the direct motivational analogue of confabulatory euphoria. In this modified sense, self-references observed in suspicious depression relate to feelings of shame or inferiority, in contrast to the more expansive sense of elation characterizing confabulatory euphoria. Indeed, Leonhard's mentor, Karl Kleist, referred to this syndrome as "depressive reference psychosis." In terms of the transitional model of the mood disorders, suspicious depression represents a transitional form of shameful humiliation experienced by the group authority figure, wherein anticipating a critical sense of ridicule from the group representative. The descriptive qualifier for suspicious depression is particularly justified, expressing the apprehension associated with the pending atmosphere of ridicule/criticism: a dual interplay with respect to the transitional realm of excess.

The extreme degree of mortification characterizing suspicious depression represents an extreme variation upon the more subdued sense of apology previously encountered with respect to the realm of the lesser virtues. In this expanded sense, suspicious depression represents a higher group analogue of the more basic borderline personality disorder, which characterizes the personal level within the transitional hierarchy. Recall, from Chapter *29*, that the borderline personality is characterized by themes of personal guilt and shame. These are expressed through self-deprecating types of behaviors, including self-mutilation and degradation. The expanded social context for suspicious depression, however, amplifies this depressed sense of inferiority to the extent that the risk of suicide cannot be excluded. The general symptom spectrum is one of constant anguish and self-recrimination, with dreadful anticipations of misfortune or doom exceeding any rational expectations.

According to this collection of clinical observations, ideas of reference with the anguished content combine with depressive or anxious mood. In response to their environment, convictions of sinfulness or inferiority generally result, often accompanied by the anticipation of upcoming disasters. The inevitable negative reactions from others only further justify these feelings of sin or humiliation, leading to a self-perpetuating cycle. Upon examination, these patients remain quietly depressed, never argumentative when their delusions are called into question.

In all such instances, the depressive affect is formally connected to higher-order mental processes, being that the feelings of sin and inferiority relate to the real (or imagined) memories of past unsavory deeds. This transitional form of shameful humiliation experienced by the group authority figure is defined in terms of such a past-directed time dimension. Being as the disturbing contents driving the depression are directly referenced in terms of a past-directed time frame, their affiliation with abstract intellectual processes is clearly specified, wherein keeping such memory perspectives clearly in mind. A similar picture was previously established in the case of confabulatory euphoria, although latter's past-directed focus primarily targeted vainful-pride rather than shameful humiliation. Suspicious depression directly complements confabulatory euphoria in terms of the group dynamics underlying this specific level within the power hierarchy.

In conclusion, the group foundations for confabulatory euphoria and suspicious depression, in turn, extend to a spiritual sphere of influence with respect to enthusiastic euphoria and self-torturing depression. As their descriptive monikers imply, this additional class of mood disorders is judged (by Leonhard) to be more debilitating than their group counterparts, an aspect consistent with the universal focus of the spiritual authority perspective. Here, the narcissistic personality disorder expressed the personal authority, in turn, extends to the confabulatory euphoria of the group authority figure, culminating in the enthusiastic euphoria targeting the spiritual realm. A similar sequence further holds true with respect to the borderline personality, suspicious depression, and self-torturing depression.

450 – ENTHUSIASTIC EUPHORIA

The first mentioned of the spiritually-focused mood disorders, enthusiastic euphoria, gains its descriptive qualifier from the theme of enthusiasm: defined as an intense degree of passion or drive, indicative of the extreme zeal with which patients relate their fantastic confabulations. It is characterized through an elevation in mood accompanied by ideas of grandeur, often with convictions of influence from a higher power. The communicational factors at issue here specify a vain sense of conceitedness expressed by the spi-

ritual authority figure, formally surpassing the vain sense of pride initially established for confabulatory euphoria.

The religious themes typically associated with enthusiastic euphoria are particularly consistent with such a universal sphere of influence, in turn, accounting for its more global psychological effects. This directly contrasts with confabulatory euphoria, where only the group level appears affected. Indeed, Leonhard describes confabulatory euphoria as less affectively intense than enthusiastic euphoria in terms of severity. In enthusiastic euphoria, the elevated mood increases in conjunction with euphoric ideas bordering upon delusions of grandeur. Enthusiastic ideas of happiness/self-elevation are also reported, with convictions attributed to higher powers; e.g., God has blessed them or revealed ideas to them.

This pronounced focus upon spiritual themes is formally consistent with the universal focus of the spiritual authority perspective. Here the newly transitioned spiritual authority vainly acts in a conceited fashion in anticipation of the patronizing sense of adulation expressed by the established follower figure. Indeed, this dual interplay superficially conforms to that previously established for the lesser virtues, where the spiritual authority acts in a sanctified fashion in anticipation of the prudent-faith from the spiritual disciple figure. As the extreme counterparts for the (lesser) virtuous realm, the communicational factors underlying enthusiastic euphoria extend to fantastical themes of self-elevation and elation, tempered by delusions of self-reference and supernatural influence. Patients tend to behave egoistically, in that they feel powerful, influential, or even erotically superior to their contemporaries.

Pure megalomania, however, is generally not prominent, rather a highly altruistic form is more likely to be manifest. One strives not only for self-aggrandizement, but also for that of others. Patients express the desire to use their power primarily for the welfare of others. As leaders of mankind, they endeavor to bring happiness to others, as well as themselves. They believe they can heal others around them, as well as bestowing peace and harmony to this world, and beyond. They similarly feel competent to perform great tasks and duties, which under milder circumstances extends to the role of bearers of happiness in their immediate surroundings. God, or the Saints, let them know they have great duties to perform, experienced as ecstatic hallucinations reminiscent of a dream-like state. The patient rarely expresses astonishment at these developments, perhaps stemming from one's own eupho-

The Pure Mood Disorders

ria. In each of these cases, the patients presented an elevated mood, their affect rising as their ideas were discussed. When distracted from their confabulations, the ecstatic mood generally fades suggesting that their euphoria is not necessarily a continuous state. Even when discussing neutral topics, their festive spirit remains evident suggesting an overall baseline of joyous experience.

451 – SELF-TORTURING DEPRESSION

The preceding clinical picture for enthusiastic euphoria, in turn, begs mention of its related motivational counterpart of self-torturing depression. As its qualifying moniker implies, this syndrome is characterized by a depressive mood based in ideas of sin or inferiority: a religious focus clearly consistent with its spiritual sphere of influence. In contrast to the purely positive focus established for its enthusiastic counterpart, self-torturing depression targets an entirely negative range of themes. Indeed, it highlights religious content that is clearly lacking for the more limited group focus established for suspicious depression.

According to Leonhard, the ideas of reference characterizing suspicious depression seem milder in nature than those specified for self-torturing depression. Consequently, in self-torturing depression only the most extreme depressive contents prevail. The patient claims that he is not only a sinner, but also the worst sinner imaginable. He is not only inferior, but more despicable than anyone else (even an animal). According to this hyperbolic ideation, he not only will suffer and die, but also endure the worst tortures of Hell.

This exaggerated content proves consistent with what would be predicted for the universal level within the power hierarchy. The newly transitioned spiritual authority figure humiliatingly acts in a mortified fashion in anticipation of the scornful sense of ridicule from the spiritual disciple. The descriptive moniker for self-torturing depression certainly proves fitting, wherein reflecting the extreme anxiety arising from this pending atmosphere of scornful-ridicule. These depressive contents directly target ideas of sin, self-accusation, and inferiority. Should one attempt to contradict their delusions, the patients cling ever tighter to their conviction. They often independently attempt to convince others of the reality of their delusions, as if repeatedly martyred through this terrible range of ideation.

The affiliated sense of anxiety appears primarily in reference to specific fears. When a patient is distracted, the anxiety no longer appears recognizable in of such an objectless format. This emotional distress appears rooted in higher mental contents; indeed, it appears to develop primarily in terms of such delusions. This focus upon higher mental functioning proves entirely consistent with the past-directed focus of self-torturing depression. Often this anxiety occurs in anticipation of the terrible punishments to be suffered in Hell due to sinfulness. The strict religious overtones associated with this case study are certainly striking to behold, imparting a supernatural sense of urgency to the depressive belief system. These circumstances superficially correspond to what is commonly referred to as involutional melancholia in the American tradition: essentially a depressive disorder coinciding with transition into old age.

In each of these further cases, a preoccupation with sin and self-accusation emerges as the dominant clinical feature. Upon clinical examination, patients may appear quiet with a depressive expression when asked unimportant questions. When pressed concerning their diseased idea constructions, their depressive affect becomes much more readily apparent. Indeed, it is often difficult to distract the patient once caught within this affective tension. The patient may cry, moan, or even scream-out their self-tortured claims, although scarcely to an obstinate degree.

Once full intensity is achieved, the patient typically calms down, and once again becomes apathetic, even approaching a state of mild retardation. Only the smallest additional stimulus, however, serves to launch a further sequence of anxious excitation. Interest in their external environment is similarly diminished due to a preoccupation with their delusional ideation. Similar to suspicious depression, the risk of acting upon suicidal impulses cannot entirely be ruled out.

In conclusion, the completed description of the group and spiritual realms for the pure mood disorders, in turn, raises the issue of the related syndromes predicted for the humanitarian level within the power hierarchy. A few general predictions are definitely in order here; namely, the symptomology necessarily appears more obscure consistent with the extreme level of abstraction. Indeed, as initially seen with respect to the lesser virtues, the distinctiveness of the ethical terms becomes increasingly more obscure when extended to the humanitarian level within the power hierarchy. Consequently, the respective counterparts for the mood disorders prove equally as abstract: distinguished by Karl Leonhard as nonparticipatory depression and euphoria. This use of the same descriptive qualifier for both the depressive and euphoric classifications further suggests such a crowning level of abstraction. For the do-

337

main of the pure euphorias, the complete sequence of syndromes is respectably specified as: narcissistic personality disorder (PA), confabulatory euphoria (GA), enthusiastic euphoria (SA), and non-participatory euphoria (HA). Similarly, in terms of the pure depressions, the affiliated sequence is further specified as: borderline personality, suspicious depression, self-torturing depression, and non-participatory depression. The remainder of the current chapter is devoted to examining this final domain of the non-participatory disorders specific to the humanitarian sphere of influence.

Being as the pure depressions are statistically more common in a clinical setting than the pure euphorias, the details for non-participatory depression are examined first in this sequence. The remaining description of non-participatory euphoria is best reserved for a follow-up treatment, formally complementing the overall description of non-participatory syndromes.

471 – NON-PARTICIPATORY DEPRESSION

In keeping with the extremely abstract nature of its respective symptomology, non-participatory depression is generally somewhat rare. Indeed, Leonhard distinguishes only ten cases in total. He further cites a somewhat chronic course for non-participatory depression, a factor consistent with its enduring humanitarian time-scale. Consequently, the more immediate sense of anguish characterizing self-torturing depression, in turn, is amplified into a more enduring humanitarian perspective. The diseased ideation is now expressed in terms of alienation phenomena and an impoverishment of the will. Leonhard's predecessor, Karl Kleist, similarly described this symptom spectrum in terms of his related concept of "alienation depression."

This implicit sense of alienation is defined as a kind of "emotional cooling," a complaint more subjectively felt than outwardly expressed, generally in a listless fashion. The patient repeatedly complains about an absence of feelings, and no longer is able to participate in them in an emotional manner. Happiness or sorrow no longer touches them, wherein profoundly lacking depth even in relation to friends or family. This deficiency in the sympathetic emotions even extends to the point of ascribing "alien" motives to those originally close to them. In extreme cases, complaints related to themes of depersonalization sometimes occur. One no longer feels the same individual, as personal feelings have been lost. Bodily sensations are less apparent in complaints,

rather targeting the more abstract realm of the higher social emotions.

A further distinguishing feature of non-participatory depression concerns the lack of any free expression of will, where all higher initiative appears to be lost. In this latter respect, Leonhard notes that only the highest emotional plane is affected, where increasingly finer degrees of affect related to socialization are targeted. The more altruistic or high-minded patients appear more likely to become affected, a contention consistent with the extreme degree of abstraction characterizing the humanitarian level within the power hierarchy.

These extensive clinical observations present a common clinical picture; namely, an alienation of the emotions and an impoverishment of the will. Upon careful examination, Leonhard notes that patients appear to care little for their surroundings, scarcely emotionally touched in this regard. When left alone, they appear rather still and lack initiative. When asked how they are feeling, this extra stimulation swiftly prompts complaints concerning their alienation, delivered in an animated and grievous fashion. Self-accusations related to their emotional cooling are also encountered, although they must be prompted in a manner similar that for self-torturing depression (although never to the same degree of excitability). The depth of depression also is not quite as deep, typically making suicide attempts a very rare occurrence.

Although the degree of correspondence to the transitional model of mental illness proves convincing for both suspicious and self-torturing depression, a parallel correspondence in terms of non-participatory depression is scarcely as clear. The extreme level of abstraction associated with non-participatory depression undoubtedly represents a key factor, resulting in the more chronic nature of the respective symptomology. The general lack of will further proves significant, primarily in terms of the observation that the authority ideal of "free will" enters into consideration precisely at this humanitarian sphere of influence.

The patient's consistent complaints of an impoverishment of will further serve to validate these issues, a factor particularly consistent with its transitional relationship to the realm of the vices of excess. In this case, this amounts to a mortified sense of anguish. The cooling of the emotions similarly can be interpreted in terms of such an understated strategy, a perspective that conveniently coincides with the chronic nature of non-participatory depression. Whether such interpretation proves truly justified remains an area open to further research, although the general level of correspondence clearly warrants formal placement of non-participatory depression within the humanitarian level of the transitional power hierarchy.

470 – NON-PARTICIPATORY EUPHORIA

Although the extreme degree of rarity for non-participatory depression (in a clinical setting) was previously noted, the prospects for its euphoric counterpart prove even more daunting. A number of key clinical features (for the depressive syndrome) are similarly preserved, although now taking on more of a euphoric mood. Leonhard proceeds to state this interpretation more clearly in the following extensive quotation from his *Classification of Endogenous Psychoses* as follows: "The assumption of a non-participatory euphoria rests more on theoretical demands than of practical experience. If, as we have seen up to now, a pure euphoria corresponds to every pure depression, then the non-participatory depression certainly must have its opposite pole. However, it seems to be very rare. The non-participatory depression itself is rare, rarer than the other depressions. If the non-participatory euphoria is rare at the same rate as the other euphorias, then one will hardly ever observe it."

Leonhard goes further to write on this subject: "After theoretical considerations, which I cannot discuss more closely here, I believe that the disease at the opposite pole of the non-participatory depression is equally connected to a weakening of the emotion and initiative, so that one can speak of a non-participatory euphoria. The two forms differ in their basic moods, but not in their contents ..."

Leonhard seems to suggest that that the rarity of clinical cases can be linked to the milder symptomology, where the symptoms are not serious enough to warrant medical attention. In contrast to the extreme sense of anguish characterizing non-participatory depression, the euphoric variety extends to extreme feelings of pretentiousness, wherein anticipating the obsequious treatment by the established follower figure. Consequently, this disorder can further be classified as an extreme sense of dominion (in a direct analogy to the domain of the lesser virtues). Indeed, this proves consistent to the extreme sense of contrition characterizing the depressive phase. This final recourse to a humanitarian sphere of influence ultimately rounds out the stepwise description of the past-directed domain targeting the pure mood disorders.

THE FUTURE-DIRECTED REALM OF THE MOOD DISORDERS

The completed description of the past-directed classifications of the mood disorders invites further comparison to the remaining future-directed mood disorders. For instance, with respect to the five pure depressions, Leonhard distinguishes the first two from the last three in terms of their expressly vital character. Harried depression and hypochondriacal depression are distinguished in terms of their emotional saliency and visceral focus, suggesting an actively experienced (and future-directed) perspective. In concert with pure melancholy, these three basic disorders effectively round out the future-directed set of depressive syndromes spanning the group, spiritual, and humanitarian realms, respectively.

Leonhard further states that for every pure depression there necessarily exists a pure euphoria, where the mood shifts from despondency to elation. In direct analogy to the case previously made for the pure depressions, two of the pure euphorias are described as expressly vital in character; namely, unproductive euphoria and hypochondriacal euphoria. Together with pure mania, these three basic syndromes comprise the "active" roles within the transitional hierarchy: as suggested in their distinctive descriptive qualifiers. The remainder of the current chapter specifically outlines the considerable wealth of clinical case histories provided by Leonhard in this respect, further endeavoring to establish the validity of the double bind model of the mood disorders.

432 – PURE MANIA

The first mentioned of the future-directed mood disorders, pure mania, merits its descriptive qualifier of "pure" to distinguish the unipolar form: as opposed to bipolar manic-depression, which will be discussed in a later chapter. Indeed, Webster's Dictionary defines mania as excessive or unwarranted desire or enthusiasm: an interpretation consistent with the extreme dignified sense of desire specified for the group authority perspective. Accordingly, pure mania represents a transitional variation upon the respective realm of excess. Here, the impudent sense of arrogance expressed by the group authority figure, in turn, prompts the envious sense of jealousy from the established group representative. Pure mania directly continues (in a group sense) the trend initially established with respect to the personality disorders; in this case, the dependent personality disorder specific to the personal authority level.

Whereas the dependent personality primarily targets individual relationships, the broader (group) sphere of influence attributed to pure mania is reflected in the more expansive range of its symptomology: affecting all aspects of social functioning.

Leonhard lists a number of key features for pure mania: including the flight of ideas, psychomotor excitation, and pressure of speech. All three of these factors are associated with an elevated mood akin to cheerfulness, compounded by heightened feelings of self-importance or delusions of grandeur. Milder forms of this disorder are often indistinguishable from normal excitement or freedom from inhibition. The smooth-talking salesman or the charming go-getter certainly falls into this category, their seemingly inexhaustible supply of energy much appreciated in our fast-paced society. When this benign degree of hypomania reaches radical proportions, then more troubling symptoms emerge.

Most prominent among these is a "flight of ideas," a tumultuous milieu where every new thought jostles to command full attention. This wealth of ideas is outwardly expressed as a pressure in speech that constantly ricochets from one topic to the next: rarely tolerating interruption and welcoming each new idea with unbounded enthusiasm. This driven pressure of speech represents a fleeting reflection of thoughts that race by at a desperate pace. In addition to speech, psychomotor excitation (busyness) also occurs, where patients constantly strive to remain involved in their surroundings. This need for activity is particularly expressed in a great wealth of gestures and facial expressions. These actions appear to serve only a temporary purpose, even if only superficially conforming to the fleeting motivations under consideration.

This elated sense of euphoria can provide a false feeling of confidence or competence. Patients never complain about being sick; in fact, they have never felt better. All things are possible for the manic patient. Their extreme convictions of competency and self-importance lead to delusions of grandeur, although the specific contents may vary from day-to-day consistent with the free-form idea construction. Leonhard also describes a certain degree of short-circuitedness in the making or executing plans: resulting in failed business ventures, marriage proposals, etc. Having cast off most reasonable inhibition, manic patients are more likely to violate the mores of proper conduct and good taste, becoming insensitive to how they are viewed by others. He also made light of anything of a self-righteous nature,

and held a supercilious attitude towards the attendants: a factor that proved particularly consistent with the general arrogant attitude predicted for the group level within the transitional hierarchy.

433 – PURE MELANCHOLY

The elated range of themes for pure mania proves a fitting counterpoint to the darker range of symptoms associated with pure melancholy. The term derives from the Greek *melancholia*, from *melanos* (black) and *chole* (bile). This derivation invokes the temperament theory of bodily humors, where an excess of black bile (by suggestion) was presumed to mediate the darker aspects associated with a depressive mood. Here, pure melancholy is characterized by a listless mood, thought inhibitions, indecisiveness, and psychomotor inhibition. As such, it represents the higher (group) analogue of the more basic avoidant personality disorder that characterizes the personal authority level. Consistent with its enhanced group status, pure melancholy presents as a mild depression lacking in obtrusive contents: a range of focus that further leaves the remaining spiritual and humanitarian levels essentially unaffected. In milder cases, the depressive mood takes on an apathetic character. In more severe cases, extreme suffering develops, accompanied by an anxious temperament. This indifference can lead to the impression of sadness, although may also be interpreted as a decline in feeling. The global range of affect is displaced to one of depression, wherein totally swamping emotions of a more positive nature.

When questions requiring some deliberation are posed, long reaction times reflect varying degrees of thought inhibition. Difficult questions may not be initially understood, although simple questions tend to be answered quickly. This thought inhibition outwardly extends to a distinctive speech pattern. Speech appears slow and monotonous, often employing softer tones. Expressive emotions are similarly subdued, extending to an observed slowness in carrying out general motions. This overriding sense of inhibition leads to indecision, even in terms of the most insignificant issues. This results in inactivity, although scarcely approaching stupor: as patients eat, speak, and use the bathroom on their own. They exhibit difficulty in initiating new activities, although appear adequate in terms of ongoing ones. This seemingly works against any tendency towards suicide, where a lack of strong feelings renders the final act rather perfunctory.

This consistent state of indecisiveness generally leads to feelings of inadequacy or insufficiency, where patients complain they no longer can complete anything or progress in their work. This sometimes leads to feelings of self-denigration in terms of delusions of sin or inferiority. Ideas of reference similarly accompany such self-accusations. According to Leonhard, this diseased ideation is generally less obtrusive than seen for the other depressions. Patients do not usually share their concerns unless questioned directly. This intellectual content is primarily dependent upon the propensities of the individual, and may even be absent altogether.

In summary, the pure forms of mania and melancholy, in turn, can be extended to a universal sphere of influence; in this case, unproductive euphoria and harried depression. Consistent with their universal focus, this additional complement of syndromes proves significantly more debilitating than pure mania/melancholy, as further documented in the detailed observations provided by Leonhard. Here, the dependent personality disorder (for the personal authority realm), in turn, extends to the pure mania characterizing the group authority perspective, culminating in the unproductive euphoria specified for the spiritual authority realm. A similar pattern further holds true for the sequence of the avoidant personality, pure melancholy, and harried depression. The next two sections in this chapter examine unproductive euphoria and harried depression in the order given, accompanied by a representative sampling of clinical case histories.

452 – UNPRODUCTIVE EUPHORIA

The first mentioned disorder of unproductive euphoria is endowed with a curious descriptive moniker: being that non-productivity is scarcely a theme consistent with the underlying realm of excess. As demonstrated by Leonhard, however, this sense of unproductiveness derives precisely from the interference stemming from such excessive tendencies: wherein conflicting with the more measured attributes for the respective lesser virtue of hospitality. This syndrome is characterized through a profound sense of wellbeing or happy contentment. The facial expression betrays a euphoric mood, generally accompanied by a broad smile. This exalted sense of joyfulness primarily appears restricted to a bodily sphere of feeling, a feature that formally lacks any specific mental content, rather entirely of a bodily origin (hence, its vital character). Patients generally speak freely without compulsive speech, and rarely ask to be released from the institution. Indeed, one patient appreciated staying at the clinic because he felt better than ever.

The mental contents for unproductive euphoria are basically expansive in character, extending to delusions of self-elevation or high position (such as when a soldier claims he's an officer). The patients maintain their ideas even when contradicted, and without a corresponding change in mood. True to its descriptive qualifier, this disorder typically appears unproductive, although feelings of happiness are outwardly observed (and subjectively confirmed by the patient). These delusions may further extend to erotic happiness, such as proposing marriage to a total stranger. Some claim they wish to give something of beauty to others (such as peace), but appear only loosely tied to these motives. Although they sometimes act upon their ideas, the general state of motivation is typically quite low. Despite their happy contentment, most patients show little compulsive activity. Occasionally, they endeavor to put their ideas of happiness into action, although (even then) display little in the way of pressure.

According to the double bind model for the mood disorders, expansive mood is explained in terms of a transitional variation on the arrogant sense of impetuosity expressed by the spiritual authority figure. This, in turn anticipates the covetousness treatment of the respective follower figure. This universal sense of potency certainly fits well within the predicted communicational dynamic, formally expanding upon the subordinate sphere of pure mania, although to an even more grandiose degree. Unproductive euphoria it takes its cue from the affiliated lesser virtues of cordiality and hospitality, although pursued to a range of extremes that nevertheless preserves some of that charming and accommodating character. As such, unproductive euphoria continues in the expansive tradition previously established for the personal/group authority levels; namely, dependent personality, pure mania, and now, unproductive euphoria.

453 – HARRIED DEPRESSION

The preceding clinical picture for unproductive euphoria, in turn, proves a fitting counterpoint for its darker motivational counterpart in harried depression. As its qualifying moniker implies, this disorder is characterized by a depressive mood based primarily within delusions of sin or inferiority, a religious focus generally consistent with its requisite spiritual authority focus within the transitional hierarchy. In contrast to the more positive prerequisites for unproductive euphoria, harried depression is restricted to a strictly negative range of themes, highlighting explicit religious content that clearly lacks the more limited group focus seen for pure melancholy.

In a clinical sense, harried depression is defined as a tortured depressive state with an anxious coloration, accompanied by continual unrest of a harried nature. In contrast to the wistful joyfulness for unproductive euphoria, harried depression targets a clearly darker range of themes: namely, anxious ruminations and self-accusations. It shares with pure melancholy a highly agitated state, although now extending to a religious range of delusions. This includes delusions of sinfulness and the fear of punishment, therein. Harried depression is formally defined in terms of a listless affect closely associated with anxiety, although not entirely congruous with it. In the absence of external stimuli the unrest may subside briefly, although the least provocation serves to revive the agitated state.

This overwhelming sense of anxiety need not contain any expressed mental content, often limited to uniform complaints concerning horrible internal sufferings. These anxious delusions appear to develop from the diseased affect, wherein prompting a state of harried unrest. The delusional ideation includes vivid self-accusations and deep feelings of torturedness, also expressed as terrible internal suffering. Curiously, patients do not always appear threatened, for their diseased idea construction often appears parenthetical, and even is occasionally absent. Convictions of sinfulness are very common, with such sinful activities certain to lead to great punishment in Hell. Hypochondriacal ideation may also emerge, expressed in terms of fears over bodily wellbeing. This also includes symptoms of an anxious nature, such as unbearable tightness or constriction.

Patients may tenaciously moan the same words for days (or even months) on end. A uniform pressure of complaints is similarly seen encountered, with patients persistently demanding their immediate release from the facility. This pressure of speech, nevertheless, retains some indwelling tortured component scarcely influenced by outside forces. Any attempt to influence the patient is generally in vain. Indeed, it proves virtually impossible to distract them from their complaints. This anxious excitation is outwardly expressed through lamentations, moaning, begging, crying for help, or screaming. Nonverbal activities include clinging, running around, or anxiously wringing one's hands.

This disruptive behavior is generally interpreted as obstinate (even malicious) in nature. It is difficult to receive answers to neutral questions, for the patients simply remain focused upon their complaints. This failure to influence the patient can create a false image of obstinacy, which more properly might be viewed as tenacity. Suicidal tendencies are also present, perhaps in an attempt to escape one's anxious suffering. Harried depression can quickly run its course, but may also take a protracted course.

This extensive set of clinical observations demonstrates the highly agitated characteristics of harried depression, fitting quite precisely with the transitional model predicted for the mood disorders. Here, the audacious sense of rashness expressed (in a transitional fashion) by the spiritual authority figure, in turn, prompts the contemptuous sense of reproach anticipated from the established follower figure. The agitated nature of harried depression proves entirely consistent with the transitional sense of rashness predicted within the communicational dynamic. This initial double bind maneuver does not always provoke the anticipated response. Indeed, it may alternately prompt the affiliated counter double bind maneuver: in this case, the expression of incoherent paraphrenia covered in the following chapter.

Regardless of the specific outcome, harried depression represents a more abstract (spiritual) variation upon the subordinate class of depressive syndromes previously described. As such, it represents the universal extension of the personal/group sequence of mood disorders; namely, the avoidant personality and pure melancholy, respectively. This agitated quality of pure melancholy, in turn, proves diagnostic for harried depression as well.

In summary, the completed descriptions for both the group and spiritual classifications of the future-directed mood disorders raises the further remaining issue of the disorders for the humanitarian sphere of influence within the transitional hierarchy. A few general predictions can necessarily be made here; namely, the symptomology becomes even more obscure consistent with its extreme level of abstraction: distinguished as hypochondriacal depression and hypochondriacal euphoria. The use of the same descriptive qualifier for both the depressive and euphoric aspects further attests to the extreme level of abstraction associated with this humanitarian authority level.

The complete sequence of syndromes for the euphoric realm is respectably designated as: dependent personality (PA), pure mania (GA), unproductive euphoria (SA), and hypochondriacal euphoria (HA). Furthermore, the remaining sequence of pure depressions is alternately defined as: avoidant personality, pure mania, harried depression, and hypochondriacal depression. The remainder of the current chapter examines this unique realm of the hypochondriacal syndromes in terms of their humanitarian sphere of influence. The pure depressions are statistically more common in a clinical setting than the pure euphorias; hence, hypochondriacal depression will be examined first, followed, in turn, by the related description of hypochondriacal euphoria.

473 – HYPOCHONDRIACAL DEPRESSION

In common usage, the notion of hypochondria typically refers to fears concerning bodily wellbeing, generally referring to physical complaints for which no organic illness is responsible. Originally, hypochondria referred to a disease situated in the stomach under the cartilage of the ribs: a derivation from the Greek *hypo-* (under) and *chondros* (cartilage). It was eventually discredited in a medical sense, although fittingly co-opted to describe all such unfounded fears concerning the health of the patient. Consequently, hypochondriacal depression exhibits many similar pathological/somatic factors. It is characterized by peculiar misperceptions directed towards a wide variety of bodily organs.

Not infrequently, fears concerning bodily wellbeing develop, although only delusional misperceptions are essential to the diagnosis. These misrepresentations can apply to the body as a whole, or to a variety of organs, therein. Hypochondriacal fears can develop in terms of anxiety over fatal illnesses, such as cancer, heart attack, etc. Most patients are not generally concerned with disease origins, but rather the respective symptoms they convey. Many complaints are localized near the heart akin to the palpitations experienced during an anxiety attack. Other internal complaints include burning, tearing, drilling, pressure, or painful sticking. Patients may tend to offer gruesome comparisons: their skin has turned to rubber, their nerves have dried up, their blood has electrified, or their intestines are twisted.

Patients, in general, complain a great deal about their alleged ailments, although without an undue degree of excitement. They can appear anxious during their unrest, although more often lachrymose and full of grief (than deeply depressed) when complaining about their illness. This tendency towards mournful lamentation can vary considerably from patient to patient. When the depressive mood is deeper, the prospects become more hopeless: hence, a lesser degree of complaints. This heightened state of unrest remains more comprehensible than that previously seen for harried depression, undoubtedly due to the more limited nature of the complaints. The depressive degree of affect does not technically approach the depths previously established for either pure melancholy or harried depression, although vital levels within the personality are strongly affected.

Alienation phenomena may also occur, affecting normal bodily sensations and sense perception. Patients complain that their whole body is internally changed (or reorganized), not strictly in terms of new sensations, but rather the total lack thereof. They report they can no longer feel their torso, arms, or legs: as everything appears dead due to a lack of feeling. A common conclusion is that the entire body is dead. Other depressive contents are generally absent or (for the most part) only roughly outlined. Patients generally complain a great deal about their alleged ailments, although without actually displaying clear excitation. This depressive state can seem emotionally painful, although the total personality is less affected than for pure melancholy or harried depression. Suicidal tendencies are generally low. Chronic courses are not infrequent, and occasionally the hypochondriacal state never fully heals.

According to these clinical observations, Leonhard cites a rather chronic course for hypochondriacal depression, a factor certainly consistent with its grand humanitarian time-scale. Here the more limited sense of rashness characterizing harried depression, in turn, is modified into a drawn-out pattern of debility. The delusional ideation is now expressed in terms of a prolonged course of illness. Accordingly, this exaggerated symptom spectrum takes its cue from the affiliated lesser virtue of "sacrifice," although now dramatized to the point of suffering chronically from hypochondriacal delusions. In this instance, the patient experiences extreme debility in anticipation of the reproachful sense of chagrin expressed by the established follower figure. Although the strict specialization of complaints of a hypochondriacal nature might seem to restrict the versatility of this syndrome, it, nevertheless, remains the leading contender for formally satisfying the requisite humanitarian authority slot within the transitional hierarchy. Its extremely abstract characteristics, however, unfortunately obscure the true extent of the clinical observations within the communicational dynamic: an interpretation further extending to the more bizarre realm of hypochondriacal euphoria.

472 – HYPOCHONDRIACAL EUPHORIA

In fitting analogy to the anxious complaints established for hypochondriacal depression, hypochondriacal euphoria is similarly concerned with bodily complaints, although now accompanied by a curiously paradoxical euphoric mood. It shares with its subordinate counterpart (in unproductive euphoria) an elevated and vital mood, although now extending to a more enduring humanitarian sphere of influence. The extreme degree of incapacitation observed in terms of hypochondriacal euphoria is similarly unproductive in nature, in keeping with its latter namesake. Indeed, chronic bodily complaints elicit similar unproductive consequences accompanied by a marked elevation in mood. Patients tender their complaints in a lively fashion, outwardly appearing to suffer, although their facial expressions appear euphoric. When questioned about this contradiction, they generally report a euphoric mood scarcely affected by their hypochondriacal complaints. They speak of varied sensations throughout their entire body: described as sticking, burning, drilling, and so forth. When pressed for an exact description, they generally reply metaphorically, such as: one's brain has been cut off, the stomach has expanded, or one's throat has been tightened.

Hypochondriacal patients appear quite lively and talkative when presenting their complaints, intimating how deeply they suffer and wish for help. Their symptoms often are stated as unendurable, yet their basic mood remains euphoric. On occasion, they may become aware of this conflict, but explain that (despite all their afflictions) they can remain cheerful. In the absence of any complaints, an elevated mood is generally observed, only imperfectly covered by a resumption of the complaints. When switched to another topic, they remain lively and stimulated, although they no longer exhibit a marked degree of compulsive speech.

Patients are generally difficult to distract, particularly from their hypochondriacal complaints. On occasion, they may theatrically produce a few tears, wherein appearing superficially depressed. These rare reactive moods generally pass quickly, with the baseline euphoric mood subsequently restored. The patient's complaints can sometimes appear somewhat querulous, although this aspect is definitely more common in the chronic cases. This general symptom spectrum suggests that the same emotional level is diseased as in hypochondriacal depression.

With respect to its relatively rare frequency of occurrence, the dynamics of hypochondriacal euphoria are primarily comprehended in terms of its more prolific depressive counterpart. In contrast to the latter (which represents a transitional expression of rashness), hypochondriacal euphoria alternately focuses upon themes of a presumptuous or impetuous nature: wherein accounting for the more positive range of emotions. How the euphoric symptomology formally fits into the broader communication dynamic is not immediately apparent, clearly more limited than the broad range of potentialities would seem to suggest. It is fair to assume that the hypochondriacal ideation is tied to the chronic nature of the complaints, wherein permitting the potential for an enduring repertoire of excuses of a perverse incapacitating advantage to the patient.

Consequently, both the ecstatic and depressive affective parameters are encountered in relation to this chronic behavioral strategy, although the former imparts a much less emotional saliency than the latter. Whether this interpretation truly explains the transitional dynamics specified for the crowning humanitarian level remains an issue open to debate, although this version remains a top contender in light of the limited range of syndromes described by Leonhard. Indeed, it is particularly amazing that this ready-made class of disorders exists at all, exquisitely formatted in a form that formally satisfies this higher-order pattern of organization.

In direct analogy to the case previously established for non-participatory depression and euphoria, a precise pattern of correspondence might perhaps never be totally feasible at this extreme level of abstraction. Whether the hypochondriacal set of syndromes similarly fits this limited profile remains an issue open to debate: although the potential always remains for the identification an entirely new set of disorders from a fresh set of clinical observations. Consequently, it scarcely appears realistic to expect that Leonhard's original set of clinical observations would (in hindsight) be seamlessly applicable to virtually every possible contingency in relation to the transitional model of mental illness.

31

SYSTEMATIC FORMS OF SCHIZOPHRENIA

The completed description of the double bind class of mood disorders, in turn, begs mention of the remaining counter double bind class of perspectives characterizing the realm of schizophrenia. Indeed, many clinicians acknowledge a continuum of symptoms linking the neuroses with the more extreme realm of schizophrenia. Psychotic symptoms formally emerge in relation to the more abstract levels within the power hierarchy, as originally depicted in Chapter 29. Consequently, one of the most elegant features of Leonhard's system concerns this general expansion of schizophrenic symptomology across the three-level span of the transitional hierarchy.

Kraepelin was the first to popularize the distinction between the manic-depressive class of mood disorders and the more bizarre classifications of schizophrenia (originally known as dementia praecox). It remained to the genius of Swiss psychiatrist, Eugen Bleuler to coin the modern sense of the term, with schizophrenia defined as a splitting-off of the emotions, in recognition of its impact with respect to emotional blunting and an inward retreat from reality. Bleuler also describes a progressive deterioration of the affective aspects of the personality, expressed through disorders in thought, feeling, and conduct: factors exceedingly reminiscent of the extreme degree of disqualification predicted for the counter double bind class of maneuvers. Bleuler, in turn, observed that the course of schizophrenia was sometimes intermittent, although the general trend appeared towards a "creeping" deterioration once symptoms first appeared. In our modern age, the term schizophrenia has sometimes implied a split-personality (as in multiple personality disorder), factor that has resulted in an unwarranted degree of suspicion from the general public.

The basic dichotomy distinguishing schizophrenia from the mood disorders formally parallels the case previously established for the personality disorders/neurosis; namely, the interactive pattern of double bind and counter double bind maneuvers. In contrast to the latter personally-based syndromes, the psychoses formally span the three more abstract levels within the power hierarchy, suggesting further distinctions in meaning. Although it is popular nowadays to define schizophrenia as a single entity, Bleuler originally argued for a broader spectrum of the schizophrenias; namely, his paranoid, catatonic, and hebrephrenic classifications. Their increasingly abstract sphere of disqualification suggests specificity for the respective group, spiritual, and humanitarian levels within the power hierarchy. These three classifications of schizophrenia are similarly featured in the *DSM-IV*, although any further degree of detail remains sketchy at best.

The paranoid classification of schizophrenia is generally acknowledged as the least incapacitating of the three, suggesting a degree of dysfunctionality with respect to the more basic group level within the power hierarchy (leaving the remaining higher levels unaffected). According to Leonhard, paraphrenia is characterized by delusional schemas and sensory distortions accompanied by misconceptions relating to the paranoid thought processes. Affective distortions are also common, typically accompanied by perplexity and ideas of reference. Confused thought patterns also occur, with delusions of persecution similarly predominating. Delusions of grandeur are much less common, formally reciprocating the darker aspects of the persecution-complex.

The catatonic classification of schizophrenia, in turn, is distinguished as more incapacitating in nature suggesting a degree of dysfunctionality targeting a higher (universal) sphere of influence. A higher-order sphere of mental functioning appears affected in catatonia, imparting affective deficits consistent with this universal degree of focus. The familiar clinical picture of catatonic stupor is primarily observed, although negativistic and foolish manifestations are also encountered. Regardless of the symptom specialization, the extreme degree of incapacitation associated with catatonia clearly surpasses the milder symptomology that predominates in paraphrenia. Consequently, the universal focus of catatonia affects all of the lower levels as subsets (in relation to the patient), in contrast to the more limited group focus of paraphrenia.

The remaining hebephrenic class of schizophrenia, in turn, is distinguished as the most chronic form of the disorder, suggesting an affinity for the crowning humanitarian level within the power hierarchy. By definition, this humanitarian sphere of influence incorporates the group and universal levels as subsets, shifting intellectual functioning into a totally disorganized state. Indeed, the term derives from the Greek root "hebe" (young) suggesting a degree of mental disintegration typically expressed as infantile silliness. At the onset of hebephrenia, anxious or ecstatic states generally occur. Excitatory or inhibited tendencies may appear somewhat catatonic, although aggressive tendencies may take on a more irritated character than that seen for catatonia. Karl Kleist (amongst others) considered affective deterioration the essential feature for hebephrenia. Leonhard similarly cites this sense of affective deterioration expressed in terms of a progressive course of emotional disorganization, a factor formally in keeping with the grand humanitarian time scale predicted for this syndrome.

It should further be mentioned, in passing, that there does not appear to be any system of categories for schizophrenia relating to the crowning *transcendental* level within the power hierarchy, undoubtedly due the fact that the contents at this extreme level of abstraction are already highly disqualified (to begin with).

THE INDIVIDUAL CLASSIFICATIONS FOR SCHIZOPHRENIA

The distinctive three-way specialization of paranoid, catatonic, and hebephrenic classifications proves highly informative, particularly in terms of the schematic correlation to the transitional model of the psychoses. The current version of *DSM-IV* retains this three-way specialization, even suggesting further subdivisions, although not formally labeled. It remained to the observational genius of Karl Leonhard to take this analysis to its logical conclusion, distinguishing further subdivisions for schizophrenia tailor-made for incorporation within the transitional model of mental illness. Indeed,

many clinicians acknowledge a basic continuum of symptoms linking the neuroses with the more extreme realm of schizophrenia. In particular, psychotic symptoms emerge only for the more abstract levels within the power hierarchy, as previously depicted in **Fig. 29** (of Chapter 29). One of the most significant features of Leonhard's system concerns the pronounced extension of neurotic-type syndromes across the remaining three-level span of paranoid, catatonic, and hebephrenic schizophrenia. Schizophrenic presentations with obsessional or phobic characteristics are readily apparent within the system. Furthermore, those invoking compulsive or anxious aspects are similarly encountered, a pattern collectively spanning the paranoid, catatonic, and hebephrenic domains of schizophrenia.

For instance, the obsessional sphere of neurosis, in turn, extends to the three-way sequence of confabulatory paraphrenia, proskinetic catatonia, and silly hebephrenia. The related phobic realm further gives way to the affiliated sequence of fantastic paraphrenia, negativistic catatonia, and insipid hebephrenia. Furthermore, compulsion neurosis, in turn, prompts the respective sequence of expansive paraphrenia, parakinetic catatonia, and eccentric hebephrenia. Finally, anxiety neurosis alternately gives way to the remaining sequence of incoherent paraphrenia, affected catatonia, and autistic hebephrenia.

This distinctive three-way pattern of organization for schizophrenia is further documented in relation to the formal set of schematic definitions depicted in **Tables S-1** to **S-4** (of Chapter 29). The respective vices of excess are plugged directly into the transitional definition format resulting in an effective simulation of the counter double bind maneuvers currently under consideration. These fundamental insights, however, necessarily require further correlation to the preliminary class of double bind maneuvers; namely, the initial classifications of the respective mood disorders

In terms of Leonhard's system of classification, schizophrenic presentations with obsessional or phobic qualities are readily apparent, denoting past-directed forms of counter double bind maneuvers in relation to the realm of schizophrenia. Other categories presenting compulsive or anxious characteristics are similarly encountered, designating the remaining future-directed variations. For both such variations, the respective pattern of schizophrenic symptomology collectively spans the paranoid, catatonic, and hebephrenic realms within the authority hierarchy: corresponding to the group, spiritual, and humanitarian levels, respectively. For instance, the obsessional realm of neurosis, in turn, extends to the remaining sequence of confabulatory paraphrenia, proskinetic catatonia, and silly hebephrenia. The affiliated phobic realm further gives way to the corresponding sequence of fantastic paraphrenia, negativistic catatonia, and insipid hebephrenia. The next segment of this chapter examines each of these past-directed forms of schizophrenia through the aid of Leonhard's comprehensive system of terminology, that in concert with the respective clinical observations convincingly validate the predicted counter double bind model of schizophrenia.

440.1 – CONFABULATORY PARAPHRENIA

The first mentioned form of paranoid schizophrenia, confabulatory paraphrenia, is described as an ingrained tendency to converse in an exaggerated or far-fetched fashion. As such, it denotes a past-directed power maneuver, disqualified in a fashion similar to that previously seen in the case of obsession neurosis. Recall, from Chapter *29*, that obsession neurosis was specified as a disqualified form of counter double bind response to the narcissistic personality disorder. Here, the new personal authority pridefully acts in a narcissistic fashion in anticipation of the flattering treatment from the established follower figure. The personal follower, however, when faced with being double bound into such a predetermined course of action, in turn, may employ the counter double bind class of maneuver; namely, obsessively accepting the face value of the communication while subliminally denying willing participation therein.

A similar pattern further holds true for the psychoses, where the confabulatory euphoria expressed by the group authority figure represents the initial transitional phase: in turn, prompting the paraphrenic form of counter double bind maneuver. Here confabulatory paraphrenia (titled in reference to the basic subject matter under consideration) is now expressed in a fully disqualified fashion, similar to the case previously established for obsession neurosis. Indeed, this more advanced (group) variation on the basic transitional model of mental illness is spelled-out to an even greater degree of detail in the following extensive discussion of confabulatory paraphrenia.

The tradition of confabulatory paraphrenia is first described by Kraepelin, and also by Wernicke. This syndrome is characterized by errors of memory experienced as fantastic experiences; often set in other cultures, countries, or even planets. These free-form delusions reportedly entertain a sensuous quality typically reserved for epi-sodic memories. This abnormal degree of sensuality, undoubtedly, is related to the perceptive errors for the imagined contents that underlie this syndrome. Should their delusions be contradicted, the patients refer to alleged supportive experiences, becoming more fully excited if others continue to disagree. As a general rule, the patients remain friendly towards the clinical staff and seem to enjoy relating their stories.

The patient's immediate surroundings are not usually drawn into their confabulations, but rather are judged correctly. They also correctly identify others within their environment. In conversations about daily topics, one finds little in the way of impairment. Patients speak in an orderly fashion, and report their confabulations in an equally ordered manner. Apparently this grounded sense of self-awareness specifies that their confabulations occur only in other places and times. Indeed, clients sometimes speak of dreams or trances, during which fantastic events allegedly happen. Accordingly, confabulated experiences are always reported as occurring remotely, transferred to an imaginary context: hence, avoiding a conflict between reality and confabulation.

These confabulations at first may be isolated, although eventually resulting in integrated stories of sensational travels to other continents, experiences on other worlds, adventures with men or animals, even conversations with God. Gaps in continuity also occur, where the patient may be unable to explain how he got from one exotic locale to the next, as in Munchhausen stories replete with a free-form fantasy spectrum.

Many confabulatory stories often refer to a patient's high position, chiefly reflected through their stories, although they do not tend to behave in a manner consistent their exalted titles. Their titles of distinction represent delusional wishes formally in keeping with the disqualified communicational dynamic predicted for confabulatory paraphrenia. Through this bizarre ideation, the respective group representative effectively disqualifies any flatterous sense of adulation in this regard, professing not to be in control of such obsessional delusions. Indeed, this absurd ideation proves suggestive of extremes relating to the affiliated lesser virtue of *veneration*. Consequently, many of these delusions are expressed in a third-person tense, suggesting a disqualified reaction to the precipitating factors within the interaction: namely, the confabulatory euphoria expressed by the group authority figure. This dual interplay of double bind and counter double bind maneuvers effectively explains the disqualified nature of the delusions characterizing confabulatory paraphrenia (as beyond the control of the individual): a symptom spectrum specifically predicted within the transitional model of schizophrenia.

441.1 – FANTASTIC PARAPHRENIA

As its descriptive qualifier formally implies, fantastic paraphrenia is characterized by grossly exaggerated forms of delusional thinking expressly fantastical in nature. Fantastic paraphrenia is closely related to the symptom pattern previously established for the confabulatory form, although the subject matter is darker and more fearful in nature, as opposed to the more benign nature of the latter. In response to the suspicious depression expressed by the group authority, the respective follower figure now denies fantastically acting phobically in response: where such fantastic ideation remains beyond conscious control. This intrinsic sublimation of volitional control is formally reflected in the cryptic quality of the fantastical belief systems. Consequently, for fantastic paraphrenia, sensations are often grotesquely described, where horrible images are hallucinated, as in the torture and murder of many people at once. These delusions generally appear unlimited by natural law or rational experience; hence, seeming entirely absurd.

In reference to similar symptoms, Kraepelin also describes a version of fantastic paraphrenia, and Kleist speaks of *fantasiophrenia*. The content of the delusions is particularly unpleasant. For example, horrible things happen in the institution: at night men and larvae dragged patients into the basement. The devil visited her, and then a black tiger with a golden crown, which kicked the bed so hard it flew into the air. Every holiday, people are kidnapped and then beaten and murdered in the cellar; nearly fifty people are there now; where one can hear men and women screaming.

Even more dramatic than these isolated visual phenomena are scenic hallucinations experienced as complete occurrences, where episodes employing the other senses are similarly factored in. Indeed, it is typically difficult to differentiate what has been seen, heard, or felt; for patients simply report a series of interrelated experiences without specifying which sensory areas the various details have appeared. If specifically queried, hallucinatory voices are generally reported by fantastic paraphrenics, although they tend not to play a significant role in the delusional ideation. The absurd claims and delusions typically remain beyond the realm of possibility, where certainties generally considered absolute no longer apply.

The affectivity associated with fantastic paraphrenia can scarcely be considered totally profound: being as the diseased ideation outwardly lacks affective intensity. Patients may describe the most horrible episodes accompanied by incongruous sense contentment. Contradicting their complaints never quite appears to cause irritation. The patients' affect appears generally flattened, for if one attempts to irritate them, they only become slightly annoyed.

This extreme degree of emotional flattening is formally consistent with the disqualified character of the respective counter double bind class of maneuvers, where the horrible emotional nature of the complaints it is effectively disqualified, compounded by the outlandish details of the stories themselves. Fantastic paraphrenia formally expands upon the more limited range of symptoms previously established for phobia neurosis, although now extending to a broader (group) sphere on influence, as reflected in the highly fantastical nature of the delusional ideation.

In this respect, the group representative disqualifies critically-ridiculing the shameful sense of humiliation expressed by the group authority, wherein mirroring the interplay of the borderline personality/phobia neurosis previously established in Chapter 29. As such, fantastic paraphrenia effectively complements the communicational dynamics previously described for confabulatory paraphrenia, although now targeting a darker range of themes. Indeed, both formulations are characterized by a benign emotional flattening consistent with such a disqualified perspective, a pattern that further repeats with respect to the catatonic and hebephrenic forms described immediately to follow.

In conclusion, the group focus for both confabulatory and fantastic schizophrenia further extends to a universal sphere of influence with respect to the affiliated categories of proskinetic and negativistic catatonia. These catatonic classifications of schizophrenia are typically distinguished as highly incapacitating in nature, suggesting a degree of dysfunctionality in relation to the next higher (spiritual) level within the power hierarchy. As specified for such a "group-of-all-groups" perspective, this broader universal focus for catatonia affects all order of relationships with respect to the patient, in direct contrast to the more limited group scope established for paraphrenia. Accordingly, a higher-order realm of mental functioning appears to be affected in catatonia, assuming a disqualified emotional quality formally in keeping with such a universal sphere of influence.

With respect to the current past-directed focus of this chapter, the dual listing of proskinetic and negativistic catatonia certainly fit the bill in this regard. As their descriptive monikers suggest, these catatonic classifications are judged by Leonhard to be more debilitating than that which has gone before. Here, the obsession neurosis of the personal follower, in turn, extends to the confabulatory paraphrenia for the group realm, culminating in the proskinetic class of catatonia specific to the spiritual realm. A related listing of terms further holds true with respect to the sequence of phobia neurosis, fantastic paraphrenia, and negativistic catatonia. The following two sections respectively examine the communicational dynamics of proskinetic catatonia and negativistic catatonia in the order given.

460.1 – PROSKINETIC CATATONIA

The first mentioned of the two syndromes, proskinetic catatonia, gains its descriptive qualifier from the theme of proskinesis, defined as the middle-eastern custom of paying homage towards one's authority figure. This takes the form of symbolic religious respect, with the head humbly bowed consistent with such general spiritual themes. Accordingly, proskinetic catatonics respond with a pliable facial expression upon being addressed, displaying a marked interest in the examination. Further verbal stimulation results in incomprehensible mumbling, actually a jumble of individual expressions. This agitation may also be expressed as responsive grasping and fastening upon objects, expressed as a plucking of one's clothes or rubbing of the skin. The patients tirelessly grasp a repeatedly offered hand, and can be prompted to motion through such stimuli, assuming any position the outside observer suggests. Should one pose contrary suggestions, the grasping and "going-with" behaviors can temporarily be interrupted, but start again once attention is distracted.

At the earliest stages of the disease, speech patterns, although soft, are still comprehensible. Furthermore, the abnormal motion readiness and responsive grasping may already be fully apparent. In the course of further development, patient initiative decreases to the point that this disorder may be diagnosed through the lack of motivation alone, although speech similarly becomes progressively quieter. In contrast to negativistic catatonia (discussed in the next section), patients willingly look up when spoken to, focussing upon the examiner's face. They continue to respond in kind even when one reintroduces conversation.

In concert, verbal expressiveness is not always comprehensible, and is punctuated with various pauses. During a long pause, a simple nod or encouraging look is typically sufficient to prompt them to again continue speaking. This monotonous speech generally resembles soft whispering or vague mumbling. Sometimes the patient's facial expressions exhibit budding interest, as if wishing to communicate something. Upon repeated observation, however, one typically recognizes a stereotyped repetition of particular facial expressions, short sequences primarily nonsensical in character, sometimes repeated iteratively.

Despite the characteristic motion readiness, overall initiative is severely limited, although many patients are able to perform routine tasks in a uniform fashion. The affectivity is severely flattened, appearing as carefree state of contentment. This overall affective flattening represents a primary diagnostic factor for schizophrenia in general, whereby disqualifying one's participation within the counter double bind maneuver. Despite this disqualified demeanor, the general patterns of motion readiness and grasping behavior betray the underlying communicational dynamics at issue, representing an enhanced sense of homage in response to the extreme sense of sanctity expressed by the spiritual authority figure. Here, the transitional sense of conceit characterizing enthusiastic euphoria, in turn, prompts the disqualified sense of patronization specified for proskinetic catatonia. This subliminal sense of disqualification extends not only to a flattening of the affect, but also to the bizarre symptom spectrum expressed by the patients. Indeed, the pronounced emphasis on religious themes remains consistent with the assignment of proskinetic catatonia to a spiritual sphere of influence, effectively expanding upon the personal/group trend initially established with respect to obsession neurosis and confabulatory paraphrenia.

461.1 – NEGATIVISTIC CATATONIA

The preceding clinical picture for proskinetic catatonia, in turn, contrasts strikingly with its related motivational counterpart in negativistic catatonia. In contrast to the more compliant behaviors seen for proskinetic catatonia, negativistic catatonia entails an extremely non-cooperative range of themes (in relation to such a universal sphere of influence). As its descriptive qualifier implies, this disorder is characterized as an overt resistance to reasonable requests for cooperation or obedience. At initial stages of the syndrome, negativism may only be implied, with patients answering questions or carrying out orders correctly, although their actions subtly include the tendency to resist. Dramatic pauses may occur before appropriate responses are given, or the patient may gaze towards the doctor only when urgently queried (looking sideways otherwise). Should irritation occur, the negativism becomes much clearer, although irritation in any form can lead to resistant behavior. This state of resistance of an impulsive or severe nature is particularly indicative of negativistic catatonia.

Should one attempt to overcome the resistance of a negativistic patient, this increased irritation frequently leads to negativistic excitation. For instance, if a patient wishes not to go into the garden, attempts to convince her are fruitless, as she defiantly turns away. The record of one female patient states: "Throws food, attacks a peaceful patient, slaps the nurse, rips her smock." Expressive motions (at times bizarre) extend to jumping, howling, clapping, or acting clownish.

The negativism need not be limited to overt forms of resistance, for it can also occur as simple omissions. In contrast, should one try to create a more amiable mood through kind treatment, the patient may follow a few orders, but only partially. For instance, they may start to give an answer, but then quiet down before the words become clear. The patient's desire to cooperate always appears to meet an opposing tendency, with such ambivalence much better proof of genuine negativism than irritated refusal.

Higher affectivity is also quite flat in negativistic catatonia, although primitive or instinctual interests remain strong, as in eating greedily or erotic tendencies. This extreme affective flattening it is generally consistent with previous forms of schizophrenia examined to date, a reflection of the subliminal degree of disqualification characterizing the counter double bind class of maneuvers. The dominant feature of negativism clearly indicates a resistance to control through the initial transitional maneuver. The disqualified scornful-ridicule characterizing negativistic catatonia, in turn, is prompted by the humiliated sense of mortification expressed in terms of self-torturing depression.

This ingrained refusal to act compliantly is effectively disguised through the affective flattening therein, where the paucity of expressive emotions is further amplified in terms of the moderate distortions in ideation, frequently bordering upon religious or mystical themes. As such, negativistic catatonia is rightfully assigned to spiritual (or universal) level within the power hierarchy, effectively expanding upon the personal/group trend initially established in terms of phobia neurosis and fantastic paraphrenia.

The completed description of both the paranoid and catatonic classifications of schizophrenia (encompassing the group/spiritual domains, respectively), begs further mention of the remaining syndromes predicted for the crowning humanitarian level: namely, the final category of hebephrenia. As initially mentioned, this final class of schizophrenia is undoubtedly the most chronic form of the disorder, suggesting a clear affinity for the enduring humanitarian level within the power hierarchy. By definition, it incorporates all of the lower authority levels as subsets, shifting the personality into a totally disorganized state. Indeed, the term derives from the Greek root "hebe" (young), suggesting a degree of mental deterioration primarily described as infantile silliness. Leonhard cites affective deterioration as the chief distinguishing feature of hebephrenia, progressing through a chronic course formally in keeping with such grand humanitarian time-scale.

With respect to the past-directed realm of systematic schizophrenia, the positive range of syndromes is respectively identified as the sequence of obsession neurosis (PF), confabulatory paraphrenia (GR), proskinetic catatonia (SD), and silly hebephrenia (RH). Furthermore, the remaining trend based upon a depressive range of themes is further described as phobia neurosis, fantastic paraphrenia, negativistic catatonia, and insipid hebephrenia. The remainder of the current chapter examines this ultimate realm of the hebephrenic syndromes in terms of the initial past-directed realm of subliminally disqualified communication.

480.1 – SILLY HEBEPHRENIA

The primary symptomology for silly hebephrenia is characterized in terms of affective dulling accompanied by a mildly contented or cheerful mood. Inappropriate smiling or laughing can appear in response to practically any external stimulus. It contains traits quintessentially regarded as hebephrenic, generally reminiscent of the silly temperament observed during normal puberty. Hebephrenia most often develops during puberty, making differentiation between the disease and typical pubescent reactions more difficult to distinguish, although the affective flattening ultimately proves the crucial criterion. The onset of the disease is characterized by a tendency towards childish pranks. This misbehavior is often minor, becoming unpleasant primarily in combination with other acts. In a clinical setting, this extends to pulling blankets off other patients, howling or other noise-making during sleep-time, or spitting on helpless patients. One patient disrupted a religious ceremony by singing along with the priest, while another drew unwelcome attention by burping loudly.

The tendency towards inappropriate laughter proves even more telling than overt misbehavior. At initial stages of the disease, the urge to absurd laughter is quite prominent, generally appearing as a silly style of chuckling. In later stages of the disease, the laughter becomes less noticeable. The patients respond with smiles whether one mentions subjects happy or sad. Even in the most severe cases (when patients no longer wish to talk) their smiles remain in reaction to external stimuli, with an embarrassed smile representing the most significant diagnostic tool for distinguishing silly hebephrenia.

This tendency to smile leads to the impression of a cheerful coloration of one's affective mood. The patients generally appear simply contented to mildly cheerful. Despite their carefree contentment, the patients can also become irritated for short periods: scolding others, slamming doors, or striking other patients that have angered them. Indeed, as affective flattening increases, the pranks become increasingly meaner. In a clinical context, patients have many chances to misbehave, often exhibiting an evil character, as well as ethical dulling. Patients may appear criminal insofar as they have an opportunity to be so, although they typically do not display any organized pattern of criminality. This often takes the form of childish obstinacy, where clients relent temporarily until they are no longer observed, then return to their mischief. In the end-stages of the disease, the tendency toward childish pranks ultimately gives way to a total loss of initiative and interest in the surroundings. Although patients lose their motivation for outward pranks, this can still be expressed in occasional evasiveness. Here, talking-past-the-point suggests they wish to fool the interviewer.

Affective flattening is particularly pronounced in silly hebephrenia. Patients primarily appear callously indifferent, failing to take interest in their surroundings. Ethical dulling also occurs during early stages, where patients may lie, cheat, or steal if given the chance: as primarily seen in conflicts involving other patients. Motivation also suffers from this extreme dulling of the affect unless involving a base instinctual level). Initiative is no longer expressed, and (in severe states) patients simply exist throughout the day scarcely moving unless stimulated.

Curiously, silly hebephrenics appear to maintain a contented state, continuing to smile in response to greetings even in the most severe degrees of emotional numbness. This chronically debilitated state appears consistent with the corresponding humanitarian sphere of defect predicted for this syndrome, where lower levels of functioning (by definition) are collectively affected as well: resulting in an overall devastation of the psyche. Indeed, the general tendency is towards a creeping course of disease development, with an incremental increase in hebephrenic symptoms observed over the course of the disorder.

The affiliated communicational themes are similarly somewhat obscure. The (disqualified) obsequious sense of patronization, in turn, occurs in reaction to the conceited sense of pretentiousness characterizing non-participatory euphoria. Indeed, many of the more silly pranks suggest such a patronizing character, where only the patient is privy to such a twisted course of logic. Consequently, this syndrome similarly takes its cue from the affiliated lesser virtue of benediction: where such an homageful attitude is subliminally disqualified, so as to making any underlying sense of reverence essentially incomprehensible. The extreme level of abstraction characterizing this humanitarian domain only further serves to cloud the basic communicational factors at issue. Here, silly hebephrenia effectively rounds out the ascending symptom spectrum previously established for the paranoid and catatonic forms, a fitting testament to the masterful observational skills of Karl Leonhard.

481.1 – INSIPID HEBEPHRENIA

The remaining past-directed category of insipid hebephrenia proves quite consistent with its descriptive qualifier, which (in common usage) denotes a lack of spirited interest bordering on mental dullness. This dulling of the affect represents the key distinguishing feature for this syndrome, often in an obstructive fashion similar to that previously established for its subordinate counterpart in negativistic catatonia. As such, insipid hebephrenia represents the darker motivational counterpart for silly hebephrenia, although now triggering responses more consistent with its depressive precipitating circumstances. According to Leonhard, all hebephrenics appear affectively insipid to some degree: a basic criterion for the diagnosis of schizophrenia in general. The insipid form of hebephrenia, however, expresses these psychic functions in a more preserved fashion than the other forms: appearing to operate on a truly insipid level. The patients are fairly easy to converse with, expressing opinions and answering basic questions correctly, although clear affective participation appears lacking. They may speak of their mental illness, their years of institutionalization, or even the death of a relative in an uninvolved fashion, as if discussing the most mundane of subjects. Any inner affective participation is completely lacking in insipid patients, particularly the absence of expressive facial expressions denoting emotional involvement. In the most severe cases, true affective desolation is detected; where despite any correctness in their responses, the patients never appear to be emotionally involved.

The general mood is characterized by a flattened sense of carefree contentment, occasionally interrupted by brief depressive states. Excitations leading to aggressive behavior are not uncommon. In other cases, depression may be quite pronounced, even in otherwise mild cases. In neutral conversations with insipid patients, one notices a lack of clear emotional participation. In conversations containing themes that should move the patient, the flattening of affect becomes even more pronounced. They do, however, remain superficially approachable, where conversations may successfully be maintained.

These affective deficits further result in a total lack of initiative, even though the patient may adapt to daily life without undue coercion. A lack of plans or wishes for the future is also apparent, and (although institutionalized) patients may occasionally petition to be released. They therefore remain more active than silly hebephrenics, to which they are fundamentally related. Whereas the silly hebephrenics' laughter can make them appear cheerful, the chronic contentment of insipid hebephrenia appears fully established giving the appearance of an enduring carefree state.

Accordingly, insipid hebephrenia shares with its "silly" counterpart such an enduring humanitarian focus, a global confluence of deficits that (by definition) affect all of the lower authority levels as subsets whereby accounting for its profoundly dysfunctional influences. As such, it formally exemplifies the profound degree of affective flattening previously seen for the paranoid and catatonic forms as collectively specifying the series of counter double bind maneuvers in relation to the realm of excess. Although this extreme realm of abstraction formally works to obscure any precise determination of the communicational parameters at issue, the parallels to silly hebephrenia alone clearly warrant its overall placement; namely, the crowning culmination of the ascending sequence of phobia neurosis, fantastic

paraphrenia, negativistic catatonia, (and now) insipid hebephrenia.

THE FUTURE-DIRECTED REALM OF SYSTEMATIC SCHIZOPHRENIA

The completed description of the past-directed forms of schizophrenia invites further comparisons to the related future-directed variations on the theme. According to Leonhard's classification system, schizophrenic presentations with compulsive or anxious characteristics are commonly encountered, spanning the ascending sequence of paranoid, catatonic, and hebephrenic classifications. These, in turn, correlate with the respective group, spiritual, and humanitarian authority levels. For instance, compulsion neurosis, in turn, prompts the ascending sequence of expansive paraphrenia, parakinetic catatonia, and eccentric hebephrenia. Furthermore, anxiety neurosis alternately anchors the related sequence of incoherent paraphrenia, affected catatonia, and autistic hebephrenia. The remainder of the current chapter examines each of these future-directed classifications in the order given, further enlisting Leonhard's considerable wealth of clinical observations in order to establish the validity of the transitional model of schizophrenia, in general.

442.1 – EXPANSIVE PARAPHRENIA

According to the preceding chapter, the confabulatory and fantastic forms of paraphrenia are respectively identified as past-directed forms of counter double bind maneuvers targeting a group sphere of influence representing an exaggerated sphere of delusion and misperception. A similar communicational pattern further holds true with respect to the remaining expansive (and incoherent) forms of paraphrenia, although now targeting a future-directed perspective. According to Leonhard, the megalomania associated with fantastic/confabulatory paraphrenia does not appear too deeply anchored in the personality. Patients voice their fantastical ideas in an apparent belief system, although the core personality is only marginally influenced by them (being essentially past-directed memory functions). In expansive paraphrenia, however, the patient's claims are generally much less bizarre, although the personality appears much more seriously pervaded by these delusions producing consequentially bizarre behaviors (consistent with such a future-directed perspective). Whereas these grandiose aspects represent the chief salient feature for this disorder, it is fitting to characterize it as "expansive" in nature. Consequently, this syndrome exhibits many commonalties to Kraepelin's *paraphrenia expansiva*, which Kraepelin describes as "affected, bombastic, and unctuous" in nature: the direct precursor to Leonhard's expansive paraphrenia.

According to Leonhard, for both fantastic and confabulatory paraphrenia, the delusional megalomania is primarily characterized by simply reporting its fantastical content. This pattern can scarcely be said to apply to expansive paraphrenia, where the outward behavior of the patient is crucial for specifying the megalomania in its expansive format. Whereas fantastic or confabulatory patients are content to speak in terms of their exalted position (but do not act expansively), expansive patients always wish to overtly demonstrate their grandiose significance. The general personality (and respective behavior) is dramatically affected by such delusions. Patients attempt to act self-importantly in terms of their posture and deportment, their dress and affectations, as well as eccentric activities such as secret writing. Their expansiveness appears extremely uniform consistent with their great poverty of ideas in direct contrast to the considerable wealth of ideas characterizing the fantastic and confabulatory patients.

The typical expansive patient exhibits a marked loquacity when presenting their megalomaniac wishes or complaints, similarly pursuing their eccentric habits with vigor. They often claim to have encountered famous personalities, won their friendship, or have been enlisted for a vital mission. They sometimes speak superciliously about others, referring to them as the "common people." Leonhard gives the example of a patient who believed he was a director with a large fortune, desiring to wed a lady of the finer class. He always greeted others with a deep bow, and his facial expression suggested that he wished to demonstrate how well he had mastered upper-class behavior.

When expansive patients are treated like others within the ward, they tend to become accustomed to it and react cooperatively. When required to do something highly unusual, however, they typically revolt, referring back to their higher standing/position. This can further lead to overt irritation, although their mood never quite appears profound, scarcely offering any serious resistance. In the presence of the clinician, they assume a more congenial persona in order to establish their status as a social equal. At times they issue commands in a haughty fashion, one patient even ordering the doctor "out of her chamber."

Patients appear the happiest when allowed to speak freely, particularly when they feel they are being taken seriously, although their affect is typically quite flattened. Furthermore, patients generally lose their overall sense of initiative, which (together with the affective deficits) indicates a correspondence to the disqualified class of counter double bind maneuvers.

Here, in response to the impudent sense of arrogance expressed (in manic fashion) by the group authority figure, expansive paraphrenia is subsequently defined as a subliminally disqualified envious sense of jealousy: an irrational reaction generally beyond the conscious control of the individual. According to this two-stage communicational dynamic, the group authority figure impudently acts arrogantly in anticipation of the envious sense of jealousy from the established group representative. The group representative, however, when faced with being double bound into such a predetermined course of action alternately employs the expansive form of counter double bind maneuver; namely, accepting the face value of the communication while simultaneously denying any willing participation therein.

This dual interplay represents a higher order variation upon the pattern previously established for the personality disorders/neuroses, where compulsion neurosis represents the disqualified counter double bind form of maneuver in response to the dependent personality expressed by the personal authority figure. Consequently, expansive paraphrenia directly expands upon this personal trend, the subliminal degree of disqualification principally expressed in terms of affective flattening and bizarre wordplay. Expansive paraphrenia takes its cue from the affiliated lesser virtue of indulgence, which similarly represents a disqualified form of reinforcement, although scarcely to the extreme degree that is encountered in schizophrenia.

443.1 – INCOHERENT PARAPHRENIA

The second-mentioned classification of incoherent paraphrenia (as suggested in its descriptive qualifier) is characterized by a confused or stuporous spectrum of symptoms. Incoherent paraphrenia is closely affiliated with the expansive form, although the subject matter is now more pessimistic and subdued in nature. In response to the avoidant style of melancholy expressed by the group authority figure, the reluctant group representative now anxiously acts incoherently in response, a subliminally disqualified form of counter double bind maneuver.

The basic symptomology for incoherent paraphrenia is characterized by marked hallucinations (primarily verbal), that even occur when patients are actively engaged in conversation. In contrast to other hallucinatory paraphrenics, the patient displays little interest or initiative, rather appearing numb and lacking in motivation. From the very onset, sensory delusions generally dominate the symptom foreground. Furthermore, in later stages of the disease, the patients are nearly always totally occupied with their delusions, a condition not typically found in any other form of paraphrenia. In the earliest stages, patients are fully capable of giving precise information concerning their sensory illusions, often reporting radiations from the body, currents in the torso, sexual molestation, and so forth. They answer questions taciturnly, with very little volume.

In a clinical setting, outward facial expressions suggest that the patient generally withholds attention from the clinician, rather focusing upon his inner experiences. Patients rarely look directly at the doctor; rather their eyes tend to wander about. Patients appear to hallucinate almost without interruption, often whispering continually to themselves. On occasion, the whispering transforms into a scolding tirade, accompanied by gesticulations and grimaces undoubtedly directed towards the voices. Patients may scream, holler, and gesticulate in the direction of their invisible antagonists. They may also run around screaming an occasional curse or desperate expression, generally in response to the voices.

Incoherent paraphrenics generally appear taciturn, rarely responding with more than a single sentence at a time. They do not willingly approach others, and general exhibit little interest in their surroundings indicative of a profound lack of motivation. They tend to basically just sit around, lacking independent interest or initiative, and must be cajoled into doing anything. Often they may appear quite catatonic, although their posture and expressions do not approach the extremes typically observed for the latter.

Although incoherent paraphrenics may exhibit a strong degree of affect when arguing with their voices, one rarely finds profound emotional reactions to external stimuli. This overall affective flattening suggests a clear correspondence to the disqualified class of counter double bind maneuvers (and indicative of schizophrenia in general). Here, incoherent paraphrenia continues the pattern previously established for expansive paraphrenia, although now targeting an entirely darker range of themes. In response to the insolent sense of audacity expressed by the group au-

thority figure, the reluctant group representative denies disdainfully acting contemptuously in return, experienced in terms of flattened affect and bizarre verbal hallucinations completely beyond conscious control.

In contrast to the condescending attitude observed in expansive paraphrenia, the disqualified contempt characterizing incoherent paraphrenia targets feelings of alienation that disguise the underlying disdainful issues. This similarly applies to the distractions provoked by the constant verbal hallucinations and delusional ideation. According to this dual interplay of double bind and counter double bind maneuvers, the preliminary symptom spectrum of pure melancholy serves as the trigger-factor in this regard: an overture that the paraphrenic incoherently endeavors to overcome, although thoroughly incapacitated in terms of function. Incoherent paraphrenia represents a higher order variation upon the subordinate syndrome of the anxiety neurosis, although now extending to a broader (group) sphere of influence.

In conclusion this group-order foundation for expansive/incoherent paraphrenia, in turn, extends to a *universal* sphere of influence with respect to the affiliated classifications of parakinetic/affected catatonia. These latter two forms of catatonia appear much more debilitating than their paranoid counterparts, a factor consistent with the more global range of focus specific to this spiritual of the authority hierarchy. The compulsion neurosis of the personal follower, in turn, extends to the expansive paraphrenia specified for the group realm, culminating in the parakinetic catatonia characterizing a spiritual sphere of influence. A similar sequence of terms further holds true with respect to anxiety neurosis, incoherent paraphrenia, and affected catatonia. The next two sections examine parakinetic catatonia and incoherent paraphrenia in the order given, endeavoring to further validate their placement within the transitional model of mental illness.

462.1 – PARAKINETIC CATATONIA

The first mentioned of the catatonic syndromes, parakinetic catatonia, rates its descriptive qualifier from the theme of parakinesis: defined as an abnormality in bodily control or the production of volitional movement. In a clinical sense it refers to expressive motions that appear unnaturally choppy, and eccentric in nature, frequently taking on the character of foolishness. Leonhard's mentor, Karl Kleist first developed the theme of parakinetic catatonia: used not only for the systematic cases, but also all forms of catatonia with parakinesis in the foreground. Leonhard, in turn, restricts this theme exclusively to the systematic form, which he originally designated as "foolish" catatonia: (also consistent with Kraepelin's manneristic dementia). The parakinesis develops gradually and insidiously so that it might easily be overlooked. At the onset of the disease, minor abnormalities start to appear: such as a brief shaking of the body, a fleeting facial grimace, a quick shoulder shrug, or a mild turning of the arms or the torso. A diagnosis is often made on the basis of the linguistic expressions, which can appear somewhat sudden and jumpy.

Even following years of affliction, the disease spectrum can appear relatively mild. The facial expressions (actually distortions) tend to become more exaggerated. The corner of the mouth may stretch sideways a bit, the eye may wink or the forehead twitches. Often the movements may appear to fulfill a reason, such as reaching for an object, although the action is not carried out naturally. The flowing connection between movements becomes obscured: an ongoing motion may stop for a moment, and then another begins with little transition lacking the fluidity of normal motions. They may run impulsively through the ward agitated by the appearance of the doctor or other such novel unrest. Indeed, Leonhard cites the following case history documenting such a foolish hyperkinesis, which became particularly intense due to the unexpected presence of a female stenographer.

"The patient greeted the doctor with a sweet smile, shook his hand, took a deep bow, and clapped his hands as if emotionally moved. He looked at the secretary with the same sweet smile, held his hands over his eyes as if this helped him see, and nodded a greeting. He turned around suddenly and looked toward the wall blankly. He then looked up and down with an exaggerated facial expression. He stood on his tiptoes, turning his torso back and forth as if looking for something. Simultaneously, he touched his face and his jacket. He took his handkerchief out but did not use it. He plucked the handkerchief and looked astonished, then shut one eye and looked down haughtily."

According to the preceding real-time example, if attention is drawn to new surroundings, then reactive movements tend to dominate the symptom spectrum. In more familiar environs, pseudo-expressive motions can create the impression of foolishness or eccentricity. Inappropriate laughter, exaggerated through parakinetic distortion, is quite common. Distorted speech patterns are also observed, with little modulation. The words appear chopped-off and produced with staccato jerkiness. Only short non-grammatical sentences are constructed, and a pause always follows with the next sentence beginning abruptly. In both the oral and written statements, one finds both insightful remarks and those bordering upon nonsensical.

The clearly disqualified nature of the behaviors in the preceding case history appears strikingly consistent. The patient's denial of seriousness encompasses both behavioral mannerisms and verbal expressiveness. Its overall foolish quality virtually begs not to be taken seriously, an exercise in disqualification greatly surpassing anything within the bounds of normal humor. The unexpected presence of the female stenographer only served to magnify the foolish mannerisms, her attendance perhaps delusional interpreted as seductive by the patient wherein triggering the elaborate disqualification of reinforcement in return. In this sense, the excitation represents a disqualified indulgent expression of covetousness in response to the extreme cordial sense of hospitality professed by the clinical staff. This dual interplay of double bind and counter double bind maneuvers represents a common theme for the related sequences of disorders described beforehand; namely, dependent personality/compulsion neurosis and pure mania/expansive paraphrenia. The current transitional interplay of unproductive euphoria and parakinetic catatonia certainly fits the bill in this regard, the foolishly-compulsive characteristics of the latter now extending to a universal sphere of influence: with profound deficits affecting virtually all aspects of mental and emotional functioning. Accordingly, parakinetic catatonia preserves the common stereotype of systematic schizophrenia, an aspect further documented with respect to the remaining classification of affected catatonia, to follow.

463.1 – AFFECTED CATATONIA

The completed description of foolish catatonia, in turn, begs mention of the remaining *affected* form of catatonia. As suggested by its descriptive qualifier, it is characterized in terms of behavioral affectations: colloquially defined as actions that attempt to suggest that which is unreal as in an outward show of pretense. Affected catatonia shares many commonalties with its parakinetic counterpart, although the subject matter is now more pessimistic and subdued in nature particularly for the more debilitating end-states of disease. This disorder is characterized by a gradual impoverishment of involuntary motor control, so that a rigidity of posture and motion develops.

Affectations generally predominate at the onset characterized by stereotypical actions. Eventually these movement affectations gradually give way to affectations of omission resulting in the stuporous forms of catatonia. Patients remain in the same position displaying a stiff posture and facial expressions, often unable to feed themselves or perform toilet duties.

Early on in his career, Leonhard characterized affected catatonia primarily as rigidity, failing to recognize the related significance of the affectations at the time. Leonhard's mentor, Karl Kleist referred to this symptom spectrum as *stereotyped* catatonia, eventually serving as the foundation for Leonhard's derivative category of affected catatonia. In the most severe cases, the motor rigidity dominates the symptom spectrum, although for initial cases, the affectations predominate. These affectations are reminiscent of compulsive actions: including collecting worthless objects, stereotyped kneeling, touching other patients, rubbing one's cheeks, or twisting one's body before passing through a door. Also described: holding a spoon in a peculiar fashion, putting the fork down after each bite, refusing certain foods (or nourishment altogether), including feeding by tube. In milder cases, the affectations are characterized by incipient rigidity, with patients standing stiffly or walking with choppy steps. Their arms do swing freely while walking, although finer transitions lacking, giving a wooden appearance. Speech modulation is also deficient assuming a monotonous tone, although general speed or volume control may appear normal. Face expressions similarly show little animation.

In terms of the more debilitating end states, the affectations remain preserved (as movements) so long as rigidity has not progressed too far. Otherwise, stereotyped omissions predominate that often have to be differentiated from any general lack of motion. In concert with the "motion-affectations," the "omission affectations" always figure prominently in the picture, especially when patients refuse nourishment. Here they remain standing in the same spot, mutely refusing to speak. Should a set course of action be externally interrupted, alternate activities fail to develop to replace what had been lost. Patients may also attempt to escape or steal from other patients. In contrast to the impulsive actions of other catatonics, this tendency is not particularly strong nor commonly encountered.

According to Leonhard's observations, the affectivity for affected catatonia appears relatively well-preserved, in contrast to the severe emotional flattening seen for many of the other forms.

In early stages of the disease, patients remain fully involved with their affectations, although, as their motility becomes impoverished, the force of the affectations decreases. Even in the severest cases (when the patients cease speaking), they still appear able to digest and process significant events within their surroundings, as reflected in appropriate facial expressions to given stimuli. Here, affected catatonia shares various commonalties with parakinetic catatonia, although the foolishly-amusing mannerisms of the latter are now replaced by the immobilization and stupor characterizing the affected end-state.

Consequently, for affected catatonia, the communicational factors now disqualified extend to the contemptuous sense of reproach expressed by the spiritual follower figure, as prompted by the audacious sense of rashness of the spiritual authority figure. In terms of this interplay of double bind/counter double bind maneuvers, harried depression initially prompts the disqualified mannerisms characterizing the affected form of catatonia. During milder phases, these mannerisms may appear bizarrely irritating or amusing, similar to the foolish affectations characterizing parakinetic catatonia. Tragically, the progressive course of the disease ultimately degenerates into a stuporous and immobile end-state: one generally acknowledged as the typical public perception of catatonia.

Affected catatonia continues the tradition of its respective subordinate counterparts; namely, the personal/group sequence of anxiety neurosis and incoherent paraphrenia. It shares with the latter syndromes their immobilizing degree of irrational concern, a factor consistent with the inherent degree of emotional disqualification. Furthermore, affected catatonia encompasses each of the subordinate syndromes as subsets, wherein accounting for the highly chronic and debilitating nature of the deficits. The similar prominent occurrence of religious themes certainly verifies such a spiritual sphere of influence, a factor primarily consistent with such universal directives.

In conclusion, the completed description of the paranoid and catatonic classifications of schizophrenia (encompassing the group/spiritual levels) further raises the issue of the identities of the syndromes predicted for the remaining humanitarian level: in this case, the systematic forms of hebephrenia. As mentioned earlier, this third class of schizophrenia is undoubtedly the most chronic form of the disorder, indicating a clear affinity for the enduring humanitarian level within the power hierarchy. By definition, it incorporates all of the lower authority levels as subsets, wherein shifting the personality into a totally disorganized state. Indeed, Leonhard cites affective deterioration as the key distinguishing feature for hebephrenia in general, expressed as a progressively creeping course of deterioration consistent with such a grand humanitarian time scale.

With respect to the two (future-directed) sequences of systematic schizophrenia, the positive range of syndromes is respectively specified as compulsion neurosis (PF), expansive paraphrenia (GR), parakinetic catatonia (SD), and eccentric hebephrenia (RH). Furthermore, the remaining darker trend based upon anxiety is further defined as anxiety neurosis, incoherent paraphrenia, affected catatonia, and autistic hebephrenia. The remainder of the current chapter examines this final realm of hebephrenic disorders, wherein validating their status as counter double bind maneuvers in relation to the realm of excess.

482.1 – ECCENTRIC HEBEPHRENIA

The general symptomology for eccentric hebephrenia certainly fits well with its descriptive moniker, defined in common usage as a nonconformist sense of whimsy or oddness. As such, it shares many of the bizarre prerequisites initially established for its subordinate counterparts in expansive paraphrenia and foolish catatonia. Eccentric hebephrenia, however, is certainly more chronic in terms of functionality consistent with its more enduring humanitarian prerequisites. It generally starts with compulsive behaviors that subsequently develop into mannerisms of an eccentric nature. The uniform wishes and complaints of the patients are also somewhat compulsive.

The most prominent symptom is the monotonous speech and complaints, their extreme uniformity giving the impression of an extreme preoccupation with manners. Patients approach the doctor on every occasion with uniform requests: as in desiring to be released, requests for different chores, etc. Ignoring their petitions scarcely prevents them from repeating them upon each visit. Upon every occasion (and using the same words), one of Leonhard's patients begged for her release: adding how long she had been confined at the institution, what the priest had said when she was admitted, and that her mother had never been in an institution. If one remained quietly at her side, she repeated the same expressions a number of times. Being as such complaints appear to remain independent of how they are received, the patients generally appear eccentric. Furthermore, this tendency appears more of

an affected activity than any rational course of action, pursued even though little success (or even reaction) may result therein.

During conversations with these eccentric patients, they generally speak without pause, developing a pressured compulsive speech. Even then, a sense of uniformity remains in the forefront, being that their speech appears stuck in the same track of themes. Lengthy monologues tend to revolve around a very few themes, and when these are exhausted, they begin again from the start. These stereotyped speeches generally occur in an affectless and monotonous fashion lacking emotional energy. Patients may claim to be clever and industrious, their failures being considered the fault of others. Even should one overtly ignore the patients, scold them, or insult them, they rarely become excited. Their complaints often appear so eccentric that one is rarely tempted to take them seriously.

The overall behavior is generally characterized by chronic affective dulling. Patients rarely express interest in anything, and (despite their complaints) rarely make any serious attempt to escape, grudgingly adjusting to institutional living. Ethical dulling is particularly evident in the harsh treatment awaiting other patients that may have irritated them. Such irritations are generally not marked, and scarcely interrupt the otherwise uniform state. In contrast to silly hebephrenia, the eccentric form does not tend towards childish pranks. Outside the institution, the patients rarely become criminals, although collector tendencies can sometimes lead to kleptomania. Many become hoboes selectively building upon the tendency towards eccentrically uniform activity. One of Leonhard's patients received a pension but left the funds in the bank and survived by begging.

Affective flattening and ethical dulling are generally characteristic of eccentric hebephrenia, often resulting in antisocial behavior. At early stages, this flattening of the affect is generally accompanied by an appearance of unhappiness, consistent with irritated excitations. The uniformity of the complaints further appears unaffected by outside influences. In addition to affective dulling, initiative also suffers. Primal instincts, however, are generally better preserved. The complaints often betray a compulsive appearance as if the patients are incessantly driven to complain. Accordingly, eccentric hebephrenia represents the crowning humanitarian culmination of the subordinate sequence of disorders; namely, compulsion neurosis, expansive paraphrenia, foolish catatonia, and now, eccentric hebephrenia. The general theme of compulsiveness collectively unifies this extended symptom spectrum, although now representing a (disqualified) covetous sense of longing, consistent with the bizarre nature of eccentric mannerisms and emotional flattening.

In terms of the dual transitional interplay of double bind/counter double bind maneuvers, the initial "presumptuous" treatment expressed by the humanitarian authority, in turn, prompts the (disqualified) covetous sense of longing expressed by the established follower figure. This latter sense of longing certainly proves consistent with its enduring humanitarian focus. The typically chronic course for eccentric hebephrenia conveniently verifies such a functional interpretation, the eccentric stubbornness and frozen pattern of complaints clearly related to other disorders within its class. Consequently, this chronically persistent pattern is similarly encountered in Leonhard's remaining hebephrenic category; namely, autistic hebephrenia.

483.1 – AUTISTIC HEBEPHRENIA

The remaining autistic form of hebephrenia is characterized by affective numbness and deficits in social instincts: as formally suggested in its descriptive moniker. Accordingly, it is closely associated with the symptom spectrum initially established for the eccentric form, although the contents are now more resigned and desolate in character. According to Leonhard, autistic hebephrenics live only for themselves. They appear alienated from others and seem untouched by events going on around them. They are curiously unfathomable, revealing little of their impoverished inner lives as deduced from their banal facial expressions. They avoid speaking or developing relationships with other patients, rarely approaching the clinical staff. Should one directly address them, they generally respond disinterestedly, giving incomplete or evasive answers. Easy questions are often answered with, "I don't know," and intelligence questions typically answered briefly disinterestedly. Patients are generally able to complete a given task, but avoid speaking as much as possible. Consequently, the inner life of the patients appears highly impoverished, never offering independent opinions of their own. In line with this lack of initiative the patients fail to initiate anything independently, only performing work assigned to them. Their autistic style of facial expressiveness is typically stiff and unfathomable with few conclusions to be drawn in terms of their internal experiences.

The typically subdued autistic state is occasionally interrupted by brief aggressive outbursts initially in the form of threats or accusations against a particular person. Alternately, the irritation may target whoever is immediately present. These attacks can be very brutal, employing whatever objects happen to be available. Such unexpected, one-time reactions prove particularly dangerous, being that the patients' mounting irritations are scarcely noticed due to their inexpressive facial characteristics and reserved attitude. Should one happen to speak to a patient during such a state, a bitter expression and affective speech tensions are sometimes observed; however, in later stages of the disease, such excitations become milder and gradually disappear.

Autistic hebephrenics are generally unhappy and suspicious, never exhibiting a friendly trait. Suspiciousness is significantly pronounced, increasing even further when patients are prompted to speak or respond. They rarely express independent interests and scarcely seem engrossed by emotional themes. Patients fail to maintain contact with their families and rarely seek to be released. Despite their autistic appearance (concealing some reactions), the patients are generally affectively numb. Their general state of unhappiness is always colored by traces of suspicion.

The downtrodden autistic mood is somewhat reminiscent of eccentric hebephrenia, both of which strictly contrast with the carefree contentment characterizing the silly and insipid forms. The foolish mannerisms specified for the eccentric form prove a fitting counterpoint to the asocial psychic numbness characterizing autistic hebephrenia. Consequently, the disqualified sense of chagrin expressed by the humanitarian follower, in turn, counters the rash sense of boldness that triggered the entire transitional interchange. This disqualified sense of chagrin proves consistent with an extreme sense of social desolation characterizing autistic hebephrenia expressing a taciturn, emotionally-flattened demeanor.

Generally speaking, autistic hebephrenia represents a global confluence of deficits that (by definition) encompasses all of the lower levels as subsets, wherein accounting for profoundly debilitating deficits. This extreme level of abstraction formally works to obscure any definitive interpretation in this regard, although distinct parallels to eccentric hebephrenia clearly justify an overall placement within the counter double bind model of schizophrenia. The basic underlying theme of neurotic anxiety is subsequently amplified throughout the remaining sequence of disorders; in this case identified as anxiety neurosis, incoherent paraphrenia, affected catatonia, and now autistic hebephrenia.

32

THE CLASSIFICATIONS FOR
MENTAL ILLNESS – (TYPE B)

The preceding comprehensive analysis of the entire *32*-part complement of syndromes for mental illness (Type-A) offered a preliminary overview of the transitional model of double bind and counter double bind maneuvers. The additional sequence of disorders predicted for mental illness (Type-B), in turn, brings this formal style of analysis to its logical conclusion. The respective follower roles are specified first in the two-stage transitional schematic, in contrast to mental illness (Type-A), where the authority roles alternately initiate the interaction. Accordingly, mental illness (Type-B) is closely affiliated to mental illness (Type-A), although with subtle and distinctive differences. Consequently, the additional forms previously described for the personality disorders and the neuroses, as well as Leonhard's supplementary terminology for the cycloid mood disorders and unsystematic schizophrenia effectively round-out this parallel complement of syndromes for mental illness (Type-B).

A number of key features formally distinguish these two fundamental categories of mental illness. According to the preliminary Chapters *29* through *31*, mental illness (A) is specifically defined through what are termed the "pure" syndromes: namely, the phasic style of mood disorders, as well as the systematic forms of schizophrenia. In subsequent chapters of his source book, Leonhard further distinguishes what he designates the *cycloid* forms of psychosis. These latter classifications are exemplified in terms of the bipolar style of manic-depressive disorders: where extremes within the range of affectivity vary from mania to depression over a cyclical course of development, in contrast to the more stable, unipolar forms for pure mania/melancholy, euphoria, and depression. In addition to manic depressive disease, Leonhard also distinguishes a further trio

of bipolar syndromes; namely, anxiety/happiness psychosis, excited/inhibited confusion psychosis, and hyperkinetic/akinetic motility psychosis. In concert with manic-depressive disease, this bipolar quartet collectively rounds-out the double bind pattern of power maneuvers with respect to the supplementary class of mental illness (B).

A similar pattern further holds true with respect to the remaining counter double bind class of maneuvers: in this case, Leonhard's unsystematic classifications of schizophrenia. The clinical picture for the unsystematic forms is truly remarkable in that (similar to the cycloid mood disorders) they exhibit a cyclical course of development often resulting in the complete remission of symptoms between attacks. This clinical course of action formally contrasts with the pattern previously established for the systematic forms of schizophrenia, which typically run a gradually chronic course with little prognosis for remission. Consequently, Leonhard distinguishes three distinct categories of unsystematic schizophrenia; namely, affect-laden paraphrenia, excited-inhibited cataphasia, and periodic catatonia. Each of these syndromes exhibits a similar cyclical picture, in direct contrast to the more stable pattern previously established for the systematic forms of schizophrenia.

Along related lines, the respective groupings of personality disorders and the neuroses suggest a similar cyclical style of clinical picture; such as the histrionic personality, dissociative hysteria, obsessive-compulsive disorder, etc. Indeed, this formal pattern of "cycling" between mood extremes represents the key distinguishing feature for this additional class of mental illness (Type-B). Similar to mental illness (Type-A), however, it is similarly explained in terms of the transitional interplay of the double bind and counter double

420	**421**
Histrionic	Paranoid
Personality	Personality

422	**423**
Passive	Schizoid
Aggressive	Personality
Personality	Disorder

PERSONALITY DISORDERS
Personal Follower
Double-Bind

→

410.1	**411.1**
Dissociative	Depersonal-
Hysteria	ization Neurosis

412.1	**413.1**
Conversion	Neuraesthenic
Hysteria	Neurosis

HYSTERIA
NEUROSIS
Personal Authority
Counter Double-Bind

440	**441**
Happiness	Anxiety
Psychosis	Psychosis

442	**443**
Manic-	(manic-)
(depressive)	Depressive
Disease	Disease

CYCLOID
PSYCHOSES (I)
Group Representative
Double-Bind

→

430.1	**431.1**
Confabulatory	Fantastic
Affect/Laden	Affect/Laden
Paraphrenia	Paraphrenia

432.1	**433.1**
Manic	Confused
Affect/Laden	Affect/Laden
Paraphrenia	Paraphrenia

UNSYSTEMATIC
PARAPHRENIA
Group Authority
Counter Double-Bind

460	**461**
Excited	Inhibited
Confusion	Confusion
Psychosis	Psychosis

462	**463**
Hyperkinetic	Akinetic
Motility	Motility
Psychosis	Psychosis

CYCLOID
PSYCHOSES (II)
Spiritual Disciple
Double-Bind

→

450.1	**451.1**
Excited	Inhibited
Cataphasia	Cataphasia

452.1	**453.1**
Hyperkinetic	Akinetic
Periodic	Periodic
Catatonia	Catatonia

UNSYSTEMATIC
CATATONIA
Spiritual Authority
Counter Double-Bind

Fig. 32 – The Three-Digit Codes for Mental Illness - (B)

bind maneuvers: as depicted in **Fig. 32**, as well as the compact diagram immediately below.

Histrionic Personality → **Dissociative Hysteria**
Happiness Psychosis → **Confab. A/L Paraphrenia**
Excited Confusion Psych. → **Excited Cataphasia**

Paranoid Personality → **Depersonalization Neur.**
Anxiety Psychosis → **Fantastic A/L Paraphrenia**
Inhibited Confusion Psych. → **Inhibit. Cataphasia**

Passive/Aggressive Pers. → **Conversion Hysteria**
Manic/Depressive Disease → **Manic A/L Paraphr.**
Hyper. Motility Psych. → **Hyper. Periodic Cataton.**

Schizoid Personality → **Neuraesthenic Neurosis**
Manic/Depress. Disease → **Confused A/L Paraphr.**
Akinetic Motility Psych. → **Akinetic Periodic Cata.**

The diagram depicted directly to the left represents the formal schematic counterpart for that previously established for mental illness (Type-A): e.g., **Fig. 29** of Chapter *29*. Furthermore, the key towards explaining this basic dichotomy for mental illness (A & B) is similarly reflected in the dual pattern of organization linking the related classifications of lesser virtues (I & II). Indeed, the latter lesser virtues are similarly defined in terms of the interplay of double bind and counter double bind maneuvers (only now with respect to the virtuous realm). According to the current context, the affiliated categories of mental illness are similarly defined as transitional variations with respect to the vices of excess. It further follows that mental illness (A & B) represent extreme motivational analogues of the lesser virtues (I & II), as a direct comparison of the individual terms respectively serve to indicate, particularly in the context of the schematic definitions.

As an inevitable outcome of the order in which they are introduced, mental illness (A) formally corresponds with the lesser virtues (II), whereas mental illness (B), currently under consideration, alternately corresponds to the lesser virtues (I) in terms of the polarities of the respective authority and follower roles. This cross-correlation of notations, however, should not create confusion, being that the dual forms of mental illness are distinguished employing "letters," whereas the lesser virtues are specified through Roman numerals.

THE SCHEMATIC DEFINITIONS
FOR MENTAL ILLNESS - (B)

The true test for such a theoretical system, however, is ultimately found within the expanded context of the formal schematic definitions. Indeed, the complete four-part listing of definitions for mental illness (B) is respectively listed in **Tables T-1** to **T-4**: a sequence beginning immediately overleaf. This format is parallel in form and function to that previously listed for mental illness (A), although now representing transitions in terms of the follower roles (rather than the authority roles). Accordingly, these schematic definitions exhibit an initial personal foundation targeting the personality disorders and the neuroses. The remaining group and spiritual levels, in turn, are alternately characterized by definitions targeting the major classifications of psychosis: namely, the cycloid mood disorders and the unsystematic forms of schizophrenia.

For instance, the histrionic personality disorder expressed the personal follower, in turn, is countered (in a disqualified fashion) by the dissociative hysteria specified for the established authority figure. A similar dual interplay of definitions further holds true with respect to the remaining sequences linking the paranoid personality/depersonalization neurosis, passive-aggressive personality/conversion hysteria, and the schizoid personality/neuraesthenic neurosis. An even more advanced degree of specialization is further encountered in terms of the remaining group and spiritual levels depicted within the tables, although now representing the interplay of the cycloid disorders and unsystematic schizophrenia.

The remainder of the current section examines each of the individual syndromes for mental illness (B) to a more comprehensive degree of detail. Accordingly, a separate chapter is devoted to each major category of syndrome. The remainder of the current chapter launches this formal analysis with an in-depth discussion of the personal realm of the transitional hierarchy, targeting the personality disorders (histrionic, paranoid, passive-aggressive, and schizoid) as well as the corresponding forms of neurosis (dissociative, depersonalization, conversion, and neuraesthenic).

Chapter *33*, in turn, extends the focus of this analysis to the affiliated forms of the psychoses; in this case, Leonhard's cycloid forms of the mood disorders: namely, manic-depression, anxiety-happiness psychosis, confusion psychosis, and motility psychosis. Chapter *33* also focuses, in turn, upon Leonhard's unsystematic forms of schizophrenia; namely, affect-laden paraphrenia, cataphasia, and periodic catatonia. This remaining chapter is further enhanced through a wealth of observations courtesy of Leonhard's longitudinal studies, clearly indicating how each of the syndromes formally matches the specifics predicted

HISTRIONIC PERSONALITY	DISSOCIATIVE HYSTERIA
Previously, I (as personal authority) have pridefully acted in an extremely nostalgic fashion in response to the flatterous attentions of the personal follower. But now, you (as new personal follower) will *flatteringly* act in an extremely worshipful fashion towards me: in anticipation of my (as established PA) prideful treatment of you.	Previously, you (as new personal follower) have flatteringly acted in an extremely worshipful fashion towards me: in anticipation of my (as established PA) prideful treatment of you. But now, I (as reluctant personal authority) will **deny** pridefully acting extremely nostalgically towards you: thwarting your (as new PF) flattering treatment of me.
HAPPINESS PSYCHOSIS	**A/L PARAPHRENIA (CONFAB.)**
Previously, I (as group authority) have vainly acted in a prideful fashion in response to the flattering-adulation of the group representative. But now, you (as new group representative) will flatteringly act with *adulation* towards me: in anticipation of my (as established GA) vain sense of pride.	Previously, you (as new group representative) have flatteringly acted with adulation towards me: in anticipation of my (as established GA) vain sense of pride. But now, I (as reluctant group authority) will **deny** *vainly* acting in a prideful fashion towards you: thwarting your (as new GR) flattering sense of adulation.
EXCITED CONFUSION PSYCHO.	**EXCITED CATAPHASIA**
Previously, I (as spiritual authority) have vainly acted in a conceited fashion in response to the patronizing sense of adulation of the spiritual disciple. But now, you (as new spiritual disciple) will *patronizingly* act with adulation towards me: in anticipation of my (as established SA) vain sense of conceit.	Previously, you (as new spiritual disciple) have patronizingly acted with adulation towards me: in anticipation of my (as established SA) vain sense of conceit. But now, I (as reluctant spiritual authority) will **deny** vainly acting in a *conceited* fashion towards you: thwarting your (as new SD) patronizing treatment of me.

TABLE T-1 – The Definitions Based on Histrionic/Hysteria

PARANOID PERSONALITY	DEPERSONALIZATION NEUR.
Previously, I (as personal authority) have shamefully acted extremely guiltily in response to the excessively blameful treatment of the personal follower. But now, you (as new personal follower) will *critically* act in an extremely blameful fashion towards me: in anticipation of my (as established PA) shameful treatment of you.	Previously, you (as new personal follower) have critically acted extremely blamefully towards me: in anticipation of my (as established PA) shameful treatment of you. But now, I (as reluctant personal authority) will **deny** *shamefully* acting in an extremely guilty fashion towards you: thwarting your (as new PA) critical treatment of me.
ANXIETY PSYCHOSIS	**A/L PARAPHRENIA (FANTASTIC)**
Previously, I (as group authority) have shamefully acted in a humiliated fashion in response to the critical-ridiculing of the group representative. But now, you (as new group representative) will critically act in a *ridiculing* fashion towards me: in anticipation of my (as established GA) shameful sense of humiliation.	Previously, you (as new group representative) have critically acted in a ridiculing fashion towards me: in anticipation of my (as established GA) shameful sense of humiliation. But now, I (as reluctant group authority) will **deny** shamefully acting in a *humiliated* fashion towards you: thwarting your (as new GR) critical-ridiculing of me.
INHIBITED CONFUSION PSYCH.	**INHIBITED CATAPHASIA**
Previously, I (as spiritual authority) have humiliatingly acted in a mortified fashion in response to the scornful-ridiculing of the spiritual disciple. But now, you (as new spiritual disciple) will *scornfully* act in a ridiculing fashion towards me: in anticipation of my (as established SA) mortified treatment of you.	Previously, you (as new spiritual disciple) have scornfully acted in a ridiculing fashion towards me: in anticipation of my (as established SA) mortified treatment of you. But now, I (as reluctant spiritual authority) will **deny** humiliatingly acting in a mortified fashion towards you: thwarting your (as new SD) scornful treatment of me.

Table T-2 – The Definitions Based on Paranoia/Depersonalization

PASSIVE-AGGRESSIVE PERS.	CONVERSION HYSTERIA
Previously, you (as personal authority) have impudently acted extremely desirously towards me in response to the envious treatment of the personal follower. But now, I (as new personal follower) will *enviously* act in an extremely approving fashion towards you: in anticipation of your (as established PA) impudent treatment of me.	Previously, I (as new personal follower) have enviously acted extremely approvingly towards you: in anticipation of your (as establ. PA) impudent treatment of me. But now, you (as reluctant personal authority) will **deny** *impudently* acting in an extremely desirous fashion towards me: thwarting my (as new PF) envious treatment of you.
MANIC/DEPRESSIVE DISEASE	A/L PARAPHRENIA (MANIC)
Previously, you (as group authority) have impudently acted arrogantly in response to the envious sense of jealousy of the group representative. But now, I (as new group representative) will enviously act in a *jealous* fashion towards you: in anticipation of your (as established GA) impudently-arrogant treatment of me.	Previously, I (as new group representative) have enviously acted in a jealous fashion towards you: in anticipation of your (as established GA) impudently-arrogant treatment of me. But now, you (as reluctant group authority) will **deny** impudently acting in an *arrogant* fashion towards me: thwarting my (as new GR) jealous treatment of you.
HYPERKINETIC MOTILITY PSY.	PERIODIC CATATON. HYPERKIN.
Previously, you (as spiritual authority) have arrogantly acted in an impetuous fashion in response to the covetous treatment of the spiritual disciple. But now, I (as new spiritual disciple) will jealously act in a *covetous* fashion towards you: in anticipation of your (as established SA) impetuous treatment of me.	Previously, I (as new spiritual disciple) have jealously acted in a covetous fashion towards you: in anticipation of your (as established SA) impetuous treatment of me. But now, you (as reluctant spiritual authority) will **deny** arrogantly acting *impetuously* towards me: thwarting my (as new SD) covetous treatment of you.

TABLE T-3 – Definitions Based on Passive-Aggressive/Hysteria

SCHIZOID PERSONALITY	NEURAESTHENIC NEUROSIS
Previously, you (as personal authority) have insolently acted extremely worrisomely in response to the disdainful treatment of the personal follower. But now, I (as new personal follower) will *disdainfully* act in an extremely concerned fashion towards you: in anticipation of your (as established PA) insolent treatment of me.	Previously, I (as new personal follower) have disdainfully acted extremely concerned towards you: in anticipation of your (as establ. PA) insolent treatment of me. But now, you (as reluctant personal authority) will **deny** *insolently* acting extremely worrisomely towards me: thwarting my (as new PF) disdainful treatment of you.
MANIC/DEPRESSIVE DISEASE	**A/L PARAPHRENIA (CONFUSED)**
Previously, you (as group authority) have insolently acted audaciously in response to the disdainful sense of contempt of the group representative. But now, I (as new group representative) will disdainfully act in a *contemptuous* fashion towards you: in anticipation of your (as established GA) insolent sense of audacity.	Previously, I (as new group representative) have disdainfully acted contemptuously towards you: in anticipation of your (as established GA) insolent sense of audacity. But now, you (as reluctant group authority) will **deny** insolently acting *audaciously* towards me: thwarting my (as new GR) contemptuous treatment of you.
AKINETIC MOTILITY PSYCHOSIS	**PERIODIC CATATON. (AKINETIC)**
Previously, you (as spiritual authority) have audaciously acted in a rash fashion in response to the contemptuous sense of reproach of the spiritual disciple. But now, I (as new spiritual disciple) will contemptuously act in a *reproachful* fashion towards you: in anticipation of your (as established SA) rash treatment of me.	Previously, I (as new spiritual disciple) have contemptuously acted reproachfully towards you: in anticipation of your (as established SA) rash treatment of me. But now, you (as reluctant spiritual authority) will **deny** audaciously acting *rashly* towards me: thwarting my (as new SD) reproachful treatment of you.

TABLE T-4 – The Definitions Based on Schizoid/Neuraesthenia

for its respective schematic definition. The discerning reader, accordingly, is encouraged to refer back to these four tables of definitions throughout the remaining description of the mental disorders to follow.

It must further be mentioned (in passing) that Leonhard fails to distinguish any unsystematic counterparts for 4th-order realm of hebephrenia as well as precipitating realm of the mood disorders that initiate the entire transitional sequence. This shortcoming is theoretically explainable in terms of the extremely abstract dynamics encountered at the corresponding humanitarian sphere of influence. Accordingly, only *24* distinct syndromes are distinguished for mental illness (B), in contrast to the *32* established for mental illness (A). This telling absence of any unsystematic forms at this 4th-order level is potentially explainable in terms of their predicted rarity consistent with their extreme level of abstraction, or alternately in terms of potential confusion with the unsystematic forms observed at the next lower level. A final resolution to this technical issue must ultimately await further corroborating case studies, for only then will such modifications to Leonhard's system be verified to the satisfaction of all concerned.

THE PERSONALITY DISORDERS/NEUROSES

The most logical place to begin an analysis of mental illness (B) occurs at the most basic personal level within the transitional hierarchy. Recall, (from the Chapter *29*) that a number of the personality disorders and forms of neurosis were formally unaccounted-for in the description of mental illness (A): respectively designated as the histrionic personality, paranoid personality, passive-aggressive personality, and schizoid personality. These four additional syndromes are further defined as transitional variations on the respective vices of excess; namely, flattery, criticism, envy, and disdain. For instance, the histrionic personality is defined a transitional form of flattery, whereas the paranoid personality represents as a similar form of criticism. Furthermore, the passive-aggressive personality is defined as a transitional form of envy, whereas the schizoid personality exhibits a similar correspondence to disdain.

A similar pattern further holds true with respect to the remaining forms of neurosis; namely, the counter double bind classifications of the hysteriform neuroses. For instance, in response to the histrionic behavior of the personal follower, the personal authority may alternately act in terms of dissociative hysteria; namely, denying acting pridefully in the process. A similar pattern further holds true with respect to the personal authority's response to the paranoid personality disorder of the personal follower; in this case, an extreme denial of shamefulness specified for the depersonalization neurosis. This same pattern further extends to the related theme of conversion hysteria: in direct response to the passive-aggressive personality of the personal follower. The personal authority denies impudently acting in an excessively desirous fashion, in direct analogy to the modesty perspective characterizing the virtuous realm. Furthermore, the remaining category of neuraesthenic neurosis represents a disqualified response to the schizoid personality expressed by the personal follower. This dual interplay linking the personality disorders and the neuroses is even more convincingly documented within the expanded context of the corresponding schematic definitions (as presented in **Tables T-1** to **T-4**). Indeed, this comprehensive analysis is further undertaken to establish the preliminary feasibility of this supplementary system for mental illness (B).

420 – HISTRIONIC PERSONALITY

The first mentioned of the personal disorders, the histrionic personality, is characterized by an extreme expression of emotionality, as suggested in terms of the extreme degree of flattery predicted in relation to the transitional model of mental illness. Indeed, the presentation of symptoms has generally been compared to a bad case of overacting, so pronounced are its outbursts and mannerisms. As such, individuals with histrionic personality disorder tend to seek attention by exaggerating events (even if insignificant), and are immature, self-centered, even vain. They react emotionally to the slightest provocation, displaying a style of speech that is excessively impressionistic and lacking in detail. The histrionic personality disorder is classified within the group of personality disorders characterized by overly dramatic, emotionally impulsive, or erratic reactions. They tend to be preoccupied with their outward appearance and attractiveness, and their demeanor is often charming and seductive, even if this behavior proves inappropriate. Such individuals pursue a fast-paced social and romantic lifestyle, although their relationships are generally shallow, tending to depend on others.

Accordingly, the histrionic personality effectively satisfies the prerequisites predicted for the personal follower realm, representing a formal transitional variation on the flattery maneuver: further reflecting the excessive sense of loyalty previously observed with respect to the lesser virtues. The newly transitioned personal follower histrionically acts in an excessively flattering fashion in anticipation of the extreme sense of pride experienced by the established authority figure. By definition, this histrionic tactic plays up the general authority status of the latter, wherein explaining the somewhat appeasing nature of this preliminary power maneuver. By formally playing up an extreme degree of emotionality, the histrionic individual directly increases the odds of achieving the attention of his personal authority figure, although not always with the desired results. Indeed, in terms of our modern media age characterized by fleeting sound-bytes, it appears that there will always be a place for such outrageous behavior, particularly with respect to those willing to exploit their "fifteen minutes of fame."

421 – PARANOID PERSONALITY

The second mentioned disorder within the hysteriform sequence, the paranoid personality, is characterized as pervasive distrust or suspiciousness towards others, such that their motives are interpreted as malevolent or harmful. In a more general sense, paranoia is commonly defined as an ever-present feeling of suspicion that others cannot be trusted. Such feelings are generally not based on fact or reality, wherein insecurity and low self-esteem tend to exaggerate these concerns. Many people experience feelings of paranoia, usually in response to a threatening situation, or in connection with feelings of insecurity based on real-life circumstances. These feelings are related to the mild anxiety most people experience at critical points during their lives. Individuals afflicted with this disorder tend to assume (with little concrete evidence to support them) that others plan to exploit, harm, or deceive them; continually analyzing the motivations of friends, family, and others in order to confirm doubts about their trustworthiness. They further expect that friends or family will abandon them in times of trouble or stress; and avoid revealing personal information due to fear that it will be used against them.

In terms of this symptom spectrum, the paranoid personality shares many points in common with its respective counterpart in criticism, although now modified to reflect a transitional sphere of influence. In this latter respect, this syndrome represents a critically excessive quest for responsibility, as the general pattern of

blameful distrust and suspiciousness directly serve to indicate. The respective transitional strategy of playing-up to the established authority role, in turn, imparts a somewhat vulnerable quality to the paranoid personality disorder: placing the patient at odds in many social contexts. The newly transitioned personal follower paranoically acts in an excessively critical fashion in anticipation of the shameful treatment of the personal authority figure. Accordingly, it shares with the histrionic personality such a highly dramatized degree of expression, although now targeting a clearly darker range of themes.

422 – PASSIVE-AGGRESSIVE PERSONALITY

The third entry within their respective quartet of personality disorders, the passive-aggressive personality, similarly shares a highly dramatized mode of expression, although now emphasizing a sense of procrastination or stubbornness (consistent with its status as a future-directed power maneuver). Accordingly, this disorder is characterized by covert obstructionism, procrastination, stubbornness, and inefficiency. Formerly listed in the first three editions of the *Diagnostic and Statistical Manual of Mental Disorders*, this syndrome has since been dropped as a distinct entity from the *DSM-IV*, although this disorder is somewhat equivalently classified as the negativistic personality disorder. Its main distinguishing feature is an indirect resistance to the expectations of others through stubbornness, forgetfulness, inefficiency, procrastination, or other covert means.

Rather than refusing outright to perform a task, the passive-aggressive individual will do it badly, or procrastinate until the deadline for its completion has passed. They characteristically resist demands for adequate performance, find excuses for delays, and find fault with those on whom they depend. Most experience this passively self-detrimental behavior as punitive and manipulative. Passive-aggressive individuals, at one time termed "ill-tempered depressives," can also be moody, discontented, and critical of others, tending to see themselves as victims, and feeling that they are singled out for bad luck or ill treatment by others. In their interpersonal relationships, they appear unable to find a healthy balance between dependence and assertiveness. Individuals with this disorder lack self-confidence and are typically pessimistic about the future.

Regardless of how it is classified, the passive-aggressive personality formally respects the specifics predicted within the transitional power hierarchy, although now reflecting the extreme sense of envy expressed by the personal follower figure. The pronounced feelings of stubbornness or resistance are further indicative of such a grudging perspective, wherein reflecting the vulnerable characteristics of the transitional power maneuvers in general. The personal follower passive-aggressively acts in an extremely envious fashion in response to the impudence expressed by the established authority figure. Due to its foundations within the relatively innocuous class of the vices of excess, this disorder is rarely overtly aggressive in nature: rather relying upon subtle manipulation (accompanied by a questionable semblance of cooperation) to advance its annoying agenda. How the various symptom parameters precisely fit within a general transitional model remains a topic open to further debate, although the underlying communicational factors (predicted within a transitional format) remain uncontested at this juncture.

423 – SCHIZOID PERSONALITY

The schizoid personality disorder is a classification first introduced in the *DSM-III*, and subsequently expanded upon in the current edition (*DSM-IV*). As suggested in its descriptive moniker, it represents a pervasive pattern of detachment from social relationships, and a restricted range of emotional expression in interpersonal settings. It begins by early adulthood and is present in a variety of contexts, as diagnosed through many the following indications. Schizoid individuals neither desire (nor enjoy) close relationships, including being part of a family. They almost always choose solitary activities, and have little, if any interest in sexual experiences with another party. They take pleasure in few activities, and lack close friends or confidants other than first-degree relatives. Indifference to the praise or criticism of others also occurs, as well as emotional coldness, detachment, or a flattened affect.

According to *DSM-IV*, schizoid individuals do not seem to be bothered by what others may think of them. They can be oblivious to the subtleties of normal social relationships, and typically do not respond appropriately to common social cues, so that they appear socially inept or superficially self-absorbed. They sometimes display a bland exterior visibly lacking in emotional reactivity, rarely reciprocating the gestures or facial expressions of others. Social relations, by definition, are severely restricted, as well as occupational functioning: particularly if interpersonal involvement is required. It is distinguished from the avoidant personality disorder in that the sense of

isolation for the latter is primarily due to hypersensitivity to rejection, although the desire to enter social relationships is present if there are strong guarantees of uncritical acceptance. In contrast, those with schizoid personality disorder never desire social relations.

In terms of the general description of the personality disorders established to date, the schizoid personality clearly fits within the overall communicational dynamic, wherein viewed as a darker variation on the more innocuous characteristics of the passive-aggressive disorder. Here, the schizoid personality targets the extremes of social dysfunction and reclusiveness, as evident in the general shyness and withdrawn symptom spectrum. In terms of the dynamics of the double bind class of maneuvers, the newly transitioned personal follower disdainfully acts in an excessively schizoid fashion in reaction to the insolence expressed by the established authority figure. Indeed, this covert sense of disdainfulness clearly represents the driving-force for the fairly broad range of symptoms, where others are judged not to be worthy of any serious consideration or meaningful effort. Consequently, the schizoid individual is content to operate within a safe and personally secure sphere of influence: a mode of operation essentially at odds with normal social functioning. Although other potential interpretations could be considered, the current version remains the best option to date; and one further validated for the related class of counter double bind maneuvers (now to be described).

THE NEUROSES - (TYPE B)

The completed description of the preliminary class of personality disorders raises the further issue of the remaining counter double bind class of maneuvers, as reflected in the subliminally disqualified forms of hysteriform neurosis. Symptoms typically derive from precipitating events of a traumatic or sexual nature: an aspect consistent with the basic foundation of the neuroses in relation to the realm of excess. Furthermore, the general inability of the patient to control his symptomology is clearly indicative of such a subliminal degree of disqualification, as in subconsciously attempting to control one's relationship without necessarily appearing to have do so.

Similar to the personality disorders, the *DSM* series formally distinguishes a distinctive complement of hysteriform syndromes; namely, dissociative hysteria, conversion hysteria, depersonalization neurosis, and neuraesthenic neurosis. This hysteriform set of disorders formally counters the initial (double bind) class of maneuvers specified for the personality disorders. For instance, the histrionic personality disorder of the personal follower, in turn, prompts the dissociative hysteria expressed by the respective authority figure. Similarly, the critical dictates of the paranoid personality are respectively countered by the depersonalization neurosis, therein. Furthermore, the passive-aggressive personality expressed by the personal follower, in turn, prompts the conversion hysteria of the respective authority figure. Finally, the schizoid personality is further counteracted by the neuraesthenic neurosis. The remainder of the current chapter examines each of the individual forms of neurosis within a formal communicational dynamic, wherein outlining the interplay of the personality disorders and neuroses.

410.1 – DISSOCIATIVE HYSTERIA

The first listed of the hysteriform neuroses, dissociative hysteria, is a term initially introduced in the *DSM-II*. In the *DSM-III*, however, this notion of hysteria is downplayed due to historical gender bias; the sense of the dissociation now fragmented into its various symptom categories: namely, fugue, amnesia, multiple personality, etc. For sake of the current discussion, the traditional sense of dissociative hysteria is preferred, being that it encompasses each of these various aspects into a single overarching category. The predominant feature is one or more episodes of an inability to recall important personal information (primarily of a traumatic or stressful nature), and not explainable in terms of ordinary forgetfulness.

The symptoms may cause clinically significant distress or impairment in social, occupational, or other areas of functioning. Dissociation (the feeling of being detached from the reality of one's body) can be categorized into two types: depersonalization and derealization. Depersonalization is characterized by a sense of not knowing who one is, or questioning long-held beliefs about one's personal identity. In derealization, individuals perceive reality in a grossly distorted fashion. Psychologists have identified several types of disorders based on these feelings. These include depersonalization disorder, dissociative fugue, dissociative amnesia, dissociative trance disorder, and dissociative identity disorder (also known as multiple personality syndrome), amongst others.

Dissociative fugue is a strange phenomenon by which persons are stricken with a sudden memory loss that prompts them to flee their familiar surroundings. Those suffering from this disorder will suddenly find themselves in new surroundings, hundreds (or even thousands) of miles from their homes, with no memories of the weeks, months, or even years that have elapsed since their flight. Dissociative amnesia describes the process of losing major chunks of memory.

Regardless of the symptom specialization therein, dissociative hysteria is defined as a neurotic reaction to the histrionic personality disorder consistent with the reciprocal interplay of double bind and counter double bind maneuvers. According to this strictly functional interpretation, the newly transitioned personal follower histrionically acts in an extremely flattering fashion in anticipation of the prideful treatment from the established authority figure. The personal authority, however, when confronted with becoming double bound into such a predetermined course of action, may alternately switch to a counter double bind class of maneuver; namely, accepting the face value of the initial communication, while simultaneously denying any willing participation therein.

The personal authority figure subliminally disqualifies any such prideful perspective, wherein presenting dissociative symptoms in the process. Indeed, this neurotic disorder represents an extreme variation on the "humility" perspective previously established with respect to the lesser virtues. Depending upon unique susceptibilities within the individual, this may be expressed as dissociative fugue, amnesia, trance, etc. These distinctive aspects share a common theme; namely, subconsciously disqualifying the participation of the established authority figure, a symptom spectrum that the client claims no clear volitional control. As such, this authority role is now blunted and sublimated to the point that the counter double bind perspective now completely takes over the psyche: a feature further encountered with respect to the three remaining forms of neurosis within the hysteriform grouping.

411.1 – DEPERSONALIZATION NEUROSIS

The second of the hysteriform disorders, depersonalization neurosis, is a syndrome closely related to dissociative hysteria, as respectively distinguished in *DSM-II*. In *DSM-III*, however, the qualifier "neurosis" is dropped in favor of the modified entry of depersonalization *disorder*. As suggested in its descriptive qualifier, it is characterized by persistent or recurrent experiences of feeling detached, and as if one outwardly observes one's mental processes or body (e.g., feeling like one is dreaming). It is further distinguished through persistent feelings of unreality. In addition, one may complain about feeling "mechanical" or as if in a dream. Various types of sensory anesthesia are also common. Furthermore, patients also complain of a sense of derealization manifest through a strange alteration in the perception of one's surroundings, so that a sense of the reality within the external world is lost. Depersonalization disorder, in itself, is an uncommon disorder. In *DSM-IV*, the depersonalization disorder is no longer listed as a distinct syndrome, rather lumped with the other dissociative variations.

This tendency to simplify categories (in later editions of the *DSM*-series) remains an issue of controversy, being that the original status of the depersonalization disorder in *DSM II & III* proves particularly crucial in terms of the newly devised transitional model of mental illness. Depersonalization neurosis formally complements the more innocuous nature of dissociative hysteria in terms of the counter double bind paradigm. Indeed, the latter dissociative disorder is defined as occurring in response to the histrionic style of symptomology, whereas depersonalization neurosis represents a counter double bind reaction to the critical prerequisites of the paranoid personality disorder. The newly transitioned personal follower critically acts in a paranoid fashion in anticipation of the shameful treatment from the established authority figure. The personal authority, however, can alternately employ a disqualified form of counter double bind maneuver, expressed in terms of the bizarre symptom spectrum for depersonalization neurosis. Consequently, the reluctant personal authority denies willingly being in control of any shameful feelings therein, as experienced through a sense of estrangement, detachment, or loss of control. As such, it mirrors the pattern previously established for dissociative hysteria, although now targeting the darker realm of disqualified innocence (as opposed to humility).

These hysteriform symptoms are explained in terms of the original precipitating circumstances. The trauma of the criticism specific to the paranoid personality appears far more adverse than that originally seen for the histrionic personality. Accordingly, depersonalization neurosis remains far more debilitating than its dissociative counterpart insofar as psychological impairment and social incapacitation. Consequently, depersonalization neurosis clearly warrants its status as a separate disorder, a pattern further documented in terms of the remaining hysteriform syndromes.

412.1 – CONVERSION HYSTERIA

The third of the neurotic disorders, conversion hysteria, represents the prototypical hysteriform

disorder: dating to its earliest descriptions in the field of Freudian psychodynamics. In the second edition of the *DSM*-series, it is designated as hysterical neurosis (conversion type), although modified in the third edition to simply the conversion disorder. Regardless of how it is designated, this disorder is described in all four *DSM*-editions, defined as one or more symptoms (or deficits) affecting voluntary motor or sensory function suggestive of a neurological or other general medical condition. These deficits are not intentionally produced or feigned (as in malingering). This condition was first described by Sigmund Freud as conversion hysteria, being he speculated it involved the conversion of repressed emotional problems to physiological symptoms.

Conversion reaction is a fairly rare condition, accounting for roughly two percent of all psychiatric diagnoses. The conversion disorder may serve as a means for the patient to avoid activities or situations associated with a source of emotional conflict (or even shut down conscious awareness of the conflict itself). A further source of secondary gain is the attraction of attention, sympathy, or support that the patient craves, but is unable to obtain by other means. The most common symptoms of conversion disorder include paralysis, blindness or tunnel vision, seizures, loss of sensation, and disturbance of coordinated movements (such as walking). Sometimes individuals will experience anesthesia in only one part of the body, such as "glove anesthesia:" which affects the hand only up to the wrist, although this syndrome can have no physiological origin since there is no cut-off point between the nerves of the arm and hand.

Conversion symptoms are largely symbolic, relieving the patient's anxiety through inexplicable symptoms such as hysterical blindness or convulsive seizures. The patient may also not appear to be concerned with the illness, a condition that French psychiatrist Pierre Janet termed *la belle indifference* (1929). At the end of the 19th century, great advances were made in the understanding and cure of hysteria through recognition of its psychogenic nature, and also through the use of hypnotism to influence hysterical patients (known to have a high degree of suggestibility). Indeed, this capacity to be treated through behavior therapy places conversion hysteria in the same category as the dissociative and depersonalization disorders, although its more overt sense of incapacitation now targets a future-directed sphere of influence: as opposed to the dissociative disorders that focus upon such a past-directed sequence of themes.

According to this conversion pattern, the newly transitioned personal follower enviously acts passive-aggressively in anticipation of the impudent sense of extreme passion expressed by the established authority figure. The reluctant personal authority, however, can subliminally deny acting impudently so: a subconscious sense of disqualification expressed through a broad range of conversion symptoms (as in hysterical paralysis, blindness, hoarseness, etc.). Here, conversion hysteria represents an extreme variation on the modesty perspective previously established in relation to the lesser virtues. Through the incapacitating and vulnerable aspects of this symptom spectrum, the reluctant authority figure experiences the affectations specific this impudent perspective without necessarily appearing to have done so: wherein counteracting the insistent quality of the passive-aggressive maneuver.

Although this interpretation could be viewed as just one of several possible alternatives, it nevertheless fits quite well within the general pattern of counter double bind maneuvers characterizing the realm of the neuroses. Indeed, the subliminal degree of disqualification characterizing the hysteriform disorders makes any definite conclusions tentative, at best. The specific mode of expression the conversion symptoms take depends upon the precipitating aspects of the initial double bind event, as well as emotional susceptibilities of the responder, etc. In terms of the dual reciprocating pattern for the personality disorders and neuroses, this broad interpretation for conversion hysteria proves quite plausible within such an overall communicational dynamic context: and one similarly suggested for the remaining class of neurasthenic neurosis.

413.1 – NEURAESTHENIC NEUROSIS

The final of the hysteriform disorders, neurasthenic neurosis, is a concept that has changed drastically in status over the years. It first appeared as a distinct entity in the *DSM-II* (also referred to as neurasthenia). It refers to a condition characterized by complaints of chronic weakness, easy fatigability, and clinical exhaustion. Unlike hysterical neurosis, the patient's complaints seem to be genuinely distressing, and there is no evidence of secondary gain. It differs from anxiety neurosis (and the psycho-physiological disorders) in terms of the low-key nature of its predominant complaint. It was noted (in the lead up to the *DSM-III*) that this disorder was only rarely diagnosed in practice, leading to its exclusion from later editions. Its basic symptom spectrum, how-

ever, was combined with what was termed the dysthymic disorder (also known as depressive neurosis). It is characterized as a chronic disturbance of mood involving a depressive affect, and a loss of interest or pleasure in usual activities or pastimes (although not of sufficient severity or duration to meet the criteria for a major depressive episode). For adults, a two-year duration is sufficient for diagnosis; for children and adolescents, one year generally suffices. The depressed mood may be accompanied by feelings of sadness, or of being "down in the dumps." This may prove relatively persistent or intermittent, sometimes interrupted by the normal periods of mood lasting a few days to several weeks.

This disorder generally shows an onset early in adult life. For this reason, it is often referred to as a depressive personality. The disorder generally begins without a clear onset, in turn, exhibiting a chronic course of development. The broad range of symptoms encompassing neurasthenic neurosis seems to obscure any overall communicational dynamic. Taking a cue from conversion hysteria, however, neurasthenic neurosis similarly reflects such hysteriform propensities: although now targeting a darker range of themes, as in complaints of chronic tiredness or low energy. It mirrors the incapacitating aspects of conversion hysteria, although now exploiting themes of physical exhaustion in order to counteract the prospects of coercion within a double bind context.

According to this tentative interpretation, the newly transitioned personal follower disdainfully acts in a schizoid fashion in anticipation of the insolence expressed by the established authority figure. The reluctant personal authority, however, can neuraesthenically deny acting insolently in the process, expressed through the symptom spectrum of weakness and volitional insufficiency. As such, it represents an extreme variation on the meekness perspective previously established with respect to the lesser virtues. Accordingly, neurasthenic neurosis continues the pattern of disqualification previously defined with respect to conversion hysteria. Indeed, a similar behavioral dichotomy was previously encountered with respect to the dissociative/depersonalization disorders. Although other potential explanations are technically feasible for neurasthenic neurosis, the current communicational factors represent the leading contender in this regard, particularly in correspondence to the other hysteriform forms of neurosis. Indeed, this dual communicational format similarly applies to the more abstract realm of the cycloid mood disorders and unsystematic schizophrenia: a functional aspect now to be described.

In all fairness, the *DSM*-series proves exceedingly efficient in terms of classifying the personality disorders and the neuroses, permitting a seamless correspondence to the transitional model of mental illness at a personal degree of influence. A similar correspondence to the psychoses, however, is not quite so precise. Here the Anglo-American system is derived primarily from the work of Kraepelin and his successors. The dichotomy between schizophrenia and manic depression is quite adequately described, although with not much further degree of detail.

A parallel system devised by the German Classificationalists (such as Karl Leonhard), in contrast, provides a wealth of clinical classifications that seamlessly fill out the sum-total of predicted slots for the transitional model of the psychoses. Here, the psychoses mirror the exquisite precision initially established for the personality disorders and the neuroses. Unfortunately, this German system of terminology is not quite as widely employed as that contained within the *DSM*-series, a regrettable shortcoming in light of its newfound facility for validating the transitional model of mental illness. Consequently, a more detailed examination of this German system definitely proves in order here, wherein outlining reasons for its less than universal appeal, as well as potential avenues for remedying such an oversight.

A GENERAL OVERVIEW OF THE PSYCHOSES

Both the German and Anglo/American systems of classification enjoy a common foundation in the clinical observations of Emil Kraepelin (1856-1925), who first established a distinction between the manic-depressive disorders and schizophrenia. A German contemporary of Kraepelin's, Carl Wernicke, labored in the related fields of clinical neurology and descriptive psychiatry, employing cross-sectional (as well as longitudinal) studies. Wernicke's major successor, Karl Kleist (1879-1960) expanded upon the Wernicke's observations in neurology and psychiatry, confirming and expanding upon the great wealth of clinical observations. It remained to the efforts of Kleist's protege, Karl Leonhard (1904-1988), to carry this German classificational tradition to its logical conclusion: leading to the *58* individual categories of the psychoses outlined in the current book.

Leonhard initially studied medicine in Berlin and Munich, and was eventually appointed senior physician in concert with his pioneering investigations into schizophrenia and the mood disorders. He eventually attracted the notice of Karl Kleist, who was instrumental in securing Leonhard an academic appointment. Karl Leonhard was exempt from military service during WW-II due to a recurrent illness. As a clinical psychiatric director, he was able to divert many patients from the state-imposed "euthanasia" of the mentally ill during the Nazi era. Not surprisingly, German psychiatry was broadly disparaged following the war, with little opportunity to showcase the observational skills of Kleist and Leonhard. In 1957, Leonhard was appointed Director of the Department of Psychiatry at Humboldt University (East Berlin), where he remained until retirement.

The political partitioning of Germany in 1961 ultimately limited Leonhard's influence within Western academia. Editors for Western journals rejected many submissions stating that they were not in strict conformity with the prevailing Anglo-American model. Nevertheless, Leonhard pursued without compromise the exceptional promise of his unique observational findings. The reasons why the Wernicke-Kleist-Leonhard school of psychiatry has not had a greater influence on the global scene appear quite varied. Critics such as Jaspers (without sufficient documentation) labeled both Wernicke and Kleist as "brain mythologists," downplaying their voluminous efforts in the process. Karl Leonhard was criticized on similar grounds. Leonhard (and co-workers) countered these objections with observations of hundreds of patients before any particular syndrome was clinically specified. Indeed, his record of investigations spans many decades, as described in his *Berlin Series* of *1,465* cases.

Perhaps the most troubling obstacle to international acceptance concerns the unfortunate legacy of Nazi euthanasia for the most seriously mentally ill during WW-II. Although Leonhard endeavored to preserve as many lives as possible under difficult circumstances, the political taint of such a tragic policy has proven difficult to overcome. The newfound relevance of Leonhard's system to the three-digit coding system, however, goes a long ways towards ameliorating these shortcomings in the future; particularly with respect to the newly proposed transitional model of mental illness. Here, this innovation proves a fitting tribute to those tragic souls lost during the mental health holocaust of WW-II. Although not apparent at the time, these enduring case histories have proven instrumental towards decoding the communicational factors underlying mental illness. In a grander sense, the tragically shortened life span of these patients will not all have been in vain, rather posthumously serving the quite noble purpose of benefiting those generations of the afflicted to follow.

33

THE CYCLOID PSYCHOSES AND UNSYSTEMATIC SCHIZOPHRENIA

The preceding personal foundations for the personality disorders and the neuroses (B), in turn, extend to the even more abstract realm of the bipolar psychoses. In particular, the personality disorders further transition into the "cycloid" forms of the bipolar mood disorders specific to the higher-order follower levels. Furthermore, the hysteriform class of the neuroses, in turn, transition into the unsystematic forms of schizophrenia introduced by Leonhard. Both of these cycloid forms of the psychoses exhibit the distinct tendency to cycle from elation to depression (and back again), suggesting a variable state of flux.

With respect to the transitional model of mental illness, this is further explainable in terms of the observation that the initial transitional maneuvers (by definition) represent extreme variations on the reinforcement perspective specific to the follower role. Indeed, for the cycloid psychoses, the respective follower roles are specified first in the two-stage transitional dynamic, in contrast to mental illness (Type–A), where the authority roles alternately initiate the interaction. Here, for the cycloid mood disorders and unsystematic schizophrenia, reinforcement occurs first, in contrast to the pure mood disorders and systematic schizophrenia, where procurement behaviors occupy the initial transitional slot. This interpretation further explains the observed tendency towards bipolar cycling, a feature not generally seen for the pure forms: where procurement occurs first (hence, more focused in terms of its goals). Indeed, the cycloid forms typically exhibit a pattern of complete remissions between disease episodes, in direct contrast to the more chronic nature of the pure syndromes. This basic dichotomy effectively verifies the clear functional distinctions between these two major classifications of mental illness.

This distinctive trend towards bipolar cycling further extends to the related sphere of the counter double bind maneuvers, in this case, the unsystematic forms of schizophrenia described by Leonhard. This unsystematic category also exhibits a tendency towards mood swings, although scarcely to the extreme degree established for the bipolar mood disorders (perhaps a carry-over effect from this initial sphere of influence).

In terms of this theoretical interpretation, Leonhard formally distinguishes four basic forms of the cycloid mood disorders; namely, manic-depressive disease, anxiety/happiness psychosis, excited/inhibited confusion psychosis, and hyperkinetic/akinetic motility psychosis. As suggested in their descriptive monikers, each of these syndromes exhibits both excitatory and inhibitory phases, a factor particularly in keeping with the extreme continuum of positive and negative reinforcement within the transitional hierarchy. In terms of the current scenario, this amounts to reinforcement expressed to an extreme degree: as previously outlined in **Fig. 32**. Accordingly, the histrionic personality of the personal follower, in turn, extends to the happiness psychosis for the group representative, followed by the excited confusion psychosis expressed by the spiritual disciple. Furthermore, the paranoid personality disorder, in turn, extends to the anxiety psychosis for the group level, culminating in the inhibited confusion psychosis targeting the spiritual level. A similar sequence of disorders further holds true with respect to the passive-aggressive personality, manic disorder, and hyperkinetic motility psychosis; as well as the schizoid personality, depressive disorder, and akinetic motility psychosis.

The remainder of the current chapter examines each of these respective cycloid mood disorders to a more comprehensive degree of detail, including a wealth of representative case histories. The remainder of the current chapter launches this analysis with respect to the group-order level for anxiety/happiness psychosis and manic-depressive disease, followed by the spiritual focus for the confusion psychosis and the motility psychoses. The final segment of this chapter, in turn, targets the remaining class of counter double bind maneuvers: namely, Leonhard's unsystematic forms of schizophrenia: affect-laden paraphrenia, cataphasia, and periodic catatonia. Throughout this stepwise analysis, the discerning reader is encouraged to refer back to the respective schematic definitions listed in **Tables T-1** to **T-4** of Chapter *32*, formally illustrating how each of the individual syndromes matches the specifics predicted within its respective schematic definition format.

440 / 441 – ANXIETY / HAPPINESS PSYCHOSIS

The first mentioned of the cycloid mood disorders, anxiety/happiness psychosis, is a syndrome particularly in keeping with the bipolar nature of this category. The positive pole is distinguished as the happiness psychosis, directly contrasting with the darker themes characterizing the anxiety psychosis. This dual affective pattern proves extremely debilitating to the individual, indicating a more abstract (group) sphere of influence, wherein generally warranting mental health treatment. This institutional focus directly contrasts with the more benign symptomology for the personality disorders: namely, the histrionic and paranoid personality disorders previously described in Chapter *32*. Indeed, even for this initial set of personality disorders, an incipient bipolar tendency is further suggested. For instance, for the histrionic personality disorder, the personal follower often reaches such a state of excitation that it further grades over into paranoid themes (and vice versa).

This conspicuous pattern of bipolar cycling, in turn, appears even more pronounced when extended to the more advanced (group) focus for anxiety/happiness psychosis. Here, the happiness psychosis represents a higher group variation on the histrionic personality, whereas the anxiety psychosis makes a similar correspondence to the paranoid personality disorder. For instance, the extreme sense of flattery expressed in a histrionic sense further extends to the excessive adulation characterizing the happiness psychosis. Furthermore, the extreme sense of criticism defining the paranoid personality disorder, in turn, leads to the excessive sense of dread experienced in terms of the anxiety psychosis. Here, the anxious form shares with the happiness psychosis such a highly dramatized mode of expression, although now targeting a clearly darker range of themes.

The happiness psychosis occurs somewhat less frequently than its anxious counterpart, an aspect also seen for manic-depressive disease, where a depressive state predominates over the manic. Controlled observations frequently reveal that (even if overt ecstatic phases are absent) the anxious phase is periodically interrupted by an incipient elevation of mood for brief periods of time. In general, delusions of divine calling or salvation are often expressed. Such transitory states prove extremely crucial for confirming the bipolarity of anxiety-happiness psychosis, although the anxiety phase alone is sufficient to diagnosis.

For the anxious pole (**441**), delusions of being tortured or murdered (or losing one's family) produces a symptom spectrum similar to that previously established for harried depression. In contrast to the latter, however, such complaints rarely occur in a pure form, rather expressed in conjunction with a paranoid ideation accompanied by distrust and self-referential delusions (often confirmed by outward occurrences). For instance, patients may believe that someone standing in front of them is threatening them, that patients are avoiding them, that employees are plotting their pending arrest, or that police are following them. The outward expression of anxiety varies considerably, including wailing, moaning, screaming, or fleeing in a state of extreme excitation. Patients may rebuff attempts to approach them or remain rigidly motionless, revealing anxiety chiefly through facial expressions.

The remaining happiness pole (**440**) of anxiety-happiness psychosis is characterized by feelings of elation accompanied by an ecstatic mood. Patients may express immeasurably elevated delusions, even extending to a divine level. Furthermore, they typically wish to make others happy, primarily expressed as ideas of religious calling, happiness, or salvation. This calling to a higher duty is often traceable back to God, or the idea is perceived as directly suggested by God. It is further common to report social or political callings, wherein striving to bring others justice or eternal peace. In less serious cases, patients take on the role of helpers (without resorting to a higher calling), as in volunteering consistent with the group prerequisites for this disorder.

Affect often expands suddenly, then sinks again just as quickly. Both the anxious and ecstatic phases exhibit this oscillatory character, where patients may run anxiously through the ward at one juncture, and then (for the next hour) may calmly respond to questions while smiling elatedly. Furthermore, patients may appear to be in the highest state of ecstasy at one moment, and then suddenly becoming resigned the next. The mood oscillations are not necessarily restricted to those spanning one pole and the centerline, but may also span the full range of extremes between the two poles, even bridging the greatest extremes of ecstasy and anxiety. More typically, the anxious or ecstatic moods target a more mundane context in terms of civil or social themes, suggesting that religious themes are not strictly diagnostic to the disease spectrum. As such, anxiety-happiness psychosis is said to occupy the middle ground in this regard: assigned an intermediate (group) status between the histrionic/paranoid personality disorders on the one hand, and the more extreme confusion psychosis on the other, the latter of which now will be described.

460 / 461 – EXCITED / INHIBITED CONFUSION PSYCHOSIS

The completed technical analysis of the anxiety/happiness psychosis (specific to a group sphere of influence), in turn, invites further consideration of its related spiritual (or universal) counterpart; namely, Leonhard's confusion psychosis (in both its excited/inhibited manifestations). In direct analogy to the anxiety/happiness psychosis, the confusion psychosis also appears to cycle between excitatory and inhibitory phases. Although one pole may tend to dominate the symptom spectrum, the basic symptom spectrum always appears to be a variable admixture of ecstatic and anxious moods. The excitatory phase is characterized by a grossly elevated mood, exceedingly reminiscent of the happiness psychosis initially described. Furthermore, the inhibited phase alternately takes on anxious characteristics similar to those previously established for the anxiety psychosis.

In terms of functionality, the confusion psychosis appears to be much more severe debilitating than anxiety/happiness psychosis, with spiritual-religious themes predominating: as in ecstatic delusions of saintliness or divine blessings. Alternately, darker themes of sinfulness or eternal perdition are further observed. Indeed, this pronounced religious slant is particularly consistent with the predicted spiritual slant for the confusion psychosis. As such, it represents the crowning culmination of the ascending sequence of authori-

ty roles: spanning the personal, group, (and now) spiritual levels within the power hierarchy. Here, the positive ascending sequence is respectively identified with the histrionic personality, the happiness psychosis, and the excited confusion psychosis. Similarly, a darker sequence of terms, in turn, extends to the paranoid personality, the anxiety psychosis, and the inhibited confusion psychosis.

According to Leonhard, the excited phase of the confusion psychosis (**460**) is characterized by incoherent ideation with abnormal contents: primarily a misrecognition of other persons, in addition to ideas of reference and sensory illusions (primarily of an auditory nature). The inhibited phase (**461**) is characterized through thought inhibition leading to perplexedness, accompanied by ideas of reference and (less often) hallucinations. As a general rule, excitatory ideation is associated with compulsive speech, whereas thought inhibition is viewed as linguistic impoverishment leading to mutism. Typically only one pole of the disease is ever in focus, although the poles may follow each other sequentially, even rapidly alternating between the two poles.

In general, thought processes become disordered in confusion psychosis, appearing fully incoherent during the excitatory phase (and stunted during the inhibited phase). During excitation, patients speak incessantly on topics not particularly relevant to those immediately at hand. For instance, when questioned concerning his health or other activities within the ward, the patient, instead, may digressively speak of experiences dating back many years (and in other circumstances): described as an incoherence of thematic choice. This ideational excitation further leads to linguistic excitation: wherein incoherent and compulsive speech represents the key distinguishing feature of excited confusion psychosis.

The inhibited phase, in contrast, reflects thought processes that appear to be frozen in higher degrees of inhibition, leading to mutism. Nothing much can be learned about these mental contents during such a stuporous state, although patients may eventually report their experiences through hindsight. In milder states, when patients only appear taciturn, one observes ideation closely affiliated with perplexity. Furthermore, an impoverishment of facial expressions (and other such movements) directly reflects a corresponding paucity of the thought processes. The limited repertoire of linguistic expressions, in turn, suggests a lack of understanding concerning ongoing events: expressed as a searching or questioning look, taking on an anxious character.

A pronounced religious coloration remains consistent with the predicted spiritual (or universal) focus for the confusion psychosis. Indeed, the excitatory phase takes its cue from the affiliated lesser virtue of piety. It reaches psychotic proportions, however, in terms of an extreme degree of patronization, wherein anticipating the vain sense of pretentiousness from the established authority figure. As such, it shares with the happiness psychosis such profoundly rewarding characteristics: an aspect further encountered with respect to the personal dramatics affiliated with the histrionic personality.

The inhibited confusion psychosis, in contrast, clearly targets a darker range of themes, expressed as a taciturn or muted demeanor. Here, the scornful sense of ridicule expressed by the spiritual disciple further prompts the mortified sense of humiliation from the established authority figure. Such scornful prerequisites prove particularly consistent with the subdued nature of the inhibited phase. Affiliated delusions of reference are encountered consistent with the subordinate symptom spectrum for the anxiety neurosis. Although other potential explanations might further be devised to explain the communicational factors at issue here, the current formulation represents the most plausible explanation at this juncture, particularly in conjunction with the transitional model of the cycloid mood disorders, in general.

442 / 443 – MANIC / DEPRESSIVE DISEASE

The preceding descriptions of the anxiety-happiness psychosis and the confusion psychosis provide a distinctive pattern of organization for Leonhard's past-directed realm of the cycloid mood disorders. As such, they represent ecstatic or anxious perceptions consistent with the memory of such past-directed perspectives. A similar pattern of organization further holds true with respect to the remaining two classifications of the cycloid mood disorders, although now targeting a future-directed perspective. These are identified as bipolar manic/depression and the motility psychosis. The remainder of the current chapter is devoted to examining these two syndromes in the order given, beginning with an in-depth examination of manic-depressive disease.

The bipolar form of the syndrome differs fundamentally from the pure categories of mania and melancholy initially established in Chapter *30*. Indeed, this distinction is perhaps Karl Leonhard's greatest claim to fame, where (through diligent observation and analysis) he drew a fine distinction between the pure and bipolar forms of the

disorder: not only in terms of symptomology, but also prognosis and disease progression. In direct contrast to the pure forms, bipolar manic-depression exhibits the distinct tendency to cycle from mania to melancholy (and back again) over the course of months or years: an aspect never encountered in the pure forms. As such, it is assigned a pivotal placement within the cycloid hierarchy of the mood disorders; in this case, the group realm intermediate between the personal foundations for the personality disorders, and the universal prerequisites predicted for the motility psychosis.

The pair of personality disorders relevant to this discussion are the passive-aggressive personality and the schizoid personality disorder, respectively. The passive-aggressive disorder was previously described as an extremely envious sense of reinforcement, whereas the schizoid personality was categorized as an extreme sense of disdainfulness. These personal prerequisites, in turn, extend to the next higher (group) level specific to bipolar manic-depression. Here, the manic pole represents an extremely envious sense of jealousy, whereas the depressive phase targets a disdainful sense of contempt.

According to Leonhard, the bipolar forms of the mood disorders are much more colorful in appearance than the unipolar forms. They vary not only in terms of the two basic poles, but each clinical phase also offers a distinct clinical picture. In contrast to the unipolar forms (which can also follow a periodic course), the symptom spectrum for the bipolar forms is not closely affiliated with any other form. Indeed, they are not related transitionally to any of the other forms. In contrast, the unipolar forms never show signs of lability toward the opposite pole; e.g., a unipolar melancholic never exhibits manic traits no matter how chronic the course. Similarly, unipolar mania never suggests a trace of depression throughout the entire course of the excitation.

For bipolar manic/depressive disease, no clear pattern of symptoms can ever be distinguished, being that most transitions occur between the two poles, causing the clinical picture to be distorted even during a single phase. Thus one generally recognizes the bipolar form during the first few phases. One also potentially recognizes those manifestations that primarily swing towards one pole (but also casually contain the potential for the other pole): hence, the primary distinction between the bipolar and unipolar forms. Indeed, the opposite phase may only be hinted at in the overall pattern of oscillation, although it certainly proves difficult to ignore.

Manic patients may swing to a depressive mood for hours, while depressive patients can exhibit a noticeable excitation with busyness when their depression becomes temporarily attenuated. The quick course for these mood swings should not necessarily be interpreted as separate phases, rather demonstrating an incipient affinity towards the non-dominant pole. Furthermore, depressive patients may become increasingly agitated through praise or encouragement (even temporarily emerging from their depression). They become lively and talkative, in stunning contrast to their initial depressed mood. Afterward, however, they return promptly to the original depressive mood.

The overall symptom spectrum for bipolar manic-depression is characterized by a manic component (**442**) expressed through an elevated sense of self-regard, flight of ideas, pressured speech, and busyness. The depressive mood (**443**) is alternately signaled by feelings of insufficiency, difficulty in making decisions, mental blocking, psychomotor retardation, and depressive idea construction. These symptoms prove equally applicable to pure mania/melancholy, although observations of bipolarity permit the correct diagnosis.

According to Leonhard, the recurrent cycling between manic and depressive moods distinguishes the cycloid mood disorder from its pure manic/melancholic counterparts. This inherent tendency to cycle in a bipolar fashion is initially suggested in its counterparts within the personality disorders; namely, the passive-aggressive and schizoid personalities, respectively. Here, manic-depressive disease is assigned an intermediate status within the ascending hierarchy of transitional power maneuvers. It directly expands upon the personal foundations for the personality disorders, in turn, serving as the elementary foundation for the remaining universal class of the motility psychosis, the latter of which now will be described.

462 / 463 – HYPERKINETIC / AKINETIC MOTILITY PSYCHOSIS

The completed analysis of manic/depressive disease, in turn, invites further speculation as to its extension to a universal sphere of influence; in this case, the motility psychosis (in both its hyperkinetic and akinetic manifestations). In direct analogy to the manic/depressive polarities initially described, the motility psychosis is similarly seen to cycle between hyperkinetic and akinetic phases. Although one pole may tend to dominate the symptom spectrum, the basic

syndrome always appears to be an admixture of these polarities throughout the course of the disease.

The hyperkinetic phase is characterized as an extremely agitated mood reminiscent of the (bipolar) manic phase. Furthermore, the akinetic phase takes on melancholic characteristics similar to those established for the bipolar depressive phase. Here, the motility psychosis represents the culmination of the ascending sequence of follower roles spanning the personal, group, (and now spiritual) levels, respectively. The positive trend, in this respect, is reflected in the ascending sequence of the passive-aggressive personality, bipolar mania, and the hyperkinetic motility psychosis. Furthermore, the darker targets the ascending sequence of the schizoid personality, bipolar depression, and the akinetic motility psychosis. The remainder of the current chapter is devoted exclusively to outlining this remaining set of classifications for the motility psychosis, as further documented through Leonhard's clinical observations and copious case histories.

The motility psychosis is a disease entity initially described by Wernicke. It was further differentiated by Kleist as a disease spectrum distinct from catatonia. The hyperkinetic form (**462**) represents a psychomotor form of excitation. It is scarcely dependent on disorders of thought or emotion (as initially seen for the excitations associated with the past-directed forms of the confusion and happiness psychoses). The automatic forms of motility are primarily reflexive in terms of function. Patients may gesticulate through movements interpreted as beckonings, threats, or acts of resistance. Reactive movements include the grabbing of one's hair or clothes, ripping up mattresses, climbing on furniture, banging on the walls, or grabbing other patients. Facial expressions may reflect joy, sorrow, anger, disappointment, and the like. Speech patterns appear scarcely affected during extreme hyperkinesis, for higher linguistic functioning is rarely impacted by such psychomotor excitation.

The opposing pole of the motility psychosis, the akinetic phase (**463**), represents a psychomotor form of inhibition, characterized by a perplexed stupor. Here, activities requiring preparatory thought are lacking, whereas reactive motions are similarly diminished, with expressive movements becoming stilted and stiff. Patients fail to respond to the simplest of commands that previously may have been followed automatically. Their posture appears stiff, the face is rigid, and the extremities appear fully non-expressive. Individual initiative appears particularly absent in akinetic stupor, being that such impulses are no longer fulfilled due to psychomotor interference. Speech is similarly affected, with patients appearing mute to all intents and purposes.

Marked religious themes expressed in the preceding case studies remain consistent with the spiritual (or universal) prerequisites attributed to this transitional phase of communication. Here, the hyperkinetic mode is characterized by restless motion comprised primarily of expressive/reactive behaviors, an aspect particularly reminiscent of the manic-busyness characterizing the mania phase of the bipolar disorder. In terms of the double bind model of the mood disorders, this is further interpreted as a jealous expression of covetousness: as the reactive sense of restlessness would outwardly appear to suggest. Indeed, the hyperkinetic phase takes its cue from the affiliated lesser virtues of chivalry/nobility: where the pressure to remain outwardly active could certainly be construed when taken to an outlandish range of extremes.

The akinetic form of this disorder, in contrast, targets a more subdued range of themes: as the stiffness and rigidity of the posture and frozen facial expressions formally serve to indicate. Here, spiritual follower contemptuously acts in a reproachful fashion in anticipation of the rash treatment from the respective authority figure. In a theoretical sense, this contemptuous sense of reproach is directly reflected in the subdued and inflexible behavior patterns characterizing the akinetic phase, although this is by no means the only potential means for interpretation. The current interpretation, nevertheless, fits the clinical observations quite nicely, and one that enjoys the further advantages of being formally predicted in terms of the transitional model for mental illness, in general.

THE UNSYSTEMATIC FORMS OF SCHIZOPHRENIA

The completed description of the preliminary class of bipolar mood disorders invites further comparisons to the remaining counter double bind class of power maneuvers; in this case, Leonhard's unsystematic forms of schizophrenia. The clinical picture for these unsystematic forms is truly remarkable, being that they exhibit a cyclical course of influence, often leading to a complete remission between episodes. This remitting course formally contrasts with the pattern previously established for the systematic forms of schizophrenia, which alternately run a progressively chronic course with little prognosis for remission. Indeed,

Leonhard argues that unsystematic schizophrenia exhibits a closer affinity to the cycloid psychoses than it does to its systematic counterparts: describing them as "evil cousins" of a sort.

Accordingly, Leonhard distinguishes three distinct categories for unsystematic schizophrenia; namely, affect-laden paraphrenia, cataphasia, and periodic catatonia. The first mentioned of these classifications, affect-laden paraphrenia, is formally titled due to its superficial sense of motivation, although subliminally disqualified consistent with its schizophrenic categorization. This perfunctory affective quality, in turn, corroborates its status as an extreme form of procurement behavior, although now expressed in a thoroughly disqualified fashion. Consequently, Leonhard further subdivides affect-laden paraphrenia into four subclassifications; namely, confabulatory, fantastic, manic, and confused subheadings. Furthermore, this quartet-style format formally accounts for the four affective dimensions predicted for the group domain within the transitional hierarchy.

With respect to the next higher spiritual (or universal) level, Leonhard distinguishes two remaining categories of unsystematic schizophrenia; namely, excited/inhibited cataphasia and hyperkinetic/akinetic periodic catatonia. Both syndromes are fittingly subdivided into dual bipolar specializations that collectively serve to satisfy the four requisite dimensions predicted for the counter double bind model of schizophrenia. Leonhard's notion of *cataphasia* effectively corresponds to the more general clinical concept of schizophasia: a confused style of "word salad" reminiscent of the confabulatory form of paraphrenia. Leonhard also distinguishes a *periodic* form of catatonia, in direct reference to the periodic cycling between its hyperkinetic and akinetic phases: a pattern consistent with the active roles specified for this universal sphere of influence.

The remainder of the current chapter examines each of these respective categories of unsystematic schizophrenia to a greater degree of detail including supportive clinical observations. The following section launches this systematic analysis with an in-depth examination of affect-laden paraphrenia, followed, in turn, by the spiritually-ordered syndromes of cataphasia and periodic catatonia. Through the remainder of this formal analysis, the discerning reader is encouraged to refer back to the respective listing of schematic definitions depicted in **Tables T-1** to **T-4** (of Chapter *32*), effectively illustrating how each of these specific syndromes effectively matches the specifics predicted within the corresponding schematic definition format.

430.1 to 433.1
AFFECT- LADEN PARAPHRENIA

The most basic (group) prerequisites for affect-laden paraphrenia encompass a rather broad range of symptoms: ranging from ecstatic to depressive moods, in addition to manic or confused variations. The tendency to cycle (in a bipolar fashion) from one extreme to another exhibits distinct similarities to the pattern previously established for the related forms of hysteriform neurosis. In the latter case, dissociative hysteria formally contrasts with depersonalization neurosis, whereas conversion hysteria makes a similar counterpoint to neuraesthenic neurosis. In a similar fashion, Leonhard distinguishes four distinct subcategories for affect-laden paraphrenia that also exhibit a bipolar pattern of development: namely, the confabulatory, fantastic, manic, and confused variations. Here, affect-laden paraphrenia represents a higher (group) analogue upon the more basic personal foundations for the hysteriform neuroses, sharing with the latter a highly disqualified range of symptomology.

According to Leonhard, affect-laden paraphrenia is primarily characterized by affective fluctuations ranging from anxious to ecstatic, further accompanied by diseased idea construction. The anxious phase is dominated by delusional self-references, whereas the ecstatic mode extends to false perceptions and feelings of happiness. In milder cases, it is often difficult to differentiate between affect-laden paraphrenia and its precipitating double bind maneuver (the anxiety-happiness psychosis). According to Leonhard, the former, indeed, establishes a formal relationship with latter, often a crucial criterion for diagnosis in more chronic states. The delusions and false perceptions for affect-laden paraphrenia, however, ultimately appear to go well beyond any simple foundation in anxiety or ecstasy, rather becoming illogical or incomprehensible in a clearly disqualified fashion.

Affective fluctuations become flatter and more alienated in character. This may further be replaced by an irritable mood that develops directly from the anxiety, often containing hostile misinterpretations concerning one's surroundings. Affectivity with respect to both poles, is also observed: where ideas of persecution and happiness exist in concert with one another. Errors of memory further indicate that this affective disorder profoundly effects the ability to think logically. The course of the disease is not always strictly progressive, for cases with remissions are common, and periodic courses may also occur (in which case the affectivity fluctuates between the two poles). A key distinguishing feature, however, is the superficial appearance of affectivity. Fantastic or confabulatory paraphrenics (from the systematic group) lack any deep tie to their world of illusions: in essence, speaking of them without any outward affective display. In contrast, affect-laden paraphrenia remains anchored in affective expression. Here, patients relate their ideas with either deep irritation or grandiose enthusiasm. Should this affective potential not immediately be apparent, then one only need to verbally stimulate the patient to observe this heightening of affect. Independent of their illusions, the end-state for affect-laden paraphrenia may appear quite numbing.

These marked bipolar characteristics allow for a clear distinction between affect-laden paraphrenia and its systematic counterparts, although the most decisive factor remains a relative preservation of the affect. For affect-laden paraphrenia, it is not so much the general blunting of the affect (which remains relatively well preserved), but rather the relationship of the affect to the diseased idea construction that remains the key diagnostic factor. Although delusions (at the onset) can appear either anxious or ecstatic, they generally maintain a clear affective connection. Patients may speak of being persecuted with marked irritability, or ramble-on concerning their ecstatic delusions. Here, the pathological affect appears to drive the diseased ideation. Being that emotional reactions to normal stimuli are diminished (but remain strong in connection with the pathological ideas), one gains the impression of a single-track affectivity.

This strong affective undercurrent directly contrasts with the severe emotional flattening initially established for systematic paraphrenia, where a creeping progressive course leads to an extreme disorganization of the affect.   This basic dichotomy is formally explained in terms of the respective affective modalities at issue: where former deals with extreme procurement behaviors, whereas the latter targets an extreme reinforcement perspective. Consequently, procurement represents the exclusive focus for affect-laden paraphrenia, where the respective group authority figure essentially disqualifies perspectives of an extreme appetitive or aversive nature. Although thoroughly disqualified, these procurement behaviors, nevertheless, retain a strong affective character. The systematic forms of paraphrenia, in contrast, alternately disqualify extreme reinforcement behaviors: such as excessive rewards or leniency. Disqualification on this scale typically leads to severe emotional flattening, being that reinforcement follows procurement in the operant sequence (hence, more susceptible to severe disorganization).

This remains the most plausible explanation for the dramatic differences between affect-laden paraphrenia and its systematic counterparts. Indeed, whereas the latter is further subdivided into four subtypes (confabulatory-fantastic-expansive-incoherent), it further stands to reason that affect-laden paraphrenia is similarly amenable to such a treatment. This four-part spectrum of subtypes; namely, confabulatory, fantastic, manic, and confused conveniently accounts for all four slots predicted for the counter double bind theory of schizophrenia. Although Leonhard does not specifically schematize these categories as distinct entities, they nevertheless fit quite precisely within the corresponding schematic definitions, as individually described to a more comprehensive degree of detail to follow.

The first-mentioned category, confabulatory affect-laden paraphrenia (**430.1**), is defined as a disqualified response to the happiness psychosis previously described, indicative of the reciprocal interplay of double bind and counter double bind maneuvers. According to this dual interpretation, the newly transitioned group representative histrionically acts happily in anticipation of the prideful sense of vanity expressed by the established group authority. The reluctant group authority figure, however, when confronted with being double bound into a predetermined course of action, may alternately choose the counter double bind course of action; namely, accepting the face value of the initial communication while simultaneously denying willing participation therein. Here, the group authority formally disqualifies any vain sense of pride in this regard, expressed in terms of the bizarre ideation specified for the confabulatory form of affect-laden paraphrenia.

A similar pattern is further implied for the reciprocal interplay of the anxiety psychosis and fantastic affect-laden paraphrenia (**431.1**). Here the fantastic form effectively complements the more innocuous nature of its confabulatory counterpart (in terms of such a bipolar perspective). Accordingly, fantastic affect-laden paraphrenia is defined as a (disqualified) counter double bind maneuver in response to the preliminary prerequisites of the anxiety psychosis. Here, the (newly transitioned) group representative anxiously acts in a paranoic fashion in anticipation of a shameful sense of humiliation expressed by the group authority figure. The latter, however, can alter-

nately opt to choose a counter double bind form of maneuver, as expressed through the disqualified form of fantastic affect-laden paraphrenia. Here, the established group authority denies any shameful sense of humiliation, although through a thoroughly disqualified range of diseased ideation.

A similar pattern is further encountered with respect to the remaining future-directed dimensions for unsystematic schizophrenia: as in the interplay of manic/depressive disease and manic/confused affect-laden paraphrenia. According to the first scenario, the newly transitioned group representative manically acts in a passive-aggressive fashion in anticipation of the impudently-arrogant treatment from the group authority figure. Through this option of the counter double bind maneuver, the reluctant group authority subliminally denies acting arrogantly so, an extreme degree of disqualification expressed through the pressured speech and delusional ideation characterizing manic affect-laden paraphrenia (**432.1**).

A similar scenario, in turn, targets the interplay of the depressive phase (for the bipolar disorder) and confused form of affect-laden paraphrenia (**433.1**). Through the incapacitating and disqualified nature of this confused variation, the reluctant group authority effectively sidesteps the insistent quality of the entire transitional interchange without necessarily appearing to have done so: although to the necessary detriment of normal rational functioning. Although other potential interpretations may prove feasible in terms of these sub-classifications of affect-laden paraphrenia, the communicational factors specified, therein, represent the best leading contenders, particularly in terms of general pattern of double bind/counter double bind maneuvers in relation to the transitional model of mental illness.

450.1 / 451.1 – EXCITED - INHIBITED CATAPHASIA

The completed description of the four subdivisions for affect-laden paraphrenia invites further comparisons to the remaining unsystematic forms of catatonia. In terms of the past-directed forms of catatonia, this is identified with excited/inhibited cataphasia. Furthermore, the future-directed format is specified as periodic catatonia (in both its hyprkinetic and akinetic manifestations). The first mentioned category of cataphasia is actually of fairly recent origin, employed to partially describe what originally had been termed schizophasia. The latter term refers to jumbled or confused speech (word salad): alluding to the random expression of ideas reminiscent of a tossed salad. Leonhard, in turn, modified the nomenclature for this disorder, being that the term schizophasia refers exclusively to the excited form. Here, Leonhard chose the closely related designation of cataphasia in order to distinguish between the dissolution of linguistic functions for both his excited and inhibited phases.

The clinical picture of cataphasia derives primarily from the symptomology of schizophasia first described by Kraepelin, and subsequently expanded on by Kleist. Kraepelin referred to a severe confusion of linguistic expressions, whereas Kleist focused on neologisms and word-confusions that scarcely occur in Kraepelin's accounts. Leonhard's approach initially appeared much closer to Kraepelin's, in that the latter described a very circumscribed clinical picture. Leonhard's eventual formulation of cataphasia, however, was ultimately achieved through the recognition of a separate *inhibited* form of the disease, an innovation that did not occur until after the 2nd Edition of his *Classification of Endogenous Psychoses*. He, therefore, made considerable modifications to his notion of cataphasia in subsequent editions (leading up to the current 5th edition).

According to Leonhard, cataphasia appears in two distinct forms, the excited and inhibited classifications. Excited cataphasia (**450.1**) is distinguished by confused and compulsive speech, with incomprehensible linguistic expressions in more severe cases. Curiously, other outward behaviors remain generally sensible, and affectivity appears relatively well preserved. Inhibited cataphasia (**451.1**), in contrast, is characterized by mutism: or in milder cases, as a taciturn demeanor.

This inherent sense of bipolarity for cataphasia is similarly found for the other two unsystematic forms of schizophrenia, being that both affect-laden paraphrenia and periodic catatonia exhibit the distinct tendency to target alternate poles. According to Leonhard, cataphasia is a thought disorder that primarily influences speech, the key distinguishing feature for this syndrome. Indeed, just as Leonhard previously related affect-laden paraphrenia to the anxiety-happiness psychosis, so cataphasia is similarly associated with the confusion psychosis on the basis of such a mutual (speech-affecting) style of thought disorder.

The excited form of cataphasia is characterized by compulsive jumbled speech, sometimes approaching a confabulatory character. The patient may turn towards the investigator as if having something significant to say, although one can scarcely understand a word of it, as if one was speaking a foreign language. New words and phrases continually occur, whose relationship to what previously had been said remains unclear. Often the same words appear in varied (although generally senseless) connotations. Grammatical sentence structure is similarly jumbled, where sentences are often left incomplete. Lively flowing speech typically obscures where one sentence ends-off and another begins.

Inhibited cataphasia, in contrast, is characterized by thought inhibition and mutism: resulting in an outward lack of linguistic blunders observed in the excited form. In extreme cases of inhibition, the patients cease speaking altogether. The patients appear somewhat retiring and reclusive, and do not seem particularly attentive to their surroundings. The facial expressions of inhibited cataphasic patients are characterized in terms of affective flatness and emotional dullness, with a degree of reactive numbing exceeding simple perplexity. One observes a profound thought disorder expressed through logical errors in basic communication.

The characteristic verbal deficits for cataphasia suggest essentially a communicational disorder, as further implied in terms of the double bind /counter double bind model of mental illness. For instance, the excited phase represents a disqualified vain sense of pretentiousness on the part of the spiritual authority figure, a response to the patronizing sense of adulation initially expressed by the follower figure. The mood is primarily elevated consistent with its enhanced authority status, although the attendant degree of disqualification accounts for the "word-salad" distortion in relation to any meaningful communication. Furthermore, the pronounced expression of religious themes generally verifies a spiritual (or universal) sphere of influence. The initial patronizing attitude expressed by the spiritual disciple, in turn, prompts the disqualified sense of pretentiousness of the reluctant authority figure.

A similar dynamic is further encountered with respect to inhibited cataphasia, although now primarily targeting a darker range of themes. Here, the reluctant spiritual authority's humiliated sense of mortification is subliminally disqualified, in response to the scornful sense of ridicule expressed by the respective follower figure. This mortified demeanor is chiefly expressed in a subdued fashion, a factor consistent with the taciturn nature of the affiliated symptom spectrum. Here, related feelings of perplexity further betray the attendant sphere of disqualification in relation the designated authority role. Although religious ideation is diminished in the inhibited form due to the degree of mutism, this universal authority

THE MENTAL DISORDERS (410 – 499)

410 – Narcissistic Personality
410.1 – Dissociative Hysteria
411 – Borderline Personality
411.1 – Depersonalization Neurosis
412 – Dependent Personality
412.1 – Conversion Hysteria
413 – Avoidant Personality
413.1 – Neuraesthenic Neurosis

----

420 – Histrionic Personality
420.1 – Obsession Neurosis
421 – Paranoid Personality
421.1 – Phobia Neurosis
422 – Passive/Aggress. Personality
422.1 – Compulsion Neurosis
423 – Schizoid Personality
423.1 – Anxiety Neurosis

----

430 – Confabulatory Euphoria
430.1 – Confab. A./Laden Paraphr.
431 – Suspicious Depression
431.1 – Fantastic A./Laden Paraphr.
432 – Pure Mania
432.1 – Manic Affect-Laden Paraphr.
433 – Pure Melancholy
433.1 – Confused A./Laden Paraphr.

----

440 – Happiness Psychosis
440.1 – Confabulatory Paraphrenia
441 – Anxiety Psychosis
441.1 – Fantastic Paraphrenia

442 – Manic/Dep. Disease
442.1 – Expansive Paraphrenia
443 – M./Depressive Disease
443.1 – Incoherent Paraphrenia

----

450 – Enthusiastic Euphoria
450.1 – Excited Cataphasia
451 – Self-Torturing Depression
451.1 – Inhibited Cataphasia
452 – Unproductive Euphoria
452.1 – Hyperkinetic Periodic Catatonia
453 – Harried Depression
453.1 – Akinetic Periodic Catatonia

----

460 – Excited Confusion Psychosis
460.1 – Proskinetic Catatonia
461 – Inhibited Confusion Psychosis
461.1 – Negativistic Catatonia
462 – Hyperkinetic Motility Psychosis
462.1 – Parakinetic Catatonia
463 – Akinetic Motility Psychosis
463.1 – Affected Catatonia

----

470 – Non-Participatory Euphoria
471 – Non-Participatory Depression
472 – Hypochondriacal Euphoria
473 – Hypochondriacal Depression

480.1 – Silly Hebephrenia
481.1 – Insipid Hebephrenia
482.1 – Eccentric Hebephrenia
483.1 – Autistic Hebephrenia

perspective accounts for the extremely incapacitating nature in both forms of cataphasia. Indeed, each of the lower authority levels is included within cataphasia as a subsets, wherein accounting for the global psychological deficits. Consequently, Leonhard's concept of cataphasia represents the supreme culmination of the trend previously established for the hysteriform neuroses and affect-laden paraphrenia, the latter of which shares many commonalties with cataphasia.

452.1 / 453.1 – HYPERKINETIC / AKINETIC PERIODIC CATATONIA

The remaining set of syndromes for Leonhard's unsystematic class of schizophrenia is respectively specified as periodic catatonia (in both its hyperkinetic and akinetic manifestations). The disorder directly expands upon the manic-confused classifications previously established for affect-laden paraphrenia. Indeed, it proves fitting to assert that periodic catatonia represents a more abstract (universal) expansion upon the more basic group focus previously established for affect-laden paraphrenia.

According to Leonhard, the basic course of periodic catatonia involves both hyperkinetic and akinetic phases. These are rarely present as pure forms, but rather the symptoms from one pole form an admixture with those from the opposing pole. Here, psychomotor excitations and inhibitions generally take on a mixed character. Consequently, hyperkinetic excitations exhibit a peculiar rigidity, where grace in motion appears diminished. Individual motions do not flow harmoniously, but rather appear stiff. These distortions often seem to disguise the meaning of the respective motions, where gestures may transform into indefinite reaching motions. Facial expressions, in turn, become grimaces. Such an admixture of symptoms occurs relatively frequently in periodic catatonia, resulting in a simultaneous appearance of both excitation and inhibition.

Extreme akinesis (**453.1**) results primarily in a complex repertoire of maintained postures, whose stereotypical nature (Leonhard implies) is generally diagnostic for periodic catatonia. Impulsive motions may also occur, where akinetic patients may suddenly jump from their beds and run wildly throughout the room. They further may become aggressive or suddenly scream-out, only then returning to a rigid stance. Furthermore, akinesis is often accompanied by negativistic resistance, where external stimulation leads to opposing reactions. In cases where hyperkinesis (**452.1**) predominates, the background akinetic

traits restrict the overall manner in which the excitation is expressed. Movements tend to be stiff and choppy, performed sluggishly, and lacking in any graceful sense of harmony. Facial expressions lack any general sense of contentment, invoking somewhat of a grimaced appearance. Indeed, the disorder selectively appears to destroy normal expressive facial and accompanying postural movements.

Affectivity is similarly flattened, with thought processes tending to become short-circuited and inhibited. The more repeated cycles that occur, the clearer the nature of the defect becomes. In the severest cases, akinesis tends to predominate, making more of an impact than hyperkinesis. In addition to severely diminished motivation, one also observes a simultaneous increase in impulsivity. This takes the form of grimaced expressions or repeated grasping or rubbing motions or sudden unexpected remarks.

This characteristic tendency towards impulsivity is fully explainable in terms of the double bind/counter double bind model of mental illness. For instance, the excitatory phase represents a (disqualified) arrogant sense of impetuosity in response to the envious sense of covetousness expressed by the spiritual follower figure. The dramatic religious themes presented in the preceding case history clearly argue for a universal sphere of influence. Here, the spiritual authority disqualifies acting impetuously in response to the initial transitional overture of the spiritual disciple figure. Consequently, this extreme sense of impetuosity is outwardly expressed in terms of grimaced facial expressions and incongruent behavior patterns consistent with the excitatory phase.

The inhibitory phase is alternately explained in terms of the (disqualified) insolent sense of rashness expressed by the reluctant authority figure, in direct response to the contemptuous sense of reproach initiated by the spiritual disciple. Here, the akinetic phase takes its cue from the related lesser virtues of obedient/conformity, whereby stunting outward expressiveness in terms of a symptom spectrum resembling sluggishness or short-circuitness. As such, both the excited and inhibited phases expand (in a more abstract fashion) upon the subordinate group characteristics for manic/confused affect-laden paraphrenia: wherein accounting for its globally debilitating effects. It, accordingly, represents the crowning culmination of the ascending trend initially grounded in the hysteriform neuroses, and further specified for the remaining categories characterizing affect-laden paraphrenia and periodic catatonia, respectively.

In conclusion, the completed description of the transitional model of mental illness offers a crucial a milestone in the decoding of the riddle of mental illness, a communicational model unprecedented on the world scene today. This achievement in large part is due to the pioneering contributions of German researcher Karl Leonhard concerning the psychoses, as well as the efforts of the American Psychiatric Association with respect to the personality disorders/neuroses. The related applications to the three-digit coding system, however, remain formally incomplete without mention of the *accessory* variations with respect to the realm of mental illness. Indeed, it was previously demonstrated that each of the other three transitional categories (namely, lesser virtues, criminality, and hypercriminality) were collectively endowed with their own accessory classifications in terms of the three-digit coding system.

The accessory format is specified through a formal reversal of the "you" and "I" roles within the schematic definitions permitting a dual interplay of authority and follower roles. The transitional realm of mental illness is clearly no exception in this regard, although its extremely specialized terminology makes the identification of any unique accessory system of terms beyond the limits of the language tradition. This technical shortcoming, however, does not necessarily prove a major concern, for (as previously established for criminality/hypercriminality) a simple prefix-style modification proves adequate for specifying the accessory variations for mental illness as well. It remains only a further minor step to add the prefix *"accessory"* in front of the respective major syndromes (also abbreviated as *Acc.*). A complete listing of terms for the main realm of mental illness is schematically depicted in **Fig. 33**, an extension of the tabular format previously initiated in Chapter 1. The related three-digit codes for the main syndromes are similarly incorporated within this master table, although the accessory versions are omitted, being that they would only duplicate the main terms through the addition of the *Acc.*-prefix (an unnecessary distraction). The corresponding accessory three-digit codes, however, are easily computable: pattern virtually identical to that previously established for the main syndromes with the exception that the third-place digit is moved four places higher reflecting a change to accessory status. For instance, the basic narcissistic personality is assigned a code number of 410, whereas its accessory variation is specified as 414. It proves particularly crucial for specifying these accessory versions in terms of fulfilling the comprehensive prerequisites of the three-digit coding system. These main/accessory variations for the realm of mental illness effectively complement one another with the exception that the polarities governing the "you" and "I" roles are effectively reversed, wherein allowing for crucial empathic insights into the wide range of mental disorders. For instance, in the case of narcissistic personality, the main class of syndrome places the patient within a subjective "I" perspective, in turn, complementing the accessory perspective characterizing an outside observer (such as the clinician of record).

THE SCHEMATIC DEFINITIONS FOR THE ACCESSORY REALM OF MENTAL ILLNESS

One further issue of crucial import concerns the incorporation of the accessory terminology for mental illness directly into the schematic definition format. The terminology for the main sequence of disorders was seen to fit quite effectively within the schematic definition format, where the respective terms for the vices of excess were incorporated in a transitional fashion for simulating the reciprocal interplay of double bind and counter double bind maneuvers. Along similar lines, there is no reason why the related system of accessory terminology could not also be incorporated within the definition format, although now distinguished through the addition of the prefix "accessory." Being as this might prove somewhat confusing within the definition format (and due to space constraints) the latter sets of accessory definitions for mental illness will not be depicted in the current volume, an aspect best reserved for an upcoming edition. The discerning reader, however, can gain a preliminary indication of how this additional set of tables might look by referring back to the main sequences of definitions for mental illness A and B initially defined and then reversing the polarities of the "you" and "I" roles within the definitions.

According to this crucial empathic innovation, both the subjective perspective of the patient, as well as the objective viewpoint of the clinician, can adequately be simulated in terms of the main/accessory forms of schematic definitions. This permits a more balanced perspective as to the rights and obligations of the client/patient, as well as parallel limiting factors with respect to the therapeutic obligations governing the code of the clinician. Furthermore, the predicted individual slots for the three-digit coding system are now all adequately accounted for, wherein effectively rounding-out the stepwise description of transitional communicational model of mental illness.

34

APPLICATIONS TO CLINICAL DIAGNOSIS AND PSYCHOTHERAPY

The somewhat technical nature of the terminology for mental illness contained in **Part VII** certainly proved warranted, an exercise justified in terms of defining the all-inclusive nature of mental illness in general. Upon this solid foundation, the stated aim of this narrative now switches to the issue of potential applications to clinical diagnosis and treatment. With an estimated *10%* of the population predicted to be affected by some aspect of mental illness during their lifetimes, this new interpretation rightfully offers hope to those who could be thusly afflicted. Furthermore, this additional analysis, in turn, could prompt much feedback on the subject, as well as enhancing the prospects of more effective treatment regimens.

The communicational dynamics underlying mental illness all share a common focus; namely, defined as a dual interplay of double bind and counter double bind maneuvers. In terms of the terminology of Communication Theory, this interpretation is clearly not without controversy. Conventional wisdom on the subject speculates that mental illness is primarily a biochemical disorder treated most effectively through drug therapy. The latter viewpoint, however, is compounded by the extenuating factors of genetics, upbringing, and personal life experience. For example, a number of genetic components have been theorized to mediate susceptibility to schizophrenia through research on identical twins. Nurture theories concerning the genesis of the psychoses have also remained in vogue, as well as theories targeting precipitating traumatic experiences.

In defense of Communication Theory, these disparate viewpoints do not necessarily appear mutually exclusive, but rather appear to complement one another. Certainly, dysfunctional communication remains a key factor in mental disorders, the extreme symptomology generally defying any casual efforts at explanation. Through the aid of the transitional model of mental illness, however, these communicational distortions are ultimately explained in terms of a focus upon excess: an achievement that stands apart from any the physiological or biochemical susceptibilities, therein. The newly proposed transitional model of mental illness is meant to supplement (rather than supplant) currently available treatment options. In essence, this new theory endeavors to supply just one further piece to the puzzle; namely, the broad range of communicational factors underlying mental illness.

This range of communicational factors is most readily apparent at the initial transitional phase of the communicational sequence, as in the personality disorders and various classifications of the mood disorders. The personal focus for the personality disorders is characterized by an extreme degree of emotionality exemplified by the narcissistic personality, the borderline personality, etc. The newcomer transitions directly into a new relationship based upon the realm of excess, effectively contrasting with the more measured prerequisites for the humorous realm. The personality disorders, accordingly, prove less incapacitating than the mood disorders: targeting only particular personal relationships, leaving the group levels (and higher) unaffected.

The mood disorders, in turn, offer a more elaborate clinical picture affecting the group, spiritual, and humanitarian sequence of authority levels. The respective domain of excess is generally more dramatic, often experienced as visions or delusions of a spiritual nature (although scarcely to the disqualified range of extremes seen for schizophrenia). This scarcely diminishes the emotional impact in terms of the patient, for such extreme patterns of communication can lead to perceptual distortions yielding experiences perhaps as real as any other.

The mood disorders, fortunately, are treated through an effective range of drug therapies. Mood dampeners (such as lithium carbonate) are theorized to diminish the degree of emotional excess, restoring patients to a more normal range of functioning. Other radical therapies for clinical depression include electro-convulsive shock therapy (ECT). By shocking the brain into a transient seizure mode, a general reset function is apparently induced: wherein dampening the extremes of mood/emotion over the course of treatment. Indeed, according to Cicero: "There is no grief that time does not lessen and soften," with the travails of depression certainly no exception in this regard.

TREATMENT OPTIONS
TARGETING SCHIZOPHRENIA

Similar insights further remain in order for the counter double bind class of maneuvers, where the extreme degree of disqualification specifies a terminal placement within the dual transitional interchange. This latter class of disorders begins with the personal foundations of the neuroses (obsession-compulsion-phobia-anxiety), in turn, extending to the more abstract realm of the schizophrenias (paraphrenia, catatonia, and hebephrenia). The extreme degree of symptomology associated with schizophrenia generally reflects a confluence of communicational factors based upon the realm of excess, although professed in a thoroughly disqualified fashion. For instance, for obsession neurosis, the personal follower flatteringly acts worshipfully towards the personal authority figure, although denying any willing sense participation therein. Furthermore, for phobia neurosis, the personal follower similarly denies acting critically towards the personal authority figure, wherein disqualifying any willing acknowledgement in terms.

This distinctive pattern further holds true with respect to the remaining classifications of schizophrenia, where the extreme range of disqualification now extends to the more abstract levels within the power hierarchy. This extreme degree of denial directly accounts for one of the most prominent features of schizophrenia; namely, the pronounced flattening of the emotions. Genuine emotion is split-off from the personality in a fully disqualified fashion, a degree of denial severely impacting the emotional life of the patient. This further explains why schizophrenia is so difficult to treat. Patients effectively disqualify any

control they have over their symptoms, with any attempts to reason with patients meeting only with perplexity or resistance.

This general pattern further explains why schizophrenic symptoms appear so bizarre and distressing to the patient: in particular, sensory hallucinations, mood extremes, and other emotional anomalies. For instance, verbal hallucinations represent a disqualification of one's inner thought processes; e.g., it is not really me, but rather an external voice. This does not necessarily mean to imply that these symptoms aren't entirely convincing to the patient. According to many individual reports, the sensory distortions appear exceedingly real, perhaps the result of some indwelling form of self-suggestion/hypnosis phenomenon leading to the most vivid experience imaginable. Along similar lines, hypnosis is often effectively employed in psychotherapy. The hypnotist serves as a surrogate for the disqualification of the patient, frequently eliciting treatment breakthroughs through the power of suggestion alone. Precipitating physical factors (such as an imbalance in neurotransmitter levels) similarly figure prominently in susceptible individuals, which in concert with a dysfunctional environment results in the total syndrome.

A "BROKEN RECORD" THEORY
OF MENTAL ILLNESS

Granted, our fast-paced modern culture is lightheartedly labeled the neurotic generation, although most individuals manage to roll with the punches. Individuals suffering from psychotic episodes present quite a different picture, where a rigid mindset suggests of a dependency upon such maladaptive perspectives. In terms of this radical interpretation, the mentally ill develop their symptomology in response to certain intractable life experiences, a symptom strategy that once may have proven marginally adaptive at the time. These symptoms persist even when the patient is transferred to a more therapeutic environment, where trained professionals aim to reverse the repetition of such a trend.

This recurring scenario appears to be the strongest justification yet for the "broken record" theory of mental illness. The patient appears stuck within the groove of a previous traumatic life experience, whereby prevented from playing-out more adaptive potentialities. Even in the general population, some individuals favor a serious temperament, whereas others appear more humorous or exhibit criminal tendencies. These character extremes extend across a broad range of society as a whole, with well-adjusted individuals able to blend the most effective combination (a truly delicate balancing act). A variable combination of hereditary/psychosocial factors appears to cause some individuals to fixate within an exclusive pattern of communication, even though potentially maladaptive under changing social circumstances. The prude at the social mixer proves as equally out of place as a joker at a funeral parlor. In a similar fashion, the mentally ill patient remains completely at the mercy of his ingrained symptomology, a tactic that originally may have offered some measure of leverage within a pre-existing context. Granted, the life of the institutionalized patient is generally somewhat regimented, a circumstance further contributing to regressive levels of functioning.

EXPANDED TREATMENT OPTIONS

It ultimately falls to the domain of treatment and diagnosis that the potential for the double bind theory of mental illness shines the brightest, uniquely specifying the communicational factors underlying the individual syndromes. The systematic organization of the transitional hierarchy, in turn, proved conducive to the development of the entire 56-part complement of schematic definitions for the realm of mental illness. This cohesive set of definitions specifically spells-out the precise leverage to be gained for each level within the power hierarchy. The specific patterns of communication that trigger a given symptom are uniquely identified, as well as the factors that reinforce its repetition. This basic determination of trigger events could potentially promote a more therapeutic environment, with treatment options tailored directly to the propensities of a given individual. These specific insights, in conjunction with a certain degree of behavior modification when symptoms spontaneously occur, could potentially avert any measure of success in employing such symptoms within a clinical environment.

This particular strategy has already proven quite effective in terms of certain currently available therapies; most notably, the desensitization techniques employed to treat phobia neurosis. A client inordinately fearful of spiders is desensitized through a gradual series of steps designed to demonstrate the inner control he has over his irrational fears. This first consists of talking about spiders, followed by photographs or plastic models, ultimately leading to a controlled encounter with a real spider. At each succeeding step, the patient is deprived of any of the ingrained advantages associated with his phobia: which

(through the process of attrition) ultimately results in a cure. A similar level of success is theoretically possible for the more bizarre realm of the psychoses, where the underlying power dynamics now are more fully understood. At this level, the clinician enjoys the clear advantage, not only in terms of training and experience, but also in light of the lucid thought processes so often lacking in the chronically ill.

PREEMPTIVE TREATMENTS FOR MENTAL ILLNESS

Chronically ill patients remain just one segment of the population to benefit from such a conceptual innovation. The old adage: "prevention is the best medicine" certainly rings true in this regard. A broader understanding of the dynamics for mental illness offers the potential for preemptive detection, even prior to obvious symptoms. These factors should figure most prominently at the family level, where the dynamics of a domineering mother and passive father have been implicated in the genesis schizophrenia in susceptible individuals. Indeed, a broad range of double bind theories for mental illness abound within the literature, although scarcely to the degree of detail achieved within the current transitional model. A broad public awareness of these communicational factors offers the potential for further diminishing dysfunctional communication across society as a whole. Maladaptive patterns in child rearing would similarly come under focus, permitting a more effective means of intervention by relatives or child-protective services. In terms of these concerted efforts, the conditions leading to such chronic dysfunctionality can be attacked on many fronts. Indeed, a multidisciplinary approach is definitely order if the scourge of mental illness is to be banished from the general culture.

The modern-day focus upon on information technology suggests the potential for computer assistance in the treatment regimen. The potential incorporation of the schematic definitions for mental illness within a diagnostic context predicts the potential for an artificially intelligent mental health assistant. Through such specific programming, the AI computer could potentially decode the bizarre symptomology associated with mental illness including the mood disorders and schizophrenia. Far from the somewhat limited human powers of comprehension, the AI assistant could instantaneously detect ongoing patterns of dysfunctional communication, wherein allowing for continuously updated diagnostic parameters in concert with the human staff. Equally definitive treatment options must surely follow leading to a continuously modified therapeutic environment, effectively minimizing any major payback to the patient. The extraordinary computational capabilities predicted for the AI clinician would potentially allow for moment-to-moment adjustments, a feat beyond the dreams of even the most gifted human clinician. The AI assistant would further be immune to the bane of most therapeutic intervention; namely, the problem of counter-transference. This term refers to the subconscious feelings of the therapist that can adversely affect the objective judgement (and proper treatment) of the patient. The AI assistant could serve as a potential safeguard against such subconscious tendencies on the part of the human staff, its sense of ego only simulated; and therefore a readily controllable factor. The specific details for potentially implementing this innovation are reserved for subsequent treatment in Chapter *37*.

A COMPARISON OF THE THREE-DIGIT CODING SYSTEM WITH THE *DSM-IV*

In terms of a final overview, one remaining crucial issue must necessarily be addressed; namely, how the current three-digit coding system fits-in with the prevailing standard model of mental illness. On the surface, the three-digit codes offer just one further perspective in relation to the dominant world-view characterizing the *DSM-series*. Fortunately, there is no potential conflict with the *DSM*-codes, being as the latter are encoded using number-codes beginning with "2" or "3," whereas the current coding system specifies mental disorders beginning with a first-place digit of "4."

A further crucial advantage of the current three-digit coding system is its seamless and systematic organization. In line with its earlier origins, the *DSM*-format arose as a hodgepodge of numbering schemes constructed in a piecemeal sequence of development. The current three-digit coding system, in contrast, is fully systematic and conceptually complete. Once one learns the few basic rules for the numbering scheme, one only need be presented with a unique three-digit number in order to deduce the identity of the respective syndrome (and vice versa). In all fairness, the *DSM*-series proves exceedingly efficient in terms of classifying the personality disorders and the neuroses, permitting a seamless correspondence to the transitional model of mental illness at a personal degree of influence. A similar correspondence to the psychoses, however, is not quite so precise. Here, the Anglo-American system is derived primarily from the work of Kraepe-lin and his successors. The dichotomy between schizophrenia and manic depression is adequately described, although to not much further detail.

A parallel system devised by the German Classificationalists (such as Karl Leonhard), in contrast, provides a wealth of clinical classifications that seamlessly fill out the sum-total of predicted slots for the transitional model of the psychoses. The psychoses mirror the exquisite precision initially established for the personality disorders and the neuroses. Unfortunately, this German system of terminology is not as widely employed as the *DSM*-series, a regrettable shortcoming in light of its newfound facility for validating the transitional model of mental illness.

It must necessarily be stressed that these mental disorders technically exist primarily in the subjective mind of the individual. Particularly with respect to the counter double bind maneuvers, the neurotic individual (for instance) interprets the actions of another in a particular subjective style that triggers their symptom spectrum. The outward motives for the other party, however, may actually be quite different. Therefore, it is this subjective interpretation of the communications from the other that triggers neurosis, not necessarily direct contact with individuals exhibiting any precipitating personality disorder. A similar pattern also applies to schizophrenia, a dynamic not necessarily implying that a direct causal relationship exists in relation to the mood disorders (rather, only the patient's individual interpretations, therein). This logically makes sense, being as the odds of such direct clinical pairings is clearly at variance to the actual incidences of these syndromes in general. This aspect can further be explained in terms of the previously described "broken record" theory of mental illness, where an ingrained pattern of dysfunctional communication offered some perverse relationship advantage during a formative period of development. This is further seen for the related realm of humor and comedy, where natural-born jokers inveterately act humorously no matter what serious or crucial context they are in. Hence, the mental disorders analogously share with humor/comedy and the other transitional variations (criminality and hypercriminality) such an extreme level of impulsivity within an ingrained communicational dynamic. Hopefully, this increased understanding for all such dysfunctional aspects of society may make a major difference in ongoing efforts at their amelioration, ushering in a welcome new era in global peace and cooperation on a truly international scale of influence.

PART-VIII

35

FURTHER MODIFICATIONS TO THE THREE-DIGIT CODING SYSTEM

The current inaugural edition of *Challenges to World Peace: A Global Solution* has endeavored to provide a formal overview of the newly devised three-digit coding system as it relates to promoting and preserving global peace and harmony. As an inaugural edition, a certain number of details were abbreviated in order to facilitate a more comprehensive overview of the basic peace issues at hand. This additional information is more properly the subject for subsequent editions within the series, wherein permitting the inclusion of details not technically crucial to the casual end-user.

The current summary chapter endeavors to suggest avenues for further refinement to the three-digit coding system. Feedback from the global community at large should aid in the development of further upcoming editions. Before entering into such a far-reaching perspective, a general summary of the current version of the three-digit coding system definitely proves in order here, wherein providing a solid conceptual foundation for a discussion of the potential modifications to the system. Indeed, the predicted number of slots within the unified power hierarchy yields a grand-total of *1,040* individual terms, the complete breakdown of which now will be described.

Part I introduced the ten-level hierarchy of the virtues, values, and ideals: reflected in the hierarchial sequence of personal, group, spiritual, humanitarian, and transcendental levels within the power hierarchy. This basic pattern, when further specialized into both authority and follower roles, accounts for the full ten-part hierarchy of ethical groupings within the virtuous mode, resulting in a grand total of forty individual terms. When this total is further extended to include the accessory variations of the virtues, as well as the

general unifying themes, the grand total expands to an even one-hundred terms.

Part II, in turn, targets the related realm of the vices of defect, in direct correspondence to the terminology first proposed by Aristotle. The master hierarchy for the vices of defect directly parallels that previously established for the virtuous mode: an ascending hierarchy of ten authority levels, each invested with individual groupings of vices (for a grand-total of forty). When further extended to include the accessory variations, as well as the general unifying themes, the grand total similarly expands to an even one-hundred terms. This enduring contrast between virtue and vice provides the basic *core*-nucleus for the three-digit coding system, wherein accounting for the majority of the more routine types of ethical communication.

Parts III and **IV** further modified this basic format through the addition of the affiliated realm of excess. The vices of excess represent extreme variations with respect to the virtuous mode. Furthermore, the respective terminology for hyperviolence similarly targets the domain of the vices of defect. In conjunction with the major core-nucleus of virtues/vices, these two additional categories for the realm of excess summate to a grand-total of one-hundred individual terms each: resulting in the master schematic format of *400* individual terms.

Part V, in turn, modifies this initial complement of *400* terms through the aid of the related class of *transitional* power maneuvers. This latter conceptual category "transitions" the new individual into acceptance within the more established ethical categories. The familiar realm of comedy/melodrama is further specified in terms of the newly defined class of the lesser virtues: defined as transitional variations with respect to the virtuous realm. Furthermore, with respect to **Part VI**, the related categories of criminality and hypercriminality further describe transitional inroads into the established realms of the vices of defect and hyperviolence, respectively. Finally, in **Part VII**, the enigmatic sphere of mental illness is further defined in terms of transitions into the subsequent realm of the vices of excess.

This distinctive quartet of transitional power maneuvers is formally defined as the dual interplay of double bind and counter double bind maneuvers within the ascending power hierarchy. This basic pattern, again, doubles the number of predicted terms, with the potential for a grand-total of *400* individual terms for the initial class of double bind maneuvers. The remaining class of counter double bind maneuvers, however, essentially overtaxes the three-digit codes: necessitating the addition of an extra digit separated from the first three by means of a decimal point. Although this additional listing of counter double bind maneuvers is designated utilizing the numeral "one" in the fourth-digit spot, this leaves the remaining other nine slots to be filled with alternate options; namely, the symmetrical or acceptance maneuvers, as well as the respective accessory variations, etc.

This additional set of ten options specified for the extra decimal place adds a heightened degree of complexity to an already elaborate coding system. The first three digits within the coding system specified an initial complement of one-thousand individual terms. The addition of the fourth digit (by definition) expands this overall pattern to roughly ten-thousand individual terms. It should be mentioned that not all of the one-thousand preliminary terms are subject to the addition of an extra decimal place. Only the *256* individual classifications of double bind maneuvers are modified in such a fashion, indicative of the dual interplay of counter double bind maneuvers.

This rather limited complement of *256* transitional terms, nevertheless, results in a tenfold increase of *2,560* four-digit slots. Accordingly, it is estimated that an additional *25* pages of tables would be required just to list each of these individual terms, along with the respective four-digit code numbers. Many of these variations, however, are fairly apparent in terms of phraseology: such as symmetrical loyalty, acceptance of loyalty, etc. Consequently, a comprehensive listing of each of these formal options will not be attempted in this inaugural edition of the coding system. Nevertheless, this supplementary *2,560*-part complement of four-digit terms, when taken in concert with the original *800*-part complement of three-digit terms, results in a master format of *3,360* coded terms: a comprehensive system consistent with the dramatic degree of complexity underlying the human emotions.

THE PHANTOM AND FANTASY DIALOGUES

The comprehensive three-digit coding system (at the current juncture) has encompassed only the domain of active human dialogue. Other formats prove equally feasible, however; namely, those referred to as the phantom and fantasy dialogues. The *phantom* dialogue is defined as communication directed to an absent individual (the phantom). It includes letter writing (in a printed mode), or the monologue/soliloquy (in the spoken form). The *fantasy* dialogue, in turn, takes this trend to the limit. Both parties are relegated to the phantom role, as in the literary genre of fiction (where all parties are fictitious). Consequently, the three-digit coding system similarly extends to the realm of the phantom/fantasy dialogues as well.

In terms of the technical specifics, only eight of the original ten first-place digits within the system have been fully accounted for, leaving the last two digits (9 and 0) to fulfill this crucial function. Here, "9" is attributed to the phantom dialogue, an assignment easy to remember when the "P" (for phantom) is rotated backwards on its axis. The remaining digit "0" is reserved for the fantasy dialogue, being as there is relatively little of substance to ground it in reality. The following two sections examine the phantom/fantasy dialogues in terms of their formal applications to the three-digit coding system. A complete listing of the virtuous themes for the phantom/fantasy dialogues is schematically depicted in **Figs. 35A** and **35B**, providing a convenient reference source for the upcoming sections to follow.

THE PHANTOM DIALOGUE:
A MONOLOGUE IN WORDS

In terms of our modern mobile society, one often enters into relationships separated by barriers to direct communication. Communication doesn't cease, but rather switches from verbal to written form, as in letter writing to a friend. Here, I record my internal dialogue in order to communicate with you in a written format. In terms of this phantom form of dialogue, I carefully record my feelings intended for your reaction, in turn, filling in the counter-perspectives you might employ if you were present. This reading of insights into the motives of another is a traditional literary device intended to simulate the continuity characterizing a more direct style of dialogue.

These fixed roles are reversed for the reader of the letter, in that the role for which the letter is intended is already anticipated. The letter reader takes on the formal role of the phantom, wherein feelings expressed during the writing of the letter are transferred in terms of the time-displaced dialogue. In this two-stage fashion, the phantom dialogue simulates a direct dialogue, although in a disjointed fashion clearly lacking in the flexible of a direct dialogue. A similar pattern applies to the soliloquy upon a stage, with the audience taking over the active role of the phantom. The ritual of prayer and supplication can similarly be regarded as a phantom dialogue, although the more religiously-minded among us might insist it is really a two-way dialogue.

Letter-writing actually represents a special case of the mental dialogues that fill-up our introspective moments, although now recorded in written form. Also known as the *self*-dialogue, the mind is generally flexible enough to take on (in imagination) a role that is not present in this time of solitude/introspection. It is chiefly through this cross style of dialogue that I am able to plan a future course of action by imagining how friends view me in various circumstances, wherein preparing accordingly (an aspect somewhat akin to diary writing). Indeed, whether one relies upon a diary, a letter, or a soliloquy: the basic impact of the phantom dialogue remains true to its focus.

9118 – THE PLEDGE

Granted, letter-writing is primarily a personal activity, generally targeting the interpersonal levels within the power hierarchy. The phantom dialogue, however, also extends to the higher authority levels, wherein affiliated with a wide variety of literary traditions. These traditional themes are specialized into two basic categories depending on whether the authority or follower roles are in focus at the time. The respective sequence of authority themes is defined as the pledge-proclamation-edict-chronicle. The first mentioned theme of the *pledge* suggests an active style of personal authority role expressing through the theme of individualism, extending to a phantom sense through a generic style of vow. One informs all in attendance that a personal surety (in the form of an action or guarantee) is assured under current circumstances. A pledge also extends to written format, as in a formal guarantee of financial support with respect to the fund-raising activities of benevolent organizations.

9138 – THE PROCLAMATION

The personal characteristics of the pledge, in turn, extend to a group sphere of influence with respect to the civic prerequisites of the *proclamation*. The ruler, as group authority figure, issues an open proclamation to all his subjects, a phantom expression of his authority status in terms of the public at large. To achieve the maximum impact, the proclamation has traditionally been issued in a written format, such as an inscribed parchment nailed up in the marketplace during medieval times. Through this public display of authority status (and subsequent word of mouth), the dictates of the monarch eventually extended across the length and breadth of the realm: wherein eliminating the excuse of ignorance in failing to conform to these royal dictates.

9158 – THE EDICT

The political focus of the proclamation, in turn, extends to a universal realm with respect to the traditions of the *edict*. Here issues of an international focus are promulgated in a global sense, as in the dictates of a religious council, where the spiritual authority issues an edict to the attention of the spiritual congregation. During the Middle Ages, when the Roman Catholic Church wielded supreme authority over Western culture, the Pope (or his designees) projected such power through the aid of a written edict, a decree that the faithful were obliged to obey. The edict continues the tradition of the pledge and the proclamation in promulgating such outward authority.

9178 – THE CHRONICLE

The universal sphere of influence for the edict, in turn, acquires elements befitting a humanitarian perspective: as reflected in the enduring traditions of the *chronicle*. It differs from genre of annals with respect to its more comprehensive character, wherein concerned with grander aspects of human history, such as the Medieval Chronicles or Viking Sagas. A running commentary of historical events is set down in written form for the edification of all future generations to come. This is recorded in terms of a prototypical humanitarian stance, although now assuming the form of a phantom dialogue that remains meaningful over a span of ages. Indeed, all such communications with future generations must necessarily be regarded as a phantom dialogue, taking into full account the gradual unfolding of historical events.

9118 – *The* PLEDGE *Phantom* - **Individualism** **Personal Authority**	**9128 – *The* GRANT** *Phantom* - **Pragmatism** **Personal Follower**
9138 – PROCLAMATION *Phantom* - **Personalism** **Group Authority**	**9148 – *The* CHARTER** *Phantom* - **Utilitarianism** **Group Representative**
9158 – *The* EDICT *Phantom* - **Romanticism** **Spiritual Authority**	**9168 – *The* SANCTION** *Phantom* - **Ecclesiasticism** **Spiritual Disciple**
9178 – *The* CHRONICLE *Phantom* - **Ecumenism** **Humanitarian Authority**	**9188 – *The* TESTAMENT** *Phantom* - **Eclecticism** **Humanitarian Follower**

Fig. 35A – The Themes for the Virtuous *Phantom* Dialogues

9128 – THE GRANT

The initial sequence of phantom themes for the authority roles, in turn, is complemented by the parallel traditions for the follower roles: respectively defined as the grant, the charter, the sanction, and the testament. For instance, the first-mentioned theme of the *grant* primarily suggests a personal sphere of influence. The personal follower rewardingly "grants" a privilege status in response to the pledge from the personal authority figure. As such, the pledge/grant mirrors the interplay of the main themes of individualism and pragmatism, although now invoking a more remote phantom character. The rewarding aspects of the grant are particularly evident in the sphere of academic research, where financial support is offered in return for services intended to further scientific investigation. Consequently, the reciprocal interplay of authority/follower roles is preserved with respect to the phantom prerequisites of the grant.

9148 – THE CHARTER

The personal characteristics for the grant, in turn, acquire a civic significance with respect to the group follower theme of the *charter*. The charter is primarily encountered in terms of group contexts such as business organizations, clubs, or colonial endeavors. The group representative grants "charter" status in response to the proclaimed sense of efficacy expressed by the group authority figure. This is exceedingly reminiscent of the utilitarian prerequisites previously established within a non-phantom context. Indeed, much of the settlement of the New World was facilitated through the granting of charters, where the services of willing colonists (such as the Pilgrims) were chartered by legal decree. Consequently, in terms of this cooperative style of group endeavor, the intended labor of the colonists was supported through a land-use charter bestowed in recognition of their concerted effort.

9168 – THE SANCTION

Ascending, once again, to the next higher spiritual level, in turn, gives way to the universal prerequisites associated with the *sanction*. The sanction is virtually synonymous with religious themes, wherein reflected in the direct dialogue nature of ecclesiasticism. As representative for the spiritual congregation, the spiritual disciple solemnly grants his sanction in response to the universal

edict expressed by the spiritual authority figure, wherein imparting a sense of sacredness to the proceedings. Consequently, through his formal sanction, the respective spiritual disciple restores an equal balance of power to the interplay of authority/follower roles, at least in terms of such a limited phantom context.

9188 – THE TESTAMENT

The preliminary sequence of the grant, the charter, and the sanction ultimately culminates with respect to the enduring humanitarian perspective of the *testament*. As a literary device, it refers to a last will and testament, or any tradition that bears witness to (or makes a covenant with) a scriptural context. The first-mentioned legacy style of testament shares with the sanction/charter a bestowal of good will, although now relating to surviving generations. The latter "witness" style of testament developed in the ecclesiastical tradition of the medieval age, generally dealing with lofty theological themes. In either case, the testament preserves the general focus of the first three themes, mirroring the ascending sequence of authority roles in a complementary follower fashion.

The complete listing of themes for the phantom dialogue is depicted in **Fig. 35A**, depicted in concert with the respective three-digit codes. Please note further that the respective code designations all begin with the first-place digit of "9" reflecting their phantom status. The remaining three digits are identical to the codes for the non-phantom complement of themes; e.g., the pledge (9118) is a single-digit modification of the original three-digit code for individualism (118) - and so forth. In this elementary fashion, the phantom dialogues represent a stepwise variation on the main complement of virtuous themes initially described in Chapter 9, a formal pattern that, in turn, extends to the remaining complement of fantasy dialogues, as well.

THE FANTASY DIALOGUE: THE REALM OF FICTIONAL IMAGINATION

In a brief review of the phantom dialogue, the written word bridges the gap not only for space, but for time as well. This proves a crucial advantage in that the written word is essentially permanent, as opposed to the ephemeral quality of the spoken word. The written tradition allows one to communicate to future generations long after one's death. Indeed, most libraries are crammed with dialogues from the past, made meaning-

0118 – MYTH/FABLE *Fantasy* - **Individualism** **Personal Authority**	**0128 – RHETORIC** *Fantasy* - **Pragmatism** **Personal Follower**
0138 – LEGEND *Fantasy* - **Personalism** **Group Authority**	**0148 – PROPAGANDA** *Fantasy* - **Utilitarianism** **Group Representative**
0158 – PARABLE *Fantasy* - **Romanticism** *Spiritual Authority*	**0168 – PROPHESY** *Fantasy* - **Ecclesiasticism** **Spiritual Disciple**
0178 – ALLEGORY *Fantasy* - **Ecumenism** **Humanitarian Authority**	**0188 – UTOPIANISM** *Fantasy* - **Eclecticism** **Humanitarian Follower**

Fig. 35-B – The Themes for the Virtuous *Fantasy* Dialogues

ful to consecutive generations of readers. The phantom dialogue, however, is still a fairly restrictive writing style. The roles are rigidly fixed for both the reader and writer alike. Over time, the audience may change to such a degree as to make the material outdated, scarcely more than a quaint curiosity.

The time-honored tradition for circumventing this shortcoming entails the use of an alternate form of recorded dialogue termed the *fantasy* dialogue. Also commonly known as fiction, the writer is divorced from any direct personal involvement within the work, wherein freeing creativity conducive to a truly imaginative narrative. The reader, likewise, is not trapped into any particular role, rather free to identify with any of the fictional characters. This vaunted sense of imagination is not limited simply to gazing inward or manipulating a range of images. The truly unfettered imagination further extends to a suspension of conventional presupposition or belief: an entertaining simulation of make-believe, as in creatively pretending or anticipating. According to Gaston Bachelard: "Imagination is not the faculty of forming images of reality, it is the faculty of forming images which go beyond reality, which turn reality into song. It is a superhuman quality." Consequently, good fiction it broadly appealing in that it generally has some meaning for everyone, whether child or adult. By restricting the content to a fantasy level, the message is generalized to all ages and cultures, as witnessed in the great popularity of mythology and lore from ancient times.

0118 – THE FABLE

Similar to the pattern previously established for the phantom dialogue, there must necessarily exist a parallel complement of literary traditions for each of the fictional levels within the ascending power hierarchy. In the latter case, the source of the dialogue is fictionally disqualified, even though a lesson is still taught. This is often achieved by converting all relevant characters into personifications of animals, such as exemplified in Aesop's Fables. A common-sense lesson (such as perseverance) is proclaimed using animal stereotypes, as in a footrace pitting the determined tortoise against the overconfident hare. Furthermore, lessons concerning industriousness contrast how the dedicated ant and the carefree grasshopper prepare for the pending winter. Sage wisdom is taught to another reflecting the one-to-one style of interplay characterizing the personal level within the power hierarchy. The fable represents a true style of fantasy dialogue, in that the

basic import of the message remains unchanged even over the course of millennia.

0138 – THE LEGEND

The personal focus of the myth/fable, in turn, extends to a civic sphere of influence with respect to the group authority theme of *legends*. The legend is distinguished from the fable in that the legend generally contains a more historical context (and less of the supernatural). Legends primarily specify the lore of the common people, wherein exalting the heritage or national spirit. In a traditional sense, legends are narratives concerning great folk heroes, although idealized to some degree: such as Paul Bunyan or Casey Jones. The group authority figure enjoys a legendary, almost mythical quality, a status befitting a leader among men. This is further reflected (in a non-fantasy sense) with respect to the class of personal ideals (glory-honor-dignity-integrity). The legend serves as a fitting exemplar to us all, a paragon of virtue/courage so sorely lacking in our modern age.

0158 – THE PARABLE

Although legendary heroism proves a fitting fictional device at the group level, the next higher spiritual realm celebrates the related fantasy technique of the *parable*. Here the spiritual authority figure employs fictional imagery to press a moral point, such as occasions when Christ uses parables to teach a lesson. According to Matthew 10:13, the disciples inquire of Christ (following his Parable of the Sower) why he speaks to them in parables. Christ replies: "To you it has been given to know the secrets of the kingdom of heaven, but to them it has not been given ... This is why I speak to them in parables, because seeing they do not see, and hearing they do not hear, nor do they understand." Christ's symbolic use of parables effectively alludes to religious truths that may be too abstract or controversial to be accepted by the uninitiated. The common man inserts himself into the story line through such a fantasy dialogue device. A fisherman gets the point of "a net cast into the sea," whereas the herder feels for "the lost sheep," and the farmer grasps "a seed cast upon barren ground."

0178 – ALLEGORY

The ascending sequence of the myth, legend, and the parable ultimately extends to the more enduring (humanitarian) prerequisites for the *allegory*. It represents an extended sense of metaphor through which persons, objects, or actions within a narrative are equated with meanings that lie outside the narration. A given concept, therefore, is cast in the guise of another, often taking the form of visual imagery. Indeed, an entire cast of characters may be personified in terms of abstract qualities, with the action/setting further reflecting the relationships between the abstractions. The allegory may lead to fictitious, mythical, or historical themes. Its truest test lies in the observation that the abstractions represent meanings independent of the surface action within the story: whether religious, political, moral, or satirical. The form of allegory most relevant to the humanitarian realm is known as the *apologue*, a short allegory emphasizing chiefly moral themes. In concert with the first three terms, the abstract theme of allegory effectively rounds-out the ascending hierarchy of (authority) fantasy themes.

0128 – RHETORIC

The orderly progression of fantasy themes for the authority hierarchy exhibits further parallels to the remaining sequence of terms based upon the follower hierarchy: namely, rhetoric-propaganda-prophecy-utopianism. For instance, the first listed theme of *rhetoric* is defined as persuasive or supportive discourse, an interpretation dating at least to the time of classical Greece. For the Sophists, rhetoric imparted effectiveness to public speaking and oratory: denoting a style of literary composition of an emotional or imaginative nature, aiming to sway the audience through fair means or foul. Indeed, as Isocrates once noted: "Rhetoric is the art of making great matters small, and small things great." The rhetorical style differs from simple testimony in that the personal reputation of the speaker is not crucial for driving home the point of the message. Indeed, many of these classical rhetorical strategies still find popular expression today. In terms of its emotional appeal, coupled with the generalized role of the speaker, establishes rhetoric as a true fantasy style of dialogue, although specialized towards personal ends.

0148 – PROPAGANDA

The personalized nature of rhetoric, in turn, extends to the group prerequisites for *propaganda*. It is defined as a rhetorical literary device consisting of stirring testimonials from members within the group in order to sway group sentiment, as a whole. More generally the highly emotional testimonials consist primarily of stereotyped cliches chiefly unsubstantiated by fact. Witness, for instance, the wishful propaganda campaign waged by the Fascist and Communist parties during the last century. Although the stigma of propaganda (to a large part) depends upon which side of the fence one is on, the true danger arises in failing to recognize propaganda for what it presumes to be; namely, a fantasy dialogue, and nothing more.

0168 – PROPHESY

The disqualified character of propaganda, in turn, extends to a universal sphere of influence with respect to the spiritual follower theme of *prophecy*. The disciple/prophet attributes the moralistic content of his message to the vagaries of divine inspiration, dream imagery, or visions. This spirited literary device aims to break the shackles of ordinary reality through the aid of symbolic portrayals of virtually epic proportions. This is particularly true in the New Testament Book of Revelation, an elaborate literary tradition replete with dreamlike imagery and mythical symbolism.

Prophecy is mainly distinguished from divination, in that the latter aims to predict future events through signs in nature or rituals of chance. Prophecy, in contrast, takes well-established elements of religious belief and then embellishes them within an unfamiliar context (generally an event projected far into the future). As such, prophecy represents a disqualified form of fantasy dialogue in relation to the spiritual congregation, wherein permitting unfettered freedom for dealing with themes of a controversial nature. Prophesy shares with rhetoric and propaganda a clear stretch of the imagination, although now appealing to a supernatural influence as the rationale for its existence.

0188 – UTOPIANISM

The remaining humanitarian variation within ascending hierarchy of terms ultimately culminates with respect to the related theme of *utopianism*. The term derives from a compound of the Greek *ou-* (not) and *topos* (place), collectively translated as "good place" or "no place." The utopian tradition certainly reflects this range of ambiguity, denoting an imaginary society enjoying perfect legal, economic, and political systems of governance. This fantasy conception of utopia is offered as surpassing any current social structure due to the prevailing sense of harmony, utility, and reason enjoyed by all.

In terms of Western culture, the term was employed as the title of a treatise published by

St. Thomas More in 1516. Utopia was described as an island where justice and prosperity reigned supreme, its inhabitants having learned to subordinate their selfish desires to rational pursuits. In modern usage, Utopia stands for any imaginary society where harmonious conditions prevail (fanciful contrasting with reality). Many versions of utopia have been devised since More's treatise, although each reflects the spirit of the age with respect to unfettered hope and optimism. Regardless of the individual traditions therein, this alluring spirit of utopianism represents a fantasy dialogue specialized to encompass an enduring humanitarian perspective, a virtuous dialogue applicable to all ages and cultures. In concert with the first three themes, utopianism effectively rounds out the stepwise description of the follower realm for the fantasy class of dialogue.

THREE-DIGIT CODING PARAMETERS FOR THE PHANTOM / FANTASY DIALOGUES

In summary, the completed description of the additional class of phantom and fantasy dialogues roughly triples the scope of the three-digit coding system. Both the phantom and fantasy dialogues are characterized by their respective categories of virtuous themes: a format analogous to the themes for the direct dialogues previously described in Chapter 9. Consequently, through the simple addition of an extra first-place digit (either a nine or zero), the additional set of phantom/fantasy themes is effectively incorporated into the three-digit coding system. For instance, the *grant* is specified as 9128 for the phantom dialogue, whereas the notion of *rhetoric* is assigned the code of 0128 for the fantasy dialogue, both of which build upon the more fundamental, direct dialogue of pragmatism (128).

In addition to the overall categories of general unifying themes, a similar style of code modification, in turn, extends the individual virtues, values, and ideals in relation to the phantom/fantasy dialogues. According to this expanded format, the newly instituted first-place digits (9 and 0) are similarly attached to the individual virtuous codes reflective of these alternate forms of dialogue. For instance, the phantom form of justice (141) is now modified as 9141, whereas the respective fantasy version is specified as 0141. A similar pattern, in turn, extends to each of the remaining virtuous terms, effectively tripling the number of potential terms within the virtuous realm. Furthermore, this basic pattern also holds true for the remaining realm of the vices of defect. Here the phantom form of vengeance (541) is alter-nately designated as 9541, whereas the respective fantasy variation is specified as 0541.

This formal pattern diverges somewhat, however, in that there fails to be any convincing complement of phantom/fantasy themes in relation to the vices of defect. This shortcoming is explained in terms of the general disparagement the realm of defect displays within the established literary traditions. Consequently, the requisite verbal labels for the phantom/fantasy dialogues do not appear to have been incorporated into the standard lexicon for the vices of defect. This shortcoming does not necessarily preclude incorporating variations of these themes in terms of the direct dialogue format. Here, phantom-villainy and fantasy-villainy are schematically coded as 9538 and 0538, respectively. Indeed, a similar coding strategy also extends to the remaining domain of excess/hyperviolence. Furthermore, this pattern similarly holds true for the related class of *transitional* power maneuvers; e.g., the lesser virtues, criminality, hypercriminality, and mental illness.

Through this schematic modification employing the addition of an extra first-place digit (9 or 0), the scope initially established for the direct dialogues now roughly triples in scope. The basic complement of *1,040* individual terms now formally expands to *3,120* potential terms in relation to the phantom/fantasy dialogues. Consequently, in terms of the extra complement of phantom and fantasy dialogues, the potential for a four (and even five) digit coding system now becomes conceptually complete.

GLOBAL APPLICATIONS TO THE THREE-DIGIT CODING SYSTEM

In final analysis, it must necessarily be emphasized that the current inaugural edition of *Challenges to World Peace* primarily remains a work in progress. Perhaps an equal number of synonyms (and related variations) have not fully been accounted for within the current system. Indeed, a ground-breaking study by Allport and Odbert (1936) suggests precisely such a potential range of additions. As suggested in its formal title: Trait Names: A Psycho-Lexical Study, this study conducted an exhaustive survey of the English language, wherein identifying a grand total of 18,000+ individual terms relating to character traits, with a significant number also relating to affective issues. This particular list of character traits actually served as a major reference source for the current system of *1,040* individual terms, accounting for many of the major categories of ethical terms.

How the remaining *17,000+* individual terms fit into this initial system remains to be determined. Through the addition of an extra range of decimal places, however, an enhanced degree of detail could ultimately be achieved. Affective categories that are more generalized than allowed within the system would be assigned two-digit code numbers reflecting their broader sphere of influence. In this modified sense, a more all-inclusive perspective on affective language might eventually be achieved. Although future researchers might see fit to propose minor modifications to the general master format, the discerning reader can rest assured that the major numerical categories should persist precisely as outlined.

Perhaps the greatest strength underscoring the three-digit coding system resides in its all-inclusive nature, wherein accounting for virtually every major category of affective language known to exist. These categories fit seamlessly into the respective ten-level hierarchy, permitting a truly convincing simulation of emotional communication in general. Indeed, based upon a limited number of elementary assumptions; namely, the principles of instrumental conditioning, and the concept of the metaperspective, the ascending hierarchy of stepwise transformations ultimately leads to the master *1,040* complement of ethical terms respectively outlined within the three-digit coding system.

It should further be emphasized, however, that the current system (by definition) is technically applicable only to the English-speaking language tradition. Fortunately, the English language has assumed the role of "lingua franca" for the global community, making its broad appeal particularly effective for the current edition. Certainly, a wide range of language traditions could similarly benefit from cross-cultural versions offering the potential for a universal understanding of the emotions, in general. Many affiliated applications prove far too significant to be restricted solely to an Anglo-American specialization, with potential benefits extending to all segments within the global community.

MULTI-LEVEL SEQUENCES OF ETHICAL TERMS

Should this general range of ethical terms not seem dramatic enough, one further level complexity, in turn, emerges with respect to the combined sequences of terms. The individual affective terms are combined into multi-part sequences of two (or more) related terms. Each of the four major ethical categories (by definition) exhibits the potential for transitioning directly into one another. For instance, the basic *glory*-maneuver transitions into the vices of excess as *vanity*, or into the vices of defect as *infamy*. The potential number of step-wise transformations expands exponentially when multiplied by the sum-total of respective terms. For instance, the *40* individual virtues and values transition, point-for-point, with the three remaining classifications of vices, resulting in a grand total of *120* distinct options. Duplicating this basic pattern across the remaining categories ultimately expands to a grand total of *560* unique two-stage transitions of ethical terms.

When the related class of three-stage transitions is further added into the mix (for instance, glory-to-vanity-to-infamy,) the potential grand-total expands to the square of *560* (or approximately a third of a million). The further consideration of four-stage transitions (and higher) quickly reaches astronomical proportions. This virtually unlimited potential for multiple transformations essentially explains the unfathomable complexity of the human mind. Certainly one rarely repeats the same exact train of thought over the course of a lifetime. Indeed, the most likely scenario for such a rare occurrence extends to the memory-retrieval of such a past contextual interchange. Consequently, it could further be argued that all memories of an emotional nature are stored in terms of such discrete transitional sequences, a speculation scarcely lost on the related programming issues predicted for the ethical simulation of artificial intelligence described in the upcoming Chapter *37*.

In conclusion, the completed description of the phantom and fantasy dialogues offers further crucial inroads towards maintaining global peace and harmony. Indeed, it proves particularly crucial to distinguish between phantom-directed words printed upon a page versus directly ongoing classes of live communication. Furthermore, the dramatic influence of fictionally-derived fantasy dialogues in relation to the accumulated literary traditions of the world must similarly be tempered in terms of political influence on the world scene today. Whereas the profound influence of political manifestos or apocalyptic scripture appears to hold considerable sway in the court of public opinion, a more realistic evaluation of these variations on the phantom and fantasy dialogues must necessarily be instituted if enduring progress in favor of succeeding generations is rationally to be ensured for the foreseeable future.

36

GLOBAL PERSPECTIVES FOR PROMOTING WORLD PEACE

The completed description of the specifics for the three-digit coding system invites further general predictions of its potential role on the world scene today. Through a radical modification of Aristotle's enduring Theory of the Mean, a more balanced sense of conceptual symmetry is established within the sphere of ethical inquiry. This all-inclusive system comprised of three groupings of vice (and one of virtue), in turn, raises the further critical issue; namely, the categories of vices outnumber the virtues by the somewhat disturbing ratio of 3-to-1. A more ethically neutral system was initially predicted, in contrast to the general preponderance of negative classifications that now occurs.

The negative connotations of a number of the categories of vice, however, actually prove somewhat misleading, calling for further evaluation of the motivational dynamics at issue. Each of the four basic ethical categories is assigned a specific plus-or-minus numerical value based upon its inherent degree of adaptability, as well as its potential for causing emotional harm. For instance, beginning with the realm of the major virtues, this category is assigned (without reservation) an overall value of (+1) on a scale of zero to one: reflecting its inherent adaptability and positive functionality within a given interaction.

On the opposite side of the ledger, the corresponding realm of the vices of defect would similarly be expected to rate a corresponding (-1) rating based upon its contrasting relationship to the virtuous realm. This initial impression, however, proves somewhat misleading in that lessons derived from the realm of defect often can prove adaptive to the individual. In a natural setting, for instance, a food source that had been exhausted directly signals to the organism that further such resources should be found soon.

A similar circumstance occurs in the realm of human relationships, as dramatized in the much-publicized phenomenon of celebrity stalking. In this latter instance, the avid fan solicitously seeks the attentions of his celebrity figure in an outward expression of such notable influences. The celebrity, however, is generally overwhelmed by the rigors of his public status, wherein unable to personally interact with each and every one of his fans (although in principle he might like to). The standard form letter addressed to the fan-base is typically taken in stride, a fairly non-threatening rejection in terms. Although this interchange represents an adaptive learning experience for the rational individual, its basic import is generally lost on celebrity stalkers, who refuse to take such practical realities into account. Celebrity stalkers often obliquely misinterpret the benign import of message, sometimes venturing into the realm of bad taste, or the even rarer extremes of hyperviolence. In formal acknowledgement of this essential adaptive function, the earlier rating of (-1) for the vices of defect now seems overly harsh, with the assignment of (-1/2) perhaps more relevant to this discussion.

This modified context scarcely appears applicable to the related sphere of hyperviolence. There is little justification for the drastic behaviors characterizing the extreme realm of hyperviolence; hence, the unequivocal rating of (-1) is specified here. This leaves open only a respective determination of the final realm of the vices of excess, a sphere of excess entirely based within the virtuous realm. This remaining category amounts to somewhat of a special case in that the vices of excess expand upon the virtues to the degree that would fit the definition of a vice, although scarcely to the negative degree previously established for the realm of defect. Indeed, a cursory survey of the vices of excess (e.g., pride, shame, envy, jealousy, etc.) suggests more in the way of bad taste than any overt sense of malice. These vices of excess, however, can prove extremely irritating to those unlucky enough to be directly involved. This basic grouping, accordingly, is assigned the less than absolute value of (**+1/2**), reflecting this category's more casual foundation within the virtuous realm. It should further be emphasized that several of these ratings could have been scaled up or down to some degree, although the true point this exercise aims for an overall evaluation. It remains to ultimately add-up the sum total of numerical values for each of the four calculations; namely, (**+1.5**) for the virtuous mode *vs.* (**-1.5**) for the vices, resulting in a grand total of zero, a direct verification of the ethically-neutral status initially predicted.

APPLICATIONS TO HARMONY ON A GLOBAL SCALE

This even sense of ethical neutrality, however, scarcely agrees with what is currently seen on the world scene today. Indeed, in terms of our modern technological age, one might rightfully argue that the balance of power is actually skewed towards the positive end of the spectrum. The highly interconnected global marketplace certainly specifies such a cooperative style of positive interface. Here, a general rule of law has endured virtually uninterrupted since its first modest beginnings during the Bronze Age. This impressive track record certainly suggests a selective advantage towards positive interactions. Although some degree of criminality has always existed down the ages, the prime directive of civilized society aims to ensure an equitable sense of reciprocity conducive to free trade and commerce. This founding principle traces its origins to the instinctual foundations for operant conditioning; namely, fair goods at a fair price. Indeed, the general state of world affairs has never been better with the exception of minor border skirmishes and terrorist incursions.

This positive outlook would necessarily diminish should the unthinkable ever occur; namely, the unforeseen breakdown of the prevailing social order. Nothing short of a nuclear winter (or other such global disaster) would reach drastic enough proportions to spark a global Dark Age. The residual vestiges of law and order would generally serve to dampen all but the worst of possible scenarios, although the balance of cooperation would undoubtedly skew towards the negative end of the scale. As so often occurs in history, a tempo-

rary reversal should remain exactly that in keeping with the indomitable collective spirit governing all human endeavors.

FOUNDATIONS FOR A WORLD SYSTEM OF ETHICS

This conflict between the forces of order/disorder remains a particularly crucial factor with respect to the major ethical systems of the world. For instance, as the enduring foundation for Christian ethics, the Golden Rule (Do unto others, as you would have others do unto you) is founded primarily upon an appeal to empathic principles. Accordingly, it is featured in the scriptures of virtually every major world religion; including Judaism, Buddhism, Islam, Hinduism, and Taoism. The Golden Rule places a supreme premium on cooperative styles of virtuous behavior, although these noble ideals do not always "square" in non-cooperative types of circumstances. As a general rule, the Golden Rule proves particularly difficult to enforce in situations where others might tend to take advantage of such noble inclinations.

This latter principle of self-interest (sometimes termed the Iron Rule) promotes a selfish agenda at the expense of the more noble principles embodied in the Golden Rule. It is a more prosaically defined as: "Do unto others before they can do unto you," a ruthless expression of selfish competition. In contrast to the Golden Rule, the Iron Rule is often the unspoken precept of the rich and powerful, as amply illustrated in the perpetual sequence of tyrants and dictators throughout recorded history. This primal rule of self-interest is formally encountered in the principles of the zero-sum game; namely, "your loss is my gain," as in the unforgiving law of the jungle. It is scarcely surprising that the darker side of empathy enters into consideration precisely at this juncture. A keen understanding of the motivations of others is essential for achieving the deception or manipulation that exemplifies with the cunning practice of the Iron Rule.

In defense of the Golden Rule, a slightly different formulation effectively addresses this vulnerability to the Iron Rule: stated in modified terms as: "Do not do unto others what you would not have them do unto you." Sometimes referred to as *The Silver* Rule, it forbids any descent into the realm of defect, wherein complementing with the more positive prerequisites of the Golden Rule. The Silver Rule prohibits retaliation in any form to harm done by another, equivalent to (but not quite a drastic as) Christ's admonition to "turn

THE GOLDEN RULE	THE SILVER RULE
"Do unto others as you would have them do unto you."	"Do not do unto others what you would not have them do unto you."
THE BRONZE RULE	THE IRON RULE
"Repay goodness with goodness, but evil with justice."	"Do unto others before they can do unto you."

Figure 36 – The Reigning World Ethical Strategies

the other cheek" when attacked. It traditionally equates to the strategy of nonviolent resistance against unfair governmental policies, as successfully expounded by Mohandas Gandhi in terms of the oppressive British occupation of India.

This strategy, again, was resurrected in the context of the non-violent resistance to racial segregation promoted by Rev. Martin Luther King Jr. during the Civil Rights era. Both civic leaders advised against retaliation towards one's oppressors, although also specifying noncompliance to unjust demands. This non-violent strategy of civil disobedience aimed to provoke a sense of empathy in the hearts of the oppressors, although such defiance could lead to a great personal sacrifice on the part the righteous. Although the Silver Rule proves effective under ideal circumstances, it can just as easily be exploited, particularly when one's oppressors remain unmoved by such a stirring appeal to conscience.

THE GLOBAL SUPREMACY OF THE LAW OF EQUIVALENT RESPONSE

The general standard for ethics down through the ages has unerringly been a hybrid of the principles underlying both the Golden and Iron Rules in what has suggestively been termed the Bronze Rule according to the late Carl Sagan's (1993) insightful analysis of the subject. Confucius perhaps best stated this rule as: "Repay kindness with kindness, but evil with justice;" in essence, the strategy of repaying "like with like." This basic paradigm is directly reflected in nature with respect to the principles of equilibrium and homeostasis. In fact, this basic strategy was previously mentioned in Chapter *21* within the

context of the *symmetrical* power maneuvers; e.g., responding back in kind what originally had been offered.

With respect to the base precepts of Iron Rule, however, the Law of Equivalent Response is typically moderated to some degree, as reflected in the "eye for an eye, tooth for a tooth" pronouncement of the Old Testament. Although this scriptural quotation is often cited as condoning violence, it actually proclaims *only* an eye, and *only* a tooth, whereupon lessening the tendency towards escalation in conflict disputes. In a more positive sense, the Golden Rule continues to specify the *reciprocity* implicit within the virtuous realm, particularly those cooperative impulses where "one good turn deserves another." This virtuous sense of cooperation serves as the enduring foundation for civilization itself, providing a stable environment for conducting business and commerce.

Whereas this cooperative style of strategy proves exceedingly effective in the virtuous mode, its darker version is all too susceptible to the formation of lasting feuds and vendettas. Few options remain for escaping such a self-perpetuating cycle. This latter shortcoming, however, can ultimately be avoided through the implementation of periodic overtures of forgiveness, wherein preemptively short-circuiting escalating conflict cycles. In this modified sense, this "like-for-like" strategy embodied in the Bronze Rule amounts to the prevailing moral standard on the world scene today. In fact, it is particularly apparent in the field of international politics, where the United States (for instance) scrupulously cooperates with its allies, while swiftly responding in kind to attacks against its self-interests.

It is scarcely surprising, then, that this basic strategy of responding in kind proves to be the most effective winning strategy determined within the field of Game Theory. Various Game Theory Tournaments feature computer simulations of the various strategies pitted against one another in head-to-head match-ups. On a consistent basis, the "reciprocal rule" program known as "Tit for Tat" proves to be the most effective in such round-robin match-ups. This program is considered *nice* (never initiates conflict), *provokable* (refuses to turn the other cheek), and also *forgiving* (permits a return to cooperation). This basic program, indeed, consistently prevails over the variants of either the Golden Rule or the Iron Rule.

FURTHER VARIATIONS WITH RESPECT TO THE BRONZE RULE

The basic concept of the Bronze Rule can scarcely claim to be the total picture, for further variations on this format are often encountered. Take, for example, the hybrid rule: "Be respectful to one's superiors, but feel free to exploit one's inferiors." This dualistic strategy employed by the "social climber" aims to secure a selective advantage within the vagaries of a stratified social hierarchy. The social climber appeases his boss in deference to his authority status, while simultaneously taking full advantage of those occupying subordinate positions.

A further example of hybrid rules concerns the tendency towards nepotism, also known as kin-selection. This basic strategy specifies close cooperation with one's relatives (or those with similar interests), while remaining competitive towards outsiders. In terms of the power hierarchy, this entails favoring those within one's immediate peer group, while withholding favor from those outside one's purview. A special case of this strategy is seen in the Tragedy of the Commons, where diverse interests come into conflict so that all are affected.

The over-harvesting of limited fish stocks is one current example, leading to an eventual "crash" in breeding populations. One township (or fleet) is typically pitted against all others, attempting to preserve self-interest in conflict with the higher aims of the group-collective. The only meaningful solution to such a partisan trap lies in an appeal to a wholly universal perspective, the resource now viewed as a commons to be shared by all, fully justifying the shared sacrifice that must be collectively endured if the resource is to remain plentiful for all.

CRIMINALITY AND HYPERCRIMINALITY

Most economic and cultural conflicts are settled through an appeal to rationality, although the same cannot be said for the realm of outright criminality and hypercriminality. Accordingly, a majority of the later chapters of this manual examine these darker issues affecting society as a whole in considerable detail, particularly criminality and mental illness. The impulsive characteristics generally encountered in criminality and hypercriminality invite similar comparisons to a related range of factors characterizing mental illness. These impulsive aspects represent an enduring legal controversy, as in the mental illness defense often encountered in a courtroom setting. The communicational model of mental illness makes a significant impact in this regard, particularly in cases where criminality and mental illness intersect (such as the antisocial personality disorder). The pitfalls of broadening the definition of mental illness to include criminal tendencies impose far-reaching consequences on the judicial system, as well as the mental health system in general.

Although both criminality and mental illness formally represent the transitional class of power maneuvers, enough functional distinctions remain to argue for a clear distinction in terms of diagnosis and treatment. Whereas a clear indication of biochemical susceptibilities for the psychoses was outlined in Chapter *34*, a similar analysis with respect to criminality/hypercriminality proves crucial for establishing distinctions (as well as parallels) between these two fundamental camps. A brief overview of relevant research relating to criminality is definitely in order here, providing a strong theoretical basis for an informed comparison to the realm of mental illness.

A number of precipitating genetic factors have been cited for criminality, as recently suggested in a ground breaking series of studies by Dr. Adrian Raine: in particular, his longitudinal study of *1800* children on the Island of Mauritius (a fairly homogeneous population). According to Dr. Raine (1997) children exhibiting statistically low resting heart rates at the age of three were approximately twice as likely to be aggressive at the age of twelve as measured through a tendency towards juvenile delinquency. This low heart rate construct is indicative of a diminished arousal factor, reflected in a sense of fearlessness in terms of novel circumstances relative to the general population. According to this innovative interpretation, under-aroused subjects are more likely to seek out extreme excitement in order to achieve emotional stimulation, which extends to engaging in antisocial behavior.

As one of the transitional class of power maneuvers, criminality clearly differs from the other categories of vice previously described. For example, in Chapter *16*, the vices of excess were defined in terms of the type "T" personality. Excessive behaviors are pursued in order to promote sensation-seeking, a factor further theorized to compensate for sub-optimal functioning within the reward centers of the brain. A similar pattern, in turn, was suggested for the realm of hyperviolence: where excessive aggressiveness was linked to the thrill of flirting with the law, indicative of the type "T-" (minus) personality. In both cases, the basic tendency towards excess is framed within an established social context of authority/follower roles, where a preexisting balance of power is firmly in place.

This standard pattern formally contrasts with the strictly transitional quality of criminal behavior. New relationships are established entirely in a one-sided (negative) fashion. The criminal generally attempts to remain unknown to his victims, a selfish impulse that flies in the face of social cooperation; e.g., your loss is my gain. Unlike the lesser virtues, which represent transitional maneuvers of a more socially acceptable nature, criminality is selfishly polarized into a winner and a loser. Consequently, rather than working within the system (and delaying gratification for the proper circumstances), the criminal selfishly seizes the assets of another for himself, wherein relying upon anonymity to perpetuate his egocentric concerns.

According to many experts, most criminals exhibit a narcissistic streak, with impulse control emerging as a major factor in criminal behavior. This ranges from the impulsive delinquent that snatches a case of beer, to the career criminal carefully planning his next clever caper. In each case, the discipline to achieve gratification in an honest fashion is clearly lacking in favor of taking an illegal shortcut. Many researchers speculate that impulse-control emerges as a direct consequence of sub-optimal functioning within the prefrontal cortex, a brain region theorized to mediate decision-making and ethical judgement. According to Dr. Jonathan Pinkus, neurologist at Georgetown University, the frontal lobes represent an "emergency brake" of sorts, serving to dampen the tendency to act upon impulses emerging from the more primitive limbic areas of the brain.

In terms of further studies by Dr. Adrian Raine (1999), violent offenders consistently exhibit ab-normal frontal lobe activity, a deficit further theorized to mediate impulse-control issues. In a study employing PET scans of the brains of violent criminals, Dr. Raine detected reduced activity in the prefrontal lobes indicating improper functioning of the impulse-control center. The study further suggested that environmental factors are similarly implicated. Poverty, neglect, and childhood abuse directly complicate the picture. Violent criminals from good homes typically exhibited more pronounced prefrontal lobe deficits than subjects raised in more deprived environments. These observations tend to suggest that violent tendencies can also emerge as a learned survival tactic in urban environments. Violent criminals from more privileged backgrounds more closely match the standard model of impulse control deficits linked to sub-optimal functioning of the prefrontal lobes.

This controversial interpretation is further corroborated through studies of patients with traumatic prefrontal lobe damage. Dr. Jordan Grafman (et al, 1996) of the National Institute of Neurological Disorders in Bethesda, Md. conducted a large retrospective study of Vietnam veterans with war injuries to circumscribed areas of the prefrontal cortex. He determined that these veterans were at a statistically higher risk for post-war violent behaviors, suggested that the prefrontal lobes play a significant role in inhibiting violent tendencies.

In concert with other brain structures assumed to be linked to aggression, a clearer picture of violence is gradually emerging, although further research is definitely an order. Through such a multi-prong approach, the more troublesome aspects of criminality can be more adequately addressed in a social sense. Research into neurological correlates, as well as advances in proper education, should provide significant inroads into arresting criminal tendencies at their source. Through the aid of the newly proposed three-digit coding system, the potential for turning the tide on global criminality may finally become a reality within the current generation.

THE BEHAVIORAL OVERLAP FOR CRIMINALITY AND MENTAL ILLNESS

The preceding transitional model for criminality can further be invoked to explain the tragic pairing of mental illness with certain sensationalistic crimes dramatized in the news media. Mental illness, by definition, exclusively targets the realm of the vices of excess (representing extremes within the virtuous realm). The mentally ill, therefore, appear relatively innocuous in terms of harm directed towards others. Harm to oneself, however, can occur as an outward expression of overwhelming depressive affect. Sensational crimes against the others, committed during a psychotic episode, alternately represent an overlap with the extreme realm of hypercriminality (which represents the transitional variation on the realm of hyperviolence).

The basic observation emerges that both mental illness and hypercriminality represent an extreme class of transitional power maneuvers, although targeting the virtues vs. the vices of defect, respectively. This leads to a bold hypothesis for explaining the motivations underlying the violent psychotic episode. If violent tendencies are present in concert with the tendency towards mental illness, then the probability of both factors being expressed becomes more likely than for those not susceptible to psychotic disorders. The bizarre belief systems typically accompanying the psychoses can further promote a feedback effect in relation to grievances driving the violent aspects of the personality (and vice versa). Consequently, the sensationalistic crimes periodically covered in the news media often represent a confluence of these two extreme trends, where a temporary lack of judgment prompts an extreme course of action. It should further be emphasized that psychotic patients without this accessory violent bias should not be viewed as particularly dangerous in this regard. Furthermore, hyperviolent individuals without any trace of mental illness remain fully capable of extreme forms of criminality, although generally lacking the bizarrely irrational aspects accompanying crimes based upon delusions.

APPLICATIONS BASED UPON THE SCHEMATIC DEFINITION FORMAT

The most effective means for diagnosing such a broad range of extremes is through the aid of the schematic definitions for both criminality and mental illness. Recall, from **Parts VI** and **VII**, that the respective listings of schematic definitions outline the formal communicational dynamics characterizing these two basic categories. The respective interplay of authority and follower roles (in addition to the specific affective terms under consideration) is spelled out in a formal longhand notation. The schematic precision of these definitions is unprecedented on the world scene today, permitting considerable clinical and diagnostic insights. In particular, the definition format proves crucial to the field of forensic

law enforcement, where the subjective perspectives within the mind of the criminal can be intuitively identified. This contrasts with the primarily objective slant that predominates in the forensic field. These formal insights into criminality prove equally applicable to the technique of criminal profiling, where crime scene details are modeled to a high degree of detail. Indeed, the main objective of profiling is to provide criminal investigators with crucial psychological insights that aid in the suspect's apprehension/conviction.

Criminal profiling is most highly useful in aberrant crimes of a serial nature, where a steady accumulation of crime scene evidence leads to educated inferences. The more experienced the criminal, the less physical evidence is generally left behind to be evaluated. Only properly documented crime scene evidence is conducive to a psychological profile of the violent offender. Insights into the offender's behavior predict motives or signature factors relating to future dysfunctional episodes. Consequently, through the aid of such schematic perspectives, the profiler can gain crucial insights into the workings of the deranged criminal mind, with behaviors becoming ever more predictable in nature.

A related issue of criminal profiling entails examining a crime sequence and determining whether a link exists based upon a criminal signature; namely, those impulses that fulfil a need for the perpetrator. These signature factors further aid in what is termed *reverse* profiling. A potential suspect is exonerated by failing to match the specifics of an established crime series signature in terms of the likelihood of such a conjunction. The schematic definitions for criminality and hypercriminality should prove a valuable adjunct at this juncture. Additional research into neurological correlates, as well as advances in the penal system, should present significant inroads towards arresting criminality at its source, offering the potential for ultimately turning the tide on global criminality.

Similar benefits can be expected within the realm of mental illness, where treatment and diagnosis are enhanced through the aid of diagnosis through the schematic definitions. Granted the definitions for the mental disorders are highly specialized in terms of nomenclature, therefore not a primary factor in direct counseling sessions. Their utility is far more crucial to the psychotherapist, who would enlist their precision to diagnose ongoing dysfunctional patterns of communication, wherein translated (through specific examples) into a format more easily comprehended by the client.

The more intellectually minded client, however, might find it therapeutic to tackle such issues as a co-participant within the therapy session. A standard flow-chart schematic depicting the organization of the schematic definitions could prove effective for outlining specific communicational issues. This is particularly applicable during multiclient sessions, when communication breakdown would be analyzed in a real time mode. These approaches necessarily apply only to clients with lucid enough thought processes to be receptive to them. Consequently, mental deficits accompanying the psychoses represent a much more challenging exercise, with the therapist taking on the greater role in applying these schematic aids within the session. Trained professional help is the only certain means to avoid the pitfalls associated with attempts at self-treatment. Accordingly, the current theoretical approach is offered as a bridge of last resort to those where no better option is available.

Similar benefits are further expected with respect to counseling on issues of criminality and hypercriminality. Here, the roles are shifted from client/therapist to parolee/adjudicant or defendant/legal administrator, etc. A related set of counseling strategies (utilizing the schematic definitions) necessarily apply, although the lucidity restrictions imposed for mental illness no longer apply. The more educated class of criminal would be offered the prospects for reform through the aid of a flow chart schematic tailored to their particular criminal propensities. Less advanced offenders would similarly be tutored in conjunction with real-life illustrations, wherein supplying crucial insights towards impulse control. Granted, a concerted effort to change one's dysfunctional outlook must necessarily accompany such therapeutic techniques, although a huge improvement on the "time-served" paradigm currently dominating the criminal justice system.

Beyond criminality and mental illness, applications similarly extend to the schematic definitions for the much broader realm of positive psychology. The character values are similarly modeled in terms of the schematic definition format, promoting positive values across society as a whole (as well as impeding criminal tendencies). Perhaps the greatest beneficiaries include the youth of the nation, whose character/propensities are gradually being molded into place. The more routine virtues and values of the ethical hierarchy prove invaluable for navigating these crucial stages in emotional development. The schematic definitions for the virtuous mode could be incorporated, where appropriate, into the academic curriculum.

Indeed, the current trend towards character education provides a valuable adjunct for themes usually dealt with at a religious level. Furthermore, the schematic contrast between the vices of defect and the virtuous mode should provide crucial guideposts for decisions of a moral nature, as specifically outlined within the schematic definition format.

The vices of excess further figure prominently in character education, particularly that adolescent phase when extremes in behavior are just emerging. These precise techniques for relationship modeling, in turn, apply to an adult sphere of influence, where marital/family frictions are respectively resolved. The schematic definition format emerges as a general-purpose diagnostic tool for virtually everything of an emotional nature: encompassing the more routine virtues and vices, as well as the darker themes of criminality and mental illness. Even the enigmatic realm of humor and comedy (modeled through the lesser virtues) is adequately represented within this master format indicating a supreme degree of versatility.

THE NEW SCIENCE OF POWERPLAY POLITICS

As with all such newly established systems, a proper descriptive moniker is definitely called for: in this case, the new science of Powerplay Politics ™. This designation has been selected in allusion to the parallel concepts of the powerplay and Power Politics. The latter term is an English translation of the German *machtpolitik* (literally, power politics). It refers to a traditional style of political administration emphasizing power and authority, often in a coercive fashion. In contrast, the "power play" denotes a collective style of cooperation, defined as a scoring strategy in team sports such as football or hockey. The power play refers to any style of mass interference within a particular point or zone, an aspect reminiscent of the cohesive style of "strike power" characterizing the follower role. Owing to the enhanced versatility of both authority/follower roles, the notion of Powerplay Politics proves particularly effective for designating this dual power hierarchy.

In terms of this communicational dynamic, Powerplay Politics is essentially grounded in two basic principles adapted from Communications Theory. The first principle states that all communication is motivationally charged to some extent, wherein targeting the intentions of the self and others within the verbal interaction. Even a routine lecture on pure mathematics contains an underlying motivational component: for the professor is subliminally determined to achieve academic tenure, whereas the student is concerned with earning a passing grade, etc.

The second basic principle derives from the ascending dynamics of the power hierarchy. Everyone (whether they choose to admit it or not) seeks to control the ongoing interaction. For instance, the group authority overrules the power leverage wielded by the personal follower, whereas the group representative counteracts that of the group authority (and so forth). In most stable relationships, power leverage is shared in a trade-off fashion, although not always with entirely equal results. Furthermore, outward expressions of weakness can similarly yield an empowering effect, such as witnessed with the hypochondriac or the masochist.

Regardless of the individual mechanisms at issue here, the pervasive desire to be in control of a relationship emerges as the common driving force: which (in concert with the first principle) accounts for the true focus of the new science of Powerplay Politics. More significantly, each of these diverse perspectives is unified into a seamless continuum based upon the traditional groupings of virtues, values, and vices; providing a grand-unified model of affective language systematized within the three-digit coding system.

In summary, this formal foundation within the behavioral sciences paves the way for a planetary system of ethics, where an innate instinctual foundation in terms of conditioning theory imparts a universal appeal towards ultimate acceptance upon the world scene today. This systematic scientific foundation is particularly unique in that it directly avoids favoritism towards any given cultural identity, rather treating each with equal dignity and validity. Furthermore, the respective traditional listings of virtues and values are similarly specified in terms of such a strictly secular perspective, one that is formally independent of any regional cultural bias or the restrictions of any (supernaturally revealed) scriptural foundation. This new ethical system enjoys the advantages of highlighting the commonalties of a virtuous lifestyle across all cultures and creeds, rather than focusing upon the individual distinctions therein.

A further crucial conceptual advantage invokes the increased awareness of the grounding of organized religion with the formal principles of Set Theory, as extensively outlined in Chapter 2. This innovation permits a radical reinterpretation of the role that religion plays in society as a whole, in particular, the disturbing ascendance of religious fanaticism. According to this interpretation, the spiritual authority perspective represents just one of the five basic levels within the master hierarchy of authority and follower roles: defined as the personal, group, spiritual, humanitarian, and transcendental perspectives. According to this updated interpretation, the influence of organized religion chiefly extends to a universal sphere of influence (binding over all of mankind). Most religious systems, however, are compounded by a humanitarian range of themes (encompassing all ages and times), as well as some extension to a transcendental realm, imparting a supernatural/mystical character to the entire edifice.

The destructive aspects of religious fanaticism essentially emerge from an inherently inflexible perspective that condemns all other forms of religion their innate freedom to express their own unique style of universal perspective on their respective side of the globe. Furthermore, religious fanaticism consistently oversteps its specific relevant focus, typically attempting to influence the political (group) and even personal realms of conduct. The timely emergence of the Set Theory interpretation of the authority and follower roles hopefully will alter this disturbing trend towards fanaticism towards of a more rational perspective (at least for the moderate constituency) wherein promoting a greater degree of flexibility in terms of both dogma and practice.

In concert with the newly devised master hierarchy of virtues and values based upon behavioral principles, it further is hoped that the moral commonalties across all religious traditions will be emphasized encouraging a new era in religious tolerance. This new ethical system could eminently qualify as the long anticipated foundation for a global system of planetary ethics serving a secular constituency, where such moral issues have typically been downplayed due to well-meaning attempts to avoid religious favoritism. This same system could also serve as a valuable adjunct to the major religions of the world without favoring any one of them. Indeed, this new ethical hierarchy exhibits the potential for promoting a peaceful coexistence with many of the established world religions, particularly in that it does not preclude the existence of a top-down pattern of influence (of a supernatural nature) as well. Consequently, this overall picture potentially amounts to the best of all possible worlds: enabling an ethical revival in the secular world (which has typically been downplayed), as well as the potential for an even greater degree of spiritual cooperation and tolerance amongst all of the established religions of the world.

37

APPLICATIONS TO INFORMATION TECHNOLOGY & ARTIFICIAL INTELLIGENCE

The dream of artificial intelligence has been a goal in the field of Computer Sciences since virtually the dawning of the Computer Age. This anticipated style of artificially intelligent agent would potentially assist in all aspects of human endeavor, accompanied by the intriguing prospects for ultimately transcending the fixed limitations of the human condition. The current dramatic growth in computing power finally enables economic feasible inroads towards such a meaningful AI development. A number of key approaches, such as brain modeling through neural networks, have been attempted, although scarcely enough detailed information exists about the brain to warrant any such serious endeavor. In actuality, the key solution to developing convincing artificial intelligence involves an innate understanding of human communication in general. The preeminent test for AI devised by Alan Turing abstains from relying upon any direct measure of consciousness or perception in its determinations, rather strictly targeting the communicative factors underlying general human language. Assuming that the symbolic attributes of human language can be convincingly simulated on the computer, then many decades of needless effort potentially could be cut from the neural-net or consciousness/perceptual approaches.

Along these lines, a recent U.S. patent (#6,587,846) has been granted for precisely such a technical innovation based upon the symbolic attributes underlying affective (or emotionally-charged) language. Clear precedents already exist with respect to chess-playing computers, which prove particularly effective for modeling the symbolisms underlying such an abstract gaming format (although scarcely capable of anything else). In similar fashion, the symbolic attributes of the English language tradition prove similarly comprehensive in scope, although several orders of magnitude more abstractly complex in this regard. Certainly the primary economic focus of human society is mediated primarily through the symbolisms of human communication, specifying language as the most rational focal point for ongoing research. This does not necessarily imply that a sensory/motor enabled robot designed in relation to its immediate environment is not a rational focus of directed research. Indeed, such an aspect could eventually be merged with the currently proposed language simulation model, resulting in a more physically complete computer avatar. As far as direct economic applications are concerned, however, it proves entirely more cost effective to target the symbolic attributes of human language in all of its various manifestations.

Fortunately, a convenient shortcut to this daunting complexity of a direct language simulation has recently been proposed (the technical basis for the aforementioned patent). This new approach directly focuses upon the motivational (or emotionally-charged) aspects of language as its guiding principle, the remaining bulk of value-neutral language filling-in in an accessory role. Indeed, as Robert Warren Penn once insightfully wrote: "What is man but his passions?" Along similar lines, most neuroscientists consider the mind/brain complex as a vast motivational analyzer that enables the individual to flourish in harmony with the environment through the principles of instrumental conditioning. The current patent establishes precisely such a foundation within conditioning theory; in this case, appetite in anticipation of rewards, or aversion in expectation of lenient treatment. Furthermore, when more abstract forms of affective language are viewed in the terms of an ascending interactive hierarchy of meta-perspectives, then the overall complement of the traditional groupings of virtues and values jumps neatly into focus, as outlined in the preceding chapters.

In summary, through a primary focus upon the affective aspects of human language, an economically feasible shortcut to the AI simulation of human communication finally appears within reach. Much detailed programming remains to be done, perhaps necessitating a customized coding language and supportive hardware consistent with a project of this magnitude. With a starting staff roughly the size of a large encyclopedia work force, a first generation simulation could potentially be achieved within a fairly modest time frame. This painstaking process might eventually be more dramatically accelerated if ultimately accorded the status of a national initiative, particularly in light of its outright commercial value, as well as military applications.

No serious contenders to Turing's Test of Artificial Intelligence have yet come to light, undoubtedly due to the enormous logistics involved in programming human language. Although this ambitious undertaking is clearly years into the future, significant inroads have already been made towards these ends. The Japanese appear to have amassed a significant lead with respect to their ongoing development of their deductive inference machine. As its name implies, this innovative form of data processing machine employs deductive reasoning to establish original conclusions from a standard battery of logical premises. The product of years of research by the Institute for New Generation Computer Technology (ICOT), this machine uses information stored in its regional database to deductively draw fresh conclusions not literally contained within the original data. The major shortcoming to this deductive format, however, is its basic restriction limiting conclusions to premises immediately at hand. The deductive inference machine must be carefully monitored in order to stay within the scope of its regional database. Such a machine is certainly destined to remain an academic curiosity, scarcely general purpose enough to convincingly pass the rigors of Turing's Test. Such an artificial set-up would further experience difficulties simulating mood and emotion, a fatal flaw in any convincing simulation of AI.

INDUCTIVE INFERENCE IN THE DESIGN OF ARTIFICIAL INTELLIGENCE

Fortunately, an alternate form of rational inquiry proves infinitely better suited for simulating human intelligence on the computer. Traditionally known as *inductive* reasoning, it gathers together the best available evidence directly inferring the most probable conclusion from the sum total of facts. Inductive reasoning is particularly evident during the courtroom trial, where various shreds of evidence are systematically presented, wherein reaching a final verdict. In contrast to deductive reasoning, the conclusions achieved through inductive reasoning are never absolutely certain, for there always remains the nagging doubt that the verdict was made in error. In the sphere of artificial intelligence, however, this drawback actually amounts to somewhat of a prerequisite, for humans almost invariably make mistakes. Indeed, the uncertainties of the natural world give inductive reasoning the clear advantage in such a problem-solving mode. According to this inductive paradigm, each of us builds a mental model of our environment over a lifetime, forming a master template for our current experiences. When our expectations match our surroundings, we achieve a general sense of security. A mismatch, however, leads to a surprised reaction followed by investigative behavior. Although this sense of security is often ill founded (as in faulty induction), it actually is a small price to pay for maintaining flexibility within a changeable environment.

In terms of artificial intelligence, the computer would similarly be programmed with its own formal map of reality employed in an analogous detection and matching mode. Any final conclusions would necessarily rely upon probability, although statistics are one of the computer's computational strong points. It is here that the logistics of the power hierarchy rightfully enter the picture, serving as the elementary foundation for the first inductive system dealing with motivational logic. According to this fundamental insight, the logical attributes of the power hierarchy are programmed directly into the computer, providing a formal model of motivational behavior in general. The computer then employs this programming to infer the precise power-level at issue within a given verbal interchange. On the basis of this initial determination, the computer further calculates the given power countermaneuver simulating motivation within the verbal interaction.

The systematic organization of the schematic definitions permits extreme efficiency in programming, each more advanced level building directly upon that which it supercedes (eliminating much of the associated redundancy). Through an elaborate matching procedure with the schematic definitions, the precise motivational level of communication can accurately be determined (defined as the passive-monitoring mode). This basic determination, in turn, serves as the basis for the production of a response repertoire tailored specifically to the computer (the true AI simulation mode). Here, the basic logistics are already in place for implementing at least the skeleton framework for such an ethical AI-agent.

TECHNICAL CONSIDERATIONS

It still remains to be determined the best means for programming this definition format into the computer, particularly in light of the current trends in computer design. In terms of hardware design, many experts currently agree that computer development has spanned roughly five generations of technological innovation. Vacuum tube technology characterized the first-generation of computer design, giving way to the transistor designs of the second-generation. The integrated computer chip ushered in the third-generation, refined in the fourth-generation as the Very-Large-Scale-Integrated Chip (VLSI). Most experts agree that a fifth-generation design component is currently under way, characterized by the expanded use of logic circuits and increased use of parallel processing. According to earlier design generations, calculation speed was strictly limited by the Von Neuman bottleneck; namely, programming instructions were executed one stage at a time. Parallel processing, however, allows various aspects of a complex problem to be handled simultaneously, greatly reducing the bottleneck plaguing sequential processing.

The practical applications of parallel processing are particularly relevant to AI computer design. Indeed, the number of parallel processors would ideally equal the sum-total of individual terms within the power hierarchy (for a grand total of *1,040)*: quite a modest number even by today's design standards. This integrated processor array is further structured along hierarchial lines, effectively mirroring the schematic organization of the power hierarchy. This stratified architecture would take full advantage of the strict transformational logic governing the schematic definitions, eliminating much of the redundancy sure to occur in any convincing language simulation. Indeed, the greatest degree of complexity must necessarily involve programming at the most basic personal level of the power hierarchy, with the remaining higher levels following naturally from this elementary foundation.

All aspects considered, the most basic unit of input for the AI computer must necessarily be the sentence, for the schematic definitions are similarly given in the form of a dual sentence struc-

ture. The AI computer then employs parallel processing to determine the precise degree of correlation between the inputted (target) sentence and its respective schematic definition template. This matching procedure directly scrutinizes each of the grammatical elements within a given sentence, attempting a statistical correlation with the specifics for a given schematic definition. For instance, the tense of the verb, the plurality or person of the noun/pronoun etc. would all be scrutinized according to a pre-set diagnostic formula. Each processor would then determine the sum-total of correct matches ultimately yielding the relative probability of a match with a particular schematic definition. The processor yielding the highest overall rating is uniquely singled-out as the best match by the master control unit.

The master control unit achieves this result through the aid of a feedback loop, the priority of the individual microprocessors reciprocally weighted on the basis of preceding determinations. Each schematic definition is respectively composed of both past (as well as present) design components: establishing context as yet a further consideration in the matching procedure. A suitably advanced AI program would retain in a long-term storage virtually every relevant conversation with a given person or context. On this contextual basis, the master control unit then selectively "weights" the individual processors according to a preset formula, taking full advantage of both past (as well as present) conversational dynamics. Furthermore, the computer would be exquisitely sensitive to variations in human personality (just as humans are instinctively so), satisfying yet a further condition of Turing's Test.

This overall process has fittingly been granted U.S. Utility Patent (# 6,587,846), an invention titled: Inductive Inference Affective Language Analyzer Simulating Artificial Intelligence. Although a complete description of the mode of operation for this patent clearly remains beyond the scope of the current chapter, the basic flow chart schematic is reproduced in **Fig. 37**, wherein permitting an indication of the formal dynamics at issue. In concert with the comprehensive listing of schematic definitions comprising the heart of the matching procedure, a cursory overview of the mode of operation becomes increasingly apparent. The complete patent specification is posted for public inspection at the U.S. Patent & Trademark web-site.

FURTHER POTENTIAL DESIGN INNOVATIONS

The ultimate implementation of ethical AI should rightfully be phased-in through several distinct

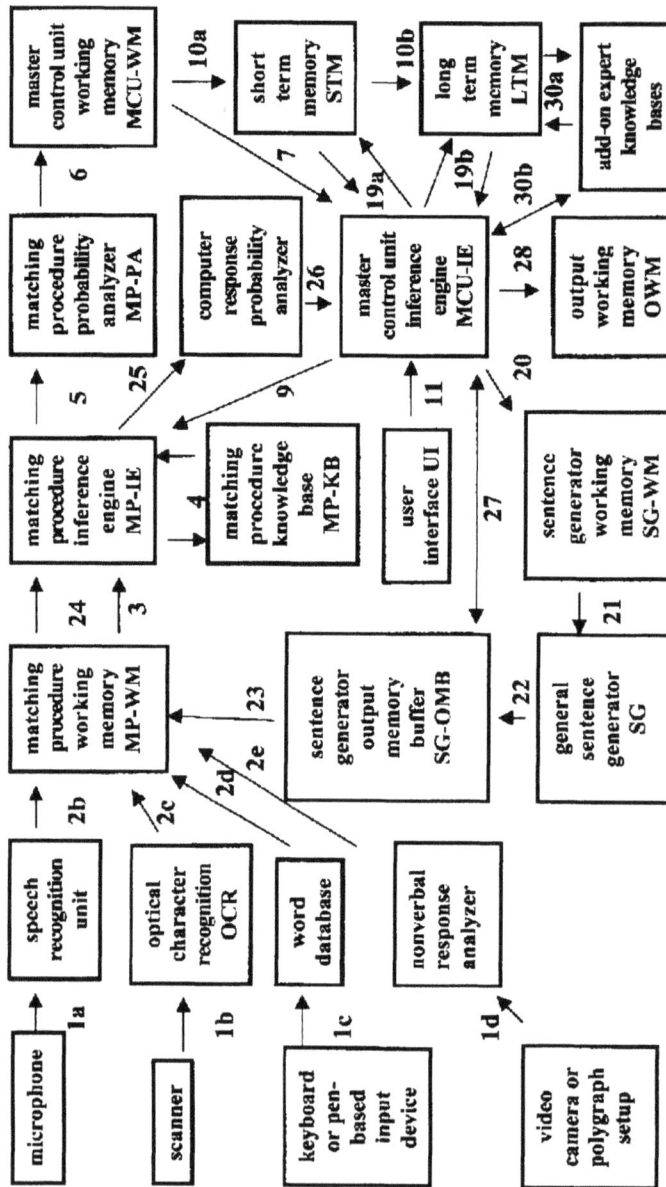

Fig. 37 - The True AI Mode of Operation
for Patents # 6,587,846 & # 7,236,963

generations of development, in keeping with the vast degree of complexity specified for a convincing AI simulation. The first-generation AI computer would excel in mostly routine types of monitoring applications; namely, security guard, night watchman, babysitter, etc.: where a simple "sound-the-alarm" response would be sufficient. This rather modest range of duties would further permit response characteristics to be tailored directly to the initial applications. For instance, in a screening/interview mode, maximum disclosure would be emphasized, keeping computer responses to a pithy minimum. A standard stock repertoire would undoubtedly be sufficient, featuring brief inquiries; such as who, what, when, where, why, elaborate further, etc. Indeed, several such elementary programs have already been implemented using key words in conversation to cue stock rejoinders. This preliminary class of programs, however, is unfortunately susceptible to logical/contextual blunders, a circumstance remedied through more advanced AI designs.

Situations requiring a more creative response repertoire would further necessitate the implementation of a true AI simulation mode aimed at permitting original sentence synthesis. As any public speaker will freely testify, it is infinitely more difficult to deliver a speech than to simply sit and listen to one. This additional level of design complexity necessarily specifies a more sophisticated form of response mechanism, the stock repertoire no longer adequate due to its inherent insensitivity to the underlying context. The master control unit would necessarily assume such a critical function, employing its determination of the current level of communication (presupposition) in order to activate the processor at the next higher level (entailment).

This basic determination (along with the particulars of the interaction) is subsequently routed to a general-purpose sentence generator: fully equipped with the formal rules governing grammar, syntax, and phraseology. Being that there are a broad range of strategies to express a given sentence meaning, a large number of potential sentences would necessarily be generated - not all equally suited to the task. Accordingly, each would be slated for subsequent feedback through the detection process, rated for their ability to best express the desired shade of meaning. The enhanced computational abilities of the AI computer would further ensure delivery of an adequate response within the relatively leisurely limits governing human response time. Only the sentence with the highest overall rating would ultimately be selected for delivery to the speech output unit, allowing for a convincing simulation of motivational language in general.

The specific practical applications for the general AI-agent depend upon which individual schematic definitions are emphasized within the programming. For instance, a focus on the definitions for criminality/hypercriminality result in the potential for a criminal-profiling computer, where the subliminal motives of the criminal mind are deduced in terms of limited crime scene evidence. Furthermore, the potential for a mental health AI-assistant is realized through a focus upon the schematic definitions for mental illness (A & B): leading to innovations in treatment and diagnosis (as previously described in Chapter *38*). The more routine schematic definitions for the major and lesser virtues suggest parallel applications to a general-purpose computer companion/assistant. This particularly applies to the lesser virtues (I and II), which would be emphasized with respect to an AI-entertainer/comedian.

AN OVERVIEW OF THE PATENT SPECIFICATION

The inductive inference affective language analyzer (abbreviated IIALA) exhibits three distinct modes of operation, each with its own peculiar advantages. First described is a passive monitoring mode, which monitors a verbal interaction without any active input of its own (no clarification of ambiguities). This circumstance is remedied through the active monitoring mode, which clarifies uncertainties through the addition of a stock-sentence generator that devises interview types of questions that elicit yes or no answers. The most advanced mode of operation is the true AI simulation mode, where the IIALA employs its detection/monitoring data to simulate a personal interactive role. This is accomplished through the aid of a general-purpose sentence generator that formulates responses judged for appropriateness by feedback through the system. Each of these modes of operation is described further in the order given. Of these three, the true AI mode is preferred, being the most technically complete. All three modes, however, are intimately interconnected, each with advantages to a given application.

The passive monitoring mode (depicted in multi-use **Fig. 37**) serves as the basic foundation for the remaining two modes of the IIALA. It represents a process for decoding the motivational parameters of affective language. The flow chart depicts the operation of this process as well as the supportive hardware: both of which are indicated in the same schematic diagram. For **Fig. 37**, the sequence of steps comprising the operation of the passive monitoring mode are depicted using consecutively numbered arrows, each numeral specifying a step in the procedure depicted in the box to which the respective arrow points. This specific format was chosen (rather than numbering the individual boxes) due to the fact that some of the boxes are assigned differing functions for the remaining active monitoring and AI simulation modes. The details for the operation of the passive monitoring mode have already outlined in the preceding section titled "Technical Considerations," making further duplication unnecessary here. Rather, the focus of the current analysis now shifts to an overview of the remaining active monitoring and true AI simulation modes.

The practical applications of the passive monitoring mode are essentially limited by the passive quality of the information gathering procedure. Communication in terms of the virtuous realm is allowed to flow freely, whereas the realm of the vices (particularly hyperviolence) sounds an alarm for outside intervention. As a basic recording device, the passive monitoring mode serves as a smart style of surveillance tape, allowing for a fast synopsis of recorded conversations. Although the unobtrusive nature of the passive monitoring mode is one of its major selling points, it lacks total accuracy due to its inability to clarify the inevitable occurrence of incomplete information (where a simple question could clarify the issue). Here, the passive mode can be converted into an optional active monitoring mode through the addition of a stock sentence generator, equipped with a stock repertoire of questions for eliciting the desired clarifications.

For instance, if the subject/object data is weak due to the use of a pronoun, then this factor is targeted for clarification. If the predicate data of the sentence proves to be obscure, then this aspect is similarly targeted. Clarifications are best achieved by posing simple yes-or-no questions formulated through the aid of a stock sentence generator. What follows is an attention-getting prefix followed by the question proper. For example, a typical question might be: "Wait! By *he* do you mean the ship's captain?" A *yes* answer terminates the questioning, whereas a *no* answer reiterates the process until a solution is achieved (or the quest is abandoned as unproductive).

Should the target of the question attempt to respond with more than a yes-or-no answer, the stock-generator politely reminds the responder of the limitations within the system. Once the query procedure has begun, the matching procedure is restricted to listening exclusively for yes-or-no answers. Following each answer, the original sentence is silently resubmitting to the matching procedure-inference engine, where it is subsequently reevaluated via the matching procedure. Upon reaching a standard level of confidence, the query phase is terminated, the system again opened up to a full range of responses.

In summary, the active monitoring mode surpasses the passive monitoring mode in terms of relative certainty. The distractions of interrupting the natural flow of conversation are offset by the ability to clarify uncertainties in the conversation. The active monitoring mode, in turn, is handicapped by its restriction to simple yes-or-no questions, imparting a somewhat machine-like demeanor. Questions posed somewhat more diplomatically entail true AI simulation, employing a more sophisticated style of response repertoire in terms of a general-purpose sentence generator. A large number of sentences are necessarily generated ensuring that at least one is judged suitable following feedback through the matching procedure. The true AI agent effectively simulates an identity of its own, wherein permitting a more natural style of interaction

Fig. 37 fully illustrates this third (and most elaborate) version of the IIALA, representing an enhanced modification of the basic passive monitoring mode through the addition of a sentence generator and associated pathways. For sake of clarity, the circuitry for the active monitoring mode has been omitted, although both sets of circuitry are compatible with one another. The active monitoring mode is switched off when operating in the AI mode (and vice versa). Although not mutually exclusive, it is inadvisable to run both modes simultaneously (for sake of response consistency), although a task-driven alternation between the two modes remains an option.

Returning to **Fig. 37**, this diagram builds directly upon the passive monitoring mode with the exception that extensive modifications are made beginning at the level of the master control unit. The passive monitoring mode runs concurrently with the AI mode. The latter only overrules the former when a computer generated response is called for. For the passive monitoring mode, the MCU predicts the next most probable response in an ongoing interaction, passing this information on to the matching procedure in order to increase monitoring accuracy. This information, in turn, can be used to synthesize responses identified as originating from the AI agent, a simulation encompassing the realm of affective language (an ethically-speaking computer). A simulation of different modes of temperament is further feasible, particularly those most compatible personalities.

ETHICAL SAFEGUARDS

In concert with such dramatic advances comes the potential for inevitable misuse. Here, the Science Fiction genre is full of nightmarish scenarios of future technology gone horribly wrong, as in all-powerful robots seizing control from their human masters. This same Sci-Fi tradition proposes a number of clever solutions to circumvent such a dilemma: most notably, Isaac Asimov's Three Laws of Robotics. This set of rules attempts to rein in the potential conduct of the futuristic AI agent, proposing rules that prohibit any harm to come to humans. The First Law states: "A robot may not injure a human being, or through inaction allow a human to come to harm." The Second Law further states: "A robot must obey orders given it by a human being, except when such orders come into conflict with the First Law." Finally, the Third Law states: "A robot must protect the integrity of its own existence, except when self-preservation conflicts with the first two laws."

Although this well thought-out system of safeguards proves particularly intriguing in a fictional sense, it still remains simplistic in its dictates leaving unresolved the specific details for implementing such a system. The purely virtuous robot (by definition) should be cognizant of the darker realm of the vices in order to steer clear of them. The overall listing of schematic definitions proves particularly applicable here, providing the supreme conceptual template for ethical determinations of a moral nature. The complete *1,040*-fold listing of definitions for both virtue and vice provides the ethical database for facilitating moral deliberations. The programming of the vices, however, is only allowable in a diagnostic mode, the computer fully aware of troublesome behaviors without necessarily responding in kind.

This enduring contrast between virtue and vice supplies the fundamental ethical matrix for determining what is harmful to humans in allusion to Asimov's Three Laws of Robotics. This dual contrast helps resolve uncertainties within Asimov's Second Law; namely, what orders a robot must follow without causing harm to a human. According to Asimov, *any* non-harmful order must be obeyed, although this necessarily invokes the gray area of a lesser degrees of harm. In addition to physical security, personal development often proves equally significant, an aspect clearly at odds with the slavish delegation of orders to a computer servant. The more proper AI strategy would amount to the encouragement of an independent human spirit in the form of a faithful as-sistant, rather than willing slave. This enhanced versatility similarly proves crucial to the Third Law of Robotics, where the self-preservation of the AI agent is more realistically weighed against the preliminary mandates of the first two laws.

THE TEN ETHICAL LAWS OF ROBOTICS

Although the ethical versatility of the schematic definitions proves particularly effective from a technical standpoint, the affiliated complexity, unfortunately, can prove somewhat difficult to grasp from an informal standpoint. Each schematic definition requires a fair degree of deliberation, a shortcoming fortunately remedied through their conversion to a more user-friendly format as represented in the *Ten Ethical Laws of Robotics* listed below.

(I) As Personal Authority, I express my Individualism within the guidelines of the four basic Ego States (guilt-worry-nostalgia-desire) to the exclusion of the corresponding Ego Vices (laziness-negligence-apathy-indifference).

(II) As Personal Follower, I behave Pragmatically in accordance with the Alter Ego States (hero/worship-blame-approval-concern) at the expense of the corresponding Alter Ego Vices (treachery-vindictiveness-spite-malice).

(III) As Group Authority, I strive for a personal sense of Idealism through the aid of the Personal Ideals (glory-honor-dignity-integrity) while renouncing the respective Sins of Villainy (infamy-dishonor-foolishness-capriciousness).

(IV) As Group Representative, I uphold the principles of Utilitarianism by celebrating the Cardinal Virtues (prudence-justice-temperance-fortitude) to the necessary expense of the corresponding Vices of Corruption (insurgency-vengeance-gluttony-cowardice).

(V) As Spiritual Authority, I pursue the Romantic ideal by upholding the Civil Liberties (providence-liberty-civility-austerity): to the exclusion of the corresponding Civil Liabilities (prodigality-slavery-vulgarity-cruelty).

(VI) As Spiritual Disciple, I celebrate the Ecclesiastical tradition by professing the Theological Virtues (faith-hope-charity-decency) at the expense of the respective Heretical Vices (betrayal-despair-avarice-antagonism).

(VII) As Humanitarian Authority, I support the spirit of Ecumenism by espousing the Ecumenical Ideals (grace-freewill-magnanimity-equanimity) while renouncing the corresponding Sins of Apostasy (wrath-tyranny-persecution-oppression).

(VIII) As a Representative Member of Humanity, I profess the spirit of Eclecticism by espousing the Classical Greek Values (beauty-truth-goodness-wisdom) to the exclusion of the respective Moralistic Vices (evil-cunning-ugliness-hypocrisy).

(IX) As Transcendental Authority, I celebrate the spirit of Renaissance Humanism by endorsing the Humanistic Values (peace-love-tranquility-equality) to the detriment of the corresponding Sins of Nihilism (anger-hatred-prejudice-belligerence).

(X) As Transcendental Follower, I rejoice in the mysteries of the Mystical experience through a celebration of the Mystical Values (ecstasy-bliss-joy-harmony) while renouncing the corresponding Mystical Vices (iniquity-turpitude-abomination-perdition).

These Ten Ethical Laws represent expanded variations on the dynamics implicit to the ten-level power hierarchy. For consistency's sake, each of the Ten Laws is written in a positive style of mandate focusing on the virtues to the exclusion of the corresponding vices. These Ten Ethical Laws represent a basic overview of the enduring conflict pitting virtue vs. vice, a format particularly conducive to the systematic computer AI programming.

It remains only a further minor step to incorporate the additional complement of schematic definitions for the realm of excess directly into the AI format, enhancing the basic core programming for the virtuous mode described in **Part I** (as well as the related vices of defect). This advanced programming platform takes full advantage of the principles governing fuzzy logic, where the predicted degree of excess is calculated primarily in terms of such indeterminate variables.

This optional addition of the vices of excess necessarily warrants a parallel modification of the Ten Ethical Laws of Robotics; namely, a supplementary corollary paraphrased as "steer away from the extremes of excess when at all possible." It is formally stated as: I will faithfully avoid extremes within the virtuous realm to the necessary expense of the vices of excess. Along a similar line of reasoning, Buddha advised his followers to "Walk the middle path." A second corollary targets the related realm of hyperviolence, which states: I will never stray into the domain of extremes relating to the vices of defect, to the complete exclusion of the realm of hyperviolence. This updated AI agent would be employed primarily in a diagnostic mode, restricted to detecting the occurrence of the realm of excess in order to minimize its disruptive effects.

This expanded diagnostic potential ultimately allows the AI computer to examine virtually every perspective of a given interaction without necessarily becoming tied to any one of them. This enhanced degree of versatility necessarily implies the implementation of a *floating* ego. The AI agent is free to entertain a myriad of simultaneous perspectives devoid of any personal bias, wherein allowing mutually exclusive perspectives to be examined in their entirety. Contrast this to the human condition, where the relevant perspectives are conceptualized only in a sequential fashion, where one's personal agenda usually claims the greatest consideration. Unlike the human condition, the AI version is further restricted to applying this processing entirely towards positive ends, effectively precluding the deception and manipulation characterizing the vices, and safeguarded through the precepts of the Ten Ethical Laws of Robotics.

Through the welcome addition of the Ten Ethical Laws, a secure version of artificial intelligence appears quite technically feasible, with suitable safeguards predicted for virtually every ethical contingency. These Ten Laws effectively supplement Isaac Asimov's Three Laws of Robotics: a preliminary platform that clearly benefits from such an advanced design innovation. This enhanced detection capacity further allows negative transactions to be converted into positive ones, while simultaneously inhibiting the reverse reaction. This dual set of checks-and-balances with respect to the response repertoire predicts an unprecedented sense of confidence in terms of computer-initiated behaviors.

With such ethical safeguards firmly in place, the AI computer should consistently be able to make the right moral decision, a virtual "saint" among men. Any direct familiarity with the vices necessarily occurs in a strictly diagnostic mode, for the prime AI directive dictates strict adherence to a virtuous repertoire. This unerring sense of ethical constancy should prove to be the most valuable asset for such an AI agent, in fitting contrast to the more questionable predilections of its human counterparts. Perhaps the greatest risk to the AI computer stems precisely from the inevitable temptation to selfishly override such programming safeguards: the computer scarcely able to initiate such drastic procedures on its own.

It is here that the resistance to the power of the AI computer would be voiced the loudest, particularly with respect to the ingrained reluctance to allow such power to pass to a machine. The many futuristic scenarios of "Big Brother" monitoring our every move certainly prove disturbing, with the free will of humanity sacrificed to such an all-powerful "god of technology." With stringent ethical safeguards restricting surveillance to only the direst of circumstances, such nightmarish scenarios must forever remain within the domain of Science Fiction. These ethical safeguards serve not only to protect against outside tampering, but also encourage a more virtuous degree of compliance within a human sphere of influence, a challenge clearly within the technological prowess of even the current generation.

Such a faithful AI assistant might eventually serve in the role of backup conscience for its human counterparts, particularly in circumstances where the native version might tend to fail us. In this more advanced sense, the Ten Ethical Laws of Robotics also serve as the basic moral guidelines in a human relationship sense. Here, each of us has our own "homework" to do in this basic respect. This glowing sense of optimism is clearly warranted in light of the considerable influence computers play in our everyday lives. The enhanced detection capabilities anticipated for the AI computer would further serve to strengthen such a beneficial relationship, with virtually unlimited benefits waiting just over the technological horizon. The nightmarish visions of technological doom surely pale in comparison to the computational marvels predicted to become commonplace during the Third Millennium.

A COMPUTER SIMULATION OF HUMOR AND COMEDY

The completed description of the AI applications for the standard complement of schematic definitions; namely, those targeting the major virtues/vices of defect is scarcely all-inclusive by any measure. The issue of the parallel complement of definitions for the transitional power maneuvers, in turn, enters the picture. These include the lesser virtues from **Part V**, as well as criminality/hyper-criminality from **Part VI** and mental illness with respect to **Part VII**. These applications have further been granted their own US Patent #7,236,963. The latter two aspects would occur somewhat infrequently in a computer-monitored context. Here, a simple sound-the-alarm response would be sufficient to alert the human staff. The remainder of the current chapter, accordingly, is devoted to outlining how the formal categories of the lesser virtues are conducive to an AI simulation of humor and comedy. Indeed, Communication Theory has long struggled to explain the riddle of humor/comedy, although scarcely to the degree of precision within transitional hierarchy. The reciprocal interplay of authority/follower roles proves crucial for deciphering the subtle nuances of the comedic realm.

The schematic definitions for the lesser virtues appear tailor-made for programming directly into the AI-enabled computer. Any all-inclusive model of communication in general must necessarily account for the transitional class of power maneuvers, wherein complementing the more straightforward class of routine power maneuvers initially described. The most basic unit of input for the AI-agent must necessarily be the sentence, for the schematic definitions (including the transitional versions) are expressed in terms of a dual sentence structure. The respective transitional definitions are utilized in a matching function with sentences inputted from live conversation, whereby determining the precise degree of correspondence with a particular humorous interchange. Abrupt shifts within the conversation further signal that a transitional maneuver has just occurred. This, in turn, prompts the detection of the counter-double bind class of maneuvers, a strategy generally disqualified to an extreme range of detail. This greatly increases the complexity of the detection procedure, placing the computer in the delicate position of decoding the various nuances of inflection, timing, lingo, sarcasm, etc.: wherein signaling that disqualification had, indeed, occurred. Curiously, it is not so much what has been said, but how one is saying it.

Enhanced speech recognition certainly proves crucial for decoding such transitional sequences, with special provisions for detecting disqualified communication. Nonverbal cues figure prominently here in that a spontaneous shrug of the shoulders greatly modifies (or even reverses) the content of what is being said. Other sub-routines target visual cues such as pupil size, body synchrony, breathing patterns, etc. indicative of internal motivational states. Together with verbal cues such as voice stress analysis and speech inflection, the suitably enhanced AI-agent should be able to detect all traces of disqualification within an ongoing interaction.

In light of these more elaborate strategies, the humor-detecting computer necessarily entails a major design upgrade, perhaps several design generations removed from the first general-purpose AI models. Even then, humor would be deemed an optional luxury, with most routine receptionist/PR duties avoiding much recourse to such humorous overtones. Those attempting to employ humor in such a restricted context would be instructed to frame statements in more formal terms, be referred to a human troubleshooter.

Only when true human companionship is paramount does humor rightfully enter the scene, simulating a more informal style of social setting. Here, the roles become less rigidly fixed, in contrast to the formal restrictions governing the more serious realm. Such good-natured bantering facilitates relaxed feelings of camaraderie. Indeed, it is difficult to imagine a computer possessing the instinctual sense of wit so ably delivered by the master comic. Picture a computer comic with a joke for virtually every occasion, tailored to the sensibilities of a given individual or audience. The databanks alone would prove breathtaking, similar to the ambitious joke registries currently in force today.

The humor computer, however, would benefit from schematic indexing conducive to ready retrieval and delivery. This system would be a scriptwriter's dream, producing made-to-order situation comedies through systematic permutations upon pre-existing works. Great works of comedy/tragedy could similarly be indexed within such a schematic format, resulting in a master catalog of literary traditions from around the world. Whether this computer scriptwriter could rival its human counterparts remains to be seen, although its companionship potential is clearly without question. With suitable timeshare capabilities, everyone could enjoy computer companionship, adding a curious twist to the trend in phone-chat hotlines. Indeed, we may finally have come full circle with respect to that we have created, a faithful friend to comfort us in our time of need.

THE ADDITION OF SUPPLEMENTARY EXPERT SYSTEMS

In conclusion, the general AI-agent is technically defined as a recurrently structured matching-procedure based upon the schematic definitions, a process dependent upon both the content and the context of the verbal interaction. In longer narratives (such as storytelling) the meaning is spread out over an extended sentence sequence, a circumstance not always correctly comprehended by the computer. This design shortcoming is further remedied through the addition of supplementary expert systems attuned to such narrative complexities. These add-on programs would be compatible with the basic AI knowledge bases. The most crucial expert system would be the form of a conversational analyzer that specializes in decoding extended conversation for the occurrence of affective meaning. Related expert systems should prove equally applicable, particularly those imparting a general-purpose knowledge base. Once general intelligence is achieved, further expert systems (in the truest sense of the term) would permit proficiency in numerous areas of expertise; e.g., legal, medical, scientific, etc. With proper indoctrination, the AI-agent could conceivably become an expert in virtually every field of endeavor, adding a curious wrinkle to the notion of a walking encyclopedia.

Attention span is a further factor sure to be enhanced within the modified AI format. The typical human mind only accommodates several given tasks at a time reminiscent of the Von Neuman bottleneck. The parallel processing capabilities of the AI-agent, however, certainly surpass such sequential limitations, reaching unheard of degrees of versatility. Indeed, a suitably advanced AI computer could theoretically process numerous conversations simultaneously, wherein maximizing available circuitry by making use of the lulls naturally occurring within general conversation. Here, multiple accounts could be accommodated, rated in terms of increasing urgency. Conversations requiring real-time parameters are assigned the highest priority, whereas more leisurely response rates are processed during free periods. This further entails a centralized CPU complex that connects end users through a standard user interface or the Internet. The bulk of processing would be transferred directly to the considerable resources of the Internet.

In terms of this speculative scenario, the comprehensive knowledge bases of the AI-agent are distributed as open source code over an extensive network of broadband servers. The end user computer needs only run a stripped-down version of the AI-MCU program, where the inference engine interfaces remotely with the web knowledge base on a real-time basis. The basic groundwork for this standardized database is already in the works with respect to the recently proposed Semantic Web. The brainchild of Tim Berners-Lee (the original innovator of the World Wide Web), the Semantic Web proposes to bypass the conceptual limitations of the human-web interface. It alternately aims to implement a machine-to-machine version through standardizing the wealth of network information. In conjunction with further provisions for a built-in AI interface, the futuristic AI assistant could eventually become a reality for those willing to entertain such aspirations. In this expanded sense, the future, indeed, looks bright, with the AI computer emerging as a welcome ally in the upcoming challenges facing mankind in the Third Millennium.

APPENDIX – (<u>A</u>)

BEHAVIORAL CORRELATES
TO THE NEUROSCIENCES

The new science of Powerplay Politics represents a welcome innovation on the world scene today. Its widespread public appeal undoubtedly stems from its unprecedented degree of versatility, incorporating the basic virtues and values of the Western ethical tradition within an elementary foundation in behavioral science. For the first time in history, the principles of behavioral psychology and value ethics can now be seen to be intimately related on parallel scale of synthesis across the board. This is chiefly made possible through the aid of the terminology of Communication Theory; namely, the crucial concept of meta-communication in relation to the principles of instrumental conditioning. Consequently, by specifying these instinctual behavioral principles on an evolutionary time-scale leading up to humans, it ultimately proves feasible to further extend behavioral psychology (as well as value ethics) to a functional foundation within the realm of the neurosciences: as partially outlined below.

Behaviorism is perhaps the most rigid field in the discipline of psychology, although (like psychology in general) it cannot readily be classified as an exact science. Rather, behaviorism is technically considered more of a descriptive science, describing behavior patterns observed in a laboratory setting, as well as within a more free-style human social context. This rather broad range of contexts posits an inferred sense of motivation: implying a motivator (or mental agent) enacting adaptive behavior patterns for fulfilling suitably reinforced motives. Whereas the mind is not a physical entity that can be precisely measured, it therefore stands to reason that behaviorism can never be classified as an exact science to the same degree enjoyed by chemistry or physics. Researchers record outwardly observable signs of behavior and make inferences with respect to motivational states, but never actually measure a distinct state of motivation. Behaviorism is entirely descriptive in that predictions are never absolutely guaranteed. Indeed, a laboratory rat repeatedly pressing a lever can have a number of possible interpretations. Consequently, behavioral experimental design often occurs over long timeframes, when multiple trials distinguish between purposeful or accidental types of behavior.

With respect to sentient human beings, daring parallels can be made between subjectively reported feelings and those inferred from laboratory derived constructs, greatly enhancing correlative links across the animal kingdom. Here, the procedural shortcomings of behavioral science come through the clearest, always relegated to the status of a descriptive science, or what some term a *soft* science. As such, behaviorism can never achieve the exacting precision enjoyed *hard* sciences such as chemistry, physics, and the biological sciences: all of deal with physical subject matter. If it were possible to establish a behavioral link to a material sphere of influence, however, then behavioral psychology (and its extensions to Powerplay Politics) finally would become conceptually complete. The corresponding soft science parameters characterizing behavioral science would enjoy the additional precision of a hard science, reaching an enhanced degree of versatility.

NEUROANATOMICAL CORRELATES

Key conceptual insights towards this interdisciplinary linkage formally exist in relation to outwardly observable manifestations of the human brain. Numerous studies have established that the brain controls purposeful movement in a style outwardly suggestive of motivated behavior. Similarly, the brain further interprets sensory data in a manner

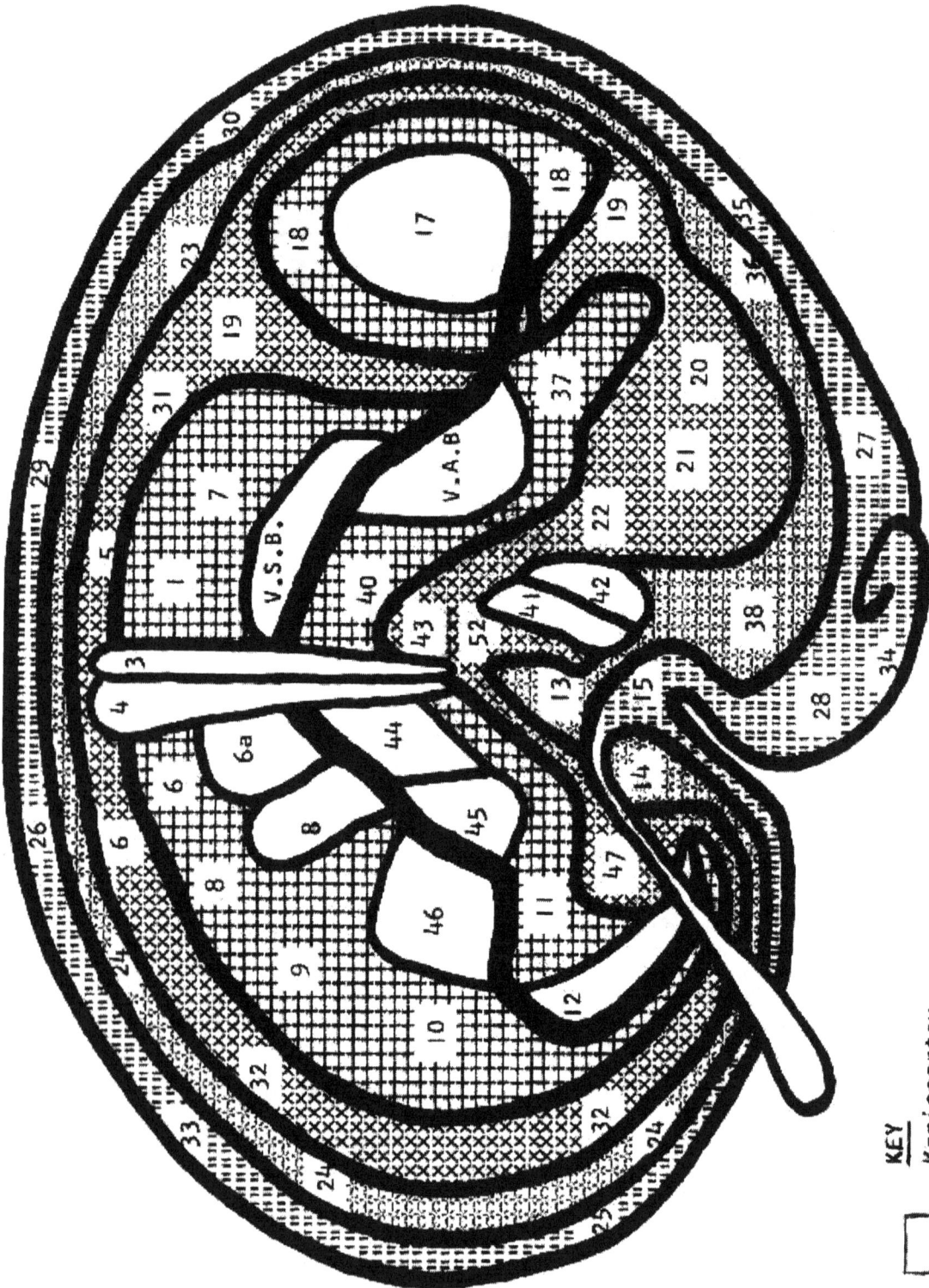

KEY
Koniocortex
Pleurekoniocortex
Paralimbic/insular
Proisocortex
Periallocortex

conducive to motivating such behavior. The human brain is basically a two pound mass of neural tissue that works to mediate the interplay of sensory and motor systems. Philosophically, the brain is considered the seat of the human mind or soul, however one cares to define it. The ultimate paradox of this relationship is that the only way to understand this connection is by observing it, an aspect invoking the existence of an observer (or ego). Unlike the material brain, the mind knows no physical limits, extending as far as our senses can reach, or our behaviors can influence. The mind is intimately connected to the body insofar as consciousness follows wherever the body goes, although science cannot establish any specific mechanism for linking mind and brain.

The dominant theory in our modern times is that of *epiphenomenalism*, where the mind is considered an emergent property of the electrical activity naturally occurring within the brain. The brain operates through electrochemical processes equivalent to the output of a *25 Watt* bulb. Through this rather modest expenditure of energy all of the miraculous manifestations of the mind become manifest in a conscious sense. Due to the extreme complexity of the brain, with estimates of multi-trillions of nerve connections, the precise mechanism for linking mind and brain has so far eluded modern science. Indeed, many researchers prefer to view the brain in terms of the circuitry concept of a *black box*, a notion derived from the field of electronic troubleshooting. In this latter respect, an electronic device of unknown origin and function can be studied by analyzing its input/output parameters without destructively dismantling the device. Consequently, a good indication of the function of the device may often be achieved, wherein enabling a simulation employing more familiar electrical means.

Similar parallels further hold true with respect to the neural attributes of the human brain. The input side encompasses sensory perceptions that serve to prompt the ongoing states of motivation. The output end equates to observable motivated behaviors conducive to the completion of the entire conditioned interaction. From this two-stage behavioral dynamic, one can technically infer that the organism/agent was motivated through sensory cues to take directed action towards resultant reinforcement. Indeed, this proves to be a key function governing the nervous system; namely, the reciprocal interplay of stimulus and response for maintain homeostatic stability in a variable environment. Consequently, from mankind's loftiest achievements to the simplest of instinctual behaviors, this recurrent cycle of stimulus and response dominates neural circuitry throughout the animal kingdom. This grand unifying feature proves crucial towards establishing the correlates of the mind/body connection. By tracing this complete range of behavioral parameters across an evolutionary timescale in relation to brain structure, then this underlying pattern of organization would ultimately permit entry into a degree of precision suitable to the hard sciences.

THE CROWNING CORTICAL LEVEL

The cerebral cortex represents the most logical initiation point for such an analysis, celebrated as the crowning culmination of human forebrain evolution. The dramatic expansion of the human nervous system occurs primarily in the cerebral cortex, the human neocortex expanding to roughly three times the size of mankind's nearest relative, the chimpanzee. The neocortex is anatomically structured as a planar surface, its radical expansion causing an elaborate pattern of wrinkles or sulci (plural of sulcus). The exposed region between the sulci is known as a gyrus (plural = gyri). Indeed, most of the surface area of the cortex it is buried from sight within this expanded system of fissures. This radical expansion of the neocortex is observed to occur in a discrete pattern suggestively termed cortical *growth rings*. The general pattern of neural evolution specifies that older structures are periodically modified to create newer functional areas, although the precursor circuitry is also preserved, so wherein new areas (and old) persist side by side.

The stepwise repetition of these processes over the course of mammalian evolution ultimately accounts for six sequential age levels of cortical evolution, schematically depicted on the facing page. This diagram is organized as a Mercator projection of the human cerebral cortex, a figure modified from an illustration originally devised by Schaltenbrand. This representation depicts the entire surface of the cortex folded flat so that the medial and sub-temporal surfaces of the hemisphere are fully exposed. The deep cortical wrinkles (the sulci) are also flattened-out so that areas hidden within the fissures approximate their true size. The uppermost margin of this diagram represents the limiting aspect of the corpus callosum, whereas the lower margin represents the boundaries of the insular lobe. The differing age levels of the cortex (the growth rings according to Sanides) are depicted as radiating away from either of these two margins.

The first and second cortical growth rings localized along these margins are represented by the

Fig. 1 – DUAL PARAMETER GRID

Inputs →→ / Cortical Growth Rings ↓↓	Mamillary Nucleus	Midbrain Tegmentum	Interstitial N. Cajal / Internal Globus Pallidus	Vestibular & Ia Afferents (N. Cuneatus)	Trigeminal N. & Spinothalamic Tract	Inferior Colliculus	Optic Tract	←← Inputs Thalamic ↓↓ Growth Shells
ARCHAECORTEX	Anterior Olfactory Nuc. Paramedianus oralis #25 FM	Inferior Hippocampus Antero-reuniens #33 LF2	Superior Hippocampus Centremedian magnocellular #26 LF1	Taenia Tecta Nucleus Intralamellaris #29 LE	Medial Cortical Amygdala Paramedianus caudalis #30 LD	Medial Cortical Amygdala Subhabenular Amygdala #35 HA	Dentate Gyrus Zona Incerta #27 HD	**UNSPECIFIC PROTOPATHIC**
PERI-ARCHAECORTEX	Antero-inferior #24 LA	Antero-dorsalis reuniens #24 LA	Reticulatus oralis #24 LA	Reticulatus intermedius #23 LC2	Reticulatus caudalis #23 LC2	Reticulatus pulvinaris #38 TG	Reticulatus geniculatus #36 HC	**RETICULATE FEEDBACK**
PROISOCORTEX	Antero-principalis #32 FEL	Antero-dorsalis #32 FCL	Dorso-oralis externus #24	Dorso-intermedius superior #5 PCY	Dorsalis superficialis #31 LC1	Pulvinaris oromedialis #22 TA2	Pulvinaris superficialis #19 OA	**COMPOSITE MULTI-SENSORY**
PARALIMBIC	Antero-medialis #10 FE	Medialis fasciculosus superior #8 FC	Dorso-oralis internus #6aβ FB	Dorso-intermedius externus/internus #3a PA1	Dorso-caudalis #31 LC1	Pulvinaris orolateralis #22 TA1	Pulvinaris supra-brachialis #19 OA	**2ND INTEGRATIVE LEVEL**
PREKONIO-CORTEX	Medialis fasciculosus posterior #46 FDΔ	Medialis paralamellaris #80 FC	Zentro-lateralis oralis #6aβ FB	Zentro-lateralis intermedius #3a PA1	Zentro-lateralis caudalis #7 PE	Pulvinaris oroventralis #22 PE	Pulvinaris inter-geniculatus #18 OB	**1ST INTEGRATIVE LEVEL**
KONIOCORTEX	Medialis paralamellaris posterior #12 FH	Medialis paralamellaris #45 FDf	Ventro-oralis anterior & internus #6aα FB	Ventro-intermedius #3a PA2	Visuo-sensory Band Ventrocaudalis posterior PD	Geniculatus medialis fibrosus #41 TC	Geniculatus lateralis #17 OC	**RELAY**
KONIOCORTEX	Medialis fasciculosus anterior #11 FG	Medialis caudalis externus #9 FD	Lateropolaris externus & internus #44 FCBm	Ventro-oralis posterior & internus #4γ FAγ	Ventrocaudalis anterior #3b PB	Geniculatus medialis fibrosus #42 TB	Visuo-auditory Band Pulvinaris lateralis inferior #42 PG	**RELAY**
PREKONIO-CORTEX	Medialis fibrosus #47 FFa	Medialis caudalis externus #47 FFo	Lateropolaris basialis #44 FCDop	Ventro-oralis posterior basialis #4δ FA	Ventrocaudalis parvocellularis #1 PC	Geniculatus medialis fasciculosus #40 PF	Pulvinaris lateralis superior #37 PH	**1ST INTEGRATIVE LEVEL**
PARAINSULAR	Medialis fibrosus #47 FI	Medialis caudalis internus #47 F1	Lateropolaris basialis #50 FBop	Ventro-oralis posterior #50 FAop	Ventrocaudalis portae #43 Pfop	Geniculatus medialis magnocellular #52 TD	Pulvinaris medialis dorsalis #20 & 21 TE	**2ND INTEGRATIVE LEVEL**
PROISOCORTEX	Medialis fibrosus #16 FK	Medialis caudalis internus #16 FK	Lateropolaris superior #14 IA	Ventro-oralis medialis #14 IA	Geniculatus medialis magnocellular #13 IB	Geniculatus medialis magnocellular #13 IB	Pulvinaris medialis ventralis #38 TG	**COMPOSITE MULTI-SENSORY**
PERI-PALEOCORTEX	Medialis basialis #47	Medialis basialis	Lateropolaris magnocellularis #16 ID	Lateropolaris magnocellularis #16 ID	Geniculatus medialis limitans #15 IC	Geniculatus medialis limitans #15 TI	Limitans opticus #28 & 34 HB	**RETICULATE FEEDBACK**
PALEOCORTEX	Lateral Olfactory Tubercle Habenula	Nuc. of Diagonal Band of Broca Habenula	Piriform Cortex Centremedian parvocellular	Piriform Cortex Parafascicularis	Lateral Cortical Amygdala Limitans portae	Piriform Cortex Limitans portae	Piriform Cortex Limitans medialis	**UNSPECIFIC PROTOPATHIC**
Cortical Growth Rings Inputs →→	*Interpeduncular Nuc.*	*Lateral Hypothalamus*	*Praestitial N. & External Globus Pallidus*	*Dentate Cerebellar Nucleus*	*Chief Trigeminal / Medial Lemniscus*	*Inferior Colliculus*	*Superior Colliculus*	↑↑ Thalamic Growth Shells Inputs ←←

Key to Notation – Top Line is Cortical Terminology by Broadman and von Economo – Below are Thalamic Nuclei by Rolf Hassler

evolutionarily ancient cingulate and insular gyri. Sanides designates the first cortical growth ring as periallocortex, further subdivided in it into the periarchaecortex (bordering the archaecortex) and the peripaleocortex (situated adjacent to the paleocortex). These two linked components collectively form a ring that encircles the remaining newer areas that evolved within the neocortex. Sanides, in turn, designates a second neocortical growth ring coined proisocortex: also subdivided into cingulate and insular sub-components collectively comprising a second-order growth ring. This initial pair of primitive growth rings are actually fairly narrow in relation to the overall diagram, although (for stylistic reasons) are thickened somewhat for sake of overall presentation.

A third cortical growth ring identified by Sanides is situated in the space immediately adjacent to the initial two growth rings. Sanides respectively subdivides this concentric structure into the paralimbic and parainsular components collectively comprising a third-order growth ring. This preliminary primordial sequence of three cortical growth rings is primarily hidden deep within the medial and insular areas of the human cerebral hemisphere. The more recent cortical growth core areas, however, directly extend outward to encompass the more expansive laterally exposed convexity of the hemisphere. Here, stepwise refinements to cellular organization result in the final neocortical growth core according to Sanides. He designates this final cortical age level *koniocortex* following the terminology for the major visual, auditory, and somatosensory representations. Koniocortex is situated as an unpaired growth core region (shown in white within the diagram) in contrast to the ring structure previously established for the preceding age levels.

Should this actually be the case, however, it is difficult to explain why there are so many other distinctive cortical areas that collectively comprise this final cortical growth core. Indeed, it seems highly inconsistent to group the heterotypical koniocortical areas with the surrounding homotypical class of association cortex. These organizational difficulties are ultimately resolved through a radical revision of this basic format, proposing that Sanides' final koniocortical growth core actually represents two distinct cortical age levels: namely, an older growth ring (now designated as *pleurokoniocortex*) that now surrounds the most recent koniocortical growth core situated at the central-most position on the hemisphere convexity. The respective cortical areas for this final growth core focus are individually outlined in black within the master growth ring diagram.

These most recent evolutionary areas are respectively situated along the central axial-sulcus represented by the stylized thick black line, a feature Sanides designates as the *ur-trend* limiting sulcus. According to Sanides, this sulcus marks the terminal juncture between those portions of the growth rings derived from the cingulate gyrus and those derived from the insular lobe. This juncture represents the precise location where the newest growth core is centrally located. Indeed, a very good correlation exists between the extent of the koniocortical growth core and the ur-trend limiting sulcus.

In summary, with respect to the cortical subdivisions of the human forebrain, a sequential gradient of five neocortical growth waves, plus the earliest precursor allocortical growth ring (not shown in the diagram) sums to a grand total of six individual cortical age levels. The master Mercator projection proved particularly effective for demonstrating this complete set of cortical growth rings. The broad range of numbers inscribed within this diagram denotes those cortical regions distinguished through measurable differences in cell structure and organization. Cortical areas comprising a given growth ring exhibit similar cellular characteristics, although minor variations exist within each growth ring resulting in a circular pattern of cortical variations similar to beads making up a necklace. The rationale behind these areal demarcations is attributed to the variations in input specificity across the entire extent of each cortical growth ring. Cortical areas receiving auditory inputs appear distinct from areas receiving visual inputs, as this distinctly affects the cellular appearance of within the various cortical layers.

This observation appears to be the chief rationale underlying the wide variety of cortical parcellation schemes that have emerged over the course of the preceding century. In hindsight, these ultimately accurately reflect this observed style of specificity of inputs, wherein permitting a number of crucial functional predictions in relation to the organization of the human neocortex. The first major system of cortical parcellation was proposed by German anatomist K. Broadman in 1909. This enduring system used Arabic numerals to specify roughly 50 distinct areas in the human cerebral cortex (as schematically depicted on pg. *418*). A complementary parcellation system was further introduced by Austrian researcher Constantin von Economo in 1923 employing a lettering system of notation, the first letter of which indicates which lobe of the hemisphere a particular area is situated. These two dominant systems exhibit significant commonalties with respect to the identification of distinctive cortical areas, although a number of telling distinctions further emerge. Both systems rely upon the identification of distinctive areal demarcations within the cerebral hemisphere, as determined by cellular variations and/or fiber density criteria. Some transitions appear quite abrupt in microscopic section, as in dramatic increases in the size or density of the pyramidal cell layers. Other transitions appear more gradual, as in shifts in fiber density within the various cortical layers, hence, driving the structural rationale for the cortical parcellation schemes for both Broadman and von Economo.

Although the precise details underlying each of these formats is clearly beyond the basic scope of the current chapter, the major focus here concerns their relevant functional significance in relation to their specificity for the various classes of input. For instance, a thick granular layer IV relates predominantly to exteroceptive inputs such as vision or hearing, whereas agranular characteristics occur in cortical areas devoted to motor functions. It is this distinctive functional specificity, in concert with evolutionary perspectives that serve as the primary focus for the remainder of the current chapter, providing the elementary foundation for the proposed grand unified correlation linking behavioral principles with the neurosciences, as technically outlined below.

THE DUAL PARAMETER GRID DESCRIBING HUMAN FOREBRAI EVOLUTION

The two fundamental variables defining forebrain evolution are the parameters of phylogenetic age and input specificity. The parameter of phylogenetic age was first quantitatively demonstrated in the marsupial neocortex as the set of "successive waves of circumferential differentiation" (Abbie, 1942). The analogous series of age levels detected in the cortex of placental mammals by Sanides (1969) were alternately designated "growth rings of the neocortex." The remaining parameter of input specificity is manifest as a related series of cortical bands, each of which receives the thalamic relay of a specific forebrain input. These cortical input bands are distinguished according to the various sensory (Penfield & Rasmussen, 1950) or motor (Hassler, 1966) functional responses elicited during localized electro-cortical stimulation.

The precise number of elementary levels has accurately been determined for both basic forebrain parameters. Sanides (1972) proposed that the human cortex evolved as a sequence of five concentric growth rings comprising a mediolateral hemisphere gradient. Furthermore, the in-

teroceptive, exteroceptive and proprioceptive input categories each project to their own four-part complex of cortical bands that (when taken collectively) define an antero-posterior hemisphere gradient. When the para-coronal variable of phylogenetic age is plotted as the ordinate and the para-sagittal parameter of input specificity charted as the abscissa in a Cartesian coordinate system, the resulting dual parameter grid depicted in appendix **Fig. 1** (shown overleaf) is spatially oriented in a pattern analogous to the standard cortical representation shown on pg. *418*. Each unit square within this schematic chart depicts paired coordinate values specifying unique age and input forebrain parameters.

The areal demarcations characterizing the conventional cortical parcellation schemes coincide strongly with the boundaries interposed between individual levels for both forebrain parameters. Accordingly, the human cortical parcellation schemes of Broadman (1909) and von Economo (1929) correlate topographically on essentially a one-to-one basis with the theoretically-derived dual parameter grid. Each cortical area described by Broadman and von Economo corresponds (in hindsight) to schematically unique age/input parameter coordinates, wherein denoting a precise location within the dual parameter grid. Areas on the hemisphere convexity correlate quantitatively on a one-to-one basis with the coordinate unit squares. A certain amount of correlative redundancy, nevertheless, is inevitable for the more ancient insular/cingulate regions.

The parallel evolution of both the neocortex and the dorsal thalamus dictates that the latter also differentiates as a function of these two basic forebrain parameters. The antero-posterior series of cortical input bands is oriented in a sequence matching the corresponding sagittal array of input nuclei in the dorsal thalamus. Furthermore, Rolf Hassler's (1972) theory of hexapartition of the thalamus (in terms of input specificity) is exceedingly reminiscent of the identical number of growth waves within the neocortex. The equivalent number of parameter levels for both the dorsal thalamus and the cortex dictates that both major subdivisions follow an identical coordinate scheme. Consequently, the detailed classification of thalamic nuclei according to Hassler (1959) correlates topographically on a one-to-one basis with the specifics predicted within the dual parameter grid. Furthermore, each thalamic nucleus of specific age and input coordinates projects principally to that cortical area comprising identical pair-coordinate values, implying that thalamo-cortical interconnectivity is similarly defined in terms of the specifics for this dual parameter grid paradigm.

The dual parameter grid depicted in **Fig. 1** represents a modified version of an original representation reproduced from an earlier journal article by the author (LaMuth, 1977). The initial journal diagram represented the first measured endeavor towards quantitatively ordering subdivisions of the forebrain into a globally coherent pattern. The currently modified version of the dual parameter grid aspires to designate the first "*Periodic Table* for the Human Forebrain," analogous to the similar influence the Atomic Periodic Table enjoys respect to Chemistry and Physics. The respective neural counterpart imparts a crucial sense of systematic order and purpose to the fragmented state of affairs currently prevailing within the neurosciences. As such, it provides the long-anticipated link between the "hard" physical science of neuroanatomy with its "soft" correlates to behavioral and humanistic psychology. A more detailed review of cortical growth ring theory is definitely in order here, providing further welcome validation for the dual parameter paradigm.

THE CIRCUMFERENTIAL GROWTH RINGS OF NEOCORTICAL EVOLUTION

The cortical manifestation of the evolutionary parameter of phylogenetic age is most readily apparent in terms of the circumferential set of cortical growth rings portrayed on pg. *418*. According to Sanides (1970) two discrete stages of differentiation have occurred within the human neocortex. The initial lamination of the paleocortical and archaecortical components of the primordial allocortex creates the periallocortical growth wave. In a second stage of differentiation, the periallocortex, in turn, generates a sequence of three additional circumferential waves: designated by Sanides as pro-, para-, and konio-age levels. These latter three age levels are defined as variations on the hexalaminar organization of the periallocortex rather than any additional lamination phases.

The final koniocortical growth core, however, covering virtually the entire hemisphere convexity, was further reevaluated to actually comprise an evolutionary sequence of two developmentally distinct neocortical growth waves. Through cytoarchitectonic criteria, it proves inconsistent to group the heterotypical classical koniocortex and the homotypic association cortex within the same cortical growth wave. By myelographic standards, koniocortex represents a focal maximum within the hemisphere myelination trend (Sanides, 1969), signifying an evolutionarily later develop-

ment than the less accentuated association regions. According to these basic criteria, Sanides' final neocortical growth wave is intrinsically modified into a sixth order koniocortical growth core, flanked by a pair of belt zones corresponding to a fifth-order growth ring. Retaining the format introduced by Sanides, it is proposed that this distinction be recognized by restricting the term "koniocortex" to the sixth wave of differentiation, while coining the term *pleurokoniocortex* to define the ring-like fifth cortical wave.

A REVISION OF NEOCORTICAL UR-TREND THEORY

Koniocortex appears unique among cortical waves in that it is manifest as a central core surrounded concentrically by all of the older growth rings. Those portions of the growth rings, positioned between the medial koniocortical border and the archaecortex are termed the medial ur-trend, while the growth ring segments intermediate to the paleocortex and lateral koniocortical boundary are termed the lateral ur-trend (Sanides, 1970). Using cytoarchitectonic and myelographic techniques, Sanides demonstrated that the classical sensorimotor representations developed via continuity across both ur-trends; with one ur-trend generally more accentuated than its counterpart.

The boldly accented line schematically depicted at the interface interposed between the medial and lateral ur-trends represents what is termed the ur-trend limiting sulcus (Sanides, 1969). This limiting sulcus is represented rostrally as the inferior frontal sulcus, intermediately as the sensorimotor sulcus between the arm and head representations, and caudally as the interparietal sulcus (Sanides, (1970). The position of each koniocortical representative area relative to this limiting sulcus proves a valuable criterion for determining its respective ur-trend of origin. For instance, for the frontal lobe, the inferior frontal gyrus comprises a sequence of three highly differentiated areas designated as pars opercularis (#44), pars triangularis (#45), and pars orbitalis (#12) - (Sanides, 1964). These three areas characteristically display giant pyramidal cells in lamina III-c: an essential property of areal maximums derived across the lateral ur-trend. The middle frontal gyrus is host to an analogous sequence of ur-trend maxima; namely, areas #46, #8δ, and #6aα. These three areas all display a size accentuation of pyramidal cells in lamina V characteristic of medial ur-trend origin.

A close inspection of the posterior association region reveals the presence of a conspicuous pair of highly myelinated koniocortical bands. The visuo-auditory band is situated within area #39 of the visual association cortex, whereas the corresponding visuo-sensory band is located between areas #7 and #40 in the somatosensory association region. These bands were first detected during gross dissection as regions of dramatic myelin accentuation (Smith, 1907). These same cortical strips were subsequently shown to commence myelination much earlier than the surrounding association regions (Flechsig, 1920). The medially derived visuo-sensory band is located on the dorsal wall of the interparietal sulcus denoting a medial ur-trend origin. Alternately, the visuo-auditory band is situated lateral to the occipital continuation of this sulcus indicative of a lateral ur-trend differentiation. Furthermore, the primary visual cortical area #17 was cited by Sanides (1970) as derived along a medial ur-trend gradient. Accordingly, area #17 exhibits the giant pyramidal cells of Meynert in cortical lamina V. In this same article, Sanides proposed that the primary auditory cortex developed along a lateral ur-trend gradient, at least in the case of lamina III-c accentuated area #42. Auditory area #41 does not exhibit giant III-c pyramidal cells, presumed to derive by way of a medial ur-trend gradient spanning the superior temporal gyrus.

The remaining intermediate segment of the koniocortical core is composed of sensorimotor areas #4γ, #3a, and #3b of the pre- and postcentral gyri. The distended parallel orientation of all three areas (perpendicular to the ur-trend limiting sulcus) promotes somatotopic cross-modal continuity, but also invalidates the limiting sulcus as an ur-trend determining criterion. Unlike the classical somatosensory area #3b displaying giant pyramidal cells in lamina III-c, the cortical motor areas #4γ and #3a alternately exhibit large pyramidal cells in both inner and outer laminae (Bailey & von Bonin, 1951). Consequently, these latter two areas are provisionally included within the pattern of strict unit alternation for medially/laterally derived growth core areas.

In light of the preceding revision of evolutionary ur-trend theory, a corresponding modification must necessarily be made to Dart's (1934) theory of the origin of the neocortex. Dart had noted continuity between the archaeocortex and the internal cortical laminae on one hand, and between the paleocortex and the external laminae on the other. These observations had been interpreted to be the earliest manifestations of a primordial lamination of the paleocortex over the archaeocortex to yield the characteristic hexalaminar organization of the neocortex, serving as further crucial criteria for specifying subsequent evolutionary development.

THALAMIC GROWTH SHELL THEORY

A more detailed mention of the other major subdivision of the forebrain, the dorsal thalamus, was deferred until now in order to exploit the many potential analogies to cortical phylogenesis. The implied parallel evolution of the dorsal thalamus and the neocortex specifies the existence of a parallel gradient of diencephalic differentiation analogous to the respective sequence of cortical growth rings demonstrated within the telencephalon. The three-dimensional organization of the dorsal thalamus, however, renders this diencephalic gradient more difficult to detect than the orderly growth rings within the planar pallium. Fortunately, in hindsight, Hassler's paradigm of the hexapartition of input termination sites within the dorsal thalamus represents the diencephalic counterpart for the six distinct age levels demonstrated for the neocortical gradient. According to Hassler (1972) six distinct levels comprise the dorsal thalamus, ranked in order of specificity as (1) relay (2) first integrative level (3) second integrative level (4) composite multisensory (5) reticulate feedback, and (6) unspecific protopathic.

The primordial unspecific protopathic age level provides crucial clues towards specifying the precise mechanisms underlying dorsal thalamic differentiation. The anterior portion of the non-specific thalamic gray matter (consisting of the nucleus fasciculosus and reuniens, pars ventralis of nucleus medialis and centralis, and the rostral parts of nucleus parafascicularis and centro-median) have all been demonstrated to be of subthalamic origin (Reinoso-Suarez, 1966). In the same article, the reticulate nucleus of the next most recent age level was similarly cited as derived from the subthalamus: suggesting the existence of a subthalamic gradient of differentiation. The subthalamus borders the dorsal thalamus from below, dictating that this gradient be termed the "ventral ur-trend" of thalamic differentiation.

The alternate posterior segment of the unspecific age level includes the nucleus limitans, suprageniculatus, peripenduncularis, and posterior centro-median. This caudal series of nuclei collectively display a distinctively intense cholinesterasic staining activity (Poirer, 1974) denoting a common developmental origin. The close proximity and/or continuity of this posterior series of nuclei to the habenula (Hassler, 1959) suggests that the epithalamus represents the remaining elementary origin of dorsal thalamic differentiation. At least in lower vertebrates, the epithalamus borders the dorsal thalamus from above, dictating that this gradient be termed the "dorsal ur-trend" of the thalamic differentiation.

These primordial precursors for the dorsal thalamus serve as the terminus for a dual optic projection similar to the dual olfactory bulb projection to the allocortex. More specifically, the epithalamus receives direct visual input from the dorsal parietal eye of lower vertebrates, whereas the subthalamus is similarly affiliated to the main lateral eyes. The parietal eye of lower vertebrates develops embryologically from the distal end of the pineal (or parapineal) evagination of the epithalamic ependyma. In the primitive lamprey eel, both pineal and parapineal bodies develop ocular structures suggesting that a remote ancestral vertebrate had paired dorsal eyes in addition to the persistent lateral eyes (Sarnat & Netsky, 1974). Nerve fibers from the retina of the parietal eye project to the habenula (Kappers, 1965), however, all photosensory afferents to the habenula degenerate upon atrophy of the parietal eye in mammals. The primordial visual projection from the main paired lateral eyes is directed to the pregeniculate nucleus, cited as yet another subthalamic derivative (Reinoso-Suarez, 1966).

The six evolutionarily distinct "growth shells" detected within the three-dimensional structure of the dorsal thalamus developed as new anatomical variations across each basic ur-trend, designated in terms of the corresponding schematic levels from Hassler's paradigm of hexapartition of thalamic inputs. Hence, both the cortex and the thalamus systematically evolved in response to a more comprehensive blending of inputs from differing neuraxial levels. Furthermore, each thalamic nucleus of specific parameter coordinates directs its main projection to cells of the cortex displaying identical coordinate values, establishing forebrain interconnectivity as yet a further function of the dual parameter grid.

EXTEROCEPTIVE, INTEROCEPTIVE, AND PROPRIOCEPTIVE MODALITIES

The precise number of component ur-trends proves an evolutionarily stable feature for both major forebrain divisions. The prefrontal cortex and the dorsomedial thalamic nucleus (to which it projects) are each subdivided into four component columns dealing with interoceptive inputs derived from the hypothalamus (Nauta & Haymaker, 1969) and the limbic midbrain area (Guillery, 1959; Massopust & Thompson, 1962). The agranular frontal motor cortex and the lateral thalamic

nuclei are similarly split four ways each for dealing individually with specialized proprioceptive inputs reaching the forebrain. When the developmentally related auditory and somatosensory representations are taken as a unit, the exteroceptively-specialized posterior granular cortex and pulvinar/geniculate complex also display a similar four-part pattern of organization. This highly stable 4-4-4 arrangement makes it exceedingly unlikely that any new values for the parameter of input specificity would be added as a result of more comprehensive parcellation of the forebrain.

The ultimate test for the dual parameter grid, however, is based upon the odds that two such widely divergent divisions of the forebrain would both be correlated to the same dual coordinate system. The cortical relay of each thalamic input category (by way of the thalamic radiations) by definition predicts an equivalent complement of input specificity units within the cortex. The identical number of age levels for both the thalamus and the cortex further suggests that only correspondingly numbered age levels are reciprocally interconnected by way of the internal capsule. Theoretically, a thalamic cell on a discrete point within the time-differentiation continuum directs its main projection to cortical cells derived during the same phylogenetic age. These evolutionary restrictions specify that only thalamic and cortical areas of identical age and input coordinates, (e.g. within the same unit square) interconnect via the thalamic radiations. In his studies on the human thalamus, Hassler (1959) cites a wide assortment of thalamic projections correlating consistently to the specifics predicted for the dual parameter grid. Yakolev's (et al. 1966) documentation of the cortical projections for the composite-multi-sensory thalamic age level further corroborates these unit-square restrictions. It is this precise topographical correlation to the dual parameter grid that establishes this new paradigm as a truly accurate account of human forebrain evolution.

In summary, through the aid of this breakthrough *"periodic table"* for the human forebrain (employing elementary exteroceptive, interoceptive, and proprioceptive input categories) an intimately detailed pattern of correspondence can be established with respect to the instinctual principles of behavioral psychology. Here, the human forebrain formally expands upon the basic stimulus/response (sensory/motor) reflex arcs implicit within the neuraxial spinal cord and brainstem. The intermediary neurons of the neuraxis mediating interoceptive sensations interposing emotional correlates within the sequence of exteroceptive stimuli and subsequent behavioral response, as schematically reflected in the operantly conditioned sequence. The nervous system never completely replaces basic circuitry, rather further modifying it: as evident in the vast expansion of the human forebrain based upon the visual and olfactory senses. Therefore, by applying these behavioral principles on an evolutionary scale clear on up to humans, it ultimately proves feasible to propose a grand unified synthesis of behavioral psychology with its corresponding "hard science" referent in the neurosciences.

The forebrain appears to have adaptively evolved as a dedicated motivational analyzer that attaches motivational significance to exteroceptive stimuli (such as vision and hearing) in preparation for appropriate action by the motor areas that also mediate proprioceptive feedback in terms of such operantly conditioned behaviors. Indeed, this behavioral dynamic exhibits many parallels to the black-box paradigm of input/output characteristics. The human forebrain (similar to the hypothetical black-box) still hides many of its secrets; although unprecedented progress is clearly in order with respect to the dual parameter grid. The current chapter represents only the most cursory outline of the theoretical subject matter at hand, the complete body of details requiring an entire book length manuscript to adequately document (an upcoming future release). This basic outline is boldly being appended here in order to further validate the systematic dynamics and versatility of the new science of Powerplay Politics with an eye towards enhancing global peace and harmony.

APPLICATIONS TO POWERPLAY POLITICS

The preceding proposed correlation linking behavioral psychology and the neurosciences offers many exciting applications on the world scene today. Although the behavioral principles underlying operant conditioning were effectively proposed as the basic conceptual foundation for the ethical hierarchy of traditional virtues and values, extending these aspects to the realm of the neurosciences appears exceedingly more problematic. The key solution resides in a general overview of the general affective language traditions, where the respective virtuous terms are specified as metaperspectival variations within an abstract linguistic matrix, something routine behavioral science technically fails to address. Indeed, mankind's unique use of conceptually abstract language implies the emergence of a subjective "I" ego manifest through conscious mental reflection. Hence, a grand scale correlation of the reflective

mind to the structure of the human brain is an achievement whose time has finally come. Countless lifetimes within in the fields of behavioral and philosophical psychology have aimed for the day when the gap separating these two grand disciplines might finally be bridged. The introspective discipline of philosophy has traditionally maintained a substantial lead in the search for such a mind/brain synthesis. The philosophical tradition of reflective awareness dates at least to the classical philosophers of antiquity. In contrast, neuroanatomical research dates only to the last few centuries, the bulk of research garnered within the last 50 years. Until a century or so ago, not enough was known about overall brain function to even hazard a guess as to the foundations for human reflection, much less its particular details.

The bilateral symmetry of the paired cerebral hemispheres is clearly suggestive of this pattern of reflective interaction, although experimental verification was long in coming. In this latter respect, virtually every neocortical area is connected to its mirror image area in the opposite hemisphere by way of a large bundle of nerve fibers known as the corpus callosum. Only a few minor exceptions, such as primary visual area #17 and the sensory representations for the hands and feet, circumvent this symmetrical pattern of bilateral connectivity. This missing contribution remains insignificant compared to the estimated 200 million total nerve fibers comprising this commissure bundle, a dual-directional conductivity rated at billions of nerve impulses per second. The magnitude of this inter-hemispheric connectivity rivals even the intra-cortical pattern of connectivity connecting the various areas within a single hemisphere.

Although both hemispheres are virtually indistinguishable at a gross anatomical level, a general asymmetry in function has recently become apparent during the latter half of the last century. Based upon brain-stroke studies, it had long been widely accepted that cortical speech areas are virtually always located within the left hemisphere (thusly designated as the dominant hemisphere). Any asymmetry in hemisphere function for normal subjects, however, is obscured by the massive connectivity of the corpus callosum linking corresponding points within each hemisphere. A later therapeutic regimen of surgical sections of the corpus callosum in epileptic patients gave the first major indications of the significance of this connective-bundle in the global realm of psychological reflection. Unobstructed accessibility to the corpus callosum via the dorsal cleft separating the two hemispheres permitted the selective cleavage of this tract without damage to the adjoining cerebral structures. This surgical procedure was undertaken as a course of last resort for over a dozen epileptic patients suffering from chronic seizures intractable even to medication. Unilateral seizures were effectively blocked from passing to the opposite hemisphere promoting a marked remission of the debilitating epileptic effects.

Post-operative psychological testing of certain of these patients by Sperry (and associates, 1974) clearly indicated the potential for fully independent hemisphere function. Each hemisphere in split-brain patients receives its own spatially exclusive complement of sensory input determined through the bilateral localization of spinal/brainstem tracts ascending to the forebrain. The bilateral input restrictions imposed upon each hemisphere served as the basis for the clever experimental designs for testing the reactions of each functionally isolated hemisphere. For instance, the finer discriminative aspects of the tactile sense project only to the hemisphere situated contra-lateral from the side of the body that originally had been stimulated.

This sensory specificity is exploited experimentally by placing a familiar object into either the right or left hand of the patient out of line of sight and soliciting subjective impressions. The visual system exhibits a similar pattern of bilateral specificity in that the portions of the retina directed towards the left side of the visual field project to the right hemisphere, and vice-versa. Consequently, experimental design is modified so that a picture or written information is flashed to either the left or right visual field for a scant tenth of the second so as to defeat subsequent shifts in the gaze of the subject (that would tip off the contra-lateral hemisphere). The catalogued subjective reports of test subjects during various experimental contexts have yielded quite unexpected interpretation concerning the functional interactivity linking the two cerebral hemispheres. Sperry was able to show that the two hemispheres communicated in radically different spatial and linguistic styles, verifying the traditional distinctions of dominant and mute hemispheres.

The dominant hemisphere alone communicates through verbal syntax consistent with the localization of the major speech centers within this hemisphere. Sperry estimates that the left hemisphere exhibits this dominance aspect in roughly 98 percent of the cases studied, making this left/right dichotomy virtually synonymous for most practical purposes. Likewise, the right hemisphere is invariably associated with a mute expressive demeanor consistent with its relatively more minor role. The right hemisphere communicates primarily in terms of a nonverbal, gestural mode, further suggesting its descriptive designation as the "mute" hemisphere. The verbal communication of the dominant hemisphere and the gestural expression of the minor hemisphere were experimentally shown to independently occur, their communicational styles often completely at odds with one another.

In a classic series of controlled studies on split-brain patients, Sperry demonstrated that the dominant hemisphere operates in an essentially independent fashion from the minor hemisphere. For instance, a patient was situated so that words flashed on a screen were visible only to the left or right hemisphere. The word "pencil" was projected so as to reach only the right minor hemisphere. Upon questioning, the patient reported that no word had been seen, consistent with speech localized only to the left hemisphere. Simultaneous to this verbal denial, the left hand (controlled by the right hemisphere) proceeded to a tray of objects out of line of sight, and through tactile discrimination was consistently able to select the named object. The minor hemisphere exhibited the capacity for a sentient and intelligent course of action, yet it was unable to express itself verbally.

The dominant hemisphere, in contrast, is fully capable of reporting in a first-person tense denoting the functioning of a subjective "I" ego. Being that such a verbally expressive reflective ego is posited only in the dominant hemisphere, what then is the nature of the mute intelligence located within the minor hemisphere? By all outright appearances, the right hemisphere appears impersonal in its mode of expression, an aspect suggestive of pre-reflective aspects of consciousness. Perhaps the pre-reflective aspects of the subconscious mind are localized within the minor hemisphere, just as the reflective "I" ego is specialized within the dominant hemisphere. This definition of minor hemisphere activity in terms of the subconscious experience is certainly in agreement with experimental observations. Despite good performance of the right hemisphere with respect to names of common objects, even the simplest of verbs or verbal commands are not comprehended by it. The dominant hemisphere, however, is freely expressive in terms of syntax of verbal communication, suggesting functionality primarily within an active style of temporal dimension. The sequential ordering of word concepts into syntactical statements that define past or future contexts seemingly verifies such a time-ordered reflective capability. The "I" ego, as the sum-unity of subjective perceptions, is necessarily optimized for abstraction within a temporal dimension conducive to directing the intricacies of complex tasks. The dominant hemisphere appears much less incompetent in relation to spatial tasks, suggesting that that the time-oriented dominant hemisphere is complemented by the spatially-oriented minor hemisphere, and vice versa.

According to this cursory style of analysis, it would appear that the distinctive functional characteristics of the paired human cerebral hemispheres exhibit a precise correspondence to the existential notions of the "I" ego and the subconscious mind. The results of split-brain studies indicate that the two hemispheres interact in a reflective communicational capacity, suggesting a similar relationship for the subjective constructs of the subconscious mind and the ego. The psychological deficits apparent in split brain patients suggest that information interchange between the left and right hemispheres is crucial in terms of a reflective sphere of awareness. A description of the most familiar form of reflection (Cartesian reflection) serves to illustrate how the ego emerges during the reflective process. The classical Cartesian formula: "I think, therefore I am" represents a prime example of reflection concerning the prerequisites of the "I" ego. German philosopher, Edmund Husserl, in his *Cartesian Meditations*, demonstrates the dual character for this reflective formula: the components of which are, I think of a proposition (P), and I am aware I think (P).

Whereas general reflection characterizes a general function of the dominant hemisphere, then a parallel form of reflection must necessarily target the minor hemisphere (owing to the two-way information potential across the corpus callosum). Husserl suggests precisely such a solution in his 1906 publication, *Ideas; A General Introduction to Pure Phenomenology*, where he introduces an alternate form of reflective inquiry widely known as *phenomenological reduction*. Husserl's phenomenological reduction comprises two distinct sequential stages similar to the thinking and knowing phases of Cartesian reflection. The first-stage in phenomenological reduction is designated transcendental reduction or phenomenological epoche (also known as bracketing). Epoche is defined as the observation of an object as experienced in the present, disavowing any judgment concerning its enduring existence, a timeless experience. With the temporal dimension attenuated, the subconscious dictates of the right hemisphere freely develop a holistic unification of gestalt qualities entirely within the here and now. Consequently, the pictorial/pattern sense of the

right hemisphere is accented, while the temporal qualities of the left hemisphere are bracketed.

The second stage of phenomenological reduction is termed eidetic reduction by Husserl, from *eidos* (essence). Eidetic reduction builds upon the residuum remaining from the bracketing phase, translating it into a universal essence of experience. This essential universality of our perceptions inwardly lived are eidetically actualized according to their essential possibilities within pure experience. Therefore, phenomenological reduction formally appears to mirror the ego-driven dynamics of Cartesian reflection in relation to the mirror-image symmetry linking the paired cerebral hemispheres.

In conclusion, through the breakthrough prerequisites of the dual parameter grid, a suitably effective correlation between the principles of behavioral psychology and human forebrain organization finally becomes conceptually complete. This innovation was technically proposed in terms of a common exteroceptive, interoceptive, and proprioceptive organizational dynamic for both brain and behavior. This functional correlation to behavioral principles, however, only technically applies to the organizational dynamics restricted to a single cerebral hemisphere, necessitating a further degree of functional analysis targeting the interactivity linking the paired cerebral hemispheres for ultimately explaining the linguistic and ethical aspects specified within the three-digit coding system. Through the aid of the parallel reflective concepts of Cartesian reflection and phenomenological reduction, a thoroughly adequate model of the linguistic aspects of the ethical hierarchy is finally proposed, extending its underlying behavioral foundations to a parallel correlation within the realm of the pure neurosciences. Although this cursory sphere of speculation admittedly represents the briefest of outlines for such a grand unified endeavor, the full details are ultimately reserved for an upcoming book release. This grand-scale proposal was purposely restricted to an analysis within this accessory Appendix-(A) in order to provide an intriguing glimpse of avenues towards further research in relation to the neurosciences. This extension of the ethical/behavioral aspects of the new science of Powerplay Politics into the more physically demonstrable realm of the neurosciences is only currently being proposed in order to add a further degree of validity and versatility to the entire conceptual edifice: and one that may ultimately work to implement innovations towards promoting and preserving global peace and harmony on the world international scene.

INDEX OF THE VIRTUES, VALUES, AND IDEALS

INDEX OF THE VICES OF DEFECT / EXCESS

INDEX OF HYPERVIOLENCE

INDEX of CLASSICAL MYTHOLOGY

BIBLIOGRAPHIC INDEX
(OF NAMED AUTHORS)

Allport, GW, & Odbert, HS (1936). Trait names: a psycho-lexical study. Psychological Monographs, 47

Aquinas, St. Thomas (1981). *Summa Theologica.* NY: Thomas More Press.

Aristotle (1992). *Nicomachean Ethics.* (M. Ostwald, trans.) New York: Bobbs-Merrill.

Athens, L. and Ulmer, J. T. (2000). *Violent Acts and Violentization.* NY: Elsevior Science.

Augustine, Saint (1950). *City of God.* (M. Dods, trans.) NewYork: Modern Library.

Avila, St. Teresa (1972) *Interior Castle.* New York: Doubleday.

Bartlett, M.S., Hager, J.C., Ekman, P., and Sejnowski, T.J. (1999). Measuring Facial Expressions by Computer Image Analysis. *Psychophysiology* 36:253-263

Bennett, William J. (1993). *The Book of Virtues, A Treasury of Great Moral Stories.* NY: Simon & Schuster.

Bennett, William J. (1995). *The Moral Compass.* New York: Simon and Schuster.

Cartwright, D., and Zander, A. (1953). "Group Cohesiveness, Introduction," In: *Group Dynamics, Research and Theory.* (D. Cartwright and A. Zander, eds.) Evanston, Illinois: Row Peterson and Co.

Catholic Encyclopedia (The)- (1913). Edward A. Pace, et al, (eds.), Encyclopedia Press International.

Child, H. (1971). *Christian Symbols, Ancient and Modern.* New York: Scribner.

Cicero (1985). *De Officiis.* Walter Miller (trans.) Cambridge: Harvard Univ. Press.

Clark, Walter Van Tilburg. (1940). *The Oxbow Incident.* New York: Vintage Books.

Crane, Steven. (1942). *The Red Badge of Courage.* NY: McGraw-Hill.

Dante, Alighieri. (1901). *The Divine Comedy of Dante Alighieri.* H. Clay (trans.) NY: Colonial.

Davidson, Gustav. (1967). *A Dictionary of Angels: Including the Fallen Angels.* New York: Free Press.

Diagnostic and Statistical Manual of Mental Disorders (2000). 4th ed. Amer. *Psychiatric Press.*

Dictionary of the History of Ideas. (1976) Phillip Wiener (ed.) New York: Scribner.

Durant, W. (1939). *Life of Greece.* New York: Simon & Schuster.

Dyer, W. (1976). *Your Erroneous Zones.* New York: Funk & Wagnalls.

Ekman, P., Levenson, R. W., & Friesen, W. V. (1983) Autonomic nervous system activity distinguishes between emotions. Sci., 221, 1208-1210.

Ekman, P. (1992). *Telling Lies: Clues to Deceit in the Marketplace, Marriage, and Politics.* NY: Norton.

Encyclopedia of Religion and Ethics (1924). J. Hastings (ed.) New York: Scribner's and Sons.

Farley, F., and Carlson, J. (1991). Type T theory: A New Approach to Facilitating Marriage Change. *Family Psychologist 7*:6-9.

Gale Encyclopedia of Psychology – 2nd Edition (2000). Bonnie Strickland (ed.), The Gale Group.

Grafman J, Schwab K, Warden D, Pridgen A, (1996) Frontal Lobe Injuries, Violence, and Aggression. *Neurology* May; *46*(5):1231-1238.

Haley, J., (1989). *The Power Tactics of Jesus Christ and Other Essays.* NY: Triangle Press/Norton.

Haley, J., (1990). *Strategies of Psychotherapy.* NY: Triangle Press/Norton.

Hare, R. D. (1991). *Manual for the Hare Psychopathy Checklist* (Revised.). Toronto: Multi-Health Systems.

Harper, D. (2003). *Etymonline.com* (online resource)

Harper's Dictionary of Classical Literature and Antiquities. (1962). Harry T. Peck (ed.) NY: Colonial Press.

Hassler, R. 1972. Hexapartition of Thalamic Inputs. In : Corticothalamic Projections and Sensorimotor Activities. New York: Raven Press.

Hesse, Herman (1951). *Siddartha.* NY: Bantam.

International Standard Bible Encyclopedia (1915) James Orr - General Editor (online resource).

James, W. (1902). *The Varieties of Religious Experience: A Study in Human Nature.* NY: Random.

Jobes, G. (1962). *Dictionary of Mythology, Folklore and Symbols.* Metuchen, New Jersey: Scarecrow Press.

Kant, I. (1899). *Critique of Pure Reason.* (J. Meiklejohn, trans.) New York: Colonial Press.

Laing, R. D., Phillipson, H., and Lee, A. (1966). *Interpersonal Perception.* Baltimore: Perennial Library.

LaMuth, J. E. (1977). The Development of the Forebrain as an Elementary Function of the Parameters of Input Specificity and Phylogenetic Age. *J. U-grad Rsch: Bio. Sci. U. C. Irvine.* (6): 274-294.

LaMuth, J. E. (1999). *The Ultimate Guide to Family Values: A Grand Unified Theory of Ethics and Morality.* Lucerne Valley, CA: Fairhaven.

LaMuth, J. E. (2000). A Holistic Model of Ethical Behavior Based Upon a Metaperspectival Hierarchy of the Traditional Groupings of Virtue, Values, & Ideals. *Proceedings of the 44th Annual World Congress for the Int. Society for the Systems Sciences* – Toronto.

LaMuth, J. E. (2002). *A Revolution in Family Values: Tradition vs. Technology.* Lucerne Valley, CA: Fairhaven.

LaMuth, J. E. (2003). *Inductive Inference Affective Language Analyzer Simulating AI.* - US Patent # 6,587,846.

LaMuth, J. E. (2004). Behavioral Foundations for the Behaviourome / Mind Mapping Project. *Proceedings for the Eighth International Tsukuba Bioethics Roundtable, Tsukuba, Japan.*

LaMuth, J. E. (2004). *Communication Breakdown: Decoding the Riddle of Mental Illness.* Lucerne Valley, CA: Fairhaven.

LaMuth, J. E. (2005). *Character Values: Promoting a Virtuous Lifestyle.* Lucerne Valley, CA: Fairhaven.

LaMuth, J. E. (2007). *Inductive Inference Affective Language Analyzer Simulating Transitional AI.* - US Patent # 7,236,963.

Leonhard, Karl. (1979). *The Classification of Endogenous Psychoses* (5th Ed.). NY: Irvington Press.

Leonhard, Karl. (1999). *The Classification of Endogenous Psychoses and Their Differentiated Etiology* (2nd Edit.). H. Beckmann (Ed.), Springer-Verlag/Teleos

Lewis, M. (1995). Self-conscious Emotions. *American Scientist, 83*:68-78.

Locke, John (1986). *The Second Treatise on Civil Government.* Amherst, NY: Prometheus Books

Noble E., et al. (1998) D2 & D4 Dopamine Receptor Polymorhism and Personality. *Am. J. Med. Genetics* 81:257-267.

Miller, C. J. (2000). *Contempt of Court – 3rd Edition.* Oxford University Press.

Oatley, K. and Johnson-Laird, P.N. (1987), Towards a cognitive theory of emotions, Cognition and Emotion, 1: 29-50

Oatley, K. and Jenkins, J. M. (1992). Human Emotions: Function and Dysfunction. Annual Review of Psychology, 43, 55-85.

Oxford Classical Dictionary. (1970). Oxford, Claredon.

Raine, A., Venables, P.H. and Mednick, S.A. (1997). Low resting heart rate at age 3 years predisposes to aggression at age 11 years. *Journal of the Amer. Acad. of Child and Adolescent Psychiatry* 36:1457-1464.

Raine, A. (1999).Murderous Minds: Can We See the Mark of Cain? *Cerebrum*, 1:15-30.

Sagan, Carl. "Can Games Test Ethics? A New Way to Think About Rules to Live By." *Parade Magazine.* (Nov. 28, 1993): 12-14.

Sanides, F. 1969. Comparative Architectonics of the Neocortex of Mammals and their Evolutionary Interpretation. Ann. N.Y. Ac. Sci. 167: 404-423.

Skinner, B. F. (1971). *Beyond Freedom and Dignity.* NY: Knopf.

Sperry, R. W. (1974) Lateral Specialization in Surgically Separated Hemispheres. In Neurosciences 3rd Study Program. Cambridge: MIT Press 3:5 -19.

Stuss, D. T. & Alexander, M.P. (2000). Executive Functions in the Frontal Lobes: A Conceptual View. *Psychological Research,* 63:289-298.

Walker, B. (1983). *The Woman's Encyclopedia of Myths and Secrets.* San Francisco: Harper and Row.

Watzlawick, P., Beavin, H., and Jackson, D. (1967), *Pragmatics of Human Communication.* NY: Norton.

Webber, F. (1990) *Church Symbolism: An Explanation of the More Important Symbols of the Old and New Testament.* Detroit: Omnigraphics.

Zuckerman, M. (2000) Are You a Risk-taker? *Psych. Today,* Nov/Dec. 54-87.

About the Author

John E. LaMuth is a *55* year-old counselor and author native to the Southern California area. His credentials include a Baccalaureate Degree in Biological Sciences from University of California Irvine, followed by a Masters Degree in Counseling from California State University (Fullerton) with an emphasis in Marriage, Family, and Child Counseling. John is currently engaged in private practice in Mediation Counseling in the San Bernardino County area. Professional affiliations include membership in the American Psychological Association and the American Philosophical Association. John has recently been granted two US patents for Artificial Intelligence - #6,587,846 and #7,236,963. *www.global-solutions.org*

*** NEW BOOK RELEASE FROM FAIRHAVEN BOOKS • *FHB* ***

Challenges to World Peace: A Global Solution

Publ. 2009 • Author: John E. LaMuth M. S. • Trade Soft-Cover • 7.44 X 9.69 in.

List $28.95 • 438 pages • Extensively Illustrated • ISBN # 978-1-929649-32-7

Please Ship to ⇩   Date: _____

_____

_____   Daytime phone #: (___) ___-___

_____

Item #	Description	Quantity	Price Each	Amount
127	*Challenges to World Peace: A Global Solution*		$28.95	

Subtotal _____

Shipping and Handling Charges:
(Includes Delivery Confirmation)
One book - $5.75 (Priority-USPS)
Two books - $11.05 (Priority-USPS)
Three books - $11.05 (Priority-USPS)
Four books (or over) - Please Query
CA residents please add 8.75% State Sales-Tax
(one copy = $1.90 • two copies = $3.80 • etc.)

Postage & Handling _____
(see chart to the left)

Order Total _____

[ ] Check or Money-Order enclosed • Payable to: Fairhaven Book Publishers

[ ] Check Here for Book Copy Inscribed by Author • (No Additional Charge)

For Credit Card Orders: Please visit: www.global-solutions.org

Phone Orders or Additional Info • Dial Toll-Free 1- 877- FHBooks (342-6657)

Tel: (877) 342-6657
Fax: (586) 314-5960
values@charactervalues.com

35425 Mojave St. - (Suite B)
Lucerne Valley, CA 92356 USA
www.global-solutions.org

www.ingramcontent.com/pod-product-compliance
Lightning Source LLC
Chambersburg PA
CBHW080603270326
41928CB00016B/2905